# SERVING PROUDLY

# Serving Proudly

## A HISTORY OF WOMEN IN THE U.S. NAVY

Susan H. Godson

NAVAL INSTITUTE PRESS
ANNAPOLIS, MARYLAND

NAVAL HISTORICAL CENTER
WASHINGTON NAVY YARD, D.C.

Naval Institute Press
291 Wood Road
Annapolis, MD 21402



Library of Congress Cataloging-in-Publication Data
Godson, Susan H.
Serving proudly : a history of women in the U.S. Navy / Susan H. Godson.
p. cm.
Includes bibliographical references and index.
ISBN 1-55750-317-6 (alk. paper)
1. United States. Navy—Women. I. Title.
VB324.W65 G63 2001
359'.0082'0973—dc21
2001031279

Printed in the United States of America on acid-free paper ♾
08 07 06 05 04 03 02 01 9 8 7 6 5 4 3 2
First printing

*To the women who have served so valiantly*
*in the U.S. Navy*

*The highest award I have received is serving proudly in the U.S. Navy.*

REAR ADM. GRACE M. HOPPER, USNR

# Contents

# Foreword

This volume presents a comprehensive study of service by American women with the United States Navy from the early days of the Republic almost to the end of the twentieth century. Susan Godson relates how women, many of whom went to sea during the nineteenth century as the wives of male mariners or even as combatants, eagerly accepted the nation's call in the twentieth century to serve in the Navy. Thousands of women joined the Nurse Corps in the decades after its establishment and rallied to the colors as enlisted yeomen (F) in World War I. The nation's obvious need in a hard-fought global war and the desire of many Americans to defend freedom from attack by Nazi Germany and militarist Japan led eighty-six thousand women to serve in the WAVES during World War II. Overcoming social and institutional biases in the postwar era, women pressed for and won the right to serve in the regular Navy. Navy nurses were on hand to ease the pain and suffering of wounded American fighting men during the conflicts in Korea and Vietnam and in the Persian Gulf War. Despite periodic setbacks to their advancement, female sailors eventually took command of U.S. naval forces, piloted fighter planes in combat, and crewed warships alongside their male compatriots. Throughout this work, Godson has richly described how Esther Voorhees Hasson, Joy Bright Hancock, Grace Murray Hopper, and thousands of other Navy women have served with distinction and dedication in the United States Navy, as they do to this day.

Godson's work is based on numerous interviews she conducted during the last decade with former and current members of the Navy Nurse Corps, WAVES, and the Navy in general; on the official records maintained in the National Archives, Navy Operational Archives, Bureau of Medicine and

Surgery, and the Marine Corps Research Center; on congressional reports and documents; on hundreds of books and articles catalogued in the collections of the Library of Congress and the Navy Department Library; and on personal papers held in special collections around the country.

The author of this thorough work, Susan Godson, brought to the project impressive credentials. She earned a bachelor's degree in history from George Mason University and a master's and doctorate degree in history from American University. In 1982, the University Press of America published her *Viking of Assault: Admiral John Leslie Hall Jr. and Amphibious Warfare*. Godson is also the coauthor of *The College of William and Mary: A History*. She has published numerous articles on naval, women's, and educational history, and presented relevant lectures at institutions of higher learning.

Many individuals are responsible for publication of this important work, including professional staff members of the Naval Historical Center. Special credit should go to my predecessor, Dean C. Allard, who recognized the need to publish a history of women in the Navy and strongly supported the project during his tenure as director of Naval History. To many deserving persons go my sincere thanks.

*William S. Dudley*
*Director of Naval History*

# Preface

A formal, written account of the history of women in the U.S. Navy is long overdue. When the Naval Historical Center assigned me the task of writing such a book in 1993, it specified that I cover both women of the line, called WAVES (Women Accepted for Volunteer Emergency Service) until 1972, and the Navy Nurse Corps. This dual coverage proved challenging because the two groups performed different functions in the Navy, yet their progress often followed parallel courses.

Research included a variety of secondary sources, official reports, and government documents. Primary materials for both groups in this study are mainly in the Operational Archives of the Naval Historical Center in Washington, D.C. Additional documentary sources are at the Bureau of Medicine and Surgery, the National Archives and Records Administration, and the Smithsonian Institution.

Of immense value to the work were the oral history interviews that I conducted with numerous present and former members of the Navy. Because I am a historian by training and experience but have never served in the Navy, these conversations increased my understanding of "Navy ways" and of women's motivations, problems, and achievements in the service.

The views expressed herein do not necessarily reflect the opinions of the Department of Defense or the Department of the Navy. Any errors in fact or interpretation are mine alone.

# Acknowledgments

My debt of gratitude for assistance with this book extends to numerous people and organizations. My sincere thanks go to many at the Naval Historical Center, including William S. Dudley, Director of Naval History; Bernard F. Cavalcante, head of the Operational Archives Branch, and his helpful staff; John C. Reilly Jr., head of the Ships History Branch; and Charles R. Haberlein, head of the Photographic Section. Everyone in the Navy Department Library always willingly and enthusiastically helped in many ways, and I thank especially Jean L. Hort, Glenn E. Helm, David Brown, and Davis Elliot. The editing talents of senior editor Sandra J. Doyle and copy editor Laura Matthews kept the manuscript on course, while Ruby D. Hughlett oversaw contract execution. Acting as an in-house review committee, historians Robert J. Schneller and Regina Akers read early drafts of the manuscript.

The story of the Navy Nurse Corps would have been impossible without the guidance, knowledge, and encouragement of Jan K. Herman, historian for the Bureau of Medicine and Surgery. Capt. Mary A. Gardner, NC, kindly gave me access to the records in the Nursing Division held at the bureau in Washington, D.C. Harold D. Langley, formerly of the Smithsonian Institution, provided material on the Yeomen (F). The College of William and Mary reference and government documents librarians and the Mariners' Museum staff offered their expertise and assistance.

Special thanks go to the people who allowed me to interview them for this project. I am grateful for their willingness to share—often candidly—their experiences with me.

Finally, as the work neared completion, four highly qualified professional historians reviewed the manuscript and offered a welter of sound advice and constructive suggestions. These reviewers were Dean C. Allard, former Director of Naval History; D'Ann Campbell, professor of history and Vice President for Academic Affairs, the Sage Colleges; Jan K. Herman; and Edward J. Marolda, Senior Historian, Naval Historical Center.

# Abbreviations

| | |
|---|---|
| ACNP(W) | Assistant chief of naval personnel for women |
| AID | Agency for International Development |
| *AJN* | *American Journal of Nursing* |
| ANA | American Nurses Association |
| bio | Biography/biographical |
| *BNPIB* | *Bureau of Naval Personnel Information Bulletin* |
| BuAer | Bureau of Aeronautics |
| BuMed | Bureau of Medicine and Surgery |
| BuNav | Bureau of Navigation |
| BuPers | Bureau of Naval Personnel |
| BuS&A | Bureau of Supplies and Accounts |
| CINC | Commander in chief |
| CNO | Chief of naval operations |
| CNP | Chief of naval personnel |
| CO | Commanding officer |
| CPO | Chief petty officer |
| CWO | Chief warrant officer |
| DACOWITS | Defense Advisory Committee on Women in the Service |
| *DANFS* | *Dictionary of American Naval Fighting Ships* |
| DCNO | Deputy chief of naval operations |
| DOD | Department of Defense |
| DUINS | Duty under instruction |
| ERA | Equal Rights Amendment |
| GAO | General Accounting Office |
| HC | Hospital Corps |
| JAG | Judge advocate general |

| | |
|---|---|
| *JAH* | *Journal of American History* |
| *JMH* | *Journal of Military History* |
| LC | Library of Congress |
| LDO | Limited duty officer |
| *MCG* | *Marine Corps Gazette* |
| MSC | Medical Service Corps |
| MSTS | Military Sea Transport Service |
| NAACP | National Association for the Advancement of Colored People |
| NARA | National Archives and Records Administration |
| ND | Nursing Division |
| NHC | Naval Historical Center |
| NNC | Navy Nurse Corps |
| NROTC | Naval Reserve Officer Training Corps |
| OA | Operational Archives |
| ONOP | Office of Naval Officer Procurement |
| *ORN* | *Official Records of the Union and Confederate Navies in the War of the Rebellion* |
| RN | Royal Navy |
| ROC | Reserve officer candidate |
| SecDef | Secretary of Defense |
| SecNav | Secretary of the Navy |
| USMC | United States Marine Corps |
| *USNIP* | U.S. Naval Institute *Proceedings* |
| USNRF | United States Naval Reserve Force |
| WR | Women's Reserve |

# SERVING PROUDLY

# 1

# The Eighteenth and Nineteenth Centuries

*During the eighteenth and nineteenth centuries,* women sailed in ships of every sort—hospital, whaling, merchant, pirate, privateer, clipper, and war—and often learned the intricacies of shiphandling and seamanship. At the same time, they provided the gentle nursing care so essential to sick and injured men, often using their talents in military settings. These two elements, familiarity with ships and maritime matters and nursing skills, would provide the foundation for women's twentieth-century participation in the U.S. Navy.

## 1776–1815

Even before there was a U.S. Navy, women had helped gain the country's independence during the American Revolution. Twenty thousand females assisted the Continental Army, some as camp followers, spies, or nurses who provided rudimentary care to the sick and wounded. The legendary Molly Pitcher was a water carrier, and Deborah Sampson enlisted, disguised as a man. Others, in the heat of battle, fired the weapons of their fallen husbands.[1] Several women saw service in the states' navies during the war. In 1776 the Pennsylvania Navy had women onboard some of its galleys; the next year the Maryland Navy's ship *Defence* hired Mary Pricely as a nurse.[2] Even John Paul Jones, when he captured the British sloop *Drake* in 1778, included the cook's wife among his prisoners, taking her onboard his ship, the Continental Navy's sloop of war *Ranger.*[3] Other than these isolated examples, however, women apparently did not play a significant part in naval operations during the American Revolution.

The Continental Navy provided some care for sick and wounded men onboard warships, and the 1775 naval regulations specified that a part of each ship would be set aside as a sick bay. A surgeon, a surgeon's mate, and often crew members would nurse the infirm. Two years later, Congress mandated professional examinations for all naval surgeons and surgeons' mates, a step toward improving the Medical Department.[4]

After the war the Continental Navy disbanded and its ships were sold. The country was left without a navy. By 1794, however, Barbary pirates were prowling the Mediterranean and venturing out into the Atlantic, seizing American merchantmen and their crews. Rather than pay ransom for these prisoners, Congress established a naval officer corps and authorized construction of six frigates to protect American commerce. Each new ship would carry a surgeon onboard. Although the United States and Algiers reached an agreement the next year to end the piracy in exchange for almost $1 million in bribes and naval supplies, Congress begrudgingly authorized completion of three frigates—the *Constitution, United States,* and *Constellation.* Not completed until 1798, these ships became the nucleus of an American naval force hastily assembled during the Quasi War with France (1798–1801). During this crisis, Congress wrenched control of naval affairs from the War Department and established the Department of the Navy in April 1798. The department had two administrative officers—secretary and accountant—and several clerks. President John Adams named Benjamin Stoddert the first secretary of the Navy, and under Stoddert's leadership the Navy grew to fifty-four ships, 750 officers, and 6,000 men.[5]

The end of the Quasi War and the election of Thomas Jefferson to the presidency in 1801 brought a reduction of the American naval establishment to thirteen frigates and one schooner. Jefferson hoped to disband the Navy, but the Barbary pirates dashed this hope by renewing their attacks on American shipping. Then Tripoli declared war on the United States. Determined to defeat the Barbary nemesis, Jefferson dispatched a squadron to the Mediterranean. Following several years of skirmishing, the United States and Tripoli signed a peace treaty in 1805, and American warships soon returned home. Another ten years would pass before the country completely resolved the problem of the Barbary corsairs.[6]

The Quasi War and the need to resist the Barbary depredations of American commerce had given the U.S. Navy permanent status in the eyes of the nation, and with this permanency came traditions and standards for the fledgling naval force. Since 1775 the Navy had had rules that were patterned largely after those of Britain's Royal Navy. In 1802 a new set of regulations detailed the responsibilities of squadron commanders, ships' officers, and crew members. A ship captain's duties included ensuring his vessel did not transport "any woman to sea, without orders from the navy office, *or the commander of the squadron*."[7] A woman's presence onboard naval vessels must not have been unusual for such a regulation to appear. If so, the American Navy again borrowed customs from the Royal Navy, whose eighteenth-century warships regularly carried wives, "loose women," children, and animals to sea.[8]

As early as April 1802, Commo. Richard V. Morris in the frigate *Chesapeake* applied the regulation when he led his squadron to the Mediterranean to protect American merchantmen. Morris must have granted himself permission, for he brought on the voyage his wife, his infant son, and a black maid. Other wives came, too, and one went into labor. The ship's doctor, hoping to speed the delivery, ordered her placed near the broadside guns and a volley fired. The remedy was successful, and a "son of a gun" was born. Another wife stood in for the mother at the baby's christening, and three other women not invited to the ceremony got drunk in their quarters.[9] Commodore Morris was an ineffective squadron commander (whether because of all the domestic squabbles is speculative); Jefferson relieved him in 1803, and the Navy subsequently dismissed him. Nevertheless, the practice of carrying women in warships continued.

As the problems with the Barbary pirates subsided, other threats to American rights on the high seas increased. Between 1799 and 1812, Britain impressed some ten thousand American sailors and interfered unchallenged with trade. After the unprovoked attack on the *Chesapeake* in June 1807, war fever swept the country, but the United States was woefully unprepared for another confrontation with Britain. President Jefferson had stressed coastal defenses, and the Navy had only two active frigates and about 172 coastal gunboats—hardly sufficient to ward off Britain's massive sea power. Following James Madison's inauguration as president in 1809, economic measures still failed, and the country edged toward another war.[10]

The U.S. Navy would play a crucial part in the coming war, and casualties were inevitable. The Act of 1798 had established a Navy Hospital Fund by deducting twenty cents a month from the pay of merchant seamen, and the next year the benefit expanded to the naval service. In February 1811 Congress passed an act establishing naval hospitals.[11] Secretary of the Navy Paul Hamilton later asked William P. C. Barton, a young naval surgeon, to compose a set of regulations for governing these hospitals. Barton was well aware of the shortcomings in Navy medical care. Shipboard facilities were primitive, and there were no permanent hospitals ashore, only temporary ones in Navy yards.[12] Surely the Navy could provide for its own. As early as 1695 the Royal Navy had emphasized professional care of its sick by building hospitals at Greenwich, Haslar, and Stonehouse; the Continental Army had hospitals with matrons and local women "nurses" during the Revolution.[13]

Borrowing heavily from the work of naval surgeon Edward Cutbush, who had published a book in 1808 on sailors' health and hospital administration, Barton drafted rules for governing naval hospitals. The Navy Department submitted them to Congress in 1812. Each hospital accommodating at least one hundred men should maintain a staff including a surgeon, who must be a college or university graduate; two surgeon's mates; a steward; a matron; a wardmaster; four permanent nurses; and a variety of servants. Barton delineated the duties of each medical care provider. Of particular interest is the role of matron, who ideally, Barton noted, should be the steward's wife. She would be responsible for keeping patients and wards clean, carrying out the surgeon's directives, and supervising nurses and servants. Barton's report did not specify whether nurses were to be male or female and made little mention of duties, except that one should avoid displeasing the hospital surgeon. An addendum recommended specific rank for surgeons and the same pay and emoluments as Army surgeons received. As for building sites, eight to ten acres were necessary for each hospital, and at least fifteen acres if an asylum was added.[14]

Not satisfied with the hastily drafted suggestions, Barton expanded his theories in a treatise published in 1814. In discussing his proposed internal organization and government of marine hospitals and staff duties, Barton further defined the matron's characteristics: she should be "discreet . . . reputable . . . capable . . . neat, cleanly, and tidy in her dress, and urbane and tender in her deportment." She would supervise the nurses and other attendants as well as those working in the laundry, larder, and kitchen, but her main function was to ensure that patients were clean, well-fed, and comfortable. Barton made no mention of the matron's providing any type of medical care.[15]

Barton's treatise increased the responsibilities for nurses, now described as "women of humane dispositions and tender manners, active and healthy . . . neat and cleanly . . . and without any vices of any description." They would dispense medicines and diets to the sick, keep the wards clean, and watch the sick—even sitting up with them at night. In addition, there should be "orderly-men," or male nurses. These men were to assist the female nurses and could perform duties in caring for the sick "that women could not decently attend to."[16]

Although Barton showed foresight in proposing the extensive use of women in caring for the sick, he envisioned their filling the customary nurturing roles in society: keeping the infirm clean and comfortable and following doctors' orders. He made no mention of any specialized training or education for these "nurses," which is not surprising. In 1814 there was no professional training for nurses in the modern sense. Barton's nurses would merely perform women's usual duties in a military setting. Unfortunately, Barton's suggestions for female nurses did not materialize.

Two years before Barton's *Treatise Containing a Plan for the Internal Organization and Government of Marine Hospitals* was circulated, the United States and Great Britain were at war. After a number of single-ship victories, the U.S. Navy found itself boxed in by a Royal Navy blockade of the East Coast.[17] Commo. Stephen Decatur planned to run his squadron of frigates *United States* and *Macedonian* and sloop-of-war *Hornet* from New York through the blockade in May 1813. Believing there would be heavy casualties, Decatur took two women onboard the *United States* as "nurses." Both were wives of crewmen and had no medical training. Mary Allen accepted Decatur's offer of accompanying her husband, John, on condition that she serve as a nurse. The second woman, Mary Marshall, the wife of another seaman, also acted as a nurse. The ship's log for 10 May 1813 lists the women as supernumeraries.[18]

Although Decatur never broke through the blockade, he kept the "nurses" onboard for months. Mary Allen's naval service ended in October, when her husband drowned and she secured permission to leave the ship. Mary Marshall might have remained on *United States* until her husband was reassigned the following spring, or she might have left with Mary Allen.[19] These two women, the first documented hired "nurses" serving on a U.S. Navy warship, were early predecessors of nurses in ships during the Civil War and the Spanish-American War.

The War of 1812 inspired another form of feminine patriotism: a woman disguising herself as a man in order to serve on a U.S. Navy warship. Ever since the alleged voyages of Lucy Brewer in the *Constitution,* naval historians have had to confront the persistent story of her service and have been thwarted by a lack of hard evidence either supporting or refuting the tale.

True or not, Brewer's exciting adventures had ample precedent in European, especially British, navies and in popular literature and song. Appealing primarily to lower-class women, British ballads extolling female warriors enjoyed great popularity from the mid-seventeenth century to Victorian times. Typically, the "warrior" had been separated from her man by war or by her irate father, dressed as a male, and went to sea or to war. She was always an exemplary, fair, and virtuous heroine.[20]

There was just enough fact to sustain these stories and songs. In the eighteenth century, the Royal Navy carried a marine named William Prothero in the *Amazon.* William turned out to be an eighteen-year-old Welsh girl.[21] Another female Royal Marine sustained twelve wounds while fighting against the French in India.[22] Among the most famous of these transvestite warriors was Hannah Snell, who served in both the British army and navy from 1745 to 1750 as James Gray. After she retired with a government pension, Snell's exploits became widely known through her biography, *The Female Soldier.*[23] Equally renowned was Mary Ann Talbot, who published her own memoir of her service as a servant, a drummer, and a sailor in a French privateer and finally in three British warships. She, too, collected a pension at retirement.[24] Even more relevant for American women were the Revolutionary War exploits of Deborah Sampson, which were published in 1797 as *The Female Review.* The Massachusetts native would be a compelling role model for Lucy Brewer.

According to her autobiography, Lucy left her family's home forty miles west of Boston when she was sixteen years old, after being seduced and betrayed by a lover. Not wanting to disgrace her family, the pregnant girl quickly found work in a Boston brothel. Her baby died at birth, and Lucy continued in the world's oldest profession for three more years. In 1812 a young naval lieutenant, presumably a customer, told Lucy the story of Deborah Sampson, suggesting that Lucy disguise herself as a man and sign on to the frigate *Constitution*, then in port.[25] Living in a busy seaport, Lucy undoubtedly would also have been familiar with barroom ballads about female warriors.

Lucy dressed in a sailor's suit and volunteered as a marine in *Constitution*. In those days many young boys served in various capacities onboard American ships, and the average sailor was relatively small.[26] Lucy would have had little trouble passing as a male. She learned to handle firearms as well as any recruit and took part in three major engagements.[27] After the War of 1812, Lucy reverted to feminine dress, returned to her parents' home, and wrote her memoirs, which went to three printings.

Lucy's memoir is the only written account of her adventures. There is nothing about them in any official documents. Ignored or dismissed by most naval historians, the story has lingered with astonishing persistency and was the topic of a book published during the country's bicentennial.[28] Fictional or not, the story of Lucy Brewer left an enduring legacy of a woman serving in a combatant ship.

## 1815–1860

As Lucy Brewer entered married life, she became a part of the cult of domesticity, a trend that lasted throughout the nineteenth century. In sharp contrast to earlier times, when they had filled skilled occupations as school mistresses, shopkeepers, and silversmiths, women were increasingly denied jobs, training, and education. Urbanization and industrialization caused men to move from rural and small-town America to the cities and to more professional occupations, a trend that left many middle- and upper-class women isolated within their homes and bound by their duties as wives and mothers. Markedly influenced by European ideas of womanhood, "fashionable" American women accepted their place in the domestic sphere.[29] Cautioned against any pursuits outside the home that might cause the loss of "femininity," women's only public role was through their husbands and families. After all, women's "special" nature endowed them with patience, endurance, passive courage, and higher moral qualities, such as piety, submissiveness, and nurturance, attributes that made women supremely fit to reign within the domestic sphere.[30]

Social reform movements, which began in the 1820s, allowed proper women to contribute their special talents to the outside world. Led by churches and benevolent societies, movements and their causes proliferated. Here, certainly, were respectable outlets for women's energies. Within reform groups women demonstrated their leadership capabilities and formed associations that trained them for larger roles in society.[31]

One such reform movement was evangelical Christianity, which preached the urgent need for salvation, as manifested by good works, temperance, and the end of corporal punishment. The U.S. Navy was a ready target. To reform and uplift sailors, the Boston Society for the Religious and Moral Improvement of Seamen was established in 1812, followed five years later by the Marine Bible Society. These two societies soon spawned such auxiliaries as the Female Seamen's Friends societies. Founded in 1820, the Society for the Relief of Families of Sailors Killed While in Service was the forerunner of the Naval Relief Society of 1904. In 1826 the American Seamen's Friend Society organized with branches in port cities in the United States and abroad. It spawned the Seamen's Bank for Savings and published the widely read *Sailor's Magazine*. These groups tried to improve sailors' living conditions ashore by setting up boardinghouses (alternatives to brothels) and encouraging savings. They also maintained employment registries, libraries and reading rooms, and training schools and sent chaplains to foreign ports. The reformers were instrumental in the drive to abolish flogging in the Navy and in commercial vessels. This inhumane punishment ended in 1850. Drunkenness, the major cause of flogging, decreased as the Navy slowly reduced its grog ration, but it was 1862 before Congress prohibited alcoholic spirits onboard naval ships.[32]

Although women were active in the American Seamen's Friend Society, they were frozen out of most leadership roles in major reform movements such as abolition (it was not ladylike to speak in public), and their anger and resentment mounted. Finally, in 1848, the first Women's Rights Convention met at Seneca Falls, New York. Its 240 delegates, led by abolitionists Elizabeth Cady Stanton and Lucretia Mott, enumerated their grievances, which had resulted from men's "absolute tyranny" over women. In the Declaration of Sentiments and Resolutions, they demanded equal moral, political, and economic rights and privileges. Most people regarded these early feminists as radicals, and they attracted only a scant following. They did, however, challenge the prevailing ideology that women's only place was in the home, and they paved the way for the nascent antebellum women's rights movement of the 1850s.[33] But most women remained contentedly in their defined sphere; it would take a war to release them from the cult of True Womanhood.

While women debated their rights, or lack thereof, the United States enjoyed more than thirty years of peace. The Navy's primary missions became protecting American commerce against pirates, showing the flag around the globe, opening new markets, and charting seas and coastlines. To achieve these goals, Congress authorized increased ship construction; and the Navy established the Pacific, Brazil, West Indies (later, Home), East Indian, and African Squadrons in addition to its old Mediterranean Squadron.[34] Worldwide expansion and far-flung stations required better administrative procedures, first overseen by the Board of Navy Commissioners (1815) and then by five naval bureaus (1842). By the early 1840s, a new generation of naval leadership grudgingly accepted such innovations as steam-powered warships, and the Corps of Engineers was formed.[35]

During these same years, naval leaders instigated means for improving officers' professional standards. To disseminate knowledge, they established the U.S. Naval Lyceum (1833), the *Naval Magazine* (1836), and the American Historical Society of Military and Naval Events (1836). The Navy Department set up the Depot of Charts and Instruments, forerunner of the Naval Observatory and Hydrographic Office. In 1845, Secretary of the Navy George Bancroft convinced Congress to establish the U.S. Naval Academy for training potential officers. Ten years later, the Naval Efficiency Act introduced a retirement process for incapable officers. In 1861 all had to retire at age sixty-two or with forty-five years' service.[36]

In military operations, the Navy helped remove the Seminole Indians from the Florida Everglades in the mid-1830s, getting its first taste of riverine warfare. When the Mexican War began in 1846, the Navy blockaded ports in the Gulf of Mexico, staged the amphibious invasion of Veracruz, and played a major role in the conquest of California.[37] As peace returned, the Navy continued opening foreign markets for American commerce. In the mid-1850s Commo. Matthew C. Perry, through astute diplomacy and a grand display of naval force, opened the door for trade with Japan.[38] Simultaneously, Secretary of the Navy James C. Dobbin convinced Congress to launch a shipbuilding program, and by 1860 there were thirty-eight steam vessels and forty-four sailing ships in the fleet.[39]

As the Navy itself underwent change and growth, so did its Medical Department. After passage of the act establishing naval hospitals in 1811 and William P. C. Barton's ambitious plans for them, little progress occurred for twenty years. The Navy maintained temporary, and primitive, hospital facilities in Navy yards at Washington, Philadelphia, New York, and Boston. During the 1820s the Navy acquired the necessary land, and in the following decade built permanent hospitals at Portsmouth, Virginia; League Island, Philadelphia; Portsmouth, New Hampshire; Chelsea, Massachusetts; Pensacola, Florida; and Brooklyn, New York. The hospital at Philadelphia also had an asylum for disabled veterans. Later hospitals followed at Newport, Rhode Island; Washington; and Annapolis.[40] No one suggested matrons or women nurses for these hospitals.

Afloat, surgeons served in major warships around the globe. Although separate hospital ships had been recommended as early as 1808, none was built.[41] The ship's sick bay continued to be the place of patients' recovery. The surgeon, his assistant, and crew members called loblolly boys (possessing no medical training or experience) provided rudimentary care.[42]

In an early, short-lived attempt at improving the professional quality of medical personnel, physician Thomas Harris set up a school in 1822 to teach new medical officers about naval hygiene, customs and usage, and the military. Another stride toward better medicine was the Navy Laboratory, opened at the Naval Hospital at Brooklyn in 1853. The lab provided pure drugs, especially the new ether and chloroform, to the Medical Department. In the 1870s the Naval Hospital at Brooklyn briefly gave a two-year course in naval medicine, and in 1893 a similar three-month program began at the Naval Laboratory and Department of Instruction at Brooklyn. These were the forerunners of the Naval Medical School, established in Washington, D.C., in 1902.[43] Other means of upgrading the professional quality of naval medical personnel were examinations for surgeon's mates in 1824, for assistant surgeons in 1828, and for surgeons in 1829.[44]

An advance for naval medicine came with the Navy's establishment of the Bureau of Medicine and Surgery in 1842. Named chief of the bureau was surgeon William Barton, who, thirty years after devising a plan for naval hospitals, had the opportunity to direct the Navy's medical program. During his two years as chief, Barton insisted on high professional standards for the physicians of the Medical Corps, advocated better recruiting procedures, established medical libraries at each naval medical facility, supplied naval surgeons with well-known medical journals, and advocated abolishing liquor onboard ships.[45]

Barton's grand plans were limited by congressional action in 1842, which capped the number of surgeons at sixty-nine and the number of assistant or passed surgeons at eighty. In 1846 Secretary Bancroft awarded military rank to medical officers. Although the Navy grew during the next fifteen years, the number of medical personnel remained fixed, and by 1860 fully one-sixth were too old to serve afloat.[46]

Like medicine itself in the antebellum era, naval medical practices showed sporadic and uneven advances. It was an age when diseases such as scurvy, smallpox, cholera, and yellow fever ran rampant and standard treatments consisted of bloodletting, purgatives, and emetics.

Until 1847 there were no female health-care professionals, that is, women trained as nurses or doctors. That year one woman, Elizabeth Blackwell, was admitted to the all-male Geneva Medical College in western New York and became America's first formally trained woman doctor. Medical schools remained male bastions, however, so several such colleges for women opened in the 1850s.[47] But with the exception of Roman Catholic religious orders, especially the Sisters of Charity, which taught their own members how to care for the sick and the poor, most people thought there was no need for either female doctors or nurses because women without special training had always taken care of the sick.[48] Some basic instruction began in 1839 at the Nurse Society of Philadelphia, which taught lay women how to help with home maternity cases.[49] Little else was done.

Suddenly, the Crimean War shown a spotlight on the need for nurses, and one woman's efforts in that war would revolutionize nursing. In 1854, Great

Britain, France, the Ottoman Empire, and Sardinia allied to halt Russian expansion in the Black Sea area, and the Crimean Peninsula became the battleground. As British army casualties mounted, many wounded and dying soldiers suffered from lack of medical care and supplies, so the British secretary of war asked Florence Nightingale, daughter of a wealthy and distinguished family, to become general superintendent of nursing for the Army hospitals in Turkey. Nightingale had studied nursing in Kaiserwerth, Germany, and in France (unheard of for a young woman of her social standing) and had become superintendent of a women's hospital in London. After recruiting thirty-eight other nurses, she went to Scutari, where the deplorable, filthy Turkish barracks serving as a hospital for British troops needed her energetic direction. Responsible for the nursing system, Nightingale also supervised the diet kitchens, laundries, and sanitary facilities and obtained supplies and laboratory equipment. Sent in early 1855 to report on and rectify the disease-spawning conditions at Scutari, the Sanitary Commission soon joined in the cleanup.

Although administrative duties took up most of her day, Nightingale trudged through miles of hospital corridors at night to nurse the ill and wounded soldiers, who fondly named her "the Lady with the Lamp." The British soon put her in charge of nursing at all military hospitals in Crimea, and the death rate there fell from 42 to 2.2 percent. Thanks to Nightingale's heroic efforts, modern military nursing had begun, in turn leading to the development of professional nursing. After the war a grateful public gave her funds, and in 1860 she established the Nightingale Training School for Nurses at London's St. Thomas's Hospital. Nurses would be taught and then sent to outlying hospitals to teach others. The control and instruction of nursing was to be handled by women nurses, not by male doctors, a novel concept for the times.[50] For generations, the "Nightingale System" would influence nursing education in Europe and the United States.

Before the Crimean War, neither nurses nor any other women had a place *in* the U.S. Navy, but there were activities involving women *with* the Navy. In 1827 the first recorded instance of a woman's christening a ship occurred when "a young lady of Portsmouth" christened sloop-of-war *Concord.* No one knows her name. In 1846 Lavinia Fanning Watson of Philadelphia christened sloop-of-war *Germantown* at the Philadelphia Navy Yard. Women sponsored more and more ships as the nineteenth century went on, but men also continued to christen vessels.[51]

Women, and often children, had always taken passage in naval ships when there was sufficient cause for transporting them. The most common reason was carrying diplomats and their families to foreign posts, a practice that continued throughout the nineteenth century.[52] For transporting passengers, naval regulations had always required authorization from the Navy Department, secretary of the Navy, or the fleet or squadron commander in chief when in foreign waters. Such passengers were not to interfere with operation of the ship.[53]

Officers' wives presented another set of problems. Ever since Commodore Morris's chaotic 1802 voyage in *Chesapeake*, with a large complement of wives onboard, the Navy had slowly tightened the rules about carrying families. Sailors complained about the women, and a young midshipman in *United States* in 1832–33 wrote in his diary that the officers had wished Commo. Daniel Todd Patterson's wife and daughter home a thousand times. The final straw came when Commo. Isaac Hull, commanding the Mediterranean Squadron in 1838, took his wife Ann and her sister Jeannette Hart to sea onboard *Ohio*. Ann had always accompanied Hull during their twenty-five years of marriage, but Jeannette proved a disruptive influence. The wardroom officers rebelled against the women's presence, and riots, desertion, and insubordination marred the cruise.[54]

In 1842 Congress passed a joint resolution asking Secretary of the Navy Abel P. Upshur to prepare new rules and regulations for the U.S. Navy. Among Upshur's recommendations was a specific prohibition: "In no case shall a commander-in-chief, or commander of a vessel, take his wife to sea in a public ship."[55] Finally, by 1881, all women were barred from either residing on or taking passage in any naval ship.[56]

Women may have worn out their welcome in naval ships, but they continued a long tradition of sailing on pirate, privateer, clipper, and whaling vessels.[57] The most flamboyant were the lady pirates, who left a trail of robbery and murder rivaling that of their male counterparts. In American piracy, for example, Rachel Wall and her husband, George, operated off the New England coast in the late eighteenth century. Their modus operandi called for taking their vessel into the shipping lane after a storm while feigning damage and distress. Well-meaning traders stopping to offer assistance promptly had their throats slashed and their money and merchandise stolen. Afterward, the Walls sunk the rescue ships. Their profitable business continued until George misjudged a storm's fury, was swept overboard, and drowned. Rachel settled in Boston, where she worked as a servant while moonlighting in petty larceny. She was hanged in 1789 for robbery.[58]

The same techniques, and often the same crews, used in these high-seas robberies appeared in privateering, the government-sanctioned version of piracy. Just before the American Revolution, Fanny Campbell of Lynn, Massachusetts, disguised herself as a man and became second officer in the British brig *Constance*. Fanny led a mutiny and became commander of the brig. Having stolen the ship, she and the crew were now pirates. After *Constance* encountered and captured several British ships, the female commander returned to Marblehead with her prizes. Along with her new husband, William Lovell, and most of her crews, she received a commission as a privateer. Fanny immediately retired to raise her family and left the privateering to William for the rest of the war.[59]

Women onboard merchant ships were not as unusual as female pirates and privateers, and during the nineteenth century it became standard practice for captains to take their wives and families to sea. Many wives learned navigation and were able to chart the ship's course; others were proficient in bookkeeping and served as pursers. Captains' children who had grown up at sea learned these same skills; the sons also mastered shiphandling, and some daughters later became captains themselves.[60]

Most glamorous of the nineteenth-century merchant vessels were the giant clipper ships that raced around Cape Horn to California or China. During the 1850s women briefly commanded two of these. Hannah Burgess of Boston, wife of William, who was captain of the large clipper *Challenger*, went to sea with him in 1855. She was an expert navigator. The following year, when William fell ill and died, she commanded the ship for three weeks until she made port at Valparaiso.[61] That same year another New England wife, Mary Patten, accompanied her husband, Joshua, captain of the clipper *Neptune's Car*. After they sailed from New York, Joshua fell critically ill with brain fever. The first mate was in the brig, so Mary, pregnant and only nineteen years old, took command of *Neptune's Car* and after fifty-two harrowing days, got her around Cape Horn to San Francisco. The ship's owners rewarded Mary's heroism, giving her one thousand dollars for bringing their ship and its cargo to safety.[62]

During these years, whaling vessels prowled the seas searching for the mammals that provided oil for machinery and lamps and whalebone for clothing and household use. These voyages often lasted four or five years, such separations playing havoc with family life. Whaling captains began taking their wives and families to sea, and the ships with women onboard became known as "petticoat whalers." The trend grew rapidly, and by midcentury about 20 percent of whaling captains were bringing their families with them.[63] These families often kept diaries and journals, which have provided abundant information about petticoat whalers.[64] The most famous whaling wife was Mary Brewster, who sailed with her husband, William, in *Tiger* in 1845. She went around Cape Horn and cruised off the California coast, reaching such exotic places as Samoa, the Cook Islands, and the Sandwich (Hawaiian) Islands. In 1849 she was the first American woman in the western Arctic.[65]

On shore, however, the whaling industry was changing. When Nantucket had been the center of whaling, wives left behind demonstrated an independence enabling them to handle business matters and provide for their families. By the 1830s the center had moved to New Bedford, where the change brought a melding of maritime and land affairs into the pattern of industrialization.[66] In this milieu, women had less opportunity to act independently.

## The Civil War, 1861–1865

When the Civil War tragically divided the nation in April 1861, the U.S. Navy had two primary missions: blockading the Southern coasts and controlling the Mississippi River and its tributaries.[67] In carrying out these tasks, Secretary of the Navy Gideon Welles oversaw the expansion of the Union Navy from 90 vessels, 1,300 officers, and 7,600 men in 1861 to 671 vessels, 6,700 officers, and 51,500 men by late 1864. To help administer the growing Navy, the number of naval bureaus increased to eight in 1862.[68]

As war continued, casualties mounted on both sides. By 1865, 618,000—

360,000 Union and 258,000 Confederate troops—had died from battle or disease.[69] Evacuation of the sick and injured by ship, as well as by railroad and wagon, became commonplace. Both on land and on water, women played an increasingly visible and effective role in caring for these casualties.

Anticipating a great need for medical care, Secretary of War Simon Cameron appointed Dorothea L. Dix superintendent of the Army nurses.[70] Dix, a Boston schoolmistress, had worked diligently during the 1840s and 1850s for reforming the treatment of the mentally ill. Dix set strict standards for Army nurses: they must be between thirty-five and fifty years of age, plain looking, and possessed of good morals. Only brown, gray, or black clothing without ornamentation was acceptable. Dix sent about one hundred women volunteers for one month's orientation at Bellevue Hospital in New York; it was their only medical training.[71]

Eventually, Dix appointed 3,214 of the approximately 9,000 nurses in more than two hundred of the Army's permanent and field hospitals.[72] These untrained nurses performed invaluable service caring for the sick and wounded under primitive and grueling conditions. Women volunteered for nursing duty in the South as well, although cultural beliefs about such activity limited their numbers to about 1,000 who served in hospitals. Countless others nursed Confederate casualties in private homes.[73]

Still another woman, Clara Barton, directed nursing as well as independent relief operations, first from Washington, D.C., later in South Carolina. She collected and carried wagon loads of supplies directly to battlefields, nursed and comforted the wounded and dying, fed the hungry, and assisted in medical care and procedures. The philanthropic work of this "Angel of the Battlefield," as Barton became known, would have lasting consequences.[74]

Doctors and military men were bitterly opposed to the presence of these nurses because they did not believe ladies should be tending male patients. Nurses often discovered and exposed gross malfeasance, dishonesty, and incompetence among hospital staff members, who, in turn, determinedly tried to rid the Army of these nuisance women.[75] Military surgeons sometimes met their match when pitted against such a formidable woman as Mary Ann "Mother" Bickerdyke, who traveled from one battle zone to another organizing hospitals, enforcing standards of cleanliness, ministering to patients, and supervising diet kitchens.[76]

Early in the war it became apparent that the Army Medical Department would be inadequate to handle the growing carnage on the battlefields. In helping alleviate the inevitable suffering and death, Northern women expeditiously set up soldiers' aid societies and the Women's Central Association of Relief in New York City. The U.S. Sanitary Commission, established in June 1861, coordinated these relief efforts. Southern women also organized aid societies, but on a local rather than regional basis. Borrowing from British experience in the Crimean War and their subsequent sanitary commission sent to improve army hospitals in Crimea, the U.S. Sanitary Commission initially dispatched physicians to investigate conditions in U.S. Army hospitals and camps. The commission's scope widened, and it became the largest welfare organization of the war. Although men were involved in the commission, most members and leaders were women. The group distributed food, clothing, and medical supplies, raised funds, and served as hospital nurses or aides.[77]

As the fighting moved to the Virginia Peninsula in 1862, the Sanitary Commission converted some idle transport steamboats into floating hospitals for evacuating the wounded. The commission paid the cost of refitting the ships and staffed them with surgeons, dressers (often second-year medical students), male and female nurses, and various servants. Women onboard prepared food, stocked shelves, and made the infirm as comfortable as possible.[78] After evacuating about eight thousand men from the peninsula, the commission's hospital transports carried the sick and wounded along the Atlantic coast throughout the war. The commission also sent supplies and delicacies for the sick to at least twenty-three naval ships and furnished medical supplies for a fleet hospital at Pilot Town near New Orleans.[79] Although the commission had offered its services to the Navy, that arm of the military had no need of their transports in the East. The Navy's ordnance ship *Ben Morgan* served as an emergency hospital off Hampton Roads, Virginia, from February to June 1862. There were no other hospital facilities afloat for the North Atlantic Squadron except ships' sick bays.[80]

In the West a separate organization performed relief services. Established in September 1861 and based in St. Louis, the Western Sanitary Commission assisted armies near the Mississippi River. It set up four large hospitals, started soldiers' homes, fitted out hospital transports, and sent medical supplies to naval gunboats.[81] As in the East, the Western Sanitary Commission chartered steamers for transporting the wounded to shore hospitals. Women served as nurses onboard these ships, and the indomitable Mother Bickerdyke took charge of the *City of Memphis*.[82]

The most effective female nurses in the commission and in the military were the more than six hundred sisters from twelve Roman Catholic religious orders, especially the Sisters of Charity and the Sisters of the Holy Cross. Although they had no formal nursing training, they were accustomed to strict discipline and obedience, so the sisters readily fit into the male-dominated medical and military worlds.[83] On 21 October 1861 Indiana governor Oliver P. Morton appealed to Father Edward Sorin, superior of the Sisters of the Holy Cross, for nuns to serve as military nurses. The next day Mother M. Angela and five others left for the hospital at Cairo, Illinois, and then went to the Army hospital at Mound City, Illinois. Eventually, about eighty members of this order served as nurses in military hospitals.[84]

On 7 April 1862 a federal gunboat captured the 786-ton Confederate side-wheel river steamer *Red Rover* at Island Number Ten on the Mississippi. The Army had her refitted as a hospital ship, and the Western Sanitary Commission furnished thirty-five hundred dollars in medical supplies and provisions. The new floating hospital was the most modern of its kind: it had a 300-ton-capacity ice box, bathrooms, a laundry, an elevator, nine water closets, gauze window blinds, two kitchens, and a "regular [male] corps of nurses." George H. Bixby was the senior surgeon onboard.[85] The *Red Rover* went into service in June, and among her first patients were men wounded in an explosion on the gunboat *Mound City*. Suffering from severe burns and scalding, the injured were taken to the hospital at Mound City.[86] Seeing victims of the *Mound City* disaster, Sister Athanasius, a nurse at the Mound City hospital, volunteered for duty in *Red Rover* and spent the rest of the summer there. Mother Angela offered to provide nurses for the Navy, an offer the Navy later accepted.[87]

In September *Red Rover* arrived at St. Louis for fitting out for the winter, and Sister Athanasius left to take charge of a Washington hospital. The *Red Rover* had been a captured vessel, so the Illinois prize court sold her to the U.S. Navy on 30 September for $9,314. The Navy had its first authentic hospital ship.[88] The next day the western flotilla gunboats under Army control were put under naval command and became the Mississippi Squadron, which now included *Red Rover*.[89]

The *Red Rover* remained at St. Louis for three months, and while being refitted, she took on patients from the overcrowded Mound City hospital. Ordnance steamer *Judge Torrence* also served as a temporary hospital until *Red Rover* was ready. Finally, *Red Rover* was commissioned in the U.S. Navy on 26 December 1862. She carried twelve officers, thirty-five enlisted men, and about thirty people in the medical department.[90]

Among the medical personnel were four nuns from the Sisters of the Holy Cross, the same order that housed Sister Athanasius, the first nurse in *Red Rover*. On Christmas Eve, Sisters Veronica, Adela, and Callista came onboard, and in early February, Sister St. John of the Cross joined them. Five black women—Alice Kennedy, Sarah Kinno, Ellen Campbell, Betsy Young, and Dennis Downs—assisted the nuns. During the course of the war, more than twelve members of this religious order served in *Red Rover*, and Sisters Adela and Veronica remained onboard the entire time.[91]

The *Red Rover* sailed on 29 December 1862 and became a familiar part of the Mississippi Squadron.[92] Always near the flagship and close to the scene of operations, *Red Rover* carried 2,497 patients, both Union and Confederate, to shore hospitals. The Sisters of the Holy Cross alleviated the suffering of the sick and wounded as well as they could. They even prepared delicacies such as herb tea, meat broth, and custard for men too ill for standard rations of cold beans and hardtack.[93] The nuns demonstrated both women's ability to serve during wartime in a naval ship and the advantages of the then fashionable womanly virtues of gentleness and compassion. Unintentional pioneers, these Catholic sisters were, in effect, the forerunners of the Navy Nurse Corps. In gratitude Congress belatedly voted a pension for them in 1892, but only sixty-three were still alive. In 1906 the Grand Army of the Republic awarded the bronze medal to the nineteen surviving sister-nurses.[94]

As war slowed on the Mississippi after the fall of Vicksburg in July 1863, *Red Rover* continued her river trips. She tied up permanently at Mound City in late 1864. Surgeon Bixby and two sisters remained onboard until the ship was decommissioned on 17 November 1865. She was soon sold at public auction for forty-five hundred dollars. The Navy's use of a fully equipped floating hospital at the scene of operations had been a success. Except for sailing ship *Idaho*'s brief stint as a hospital and store ship for the Asiatic Squadron in 1868–69, there would be no other hospital ship until the Spanish-American War.[95]

During the Civil War, nurses and all other medical personnel had more work than they could handle, for casualties included more victims of disease than of gunfire or explosions. The leading causes of death were dysentery, typhoid, malaria, pneumonia, and smallpox. Sweltering heat in the Mississippi area exacerbated any medical condition, and the still primitive state of medical care guaranteed a high mortality rate.[96]

To relieve overcrowding at Army hospitals, the Navy established a temporary hospital in a Memphis hotel and later opened another hospital at New Orleans. But naval hospitals provided rudimentary care at best. One young acting ensign, Robley D. Evans, wounded at Fort Fisher, described the sordid conditions at the Norfolk Naval Hospital. Riddled with vermin, the hospital had no modern equipment or trained nurses. A diet of bacon and cabbage was meant to sustain the patients. Evans fought off the surgeon's attempt to amputate his shattered legs, developed an infection and a fever, and nearly died. After months in the hospital, he recovered sufficiently (in spite of the medical attention) to go home to Philadelphia.[97]

Nurses had played an important role during the Civil War, but other women found different ways to assist the U.S. Navy. On 10 January 1863 the Confederate privateer *Retribution* captured the USS *J. P. Ellicott*, a brig sailing near St. Thomas. The *Retribution* took onboard *Ellicott*'s officers and crew and later deposited them on the island of Dominica.[98] Overlooked was the mate's wife; she was left on *Ellicott* to serve refreshments to *Retribution*'s prize crew. Allegedly, her "refreshments" got the prize crew so drunk that she was able to tie them up below deck. Assuming sole command of *Ellicott*, she navigated the brig into St. Thomas and turned her prisoners and the ship over to naval authorities.[99]

Some women helped Union naval operations as lighthouse keepers. Harriet Colfax, a wartime nurse, also served as keeper of the Michigan City, Indiana, light for many years. Martha Coston, widow of naval scientist Benjamin Franklin Coston, finished developing her husband's flare signaling device and a signal code. She sold her patent to the government when the war started, and the "Coston light" enabled blockading Union ships to signal each other during the night and at long distances.[100]

As in earlier wars, many women disguised themselves as men, serving in both the Union and Confederate armies, and some later received pensions.

Others helped military operations as spies, scouts, saboteurs, messengers, couriers, and blockade runners. Many were cooks, laundresses, and sutlers. Still others worked in munitions plants. A few, such as Mary E. Walker, were licensed doctors. Walker was an assistant surgeon in the Army of the Cumberland and later received the Medal of Honor.[101]

On the home front, women replaced men in factories and in teaching. For the first time, hundreds took government jobs as clerks in the Treasury, Post Office, and War Departments as well as with the Confederate government. In 1863 bread riots in the South and antidraft riots in the North brought thousands of women into the streets. Leaders of the earlier women's rights movement banded into the Women's National Loyal League and gathered four hundred thousand names petitioning Congress to abolish slavery.[102]

All these different means of aiding the war effort, in addition to women's work in the U.S. and Western Sanitary Commissions and in nursing, opened new doors. Women had actively participated in the war, gained leadership experience, and honed their organizational skills.

## 1865–1898

Except for a war scare in 1873, when the Spanish seized the *Virginius*, the international scene was relatively calm. By 1880 the fleet had dropped from about 626 commissioned vessels to 48 outdated ships. Once again sail became important, for two reasons: steam plants in ships continued to work inefficiently and the United States did not have enough coaling stations abroad to sustain the steam engine. The officer corps dwindled and promotions were slow; enlisted men numbered only six thousand, and most were foreigners. Simultaneously, the Medical Department reflected the same stagnation and decline. It did, however, open a naval hospital at Yokohama, Japan, in 1872—the only such American facility in the Far East. Nevertheless, the Navy kept showing the flag around the world, and the United States and Korea signed a trade treaty in 1881. Exploration of uncharted seas continued.[103]

The country would need the Navy as industry and agriculture then undergoing an explosive growth looked abroad for markets. Such foreign trade required a fleet for protection. President James A. Garfield's secretary of the Navy, William H. Hunt, began campaigning in 1881 for a revitalized Navy;

and his successor, William E. Chandler, pursued the modernization goal. Two years later Congress appropriated $1.3 million for the first four ships of a new steel Navy. Two more cruisers came next, followed by the battleships *Texas* and *Maine*.[104]

Fueling the drive for expansion and modernization was the impact of Alfred Thayer Mahan and his book, *The Influence of Sea Power upon History, 1660–1783* (1890). Mahan demonstrated that control of the sea had created mighty empires in the past and called upon the United States to build a powerful battleship fleet and acquire overseas bases. Mahan's theories gained worldwide praise and meshed with the rising tide of imperialism at home. President Benjamin Harrison's secretary of the Navy, Benjamin F. Tracy, adopted the trend, and, at his urging, Congress authorized three more battleships in 1890. The nascent attempt to bring the American Navy on a par with European nations succeeded, and by 1897 the Navy had risen to respectability among the world's fleets. It was an effective fighting force of fifty-four ships, sixty-four auxiliary vessels, and twenty subsidized steamers. Five battleships, sixteen torpedo boats, and one submarine boat were under construction.[105] At the same time, the Navy continued its drive for professionalization. New offices—the Navy Department Library, Naval Intelligence, and Naval War Records—opened in the 1880s. In 1884 the Naval War College introduced its postgraduate program for officers.[106]

The Medical Department, as well, had kept pace with naval expansion, and throughout the century it had strived to professionalize its services. Although it had difficulty attracting and retaining medical officers, it maintained high standards for those entering the service. In 1893 the Naval Laboratory and Department of Instruction established a course required for junior medical officers before they began active duty.[107]

During the 1890s the Medical Department repaired, rehabilitated, and modernized naval hospitals, making them comparable to good civilian hospitals. By 1897 all naval hospitals had new aseptic operating rooms with modern furniture and appliances, bacteriological and chemical laboratories, disinfecting plants, electricity, X-ray machines, and adequate sanitary facilities. Each had an ambulance available.[108]

Aware that the practice of using seamen as nurses was unsatisfactory, the surgeon general had consistently called for a hospital corps, composed of hospital apprentices, apprentices first and second classes, and pharmacists. The U.S. Army and foreign countries and their navies had had such corps for years. Training schools for apprentices would operate at naval hospitals, so there would be an ample supply of trained "nurses" for both hospital and ship duty. The surgeon general recommended that ambulance (hospital) ships be available for all fleet actions.[109]

There was no place in this new Navy for women, but they made inroads as civilians connected with the Navy. By 1869 they worked as laundresses, cooks, and cleaning women at the Naval Asylum in Philadelphia. Before the end of the century, there were women working at the Navy's clothing factory in Brooklyn, New York. Others provided such piecework service as quilting for naval needs at the Washington Navy Yard.[110]

Although the Civil War had provided women access to jobs in government departments, the Navy was slow in hiring female clerks. One reason was that some men believed these working women had acquired the reputation of "brazen hussy" during the war.[111] By 1879, at least one woman, M. M. (Martha M.) Smith of New York, was working as a "writer" in the Hydrographic Office for seventy-five dollars a month.[112] The Navy hired more female writers in the same office; copyists, clerks, then typists in the judge advocate general's office; clerks in seven naval bureaus; and a telegraph operator in the secretary of the Navy's office. The Hydrographic Office employed several women draftsmen, a stenographer, a custodian of archives, an engraver, and even a laborer. After the Navy established the Library and Naval War Records Office in 1882, women readily found jobs there as clerks. A German-born woman became a translator in the Office of Naval Intelligence, and the Navy Pay Office in Philadelphia hired a woman stenographer. Later, the Marine Corps employed a woman clerk. By the end of the nineteenth century, at least thirty-six women worked in a clerical capacity for the naval shore establishment, primarily in Washington.[113]

Navy Department civilian workers represented only a fraction of the women escaping the confines of their domestic life during the last third of the nineteenth century. The women's rights movement, quiescent during the war, split into two organizations in 1869 because of differences in suffrage goals. To pursue their common cause, the two groups reunited in 1890 as the National American Woman Suffrage Association.[114] Another antebellum reform, temperance, resurfaced. Closely linked to suffrage, temperance crusaders became national Woman's Christian Temperance Union (WCTU) members. Organized in 1874 and led by Frances Willard, the WCTU ultimately attracted a broad spectrum of women, who, in addition to closing thousands of saloons, spread their reform efforts into other areas.[115] For example, they established the Young Women's Christian Association (YWCA) in Boston in 1867.[116]

Yet another offshoot of humanitarian reform sprang from Clara Barton's relief work during the Civil War. Barton believed that not only the military should have medical care and supplies, but natural disaster victims should as well. She established the American Association of the Red Cross in 1881, and the organization was reincorporated in 1893 as the American National Red Cross.[117]

Focused on intellectual stimulation rather than specific reform, the women's club movement started in 1868. The idea quickly spread, and women across the country united in clubs for personal enrichment and female fellowship. The General Federation of Women's Clubs, organized in 1892, saw its membership reaching 150,000 by century's end. A similar group, the Association of Collegiate Alumnae, founded in 1882, provided an intellectual community for college-trained women.[118]

In addition to association building, many young, single women joined the white-collar labor force as clerical workers. Introduction of the typewriter in the 1870s guaranteed that routine jobs as typists, stenographers, and telephone operators would fall to lower-paid women. Concurrently, the advent of department stores created a need for retail clerks, and women moved into these positions. By the turn of the century, office and sales clerks jobs were women's work.[119] Factory labor increasingly became the lot of immigrants, who, along with blacks, also filled most of the domestic-servant jobs. For these working-class women, the Knights of Labor sponsored about 270 ladies' locals and another 130 mixed local groups.[120]

As more women worked outside their homes, others acquired higher education. By 1900 about eighty-five thousand women were attending colleges. Trained beyond available professional opportunities, educated women moved into social work, elementary school teaching, and nursing. The nurturing fields had always been women's work, and now these fields were becoming professionalized.[121]

Social work became a profession in 1889, when Jane Addams and Ellen Gates Starr launched the settlement house movement by establishing Hull House in Chicago. The concept spread, and by 1900 there were about one hundred such houses across the nation. Similarly, as public schools mushroomed after the Civil War, demand for elementary schoolteachers grew apace. States opened separate teacher training schools for whites and blacks, and women filled a customary role of instructing the young.[122]

There was one woman, however, who argued against societal restrictions. Charlotte Perkins Gilman, in her 1898 book *Women and Economics*, maintained that women should be economically independent rather than in bondage to men. In thought and writings, she presaged twentieth-century feminism, declaring that young boys and girls should not be locked into the stereotyped sex roles of the dominant breadwinner male and the subordinate domestic-servant female.[123]

Still another field that became professionalized during this era was nursing. The Civil War had revealed the advantages of females as nurses in the military and in the sanitary commissions, and even physicians, who had been skeptical of women's value, soon advocated professional training. In 1868, physician Samuel D. Gross, president of the American Medical Association, called for training institutions in all major towns and cities. Three years later *Godey's Lady's Book*, a widely read magazine, popularized the idea of "lady nurses."[124]

Several training schools had already begun. In 1857 physicians Elizabeth Blackwell and Marie E. Zakrzewska started training a few nurses for six months at their New York Infirmary for Women and Children. Four years later the Women's Hospital of Philadelphia, run by two women physicians, Ann Preston and Emmelin Horton Cleveland, instigated a six-month practical training course for nurses. In 1863 the New England Hospital for Women and Children, founded by Dr. Zakrzewska, offered a similar program.[125]

After the New England Hospital for Women and Children got a new building in 1872, it launched the country's first general training school for nurses. Female physicians gave weekly lectures on medical or surgical subjects, and students received practical training in medical, surgical, obstetrical, and night nursing under the supervision of other nurses. After a year's study, one of the five students, thirty-two-year-old Linda Richards, earned a diploma, becoming the first trained nurse in the United States. The first black nurse to graduate was Mary Eliza Mahoney, who finished the course in 1879. The hospital expanded its program to two years in 1893 and to three years in 1901.[126]

Three other training schools, established in 1873, had two-year programs and were patterned after Florence Nightingale's work at St. Thomas's Hospital in London, with the superintendent being a nurse. One training school opened at Bellevue Hospital in New York, which began a class with five students under the direction of Sister Helen of All Saints Sisterhood. Next came the Connecticut Training School at the New Haven Hospital, where four aspiring nurses were under the charge of a Miss Bayard. Soon the Boston Training School at Massachusetts General Hospital operated a similar program, with four students under the superintendent, Mrs. Billings. Not surprisingly, many of the early pioneers in establishing professional training programs for nurses had themselves been nurses with the Army or had worked in the U.S. Sanitary Commission during the Civil War. Trained nurses quickly proved their worth in hospitals, and the idea of nursing schools grew. By 1880, fifteen schools instructed 323 students and had 157 graduates.[127] A few males entered the nursing field, and in 1888 Bellevue Hospital in New York City opened the Mills Training School for Men. Fifteen entered the first class; four graduated. The next year forty-four men began the training, and eighteen graduated.[128]

By the turn of the century, the general hospital movement had brought a proliferation of facilities, and the public's concept of hospitals had changed. No longer places of inevitable death, hospitals were havens of healing. More patients created a demand for more nurses, and by 1900 there were 432 hospital training schools with more than 11,000 students. Most training courses had increased to three years. Not only hospitals ran schools, but so, too, did Catholic religious orders. Separate schools, beginning with the Spelman Seminary in Atlanta, trained black nurses. The first university training class for nurses began in 1899 with a course called "hospital economics" at the Teachers' College, Columbia University.[129]

As nursing became a recognized profession, educators clamored for uniform standards of instruction. In 1893 Isabel Hampton Robb took the lead in establishing the American Society of Superintendents of Training Schools for Nurses to set up universal training criteria.[130] Three years later Robb founded the Associated Alumnae of the United States and Canada for all trained nurses. In 1900 Robb, along with other nursing professionals, launched the *American Journal of Nursing*, a periodical for and by nurses.[131]

At the same time these organizational steps occurred, two other trained nurses, Lillian D. Wald and Mary Brewster, took the settlement house philosophy to New York City's Lower East Side. They opened the Henry Street Settlement, providing nursing care and advice either at the settlement house or in the homes of the immigrant poor. In effect, they began public health nursing.[132]

By the end of the nineteenth century, trained professional nurses had earned the respect and acceptance of doctors, hospitals, and the general public. They had broken out of the restrictive cult of domesticity by going to training schools and working outside their homes, but their duties of healing, nurturing, and caring for the infirm reflected the prevailing social norms for women. Nursing was women's work.

## The Spanish-American War, 1898

The United States would soon need some of these trained nurses as the nation raced toward war with Spain in 1898. Influenced by European colonialism, the country embraced the lure of foreign markets, the cult of Anglo-Saxon superiority, a sense of national mission, big-Navy enthusiasm, and jingoism. The United States soon liberated Cubans, Filipinos, and Puerto Ricans from oppressive Spanish rule and, in turn, relieved Spain of her overseas possessions.[133]

It took little to generate war fever. In February 1898 an indiscreet letter written by Spanish minister Dupuy de Lome described President William McKinley as "weak"; the letter fell into the hands of the press. A few days later, on the fifteenth, the battleship *Maine* exploded in Havana Harbor with the loss of 266 men. A subsequent investigation and failed negotiations with Spain fanned American anger. Amid cries of "Remember the *Maine!*"

Congress declared war on 21 April, and the next day a naval force blockaded Cuba.[134] The Navy's performance during the hostilities would be decisive.

On a second front the Navy dispatched Commo. George Dewey with the Asiatic Squadron to Manila Bay in the Philippine Islands. Dewey reduced the dilapidated defending Spanish squadron to scrap without delay. His ships remained in Manila Bay until U.S. Army troops arrived, captured Manila on 13 August, and occupied the Philippines.[135] Meanwhile, Rear Adm. William T. Sampson led a squadron to Cuba's Santiago Harbor and on 3 July annihilated another major squadron of the Spanish fleet. About sixteen thousand Army troops, carried in naval transports, had landed on Cuba's southeastern coast. These forces sustained heavy casualties at El Caney and San Juan Hill but finally captured Santiago on 14 July. Other troops took Puerto Rico, and the most popular of all American wars ended on 12 August 1898.[136]

In December the peace treaty gave Cubans their independence and ceded Puerto Rico, Guam, and the Philippines to the United States for $20 million. That same year, the country annexed the Hawaiian Islands, Samoa, and Wake Island. The "splendid little war," as Secretary of State John Hay called it, produced an empire for the United States, an empire with overseas possessions and colonies, subjects, and protectorates.[137]

But the price of liberating or acquiring these possessions had been high in human terms. When the Spanish-American War began, the Army increased from 28,000 to about 200,000 troops. Lacking medical facilities and personnel to care for this large influx, the War Department accepted the offer of the National Society of the Daughters of the American Revolution (DAR) to screen potential military nurses. Physician Anita Newcomb McGee directed this examining process. Unlike the Civil War nurses, Army nurses had to be training school graduates, and eventually the service utilized 1,563 contract nurses, paying each thirty dollars a month and subsistence.[138] Other contract nurses came into Army service through the American National Red Cross, which kept a nationwide list of trained nurses. Clara Barton had offered the agency's services to the armed forces when the war began, and about 700 Red Cross nurses helped in Army hospitals.[139]

These nurses served in the United States, Cuba, Puerto Rico, Hawaii, and the Philippines, and on three ships, including hospital ship *Relief.* The Army had acquired *Relief,* a passenger liner, and used the vessel to evacuate casualties from Cuba. Six trained nurses, including Esther V. Hasson, who would later be Navy Nurse Corps superintendent, cared for 1,485 sick and wounded men aboard *Relief.*[140] These infirm were only a fraction of the Army's casualties: 968 deaths from battle, 5,438 from disease. Ravaged by typhoid, malaria, yellow fever, and dysentery, fully 30 percent of American troops were sick by August 1898.[141]

The Navy as well had its share of casualties. Adding 128 ships and raising the complement of officers and men to 26,102 increased the chances for injury and disease. During the war the Navy sustained 85 deaths: 29 from wounds or injuries, 56 from illness. Fourteen Marines succumbed to an outbreak of yellow fever at Key West, but the naval services did not suffer the severe epidemics that had decimated the Army.[142] To help care for the expanded naval force, the Medical Department took on sixty-one volunteer assistant surgeons. One of these, John Blair Gibbs, was killed at Guantanamo, the only naval medical officer to die in the war.[143]

The sick and wounded required nursing attention as well as physicians' services, and the Navy finally got its Hospital Corps in June 1898. Designed to provide a trained cadre of men willing to make a career in the naval service, the Hospital Corps soon sent "trained" male nurses and apprentices to all naval hospitals.[144] Their training lasted only several months and was not comparable to the two to three years women spent in civilian hospital training schools. The network of naval hospitals now included facilities at Portsmouth, New Hampshire; Chelsea; Brooklyn; Philadelphia; Washington; Norfolk; Pensacola; Mare Island; Yokohama, Japan; Newport; and Sitka, Alaska.[145]

Although the Hospital Corps provided "nurses," the Navy still needed professionally trained graduate nurses. Unlike the Army, however, the Navy had no authority to hire contract nurses and so turned to volunteers. Four female students from Johns Hopkins Medical School served as nurses at the naval hospital in Brooklyn. Six women from the DAR register of trained nurses volunteered for duty at Norfolk Naval Hospital and were there for an average of fifty days. Five Sisters of Charity from St. Vincent's Hospital in Norfolk joined in the work. The Navy gave them lodging, board, and transportation, but their pay came from private funds. Later, Surgeon General William K. Van Reypen described the nurses' performance as thorough and conscientious.[146] When the hospital at Portsmouth, New Hampshire, added two new pavilions for housing Spanish prisoners, the Red Cross provided one hundred cots and six trained nurses.[147] These twenty-one women were the first to serve as trained nurses in U.S. Navy hospitals.

The Bureau of Medicine and Surgery had long advocated a hospital ship to accompany fleets engaged in action, and on 7 April 1898 the Navy bought *Creole*, a new steamer operated by Cromwell Lines. Converted to the ambulance (hospital) ship *Solace* and equipped with the most modern medical supplies and conveniences, the vessel could carry two hundred patients and had four surgeons, three hospital stewards, and eight male nurses in her medical department. Throughout the summer she collected the sick and wounded from Cuban operations and transported them to military and naval hospitals in the United States. Among the patients were forty-eight Spanish naval officers and men who were taken to Norfolk Naval Hospital. On her return trips to the Caribbean, *Solace* took medical stores and supplies, as well as assorted "delicacies and comforts" donated by private individuals and societies, to the ships on station there. The *Solace* was the first American ship to meet the Geneva Convention requirements and the first to fly the Geneva cross flag.[148]

By the end of the nineteenth century, the U.S. Navy had developed into a world-class naval power with fleets to sail and colonies to administer. The Navy's evolution had been uneven and sporadic, and growth had depended on external threats or, by the 1890s, on markets to open, colonies to supervise, and primitive people to uplift. Concurrently, training and requirements for officers and men had become professionalized.

As the Navy developed, so, too, did its Medical Department. Beginning with only a few surgeons assigned to ships' sick bays, the department grew into a complex, modern health-care service with a string of well-equipped hospitals and dispensaries staffed by competent doctors. Naval medicine had kept pace with the trends in civilian medicine and employed such innovations as anesthesia, antiseptic surgery, and bacteriology. It had established the Hospital Corps to provide meagerly instructed "nurses" for hospitals and ships.

But the Medical Department still lacked a vital element: professionally trained nurses—those women who had taken two- or three-year courses in hospital training schools. Nursing, along with teaching and social work, was one of the few professions open to women. During the nineteenth century, many women emerged from their prescribed sphere and went into reform movements, clubs and associations, and higher education. And they were no strangers to the seafaring life; they had been in virtually all types of vessels, both private and naval. The Navy needed professional nurses, and such women had proven their worth during the Spanish-American War. Could the two, in fact, be mutually beneficial?

# 2

# The Navy Nurse Corps, 1900–1915

*After its Spanish-American War victory*, the United States became a full-fledged colonial power, and the exuberant nation began its experiment in imperialism. The U.S. Navy played a major part in managing the new empire, and the Navy, in turn, grew in ships and personnel. The enlarged fleet called for expanded medical care and facilities, and adhering to the most modern medical practices, the Bureau of Medicine and Surgery successfully advocated establishing a group of trained female nurses as a permanent part of naval medicine. Soon after Congress authorized the Navy Nurse Corps in 1908, these first naval women began using their healing arts in both the United States and overseas.

## The Setting

When Theodore Roosevelt became President after William McKinley's assassination in 1901, he reflected the Progressive era values and agendas that transformed American society. Order and bureaucratic efficiency were cornerstones of Roosevelt's jubilant tenure in the White House. Reform was everywhere—in politics, business, industry, labor, social humanitarianism, and women's rights.[1]

More and more women entered the world outside the home during these years. Building on foundations laid in the late nineteenth century, a new generation of women sought to escape the Victorian cult of domesticity. More women attended colleges and universities, and some even earned advanced degrees. Between 1900 and 1910, the number of females in colleges grew from 85,000 to 140,000, and the majority attended coeducational institutions.[2]

If educated women chose roles other than wife and mother, they remained within their "sphere" as elementary schoolteachers, nurses, or social workers. Few were able to break the barriers into male-dominated professions. In 1900 there were 5,319,400 women (21 percent) in the work force. The majority were poor, single, and either blacks or immigrants. Most were domestic servants, factory workers, and farm laborers. Ten years later, fully 25 percent of adult women worked outside the home.[3]

College-educated women took learning seriously as it applied to their homes and families. "Educated motherhood" became the prevailing middle-class ideology of the Progressive years. Children's best interests dominated, and women needed to be educated and trained for the important maternal role. Such thinking spilled over into social reforms, and mandatory public school education, kindergartens, and health clinics proliferated. Women activists worked for laws regulating child labor and women's wages and hours.[4] The establishment of the Federal Children's Bureau in 1912, headed by social worker and reformer Julia Lathrop, represented a giant stride in protective action by the government on behalf of children.[5]

Settlement houses, modeled after Jane Addams's Hull House, spanned the nation. Increasing from about one hundred in 1900 to more than four hundred a decade later, these havens for poor urban women were training grounds for college-educated female activists who also led fights for other reforms.[6] One agent of such reform, composed of an alliance of working-class and college-educated women, was the Women's Trade Union League, founded in 1903. Campaigns for better working conditions culminated in thirty thousand women going on strike in New York in 1909. There were about four hundred thousand women in various unions.[7]

Taking part in the labor agitation were numerous women's clubs, whose memberships continued to climb during the Progressive era. Although there were hundreds of local women's clubs, the largest national organization was the General Federation of Women's Clubs, which expanded from 150,000 members in 1900 to 1 million by 1920. Other groups with nineteenth-century roots also thrived: the WCTU had about 800,000 members; the YWCA, about half a million.[8]

All these organized groups of women joined in the greatest reform movement of the era: women's suffrage. After the merger of suffragists into the National American Woman Suffrage Association (NAWSA) in 1890, longtime feminists Elizabeth Cady Stanton and Susan B. Anthony led the group into the early twentieth century. Younger suffragists watched with keen interest as their British counterparts agitated for voting rights with marches, parades, meetings, riots, and arson. In 1900 Carrie Chapman Catt became president of the American NAWSA, giving the movement new vitality during her four-year tenure.[9] To further their cause, suffragists took up campaigning on state and national levels, and by 1914, five more states had given women the right to vote.[10]

During these Progressive years, the United States also had a duty to carry its brand of democracy to its far-flung empire and impress other nations with American power and prestige. The Navy could implement the new imperialism, and Roosevelt was its firmest supporter.[11] Heavily influenced by Rear Adm. Alfred Thayer Mahan and by a generation of highly vocal naval officers, Roosevelt pushed construction of a battleship fleet. In 1900 the United States had an active force of 292 ships, including 18 battleships. Fifteen years later there were 324 commissioned ships; 33 were battleships. The destroyer was the new ship of choice, and its numbers rose from 18 in 1900 to 53 in 1915.[12] Roosevelt's 1902 division of American naval strength into the Atlantic and Pacific Fleets touched off a series of flamboyant displays of American sea power in large-scale maneuvers and international celebrations. The most lavish of these extravaganzas was the fourteen-month, around-the-world voyage of the Great White Fleet in 1907–9.[13]

Manning these new technically advanced vessels required a marked shift in recruiting procedures. It was no longer sufficient for recruiters or ship captains to pick up hands in East Coast ports. Rather, the Navy concentrated on the Midwest, hoping to attract educated, "wholesome" American men and boys. The number of foreigners decreased; blacks were segregated onboard ship and assigned to engine rooms and messmen branches. As the composition of the enlisted force changed, the Navy improved pay scales, benefits, and service life and established training stations at Newport, Rhode Island; Great Lakes, Illinois; San Francisco; and Norfolk. These efforts helped recruit and retain a well-trained enlisted force whose numbers grew from 13,750 to 52,974 between 1900 and 1915. Similarly, the number of officers increased from 882 to 1,865.[14]

Looking for an efficient way to administer its burgeoning fleet and personnel, the Navy in 1900 created the General Board, headed by Spanish-American War hero Adm. George Dewey. The board advised the secretary of the Navy about war plans and fleet deployment, but the eight naval bureaus retained their customary powers. It was not until 1915 that Congress established the office of chief of naval operations for strategic planning and wartime readiness. Rear Adm. (later Adm.) William S. Benson was the first to fill the post. Such consolidation of authority and management seemed a progressive step toward increased administrative efficiency.[15]

Among the spoils of the Spanish-American War and annexation in the Pacific that required a sustained naval presence were the Philippines, Guam, Hawaii, and Samoa. After the Army had suppressed an independence movement in the Philippines, the Navy established a base at Cavite for coaling and for bringing in Army reinforcements. Guam, essential as a coaling station and naval base between San Francisco and Manila, came under naval administration and government in January 1899. Similarly, the United States acquired Tutuila, Annuu, and the Manua Islands, as well as the magnificent Pago Pago Harbor at Tutuila, through a treaty with Great Britain and Germany in 1899. The next year the Navy assumed control of these islands, which became Naval Station, Tutuila. The Hawaiian Islands, annexed in 1898, became an important way station and a large naval base.[16]

All these stars in the American imperial crown called for more naval personnel on ships and in shore facilities, and the need for the Bureau of Medicine and Surgery to set up hospitals or dispensaries in all of them. The early twentieth century saw triumphs in the medical field: control of yellow fever, typhoid, and malaria; isolation of infectious diseases such as tuberculosis; and increased emphasis on hygiene and sanitation. The Navy wanted its entering physicians and seasoned surgeons to keep abreast of modern medical trends, so in 1902 the U.S. Naval Medical School opened on Observatory Hill in Washington, D.C. Students went through a five-month program covering military medicine, surgery, hygiene, and their duties on land and sea. The school developed into a national center for tropical disease as the Navy pioneered in this important field. A new naval hospital, opened in 1906, became part of this medical complex.[17]

Nursing was another arm of naval medical care, and the "nurses" of the Hospital Corps, who had trained at naval hospitals since the corps was established in 1898, began attending the new centralized Hospital Corps Training School at Norfolk Hospital in 1902. After a three- to four-month training period, these "nurses" served in hospitals and ships. The training school moved to Washington in 1907, operating there for four years.[18]

Naval training of hospital corpsmen was, however, inferior to the education and practical training available in civilian life. Hospitals continued to train most nurses, and these were women. In 1900 there were 432 hospital training schools with more than 11,000 students; ten years later there were 1,129 such schools with 32,636 students. Most schools required that students have only two years of high school, so in 1901 Johns Hopkins University started a six-month preparatory course in basic sciences and nursing principles. The trend spread during the next decade as about eighty-six schools offered preparatory classes. Another advance in education occurred in 1909, when the University of Minnesota established its School of Nursing as a part of the university. Seven years later the first five-year degree program began at Teachers' College, Columbia, in conjunction with Presbyterian Hospital.[19]

With such disparate training, some type of standardization and licensure became essential. In 1903 four states passed laws requiring examinations and licensing. During the next twenty years, the remainder of the states, Hawaii, and the District of Columbia enacted similar legislation.[20] Standardization and regulation of nursing fit into the progressive pattern of upgrading professions to meet established criteria and were part of a broader reform of all medical education.[21]

Nurses became better organized during the Progressive era, and collectively they pressed for higher standards and reforms. Several groups were founded in the late nineteenth century, and two changed their names. The Nurses Associated Alumnae of the United States and Canada became the American Nurses Association (ANA) in 1911, and the following year the National League of Nursing Education replaced the American Society of Superintendents of Training Schools. Other societies—the National Association of Colored Graduate Nurses (1908) and the National Organization for Public Health Nurses (1912)—joined the organizational trend. To keep nurses advised about the profession in other countries, the International Council of Nurses first met in 1901.[22]

During these years, graduate nurses had three options for employment: hospitals, private duty, and visiting nursing. Long hours and hard work characterized the routine of the hospital nurse, who put in thirteen-hour days with little time off. Private-duty nurses were on call twenty-four hours a day in patients' homes, performing housekeeping as well as nursing services. Visiting nursing was introduced in the 1890s, when Lillian Wald and Mary Brewster began making calls in the tenements of Lower East Side New York. By 1910 there were about twenty-five hundred such nurses, who became known as public health, rather than visiting, nurses.[23]

Development and reform of nursing coincided with the early-twentieth-century women's movement, and many nurses participated in both. Some actively campaigned for suffrage and took part in parades and marches; others were even arrested for picketing in front of the White House. Radical feminist Lavinia L. Dock, the most visible and energetic of the nursing leaders, tried to convince her colleagues to support the suffrage movement. In 1907 she urged the Nurses Associated Alumnae to work for the ballot, but the next year the organization voted down such a resolution. It was not until 1915 that the group, now called the American Nurses Association, backed a constitutional amendment enfranchising women. In addition to Dock, other notables of the nursing profession—M. Adelaide Nutting, Annie W. Goodrich, and Isabel M. Stewart—worked diligently to secure women's voting rights.[24]

## Establishing the Corps, 1902–1908

Women nurses had proved their usefulness to the U.S. Army during the Spanish-American War, when 1,563 had served as contract nurses. The next year, nursing leaders, influential socialites, and congressional wives united to agitate for a permanent corps of female nurses, but Congress failed to approve such a radical measure. It did, however, authorize civilian nurses for use in Army hospitals. At the same time, the Navy's Bureau of Medicine and Surgery asked for a similar bill, approving twenty temporary nurses in its hospitals to care for special cases such as typhoid or pneumonia, but the measure went no further.[25]

In 1901 a general reorganization of the Army included provisions for the

Nurse Corps (Female) as a part of the Medical Department. The corps was to have a superintendent—a graduate of a hospital training school with at least a two-year course—and as many chief nurses, nurses, and reserve nurses as needed. All nurses had to be graduates of hospital training schools and pass the corps's professional, moral, mental, and physical examinations. The salary of the superintendent was eighteen hundred dollars a year; of nurses serving in the United States, forty dollars a month; and of those overseas, fifty dollars. Chief nurses could get an extra twenty-five dollars a month at the discretion of the secretary of war. Nurses would draw quarters and subsistence allowances, transportation expenses, medical care, and thirty days' paid leave a year. Dita H. Kinney, onetime head nurse of the Army hospital at Fort Bayard, New Mexico, became the first superintendent of the Nurse Corps (Female).[26] The Army's success in attaining a permanent corps of professionally trained graduate nurses set a precedent for the Navy's sustained efforts toward the same goal.

When Presley Marion Rixey became surgeon general in 1902, one of his immediate objectives was to establish a naval nurse corps, and he was the driving force in pressing for necessary congressional action. Rixey had entered the Navy as an assistant surgeon in 1874 and served afloat and ashore for twenty-five years while he advanced to surgeon. He became a medical inspector with the rank of commander in 1900, simultaneously directing the Naval Dispensary in Washington and acting as White House physician. Upon President McKinley's death in 1901, President Roosevelt asked Rixey to continue providing medical care for the first family. The Roosevelts and the Rixeys became close personal friends as well. In 1902, the president appointed Rixey as surgeon general, conferring on him the rank of rear admiral. During his eight-year tenure, Rixey kept up a whirlwind of activities. He increased the size of the Medical Corps, upgraded naval hospitals and built new ones, improved sanitary conditions at Navy yards and stations, installed modern sick bays in ships, and established the Naval Medical School in Washington and the Hospital Corps training school in Norfolk. Rixey had long advocated hospital ships, and in 1908 the *Relief*, acquired from the Army in 1902 and recommissioned, traveled with the Great White Fleet. The next year *Solace* joined the Atlantic Fleet. Although Rixey was an energetic and successful surgeon general, he failed to accomplish one of his major goals, a dental corps, which finally was established in 1912.[27]

Rixey consistently entreated Congress to authorize a female nurse corps. In 1902, Medical Inspector J. C. Boyd had drawn up an organizational plan for such a unit. Year after year Rixey argued that women would provide greater efficiency in naval hospitals and were inherently superior to male nurses. These graduate nurses could also instruct hospital corpsmen in nursing skills. In wartime, women could assume all nursing duties at naval hospitals, thereby releasing hospital corpsmen for duty afloat, and women could also serve in hospital ships. After all, the Army Nurse Corps (Female) had already demonstrated the value of trained women nurses. In 1907 Rixey strengthened his argument by citing the success of New York's Bellevue Hospital and its five allied hospitals in putting all nursing, even of insane and alcoholic patients, under women's supervision. In frustration and exasperation, Rixey concluded that it was "impossible to find adequate reason for the difficulty experienced in obtaining favorable congressional consideration of such a meritorious measure of relief."[28] As a stopgap measure, Rixey permitted naval hospitals to employ trained male and female civilian nurses temporarily, when "absolutely necessary" for special cases.[29]

There had been sustained opposition to a naval nurse corps, and although Congress considered bills for five years, it had taken no action. The strongest resistance came from within the Navy itself. Many older senior medical officers had never worked with women nurses as their civilian counterparts had done, and some had even entered the Navy to escape women patients and nurses (and possibly their wives). They could only envision with horror "petticoat government" in naval hospitals. Women were unwelcome in the man's world of the Navy. More opposition sprang from the other end of the naval medical hierarchy, the Hospital Corps, whose members feared that female nurses would usurp the best hospital assignments and leave the dirty work to male corpsmen. Women could also displace the men who went to sea by relegating them to lesser positions upon their return to shore duty. The underlying reason was, apparently, that hospital corpsmen did not want to be bossed by women nurses, and many predicted the demise of the corps should women enter naval service.[30] Exacerbating the conflict was higher visibility of women as a whole, especially the suffragists, whose ranks included many nurses, during the early years of the twentieth century. The Navy was no place for strident females.

After Rixey's impassioned plea in his report to Congress in 1907, that body once again considered a bill to establish a corps of trained women nurses for the Navy. Rixey had written to Secretary of the Navy Victor H. Metcalf on 29 February 1908, listing the compelling reasons for immediate action. There was a shortage of about 250 male nurses in the Hospital Corps, he noted, and as a result, needless suffering had occurred among the sick and injured. Rixey also believed that many deaths had occurred for lack of adequate nursing care. Metcalf sent Rixey's letter to George E. Foss, chairman of the House Committee on Naval Affairs, and added his own strong recommendation for the legislation. That committee amended the bill and reported favorably on it. The House and subsequently the Senate approved the measure. On 13 May 1908 the Navy Nurse Corps became reality.[31]

Mirroring the Army Nurse Corps (Female), the Navy Nurse Corps (Female) consisted of a superintendent and as many chief nurses, nurses, and Reserve nurses as necessary; all served at the pleasure of the surgeon general.Navy nurses had to have graduated from a hospital training school with at least a two-year program and qualified professionally, morally, mentally, and physically for the Navy, where they would serve in naval hospitals, on hospital and ambulance ships, and in special duties designated by the surgeon general. Nurses received the same pay and allowances as their counterparts in the Army Nurse Corps: eighteen hundred dollars a year for the superintendent, forty dollars a month for nurses, with up to an extra twenty-five dollars a month for chief nurses and ten dollars more a month for those in hospital ships or overseas. Benefits also included quarters and subsistence allowances.[32] The Navy finally had the missing component in its comprehensive plan to establish parity with Army and civilian medical standards and practices. Rixey expressed his gratitude. The Medical Department, he declared, could now operate more efficiently and improve its patients' comfort and welfare.[33] Interestingly, neither the Army nor the Navy Nurse Corps placed any age or marital restrictions on nurses. These would come later. Both services had taken important steps in professionalizing their nursing standards by employing only graduate nurses, in contrast to civilian hospitals, where students did most of the nursing work.

## The Formative Years

Long before Congress established the Navy Nurse Corps (Female), one woman applied for the superintendent's position. Julia E. Woods, an Army nurse since 1898, wrote to Rixey in January 1903, providing several letters of recommendation. Later, in July 1908, Laura A. C. Hughes, a Boston physician, also a graduate nurse, wrote directly to President Roosevelt, asking for the superintendent's job. "No one," Hughes wrote, was better qualified than she.[34]

The surgeon general, however, thought he had found a woman with even better qualifications—qualifications that combined nursing training and experience with military service. She was Esther Voorhees Hasson, a forty-one-year-old who had graduated from the Connecticut Training School for nurses in 1897. She had been an Army contract nurse, serving in the hospital ship *Relief*, during the Spanish-American War, and after the war she had served as chief nurse at the Brigade Hospital, Vigan, Philippine Islands. She received an honorable discharge from the Army in August 1901, after more than three years of service. Anticipating favorable congressional action on a Navy Nurse Corps bill in 1903, she, too, applied for the superintendent's job. When the measure failed, she went to the Isthmus of Panama in 1905 for duty in hospitals there and stayed a year and a half.[35] When the Nurse Corps (Female) was established, Hasson again applied for the superintendent's position. On 3 August 1908, a three-member board examined her knowledge of nursing, therapeutics, first aid, materia medica, and general information. She also wrote an essay on military nursing and on the administration of the Navy Nurse Corps. Notified of her successful candidacy on 17 August, she was sworn in as superintendent the next day.[36]

Hasson's administrative duties as the first head of the Nurse Corps were far-reaching. Under the surgeon general's direction, she devised and conducted a course of instruction for all entering nurses. Responsible not only for keeping office records and correspondence, as a member of examining boards for entrance and promotion she also maintained individual records and card files on each nurse's credentials. In the field, she inspected and reported on conditions at stations where nurses served and supervised the nurses' houses in Washington, D.C. She handled complaints and reports of misconduct, illness, or incompetence.[37]

The next step in establishing the Nurse Corps was recruiting qualified nurses. Aware that this first group of women would set the precedent for efficiency and high standards, the surgeon general moved cautiously. In August he sent a circular letter to thirty-three candidates, hoping to have at least twenty nurses in the corps by 1 October. Interested applicants had to provide the name of their training school, information on any postgraduate or special training, and evidence of state registration. Before final acceptance, the candidates came to Washington in September for a personal interviews and a practical examination much like those administered by training schools.[38] Hasson even emphasized intangible requirements: executive ability, cheerful disposition, quiet dignity, self-control, and the ability to get along with others.[39] A nurse's image was important.

Between 17 September and 3 November, the Bureau of Medicine and Surgery carefully selected nineteen additional nurses who, along with Superintendent Hasson, became known as the "Sacred Twenty." These women averaged thirty-four years of age, had graduated from nineteen nursing schools, and represented a broad spectrum of training and experience. Most were from the East Coast, although two came from the Midwest and one from California. Seven had been Army nurses, and three had been superintendents or heads of nursing in civilian hospitals. This group provided Nurse Corps leadership for the next twenty-five years: three were superintendents—Hasson, followed by Lenah S. Higbee and J. Beatrice Bowman—and twelve were chief nurses.[40] The Nurse Corps slowly added new members, and by the end of 1909 there were forty-four. In 1910 there were seventy-two.[41]

Upon reporting for duty, the new nurses immediately went to the naval hospital in Washington for at least three months' indoctrination and training in naval medicine. This period of familiarization with the requirements of naval service also gave the superintendent a chance to judge each nurse's capabilities and fitness and to rid the corps of unsuitable women.[42] After the brief course, the nurses were assigned to naval hospitals at Washington, New York, Norfolk, and Annapolis for duty under a chief nurse's supervision.[43] Medical officers soon requested large increases in the nurses' complement at these hospitals.[44] Hasson kept in close, albeit unofficial, contact with her nurses. Her letter book is filled with friendly, supportive, and chatty correspondence with many nurses.[45] Although nurses proved their value, old attitudes and ways lingered. One physician was anxious to retire because there were "too many . . . women nurses" in the Medical School Hospital to make it a pleasant berth anymore.[46]

Rules were strict. Nurses were required to sign up for three years but could be discharged at any time if their services were not needed, if they became disabled, or if they were guilty of misconduct. Chief nurses, selected from within the corps rather than hired from the outside, had heavy responsibilities. In addition to executing orders from the commanding officer, they had to maintain order and discipline among their subordinates, oversee their living quarters, keep a register and daybook of nurses' services, and submit quarterly efficiency reports for them. An important part of the chief nurse's job was supervising and instructing her hospital's corpsmen. All nurses, as well as other medical personnel, were forbidden to accept presents from patients or their friends and relatives for nursing services. Apart from these official regulations, nurses were expected to meet the superintendent's high standard for keeping the Nurse Corps respectable: there would be no fraternization between nurses and enlisted corpsmen or patients.[47] Hasson wanted her nurses to avoid indiscriminate associations with enlisted men, which had caused "the Army nurses to be given such low social status." She was determined that the Navy Nurse Corps would be "a dignified, respected body of women."[48] If the regulations seemed overly restrictive, they were no more so than those enforced by civilian hospitals and training schools of the time.

Offsetting these tough requirements were excellent benefits for Navy nurses, especially the eight-hour day, which contrasted to the standard thirteen hours in civilian hospitals. Moving into the forefront of protective federal and state legislation regulating women's working hours, the Navy immediately limited the workday to eight hours and night duty to one month in three. Nurses were eligible for thirty days' paid leave a year.[49] The government provided housing and subsistence for nurses, but when naval facilities were not available, it paid each nurse fifteen dollars a month as her share of a communal house and twenty-two dollars a month for subsistence. When new nurses first entered the Navy, they lived in one of the two houses that Hasson had arranged for the Navy to lease on Twenty-first Street until nurses' quarters were completed at the Naval Hospital in September 1910.[50]

Despite these benefits, recruiting slowed in 1910. "It grows harder and harder to secure desirable women for the service," wrote Hasson, who hoped a recent pay raise would entice more nurses to the Navy.[51] In March 1910 Congress had raised Army Nurse Corps salaries. Because Navy nurses received the same pay and allowances as Army nurses, their pay rose to fifty dollars a month for the first three years' service, fifty-five dollars for the second three years, sixty dollars for the third three years, and sixty-five dollars after nine years' service. They received an extra ten dollars a month for duty outside the United States, and chief nurses received an additional thirty dollars a month. The superintendent's salary stayed at eighteen hundred dollars a year.[52] Nurse Corps salaries then remained constant until World War I.

Hasson had still another idea to make it easier for qualified nurses to apply for the corps. Women had to pay their own expenses when traveling to Washington for the entrance examinations, and this expense was a hardship for many, especially if they traveled great distances. Hasson suggested, and the surgeon general approved, dispensing with the examination, instead requiring an essay from applicants. Nurses could subsequently take the written mental examination in the presence of a medical officer nearest her residence.[53]

Although there was no regulation Nurse Corps uniform when the corps was established, Hasson designed an outfit, which the surgeon general approved. Made of heavy white drill, or lawn cloth for summer, the uniforms had nine-gore skirts. Buttons were concealed in the front of tailored shirtwaists, and long sleeves with two-and-a-half-inch starched cuffs, clerical collars, and pockets measuring four by four and a half inches completed the waists. Initially, a Geneva Red Cross adorned the left sleeve, but the surgeon general discontinued this practice in 1910 to avoid confusion with the American Red Cross. A Nurse Corps pin was worn on the left breast of the ward uniform. Except for a watch or the Maltese Cross of the Spanish-American War Nurses Association, no jewelry was permissible. Completing the uniform was a pert white lawn cap with a one-inch-wide black velvet band.[54]

These prim garments did not deter one nurse, whose "indiscreet conduct" incurred the wrath of the bureau. Rumors had circulated for more than a year that the woman would leave nurses' quarters on a Saturday afternoon and return Sunday evening. Hasson had the nurse followed by detectives and learned that she had been meeting a man. Her "grave indiscretion" made her unsuitable "to uphold the dignity of the Corps." The nurse was also in constant ill health, so the bureau planned to discharge her on physical disability.[55] This was an early instance of Navy nurses having to fight rumors of sexual promiscuity.[56]

During the corps's formative years, Navy nurses first served on a warship. Although the Navy had no intention of using female nurses on any type of ship except hospital ships, the commander of the Atlantic Fleet compassionately allowed two nurses from the Brooklyn Naval Hospital to attend a critically ill man in the battleship *Michigan*. Paymaster S. P. Sackett had contracted pneumonia. Already weakened by several bouts of pneumonia and yellow fever and by a bad heart, he was gravely ill. The fleet surgeon wisely chose to keep Sackett onboard *Michigan* and to provide around-the-clock expert Nurse Corps care. Four days later the patient was strong enough to be moved to a shore hospital, and the Navy nurses returned to their post.[57]

Others were aware of the value of Navy nurses and tried to exploit them. Naval dependents often appealed to nurses at a nearby hospital for nursing services at home. Several incidents occurred at the Annapolis Naval Hospital. In one case, the hospital asked the Bureau of Medicine and Surgery to pay for two nurses for an officer's wife recovering from an appendectomy. Another episode involved the commanding officer's detailing a hospital nurse to attend a doctor's sick child. Later, several non-naval patients were admitted to the Annapolis Hospital. Undoubtedly, similar abuses took place at other naval hospitals. The bureau reacted swiftly. Hasson thought that if outside work became expected and customary, Navy nurses would have little time for their duties in the hospitals. She also feared that such practices would lead to the demise of the eight-hour day, a right jealously guarded by Navy nurses. In his annual report of 1909 and in a circular letter the following year, Surgeon General Stokes prohibited outside use of nurses without the bureau's approval—and such authorization would cover only medical emergencies and life-threatening situations.[58] Nevertheless, the problem persisted, and years would pass before the military provided medical care for dependents.

In addition to nursing duties in naval hospitals, the Navy Nurse Corps was charged with the important task of training Hospital Corps apprentices. This responsibility fell to the chief nurses, who arranged for ward nurses to instruct the corpsmen "in practical nursing and the care of the sick."[59] Navy nurses had to be teachers as well as nurses. Hasson stressed the importance of bedside instruction for apprentices because the hospital corpsmen would provide nursing services for the Navy afloat and must be carefully trained.[60] If the apprentices resented women instructors, their medical officers admonished them. Women nurses meant better nursing. After all, men could not fix a tempting tray, coax a patient to eat, rearrange pillows, or create a neat and cheerful room. The corpsmen must learn everything they could about the art of nursing from these women.[61] The hospital corpsmen also went by the title of "nurse," which generated confusion, so in early 1910 Surgeon General Rixey directed that the term would no longer apply to these men.[62]

In less than two years, Surgeon General Rixey and Superintendent Hasson had gotten the Navy Nurse Corps off to a good start, establishing the administrative structure for the corps. Rixey and Hasson shared similar goals and worked well together. After William H. Taft became president, however, he replaced Rixey with a new surgeon general, Rear Adm. Charles F. Stokes, in 1910. Hasson and Stokes had an immediate personality conflict that worsened as time passed.

Shortly after taking office, Stokes criticized Hasson because she and her eighty-five-year-old, partially paralyzed mother ate their meals in the nurses' mess. Although Hasson paid for the food, such a practice did not uphold the dignity of the superintendent's position, he said. Stokes consistently bypassed Hasson by trying to manage the Nurse Corps himself. He corresponded directly with the nurses, granted excessive leave without pay, and interfered with discipline. The nurse whom Hasson wanted discharged for "indiscreet conduct" in November 1910 was still in the corps in early 1911, at the naval hospital in Philadelphia. The bureau's inaction had caused "disagreeable gossip" about a possible relationship between the surgeon general and the wayward nurse, wrote Hasson. During the summer of 1910, Hasson apparently threatened to resign several times, and on 27 September Stokes asked for her resignation. Hasson heatedly demanded a detailed account of the charges against her. Stokes answered only that he had to make provisions for a successor. Several months passed, and on 14 January 1911 Hasson tendered her resignation to Secretary of the Navy George von L. Meyer, saying that she had "failed to receive the support, confidence, and courtesy from the Chief of the Bureau of Medicine and Surgery" necessary to perform her duties. She attached a scathing memorandum of complaints. Stokes brushed off the firestorm: "Miss Hasson is temperamentally unfitted for the position of superintendent of Nurses," he wrote. Hasson's resignation took effect on 16 January 1911.[63]

## Expanding Duties

Late in 1910 three women heard of Hasson's pending resignation and applied for the superintendent's position, but Stokes decided that one of the Navy's own nurses was best qualified. Lenah Sutcliffe Higbee became the second superintendent of the Navy Nurse Corps on 20 January 1911. The thirty-seven-year-old Canadian-born Higbee had graduated in nursing from the New York Postgraduate Hospital in 1899 and married retired Marine Corps lieutenant colonel John H. Higbee. The colonel died in April 1908, and Lenah Higbee returned to nursing and took postgraduate training at Fordham Hospital, New York. After finishing the course, she joined the Navy Nurse Corps on 1 October 1908 as one of the Sacred Twenty. She soon demonstrated her ability and became chief nurse at the Norfolk Naval Hospital in April 1909. Stokes recognized Higbee's success at Norfolk, which he attributed, in part, to her learning naval customs and ways as a Marine wife. She therefore had been able to impart the naval spirit to the nurses serving under her.[64]

Under Higbee's direction, the Nurse Corps grew from 72 members in December 1910 to 140 in late 1915. Women chose naval nursing rather than work in civilian hospitals because of more interesting and diversified career opportunities, regular eight-hour days, guaranteed pay, and "the rested look" from regular, alternating hours of duty and rest. Most important was the opportunity to provide competent medical care, either through their own efforts or through the hospital corpsmen they trained, for the men who guarded the nation's security.[65] Although pay and subsistence allowances remained constant during these prewar years, the Navy granted more realistic travel allowances in 1914. In addition to transportation, meals, and lodging, new regulations also permitted payment for baggage transfer and for taxi or carriage fares when streetcars were unavailable.[66]

Training hospital apprentices in nursing skills assumed greater importance as the Hospital Corps grew to 1,437 in 1914. Two years earlier Congress had authorized another grade for the corps: chief pharmacist. After six years in service and upon passing an examination, a pharmacist could be commissioned chief pharmacist and receive the pay and allowances of a chief boatswain. The training course at the Naval Medical School stopped in 1911, and for three years apprentices received on-the-job instruction in hospitals rather than formal training. New Hospital Corps training schools opened at Newport in 1914 and at San Francisco early the next year.[67] Teaching the rudiments of nursing care to these often disinterested young apprentices, whose ages ranged from seventeen to twenty, challenged the Navy nurses. Yet they were well aware that their charges later might be the only men available on ships or on shore with crucial, life-saving knowledge in medical emergencies. The nurses took their teaching responsibilities seriously.[68]

As the Nurse Corps expanded, its members served at more naval hospitals in the states. By 1915 Navy nurses were on duty at Washington, D.C.; Philadelphia; Annapolis; Brooklyn, New York; Norfolk; Mare Island, California; Chelsea, Massachusetts; Newport; Puget Sound; Portsmouth, New Hampshire; and Las Animas, Colorado. Surgeon General Stokes praised nurses' efficiency in ward management, hospital administration, and instruction of hospital corpsmen. Their work was "unqualifiedly excellent."[69] So excellent, in fact, that medical officers still tried to detail them to private duty for officers' families. In 1914, for example, a medical officer at Norfolk asked permission to send a nurse to the house of a Marine quartermaster in Mexico. Surgeon General Braisted immediately telegraphed his refusal: "The use of Nurse Corps outside of hospital not authorized except for temporary duty in cases of extreme emergency or to save life." He followed up with a circular letter to the commandants of naval hospitals with Nurse Corps women, prohibiting their assigning nurses to duty outside the hospitals.[70]

During these years the Nurse Corps served only in naval hospitals, although the original act establishing the corps had anticipated duty in hospital ships. The Navy had only two such ships. The *Relief*, which had accompanied the Great White Fleet in 1908, had suffered severe damage from a typhoon on 18 November that rendered her unseaworthy. The Navy kept the ship as a floating hospital at Olongapo, Philippine Islands. The *Solace* had joined the Atlantic Fleet in 1909 and steamed along the East Coast and in the Caribbean. All fifty nurses onboard were male, that is, hospital corpsmen.[71] In March 1913, however, two Nurse Corps women served briefly in the presidential yacht *Mayflower* and cruiser *Dolphin* (PG 24), assigned to the secretary of the Navy. The two ships took members of the House Naval Affairs Committee on a three-week inspection tour of Guantanamo, Colon, and Havana, Cuba. Nurse Mary H. DuBose accompanied a group in *Mayflower*, and nurse Mary M. Hickman sailed with others in *Dolphin*.[72]

## *The Tropics*

The first overseas station staffed with Navy nurses was at Cañacao, Philippine Islands. Following the Spanish-American War, the Navy established a temporary hospital at Cavite in 1899 and then built a more permanent facility at nearby Cañacao in 1905.[73] The one-hundred-bed hospital provided medical services for men of the Asiatic Station. In 1910 quarters were ready for female nurses.[74]

While she was still superintendent, Esther Hasson had initiated the process of choosing competent nurses for this detail. She selected Florence T. Milburn, one of the Sacred Twenty and then chief nurse at the Naval Hospital in Washington, as chief nurse at Cañacao and in September 1910 asked the Bureau of Navigation to assign her there.[75] Milburn and seven other nurses sailed to the Philippines in an Army transport and arrived at Naval Hospital Cañacao on 2 December 1910. After settling into their quarters, the nurses began their assignments: one as dietitian, one on night duty, two in the linen room, two as ward nurses, and one in the sick officers' quarters. No sooner had the nurses arrived than the usual clamor arose for their services for families. Physician Edward R. Stitt, commanding officer at

Cañacao, reported these events to Surgeon General Stokes, who immediately reiterated the prohibition against diverting nurses from hospital duty.[76] Soon surgeon C. S. Butler suggested that female nurses be detailed to critical positions such as those in the operating room. In that way, he continued, "the Admiral can't touch them and the organization would remain intact."[77] Since the Army administered the Philippines, the Navy did not get as involved with local medical problems as it did in two other island possessions.

Soon after the Navy nurses arrived in the Philippines, others were sent to the naval hospital at Guam in the Marianas. Since 1899, the Navy had administered Guam, one of the spoils of the Spanish-American War. The island was important as a potential mid-Pacific coaling and communications center, and Guam's naval governor was also commandant of the island's naval station.[78] Feeling obligated to better the lives of the primitive Chamorro inhabitants and also to protect the health of American Navy and Marine Corps personnel there, the Bureau of Medicine and Surgery promptly improved sanitation and water supplies. The Chamorros had an assortment of treatable ailments: tuberculosis, syphilis, parasites, scabies, elephantiasis, and dysentery. To care for the locals, the Navy established a dispensary and a hospital at Agana and furnished surgeons, hospital corpsmen, and medical supplies. By 1905, the entire population had received smallpox vaccinations. Naval doctors established leper and gangosa colonies to halt the spread of those loathsome diseases. Isolation and quarantine of infectious patients were progressive medical practices in the United States and helped prevent widespread epidemics.[79]

Private hospitals—Susana for women and children and Maria Schroeder for men and boys over twelve years of age—and a small bacteriological and chemical laboratory provided facilities for treating the locals. The senior naval medical officer oversaw all their activities. An early attempt at training young Guamanian women in the rudiments of nursing had started. When trained, these women would replace inefficient midwives, who were at the time the only nurses available. Moreover, four laborers at the hospital were training as hospital apprentices and would eventually take their skills to isolated towns and villages.[80] The Navy was teaching the locals to help themselves.

In 1909 an earthquake destroyed Susana Hospital, and the next year the Navy funded a new one-hundred-bed hospital to be combined with Maria

Schroeder and called Naval Hospital, Guam. The medical officer tried, unsuccessfully, to get the bureau's approval for hiring seven former Susana Hospital employees as nurses. The surgeon general suggested sending Nurse Corps personnel instead, and in early 1911 three nurses were en route. They would work in the women's and children's wards and instruct local women about child care.[81]

Chief Nurse Elizabeth Leonhardt, another of the Sacred Twenty, was in charge of two other nurses, Julia T. Coonan and Anna Turner. The three arrived at the naval hospital at Agana on 26 April 1911 and worked primarily with women and children. They soon established a training school for Chamorro women, with six in the first class. Leonhardt taught them some English, but most communication was accomplished through sign language. Because the school was so successful, in 1914 the surgeon general raised the complement of nurses at Guam so that the hospital could increase class size and expand training to include tubercular cases and massage therapy.[82]

But the boredom and isolation of the tiny island caused friction and dissatisfaction among the nurses. By September 1911 Turner had moved out of the rented house the three women shared and into the Susana Hospital. She took her meals with the families of two hospital stewards, violating the nonfraternization policy. In early January 1912, hospital authorities leveled five minor charges against Turner, who vigorously defended herself—to the anger of the commandant. She subsequently resigned from the Nurse Corps and left Guam a few months later.[83]

Leonhardt, however, remained chief nurse at Guam until 1914. Her replacement, Della V. Knight, devised a new way to attract the daughters of the Guamanian better classes to the school and to overcome parental objections. She hired the locally well known and highly respected Maria Roberta as "official chaperone" to the students.[84]

The remote Pacific island of Samoa generated a situation similar to that at Guam. Since 1872 the United States had maintained the right to build a naval station in Pago Pago Harbor at Tutuila, Samoa. Reaffirmed in 1878, the right was never exercised. Finally, in 1899, Great Britain, Germany, and the United States partitioned the Samoan Islands, and the United States acquired Tutuila and several smaller islands. That same year Cdr. Benjamin F. Tilley became commandant of the new Naval Station, Tutuila, and soon governor of

American Samoa. The United States now had the finest harbor, Pago Pago, in the South Seas and set about developing the naval station with a coal shed, wharf, and supply facilities.[85]

As part of administering the island's government, the Navy felt compelled, as it had in Guam, to improve living standards for the Polynesians, and health care assumed major significance. Disease abounded: yaws, filariasis, parasites, funguses, tuberculosis, trachoma, leprosy, gonorrhea, typhoid, and dysentery were endemic. Samoan medical practice encompassed primitive home remedies and, for more serious illnesses, the services of "devil doctors," so a naval surgeon set up a clinic and a temporary dispensary. In 1906 the Navy authorized funds for a permanent dispensary and medical supplies. Vaccination against smallpox was mandatory, and sewerage and water supplies were modernized. In 1911 the Samoans themselves financed and built a new hospital, but naval medical officers ran it. Two hospital corpsmen, an untrained female nurse, and a janitor made up the staff. To meet the dire need for attendants, American officials wanted to teach Samoan girls nursing skills.[86]

Surgeon General Stokes approved a training school at Tutuila and assigned two Navy nurses to administer it. In September 1913 Acting Chief Nurse Mary H. Humphrey and Nurse Corinne W. Anderson sailed from San Francisco, arriving in Tutuila on 6 October. Humphrey would be superintendent of the school, Anderson, her assistant.[87]

Soon after she arrived, Humphrey wrote about her first impressions of the primitive island. She and Anderson worked solely at the Samoan Hospital and had nursed only sick babies. Humphrey was especially excited about establishing the school to train young women in nursing. Although they were not connected with the naval dispensary, they would also have to nurse serious illnesses in the American colony.[88]

Humphrey and Anderson had no sooner arrived than they ran afoul of medical officers and a string of events threatened their assignment in Samoa. The two women took offense at various breaches of naval medical etiquette: doctors sent them orders through hospital stewards; the paymaster classified the nurses with enlisted corpsmen; the surgeon ordered Humphrey to be present while male hospital apprentices gave douches to female patients, a situation that was demeaning and humiliating; and Anderson involuntarily spent eight days attending a private obstetrical case. By mid-December the medical officers were giving the two nurses little to do, and they quickly became demoralized, especially because there had been no progress in beginning the training school. On 28 January 1914 Humphrey and Anderson requested honorable discharges from the Nurse Corps—they would "sacrifice their professional honor" if they remained. The two medical officers immediately brought charges against the nurses. The unfortunate affair escalated when the commandant, Governor C. D. Stearns, called a board of investigation, which found the nurses guilty. Stearns sent a report to Secretary of the Navy Josephus Daniels, who referred it to the surgeon general, who consulted with Superintendent Higbee, who defended her nurses. In March Daniels tossed the whole decision back to the commandant, who let the nurses remain in Samoa.[89]

Meanwhile, the training school for Samoan women started in a building next to the hospital. On 23 February 1914, four young Samoans—Anna, Corey, Winnie, and India—began a two-year course that would teach them the fundamentals of practical nursing. To help the students, the nurses put together an elementary "Care Procedure Book." After they graduated, the student nurses would go to the villages as nurses and sanitary inspectors.[90] Humphrey wrote of the difficulties in teaching the students, who had been in a missionary school for ten years but whose knowledge of English was scant. She was, however, pleased with the girls' enthusiasm and sincere efforts to learn.[91]

Running the training school as well as working eight-hour hospital shifts was overwhelming for the two nurses. Consequently, in August Humphrey asked for another nurse to help in the important task of training the Samoans. Her request was so eloquent that Secretary of the Navy Daniels authorized two additional nurses.[92] Surgeon General Braisted expressed his great satisfaction with the school's progress.[93] Feeling vindicated by the school's success, Humphrey remained in Samoa until May of 1915, Anderson about six months longer.[94] They would not be there when the first class of Samoan nurses graduated in 1916.

## *Overseas*

While some Navy nurses took American nursing standards to island possessions in the Pacific, others had different experiences in Great Britain and

Europe. When World War I began in 1914, the American National Red Cross sent sixteen hospital units to European countries to care for casualties. Each unit had three surgeons and twelve nurses. Following a policy of strict neutrality, Red Cross workers nursed the sick and wounded from all belligerent nations.[95] Several Navy nurses wanted to take part in this humanitarian activity and requested leaves of absence from the corps.

J. Beatrice Bowman, one of the Sacred Twenty and chief nurse at the Norfolk Naval Hospital, received Superintendent Higbee's blessing for such temporary duty in April 1914, and Surgeon General Stokes recommended her highly to Red Cross officials. Stokes cited Bowman's exceptional ability and training and asked that the Red Cross make use of her superior qualifications.[96] In September Bowman became a supervising nurse of Unit D, made up of Rochester and Connecticut nurses, and served at the Royal Naval Hospital, Haslar, England. The twenty-six-hundred-bed facility had a nursing staff of "sisters"—as British nurses were called—both Royal Navy sisters and Reserve sisters, supplemented by the American contingent of thirteen Red Cross nurses. Bowman remained at Haslar for six months, then returned to the Navy Nurse Corps.[97]

Another Navy nurse, Katrina E. Hertzer, also took a leave of absence to serve in Red Cross units and was on active duty in Europe for eighteen months. When she returned to the United States, Hertzer reentered the Navy Nurse Corps, assigned to special duty at Red Cross Headquarters, thus strengthening the ties between the two nursing services.[98]

The European war would soon embroil the United States, so it was fortunate that the Navy had established the Nurse Corps as part of its Medical Department. Blessed with effective, competent superintendents and supportive surgeons general, the Nurse Corps had become organized and accepted only well-trained and highly qualified graduate nurses. Its numbers grew from the original Sacred Twenty to 140 by 1915.

Establishing the corps had not been easy. Opposition to women, organizational difficulties, and bickering had often marred these early years. Perhaps because of the ambiguity and uncertainty about the nurses' status in the Navy—they had no rank although they were subjected to naval discipline and were in the chain of command—they were overly sensitive about their dignity and "place." Professional status was new to women, and the trained nurses zealously guarded their position.

Soon proving its worth, the Navy Nurse Corps dispatched members to naval hospitals in the United States and to three hospitals in the Pacific. They improved medical care by providing professional nursing services to the sick and injured. Another major contribution of Navy nurses was in teaching, first by training Hospital Corps apprentices and later by establishing training schools for local women in Guam and Samoa. A few nurses got a preview of World War I involvement by serving with Red Cross units. The Navy's experiment in making use of women was succeeding. The United States' entry into the European war would test the competence of the Navy's Medical Department and of its Nurse Corps.

# 3

# The World War I Era, 1916–1920

*When the United States entered* the European war in April 1917, the armed forces experienced an acute manpower shortage. Alone of the services, the U.S. Navy turned to a novel method of filling its requirements: enrolling women as yeomen (F) and Marine Reservists (F). Never before had women been a legitimate and official part of any uniformed service, except as nurses, and the Navy's great experiment would have far-reaching ramifications. Simultaneously, the Navy Nurse Corps grew in size, complexity, and importance as it fulfilled its wartime obligations. These were exciting times as women grasped such unprecedented opportunities.

## The Setting

Women ventured into many fields during World War I. Erosion of the Victorian concept of woman's sphere accelerated, fueled by the Progressive ethos of good management and efficiency, social justice and regulation, and specialization and professionalization. Young women flocked to colleges and universities, and between 1910 and 1920, their numbers more than doubled, from 140,000 to 283,000. They comprised 47 percent of all college students.[1]

These educated women gravitated to professions they had already claimed: elementary school teaching, social work, and nursing. A few became doctors, lawyers, and college professors or college administrators. Women quickly dominated other white-collar fields, becoming department store sales clerks, typists, and stenographers. In all professions, however, women received less pay than men for comparable work. The majority of the 25 percent of women who worked outside the home continued to be poor and uneducated and found jobs as domestics or factory workers.[2]

While these women entered the labor market, others worked through various peace organizations to forestall American participation in the European war. Some attended the International Women's Congress at the Hague in 1915, then returned home and established the Woman's Peace Party. One of the party's members, Jeannette Rankin of Montana—the first woman ever to serve in Congress—voted against the U.S. declaration of war in 1917.[3] When these movements failed and the United States entered the war, peace activists fell quiet and joined the rush to help defeat "the Huns."

Women volunteers set up relief committees that gathered and sent vast supplies of food and supplies to Europe. Hundreds of Red Cross nurses served in Europe. Other women attended national service training camps, where they drilled and studied subjects such as dietetics and agriculture. The federal government established the Woman's Committee of the Council of National Defense, an advisory group headed by suffragist Anna Howard Shaw. Clerical workers substituted for many males in government offices, notably in the War Department. Although the number of working women did not increase perceptibly, the American people became more aware of women's visible contributions to the war effort.[4]

During the war era, women continued their reform movements through such organizations as the Women's Christian Temperance Union, with eight hundred thousand members, all of whom rejoiced when the Eighteenth Amendment ushered in Prohibition in 1919. The General Federation of Women's Clubs had about one million members, membership in the YWCA reached half a million, and four hundred thousand women belonged to unions.[5] Through participation in these groups and countless others, women gained organizational and administrative experience and shook off more vestiges of Victorian subservience. They would join forces in the greatest of all their crusades: woman's suffrage.

The National American Woman Suffrage Association (NAWSA) took on new life when Carrie Chapman Catt again became its president in 1915. She had, she said, a "Winning Plan" to work at state and national levels for the necessary constitutional amendment giving women the right to vote, and membership in the NAWSA swelled to two million. A more militant group, the Congressional Union, was formed in 1913 by Alice Paul and Lucy Burns. It became the National Woman's Party (NWP) three years later and included among its members nursing leaders such as Lavinia Dock. These organizations and others campaigned through parades, speeches, and public meetings, and by distributing leaflets, picketing, and lobbying. President Wilson announced his support of woman's suffrage in 1916.[6] Finally, the House passed the Nineteenth Amendment in 1918; the Senate passed it the following year. The amendment was ratified in 1920, just in time for newly enfranchised women to vote for Warren G. Harding.[7] The long battle had been won at last; it would be years, however, before its impact and significance became clearer.[8]

Meanwhile, as women had become more active and visible, the nation had advanced toward involvement in a war that few people wanted. During the early months of World War I, President Woodrow Wilson and most Americans espoused a policy of neutrality toward the European belligerents. When German submarine warfare began taking its toll on American lives and merchant ships, the President and Congress, still hoping that they could avoid war, took faltering steps to prepare for potential U.S. involvement. In 1914 Congress passed the Naval Militia Act, and two years later a new law doubled the size of the regular Army. Similar legislation authorized a substantial increase in naval forces and shipbuilding to create a navy "second to none." To help staff the expanding Navy in a time of national emergency, the Naval Appropriations Act of 1916 also established the Naval Reserve Force.[9] Wilson's attempts to mediate among the belligerents failed, and in early 1917 Germany announced its unrestricted submarine warfare policy. There was no escape for the United States, and at Wilson's request Congress declared war on 6 April.[10]

As the country mobilized, the Navy devised a method of delivering both military supplies for the Allies and goods for humanitarian relief. Naval representatives convinced the reluctant British to use convoys for moving American soldiers and supplies across the submarine-infested Atlantic. The convoy system, under the direction of the Naval Overseas Transportation Service, was ultimately effective, enabling American ships to circumvent German submarine zones and reach Britain and France safely.[11]

Convoys meant a large increase in American merchant ships and warships, and the Naval Appropriations Act of 1916 had authorized funding for a Navy that would have few rivals. Under the direction of Secretary of the Navy Josephus Daniels, the Navy's active fleet grew between 1916 and 1919 from

331 to 752 vessels. The largest increases occurred with destroyers, the work-horses of the convoy system, whose numbers swelled from 63 to 161, and submarines, which rose from 38 to 91. The number of battleships, that pride of earlier navies, remained at 36. The fastest growing segment of naval power was the Flying Corps, which expanded from 54 planes to 2,107 aircraft, including planes, blimps, and kite balloons.[12] Manning the vastly expanded fleet demanded a huge increase in personnel, and from the declaration of war on 6 April 1917 until Armistice on 11 November 1918, the Navy grew from 5,243 to 32,483 regular and reserve officers, and from 65,789 to 469,965 enlisted men and women.[13]

Such rapid mobilization called for streamlined administration. In 1915 Congress had established the office of the chief of naval operations (CNO), who worked under the secretary's direction. Adm. William S. Benson, the first CNO, oversaw naval readiness and operations throughout the war.[14] The naval bureaus continued their customary specialized functions.

The Navy not only took part in the European war but also administered many of the country's overseas possessions and protectorates. Guam and Samoa remained under naval jurisdiction, and new responsibilities arose in the Caribbean. In 1912, U.S. Marines occupied Nicaragua to quell local disorder and protect American lives and property. Similar incursions occurred in Veracruz, Mexico, in 1914, in Haiti in 1915, and in the Dominican Republic in 1916. Additionally, the United States purchased the western Virgin Islands—notably St. Thomas, St. John, and St. Croix—from Denmark in 1917.[15]

## The Yeomen (F)

All these commitments demanded a vast increase in naval personnel. Even before the United States entered the war in April 1917, Secretary of the Navy Josephus Daniels had given careful thought to a probable manpower shortage. How could the Navy man its expanded fleet when so many able-bodied sailors remained in shore stations doing paperwork essential to the Navy at war? The Navy needed clerical help and it needed it immediately. The civil service could not provide enough clerks or process them rapidly enough. Daniels, who served as Navy secretary throughout the Wilson administration, shared many Progressive views with the president. Among these was a firm belief in woman's suffrage, and he worked tirelessly for passage and ratification of the Nineteenth Amendment.[16] Generally sympathetic toward women's aspirations and aware of their efficient clerical service in government agencies, Daniels had no difficulty justifying a role for them in the U.S. Navy.

The Naval Appropriations Act of 1916 had established the United States Naval Reserve Force (USNRF) with six different classes, composed of U.S. citizens who must enroll for four years and take an oath of allegiance. The act did not specify "men," but "citizens" and "persons."[17] Daniels seized the opportunity. "Is there any law that says a yeoman must be a man?" he asked his legal advisers. Receiving a negative reply, on 14 March 1917 Daniels ordered that women be enrolled as yeomen, radio electricians, and other useful ratings (specialties). "We will have the best clerical assistance the country can provide," he declared.[18] He authorized admitting women as part of the Naval Coast Defense Reserve—in the same category as owners of yachts and power boats and with those who could serve in coast defense vessels—and even suggested that Congress had contemplated women's enrollment when it had set up the Naval Reserve.[19]

When Secretary Daniels's decision became public, young women across the country swarmed to recruiting offices. The first to enlist was Loretta Perfectus Walsh, a civilian clerk at the Philadelphia recruiting center. On 21 March 1917, she became a chief yeoman at the naval home for disabled veterans in that city.[20] When the United States declared war on 6 April, there were 201 women in the Naval Reserve. By Armistice Day, their numbers had reached 8,997; three weeks later, 11,275. Altogether, 11,880 women served in the Navy.[21] They came from each of the forty-eight states and the District of Columbia and from American possessions such as Hawaii and Puerto Rico. New York supplied the most, 2,329, followed by the District of Columbia (1,874), Massachusetts (1,324), Virginia (1,071), and Pennsylvania (1,067).[22]

The Navy stipulated few requirements for these new sailors. They had to be American citizens between eighteen and thirty-five years of age. Recruiters sometimes looked the other way, allowing girls as young as fifteen, and in one case, fourteen, to sign up. Reservists enrolled for four years and received a retainer of twelve dollars a year. Women with high school diplomas, business school training, or clerical experience had the advantage over those less qualified. A community leader often sponsored them and attested to their good character.[23]

Joining up frequently took less than a day. Typically, a woman went for an interview at the recruiting station, where she filled out an application form and, if she had clerical skills, took a brief test. Afterward she reported to the nearest naval hospital for a cursory physical examination conducted by male physicians. Some new recruits were embarrassed by such brusque procedures, but one laughingly recalled three men peeping at the scantily clad women through the transom of a hospital examining room.[24] If a recruit passed these examinations, she took the oath of allegiance and reported for duty—usually within a week, but sometimes on the spot.

Women with different backgrounds and with varied educational or work experiences took part in the U.S. Navy's new experiment for filling its ranks. Postmaster General Albert S. Burleson's daughters, Lucy and Sidney, both college graduates, signed up. So did Caroline, the daughter of Rear Adm. Bradley A. Fiske, as well as Willie Duncan and Elsie Hepburn, both related to congressmen.[25] Sometimes a mother and daughter; or two, three, and even four sisters; or women with a husband or brother in the service would enlist. Some had taught in schools or colleges, others had worked in the business world.[26] Like many young women of that era, Joy Bright had completed a secretarial course, Helen O'Neill had a degree from a business college, and Helene Johnson had just finished a business course.[27] Most of the women had graduated at least from high school. Similar to the female reformers of the Progressive era, women who joined the Navy were white and predominately middle and upper class. They projected a refined image, one that would be important in the Navy's World War II experiences with women.[28]

There were many reasons for enlisting, but the strongest motivation for these women was patriotism, the desire to help their country in its struggle against the Central Powers. With a sense of duty, women offered their skills where needed.[29] Others joined the Navy because, in comparison to civilian employment, they found steady jobs with good pay.[30] The Navy offered challenging opportunities for women who were severely conscribed in the peacetime job market.[31] Some carried on family traditions of military service, only this time it was women who volunteered. Others joined for more superficial reasons: the uniforms were "super."[32] Perhaps an underlying and unspoken reason was the longing for excitement and adventure. These "crusaders" could help make the world safe for democracy.[33]

When women entered the Navy as yeomen, no one knew what to call them. The Navy did not designate the sex of new recruits, and some women found themselves mistakenly assigned to combatant ships.[34] Nicknames abounded: yeomenettes, yeowomen, lady sailors, petticoat pets. Finally, the Navy's brass clamped down on the terms. "I never did like this 'ette' business. . . . If a woman does a job, she ought to have the name of the job," said Secretary Daniels. Rear Adm. Samuel McGowan, paymaster general of the Navy, took up the refrain: "These women are as much a part of the Navy as the men who have enlisted. They do the same work . . . and have done yeoman service."[35] To clarify the situation, the Navy dubbed the women reservists yeomen (F), the "F" for female.

Women entering the Navy received no formal indoctrination as their counterparts in the Nurse Corps had. There was no central office to oversee the yeomen (F), no director for women's affairs. They simply reported to their designated posts and worked under the supervision of their commanding officers. Because most had clerical experience, they could easily assume the duties of male yeomen, who were needed at sea and abroad. The yeomen (F) had to learn naval office procedures and terminology, so the *Bluejacket's Manual* became their constant companion. This sturdy volume described the required knowledge for yeomen's routine duties, including correspondence, typing, and mastery of naval regulations. In addition, chief yeomen were expected to have a thorough knowledge of bookkeeping.[36] The yeomen (F) also learned close-order drill: they practiced marching in step and in straight lines. In Washington, D.C., where there was a large contingent of yeomen (F), they formed a battalion, became proficient at drilling, and prepared to march in parades.[37]

The Navy's newest yeomen could progress from third to second to first class. Exceptional women became chief yeomen, but only about a dozen attained this rate. A few qualified women entered as radio operators, and at least one had a commissary steward's rating. As the women demonstrated their efficiency, rumors abounded that some would become officers; but nothing came of the idea.[38]

Some old "sundowners" resented female intrusion into "this man's Navy."[39] Others groused that it was wrong for women to wear a regular Navy rating badge because they could not fulfill all the functions, such as sea duty, of that rating.[40] Family opposition was not uncommon. Sailors, after all, did not always enjoy the best of reputations.[41] Most men, however, gladly accepted the sorely needed clerical assistance. These women perceived no sexual harassment in the modern sense of the term. One former yeoman (F) recalled that men in her unit acted as "perfect gentlemen" toward the women.[42]

Pay and allowances for yeomen (F) were the same as for their male counterparts. Thanks to Secretary Daniels, the Navy adopted a progressive policy of equal compensation. "A woman who works as well as a man ought to receive the same pay," said Daniels—and this policy became reality.[43] A disbelieving Carrie Chapman Catt, president of NAWSA, queried Daniels about equal pay because women in the civil service usually got lower salaries than men. He assured her that the Navy would not discriminate against women and was, in fact, giving them preference for wartime clerical jobs with the same pay as men.[44]

No one would have gotten rich serving as a yeoman or in any other enlisted rating. Base monthly rates in 1917 were $60 for chief yeoman, $40 for yeoman first class, $35 for yeoman second class, and $30 for yeoman third class.[45] In addition, each yeoman received $60 for a uniform allowance and $1.25 a day subsistence.[46] The Navy provided no housing for the yeomen (F), except at the Mare Island Navy Yard, where an old Marine Corps barracks sheltered them. Most women lived at home or with friends; others had to pay for their own housing.[47]

There was no uniform for women when they first entered the service, but within a month that situation changed. Not designed to flatter the feminine figure, the uniforms were navy blue serge for winter and white drill for summer. Both had a Norfolk jacket—a single-breasted coat with patch pockets, a belt, and pleats running from the shoulders down the front and back. The skirts, fitted over the hips then flared at the bottom, came to within eight inches of the floor. White shirtwaists could be worn either buttoned or with the top button undone. When unbuttoned, the blouse was to be accompanied by a regular Navy neckerchief. Topping this severe outfit was a straight-brimmed sailor hat made of navy blue felt for winter, white straw for summer. In winter, the women could also wear an ankle-length blue serge cape.[48]

With their uniforms and in other ways, women remained distinct and apart from the regular Navy. One major distinction was in discipline for infractions of regulations or bad conduct. In December 1917 Daniels overruled the court-martial of a yeoman (F) who had left her post when she was sick. The Navy "cannot deal with women as with men," he wrote. He disapproved the deck court-martial of another woman several months later because it would be a contravention of public policy. Using this same protective reasoning, the Navy Department rejected two other courts-martial in March 1919.[49]

The vast majority of yeomen (F) performed clerical tasks such as typing, stenography, and filing. These routine yet exacting duties were vital for a navy at war, and women handled them cheerfully and competently. The largest contingent of yeomen (F), about two thousand, served in the naval bureaus in Washington. The Bureau of Supplies and Accounts, for example, employed several hundred, many as accountants. Sue Dorsey was so efficient there that Rear Adm. Samuel McGowan, the paymaster general, called her the "most valuable woman in government" and recommended that she be commissioned.[50] Other yeomen (F) filled about four hundred accounting and other jobs at the Washington Navy Yard.[51] Yeomen (F) served in all the naval districts and at training stations and navy yards across the country. New York, for example, had 615 women reservists; Boston, about 200.[52]

Although the yeomen (F) held the Navy's clerical rating, they engaged in many duties other than typing. They took over the switchboards, becoming the Navy's telephone operators. At the Office of Naval Intelligence, yeomen (F) were fingerprint experts. They learned to operate the wireless telegraph system, acted as messengers, and worked as cable decoders. Some tracked ships' movements while others were proficient draftsmen.[53] At least one became a ship's cook.[54]

Even more unusual, yeomen (F) assembled primers at the munitions factory in Bloomfield, New Jersey, and put together torpedo parts at the Newport Torpedo Station in Rhode Island. "Their deftness and quick touch make them better than men," said Secretary Daniels.[55] Still other yeomen (F) entered another field foreign to women: medical technology at naval hospitals. Some excelled in designing camouflage; others served as translators.[56]

Many yeomen (F) held high-profile billets at naval recruiting stations. Perhaps the Navy believed that attractive young women in uniform would lure more recruits into the sea service; in any case, the strategy worked. In New York City, Dorothy Frooks set a record by signing up ten thousand men.[57] Another woman achieved immortality of sorts when she rushed into the Los Angeles recruiting office in 1917 and exclaimed, "Gee! I wish I were a man. I'd join the Navy!" A noted civilian artist overheard her, and with a burst of inspiration, had her don a sailor's outfit and pose for a World War I poster that would become a classic.[58]

Equally as visible as yeomen (F) recruiters were those who had drilled to proficiency and participated in parades. They marched in Victory Loan parades and afterward sold Liberty bonds in theaters and other public places. These yeoman (F) marched when the Rainbow (42d) Division returned from war and when President Wilson came back from the Paris treaty negotiations in 1919. As an honor guard, they also welcomed him at Union Station in Washington.[59]

A few women served overseas. Yeoman (F) 1st class Edith R. Barron worked in a nonmedical position at Red Cross Base Hospital Number 5 in France and later in the transport *Agamemnon*. Chief Yeoman (F) Mary B. Davidson was stationed in Paris, and four other yeomen (F) reportedly served with hospital units in France. Another had duty with the Office of Naval Intelligence at the radio station in San Juan, Puerto Rico.[60] A few served in Hawaii, Guam, and the Panama Canal Zone.[61]

## The Marine Reservists (F)

Like the Navy, the Marine Corps experienced a severe personnel shortage as the war dragged on. Believing that 40 percent of clerical jobs could be performed by women, in July 1918 Maj. Gen. George Barnett, Marine commandant, queried local offices about the feasibility of employing women. All responded positively, although it would take three women, they said, to do the work of two men. On 12 August Secretary Daniels authorized enrolling women for Marine service in Washington and other offices in the United States.[62]

The next day eager women rushed to recruiting offices. The first to enroll was Opha M. Johnson of Washington, D.C., whose duties included looking after the welfare of other women marines (the Navy had no comparable position).[63] Soon 305 women had enlisted. The majority served as stenographers, bookkeepers, accountants, and typists in the Washington area offices of the commandant, quartermaster, paymaster, adjutant, and inspector. Others worked at recruiting stations around the country. All entered as privates but could be promoted to privates first class, corporals, and sergeants. Women Marines received the same pay and allowances as men in the same ranks, drilled regularly, and, like the yeomen (F), took part in parades and other ceremonies.[64] They, too, soon acquired nicknames: Marinettes, lady hell cats, skirt Marines, and women soldiers of the sea.[65]

## Influenza Epidemic

Many women of the Navy and the Marine Corps fell victim to the virulent influenza epidemic that swept the world in late 1918 and early 1919. One yeoman (F) recalled that the Navy dispensed a jigger of whiskey every morning to help ward off the deadly virus.[66] During the war era fifty-seven yeomen (F) died, most from influenza or its complication, pneumonia. Similarly, two Marine Reservists (F) succumbed while in the service.[67]

## Demobilization

After the end of hostilities in November 1918, the Navy slowly began releasing its reservists. By July 1919, there were 7,694 enlisted women still in the Navy; Congress soon hastened their departure. The Naval Appropriations Act of 11 July stipulated that all female reservists, except nurses, must be placed on inactive duty within thirty days, so before 1 September, most yeomen (F) and women Marines had gone. A few lingered until early 1920.[68] Many women wanted to stay in the service, and one disgruntled chief yeoman (F) who wished to remain until her four-year enlistment expired carried her protest to the highest levels. She was allowed to keep her job but as a civilian.[69]

Initially, the discharge form for women failed to specify "honorable." Some thought that women reservists should not receive such discharges, which carried a recommendation for reenlistment that was no longer possible. Highly incensed, the yeomen (F) protested loudly: omitting "honorable" would mean they had not carried out their duties satisfactorily, and that would jeopardize their chances for civilian employment. The matter went to the secretary of the Navy, who decided women's discharges would be based on individual performance.[70]

Those reservists who remained on inactive status for the duration of their enlistments continued to earn a retainer of twelve dollars a year. Many wished to go on working for the Navy and received temporary civil service appointments. Like other veterans, the women reservists got a 5 percent increase in civil service ratings for later jobs. They received the World War I Victory Medal and the Good Conduct Medal and were eligible for other benefits, such as burial in Arlington National Cemetery, government insurance, a discharge bonus of sixty dollars, and Veterans Administration medical care for service-related disabilities.[71]

The yeomen (F) and Marine Reservists (F) had made a distinct contribution to the American war effort. "These women," wrote Secretary Daniels, "were the elect of their sex, and I do not know how the business of the department, of the navy yards and stations and of the districts, could have been carried on without them." Marine commandant Major General Barnett echoed the high praise: "The service rendered by the reservists (female) has been uniformly excellent . . . exactly what the intelligence and goodness of our countrywomen would lead one to expect."[72]

## The Navy Nurse Corps

As the yeomen (F) and Marine Reservists (F) became the Navy's first enlisted women, the Navy Nurse Corps expanded its services to meet wartime demands. Established in 1908, the corps continued under the direction of Lenah S. Higbee, superintendent since 1911. She and others of the Sacred Twenty would guide the corps throughout World War I.

Navy nurses were representative of the far larger, and now universally accepted, nursing profession, which grew rapidly during the war era.[73] Hospital training schools, which provided most preparation for nurses, expanded from 1,129 schools with 32,636 students in 1910 to 1,755 schools with 54,953 students in 1920. In spite of increasing numbers of trained women, nurses put in long hours—fourteen to eighteen a day—to fulfill urgent needs. To meet the heavy wartime demand for nurses, the American Red Cross recruited them for military as well as civilian service and maintained a national registry of qualified trained nurses. In 1917 the Committee on Nursing was organized to determine ways of providing nurses for the military. Led by Adelaide Nutting, the committee included such nursing notables as Annie Goodrich, Lillian Wald, Jane Delano of the Red Cross, Lillian Clayton of the National League of Nursing Education, and Dora Thompson and Lenah S. Higbee, superintendents of the Army Nurse Corps and Navy Nurse Corps, respectively. The Vassar Training Camp, which opened in 1918, also helped alleviate the shortage of nurses. It provided a three-month preparatory course for 434 college graduates who then underwent an intensified training program at one of some thirty-three nursing schools. Five other colleges began similar programs. The Army even established its own school in 1918 at Walter Reed Hospital. Eventually, about 23,000 nurses entered the Army Nurse Corps and Navy Nurse Corps.[74]

World War I brought great changes to medical care. Modern artillery with fragmentation shells caused massive wounds; shrapnel created multiple internal injuries; steel-jacketed bullets pulverized tissue. A new method of disinfecting wounds—continuous irrigation with a chlorine solution—and better wound surgery decreased infections and amputations, while antitetanus toxins lowered mortality rates. These were, after all, the days before penicillin and antibiotics. More effective treatment of shock, blood transfusions, and reconstructive facial surgery were major advances. Additional problems confronted medical practitioners: the German use of poisonous gas and the devastating influenza epidemic of 1918–19.[75] The heavy requirements for skilled nursing care in the military and civilian communities severely stretched nursing resources.

In the Navy, wartime duties required an increased commitment afloat and ashore. To care for naval and Marine personnel, the Bureau of Medicine and Surgery set up and staffed more hospitals and dispensaries. The Navy Medical Department's major focus was, of course, the conflict in Europe, and during the war years the department's strength increased markedly. The number of regular and reserve doctors leaped from 327 to 3,074; dentists, from 30 to 485.[76]

Nursing services expanded proportionately. The Hospital Corps, authorized at 3.5 percent of Navy and Marine strength, grew from 1,585 to 14,718, and corpsmen underwent six months' training at schools in Newport, Great Lakes, and San Francisco. Corps pharmacists received special instruction at the Pharmacist's Mates' School in Hampton Roads.[77]

The great increase in doctors, dentists, and hospital corpsmen generated an urgent need for many more women in the Navy Nurse Corps, and the Bureau of Medicine and Surgery launched a massive recruiting drive.[78] When the United States entered the war, there were 160 women in the Nurse Corps. Publicity, appeals to nursing schools, active recruiting by Navy nurses, and help from the American Red Cross brought the number of women in the regular Navy Nurse Corps to 317 by November 1918. Others, 539, came in through the Naval Reserve, which had been authorized in the 1908 legislation establishing the corps but never activated until the war. Still more, 697, entered through the U.S. Naval Reserve Force. Altogether, 1,553 nurses served in the Navy. The Red Cross Nursing Service, which acted as a national reserve of registered nurses, supplied the bulk of the new recruits and was responsible for mobilizing 1,058 Navy nurses and about 18,000 Army nurses.[79] As with the yeomen (F), New York furnished the most, 227, followed by Pennsylvania (184), California (179), and Massachusetts (112).[80] Five Nurse Corps members—four chief nurses and one Reserve nurse—had served in the Spanish-American War.[81]

The Navy's requirements remained high: graduation from a large general hospital training school, state registration, American citizenship, and eligibility for membership in the American Nurses Association, plus the Navy's own professional, medical, and mental examinations. In contrast, the Army waived state registration and the Red Cross waived ANA membership. By this time, the Navy had added the stipulation that nurses must be unmarried; and the USNRF had an age restriction: its nurses must be between the ages of twenty-two and forty-four.[82]

As an incentive for more nurses to enter the corps, pay rose in 1918 to $2,400 a year for the superintendent, $60 a month with $5 increments for each three years of service for nurses, an extra $10 a month for chief nurses, and $10 more a month for those serving outside the United States. The reduction in chief nurses' pay from $30 extra to $10 extra was a congressional mistake. The following year, chief nurses' extra pay went back to $30 a month. Always in tandem with Army Nurse Corps compensation, base pay for nurses increased 20 percent in 1920. In addition, nurses received quarters and subsistence when available, or up to $4.50 a day if hospitals did not provide them. The government assumed travel costs or gave nurses an allowance to cover transportation, meals, and lodging.[83] Benefits for Navy nurses included medical care and treatment: physicians, nursing, medicine, and hospitalization. They could accumulate up to 120 days' paid leave, at the rate of 30 days a year, and 30 days' sick leave a year. A new benefit, war risk insurance, compensated up to $10,000 for death or disability from injuries or disease contracted in the line of duty.[84] The eight-hour day continued to be a magnet attracting civilian nurses (although during the influenza epidemic, the number of duty hours often extended beyond eight).

Nurses had to provide their own uniforms, although members of the USNRF received a gratuity for them. The white ward uniform consisted of a shirtwaist, a full and crisply starched skirt, and white stockings, shoes, and cap. Later in the war, explicit instructions about the cap specified a three-quarter-inch black velvet band with two gold stripes for chief nurses, one gold stripe for assistant chief nurses, and a half-inch black velvet band for acting head nurses. All others wore unadorned caps. Nurses could add garments such as a uniform suit, topcoat, cape, or hat. The insignia worn on either side of the collar of the top coat or cape changed to a gold foil anchor with a gold oak leaf and acorn on top and surrounded by "Navy Nurse Corps" in silver. An outdoor uniform was advisable but not mandatory.[85] The Red Cross provided a complete set of equipment for each nurse—Army, Navy, and Red Cross—who served overseas. This included not only uniforms but also blankets, a sleeping bag, poncho, assorted undergarments, shoes, and stockings. The organization later loaned capes to Navy nurses in the United States.[86]

Throughout the war years, the status of military nurses remained undefined. Navy nurse Lucile M. Crane, stationed in Scotland, expressed nurses' frustration: "The Navy . . . had no place for us. We had no rank and we had no status. We were neither the corpsmen nor the officers."[87] Army nurses had tried in vain to obtain military rank and had secured the support of civilian groups such as the College Equal Suffrage League and the American Nurses Association.[88] After all, in the Australian and Canadian services, nurses held the relative rank of lieutenant and received all benefits granted officers. In the Royal Navy, nurses had the equivalent of rank by the dignity, respect, and obedience rendered them.[89] Secretary Daniels and Surgeon General William C. Braisted pushed for congressional help in defining Navy nurses' status; by law, they were neither commissioned nor enlisted. When these attempts failed, the Navy established a policy considering the women as officers.[90]

## *Duty in the United States*

With the vast wartime increase in personnel came a concomitant growth in naval medical facilities. The Navy built new hospitals and dispensaries and enlarged and improved older ones so that capacity swelled from three thousand to more than seventeen thousand beds.[91] From 15 to 220 nurses served at thirty-one hospitals, and 40 others were at seven dispensaries.[92]

As hospitals' capacities stretched taut, nurses who had worked as dietitians moved to the wards. From necessity, the Bureau of Medicine and Surgery hired Red Cross–certified civilian dietitians. To enter under civil service, these women were hired as skilled laborers. Eventually, thirty such dietitians served in thirteen hospitals under Navy Nurse Corps supervision.[93]

Providing the necessary six months' training for hospital corpsmen was a herculean task.[94] Corpsmen completed their basic class work, then continued training under the supervision of Nurse Corps women at a variety of naval hospitals. Ward nurses instructed them in the practicalities of bedside care. Teaching such young and often disinterested men called for "executive ability, tact, and patience."[95] Nurses worked hard to prepare corpsmen for their wartime missions. "*Have* I taught that man everything I possibly could? *Will* he make any mistake with a life . . . because I did not teach him *how?*" wrote one chief nurse.[96]

Knowing that hospital corpsmen continued to resent them added to the nurses' teaching concerns. The corpsman, wrote Superintendent Higbee, "dislikes the Navy nurses and does not believe that they know more, if as much, as he does."[97] The negative attitude brought a stern admonition from a medical officer: the corpsman must learn "how wide is woman's sphere, how indispensable her deftness, her gentleness, her fineness of perceptions. . . . He must perceive what an art [nursing] is."[98]

## *Duty Overseas*

During World War I, 293 Navy nurses served in hospitals and base units in Britain, Scotland, Ireland, and France. Of these, 22 were regular Navy nurses, the rest were reservists or USNRF. They were far fewer than the 8,587 Army nurses in Europe.[99] Carefully chosen for their professional fitness for foreign service, the nurses must embody poise and adaptability and must, of course, uphold the dignity of the Navy Nurse Corps.[100] As the nurses prepared for duty abroad, Superintendent Higbee encouraged them to continue displaying their "splendid professional qualifications." Like a mother hen, she also admonished them against any breach of the nonfraternization rules with enlisted men or patients.[101]

The American Red Cross had set up and equipped a network of hospitals, including several that it transferred to the U.S. Navy. Fifteen Navy nurses served at the naval hospital in London, six others at a small naval hospital in Lorient, France.[102] The remainder had duty at five base hospitals, which the Red Cross had organized then released to the Navy. Medical personnel at various American hospitals formed units of doctors, nurses, and hospital corpsmen that would serve together abroad. Navy nurses joined the units when they were ready to go to Europe.[103]

Base Hospital Number 1 originated at Brooklyn Naval Hospital and sailed for Brest, France, in September 1917. It began admitting patients (mostly Marines) in December and eventually treated 9,035 cases. Under Chief Nurse Frances Van Ingen, fifty-nine Navy nurses lent their healing talents at this base hospital. Two Reserve nurses, Mary Elderkin and Jeannette McClellan, saw duty with a field hospital company near Cohen. For eight days and nights they endured air raids and shell fire while administering to the wounded. Also at Brest was Base Hospital Number 5, which had formed at the Methodist Episcopal Hospital in Philadelphia. It was the primary hospital for U.S. naval forces overseas. Chief Nurse Alice M. Garrett guided the fifty-nine nurses of this unit. Operating teams of doctors, hospital corpsmen, and nurses from this hospital also served temporarily with Army hospitals near the front lines.[104]

Base Hospital Number 2, from San Francisco's Stanford University Hospital, worked at Strathpeffer, Scotland. With Chief Nurse Elizabeth Hogue and her fifty-nine nurses, this hospital treated the sick and injured of the U.S. Navy as well as the British army and Royal Navy. In addition, the staff performed surgical procedures and provided orthopedic and neurological care. Altogether, the unit treated 83,713 patients.[105] Base Hospital Number 3, which originated at Los Angeles's California Hospital, worked in Leith, Scotland, at the Parish Poorhouse. It was in service for only five months, but during this time its staff cared for the sick of both the American and British armies and navies. Chief Nurse Sue S. Dauser and fifty-nine nurses treated about 295 patients a day. From the hospital also came three operating teams who served in Army hospitals near the front in France.[106] The last of these units, Base Hospital Number 4, from the Providence Hospital in Rhode Island, went to Queenstown, Ireland. Chief Nurse Grace M. McIntyer directed forty nurses in caring for U.S. Navy men operating on convoy duty.[107]

In spite of meritorious service in all these base unit hospitals, Navy nurses, along with canteen girls, fell victim to "scurrilous charges of immorality."[108] Although the charges against nurses were groundless, such slander would resurface in a vitriolic way during World War II.

Thirty-four Navy nurses saw duty afloat. Although the Navy had three hospital ships, nurses did not serve on them but on transports. In December 1918 Chief Nurse Sophia V. Kiel supervised six nurses accompanying President Wilson to France for peace negotiations. They, along with Navy surgeon Cary T. Grayson, sailed in the *George Washington* and were the first to have temporary duty of this nature. That same month, Chief Nurse Mary M. Robinson led six other nurses in the *Leviathan*, and in May 1919 four seagoing nurses sailed in *Imperator.* So effective were these women that commanders of ten more transports requested Navy nurses, but a growing shortage in naval hospitals precluded such assignments. The only exceptions were in ships carrying wives and children of enemy aliens back to Europe. For this purpose, four nurses sailed in *Martha Washington*, three in *Princess*

*Matoika*, two in *Powhatan*, and others in *Pocahontas*. Although Surgeon General Braisted had been apprehensive about nurses' shipboard duty, he finally realized that his fears were groundless.[109]

## *Duty in the Tropics*

The war in Europe did not prevent the Navy Nurse Corps from continuing the work it had so ably begun in the Pacific. Since 1911 Navy nurses had run a training school for Chamorro women at Guam. Chief Nurse Beatrice Bowman, one of the Sacred Twenty, arrived in early 1916 and with three other nurses conducted the two-year course in modern midwifery and practical nursing. To give the students a more professional appearance, the Navy issued them nurses' uniforms.[110] As the program expanded, especially during the war, more newly trained "nurses" provided health care to their own villages.

The expansion of Navy medical facilities on Guam included the new Tubercular Hospital, which opened in 1916. Navy nurses joined the staff here and continued their duties at the Naval Hospital and the small, private Susana Hospital in addition to upholding their teaching duties. Bowman also found time to chair the Department of Physiology and Hygiene at the new normal (teacher training) school. Nevertheless, Navy nurses at Guam maintained their cherished eight-hour day, a right not enjoyed by civilian nurses in the United States and Europe.[111]

Similarly, in Samoa, the Navy maintained its governmental control, and Chief Nurse Ada M. Pendleton, also of the Sacred Twenty, led three other nurses at the training school adjacent to the Samoan Hospital in Tutuila. This school for Polynesian teenage girls, established in 1914, graduated its first class in 1916. Its members went into outlying districts as visiting nurses and later returned to the hospital for duty and additional instruction. These nurses were the only wage-earning women on the island, aside from a few domestics.[112] One woman, Grace Pepe, had shown such exceptional ability that the Navy sent her for six months' training at the naval hospital, Mare Island. After Hannah Workman became chief nurse at Samoa, the educational mission spread to include public health classes for pastors' wives.[113]

Duty of a different sort came to the twelve nurses stationed at Cañacao,

Philippine Islands. First sent to the naval hospital there in 1910, Navy nurses administered primarily to naval personnel but also assisted with a clinic, giving both medical treatment and sanitary suggestions to the local women.[114] In 1919 another station opened to Navy nurses: Yokohama, Japan, with Mollie Detweiler as chief nurse. The hospital here had been established late in the nineteenth century and was the first such naval facility in the Far East. As in the Philippines, nurses cared for U.S. Navy men. Nurses at Guam and the Philippines rotated duty at Yokohama. Late in 1919, yet another nurses' duty station opened: Pearl Harbor. Chief Nurse Anna E. Gorham initiated the nursing service there.[115]

On the other side of the world, the Navy Nurse Corps carried its teaching mission to the Caribbean. When the United States acquired the Virgin Islands in 1917, the Navy took over as administrator, and medical officers requested nurses to train local women. Chief Nurse Alice M. Gillett and Nurse Eva R. Dunlap arrived in September, followed by four more nurses. These women began a training school at the municipal hospital at St. Thomas. Two other schools opened: one in Frederiksted and one in Christiansted, both on the island of St. Croix and later under the direction of Chief Nurse Hannah M. Workman.[116] As in the Pacific, these American nurses taught local women the basics of practical nursing and hygiene before dispatching them to outlying areas.[117] Also on St. Croix was the Richmond Institute for Lepers and Insane. The Navy Medical Department, which ran the hospital, sent a supervising nurse to make daily visits to the colony and oversee the local nurses there.[118] By 1919 the contingent of Navy nurses in the Virgin Islands had grown to nine.[119]

When U.S. Marines occupied Haiti in 1915, the Navy Medical Corps assumed control of all health care and hygiene. It soon became apparent that Haitians must learn to help themselves, so the naval commander planned to establish the Training School for Nurses at the City General Hospital at Port-au-Prince. Chief Nurse Lucia D. Jordan and Nurse Josephine Y. Raymond reached Haiti in July 1918 and opened the school in October. Soon Nurse Marie A. Lincoln joined them. Twenty-three students entered the first two-year class, and all instruction was in French.[120] The next year Chief Nurse Elizabeth D. Bushong and two other Navy nurses replaced the original nurses. But the demands of maintaining still another training school drained a shrinking Navy Nurse Corps, and in 1920 the Red Cross assumed operation of the program.[121]

### *The Great Influenza Epidemic*

Navy nurses everywhere felt the effects of the influenza epidemic, which claimed about twenty-two million lives worldwide. This modern plague ran its course from September 1918 to August 1919. Good nursing care was the only treatment for influenza and the pneumonia that often followed it, and Navy nurses frequently worked as much as eighteen hours a day to help relieve the suffering.[122] Naval hospitals admitted an astounding 91,656 patients from the end of August to the end of December 1918, and some facilities had to hire civilian nurses during the crisis to help meet demands for nursing services. Aboard transports influenza ran rampant. One Army commander described the Navy nurses: "They worked night and day in the cold and damp, on decks that were being washed by seas, without any lights whatever, exposed to the dangers of contagion with a deadly malady, and they have rendered these services most cheerfully."[123] Twenty-five Navy nurses died from the disease; eleven more died from other causes before the war officially ended in 1921. A special section at Arlington National Cemetery was reserved for Army and Navy nurses.[124]

### *Winding Down*

On 11 November 1920, Superintendent Higbee and three Reserve nurses—Lillian M. Murphy, Edna E. Place, and Marie L. Hidell, who had died during the influenza epidemic—were awarded the Navy Cross. Three chief nurses—Elizabeth Leonhardt, Martha E. Pringle, and Elsie Brooke—received letters of commendation from the Navy; another, Frances Van Ingen, received a letter for especially meritorious service from the Army. The Army also commended Mary Elderkin and Jeannette McClellan, the Reserve nurses who had served on the front lines in France. Of the nurses entitled to the World War I Victory Medal, thirty-two had died, so their next of kin received their decorations.[125]

Navy nurses remained involved with the demobilization process at the end of the war, especially because of the influenza epidemic. But by 1 July 1919, 514 nurses had returned to civilian life, leaving 1,024 on active duty. A year later there were but 533 Navy nurses.[126] All who left the service received the sixty-dollar Victory Bonus. In 1919 no more nurses could enroll in the USNRF. Two years later all inactive nurses in this group were disenrolled; the following year, the remaining USNRF nurses were either disenrolled or transferred to regular or reserve status.[127]

As the demobilization process continued, the struggle to gain rank for military nurses reached a climax. With the support of individuals and civilian organizations, the Army Nurse Corps tried once again to obtain military rank, which would give its nurses authority over enlisted corpsmen, who often failed to comply with nurses' orders.[128] After extensive hearings, Congress authorized relative rank for Army nurses in June 1920. The superintendent would be a major; assistant superintendents and directors, captains; chief nurses, first lieutenants; and other nurses, second lieutenants. These nurses would exercise authority next after medical officers in the line of professional duties. Although less than commissioned status, relative rank at least provided nomenclature and insignia and gave the nurses a place in the military hierarchy.[129]

Because Navy nurses were supposed to have the same pay and benefits as Army nurses, would the new law apply to them? Superintendent Higbee drew attention to the unsympathetic attitude within the Navy Department itself, and one of her chief nurses questioned the benefits of rank.[130] The Navy already considered nurses, in an administrative context, to be officers, and they had long held authority, just under the medical officers, in naval hospitals, said the new surgeon general, Edward R. Stitt. Rank, then, was superfluous. In September 1921, Stitt argued persuasively that Navy nurses should have relative rank, but then he changed his mind. By November, Stitt firmly opposed giving such status to nurses because it would impair the morale of the Hospital Corps. "It would certainly seem," he wrote, "that recognition of their noble calling and the chivalrous tribute to their womanhood . . . place them on a higher plane than would mere rank." Within weeks, the judge advocate general had made the final decision: Navy nurses were not entitled to relative rank.[131]

In spite of this humiliation, the Navy Nurse Corps performed admirably throughout World War I. Superintendent Higbee had directed corps development and expansion to handle strenuous wartime demands. She kept in close contact with her chief nurses, encouraging and guiding them, and refused to lower the strict standards for Nurse Corps admittance and selection of nurses for important duties. In emphasizing professional qualifications, executive ability, and dignified conduct, she relied heavily on the surviving members of the Sacred Twenty. To publicize the work of the Nurse Corps, Higbee frequently contributed articles to professional journals such as the *American Journal of Nursing* and encouraged her nurses to do the same. Participating in wider wartime nursing endeavors, she gained membership on the Navy's subcommittee of sanitation and public health, the nursing committee of the Advisory Commission of the Council of National Defense, the advisory council of the Army nurse training school, and the National Committee of the Red Cross Nursing Service. Her leadership of the Navy nurses caused Surgeon General Braisted to recognize the "splendid work of this corps, which has been self-sacrificing in its service, devotion to duty, in many instances resulting in disability and death."[132]

During World War I, the U.S. Navy grew in men and ships to address the demands of the European conflagration. How it met wartime requirements depended largely on Secretary of the Navy Josephus Daniels. Because of his vision and boldness, the Navy embarked on the temporary and unprecedented wartime expedient of bringing women into its enlisted ranks as yeomen (F) and Marine Reservists (F).

Those women who entered the naval service had no idea that they were pioneers. They joined the Navy because the country needed their talents. Realizing that their contributions were only for the duration of the war, nearly twelve thousand enlisted women worked as stenographers, typists, file clerks, and telephone operators. A few others filled more unusual billets. After the war ended, the yeomen (F) and Marine Reservists (F) left the service, still not knowing that they had paved the way for future generations of military women. Although the Navy did not want women in its ranks permanently, it followed the Progressive tenant of equal pay for equal work, at least while women served.

Simultaneously, the Navy Nurse Corps, under the steady direction of

Superintendent Lenah S. Higbee, met wartime necessities by expanding the regular corps and by drawing from the reservists and USNRF. Without compromising the high standards for Navy nurses, the corps sent nurses to naval hospitals throughout the United States and to base unit hospitals in Europe. A few served in transports. The nurses continued providing vital instruction to hospital corpsmen, who would be the Navy's nurses onboard ships and in war zones. Navy nurses taught young women in Guam and Samoa, and in Haiti and the Virgin Islands, the fundamentals of practical nursing, which they would use to help improve medical conditions among their own people.

The women of the U.S. Navy performed their duties creditably during World War I. Their jobs in clerical work, nursing, and teaching matched the prevailing professions open to women in society as a whole and locked them into these stereotypes in naval thinking. The interwar years would again bring changes to women's roles, and the Navy would have to grapple with new decisions about women's place in naval service.

# 4

# The Interwar Years, 1921–1940

*After World War I* and the demobilization process, the U.S. Navy returned to normal peacetime activities and traditional ways of meeting its personnel demands. It had no trouble determining women's place: out of the Navy. The exception was, of course, the Navy Nurse Corps, whose members cared for the sick and injured and trained hospital corpsmen and student nurses in faraway places. The character of the Navy's nurses changed during these years as well and reflected the trends in civilian medicine and nursing. "Normalcy" received a rude awakening when the Great Depression forced a cutback in naval expenditures and personnel, including nurses; but in the late 1930s, the Navy began a buildup in anticipation of entering another global conflict.

## The Setting

When the World War I era ended, the United States confronted massive domestic problems: inflation, unemployment, labor strikes, rampant racism, and a Red scare that translated to hostility toward immigrants. The nation longed to throw off the crusading fervor of the Wilson years and retreat into an isolationism that sanctioned the private pursuit of pleasure and the renunciation of global entanglements or responsibilities. Warren G. Harding was just the man to lead the country in its return to normalcy.

Women themselves generally embraced a different ideology after the tumult and fervor of World War I and the drive for suffrage. The 1920s ushered in an age of optimism. Young women, whose idol was the flapper, set out to "have fun," turning their backs on earlier generations' efforts to break out of Victorian domesticity and to gain status in the educational, political, and professional worlds. The female community, which had accomplished much through collective action and reform movements, disintegrated. In its stead came an overwhelming desire to attract a husband, bear children, and sink into domesticity (and isolation). The woman became the wife-companion in a romantic, sensual marriage and reared her children "scientifically" with advice from "experts."[1]

Reinforcing this need for marriage were women's experiences in colleges and universities, where in a communal setting they learned how to catch a man. Attendance surged: in 1920, 283,000 women went to institutions of higher learning; 481,000 went in 1930; and 601,000 attended in 1940. Most women were at coeducational schools.[2]

Once educated, these women, if they did not marry, gravitated toward traditional professions as teachers, nurses, social workers, librarians, and office workers. Only a few entered male-dominated professions such as law, medicine, pharmacology, or architecture. Less educated women found jobs as sales clerks, domestics, or factory workers.[3] In 1920, 25 percent of all women worked outside the home, universally for less pay than men. World War I and its temporary spurt of unorthodox jobs, including naval service, proved to be an aberration that afforded no real change in women's economic or professional status.[4] The number of working women held steady at 25 percent through 1930 and inched up another 2 percent ten years later. Although more women, including married ones, entered the work force during the Depression, they encountered growing hostility, especially if they deprived men of scarce jobs.[5]

Although reform movements engaged fewer women, some persevered, often with a new look and agenda. The National American Woman Suffrage Association, for example, became the League of Women Voters in 1920, with its focus on teaching women the responsibilities of enfranchised citizenship. Even Carrie Chapman Catt saw no further need for a group dedicated to women's rights. She did, however, lend her organizational talents to forming a new peace group, the National Conference on the Cause and Cure of War, in 1925. This broad coalition included members of mainstream women's groups: the General Federation of Women's Clubs, the League of Women Voters, the YWCA, the WCTU, and the American Association of University Women.[6]

In the early 1920s, two new measures were carryovers from the Progressive era's protective efforts on behalf of women and children. The Women's

Bureau of the Department of Labor, established in 1920, collected data on working women and recommended federal policy on their behalf. The following year, the Sheppard-Towner Act provided federal aid to states to reduce infant and maternal death rates, and public health nurses implemented it largely by instructing mothers. In spite of its success in reducing mortality rates, the program lapsed eight years later.[7] At the same time, Nurse Margaret Sanger launched the birth control movement, which gave women the knowledge and ability to control family size. In 1921 she organized the Birth Control Federation of America, the forerunner of Planned Parenthood. The birth rate dropped from 127 per 1,000 women of childbearing age in 1910 to 17.6 in 1933, then began rising again.[8]

Other reform-minded women joined with Alice Paul in the National Women's Party, which in 1923 proposed an equal rights amendment (ERA) to the Constitution: "Men and women shall have equal rights throughout the United States and every place subject to its jurisdiction." The redoubtable nursing leader and activist Lavinia Dock pushed for the measure, although the superintendents of the Army, Navy, Veterans Bureau, and Public Health Service Nurse Corps opposed it. Progressive opponents feared such an amendment would weaken protective legislation already in effect for women and children; others thought it would make women a separate and unequal class. Nothing came of the proposal.[9]

Although there was no central issue inspiring women to band together during these interwar years, notable individual achievements came to the forefront. On the national level, Eleanor Roosevelt, wife of the president, actively championed liberal and social causes and regularly communicated with Americans through public appearances, radio broadcasts, and newspaper and magazine columns. Her influence in New Deal social-welfare programs was crucial. Another social reformer, Frances Perkins, served as secretary of labor throughout the Roosevelt presidency. She was the first woman ever to hold a cabinet position.[10]

As the country turned away from the world beyond its shores, it had no reason to maintain a strong military, and the U.S. Navy fell victim to budget slashing. To reduce the need for expensive shipbuilding in competition with other maritime powers, the administration called the multinational Washington Conference on the Limitation of Armaments, which convened in Washington, D.C., in November 1921.[11] Secretary of State Charles Evans Hughes convinced representatives of the major seafaring nations to agree to a ten-year moratorium on capital-ship construction and to scrap parts of their battleship fleets. The resulting Five Power Treaty, signed on 6 February 1922, established a tonnage ratio of 5:5:3:1.75:1.75 for battleships and aircraft carriers of Britain, the United States, Japan, Italy, and France respectively. Two other treaties resulted from this conference: The Four Power Treaty and the Nine Power Treaty. The United States had finally reached naval parity with Britain, and the "new order of sea power" temporarily stabilized political relations by curtailing a naval arms race.[12]

When the Washington treaties went into effect in August 1923, the Navy possessed 379 active ships, including 18 battleships, 1 fleet aircraft carrier, 13 cruisers, and 69 submarines. By the time the London Treaty of 1930 was in force, extending the moratorium on capital ship construction and limiting cruiser, destroyer, and submarine tonnage, the United States had 16 battleships, 3 carriers, 20 cruisers, and 81 submarines in its 357-ship fleet.[13] During these years, naval aviation came into its own. The Bureau of Aeronautics, established in 1921, was the first new naval bureau since the Civil War. It oversaw the increase of planes and dirigibles.[14]

But twelve years of conservative Republican administrations saw naval budgets cut and personnel reduced from 9,509 active duty officers and 120,421 men in 1921 to 9,463 officers and 81,679 men by 1932.[15] Constricted by treaty limitations and a parsimonious Congress, the Navy concentrated on modernizing its ships, on converting from coal to oil, and on stressing electronics improvements and engineering changes.[16]

The stock market crash in October 1929 ushered in a decade of depression, and during Herbert Hoover's presidency, the Navy cut manpower and operations, laid up ships, and took a 15 percent pay cut. In 1932 Franklin D. Roosevelt was elected president, and a gradual turnaround began. Emergency relief funds put shipyards back to work on 32 new ships, and the 1934 Vinson-Trammell Act authorized a long-range building program. By 1938, the fleet had 346 vessels, including 15 battleships, 5 carriers, 32 cruisers, and 54 submarines. Matching this buildup, personnel expanded to 10,312 officers and 105,599 men.[17] Although the fortunes of the Navy ebbed and flowed, it had no further use for its enlisted women.

## The Yeomen (F)

After the yeomen (F) returned to civilian life, they, like countless male veterans, joined the American Legion. Established in 1919 by American officers still in France, the legion grew into a national organization with thousands of local posts. Women veterans joined the predominately male local posts, although they were not always welcome. In areas where there were large numbers of yeomen (F), the women often set up their own posts, such as the Jacob Jones Post in Washington, the first such all-female group.[18]

Yeomen (F) became eligible for various veterans' benefits, but not always without a fight. In 1923 Acting Secretary of the Navy Theodore Roosevelt Jr. wrote that the Navy favored providing government care for incapacitated women who had served their country. The judge advocate general ruled that women veterans of the Navy and Marines could receive treatment at the National Home for Disabled and Decrepit Naval Personnel.[19]

A bitter dispute developed over adjusted compensation for World War I veterans. Since the end of the war, Congress had considered various bills to give veterans a bonus and in 1923 finally passed a measure that did not include women, but President Harding vetoed it. Early the next year, the House held hearings on the McKenzie bill, which also excluded women. Interest groups mobilized. The American Legion, the Veterans of Foreign Wars, and women's organizations petitioned Congress to include women veterans, and representatives of these groups testified before the House Ways and Means Committee and lobbied senators and congressmen.[20] Finally, an amended bill including women passed both houses and was signed by President Calvin Coolidge in May 1924. The Adjusted Compensation Act defined "veteran" as any *individual* who was a member of the military or naval forces between 5 April 1917 and 12 November 1918. Women, therefore, were officially classified as veterans. This bonus act provided an extra $1.25 a day for overseas duty, $1.00 a day for domestic service.[21] Women also benefited from the Veterans' Act of June 1924, which gave honorably discharged veterans the right to hospital care and treatment as well as compensation for death and treatment for disability acquired in the service during the war period, now extended from 6 April 1917 to 2 July 1921.[22]

As if to make sure that there would be no more women to claim veterans' benefits from future wars, Congress passed the Naval Reserve Act of 1925, which limited membership in the Reserve to "*male* citizens."[23] Such pointed exclusion was not surprising in a decade that saw women willingly return to the realm of domesticity. Flappers certainly would have no interest in military service.

Later legislation gave still more benefits to women veterans. In 1929 Congress authorized the care and treatment of retired naval patients in other government hospitals if no naval hospitals were available. The next year women veterans became eligible for disability allowances for non–service-related ailments.[24]

On the lighter side, in 1925 three former Navy women posed for a composite oil portrait of a yeoman (F) in wartime uniform. Painted by Washington artist Anne Fuller Abbott, the portrait hung on display at the Philadelphia Sesquicentennial in 1926. Afterward, it went on a long odyssey: to the old Main Navy Building, to a special display at Hecht's Department Store in Washington, D.C., then perhaps to the Pentagon's Arlington Annex. After that it was lost for years, finally turning up in the Navy Recruit Training Command in Orlando, Florida.[25]

The yeomen (F), like others who shared mutual interests, realized that there was strength and camaraderie in organization, so in 1926, at the American Legion convention, women delegates established the National Yeomen (F) "to foster and perpetuate the memory of the service of Yeomen (F)." The group received a charter from the District of Columbia in 1928 and a national charter from Congress eight years later. Meeting annually at different locations around the country, the National Yeomen (F)'s membership peaked at 1,075 in 1961. The group sporadically sent out a newsletter, the *Note Book*, which printed news items, reminiscences, and notices of National Yeomen (F) events. One event that stirred patriotic memories was the 1929 inaugural parade for Herbert Hoover. About thirty-five of these veterans marched in uniform to the cadence of a prize-winning drum corps from Alexandria. During World War II, many yeomen (F) entered military service once again. As the years passed, the numbers of former yeomen (F) dwindled, and finally, in 1985, the national organization closed down.[26]

## The Navy Nurse Corps

Although the Navy no longer needed the yeomen (F), it still had worldwide administrative responsibilities. In the Pacific were Guam and Samoa; in the Caribbean, the Virgin Islands and Haiti. The Bureau of Medicine and Surgery continued to provide medical care in these, as well as other, locations overseas, at home, and in hospital ships. In 1920 an additional task came with the formation of the Veterans Bureau (which ten years later became the Veterans Administration). The Navy loaned five hospitals to the U.S. Public Health Service for the bureau's care of naval veterans. Health-care services for these veterans would strain dwindling personnel resources.

Matching the decline and resurgence of the Navy itself, the Medical Department had 886 physicians, 71 commissioned pharmacists, and 150 dentists in 1921; 904 surgeons and 198 dentists in 1932; and 881 doctors and 277 dentists in 1940.[27] To direct all medical personnel more efficiently, the Bureau of Medicine and Surgery had reorganized in 1931 and had divided its functions into divisions. The Division of Personnel included sections for each corps—Medical, Dental, Nurse, Hospital, and Reserve.[28]

The Bureau of Medicine and Surgery provided postgraduate training for about thirty doctors a year at the Naval Medical School in Washington. Here physicians received instruction in topics such as naval hygiene, gas warfare, aviation, and submarine and deep-sea diving. Other medical officers took special training at civilian postgraduate medical schools. Similarly, naval dentists attended courses at the Naval Medical School or at civilian dental schools.[29]

As the Medical and Dental Corps became more specialized and highly trained, so, too, did nursing services. The Hospital Corps, which supplied most of the Navy's "nurses," grew from 3,895 men in 1922 to 4,624 in 1932 and 10,545 in 1940. The bureau tried throughout the 1920s to secure permanent commissioned rank for chief pharmacists, because these skilled men had reverted to the Hospital Corps from their wartime commissioned status in 1921.[30] The number of women in the Navy Nurse Corps averaged about 500 during the interwar years. Like other medical professionals in the Navy, nurses took advantage of opportunities for specialized postgraduate training at the Naval Medical School and at private universities and hospitals.[31]

The move toward more education was characteristic of the entire nursing profession. Hospital training schools proliferated: in 1920 there were 1,755 schools with 54,953 students. The numbers peaked in 1927 with 2,286 schools and 77,768 students, then dropped during the Depression to 1,472 schools with 67,000 pupils.[32] The Mills School for Male Nurses, established in 1888, was the only one of its kind, but in 1912 its program shifted to training male orderlies. Ten years later, it reopened as a nurses' training school for men. In 1930 the American Nurses Association began admitting qualified male nurses.[33] Acceptance of male nurses did not extend to the Navy or Army Nurse Corps, which remained exclusively female.

Simultaneously, nursing took on more academic respectability as colleges and universities started offering nursing education. By the mid-1920s, some twenty-five institutions gave a five-year course that would lead to a bachelor's degree and a nursing diploma. By 1936, seventy colleges offered this degree program. Two universities introduced doctoral programs in nursing: in 1920 at Teachers College, Columbia, in New York, and in 1934, at New York University. Yale University opened a school of nursing in 1924—the first autonomous university department of nursing in the country. A new organization, the Association of Collegiate Schools of Nursing, established in 1933, evaluated nursing programs in colleges becoming, in effect, an accrediting agency.[34] After they finished their training courses, nurses, like physicians, often specialized in one field, pursuing postgraduate courses in anesthesia, dietetics, physical therapy, or operating room and tuberculosis nursing.[35]

The practice of nursing changed markedly during the interwar years. Private-duty nursing decreased because of improved medical technology and better general hospitals. Public health, or visiting, nursing, begun in the 1890s by Lillian Wald and Mary Brewster, became more widespread. Graduate nurses often took postgraduate courses at colleges and universities to prepare themselves for this specialized field; and the U.S. Public Health Service, the Red Cross, the Bureau of Indian Affairs, and state and local governments began utilizing such nurses in public health departments. By the mid-1920s, 3,629 agencies employed more than eleven thousand public health nurses.[36]

During the Depression, nurses joined the ranks of the unemployed, and many found novel ways of earning a living. Because the demand for private-duty nurses had diminished, nurses looking for work sometimes resorted to floor duty in hospitals, a task usually assigned to student nurses, when they could find such jobs, and often they were willing to work for room, board, and laundry. Others turned to a new field: in-flight service for major airlines. In the early 1930s, airlines hired only graduate nurses, who could reassure nervous or airsick passengers, as stewardesses. New Deal measures provided employment for numerous nurses. Beginning in November 1933, the Civil Works Administration hired more than ten thousand nurses for public health projects. This program ended the following April, but in 1935 the Works Progress Administration found employment for about six thousand graduate nurses in similar activities. That same year, the Social Security Act provided funds to train public health nurses, who then found jobs with state and local health departments.[37]

Nurses were a part of the changing medical scene during the interwar years. War-related injuries and illnesses receded, and old problems gave way to new treatments or solutions. Death rates from tuberculosis dropped; blinding trachoma yielded to modern treatment. Better education lowered maternal and infant mortality rates, and Margaret Sanger spearheaded the birth control movement. In 1936 new sulfonamide drugs attacked earlier killers such as blood poisoning, strep throat, pneumonia, and scarlet fever.[38]

Although employment for nurses may have been uncertain in the civilian sector, the Navy definitely needed them. Already firmly established as an intrinsic part of the Medical Department, the Navy Nurse Corps continued in the interwar years to demonstrate its value and usefulness under a new superintendent.

In April 1921, Secretary of the Navy Edwin Denby received a letter from the American Legion passing along news of the alleged favoritism of Superintendent Lenah S. Higbee to foreign-born, especially British, nurses. An enclosed anonymous abstract recited instances of Anglophilia in appointing such women as chief nurses. Apparently, Chief Nurse Mary H. DuBose had aired these complaints against the superintendent. The Navy rose up in arms. Denby refused to take action based on anonymous charges, but the department refuted point-by-point the allegations made against

Higbee, concluding that DuBose had acted through personal malice. Surgeon General Edward R. Stitt took the defense to the larger nursing community by sending a spirited letter to the *American Journal of Nursing*.[39] But the allegations, coupled with fatigue caused by long years of service, must have taken their toll, for Higbee resigned as superintendent on 23 November 1922.[40]

Waiting in the wings for her job was Higbee's friend and protégée, Josephine Beatrice Bowman. Bowman had asked Secretary Denby for permission to take the examination for the superintendent's position if a vacancy occurred, but not as long as there was the "slightest hope of keeping Mrs. Higbee." Higbee supported Bowman's request, and Denby made the appointment on 28 November.[41]

One of the Sacred Twenty, Bowman had excellent qualifications for the job. Born in 1881, she had graduated from the Training School for Nurses, Medico-Chirurgical Hospital in Philadelphia in 1904 and soon joined the American Red Cross Nursing Service. She entered the Navy Nurse Corps on 3 October 1908, becoming a chief nurse three years later. After working in various naval hospitals, she left the corps briefly in 1914–15 to serve in a Red Cross Unit Hospital in England. Bowman reentered the Navy and served in Guam. She was chief nurse at the large hospital at Great Lakes during World War I, then at Ft. Lyon, Colorado. In 1920 she was among the first nurses to serve in the hospital ship *Relief* (AH 1). In early 1922, she returned to the Bureau of Medicine and Surgery for a preparatory course for the superintendent's position.[42] Perhaps even more to her credit was a complaint sent to the bureau about Bowman's "domineering and autocratic manner," an attribute that might be useful in her new role.[43]

Under Bowman's administration there were 479 Navy nurses in 1922 and 529 in 1931. During the Depression and the Navy's economy drive, the number dropped to a low of 332 in 1935. After having to discharge 15 nurses because of personnel reduction, Bowman, who felt the loss keenly, tried to soften the blow by explaining the situation to all Navy nurses. As the economy improved, the number of nurses climbed to 488 in 1940.[44] Meanwhile, Reserve nurses were slowly phased out. Appointments of new reservists stopped in 1926; and five years later, all remaining in the Reserve transferred to the regular Navy Nurse Corps.[45]

Throughout the affluent 1920s, the Navy had difficulty attracting and retaining nurses because of the low pay in comparison to civilian nursing and because of the slight advantages gained in promotion—only from nurse to chief nurse. The nurses whom the Navy could attract might be of lower quality than naval service demanded. Before she resigned, Higbee had complained of the scaled-down requirements of nurses' training schools during the war and the poor caliber of graduates. These young nurses expected the government to complete their training, which put more burdens on the Navy's chief nurses.[46]

Bowman hoped to rekindle nurses' interest in naval service and spent much of her time as superintendent taking the Navy Nurse Corps's case to the public. She and her assistants presented talks and slide shows before dozens of groups of nurses, students in training schools, and professional organizations. She sent thousands of circulars to hospitals, alumnae associations, and nurses' registries, and she appealed to her friend, Clara D. Noyes, director of the Red Cross Nursing Service, for that group's help. She regularly published articles in professional journals.[47] In spite of these intense efforts, the Navy Nurse Corps rarely reached its authorized strength.

Poor pay continued to be the major deterrent. Army and Navy nurses had received a two-year, 20 percent pay hike in 1920, and when that expired, Congress refigured and raised pay and allowances for military nurses. For the superintendent, base pay, subsistence, and an extra allowance totaled $4,276; for assistant superintendents, $3,276; and for chief nurses, $2,376. For nurses, base pay and subsistence started at $1,056 and rose in three-year increments to a maximum of $1,776 after ten years. In addition, nurses got up to $480 a year for a rental allowance. Subsistence rose by $3 a month in 1924. These rates remained unchanged throughout the rest of the 1920s. The $70-a-month base pay for an entering Navy nurse compared unfavorably with $90 in civilian hospitals and $80 in the U.S. Public Health Service.[48] At the height of the Depression, Navy nurses, along with everyone else in the Navy, took a 15 percent pay cut in 1932.[49]

There were, however, compensatory benefits for Navy nurses. In 1923 they began receiving government-issued uniforms for the first time. Previously, nurses had to provide their own. Like the yeomen (F), members of the Navy Nurse Corps who had served during World War I were eligible for the veterans' bonuses provided in the Adjusted Compensation Act of 1924 and for treatment in government hospitals under the Veterans Bureau.[50] A major benefit resulted from the Retirement Act for Army and Navy nurses in 1926. The Medical Departments of both services had been trying for several years to persuade Congress to pass such legislation and among their arguments had used the precedent of the British military's providing these benefits for its nurses. In effect on 13 May 1926, the retirement law provided that nurses with thirty years' service or with twenty years' service and having reached age fifty would be placed on the retired list. They would receive up to 75 percent of their active base pay. Higher administrators got extra compensation.[51] In rapid succession, Army and Navy nurses amassed other benefits: hospital treatment or domiciliary care in the National Home for Disabled Volunteer Soldiers; care and treatment in non-naval hospitals; and in 1930, retirement for disability incurred in the line of duty, regardless of length of service.[52] By 1940, 127 Navy nurses had retired on disability.[53]

The Navy continued to provide the cherished eight-hour day (with ten to twelve hours for night duty about every third month) and thirty days of paid annual and sick leave per year. It offered attractive quarters for nurses and opportunities for travel and for diversified assignments at home, abroad, and in hospital ships, said one nurse from the interwar era. And it encouraged qualified nurses to take courses in a variety of specialties at nursing schools and universities. "It was a nice life," recalled another nurse.[54]

In 1924 Navy nurses received their official uniforms. Completely redesigned and approved by the secretary of the Navy, the uniform was mandatory by November, except for probationers (those in service less than six months) who could wear any white ward uniform.[55] Nurses were issued six white uniforms, a navy blue sweater, a blue cape lined with maroon, and summer and winter hats. They also had to don the Nurse Corps cap, white hose, and white oxfords or boots. For outdoors, chief nurses and nurses in hospital ships had to wear either a navy blue or white two-piece suit and a blue silk velour or white straw Knox sailor hat. Raincoats, not provided by the government, were optional. Stripes adorned the coat sleeves: black silk braid on the blue, white with luster braid on the white. The superintendent had three stripes—two half-inch stripes with a quarter-inch stripe between them. Assistant superintendents had two half-inch stripes, and chief nurses, one half-inch and one quarter-inch stripe. Regular nurses wore one half-inch stripe. A new insignia pin, to be worn on the collars of the ward uniform and the outdoor coat, completed the new outfit. The redesigned pin was smaller than the earlier one and consisted of an anchor and an oak leaf with the letters "N.N.C." superimposed on it.[56] This Nurse Corps uniform remained unchanged during the interwar period.

The nurses may have succeeded in getting better uniforms, but their status within the service did not improve in this era. After the Navy rejected the concept of relative rank, such as Army nurses had gained in 1920, the question remained: Were the nurses officers or enlisted? That same year, Surgeon General Braisted had ordered that nurses no longer be designated "supernumeraries" but be listed on the roles as naval personnel.[57] This action, however, did not solve the problem. Although Nurse Corps accounts were carried as those of commissioned officers, benefits were not commensurate. Superintendent Bowman felt that these women, who were trained professional nurses and teachers, should have a clearly defined status.[58] In 1924 the Bureau of Navigation took another step: nurses in transports for duty or passage would enjoy officers' status for quarters and mess.[59] That right soon applied in naval hospitals, too, where nurses were equated with officers for quarters.[60] Then, progress toward a definition of status stopped, and a series of opinions hammered home the fact that nurses were not officers. In 1927 the judge advocate general ruled again that because nurses were not officers, they were not entitled to relative rank. That same year, the Bureau of Navigation said that nurses could not be included in the *Navy Register* or the *Navy Directory*. In 1932 the same bureau would not establish rules of precedence for nurses in the *Relief* because they were "in no sense officers." The following year the comptroller general refused mileage allowances for nurses, and in 1935 the judge advocate general disallowed paying for utilities in nurses' quarters—all because nurses were not officers.[61]

In spite of the status problem, the Nurse Corps continued to maintain high standards. Nurses, the corps declared, must have graduated from approved schools of nursing and have one or two years of experience, state registration, and American citizenship. They must be between twenty-two and thirty-five years of age, unmarried, and in good physical condition. Because Navy nurses had heavy teaching responsibilities as well as nursing duties, they must have tact, dignity, and executive ability. As time passed, requirements tightened to include graduation from high school and age limits of twenty-two to twenty-eight years.[62]

Discipline was not a major problem during these interwar years, and in most cases the superintendent merely recommended releasing nurses who were not "suitable" for the corps.[63] One case, however, led to a court-martial and newspaper publicity. In April 1925 customs officials found and seized liquor in the luggage of Chief Nurse Ruth M. Anderson and Nurse Katherine C. Glancy, who were returning from duty at Guantanamo Bay, Cuba. In June, they stood trial by general court-martial at the Washington Navy Yard, and even Superintendent Bowman was summoned as a witness. The nurses pleaded ignorance: friends had given them a party the night before they left Cuba and must have placed the contraband in their baggage. The prosecution uncapped the bottles to show they did, in fact, contain liquor. The six-officer court promptly acquitted the nurses, but the whole silly episode did not subside. In August Secretary of the Navy Curtis Wilbur sent the prosecutor, a young Marine lieutenant, a letter of admonition for not pursuing the case vigorously enough.[64]

Following a trend in civilian nursing, the Bureau of Medicine and Surgery encouraged Navy nurses to take specialized postgraduate training at the bureau's expense. Bowman always believed that nursing should be a university program with hospitals accepting nurses, as well as doctors, for internships, but because this was not the case, she encouraged nurses to participate in Navy-sponsored postgraduate training. Surgeon General Braisted suggested this program in 1920, and subsequent surgeons general expanded it. After nurses completed their course work, they made use of their specialized training in naval hospitals, in giving basic instruction to other nurses, and in teaching hospital corpsmen.[65]

Beginning in October 1921, nurses started taking a wide variety of courses: dietetics at Miss Farmer's School of Cookery in Boston; laboratory skills at the Naval Medical School; the teaching of nursing at Teachers College, Columbia, and at Stanford University; tuberculosis nursing at the Veterans' Hospital, Oteen, North Carolina; physiotherapy at the Naval Hospital, Brooklyn; and anesthetics at Lakeside Hospital, Cleveland. By March 1924, sixty-one nurses had participated in specialized training courses.[66] As time passed, more schools, universities, and hospitals offered courses for nurses: Harvard Medical School; the Graduate School of Medicine and the School of Nursing, University of Pennsylvania; the New Haven School of Physical Therapy; George Washington University; Johns Hopkins University; and various naval hospitals. In five years, another sixty-seven nurses had participated in postgraduate training courses. The program slacked off during the worst of the Depression, then revived. Ten years later, at least sixty-three more nurses had taken classes.[67]

This increased professionalization of the Navy Nurse Corps occurred simultaneously with a revamping of the superintendent's duties. Bowman had regularly visited naval hospitals on the East Coast for the purpose of inspecting nursing activities and solving whatever problems nurses had. She wanted to make nursing procedures more efficient and uniform, but this required too much traveling to far-flung hospitals for one person. In January 1923, Congress authorized three assistant superintendents and one director for the Nurse Corps. The three assistants would be inspectors, conveying the Bureau of Medicine and Surgery's interest to the nurses and in turn bringing nursing problems to the surgeon general's attention. One assistant went to the Inspector of Medical Department Activities on the Pacific coast, one went to the bureau for inspection duty on the East Coast, and one went to the superintendent's office.[68] The Nurse Corps did not fill the director's slot.

Taking on the newly created assistant superintendent's positions were three chief nurses: Clare L. DeCeu (one of the Sacred Twenty), Anna G. Davis, and Betty W. Mayer. These women regularly visited naval hospitals, observed and talked with the nurses, and reported back to the superintendent. Bowman herself continued to inspect hospitals on the East and West Coasts, in the West Indies, and in the hospital ship *Relief*. In addition to making inspection trips, the assistant superintendents gave dozens of presentations at hospitals, clubs, nursing schools, and professional organizations to stimulate interest in the Navy Nurse Corps.[69]

### *Duty in the United States*

The primary job of Nurse Corps women was, of course, caring for the ill and injured in naval hospitals. Following the urgent demand for hospital facilities during World War I, the need dropped during the interwar years.

Consequently, hospitals either closed or consolidated, and five were given over for Veterans Bureau use. Navy nurses served at all remaining hospitals.

An added responsibility for the Medical Department and, consequently, for nurses, was the influx of veterans sent to naval hospitals by the Veterans Bureau. Their numbers steadily increased, and the nature of their problems often called for nursing expertise in physical therapy, tuberculosis care, and neuropsychiatric disorders.[70] Fortunately, many Navy nurses had taken post-graduate courses in these fields.

Another major domestic task for the Navy Nurse Corps was teaching hospital corpsmen, a responsibility they had assumed since their founding in 1908. After the war, training facilities consolidated: schools at Newport and Great Lakes closed, the San Francisco (Mare Island) school relocated to San Diego in 1928, and the Pharmacist's Mates School moved to the grounds of the Norfolk Naval Hospital.[71] The two remaining schools, San Diego and Norfolk, gained added recognition when the health authorities in California (1922) and Virginia (1924) placed them on their accredited lists. This meant hospital corpsmen who had completed instruction at one of the schools and had four years' naval service were entitled to examination and registration as nurses in those states.[72]

Like the Nurse Corps, the Hospital Corps had difficulty maintaining its authorized strength; and, also like the Nurse Corps, caring for Veterans Bureau patients drained its personnel resources. The Hospital Corps averaged about four thousand personnel for most of this era. When young men entered the corps, they were about eighteen years old and had completed roughly two years' high school education. They spent between four and six months in training schools conducted by doctors, other hospital corpsmen, and Navy nurses. After completing this theoretical instruction, they continued their practical training in naval hospitals, always under the watchful eye of Navy nurses. The male "nurses" then served in hospitals at home and abroad, in naval ships, and with the Marine Corps, which relied on the Navy for medical support.[73]

## *Duty Afloat*

In 1920, a long-awaited and exciting opportunity opened for the Nurse Corps: permanent duty in hospital ships. Although these nurses had served temporarily in transports in the months following the armistice and in the hospital ship *Mercy* (AH 4) on a voyage from New York through the Panama Canal to California in 1920, they had had no chance for permanent assignment afloat. In part, this may have come from then–Surgeon General Braisted's reluctance to make use of their services. He realized that no hospital was complete without them, but he feared that confinement and isolation onboard ships would cause difficulties.[74]

The Navy commissioned *Relief,* the first vessel designed and built as a hospital ship, in December 1920. Its modern facilities and five hundred beds qualified it as one of the world's finest floating hospitals, and it included quarters for female nurses. Chief Nurse Beatrice Bowman and ten others were the first Navy nurses assigned to *Relief.* In February 1921 *Relief* took part in Caribbean maneuvers and then sailed with the Atlantic Fleet for two years before permanently joining the Battle Fleet in the Pacific. The women were ecstatic at the chance to be a part of the seagoing Navy, and Bowman wrote glowingly of their experiences to Superintendent Higbee and in a series of articles for the *American Journal of Nursing.*[75] Nurses continued to be part of the ship's complement during the entire interwar period.[76] Beginning in 1938, for example, Ruth A. Erickson, who would later become director of the Navy Nurse Corps, and Mary J. Lindner served in *Relief* for eighteen months.[77] Lindner marveled at the efficiency of the floating hospital: "All necessary doctors and dentists were right there and could attend patients as soon as they came on board."[78] Nurses also saw permanent duty in *Mercy,* hospital ship of the Scouting Fleet, starting in January 1921. The commanding officer had urgently requested that the surgeon general send nurses. Stitt complied by assigning one chief nurse and four nurses to *Mercy,* and another nurse soon joined them. Women continued to serve in *Mercy* until she was decommissioned in 1934.[79]

Transports also needed nurses as the occasion demanded. In November 1921 Surgeon General Stitt approved of assigning them to the transports *Argonne* (AP 4) and *Chaumont* (AP 5) because they were carrying women and children.[80] Soon more Navy nurses served in other such ships. Chief Nurse Susie Fitzgerald wrote of a one-hundred-day voyage from Hampton Roads, through the Panama Canal, up the West Coast to Puget Sound, and back carrying several hundred women and children each way.[81] Still more nurses served in the *Henderson* (AP 1), *Kittery* (AK 2), and *Gold Star* (AG 12), and two others received letters of commendation for their service.[82]

Navy nurses sailed in *Henderson* in the summer of 1923 with President and Mrs. Harding on their twenty-one-day Alaskan trip. Nurse Ruth Powderly had cared for Mrs. Harding during a serious illness the year before, and she, along with Chief Nurse Sue S. Dauser, accompanied the presidential party at sea. Sailing from Tacoma on 5 July, *Henderson* carried her important passengers to ports in Alaska and Canada, then back to Seattle. Before the transport could pick up the Hardings again in San Diego, the president fell ill in San Francisco. Dauser and Powderly were assigned to his case, but he died on 2 August.[83]

## *Duty in the Tropics*

As they had since 1911, Navy nurses ran a training school for teenage girls at Guam. They continued teaching the rudiments of sanitation, child care, and midwifery, which the students would practice in outlying villages after graduation. The young graduates became private-duty nurses or were children's nursemaids for the whites on the island, and they acted as midwives among the Guamanians. Some were floor nurses at Susana Hospital, while others worked at the Tuberculosis Hospital. A few were school nurses. There were limited professional opportunities for nurses at Guam.[84] Nevertheless, when Assistant Superintendent Clare L. DeCeu inspected the facilities in 1925, she found the atmosphere happy and the Chamorro nurses courteous and efficient.[85]

The training school program was a two-year course until Hannah M. Workman became chief nurse in 1927. Believing that this was too brief a time for teaching students the essentials, especially because the Chamorros had difficulty with the English language, Workman extended the course to three years in 1928.[86] The next year the Training School for Native Nurses held its first graduation ceremony ever, attended by the governor and complete with pomp, circumstance, diplomas, and pins. These ceremonies became traditional and soon included the Florence Nightingale Pledge.[87] By 1934, sixty-eight young women had graduated from the training school. Chief Nurse Emily J. Cunningham and four other nurses carried on the dual tasks of nursing naval personnel and conducting the school, and the program continued throughout the 1930s.[88]

Navy nurses also carried on the training school in Samoa, which had started in 1914. The same concept, helping locals learn to improve their own health and hygiene, had led to a similar program for teaching young women the basics and sending them out as district health nurses, midwives, and infant-care experts. Others worked at the Samoan Hospital. In the early 1920s, Chief Nurse Bernice Mansfield and three of her colleagues managed the work of the Samoan Hospital Training School in Tutuila, and their students later helped improve maternal care and lower infant mortality.[89]

To encourage young Polynesian girls to enter the school, the Navy nurses relied heavily on village pastors who would supervise the graduates when they returned as district nurses. The Navy nurses also depended on the good influence of Grace Pepe, the Samoan who had gone for six months' training at the Naval Hospital, Mare Island, and had become chief nurse in Samoa.[90] Others from the outside world were also intrigued with Samoan life, and in 1926 noted anthropologist Margaret Mead visited there to study adolescent girls.[91]

Navy nurses kept the training school, which had increased its course to four years, operating. By the mid-1930s, Chief Nurse Theresa E. Wilkins reported that since the school had begun, fifty-seven student nurses had graduated. At this time, there were four Navy nurses stationed in Samoa. So effective were they that the secretary of the Navy assessed their training school as a "very valuable institution for the Samoan people."[92]

Elsewhere in the Pacific, Navy nurses had routine duty in naval hospitals. At Cañacao, Philippine Islands, their work was similar to that at any such hospital in the United States but without the veterans. The Philippines lacked the isolation of Guam and Samoa, offering instead a wide range of activities for off-duty nurses. Many used this station as a takeoff point for extended trips to China and Japan. After Assistant Superintendent Clare DeCeu inspected the station in 1925, she commended her colleagues for their continuing efficient training of hospital corpsmen there. About a dozen nurses were on duty at Cañacao throughout the interwar years.[93]

Another tropical station, Pearl Harbor, Hawaiian Islands, had opened for Navy nurses in 1919. The naval hospital, like the Cañacao facility, cared for men of the U.S. Navy, so duty was comparable to that at a stateside hospital. DeCeu had included this station on her 1925 inspection trip and commented favorably on the nurses' professional ability. Eleven worked at the hospital, and one worked in the dispensary at Honolulu.[94] Nurses at Pearl Harbor and Cañacao would be the first to suffer the onset of World War II in the Pacific. The third naval hospital in the Far East that had opened to Navy nurses was in Yokohama, Japan. Two nurses served at this post until a massive earthquake on 1 September 1923 destroyed the hospital and most of the city.[95]

In the Caribbean, as well as in the Pacific, the Navy Nurse Corps continued its teaching mission. At three hospitals in the Virgin Islands, nine nurses ran training schools set up in 1917—at the municipal hospitals on St. Thomas and at Frederiksted and Christiansted on St. Croix. Each school averaged about fifteen students a year, although fewer than half completed the three-year course.[96]

Believing that affiliation with an American nursing school and a subsequent diploma would help draw better students, the Bureau of Medicine and Surgery tried for years to arrange such an affiliation. After Superintendent Bowman's inspection trip in early 1925, she pursued the matter by contacting the superintendent of nurses at Freedman Hospital in Washington, but nothing came of it.[97] Chief Nurse Myn M. Hoffman, later superintendent of the Navy Nurse Corps, despaired of attracting a better class of girls to the schools because their parents would not let them care for "inferior" classes of patients.[98]

Nevertheless, the graduates of the three training schools worked as charge nurses in the hospitals and as district welfare nurses who visited schools, homes, and the Richmond Institute for Lepers and Insane. They practiced midwifery and worked as private-duty nurses. Their numbers were small—fewer than one hundred—by 1931, which was fortunate because job opportunities were limited.[99]

Naval administration of the islands ended in 1931, when President Herbert Hoover ordered the Department of Interior to assume their responsibility. During the summer, Navy nurses returned to the United States; the last left on 25 July.[100] As in other tropical stations, their greatest achievement had been helping poorly educated inhabitants help themselves.

Navy nurses took their healing talents elsewhere in the Caribbean. They had established a training school at Port-au-Prince, Haiti, in October 1918, but the American Red Cross took over the program two years later. U.S. Marines still served as peacekeepers in that troubled nation, and in 1921 the secretary of the Navy urged the surgeon general to send nurses to the Marine's

First Brigade field hospital at Port-au-Prince. Chief Nurse Fida Krook and Nurses Ellen M. Olson and Clara Klinksick initially handled the assignment.[101] By 1925, when Superintendent Bowman inspected the station, Chief Nurse Virginia A. Rau, who also would become superintendent, reported that there were five Navy nurses at the one-hundred-bed facility. Other members of the Nurse Corps continued this duty until the Marines left Haiti in 1934. On the same inspection trip, Bowman visited Guantanamo Bay, Cuba, where several nurses worked in the naval hospital. As in other overseas hospitals, nurses cared for Navy personnel.[102]

## *Civilian Disasters*

In addition to juggling its teaching and nursing responsibilities, the Navy Nurse Corps responded to civilian catastrophes. A thirty-inch snowfall blanketed Washington, D.C., in January 1922. As several hundred people watched a movie, the roof of the Knickerbocker Theater collapsed under the weight of the snow. Casualties were immense: 98 killed and 136 injured. The Navy sent medical teams to render emergency aid and admitted civilians to the naval hospital as supernumeraries. Two chief nurses, Anne K. Harkins and Florence M. Vevia, received letters of commendation for their efficient assistance.[103]

Disaster of another sort struck in Newport Harbor on 18 August 1925, when the excursion steamer *Mackinac*, carrying more than six hundred men, women, and children, was returning to Pawtucket in the late afternoon. As the ship passed within a mile of the naval hospital, a defective boiler exploded, showering boiling water and spraying steam on the hapless passengers. Within minutes, rescue launches from Navy ships anchored nearby began removing the injured and carrying many to the hospital landing. The hospital staff admitted seventy-nine victims, twenty of whom were treated and released. Chief Nurse Esther L. James directed both Navy nurses and countless volunteer nurses who came to help in caring for the severely injured patients. Most were badly scalded; others had inhaled the steam, while still others suffered from shock. Twenty-eight died before the next morning, forty-six within a few days. Once again, in the face of calamity, the Navy had aided civilian victims.[104]

The following year another such opportunity arose. On 19 September a ferocious hurricane bore down on Pensacola, Florida, and on the nearby naval air station and hospital. By the next day, the 120-mile-an-hour winds and torrential rains had washed out bridges connecting Pensacola and the air station, downed power and telephone lines, destroyed buildings, and uprooted large trees. Warrington, a small town adjoining the air station, was completely flooded. Refugees from the town struggled to the safety of the naval hospital, perched on a hill, and hospital staff opened the doors to some four hundred civilians. Five Navy nurses busily set up empty wards; found dry sheets, blankets, and pajamas for everyone; and tended to minor ailments as they developed. Hospital corpsmen doubled as cooks, preparing soup, Navy beans, biscuits, and coffee for the unexpected guests. The following morning the refugees began leaving the security of the hospital to start the cleanup work at home. The only hurricane-related fatalities were an Army pilot and his passenger who flew too low over the air station, hit the radio tower, and plunged to the ground.[105]

## *Changes in Leadership*

Superintendent Bowman was in her fifty-fourth year when she retired on 1 January 1935. She had been in the Navy Nurse Corps since it began in 1908 and was the last of the Sacred Twenty to leave it. With her retirement, the era of establishment, organization, development, wartime expansion, and peacetime professionalization ended. During her watch as superintendent, Bowman worked hard for her nurses—better pay (but never enough), retirement benefits, free uniforms—and tried to gain congressional action on their military status. She instigated inspections of all naval hospitals, either by herself or by her assistants, to acquire information so the corps could establish uniform hospital nursing standards and to learn firsthand the nurses' experiences and problems. Perhaps her greatest contribution was in encouraging Navy nurses to take postgraduate courses, a means of keeping themselves apprised of new developments in medicine and maintaining professional equality with civilian nurses. In addition to her Nurse Corps responsibilities, she assumed a leadership role in numerous nursing organizations.[106] When the long-awaited monument to mark the Army and Navy nurses' plot in

Arlington Cemetery was unveiled in November 1938, it was appropriate that Beatrice Bowman presided at the ceremonies.[107]

Succeeding Bowman as superintendent came Myn M. Hoffman. Born in 1883, she graduated from St. Joseph's Training School for Nurses in Denver, joined the Navy Nurse Corps in February 1917, on the eve of the United States' entry into World War I, and quickly rose to chief nurse. She served in hospitals at home and at St. Croix, Virgin Islands. Because of her exceptional ability, she became an assistant superintendent in 1934 and worked with Bowman in the Bureau of Medicine and Surgery. After replacing Bowman in January 1935, she guided the corps as it grew in personnel from 339 in 1935 to 427 three years later. Hoffman retired on 1 October 1938.[108]

Replacing Hoffman was Virginia Rau, who served as acting superintendent from October 1938 to February 1939. Born in 1889, she graduated from Buffalo General Hospital in 1906 and enrolled in the Navy Nurse Corps in 1911. A longtime enthusiast of the corps, Rau often spoke of the advantages Navy nurses enjoyed. The corps, she said, had always been directed by progressive nursing leaders. As acting superintendent, Rau kept the corps running until a new leader came on duty.[109]

## *The Approach of World War II*

By the mid-1930s, the world's efforts to maintain the fragile peace had begun unraveling. Adolf Hitler launched the Nazi regime in Germany in 1933, and that country soon walked out of the League of Nations. Japan took similar action and the following year ended its adherence to the Washington naval treaties. Disarmament was dead and rank expansionism began. Italy invaded Ethiopia in 1935, Germany went into the Rhineland the following year, and Japan invaded China in 1937. The Munich Conference led to the dismemberment of Czechoslovakia in 1938. In 1939 Italy attacked Albania. After Germany invaded Poland in September 1939, Britain and France declared war on Germany. The Axis powers appeared unstoppable. The Soviet Union moved into the Baltic states, and early in 1940 the Nazi blitzkrieg overran Denmark, Norway, the Netherlands, Belgium, Luxembourg, and northern France. That June, France surrendered. Britain stood alone in Europe against the Axis. Then, in 1941, Germany turned against its erstwhile ally, invading the Soviet Union. Meanwhile, in the Far East, Japan had allied with Germany and Italy in September 1940 and soon invaded Indochina and eyed Europe's colonial possessions in the Pacific.

As these events unfolded, the United States edged toward involvement. While isolationists battled interventionists, President Franklin D. Roosevelt cautiously nudged the country toward helping the Allies but without military action. The Neutrality Act of 1935 and its extension in 1936 set up a mandatory arms embargo against all belligerents; revisions to the act in 1939 put arms on a cash-and-carry footing, thus favoring the Allies. At the same time, the president declared a state of national emergency. The next year, Roosevelt arranged the exchange with Britain of fifty overage American destroyers for ninety-nine-year leases of bases in the Caribbean and Newfoundland. The Selective Service also started that same year. The United States placed an embargo on materials such as gasoline and scrap metal for Japan. In 1941 a series of actions tilted the country toward war: the Lend Lease Act, troops to Greenland and Iceland, escorts for convoys as far as Iceland, a shoot-on-sight policy for the Navy, and a revision of the Neutrality Act that permitted arming merchant ships.

These tense years saw changes in military preparations. In 1935 Congress approved increasing the size of the Army, and toward the end of the decade, it authorized much larger defense expenditures. Roosevelt had encouraged naval growth: the Public Works Administration got into the shipbuilding business, and the Vinson-Trammel Act authorized at least 102 new ships. The Fleet Marine Force, established in 1933, prepared for amphibious landings, while naval aviation grew in importance. In 1940, Congress appropriated $4 million for a two-ocean navy, which by then had 478 active vessels.[110]

To man this new Navy, Congress authorized more personnel, and by 1940 there were 13,162 officers and 144,824 men on active duty. In case of a national emergency, however, the Navy would need more personnel, so in 1938 Congress had established the Naval and Marine Corps Reserves, to be composed of *male* citizens. The act also provided for female nurses in the Volunteer Reserve.[111]

The Navy Nurse Corps seized this opportunity to prepare for the worst, and it was up to Superintendents Hoffman and Rau to begin arranging for supplemental nurses. Soon a new superintendent, Sue S. Dauser, directed the mobilization of the Navy Nurse Corps and guided it through the approaching war. Born in 1888, she had graduated from the California School of Nursing, Los Angeles, in 1914 and entered the Nurse Corps through the Naval Reserve in 1917. After transferring to the regular Navy, she became a chief nurse assigned to Base Hospital Number 3 in Scotland. Dauser later served afloat in the *Relief*, *Argonne*, and *Henderson* during President Harding's Alaskan trip. She served in Guam and the Philippines and in several naval hospitals in the United States.[112]

Soon after Dauser became superintendent, she brought Chief Nurse Elizabeth M. O'Brien into her office as administrator of Naval Reserve nurses. Most of the Reserve nurses came from a pool maintained by the American Red Cross Nursing Service called the First Reserve. Patriotic nurses nationwide registered with the Red Cross Nursing Service, which furnished the surgeon general with names of those who might accept appointment in the Naval Reserve Nurse Corps. The Medical Department contacted the nurses directly. Surgeon General Ross T. McIntire began exploring the possible use of Reserve nurses in Medical Reserve Specialists Units and by 1939 had assigned six nurses to each of the units. They would be called to active duty only with these units during a national emergency. Nine new nurses enrolled in the Naval Reserve Nurse Corps in 1939; 8 reported for active duty the next year. By mid-1941, there were 1,036 Naval Reserve nurses, 72 of them on active duty. These women were a nucleus available to strengthen the Navy Nurse Corps, which now totaled 670.[113]

As the corps readied itself for war, the nursing profession itself made similar preparations. In 1940 the Nursing Council on National Defense was organized to consider the needs for nurses in the approaching conflict.[114] The nation would call on thousands of them.

The interwar years saw the Navy return to normal peacetime operations and personnel procedures. Restricted in size and composition by the Washington treaties, congressional stinginess, and the Great Depression, the Navy once again began expanding during Franklin Roosevelt's presidency. However, it had no need to enroll women for yeoman jobs.

After leaving the Navy, the yeomen (F) faded from view and national consciousness. They became eligible for veterans' benefits and fought hard for inclusion in the Adjusted Compensation Act of 1924. To keep the memory of their wartime service alive, these women veterans established the National Yeomen (F) in 1926.

Simultaneously, the Navy Nurse Corps dropped in size from its wartime peak. Under the leadership of J. Beatrice Bowman for twelve of the interwar years, the corps had difficulty attracting and retaining qualified nurses because of poor pay and limited opportunities for promotion. Nurse Corps benefits compensated to some extent for these limitations.

As the civilian nursing profession emphasized postgraduate training and specialization, so, too, did the Navy Nurse Corps, and it offered its members comparable training. It provided a far greater diversity of nursing opportunities in a variety of naval hospitals at home and overseas and in hospital ships and transports. Like men, nurses could join the Navy and see the world. Navy nurses also met emergency civilian disasters with efficient and skilled assistance.

In addition to their nursing duties, Navy nurses instructed hospital corpsmen who carried their healing talents to hospitals and ships around the world. Navy nurses continued to operate training schools in Guam, Samoa, and the Virgin Islands, thereby encouraging local women to help their own people.

Navy nurses were a special breed: well trained, highly professional, adaptive to varying circumstances and living conditions, and, above all, dedicated to the service. Their dual roles—nursing and teaching—matched the prevailing societal norms for acceptable professions for women, and the Navy had no qualms about making use of their abilities.

In the late 1930s, the nation once again moved toward war, and the Navy began preparations and expansion. Similarly, the Medical Department and the Nurse Corps grew in numbers and started enrolling reservists. For women, nursing and teaching would continue to be necessary duties, but on a far larger scale. When war came, the old societal norms would crumble, and new opportunities for service would rapidly emerge.

# 5

# The WAVES in World War II

*World War II demanded* total mobilization of the United States. The armed forces called on twelve million men to defend the country, stretching manpower resources thin. Looking for ways to cover desk jobs at home so that more men could go into combat, all branches of the military turned to women to meet their personnel needs, and some 350,000 women saw military service during the war.[1] The U.S. Navy, having set the World War I precedent of employing more than 11,000 women as yeomen (F), once again turned to women for filling billets in the shore establishment as both officers and enlisted.

## The Setting

The entry of the United States into World War II gave American women an unparalleled opportunity to enter fields previously monopolized by men. As military demands drained males from the work force, employers, in desperation, turned to females for filling production goals. The federal government and the press glamorized the value of patriotic women doing their part for the war effort, and women responded in diverse ways.[2]

At the same time, higher education attracted proportionately more women. In 1940, 601,000 females comprised 40.2 percent of college students. By 1944, with campuses denuded of men, 568,603 women made up 65 percent of enrollments.[3] Educated women continued to dominate their traditional professions as teachers, nurses, librarians, and social workers.[4] Some, however, held nontraditional jobs. For example, a number of female physicists, chemists, metallurgists, biologists, and mathematicians worked on the Manhattan Project, which developed the atomic bomb.[5]

Clerical workers found unlimited job opportunities. The federal government alone hired about one million women, mostly clerks, and another two million worked in offices across the country. They were part of the more than six million women who had found employment for the first time. Between 1940 and 1945, in fact, the number of working women climbed from 27.6 percent to 36.1 percent of the civilian work force.[6]

The most dramatic breakthrough for women came in the well-paying industrial sector, now converted to wartime production. It had always been a male bastion, but here women received far higher wages than elsewhere, although usually not equal to men's pay, and they rarely held supervisory positions. Women were employed in a variety of occupations—as longshoremen and cab drivers, in shipyards and in heavy industry. At two San Francisco Bay area shipyards, for example, some forty thousand women comprised 20 percent of the labor force, and many specialized in welding. "Rosie the Riveter" appeared on magazine covers and posters in the workplace, symbolizing women's assuming skilled masculine jobs.[7] Few people objected because everyone believed that holding nontraditional jobs was only for the duration and that intruding females would go home after the war. And women, after all, were useful because they possessed the feminine traits of manual dexterity, patience, and tolerance for boredom, tedium, and repetitive tasks.[8]

To encourage young mothers to join the industrial work force, in 1942 Congress made construction funds provided by the Community Facilities (Lanham) Act applicable to building child-care centers in towns booming with war work. Appropriating just $1.5 million, the government created three thousand facilities that served only one-tenth of the children of working mothers.[9] As another means of drawing female workers, President Franklin D. Roosevelt established the Women's Advisory Commission under the War Manpower Commission, but this token group could only suggest ways for attracting and retaining women workers.[10]

The most unexpected and novel change in the feminine work force came with older, married women taking jobs—a major departure from times past, when women workers were usually young and single. During the war years, the percentage of working married women rose from 15.2 to 24. It also became acceptable for middle-class wives to work outside the home—a change that would become permanent.[11]

But what of married women who remained at home? The prevailing ideology extolled the roles of wife and mother, and the majority of women still filled these roles. Yet housewives, too, caught up with patriotic fervor, aided the war effort. They dealt with price controls, rationing, and fewer consumer goods; and they often handled household responsibilities alone because their husbands were serving their country abroad. With decades of experience as volunteers in clubs and reform groups, housewives rushed to volunteer for Uncle Sam. They planted victory gardens, canned and preserved their produce, saved scrap metal and newspapers, and sewed their families' clothing. Housewives bought war bonds, assisted in United Service Organization (USO) clubs, and rolled bandages for the Red Cross.[12]

Industry, government, and business were not the only groups frantically seeking wartime workers. Even the U.S. military scrambled to find replacements for men. The greatest shortage would be in clericals to relieve deskbound warriors, and the Navy needed such replacements as much as any service.

The Navy's part in the war was unprecedented.[13] When the Atlantic Fleet began escorting convoys carrying supplies to the Allies as far as Iceland, it ran afoul of German submarines. In September 1941, the destroyer *Greer* (DD 145) came under attack, and the next month destroyer *Kearny* (DD 432) was damaged and destroyer *Reuben James* (DD 245) was sunk. Three months later, on 7 December, the Japanese attacked the U.S. Fleet at Pearl Harbor. Japan swept through American possessions in the Pacific—the Philippines, Guam, and Midway Island. Congress declared war on Japan. Germany and Italy then declared war on the United States, and America began mobilizing its military might to roll back the Axis powers in the Pacific, North Africa, the Mediterranean, and Europe.[14]

The naval buildup had begun during the 1930s, and in 1940, President Roosevelt had successfully pushed Congress for $4 billion for a two-ocean Navy. The number of ships and craft of all kinds grew from 478 in June 1940 to 6,626 by August 1945.[15] For staffing so many vessels and concomitant shore establishments, the number of officers was increased from 13,162 to a peak strength of 325,074; the number of enlisted grew from 144,824 to 3,005,534.[16]

This powerful naval establishment required first-rate administrative procedures and personnel. At the top was the secretary of the Navy—Frank Knox from 1940 to 1944, then James V. Forrestal.[17] Directly responsible for conducting the maritime war was the chief of naval operations, a job ably handled by Adm. Ernest J. King, who was also commander in chief of the U.S. Fleet. Various deputies assisted King, and seven bureaus, some renamed, carried out the manifold duties thrust upon them.[18] The immense growth of the service generated vast amounts of paperwork, and the Navy would sorely need clerical help.

## Establishment of the Women's Reserve

Naval leaders realized that they needed a great infusion of personnel, but where would they find it? Civil service workers were not satisfactory because the Navy could not enforce discipline or impose wartime security on them; moreover, civilians could leave at any time. The Navy had to look elsewhere.

The British had a similar, but worse, dilemma and turned to women for help in meeting personnel shortages. In 1939 they established the Women's Royal Naval Service (WRNS), which was never a part of the Royal Navy but an auxiliary to it. These women relieved men as clericals, messengers, communications workers, linguists, and even cooks and stewards.[19] The U.S. Army also found itself desperately short of men for desk jobs, and in May 1941 Rep. Edith Nourse Rogers (R-Mass.) introduced legislation establishing the Women's Army Auxiliary Corps (WAAC). In spite of vigorous opposition in the House, Congress passed the bill a year later, and Oveta Culp Hobby became the corps's first director. Immediately, the auxiliary status of WAACs presented problems in discipline, command, and deployment, and WAACs did not receive the same pay and benefits as their male counterparts.[20]

The U.S. Navy, believing that it would be the next target for congressional "helpfulness," preferred to devise its own plan. In fact, Representative Rogers had phoned Rear Adm. Chester W. Nimitz, chief of the Bureau of Naval Personnel, in December 1941, asking if the Navy wanted a bill similar to the pending WAAC legislation.[21] Nimitz nimbly referred her to Secretary of the Navy Knox, but a few days later Nimitz sent queries to all bureaus, districts, and offices about the possible usefulness of women in the service.[22] With few exceptions, the replies were overwhelmingly negative. The office of the CNO was in favor of employing women to handle its wartime communications; and the Bureau of Aeronautics, long an advocate of woman power, enthusiastically envisioned twenty thousand women at work. Outside Washington, D.C., only the Eleventh and Twelfth Naval Districts and the Naval Operating Base, Norfolk, were receptive to the idea of women workers.[23]

Nevertheless, Secretary Knox seized the initiative and in February 1942 recommended a women's branch as part of the Naval Reserve. Unfortunately, the director of the Bureau of the Budget rejected the proposal unless the Navy adopted an organization similar to the WAAC—the women were to be *with*, not *in*, the Navy. The two men deadlocked. The Bureau of Aeronautics, determined to include women, appealed to an influential friend of naval aviation, Margaret Chung, who obtained the help of Rep. Melvin J. Maas (R-Minn.), who introduced a bill identical to the Knox proposal in the House on 18 March. Sen. Raymond E. Willis (R-Ind.) followed likewise in the Senate. The House passed the bill on 16 April, but the Senate resisted. David I. Walsh (D-Mass.), chairman of the Senate Naval Affairs Committee, did not want women in the Navy because it "would tend to break up American homes and would be a step backward in the progress of civilization." The committee finally recommended a naval version of the WAAC, and President Roosevelt approved it in late May. Secretary Knox promptly asked him to reconsider.[24]

As Congress debated the prospect of military women losing their femininity, the Navy turned to female educators for advice on how best to organize and administer its women's program, no matter what form it eventually took. Realizing that many admirals would have preferred "dogs, ducks, or monkeys" to women, these educators nevertheless willingly cooperated.[25] On the recommendation of Dean Virginia C. Gildersleeve of Barnard College, Professor Elizabeth Reynard of the same college became a special assistant to Rear Adm. Randall Jacobs, the new chief of the Bureau of Naval Personnel, in April 1942. Soon several female college administrators met in Washington, and on 27 April a larger group gathered at Barnard to discuss possible organization of a women's reserve. From this nucleus came the Women's Advisory Council, a group of eight notable women, with Gildersleeve as chairperson. The council began meetings with Admiral Jacobs, and plans started taking shape.[26] Raynard first visited Canada to observe the women's services there, then surveyed domestic naval establishments to determine the employment potential for women in the United States, and finally visited various college campuses to evaluate them as possible training sites. The council unanimously recommended Smith College as the ideal campus for officer training; the Navy asked for its use, and the president and trustees quickly complied.[27]

The most critical decision the council made was recommending a director for the nascent organization. It chose Mildred Helen McAfee, president of prestigious Wellesley College. Born in 1900, McAfee graduated Phi Beta Kappa from Vassar College in 1920 and earned a master of arts degree eight years later from the University of Chicago. She pursued a career in teaching and administration and became dean of women at Oberlin College in 1934. Two years later she accepted the presidency of Wellesley. In addition to being strong in academic experience, McAfee was vivacious, congenial, and possessed of a sense of humor. She would lend credence and respectability to the new naval venture.[28]

During these weeks, the Navy sought an appropriate name for its women in the event Congress enacted a law establishing such a group. In anticipation, newspapers began referring to potential female naval personnel as "goblettes" (male sailors were often called "gobs") and "sailorettes." Someone even suggested "swans." Elizabeth Reynard was asked to devise a suitable acronym. Realizing that it must have "W" for women and "V" for volunteer, Reynard came up with the nautical-sounding "WAVES"—Women Accepted for Volunteer Emergency Service. (The terms "WAVES" and "Women's Reserve" will be used interchangeably.)[29]

Meanwhile, the Bureau of Personnel again queried the bureaus, districts, and offices about jobs women might fill. As before, most replies were negative, with the exceptions of communications, intelligence, the CNO's office, aeronautics, and several naval districts. Altogether, about 150 officers' and 1,000 enlisted billets could be handled by women.[30]

The Navy had done what it could to plan for women's entrance; the next move was up to Congress. In late May, President Roosevelt had approved the Senate Naval Affairs Committee's proposal to make the women's unit an auxiliary like the WAAC. Then several strong-minded educators got involved. On 30 May, Dean Harriet Elliot of the University of North Carolina wrote Eleanor Roosevelt, urging that a women's reserve be *in*, not *with*, the

Navy. Two days later Gildersleeve penned a similar letter to the president's wife, citing security and discipline concerns. Mrs. Roosevelt forwarded Gildersleeve's letter to Undersecretary of the Navy Forrestal and shared Elliot's letter with the president. Dean C. Mildred Thompson of Vassar College also wrote the president, as did Herman Davis, president of Smith College. Both echoed Elliot's and Gildersleeve's suggestions.[31]

This outpouring possibly helped convince President Roosevelt of the Senate Naval Affairs Committee's mistake, for on 16 June he gave Secretary Knox carte blanche in organizing a women's reserve. Knox promptly asked Senator Walsh to reconsider the Navy's earlier suggestion that women be *in*, not *with*, the Navy. The senator agreed, and the bill cleared both houses and went to the president on 21 July. When he signed it on 30 July, the Women's Reserve was born.[32]

As finally approved, the legislation was the Title V amendment to the Naval Reserve Act of 1938 as amended. The Women's Reserve was a branch of the Naval Reserve; its purpose was to "expedite the war effort by releasing officers and men for duty at sea and their replacement by women in the shore establishment." Its members could volunteer for the duration of the war, plus six months, and could serve only in the continental United States. They could not go onboard naval vessels or in combat aircraft and had no command authority except within their own branch. There could be one lieutenant commander, no more than thirty-five lieutenants, and the number of lieutenants (junior grade) could not exceed 35 percent of all commissioned officers. Members must be at least twenty years old.[33] The Navy now projected a women's reserve of about one thousand officers and ten thousand enlisted.

Hard on the heels of the naval legislation came authorization for other women's services. In November 1942, the U.S. Coast Guard created its women's branch, the SPAR (Semper Paratus—Always Ready), and the following February the U.S. Marine Corps followed suit with its Women's Reserve. Congress finally rid the WAAC of its auxiliary status when it established the Women's Army Corps (WAC) in June 1943.[34] On the periphery of the military were the Women Airforce Service Pilots (WASP), established in August 1943. These civilian female pilots ferried military aircraft more than sixty million miles during the war.[35]

## Getting the Program Started

On 3 August 1942 Mildred McAfee was sworn in as "an officer and gentleman in the United States Navy." She received her commission as lieutenant commander, the first woman officer in the Naval Reserve. Two days later, Elizabeth Reynard was commissioned a lieutenant. McAfee, told to "run" the women's program, had no clear idea of what she was to do as director of the Women's Reserve. No one seemed to know. She had a separate office in the Bureau of Personnel and direct access to Admiral Jacobs, but the program was so new that this bureau chief had not formulated a plan.[36] To generate ideas for the Women's Reserve, the Bureau of Aeronautics sent Joy Bright Hancock, a World War I yeoman (F) and longtime editor and writer at the Bureau of Aeronautics, to inspect the training, utilization, and housing of the six-thousand-member Women's Division, Royal Canadian Air Force. The Navy eventually incorporated many of Hancock's suggestions into the WAVES program.[37]

During August and September, the Navy drew 108 additional women from the education and business worlds to become officers. Attracted by the prestige and credibility of McAfee and the Advisory Council, these successful women included four who would later become directors of the Women's Reserve: Winifred Quick, a personnel manager; Louise K. Wilde, a dean at Rockford College; Jean T. Palmer, a business manager; and Joy Bright Hancock. Another early officer was Dorothy Stratton, dean of women at Purdue University, who became director of the SPARs.[38]

With the exception of Stratton, these women had no indoctrination in the ways of the U.S. Navy; they just started working. At first there was no school to teach them naval traditions or the bureaus' operations and procedures or even naval vocabulary. The Navy assigned no regular officer to advise McAfee and her staff—a lack of professional assistance that caused confusion, mistakes, and friction with the operating divisions.[39]

Finally, on 16 September 1942, a concrete plan for organizing the Women's Reserve came in the form of a memorandum from Capt. Louis E. Denfeld, assistant chief of naval personnel. The director would have authority to administer the program, define policies, and coordinate women's work in the bureau's operating divisions. Each division and section would have a Women's Reserve officer acting as direct liaison with the director and keeping her informed of all activities involving women. The director would report to the chief and assistant chief of the bureau. Because the program was just beginning, it was vital to keep the director aware of various activities, wrote Denfeld.[40]

As policies solidified and operations increased, McAfee assembled an efficient and competent staff in her office. Cdr. Tova P. Wiley became assistant director, Lt. Cdr. Grace Cheney was executive assistant to the director, and Lt. Cdr. Louise K. Wilde handled public relations. Other assistants oversaw Women's Reserve matters within the bureau's own activities: Lt. Cdrs. Joy Grimm in Planning and Control, Virginia Carlin in Officer Personnel, Mary Jo Shelly in Training, Eleanor McKay in Welfare, and Jean Palmer in Enlisted Personnel. Another reservist was the traveling representative for the director's office. Carefully chosen liaison officers represented the Women's Reserve in the other bureaus.[41]

For overseeing and coordinating women's activities throughout the Navy's many geographical and occupational areas, Director McAfee detailed Women's Reserve representatives, called district directors, to each of the continental naval districts as well as to the Potomac and Severn River commands and several air training commands. Each district had a WAVES officer assigned to the commandant's staff for advising on women's policy. McAfee or one of her assistants frequently visited these districts, assessing women's progress and problems. Each year, beginning in September 1943, McAfee summoned the district directors to a conference in Washington for discussion of policies, organization, morale, uniforms, discipline, housing, and effectiveness of the reservists.[42]

### Recruiting

The most immediate task confronting McAfee was recruitment of more women. Assigned to recruiting offices in the various naval districts, women officers provided information and advice to prospective WAVES. Within a year, about eighty enlisted women with the recruiter rating had joined them. Traveling recruitment parties, including WAVES, assisted in these efforts.[43]

Associated with recruiting were public relations and promotional campaigns. Determined that the Navy's women would project a ladylike image, McAfee insisted on tasteful advertising. She was incensed when a full-page ad in a

Chicago newspaper featured a pinup girl dressed as a member of the Women's Reserve beckoning suggestively to join the WAVES or SPAR. An immediate order went out prohibiting "cheesecake" photos and illustrations. Advertising must appeal to conservative parents, schools, and churches as well as to young women themselves.[44]

The Women's Reserve chose to rely on radio and newspaper publicity, rallies, posters, brochures, personal contact, and an invitation from Admiral Jacobs to join the "large, friendly family of the USN." The Navy appealed to patriotism and emphasized its vital need for women. It stressed the training facilities at leading colleges and the stylish uniforms.[45]

The recruiting campaign produced results. By the end of 1942, there were 770 officers and 3,109 enlisted women in the WAVES. Their numbers rose steadily until the Women's Reserve reached its peak strength of 86,291, including 8,475 officers, 73,816 enlisted, and about 4,000 in training on 31 July 1945.[46] These numbers far exceeded the Navy's early projections of 1,000 officers and 10,000 enlisted. Altogether, 104,339 women saw service in the WAVES. The Navy also handled recruiting for the Coast Guard throughout the war and for the Marine Corps until 1943.[47]

The number of women reserves in other maritime services rose proportionately but on a much smaller scale than that of the Navy. The Marine Corps Women's Reserve, under the direction of Col. Ruth C. Streeter, achieved a maximum strength of 17,672.[48] The Coast Guard Women's Reserve, directed by Capt. Dorothy Stratton, had 10,000 members.[49] The largest women's service was the Women's Army Corps, led by Col. Oveta Culp Hobby. Top enrollment in WAC was 100,000.[50]

Hindering recruitment for all the women's services was a demoralizing worldwide slander campaign, launched in 1943. Word-of-mouth rumors, gossip, and innuendo suggested that military women, even nurses, were promiscuous and readily available. Adding fuel to the fire, the press picked up the speculations. After an FBI investigation ruled out Axis involvement in the adverse propaganda, that agency determined that servicemen themselves, especially enlisted, had started and perpetuated the slander. Resentful of women's intrusion into the male military world, these servicemen did not relish having women relieve them of desk jobs so they could fight. Impugning women's morals had long been a way of discouraging them from seeking male professions.[51]

## Who Joined and Why

The Navy needed women but not just any women. Like their predecessors in World War I, Navy WAVES were predominately white and middle class. They came from every state, but the largest numbers came from New York, California, Pennsylvania, Illinois, Massachusetts, and Ohio.[52] Candidates for officers had to be between twenty and forty-nine years of age and hold a college degree or have two years each of college and professional or business experience. Enlisted requirements stipulated an age range of twenty to thirty-five and a high school or business school diploma or equivalent experience. All had to be American citizens.[53] They were young: in the Ninth Naval District, for example, 76.8 percent of enlisted were between twenty and twenty-four years old; 16.2 percent between twenty-five and twenty-nine years; and just 7 percent between thirty and thirty-five years.[54] Because entrance requirements were high, Navy women were generally better educated and had more work experience than their male counterparts. The majority of officers had college degrees. Other graduates who could not secure commissions enlisted instead.[55] One such woman was Doris Locke, who had a degree in library science but wore glasses, which, at that time, barred her from being an officer.[56]

The Navy made no effort to recruit minorities, notably blacks, who had served in the WAAC since that corps's inception. Because the Navy admitted few black men except as mess attendants and stewards before June 1942, it had no need for women to replace them.[57] Finally, on 19 October 1944, under increasing pressure from black organizations and with an election looming, President Roosevelt approved accepting black women in the Reserves. Officers Harriet Ida Pickens and Frances Wills trained at Smith College, Northampton, Massachusetts, late that year; enlisted women began entering Hunter College, Bronx, New York, in January 1945. By September seventy-two blacks were in the WAVES on a fully integrated basis.[58]

As in World War I, all kinds of women joined the Navy during World War II and for a variety of reasons. Again the most compelling motivation was patriotism. "WAVES are typical, civic-minded American citizens . . . who possess . . . the urge to serve their country," wrote one.[59] "Uncle Sam needed me," said another.[60] "I know I'm doing my share to help our side win. I'm . . . part of the backbone on which the boys at the front rely," confided one volunteer to her parents.[61] A later writer rejected the widespread idea that WAVES were feminists rather than patriotic Americans.[62]

Other women were looking for adventure, or professional advancement opportunities, or the chance to train on college campuses. Some followed family traditions of military service, and some had loved ones who had been killed in action. Still others were escaping strict parental supervision or boring civilian jobs.[63]

Whatever the reasons, thousands of women volunteered to become a part of the U.S. Navy. They chose the Navy rather than the Army or the other maritime services because family members were in the Navy or because of their proximity to naval bases. Some had been directly approached through their universities. Others thought they could join the Navy at a younger age, while still others were attracted by the ladylike, educated image of WAVES. Some even joined because the designer uniforms were more attractive than those of the other services.[64]

## Training Officers

The Navy contracted to use college campuses whenever possible for training new WAVES. Colleges offered the "dignity and prestige of an academic atmosphere," genteel surroundings, and readily available space for rapid conversion to military use. They also reassured anxious parents of daughters who wanted to become sailors.[65]

Smith College was the first to agree to provide facilities for indoctrinating women officers. Designated as the U.S. Naval Reserve Midshipmen's School (WR), Northampton, Smith soon became known as "USS Northampton."[66] To command the school and its indoctrination program, the Navy chose Capt. Herbert W. Underwood, a retired officer with a distinguished career and a recipient of the Navy Cross in World War I. He arrived at Northampton on 13 August 1942 and promptly developed the curriculum and other programs for this experiment in turning women into naval officers. Underwood was an enthusiastic, good-natured administrator whose interest and efficiency inspired his staff and his trainees.[67]

The first class, which reported on 28 August, became immersed in a one-month crash course that taught them naval history, organization, administration, correspondence, law, communications, protocol, and ship and aircraft identification. They took physical education, and they drilled.[68] These were the professional women commissioned in August and slated to become the first leaders of the WAVES. They completed their indoctrination training on 30 September and immediately filled developing administrative billets.[69] One member of this first class, Lt. (jg) Winifred Quick, who would later become WAVES director, remained on staff at Northhampton for a year as personnel director.[70]

The second class, with 776 members, began on 6 October. For the first month, the trainees were apprentice seamen; for the second month, midshipmen. After finishing the two-month course, midshipmen received commissions as ensigns or lieutenants (junior grade). There were another 125 officers who, like those in the first class, took a one-month course. After the third class, all trainees were apprentice seamen until commissioned when they finished indoctrination. This training pattern remained in place until the school closed in December 1944. Of the 10,181 women enrolled, 9,477 completed the program. The Midshipmen's School trained not only WAVES but also 203 SPARs and 295 Marine Corps Reservists.[71]

The facilities at Smith soon became overcrowded, and in late 1942 nearby Mount Holyoke College agreed to accommodate the overflow. At first, this new unit handled both indoctrination and communications training, but in August 1943 it became solely an officers' specialized communications school.[72] In early 1943, other graduates of the Northampton training school went to the Supply Corps School at Harvard University, and these women lived at Radcliffe College. Upon completion of the three-month course, the new supply officers fanned out to various stations and depots.[73] Specialized training of still another sort began in July 1943 when eighty-eight highly qualified women entered the Navy's fourteen-month course in the Japanese language at Boulder, Colorado. The Bureau of Aeronautics sent women to meteorology classes at the Massachusetts Institute of Technology and the University of California at Los Angeles. Other WAVES studied aerological engineering at the University of Chicago.[74]

Specialized officer training took place in locations other than college campuses. The Bureau of Ordnance opened its schools to WAVES officers in September 1943, and courses included aviation ordnance training at the Naval Air Station, Jacksonville. Others attended the Naval Air Technical

Training Command School in Corpus Christi, while more went to the Naval Aviation Training School in Hollywood, Florida, to prepare to become air navigation instructors.[75]

These specialized training courses were coeducational rather than sex segregated. The concept had begun in the Bureau of Aeronautics and spread to the other bureaus. Joy Bright Hancock, the Women's Reserve liaison officer at the Bureau of Aeronautics, had strenuously pushed coed training because she believed that men and women who would later work together should train together.[76]

## Training Enlisted

As thousands of women prepared to become officers in the U.S. Navy, many more trained for the enlisted ratings. Once again, college campuses became the scenes of military preparation. On 9 October 1942, the first trainees reported at three colleges for a combination of recruit, or "boot," and specialized training. Oklahoma A&M (now Oklahoma State University) at Stillwater was the site for yeomen training; Indiana University at Bloomington for storekeepers; the University of Wisconsin at Madison for radiomen. Enthusiastic WAVES recruits like Eunice McConnell shared their experiences with family members. "I love it," she wrote. "I thought I loved it before I got here, I *knew* it when I got here, and I'm *more* sure of it every minute that I stay!"[77]

But soon the disadvantages of basic training in disparate locations became apparent: inexperienced instructors and a lack of naval esprit de corps. An abrupt change in training tactics and an upwardly revised estimate of how many WAVES the Navy would need led to setting up a temporary, central boot training unit at Iowa State Teachers College at Cedar Falls in mid-December. The facilities at Stillwater, Bloomington, and Madison reverted to specialized instruction.[78]

The Navy turned to yet another campus to provide boot training for all enlisted WAVES. On 1 February 1943, the Navy contracted to take over Hunter College in the Bronx. Hunter could accommodate six thousand recruits at a time. On 8 February, the college was commissioned U.S. Naval Training Center (WR), the Bronx, but became known as "USS Hunter."[79] Capt. William F. Amsden, who also held the Navy Cross from World War I, took command of USS Hunter and rapidly converted the civilian college into an efficient military training center. Amsden was a hardworking, efficient administrator who guided the largest WAVES school until it closed in October 1945.[80]

The first group of about 2,000 apprentice seamen began the six-week indoctrination program on 17 February 1943, and every two weeks another group of about 2,000 recruits reported. Subjected to a barrage of new knowledge—ships and aircraft, ranks and ratings, traditions and customs, and naval history—the recruits also marched, drilled, and underwent physical conditioning. Eventually, 80,936 WAVES, 1,844 SPARs, and 3,190 women Marines completed the training course. The SPARs and Marine Corps Reservists used the Navy's enlisted training facilities until the summer of 1943, when those services established their own boot camps.[81]

Following basic training, 83 percent of enlisted WAVES initially went to various specialized schools.[82] The earlier campuses continued to provide yeomen training at Oklahoma A&M, Stillwater, and at Iowa State Teachers College, Cedar Falls. The University of Wisconsin, Madison, taught radiomen while Indiana University, Bloomington, instructed storekeepers. The Navy's need for trained WAVES soon overwhelmed the ability of these centers to produce them. Other colleges opened their doors: Georgia State College for Women in Milledgeville and Burdett College in Boston trained storekeepers; Miami University in Oxford, Ohio, instructed radiomen. Cooks and bakers learned their skills at Hunter.[83] In all their training on college campuses, enlisted women remained segregated from male trainees. Such isolation caused women to feel that they were not a part of the naval "fighting machine."

Two bureaus, however, considered separate training units for males and females a needless duplication of resources. The Bureau of Aeronautics, always in the lead in employing women, trained them side by side with men at naval air stations and training centers.[84] Similarly, the Bureau of Medicine and Surgery sent WAVES for Hospital Corps training in seventeen naval hospitals until December 1943. Afterward, they received instruction at either the National Naval Medical Center, Bethesda, or at Great Lakes, Illinois. Although most became general duty corpsmen, others trained as therapists, technicians, and, later, rehabilitation specialists.[85]

## Working Conditions

In contrast to civilian pay practices, Navy women received equal pay for equal work. Whether male or female, a captain—a rank the WAVES director would hold in late 1943—got $4,000 a year; a commander, $3,500; a lieutenant commander, $3,000; a lieutenant, $2,400; a lieutenant (jg), $2,000; and an ensign, $1,800. Rental and subsistence allowances ranged from $1,515 to $795 a year, depending on rank. Enlisted women's base pay began at $600 a year for an apprentice seaman and rose to $1,512 for a chief petty officer.[86] The Navy took care to provide safeguards for the health, safety, and security of women by setting standards for the workplace. WAVES could work no more than fifty-one hours a week and had to have one day in seven off.[87]

Their benefits, however, were not commensurate with those of male reservists. WAVES received no death gratuity or retirement pay. Equally damaging was the comptroller general's decision in February 1943 that women reservists were not eligible for allowances for dependents. This ruling played havoc with recruiting and even forced some WAVES to leave the service for financial reasons. Finally, in November 1943, Congress rectified this mistake in part, granting them military benefits. Husbands, however, could not be dependents, and neither could children unless the father was dead or the mother was their chief support.[88]

To house WAVES, the Navy modified male barracks or built new ones. Cubicles for two or four women, adorned with their own curtains and bedspreads, afforded a little privacy. Lounges, laundry facilities, partitioned showers, and toilet stalls with doors eased the transition from civilian life. Each barracks was supervised by an officer or a specialist (S). In cities where there were no barracks, the Navy leased hotels or apartment houses for WAVES' accommodations.[89]

Marriage policies for WAVES kept changing as the war continued. At first, no member of the Women's Reserve could be married to a man in the armed forces. Women also could not marry during indoctrination or training periods. Such impractical regulations would cause the loss of well-qualified women or prevent their signing up, so the Navy amended its policy in October 1942. WAVES could marry men of any service except the Navy;

marrying a naval officer or enlisted man brought immediate discharge. In March 1943, the Navy relented and allowed its women to marry naval men, after indoctrination and training. Still forbidden were women joining the same service, after marriage, as their husbands had. By August, WAVES could marry, with permission, during specialist training.[90]

Discipline was not a major problem with the WAVES, far less than with their male counterparts. Always concerned about the image of women reservists, McAfee would not condone "behavior unbecoming a lady." Discipline depended on sex or location. Some conduct such as drunkenness or disturbance of the peace might be tolerated for enlisted men but not for women. Actions that would go unnoticed in a large city would "ruin the reputation of the Service in a small town."[91] WAVES could not be imprisoned for misconduct but were confined to their station. More serious offenses brought discharge from the Navy.[92] Despite strict standards, only 4 of a total of 10,007 officers and 3,335 out of 94,332 enlisted were involuntarily separated from the Navy.[93]

Pregnancy, whether in or out of wedlock, led to discharge for the "convenience of the government" as a physical disqualification rather than as a disciplinary measure. McAfee urged instant action by putting pregnant women on inactive duty "in the interest of the reputation of the Women's Reserve."[94] The Navy provided no medical care for maternity cases until 1945, so pregnant women had to pay their own expenses. Since naval regulations prohibited women with children under eighteen from serving, there was no possibility of returning to duty after childbirth. In March 1945, a change in naval regulations permitted women whose pregnancies had terminated to remain in the service.[95]

Another related problem was homosexuality, which the Navy had always considered a threat to good order, discipline, and security. Although the Navy denied reports that the WAVES harbored lesbians, it quietly discharged women caught in overt homosexual acts or exhibiting such tendencies. One distraught reservist wrote of the turmoil resulting from the discovery and discharge of two lesbians in her barracks: "The barracks has been so divided about the whole affair that it practically started another Civil War."[96] Few concrete estimates of the number of lesbians in the Navy emerged, but one writer found that late in the war a marked shift occurred in military policy, as homosexuals of either sex were declared unfit for service.[97]

Sexual harassment was not a defined, recognizable problem, although undoubtedly it existed. In the 1940s, young women, especially the "ladies" of the Navy, perhaps shrugged off unwanted advances or avoided compromising situations. The slander campaign of 1943 was a form of harassment but was directed against all military women rather than specific individuals. One WAVE, who served as a Link trainer operator, could recall no incidents involving sexual harassment at her station. Others, too, denied any recollection of such occurrences.[98] In contrast, one reservist wrote of vulgar, humiliating language and treatment from men.[99]

Another grievance for women was the congressionally fixed limitation on rank. At first there could be only one lieutenant commander (the director) and thirty-five lieutenants. The number of lieutenants (junior grade) could not exceed 35 percent of the total commissioned officers. These restrictions left little incentive for high-caliber women to join and provided scant opportunity for advancement. At the Navy's behest, both houses of Congress held hearings during 1943 to lift the ceiling on rank and in November passed an act allowing one captain (the director) and not limiting the number of lower ranking officers.[100]

Equally irksome was the ban on command authority except within the Women's Reserve. In April 1943 McAfee recommended to Jacobs that the director of the Women's Reserve be an assistant to the bureau chief. Jacobs concurred and on 5 May announced that the Women's Reserve as a separate division was abolished and the director would now be special assistant to the chief of naval personnel on Women's Reserve matters.[101] McAfee was thus in the chain of command, but this chain gave no authority to command men, even at training schools. McAfee then argued for changing the law and allowing women such authority, but career naval officers resisted. "Giving military authority to members of the Women's Reserve in rare instances might be considered an opening wedge which could be expanded to include the extension of military authority in all situations," wrote the director of enlisted personnel. The ban remained.[102]

Women tried to avoid stereotypical "women's work." Lt. Elsa Scharles laughingly recalled telling a male ensign that she did not know how to make the coffee, nor could she type. These "shortcomings" were "[her] saving graces throughout [her] naval career!"[103]

An undercurrent of opposition to women persisted. At first the old chiefs were reluctant to accept women until they had proven themselves capable of performing their jobs.[104] Captain McAfee captured the tone of this reluctance to allow women into the Navy except as the last resort in solving personnel shortages by citing scripture: "He cried unto the Lord saying, 'Thy wrath lieth hard upon me. Thou hast afflicted me with all thy WAVES.'"[105] Even a writer in *Our Navy*, while acknowledging that women's help was essential, maintained that their service should be temporary.[106] More WAVES noticed lingering resentment in the grumbling of enlisted men; others perceived opposition from old line officers, which manifested itself in a rigid insistence on carrying out orders and performing duties by the book. One reservist remembered resentment from another source: native girls, when WAVES arrived in Hawaii.[107]

## Uniforms

The WAVES looked professional and attractive in stylish uniforms created expressly for them. Even before McAfee became director, Mrs. James V. Forrestal, wife of the undersecretary of the Navy, had convinced the famous fashion designer Mainbocher to create uniforms for the reservists. Soon after McAfee came onboard, she attended a preview of the proposed new uniforms. To her horror, she said, she found the traditional gold braid replaced by garish stripes of red, white, and blue like a comic opera. She convinced the Navy and the designer to use light blue stripes instead.[108]

The finished product was an attractive Navy blue (white for summer) suit with a semifitted jacket, a six-gored skirt, brass buttons, and light blue braid. Black oxfords or pumps, a black leather purse, and gloves completed the outfit. The officer's hat resembled that of eighteenth-century naval hero John Paul Jones. The enlisted hat was less functional; its snap brim, turned up in back, became a moat retaining water in the rain. A garrison cap replaced it. During inclement weather, a raincoat with havelock headpiece provided protection.[109] Various changes took place as time passed, including a new gray-and-white striped seersucker work uniform for summer and permission to wear slacks or dungarees if the job demanded.[110]

## Deployment

After training, WAVES eventually served at nine hundred shore stations in the United States. Barred from assignments requiring rotation to duty afloat, women nevertheless held about 102 officers' billets, 45 enlisted ratings, 22 Hospital Corps billets, and 45 seaman billets.[111] By war's end, 18 percent of naval personnel assigned to shore duty were women.[112] In spite of their new titles, most women performed stereotypical jobs: clerical work, health care, or storekeeping.

The highest concentration of WAVES was in the Washington, D.C., area, where twenty thousand women made up 55 percent of the Navy's personnel. In the Office of Naval Operations' sensitive and highly secret Communications Division, WAVES such as Lt. Dorothy Brown were responsible for 75 percent of encoding and decoding messages. In the Bureau of Naval Personnel, WAVES comprised 70 percent of the staff.[113] In addition, WAVES handled about 80 percent of the Navy's mail service. Lt. (jg) Susan Davis, for example, served in Postal Affairs in Washington and Hawaii.[114]

A significant breakthrough for women was their increased presence in the Bureau of Medicine and Surgery. The Navy Nurse Corps had been an integral part of this bureau since 1908, but it took wartime pressure to open other opportunities. At first, female physicians could volunteer only by entering the Women's Reserve as junior grade lieutenants and awaiting assignment to the Medical Corps. Because of early rank limitations, few women doctors rushed to serve. Among the first physicians to enter the Medical Corps through the Women's Reserve were Lt. (jg) Cornelia Gaskill, who served at Bethesda, and Lt. (jg) Hulda Thelander, stationed at San Francisco. In April 1943 Congress approved directly appointing women physicians and surgeons in the Army and Navy with the same pay and benefits as men. By mid-1945, there were forty-two female doctors in the Navy. Similarly, the Dental Corps took in two women dentists, Sara G. Krout and Alice Tweed.[115] By far the largest gains occurred in the Hospital

Corps, which had been composed only of young men. About thirteen thousand WAVES entered the corps and served in naval hospitals, stations, and dispensaries. As the war ended, some of these WAVES worked at the Navy's rehabilitation centers.[116]

The Bureau of Aeronautics, with twenty-three thousand WAVES, utilized them, in Washington and around the country, often in unheard-of ways. Sue King, for example, brought her mathematical education and aeronautical training to her assignments in research in the CNO's office and at Quonset Point, Rhode Island. In addition, the Navy trained and employed about one hundred WAVES weather forecasters at naval air stations.[117] In 1942 Elsa Gardner became the only female aeronautical engineer in the Navy. The bureau was daring enough to train and assign women officers to technical billets in engineering, gunnery instruction, navigation, Link training, radio and radar, and traffic control. Enlisted women served in ratings such as aviation machinist's mate, aviation metalsmith, parachute rigger, control tower operator, and even pigeon trainer. The bureau took full advantage of women's talents and desire to serve their country.[118] And those women took vicarious pleasure in men's military successes. Mary Louise Wilkerson, an enlisted Link trainer instructor, was proud when one of her students was decorated for a direct hit on the enemy.[119]

Other bureaus made use of women reservists but on a smaller scale than medicine and surgery and aeronautics. The Bureau of Ordnance employed predominately mathematicians and technicians for work in production scheduling, parts and equipment distribution, ordnance materials inspection, negotiations with manufacturers, drafting and designing, and logistics planning. On one unusual assignment, the bureau sent Lt. (jg) Grace M. Hopper, a mathematician, to Harvard University to work on its computation project with the Mark I computer. The Bureau of Ships found billets for officers and enlisted in technical and administrative work. Officers tested ship models, developed improved navigational systems, inspected machinery, operated radio equipment, and scheduled procurement and delivery. Enlisted handled such jobs as radioman, yeoman, and statistician. In the Bureau of Yards and Docks, WAVES worked in camouflage, administration and personnel, and war plans. The Bureau of Supplies and Accounts found a multitude of duties for about one thousand officers and ten thousand enlisted WAVES who entered the Supply Corps and went to most continental naval stations. These women handled such diverse duties as accounting, disbursing, marketing, purchasing, and transportation.[120] Early in the war, these bureaus had shown no interest in women's services, but the drain of men left them no choice.[121]

Other offices also called upon women to occupy emptying shore billets. The JAG office took in WAVES who had been attorneys in civilian life and gave them similar posts. One reservist was admitted to practice before the Supreme Court. Other reservists went into the Chaplain's Corps and trained with male members at the College of William and Mary, not to minister to naval men or even women but to serve as organists and choir directors. Near the end of the war, about eighty officers, trained as air navigators, were allowed to serve on Naval Air Transport Service flights in the United States and to Hawaii and the Aleutian Islands.[122]

Commands outside the United States needed WAVES, and the Navy had tried in vain since 1942 to get Congress to revoke the prohibition against overseas service. Navy nurses had served in far-flung places since 1910, and WACs had gone abroad since late 1942. In June 1944 the Navy called upon high-ranking officers to plead its case at hearings before the House Naval Affairs Committee. Surgeon General Ross T. McIntire cited the potential usefulness of WAVES to the Medical Department abroad, and Jacobs passed along the request of Adm. Chester Nimitz, commander in chief, Pacific Fleet, for women reservists in Hawaii. After protests from conservative committee members—"If we have reached the time in the life of this country when we do not have enough men to go out and fight its battles but have to call on the women to go out and do the dirty work"—the committee agreed to the change. The amendment to the Naval Reserve Act passed both houses of Congress and became law on 27 September. Now WAVES could volunteer for service in the territories of Alaska and Hawaii and in the American area (mainly the Caribbean).[123]

In anticipation of the change, McAfee had met with WAC leaders in June to discuss problems with women's overseas duty. The CNO's office issued guidelines for localities and billets and stressed careful selection of WAVES bound for overseas. As preliminary surveys of naval units revealed thousands of jobs that women could fill, McAfee recommended policies and procedures governing the new departure.[124] Requirements were strict: only WAVES with six months' active duty; with good conduct, health, and work records; and who demonstrated maturity and emotional stability need apply. A selection board in the Bureau of Naval Personnel would determine the final cut.[125]

The most urgent request for large numbers of WAVES had come from the Fourteenth Naval District in Hawaii, so in October McAfee dispatched Lt. Cdrs. Joy Bright Hancock and Jean Palmer to that island. The two women inspected potential billets and housing, then returned to Washington and reported their favorable findings to McAfee. Soon Lt. Cdr. Eleanor G. Rigby, district director of the Women's Reserve, and Lt. Winifred R. Quick arrived in Hawaii to make necessary arrangements. Quick supervised the readying of barracks for 4,500 women and insisted on adequate recreation and bathing facilities. In December, the first contingent of WAVES sailed from San Francisco, arriving in Hawaii on 6 January 1945. Under Rigby's command, 350 officers and 3,659 enlisted eventually served in Hawaii.[126]

Hawaii was the only overseas post staffed with WAVES on permanent assignment. Duty in Alaska, the Tenth Naval District (Puerto Rico and the West Indies), Newfoundland, and Bermuda, authorized by Congress in September 1944, never materialized. One WAVES officer visited Bermuda and Puerto Rico on temporary duty in early January 1945, and another served for eleven days as a weather observer in the Aleutian Islands.[127]

## Casualties and Decorations

Although WAVES could not serve in combat zones or in combatant ships and aircraft, they nevertheless suffered casualties. Seven officers and sixty-two enlisted women died during World War II.[128] Many received awards and decorations for their contributions to the war effort. In 1944 Cdr. Elizabeth Reynard received a letter of commendation from the secretary of the Navy for her work in developing the WAVES training program. The Navy awarded the Distinguished Service Medal to Capt. Mildred McAfee in November 1945 for her efforts as director of the Women's Reserve. Two WAVES received the Legion of Merit; three, the Bronze Star; eighteen, the secretary of the Navy's letter of commendation with ribbons; and one, the Army Commendation Ribbon.[129]

Soon after the WAVES celebrated its third anniversary in July 1945, World War II ended. The Navy's experiment utilizing women to replace men in the shore establishment had succeeded. Tributes came from the highest levels. Secretary of the Navy Forrestal wrote, "Your conduct, discharge of military responsibilities, and skillful work are in the highest tradition of the naval service." Fleet Admiral King continued the praise: "The Navy has learned to appreciate the women . . . for their discipline, their skill, and their contribution to high morale. . . . Our greatest tribute to these women is the request for more WAVES." And from Fleet Admiral Nimitz: "They have demonstrated qualities of competence, energy, and loyalty."[130] Even the vast majority of enlisted men, who had been the most resistant to women in the Navy, thought they had done a good job during the war.[131]

Extraordinarily fortunate in their leadership, the WAVES owed much of its success to its director, Capt. Mildred McAfee. A resourceful, intelligent woman, McAfee took a nebulous program and transformed it into an effective, well-run means of helping the United States win the war by releasing men for sea duty and by filling additional billets in the expanded Navy. Through her career in higher education, she was aware of women's capabilities and encouraged novel uses of their talents. Diplomatic, humorous, and nonabrasive, she insisted on Navy women maintaining a "ladylike" image. She kept abreast of WAVES' activities by frequent inspection trips and conferences, and she worked well with the directors of the other women's services. Throughout all the uncertainties and confusion of establishing and running the Women's Reserve, McAfee enjoyed the enthusiastic support of Secretaries of the Navy Knox and Forrestal and Chief of the Bureau of Personnel Randall Jacobs.

Most women reservists viewed their naval service positively, and many have declared they would do it again under similar circumstances. Their service proved to be a growth experience that led to more self-assurance, tolerance, patience, and better skills.[132] Added maturity, development, discipline, and attention to detail paid off later in postwar careers, especially in management.[133] One officer, who had been among the first commissioned and had come from the field of education, thought that military service helped advance American women. "It was the real world," she said.[134] Few studies exist concerning the long-range effects of World War II military service, but one such work reinforces the women's own perceptions of higher achievements and greater self-esteem later in life.[135]

The Navy began to demobilize and to consider its needs in the postwar world. Many people wondered if women's participation had marked a real turning point in women's history or was just a wartime aberration.[136] The members of the Women's Reserve set the precedent, watershed or not, of providing competent service to a nation in need. Permanent change comes slowly, but these women had set in motion a process that would develop and mature. In turn, their own hopes, expectations, and perhaps dreams of a dignified naval career rested on the assurance that they had performed admirably in a new and often stressful life-style.

# 6

## The Navy Nurse Corps in World War II

*As the WAVES took over shore positions* in the United States, the Navy Nurse Corps responded to wartime demands at home and abroad. In hospitals and dispensaries, in hospital ships and transports, in medical evacuation aircraft and in prisoner-of-war camps, Navy nurses unstintingly cared for the sick and injured, and their service vastly increased the Navy's wartime efficiency. Led by Capt. Sue S. Dauser, superintendent since 1939, the corps reflected modern, progressive nursing care at its finest.

### The Setting

Navy Nurse Corps women were part of the nursing profession, which had anticipated wartime needs by organizing the Nursing Council on National Defense in 1940. Two years later the group's name changed to National Nursing Council for War Service. Made up of leaders of nursing organizations, federal agencies, and the military nurse corps, the council coordinated civilian and military programs requiring a large increase in the number of nurses.[1]

In 1941 Congress helped support nursing and nursing education by providing funds for equipment and facilities, including hospitals and nurses' housing, in areas impacted by defense activities. That same year, the Labor–Federal Security Appropriations Act allocated $1.8 million for nursing education—for refresher courses for older nurses, for specialized training, and for enlarging existing training programs. To alleviate the anticipated shortage of civilian nurses, nursing schools introduced crash courses for volunteer nurses' aides, who would help graduate nurses in hospitals.[2]

As the war progressed, still another congressional act created the U.S. Cadet Nurse Corps. Administered by the Public Health Service and directed by Lucile Petry, the program paid all expenses for accelerated training of nurses at 1,125 schools. In turn, students agreed to work in essential civilian or military nursing as long as the war lasted. Beginning in 1943, the Cadet Nurse Corps attracted about 169,443 students over the next two years.[3]

All nursing schools joined the emergency effort to provide enough trained nurses for the private and government sectors. In 1940, there had been 1,304 schools of nursing, including 131 affiliated with colleges and universities, with 97,345 students. Five years later, 1,271 schools brimmed with 112,956 students.[4]

Even with all these actions, there were never enough nurses. As the war dragged on, mounting casualties and lack of proper care for injured American servicemen led to an attempt to draft nurses for the military. President Franklin D. Roosevelt suggested the measure in January 1945, and the House passed such a bill. The Senate was more cautious, and the war's nearing an end precluded any action.[5]

During the war years, great advances in medicine kept military mortality rates at an all-time low; 96 percent of the 671,000 wounded survived. Sulphonamides had come into use in the 1930s, and soon penicillin controlled a wide variety of infections. More effective antimalarial therapy, better understanding and treatment of shock, and greater use of blood and its derivatives all contributed to lower mortality. At the same time, the introduction of the chemical DDT eradicated many disease-carrying pests. A new capability—air evacuation of the wounded from combat areas—provided swift treatment and saved lives that would have been lost. It also brought forth a new type of medical service: flight nursing.[6]

The Navy had to care for its vastly increased forces as they fought a two-ocean war, and the Bureau of Medicine and Surgery directed the expansion of health-care facilities at home and abroad. The bureau underwent several reorganizations to meet wartime demands. Between 1942 and 1945, new administration, professional, and medical statistics divisions augmented the existing eleven divisions. Such compartmentalization enabled specialists to focus on essential services.[7]

Between 30 June 1940 and 30 June 1945, the number of naval hospitals of all types in the United States grew from fifteen to fifty-four; overseas, from three to six permanent hospitals and more than forty temporary base and fleet hospitals and dispensaries. These facilities could accommodate about 130,000 patients. There had been two hospital ships, the *Relief* (AH 1) and *Solace* (AH 5), on the eve of war; by 1945, there were fifteen, twelve staffed by Navy medical personnel.[8] The opening of the new National Naval Medical Center at Bethesda, Maryland, in 1942 provided modern facilities for both the hospital and the medical school. The old buildings on Observatory Hill in downtown Washington, D.C., then housed the Bureau of Medicine and Surgery.[9]

Under the direction of the surgeon general, Rear Adm. (later Vice Adm.) Ross T. McIntire, the Medical Department saw the number of medical officers soar from 932 in 1940 to 12,790 males and 42 female reservists five years later; the number of dentists grew from 200 to 6,218, including two women. Nursing assistance expanded: the Hospital Corps, which consisted of approximately 6,000 officers and men in 1940, grew to 3,398 officers and 124,279 enlisted men and women in June 1945. Navy Nurse Corps personnel increased from 440 to 11,086 women.[10]

These medical, dental, and nursing professionals transformed naval medicine to meet the demands of a series of invasions that took the war to the enemy, and they created amphibious medicine. The sequence of care began with corpsmen on the landing beaches and progressed to aid stations, field hospitals, hospital ships, and fleet and advance base hospitals. In 1945 the special augmented hospital linked field and fleet hospitals in combat areas. So effective was this on-the-spot care that 98 percent of Navy and Marine wounded survived.[11]

## The Action Starts

Even before the country entered the war, a group of nurses experienced a terrifying preview of dangers to come. In June 1941, twenty-six Red Cross nurses, part of the American Red Cross–Harvard Field Hospital unit going to Salisbury, England, sailed in a British convoy. German submarines attacked the convoy in the North Atlantic and sank seven of the ships, including two carrying the nurses. Five nurses drowned. One of those rescued, Marion Blissett, later joined the Navy Nurse Corps.[12]

## *Pearl Harbor*

Navy nurses came under fire with the war's opening salvo when the Japanese bombed Pearl Harbor on 7 December 1941. Anticipating war in the Pacific and its inevitable casualties, both the Navy and the Army had been upgrading their medical facilities at Oahu. To bolster the capacity of its two large hospitals and scattered dispensaries, the Army Medical Department built a new hospital at Hickam Field and set up temporary wards in other existing buildings.[13] The Navy's 506-bed Pearl Harbor Naval Hospital, dispensary at Kaneohe Naval Air Station, and sick bay at Ewa Marine Corps Air Station were insufficient for projected casualties, so construction of a new hospital had begun but was not complete. The recently commissioned hospital ship *Solace* lay at anchor at Pearl Harbor. Thirty-one Navy nurses served at the naval hospital and dispensary at Pearl Harbor, and twelve more served in *Solace*.[14]

The early-morning Japanese carrier attack destroyed about 265 Army, Navy, and Marine aircraft on the ground and made a shambles of nineteen U.S. Pacific Fleet ships. American forces suffered devastating casualties—2,403 killed and 1,178 wounded. of these, the Navy lost 2,008 men, and 710 more sustained injuries.[15]

With Japanese planes still overhead, Navy nurses rushed to care for the injured. Under the direction of Chief Nurse Gertrude B. Arnest, the nurses at the naval hospital hastily tended to convalescing patients and prepared for the influx of wounded. In just three hours, 452 injured arrived; many more followed. Nearly half suffered severe burns from explosions; others were in shock. Both conditions were life-threatening. Arnest supervised nurses, hospital corpsmen, and civilian volunteers in quickly applying tannic acid to the burn victims and giving plasma and saline solutions to shock patients.[16] Nurse Ruth Erickson, who later would become director of the Navy Nurse Corps, recalled the horror and the valor of that day: "The everlasting line of severely wounded or burned patients pushed the nurses from thinking of their own peril to concentrating on the task at hand: aiding those injured men."[17] A week later, many of the wounded were moved to transports for return to naval hospitals in the States.[18]

As nurses at the hospital tended the injured, twelve others in *Solace* prepared for more. Chief Nurse Grace B. Lally had seen the Japanese planes bombing and torpedoing the nearby warships and knew the human carnage would be great. The 132 burned and mangled men, cared for by Navy doctors, nurses, hospital corpsmen, and some civilian nurses, received emergency treatment for injuries and shock.[19] In recognition of their bravery and efficiency in *Solace* and at the naval hospital, the Navy awarded its Unit Commendation to the nurses.

### *Guam*

The attack on Pearl Harbor was not an isolated case of Japanese aggression. On 8 December, enemy planes bombed Guam in the Marianas, and on 10 December Japanese forces overran the island. Among their prisoners were five Navy Nurse Corps women, who had been running the training school for Chamorro nurses. Led by Chief Nurse Marion B. Olds, the Navy nurses remained on duty at the hospital for several weeks after capture.[20]

On 10 January 1942, their captors moved the nurses to a prison camp in Zentsuji, Japan. Transferred again on 12 March to a detention house in Kobe, the five Navy nurses, along with ten American missionaries, remained for several months, sleeping on straw mats and consuming an unappetizing "weed and water" soup and a rice-wheat mixture. There was little to do but read and study. Nurse Leona Jackson, subsequently director of the Navy Nurse Corps, wrote two graphic descriptions of these troubling months.[21] Aside from poor rations and constricted activities, the women apparently suffered no harm from their captors.

Then, unexpectedly, the women learned they would go home as part of an exchange of prisoners. On 17 June they sailed from Yokohama in the exchange ship *Gripsholm*. One nurse had met and fallen in love with an American consul, also a prisoner, and she left *Gripsholm* in East Africa to marry him. The other four women returned to the United States.[22]

Guam remained under Japanese control until 21 July 1944, when American forces recaptured the island. It was another year before the Navy could reopen its training school for nurses.

## *The Philippines*

Another attack against American possessions in the Pacific took place in the Philippines. In the months before war erupted, the Army had belatedly supplemented personnel and supplies, including medical staff and equipment, to defend the islands. Sternberg General Hospital in Manila became a major medical center, augmented by five station hospitals.[23] The Navy maintained one hospital, Cañacao Naval Hospital, near the Cavite Navy Yard. Twelve Navy nurses served there, including Chief Nurse Laura M. Cobb, who was a veteran of World War I.[24]

On 8 December 1941, Japanese aircraft began systematically destroying American air defenses, bombing Clark Field and Iba Field, followed by Nichols Field the next day. Two days later, bombers leveled the Cavite Navy Yard, and more raids continued throughout the month. That same day, Japanese troops invaded Luzon and moved toward Manila.[25]

As the bombing continued, Nurse Cobb and other Navy nurses moved patients from Cañacao Hospital wards to safety under the building's reinforced concrete floor. On 11 December, Cañacao medical personnel moved all patients to Sternberg General Hospital, renamed Manila Hospital Center, which became the central medical facility for Army and Navy personnel as well as civilians.[26]

The Navy nurses then scattered, serving briefly in emergency medical units around Manila. On 2 January 1942, the capital city, as well as Cavite Naval Base, fell to the enemy. Within a week, eleven Navy nurses were Japanese prisoners. Sent to the University of Santo Tomas, which was now a prison camp for civilians, the nurses helped establish and run a makeshift hospital for thirty-five hundred internees.[27]

Santo Tomas became overcrowded, and in May 1943 the Japanese set up another camp at Los Baños. The Navy nurses formed part of the medical team sent there to open a twenty-five-bed hospital. According to Nurse Dorothy Still, Los Baños was at first the "country club" of prison camps, but conditions soon deteriorated. From early 1944 onward, malnutrition to near-starvation weakened the nurses and killed many internees. Supervised by Chief Nurse Cobb, the Navy nurses credited their survival to carrying out their duties and maintaining their dignity and sense of humor.[28]

Finally, the tide of battle turned: American forces invaded Luzon in January 1945 and liberated the prisoners at Santo Tomas and Los Baños the following month. The nurses had endured thirty-seven months of internment. After returning to the United States, they were awarded the Bronze Star for caring for the sick and wounded while they were themselves prisoners of war.[29]

The twelfth original Cañacao Naval Hospital nurse had a far different experience. When the nurses had dispersed to various medical units in late December 1941, Ann A. Bernatitus joined an Army group setting up a hospital on the Bataan Peninsula. In the face of certain Japanese victory, the U.S. Army had moved its forces, including medical facilities, to Bataan, where it built two hospitals, and to Corregidor, an island off Bataan. At General Hospital Number 1 at Camp Limay, Bernatitus and Army nurses worked feverishly in surgical teams until enemy fire forced the hospital into the jungle. Before Bataan fell on 9 April 1942, the nurses moved to Corregidor.[30]

On that island, an elaborate system of tunnels, called the Malinta Hospital, provided shelter from bombing and shelling. Relentless Japanese bombardment continued, and defeat was imminent. On 29 April two Navy PBY patrol planes brought in medical supplies and left with nineteen Army nurses among their forty-seven passengers.[31] On 3 May, submarine *Spearfish* (SS 190) slipped into Corregidor to evacuate twenty-five more, including eleven Army nurses and Ann Bernatitus, the sole Navy nurse who had gone to Bataan and Corregidor. After seventeen days at sea, *Spearfish* reached Australia and safety. Bernatitus returned to the United States in July and became the first person to receive the Navy's new medal, the Legion of Merit. Meanwhile, Corregidor fell on 6 May, and the remaining fifty-four Army nurses were captured and taken to Santo Tomas prison camp, where they remained until liberated in February 1945.[32]

Navy nurses served at still another American territory in the Pacific: Samoa. The corps had run a training school there for young Polynesian women since 1911. In their drive for supremacy in the Pacific, the Japanese shelled Tutuila on 11 January 1942 but caused no major damage.[33]

## The Call to Arms

Masterminding Navy Nurse Corps wartime activities was Superintendent Sue Dauser. Her main duties were recruiting nurses, examining and approving their qualifications, and assigning their duties.[34] A corps member since World War I, she knew personally each nurse during the interwar years. Drawing upon this prior acquaintance, she employed these nurses as an administrative nucleus for wartime expansion. She carefully assigned them to critical billets setting up nursing services in large new hospitals, in mobile hospitals, and in hospital ships.[35] From her office in the old naval hospital building, Dauser and her assistant superintendents, Cdrs. Loretta Lambert and Mary D. Towse, directed a growing staff of about nine nurses, three WAVES, and eighteen civilian clerks. Voluminous files contained nurses' records, and Dauser kept a summary of this information at her fingertips in cylindrical card files. She was vitally involved with all facets of running the Nurse Corps.[36]

### *Recruiting*

The Bureau of Medicine and Surgery had to procure enough trained nurses for its medical facilities at home and abroad, relying on several organizations to help provide them. The American Red Cross, which maintained a registry of graduate nurses, was the official recruiting agency for the Army and Navy Nurse Corps, certifying professional credentials of nurses seeking appointment to the services.[37] The National Nursing Council for War Service turned over its recruiting tasks to the War Manpower Commission Procurement and Assignment Service in 1942, and the latter group worked through state committees to recruit nurses for the military.[38] Other interested nurses sent applications directly to the Bureau of Medicine and Surgery. The bureau also urged Navy nurses to recruit among their friends by sending them pamphlets and literature.[39]

A critical shortage of nurses developed by late 1944 and precipitated the unsuccessful move to draft nurses the following January. The Navy preferred other methods of attracting nurses, and on 24 January 1945 it instructed the Offices of Naval Officer Procurement to assist in recruiting.[40] No nurses were sent as procurement officers, although some served in these offices to help examine applicants or to travel with WAVES officers on recruiting trips.[41] A few others came into the Nurse Corps through the cadet nurse program. The Navy trained 1,155 senior (third-year) cadets, and 468 completed the course. Of these, 58 actually entered the corps.[42] The program ended in 1946.[43] Through all these sources, the Navy filled its quota for nurses by March 1945 and needed to recruit only about 100 a month as replacements. Realizing that the Army Nurse Corps continued to suffer chronic shortages, Superintendent Dauser sent unneeded applications along to the Army.[44]

At peak strength in June 1945, the Navy Nurse Corps had 11,086 active duty members, up markedly from 787 on the eve of war. Of these, 1,813 were permanent Nurse Corps and 9,273 were reservists. Altogether, 14,178 women served in the corps. Far larger, of course, was the Army Nurse Corps, whose numbers reached more than 57,000.[45] American nurses led all professions in volunteering for war service. Of 242,500 registered nurses, 42.9 percent offered their skills to the military, which accepted 76,000 of them during the course of the war.[46]

## *Who Volunteered*

Maintaining its high standards, the Navy Nurse Corps had set age requirements of between twenty-two and twenty-eight years for the regular corps and between twenty-two and forty-five for the reserve nurses. By war's end, these had changed somewhat—twenty-two to thirty for the Nurse Corps and twenty-one to forty for reservists. To quality for the Nurse Corps, a woman had to be an American citizen and unmarried; she had to have graduated from high school and from an approved nursing school, qualified as a registered nurse, and passed professional and mental examinations as well as stringent physical requirements. After appointment, a nurse served a six-month probationary period to determine her fitness for naval service.[47]

Like the WAVES, Navy nurses were white, middle-class women. New York led the way with the most volunteers, followed by California, Pennsylvania, Illinois, and Michigan.[48] They were young. Of the 1,028 nurses recruited by the Office of Naval Officer Procurement in early 1945, 846 were between twenty-two and twenty-six years of age. Among all Navy nurses, 72.7 percent were younger than thirty. The great majority gained experience in institutional nursing. Two hundred eight had some college training, and 128 had taken postgraduate nursing courses.[49]

Others tried to join the corps but were unsuccessful until late in the war. Although about 500 black nurses served in the Army Nurse Corps, on a segregated basis, the Navy did not recruit black women until early 1945, when the increased need for nurses and intensified pressure from black groups led to a change in naval policy.[50] The Navy Nurse Corps soon accepted 5 qualified black nurses on a fully integrated basis.[51] Even less successful were registered male nurses, although they actively campaigned for admission. Dauser opposed proposed legislation enabling men to enter the corps, and neither the Army Nurse Corps nor the Navy Nurse Corps accepted men as nurses, but they could enlist in the Hospital Corps.[52]

Women joined the Navy Nurse Corps for many reasons. Like the WAVES, the nurses' strongest motivation was the desire to help their country win the war by giving their best.[53] With dignity and pride, Navy nurses served a "cause above self."[54] In addition to patriotism, the appeal of foreign travel, more education, and specialized training attracted many nurses. "It sounded nice," recalled one. Diverse experiences in a variety of clinical settings inspired others.[55]

Family tradition prompted many to join the Navy, rather than Army, Nurse Corps. Others joined because of Nurse Corps friends who told them of life in the naval service. Perceived as being more selective than the Army Nurse Corps, the Navy Nurse Corps, as well as the Navy itself, had a reputation for being aloof, snooty, and old-fashioned—a reputation that appealed to many talented nurses.[56]

## *Orientation and Training*

At first, there was no formal indoctrination program for incoming Navy nurses. They learned on the job. Nurse Alene Duerk, who later became director of the Nurse Corps, recalled arriving at her first assignment, receiving her nurse's cap, and beginning work on the ward at seven the next morning. "After two weeks, you were expected to take over your own ward," she said.[57] It soon became apparent that the transition from civilian to military nursing would be smoother with some type of orientation. In July 1942 the Bureau of Medicine and Surgery directed naval hospitals to conduct indoctrination courses for incoming nurses, but these programs were cursory and tacked onto nurses' regular duties.[58]

In November 1943, the Nurse Corps began sending new recruits to the Naval Hospital, Portsmouth, Virginia, for the first formal indoctrination program, a two-week course familiarizing nurses with naval terminology, etiquette, customs, procedures, and medical practices, including ward management, and, of course, military drill.[59] The nurses received a copy of *Navy Nurses Guide* to help them. The guide emphasized "honor, justice, truth, patience, charity, and refinement." A familiar theme recurred: "A nurse must be a lady."[60] The most difficult thing, recalled one nurse, was learning to take orders, especially from a nurse who was junior in years and experience but senior in rank or length of service.[61]

The Nurse Corps had always stressed specialized training for its members. Wartime demands for nurses sharply curtailed, but did not halt, the numbers sent for courses. Superintendent Dauser strongly supported advanced training and encouraged nurses to apply. Most specialized in dietetics at George Washington University, but in 1943, two nurses studied the Kenny method (application of hot packs for polio victims) at Stanford University Hospital and twelve learned operating room technique at Lahey Clinic in Boston.[62]

Early 1943 saw the first graduates in the new field of flight nursing, which developed during the war. The Army Nurse Corps graduated its flight nurses from the Army Air Forces School of Air Evacuation, after airlifting the wounded had started in the central Solomons in 1942. The Navy introduced a similar program when the Naval Air Transport Service (NATS) began carrying whole blood, plasma, and medical supplies to the Pacific and bringing home casualties on return flights.[63]

Two Navy nurses took air evacuation training late in 1943 at the Army's Bowman Field, but it was not until a year later that the Naval School of Air Evacuation at Alameda, California, offered formal instruction. Each class ran for two months and included a flight surgeon, a Hospital Corps officer, 24 nurses, and 24 pharmacist's mates. After classroom training, they received flight indoctrination on NATS hospital planes within the United States.[64] Under the supervision of the flight nurse in charge, Lt. (jg) Mary Ellen O'Connor, 110 women became Navy flight nurses. Their studies included lectures, demonstrations, practice in loading patients onto planes, flight nursing care, and emergency survival techniques.[65] O'Connor regularly informed Captain Dauser of the progress, and Dauser responded with lively interest.[66]

### *Working Conditions*

From December 1942 throughout the war, pay for Navy nurses remained constant. The superintendent received base pay of $4,000 a year; assistant superintendents, $3,500; chief nurses, $2,000; and nurses, $1,800. All were eligible for a 5 percent raise for every three years' service. When quarters and subsistence were not provided, rental allowances ranged from $540 to $1,260, depending on grade. Subsistence pay was $255.50 for everyone.[67]

Although the cherished eight-hour day failed to survive wartime demands, Navy nurses continued to enjoy thirty days a year of both annual and sick leave. Retirement benefits for age, length of service, and disability continued, as well as medical treatment in naval hospitals.[68] A breakthrough for most naval and Marine personnel came with the 1943 act providing inpatient or outpatient hospital care for dependents. Since "dependents" meant wives, unmarried children under twenty-one, or parents who were, in fact, dependents, the new law had little impact on the unmarried ladies of the Nurse Corps, although its passage meant there were more patients to care for.[69]

The ban against marriage remained strict until near the end of the war. Marriage while in the Nurse Corps had brought immediate dismissal and was an avenue women sometimes took to leave the Navy. As the military looked for ways to recruit more nurses in early 1945, the Navy turned to the obvious: allowing married women in the corps. On 10 January, Secretary of the Navy Forrestal suspended the ban on marriage by permitting retention of nurses after marriage. He soon allowed reappointment of former members of the corps who had resigned because of marriage.[70] Such latitude ended on 1 November, when the need for nurses diminished and the prohibition returned.[71] Similarly, pregnancy brought an immediate request for resignation. Late in the war, the Navy granted maternity hospital benefits for nurses, as well as WAVES, and for newborns but only for the period of the mothers' confinement.[72]

Rank, or lack thereof, had been a long-standing problem, and the war brought changes the Nurse Corps had sought. In February 1942 Surgeon General McIntire urged Knox to ask Congress for relative rank for Navy nurses. The Army Nurse Corps had enjoyed this privilege since 1920. Knox wrote Congress that the present indefinite status of the Navy Nurse Corps was "most unsatisfactory and confused" and requested legislation authorizing relative rank to increase the professional efficiency of the corps.[73] Congress obliged, and on 3 July 1942, Navy nurses gained relative rank. The superintendent would be a lieutenant commander; assistant superintendents, lieutenants; chief nurses, lieutenants (jg); and nurses, ensigns. The measure also spelled out nurses' authority: They would have authority next after commissioned officers of the Medical and Dental Corps in and about naval hospitals and other medical activities and were entitled to the same obedience from enlisted men and patients as commissioned officers received.[74]

As welcome as the new status was, the ranks were too low for the positions, so another law in December 1942 raised the superintendent to captain and assistant superintendents to commanders. Chief nurses and nurses kept their earlier ranks. These relative ranks would be in effect until six months after the war ended. Along with them came temporary pay increases.[75] On 22 December 1942, Superintendent Dauser was sworn in as captain—the first woman to hold this rank in the U.S. Navy and the first captain in the Nurse Corps.[76]

But relative rank still did not give military nursing the authority and status needed to attract and retain qualified nurses. Women could go into the reserves of any of the armed services and hold commissioned, not relative, rank. Captain Dauser had always argued that Navy nurses should have the same rank and privileges as male officers.[77] Finally, in February 1944, Congress authorized temporary commissioned rank for the Navy Nurse Corps for the war and six months afterward.[78] Their new ranks and titles brought them "honor and dignity, as well as protection, and authority consistent with their responsibilities."[79] In September rental and subsistence allowances rose for all women in the military who had dependents. Finally, to make the Nurse Corps officers' pay and allowances consistent with the regular Navy, Congress increased pay in grade for nurses on the same schedule as other naval officers. Retirement benefits would be based on all service, whether active or inactive, under appointments or commissions in the corps.[80]

In spite of their vital importance to the war effort, Navy nurses experienced opposition. It surfaced in the paternalistic and patronizing attitudes of those who had definite ideas about women's proper place in society, and in the hostility of hospital corpsmen who did not like being bossed around by women or who resented the prohibition against nurses socializing with enlisted men.[81] An unusual burst of criticism came from within the Nurse Corps itself. One disgruntled member had complained to Bess Truman, wife of President Harry S. Truman, about having to instruct hospital corpsmen, especially blacks, and care for Navy dependents.[82]

### *Uniforms*

In 1942 Navy nurses received new uniforms. A complete outdoor uniform consisting of a semifitted Navy blue jacket (or white for summer) with gilt Navy buttons down the front and gold stripes (in contrast to the WAVES' light blue stripes) on the sleeve designating rank became mandatory. An officer's cap with no visor and a corps insignia pin in the center and black (or white) shoes and hose completed the outfit.[83]

A few changes to the uniform took place in 1944. Nurses were permitted to wear naval officers' cap insignia, and the metal corps insignia worn on the lapels changed to miniature devices with "N.N.C." on one side of the collar and a metal rank device on the other. Nurses could now also wear a gray work uniform. The most dramatic change in traditional uniforms came in early 1945, when flight nurses could wear flight shirts, trousers, and visored caps.[84]

## Deployment

### *The United States*

Wherever there was a naval hospital within the United States, Navy nurses were there. By June 1945, forty regular hospitals spanned the continent, handling 84,361 patients. In addition, 176 dispensaries treated others.[85] The vast majority, 9,436 of the 11,086 Navy nurses, served in these stateside facilities, with the highest concentrations in California, New York, Virginia, Illinois, and Maryland.[86] Nurses' healing talents not only aided Navy, Marine, and

Coast Guard personnel but also dependents, who became eligible for government medical care.

At these hospitals, rehabilitation was the major goal: either return the fighting man to active duty or make him as whole as possible for civilian life. Various naval hospitals focused on specific problems. At San Diego, for example, there was a large physical therapy department where Navy nurses supervised hospital corpsmen in administering heat and massage, exercise, and physical and vocational therapies to patients. For these nurses, there was no greater feeling of accomplishment than when "an independent man says good-bye—and walks away."[87] This same large hospital also treated severe burn cases with saline solutions and reconstructive surgery and combated the shock associated with brain injuries.[88] A major breakthrough in the treatment of burn and gunshot wounds, recalled Ens. Ann Clendenin, was a procedure called pedical skin grafts.[89]

A novel program took shape at the Marine barracks dispensary in Klamath Falls, Oregon. Ten Navy nurses were part of a medical team conducting research and rehabilitation with veterans of Pacific campaigns who had contracted malaria or filariasis (filarial worms infesting the blood and lymph system, causing gross disfigurement). Reassurance, as well as medical and vocational treatment, played a major role in recovery.[90]

New to naval medicine were fourteen special hospitals, with 6,267 patients, focusing on general and surgical convalescents and neuropsychiatric and orthopedic cases.[91] Nurses trained in such specialties helped staff these convalescent facilities.[92]

Attending patients from the Pacific to the United States, nurses served in air transport duty. In early 1942, the commandant of the Twelfth Naval District in San Francisco requested Navy nurses for flights in Pan American clippers from San Francisco to Hawaii and back because these aircraft often carried pregnant women and other evacuees from Hawaii. Surgeon General McIntire readily agreed, and three Navy nurses started this service.[93]

One of the Nurse Corps's paramount tasks was training members of the Hospital Corps at six schools set up for the purpose. When the war began, training schools operated at the Norfolk, Brooklyn, and San Diego hospitals, but the great influx of new corpsmen called for more training sites. Basic theoretical training, administered by doctors, Navy nurses, and more experienced hospital corpsmen, lasted about six weeks. To teach the classes, Dauser carefully selected nurse-instructors who had university or teaching experience and who had graduated from good schools of nursing. The corpsmen took courses in materia medica, physiology, field hygiene, minor surgery, and first aid. When WAVES entered the Hospital Corps, they received their preliminary training in schools at Bethesda, San Diego, and Camp Moffett at Great Lakes. A more specialized unit, the Rehabilitation Training School, opened at Hunter College.[94]

After the classroom training phase, men and women of the Hospital Corps continued learning at naval hospitals, under the direct supervision of Navy nurses. There they mastered bedside nursing. Some corpsmen went on to more specialized training such as six months' intensive preparation to become operating room technicians. The nurses were well aware that their students would provide most of the nursing care in hospitals, ships, and aircraft, and on the invasion beachheads as a major component of amphibious medicine.[95] One nurse expressed the urgency in teaching these corpsmen: "Their failure would be her failure," and they must not fail.[96] And they did not fail. Hospital corpsmen were among the most highly decorated men of the war.

## *Overseas*

Congress was not reluctant to allow Nurse Corps women, in contrast to the WAVES, to go overseas, and these nurses followed the fighting in the Pacific and in Europe. By war's end, 1,261 Navy nurses had served in more than forty foreign posts and on twelve hospital ships.[97]

The Navy had to protect the approaches to the United States and simultaneously provide medical care for men in distant places. In June 1941, Chief Nurse Ruth Abrams and four other nurses arrived at Kodiak, Alaska. They worked in the civilian hospital run by the contractor building the naval air station, which included a new naval hospital. When it was ready in December, the nurses moved there.[98] Because the Japanese bombed Dutch Harbor in June 1942, the Aleutian Islands took on added strategic significance, and Adak became a naval operating base. Navy nurses went to hospitals at Dutch Harbor in January 1943 and to Adak and Attu later that year.[99]

The chief nurse at Adak, Lt. (jg) Lucille Hendricks, and two other Navy nurses died when their plane crashed in the Aleutians in April 1944.[100]

The southern approaches to the United States saw an increased naval presence, and with it came supporting medical facilities in the Caribbean. Late in 1941, eight Navy nurses served in the naval hospital at Guantanamo Bay, Cuba; five at St. Thomas, Virgin Islands; and four others at Coco Solo, the Canal Zone. The next year, more nurses reported to San Juan, Puerto Rico, and Trinidad, British West Indies. Later, still others served in Bermuda and in Curaçao, Dutch West Indies. The northern approaches to the country carried heavy traffic from the Atlantic Fleet, and by early 1943, Navy nurses joined the naval hospital medical staff at Argentia, Newfoundland.[101]

Two Navy flight nurses who had trained in air evacuation in late 1943 were assigned to Brazil, which was not part of the defensive ring around the United States but still in the Western Hemisphere. Lts. (jg) Stephany J. Kozak and Dympha Van Gorp went to Rio de Janeiro in January 1944 to set up an air evacuation training program for Brazilian Air Force nurses. After they helped establish a hospital unit for American servicemen within the Brazilian Air Force Hospital, they launched the air evacuation program.[102]

As the series of amphibious invasions in North Africa, Italy, and Normandy placed naval forces in the thick of battle, casualties mounted and the Navy had to provide medical care for its men. Hospital corpsmen handled nursing duties onboard ships and on beachheads, but the Navy Nurse Corps went to numerous hospitals and dispensaries. Navy nurses also served in the hospital ship *Refuge* (AH 11) as it carried the injured from Oran, Algeria, from Naples, and from Britain back to hospitals in the United States during the spring and summer of 1944.[103]

In March 1944, twenty-five nurses, under the supervision of the chief nurse, Lt. (jg) Clyde E. Pennington, arrived at the five-hundred-bed base hospital in Oran, Algiers. Within a few weeks, five of these nurses, under Lt. (jg) Susie Burns, chief nurse, moved to the large dispensary in Palermo, Sicily. In the fall, four nurses, led by Lt. (jg) Doris Davis, were transferred to the dispensary at Naples.[104] Later, eleven others served at Bizerte, Tunisia.

Larger complements of Navy nurses served in England. Anticipating the invasion of mainland Europe through France, the Navy had established throughout the United Kingdom a string of sixteen dispensaries, beginning in Roseneath, Scotland, in 1942. In March 1944 a base hospital was commissioned at Netley, England, and as German V-bombs fell, Lt. Cdr. Mary Martha Heck led ninety-eight nurses there in preparing for the inevitable casualties of the Normandy invasion.[105] Within days of D-day, American wounded arrived, and nurses Helen Ramsey and Sara Kelley were among those providing round-the-clock life-saving care.[106] The speedy and effective medical treatment of 7,877 men in four months resulted in a mortality rate of only .26 percent of combat casualties.[107]

Even more Navy nurses followed the military action across the Pacific, but their longstanding duties changed. Because the Japanese had overrun the Philippines and Guam early in the war, hospitals there had to await American liberation forces before rebuilding. The new naval hospital at Aiea Heights in the Hawaiian Islands was completed in 1942, and the following year a base hospital was built at Pearl Harbor. Navy nurses served in these posts, which later became the intermediate staging ground for evacuating wounded from battle areas to the United States.[108] American Samoa, remote from combat zones, continued to maintain its naval presence, and Navy nurses kept their school for local girls operating. As Chief Nurse Mary J. Lindner later described in an interview, Navy Seabees built a new classroom for the school. In addition, a mobile hospital for treating filariasis opened there in 1942.[109]

By late 1942, the Navy was sending nurses to the Southwest Pacific. Some worked at the base hospital at Efate, New Hebrides, where they cared for Marines injured at Guadalcanal and New Georgia as well as for numerous malaria victims. As usual, they continued training hospital corpsmen. Soon, more Navy nurses arrived at the large base hospital at Espiritu Santo, New Hebrides. Their duties were the same as those of the nurses at Efate. In addition to medical assignments, nurses looked after sagging patient morale, and they devoted long hours to occupational therapy.[110]

As these hospitals became overcrowded, the Navy built a series of new ones in 1943: another base hospital at Espiritu Santo and one each in Wellington, New Zealand; Tulagi, the Solomons; Sydney, Australia; Munda, New Georgia; and Milne Bay, New Guinea. Mobile hospitals sprang up at Auckland and Wellington, New Zealand; Brisbane, Australia; the Russell

Islands in the Solomons; Guam; and New Caledonia. As the island-hopping Pacific campaign moved closer to mainland Japan in 1944 and 1945, larger base hospitals opened from New Guinea to the Admiralties, the Schoutens, the Marianas, the Palaus, and the Marshalls. Fleet hospitals operated at Samar, Philippines, and at Guam.[111]

Designed to provide expert medical care as efficiently as possible, each hospital had up to forty Navy nurses, often more. One wrote of being with twenty-seven other nurses who reached Tinian in the Marianas in 1944. They were the first white women or nurses to come to the island with its one-thousand-bed base hospital. Here they continued their customary task of teaching hospital corpsmen as well as nursing the sickest patients.[112] Fifty more pioneering nurses arrived at the eleven-hundred-bed mobile hospital at Banika in the Russell Islands. One wrote of trying to cope with the debilitating tropical humidity as well as casualties from Saipan, Pavuvu, Guam, and Palau.[113]

At New Hebrides, a nurse described the busy hospital routine as well as continually teaching the corpsmen to give intelligent care.[114] One nurse wrote about the experiences of fifty nurses dispatched to the Solomons. Part of a contingent of 127 nurses assigned to three islands, the women experienced intense gratification as they helped their ill and wounded patients recover.[115] Two told of the fifty-nine nurses working tirelessly at the twenty-six-hundred-bed base hospital on Guam. Inundated with critically wounded soldiers, sailors, and marines from the Iwo Jima and Okinawa campaigns, the Navy nurses demonstrated "superhuman endurance."[116] Twelve nurses were part of the American triumphant return to the Philippines and served at the new one-thousand-bed (later expanded to three thousand beds) fleet hospital at Samar.[117] These women were but a small number of the hundreds of Navy nurses who served in the Pacific.

At the beginning of the war, the Navy had two commissioned hospital ships, the *Relief* and *Solace*. In 1945, there were fifteen floating hospitals plying the Pacific, and Navy nurses served on twelve.[118] Each carried a full medical contingent: about 12 physicians, 2 dentists, 13 nurses, and 130 hospital corpsmen. The *Solace* had her baptism of fire at Pearl Harbor, then she followed the fighting to the Solomons, the Marianas, Iwo Jima, and Okinawa. Typically, the hospital ship would take on wounded delivered by smaller craft, provide emergency treatment or surgery, then deliver the patients to a large base hospital like those at Tinian, Guam, and Pearl Harbor.[119] The *Relief* joined the Pacific Fleet in 1943, evacuating wounded from the Solomons, Kwajalein, Saipan, Tinian, and the Palau Islands. During the Okinawa invasion, Japanese planes attacked the hospital ship but caused only minor damage. Altogether, *Relief* evacuated approximately ten thousand men from the Pacific. Bringing these floating hospitals close to shore saved lives by administering almost immediate medical care.[120]

In 1944 three new hospital ships—the *Bountiful* (AH 9), *Refuge*, and *Samaritan* (AH 10)—arrived in the Pacific. Nurse Georgia Reynolds exulted over the amenities of *Bountiful:* "Imagine receiving . . . five hundred fresh casualties . . . in a few hours. The wonders of plasma, the sulpha drugs, and penicillin could never be better demonstrated."[121] The next year, seven more—the *Benevolence* (AH 13), *Consolation* (AH 15), *Haven* (AH 12), *Repose* (AH 16), *Rescue* (AH 18), *Sanctuary* (AH 17), and *Tranquillity* (AH 14)—joined the Pacific Fleet, and in each came Navy nurses. Three of these ships—*Rescue, Tranquillity,* and *Benevolence*—entered Tokyo Bay in September 1945.[122] Nurse Alene Duerk remembered sailing into Tokyo Bay in *Benevolence* ahead of the minesweepers and having to back up.[123] After the surrender, the three ships began evacuating Allied prisoners of war.

### *Air Evacuation*

Efficient air evacuation of wounded from battlefields to hospitals in the rear aided American wartime medical success. First used at Guadalcanal and then in other Pacific campaigns and at Normandy, rapid removal of the injured saved countless lives.[124] The Navy trained flight nurses in early 1945, and they joined three Naval Air Evacuation Service squadrons. Each squadron consisted of twelve planes, usually two-engine Douglas Skytrains, and twenty-four nurses and twenty-four pharmacist's mates. On each flight, a nurse and a pharmacist's mate worked as a team providing care for about two dozen wounded.[125] Evacuation planes traversed three major routes: from the combat area to the fleet hospital at Guam, from Guam to Pearl Harbor with an intermediate island stop such as Kwajalein, and from Pearl Harbor to the United States.[126]

Flight nurses came into the combat area at Iwo Jima on D-day +15 (6 March 1945). Ens. Jane Kendeigh was the first to touch down at Iwo Jima, amid heavy mortar fire. She and the rest of the crew took shelter in a foxhole until the attack ended. Too excited, then too busy to be afraid, Kendeigh helped load the wounded onto the aircraft, which promptly took off. Later that same day, Lt. (jg) Emily G. Purvis arrived with another air evacuation plane.[127] Two days later, Lt. (jg) Evelyn Schretenthaler came on yet another plane to gather up more wounded. She later emphasized the difficulties of nursing in an unpressurized aircraft.[128] The twelve flight nurses in their squadron continued the air evacuations.[129]

Flight nurses took part in the next amphibious operation: the invasion of Okinawa. On D-day +6 (7 April 1945), Ensign Kendeigh was again the first flight nurse to land in the combat areas; others followed. After the flight nurses helped load their cargo of wounded servicemen, they attended to them during the long flight to Guam.[130]

## *Casualties, Decorations, and Honors*

No members of the Navy Nurse Corps lost their lives in combat during the war, but nine died while stationed overseas. Thirty-one others died in the United States.[131] The nurses' valor and dedication earned them 303 military awards. Capt. Sue Dauser received the Distinguished Service Medal, and Lt. (jg) Ann Bernatitus, who had escaped from the Philippines, the Legion of Merit. Fourteen nurses earned the Bronze Star, and eleven nurses received a Gold Star in lieu of a second Bronze Star. Forty-four were awarded letters of commendation with ribbon; twelve got the Army's Distinguished Unit Badge. The Navy Unit Commendation went to 224.[132] In a gesture of appreciation to the Nurse Corps, the Navy named a destroyer after the corps's second superintendent, Lenah Sutcliffe Higbee; and in November 1944, her sister, Mrs. A. M. Wheaton, christened the *Higbee* (DD 806). The ship was commissioned in January 1945, the first combatant ship named for a servicewoman.[133]

The Navy Nurse Corps played a major role in the transformation of naval medicine into an efficient and effective means of taking health care around the world. Trained professionals, these nurses gave untiringly of their talents and of themselves in caring for the sick and wounded of the Navy, the Marines, and the Coast Guard. They came under enemy fire at Pearl Harbor, Guam, the Philippines, and in Great Britain; and some endured Japanese prison camps. Navy nurses served in hospitals and dispensaries in the United States, the Pacific, the Caribbean, Alaska and the Aleutians, Newfoundland, Europe, North Africa, and the Mediterranean. Others sailed in hospital ships or flew with air evacuation missions.

A primary mission of the Nurse Corps was teaching, especially the untrained youths of the vastly expanded Hospital Corps. Nurses realized that they must impart enough knowledge and skill because corpsmen would provide most of the nursing care in hospitals and all of it on battlefronts and in combatant ships. In addition, nurses instructed the Cadet Nurse Corps, the WAVES, and local women in Samoa and Brazil.

The quiet courage and unswerving dedication of the Navy Nurse Corps brought accolades. Adm. William F. Halsey, commander of the Third Fleet, knew well the nurses' accomplishments in the Pacific. In tribute, he wrote, "Their untiring service, their professional skill, and their ability to sustain the unparalleled morale of the wounded in their care will always reflect the highest credit to the Nurse Corps, U.S. Navy."[134] Fleet Adm. Chester W. Nimitz noted that Navy nurses brought the same high standard of the nursing service to the Pacific as they did to stateside hospitals. "Their specialized knowledge and training and devotion to duty are invaluable," he declared. The most touching praise came from General Jonathan Wainwright, when he was released from Japanese captivity: "The sight of the beautiful Navy nurses was the best medicine an American could have."[135] Proud of her nurses, Captain Dauser pointed to their spirit of "ever-ready, unselfish solicitude."[136] On a wider scale, the war brought "power and prestige" to nurses, who were part of the health-care teams that significantly affected the war effort.[137]

Dauser herself deserves much credit for the Nurse Corps's superior wartime performance. When she became superintendent in 1939, there were 442 Navy nurses. Realizing the likelihood of war, she began building both the regular and reserve Nurse Corps, which reached a maximum wartime strength of 11,086. A career Navy nurse, she insisted on maintaining high standards for the corps, even during the nurse shortage of early 1945.

She devised the requirements for various assignments and oversaw putting the right nurse in each job. Keeping in close touch with nurses in the field, she encouraged them to write detailed accounts of their experiences.[138] She supported advanced specialized training for nurses and was especially enthusiastic about air evacuation training in early 1945. Dauser vigorously pushed commissioned rank and other benefits for Navy nurses. A good administrator who surrounded herself with competent assistants, she firmly guided the Nurse Corps through the difficult years of World War II.[139]

After Allied victory, the Nurse Corps, as well as all parts of the military, faced large cutbacks. Demobilization was the first step as the postwar Navy reverted to its peacetime role. Next would come the process of determining what future role the women of the Nurse Corps and the WAVES would play in the U.S. Navy.

# 7

# The Fight for Permanence, 1945–1950

*Although most Navy women* left the military to resume civilian pursuits, a determined few wanted a permanent role in the peacetime Navy. This novel concept required convincing a sometimes reluctant Navy and an obdurate Congress of the value of women in the military. Similarly, the Navy Nurse Corps struggled for permanent commissioned rank that would give these professional women the status, pay, and benefits granted other naval officers.

## The Setting

With the victorious conclusion of World War II, American women once again stood at a crossroads. What would be their place in the postwar world? Would they maintain the advances they had achieved in the work force, including the military, or would they retreat to the domestic sphere? The answer came with astonishing speed.

When the euphoria of victory subsided, new worries came to the fore. Returning veterans demanded jobs that women had held. Rampant inflation accompanied a period of pent-up consumer demand. The Soviet Union replaced the Axis powers as the dominant threat to American safety. As the cold war, with its concomitant possibility of nuclear warfare, got under way, anticommunism became the overriding ideology.[1]

Women continued to pursue higher education, but many concentrated on acquiring the "MRS" degree. Although the number of women students rose from 568,603 in 1944 to 805,953 in 1950, their percentage of all enrolled students plummeted from 65 to 30.2. Returning veterans crowded college campuses and edged out many female students. Only 24 percent of all baccalaureates went to women, who left college in large numbers to get married.[2] Higher education, many argued, should not train women to compete with men but should prepare them to be wives and mothers.[3] Consequently, women who graduated from college and got jobs gravitated to the traditional, nurturing professions: nursing, teaching, and library and social work.[4]

Those with less education found other employment. Frozen out of high-paying industrial jobs, women workers virtually took over office, sales, and service positions. By 1950, 31 percent of women worked, but the primary change occurred in the composition of this labor force. As young, single women rushed to the altar, older married women moved into the work force and continued a trend that had begun during the war.[5]

Any semblance of an organized women's rights movement sputtered and faded, though a few women's groups, such as the Women's Bureau of the United Auto Workers and the American Friends Service Committee (AFSC), and religious organizations, such as the YWCA, espoused women's rights and equality.[6] The equal rights amendment resurfaced, but the Senate rejected it in 1946. Four years later, that same body approved the measure but with a rider guaranteeing that protective legislation for women would remain.[7] The amendment was virtually dead until it was taken up again in the late 1960s.

Most women willingly took on the roles of wife and mother. They revisited the 1920s' model of the wife-companion. Marriage rates soared to 118 per 1,000 women in 1946, up from 79 per 1,000 twenty years earlier. Median age for first marriages dropped from 21.5 years to 20.3 years for women, and from 24.3 years to 22.7 years for men. Simultaneously, birth rates skyrocketed, and mothers of the baby boom generation averaged 3.5 children.[8]

Reinforcing these biological events, an ideology extolling motherhood and domesticity arose. Following Freudian doctrine, popularizers such as Ferdinand Lundberg and Marynia F. Farnham (*Modern Woman: The Lost Sex*) emphasized such "feminine" traits as passivity and submissiveness. Women, they argued, must organize their lives around the home, their natural sphere of nurturing. A logical complement to this line of thought was the permissive child-rearing practices advocated by pediatricians Arnold Gesell and Benjamin Spock.[9]

As American women reverted to a peacetime life-style, so, too, did the U.S. Navy shed the trappings of global war. Demobilization of the giant fighting machine proceeded quickly. From a high point of 6,626 active ships in August 1945, the number of ships fell to 1,248 by the following June and dropped to 634 in June 1950.[10] Simultaneously, naval personnel, which in July 1945 had reached 3,405,525 and included 323,755 officers, 3,005,534 enlisted, and 11,086 nurses, decreased to only 381,538 by June 1950, and this number included 42,687 officers, 331,860 enlisted, and 1,954 nurses.[11] Although the size of the Navy diminished rapidly, it was able to bring home more than 2 million servicemen by May 1946. Operation Magic Carpet, as it was called, even used battleships, cruisers, and aircraft carriers as transports to speed the return of American troops.[12]

In the fast-changing postwar world, the Navy was subject to budget slashing at the same time that it shouldered new responsibilities. First among these responsibilities was Operation Crossroads, which required ships for atomic bomb tests at Bikini Atoll in the Marshall Islands in 1946. The Navy also conducted Operation Nanook, cold-weather tests in Arctic, and experimented with nuclear-powered submarines under the driving force of Capt. Hyman G. Rickover.[13]

When the cold war divided the war-weary world into communist and anticommunist camps, the Navy's role changed once more.[14] Although no longer fighting a two-ocean war, the Navy was responsible for projecting an American presence around the world. To offset Soviet threats in Eastern Europe, the Navy built up what became the Sixth Fleet in the Mediterranean. Naval aircraft took part in the airlift carrying food and supplies to West Berlin after the Soviets cut off access to the city in 1948. On the other side of the world, the Navy tried to block communist expansion by maintaining the Seventh Fleet in Asian waters. It also administered the Trust Territories of the Pacific Islands—islands wrested from Japan during the war.[15] The Navy thus served as a viable arm of American foreign policy, dedicated to containing Soviet-led communism.

As it carried out this new role, the Navy encountered problems at home. During the debate about unification of all the armed forces, the Navy feared it would become subordinate to the Army and to an independent Air Force, which claimed full credit for the capability of delivering atomic bombs. "Why should we have a Navy at all?" asked Air Force general Carl A. Spaatz. Nevertheless, in 1947 Congress passed the National Security Act unifying the armed services into a single National Military Establishment under the

Department of Defense. James V. Forrestal, secretary of the Navy since 1944, became the first secretary of defense, with secretaries of the Army, Navy, and Air Force under him. John L. Sullivan replaced him as secretary of the Navy, then Francis P. Matthews assumed the post in 1949.[16]

Louis A. Johnson took over as secretary of defense in March 1949 and within weeks rocked the naval establishment by canceling construction of the supercarrier *United States* and diverting these funds to the Air Force's B-36 bombers. Secretary Sullivan resigned in anger. The Navy's admirals resisted, protested Johnson's budget cuts to Congress, and sharply criticized the Air Force's claims of the omnipotence of the B-36. The military must be able to fight limited, as well as nuclear, wars, said the Navy. Indeed, when the Soviet Union detonated an atomic bomb in the fall of 1949, that country crashed the United States' exclusive nuclear club.[17]

## Navy Women

The uncertainty of the postwar years also affected the women of the WAVES and the Nurse Corps. They wondered what their place was in the peacetime Navy. Firmly established, the Nurse Corps would continue as a vital element in the Navy's worldwide health services, but women reservists had entered the service for the duration plus six months. Would they, like the yeomen (F) of World War I, simply be forgotten?

### *Demobilization*

Before these questions could be resolved, the Navy's women took part in the demobilization process, and most reentered civilian life. In June 1944, Capt. Mildred McAfee advocated following the men's demobilization plans, but with changes in the dependency rules. Since WAVES could not have children who were under eighteen years of age, the Navy should give more weight to women's marital status.[18] By the following June, as demobilization was getting under way, WAVES who were married to servicemen returning from overseas were allowed forty-five days' leave; those married to disabled servicemen could leave the Navy immediately.[19] In September, the Bureau of Personnel completed a point formula for releasing all naval personnel:

half a point for each month of service since September 1939, half a point for each year of age, ten points for having a dependent as of 15 August, and one-quarter point for each month of duty outside the United States. Women officers needed thirty-five points, while enlisted required twenty-nine. The Navy set a target date of 1 September 1946 for releasing three million people, including those in the Women's Reserve.[20]

In addition to thirty-two separation centers for men, the Navy established five centers for WAVES in Washington, Memphis, San Francisco, Chicago, and New York. Ten more auxiliary centers sprang up. At these centers, the women reservists spent several days undergoing physical examinations, sitting through briefings on their veterans' benefits, such as those secured by the GI Bill, settling their accounts, and collecting travel expenses to go home. The system worked efficiently: by June 1946, there were only 2,023 officers and 15,244 enlisted remaining in the WAVES. By 1 September, the date set for complete demobilization, more than 3 million naval personnel had left the service. Still, some 1,715 officers and 3,926 enlisted remained on active duty in the WAVES.[21]

Navy nurses underwent a similar demobilization process. Like the WAVES, the Nurse Corps had given prior thought to demobilization, and superintendent Sue Dauser looked to the American Nurses Association to help relocate Navy nurses.[22] During August 1945, Captain Dauser's office formulated plans to demobilize the Reserve Nurse Corps, and in September the point system and procedure for other naval personnel was put in effect for the nurses. Since there were so few nurses, they used the same separation centers as did the WAVES. The Nurse Corps sent seven women to the school for civil readjustment indoctrination at Great Lakes, then these women served at the separation centers to ease nurses' transition to civilian life.[23] In November all married nurses could leave the service. At the same time, the points required for release dropped to thirty-two and, over the following months, continued to fall to twenty-two. By June 1946, demobilization of the Nurse Corps was 75 percent complete, and corps personnel numbered 4,459. By 1 September, 3,275 nurses remained on active duty.[24]

Nurses and WAVES who left the service were eligible for the educational benefits of the GI Bill, and many took advantage of it. For example, WAVE

Elsa Scharles enrolled in graduate school, while Dorothy Ditter completed her doctoral dissertation. Nurse Alene Duerk pursued a bachelor's degree in ward management.[25]

## *Personnel Shortage*

The Navy's demobilization process was, perhaps, too efficient, for by early 1946 personnel shortages were apparent. In an about-face, the secretary of the Navy looked for ways to encourage WAVES to remain in the service until 1 September 1946. In January, spot promotions for officers agreeing to stay in the service until September took effect. To induce enlisted WAVES to remain, the Navy waived requirements and exams and advanced them one pay grade. It soon opened a reenlistment program for former WAVES.[26] In March the Navy urged WAVES to extend their service until 1 July 1947, and by that time, only 572 officers and 2,094 enlisted reservists remained.[27]

The Nurse Corps, too, sought ways to keep more women in the corps. It offered Reserve officers the opportunity to remain on active duty or to request a transfer to the regular Nurse Corps. Of the 1,210 applying for transfer, the corps accepted 809. In late 1946, the Nurse Corps renewed recruiting through the Offices of Naval Officer Procurement. Another enticement was the upgraded education program, begun in January, to train nurses in various specialties. But the number of Navy nurses fell especially low—to only 2,100—by 1 July 1947.[28]

## The Women's Reserve

The most obvious way to retain women in the Navy, as well as in the other services, was, of course, to give them a permanent place in the regular armed forces. Although the original legislation establishing the Women's Reserve had specified enrolling women for the duration plus six months, some naval leaders had thought about postwar needs. As early as December 1943, Captain McAfee wrote that it would be "inefficient" in another emergency to begin with a whole new group of women and suggested retaining a small number of WAVES in the inactive Reserve. Occasional refresher courses would keep them up-to-date. These women would be the nucleus of women's forces in any future national emergency.[29] McAfee expressed no interest in employing women in any permanent active-duty capacity.

The Bureau of Personnel took the idea a step further and recommended a permanent Women's Reserve of about five hundred officers as part of the U.S. Naval Reserve. These volunteers would undergo several weeks' training each year and take correspondence courses on regulations, duties, and the like. They would receive no monetary compensation. The bureau also suggested retaining officers involved in highly specialized work that would be useful to the peacetime Navy.[30] McAfee elaborated: a permanent reserve could be composed of interested WAVE officers under thirty-six years of age with five hundred more recruited each year. All would be on inactive duty, except six assigned to the Bureau of Personnel to make or revise plans for the Women's Reserve. McAfee believed such a policy would stimulate public interest and provide enough officers for an emergency.[31] Then, as the Navy became caught up in demobilization, it postponed any changes in women's policy.

By September 1945, Chief of Naval Personnel Randall Jacobs had surveyed the bureaus and offices and found they could easily use nearly ten thousand WAVES in the postwar Navy. The decision had been made to press for legislation to keep women in the Naval Reserve. McAfee had thought that it was not in the Navy's best interest to have women on active duty in peacetime; but if it happened, she wanted ample attention and money devoted to maintaining the WAVES' high wartime standards.[32]

But it would be incumbent upon new leaders to guide the Women's Reserve into the postwar era. Eager to return to the presidency of Wellesley College, McAfee left the Navy in December, after receiving the Distinguished Service Medal for her splendid wartime contributions. She recommended Lt. Cdr. Jean Tilford Palmer as her successor.[33]

Palmer was born in 1903 and graduated from Bryn Mawr College in 1924. After working as business manager for the Association of Junior Leagues of America and its magazine, she was among the first to join the Women's Reserve. Commissioned lieutenant in August 1942, Palmer served as executive assistant to the director and then as liaison officer with the Office of Enlisted Personnel. She received a letter of commendation with ribbon for her work. In November 1945, Palmer rose to commander and assistant director of the Women's Reserve. When McAfee left, Palmer became acting director, and on 2 February 1946, director, with the rank of captain.[34] Few knew as much about the operations of the WAVES as Palmer.

## *First Attempt at Legislation*

Palmer immediately described the pros and cons of having women on active duty in peacetime. Included in the list of advantages was superior adaptability to billets in the Hospital Corps, in communications, and in aviation jobs involving teaching or manual dexterity. Palmer urged passage of legislation authorizing careers in the regular Navy for women.[35] Within the Navy itself, especially among enlisted, opinion was sharply divided over whether women should remain. A Navy poll showed 60 percent favoring Navy careers for women, but even some WAVES thought the Navy should remain a man's world.[36]

Now the Navy had to convince Congress that women should be a permanent part of the maritime service. For this, Palmer had the expert help of Cdr. Joy Bright Hancock, who became assistant director (plans) of the Women's Reserve in February 1946. Hancock firmly believed that women should be allowed to serve in the regular Navy as a career and in both the active and inactive Naval Reserve. As she traveled around the country during the war, Hancock had listened as many women expressed interest in remaining in the postwar Navy.[37] One of Hancock's first tasks as assistant director was to help conduct a survey in early 1946 that revealed a potential use for 1,367 officers and 9,426 enlisted women, with the Bureaus of Aeronautics and Medicine and Surgery requesting the most.[38]

Hoping to secure swift congressional cooperation, Palmer, along with Capt. Ira Nunn of the judge advocate general's staff, met with the chairman of the House Committee on Naval Affairs, Carl Vinson (D-Ga.), on 25 March 1946. Although Vinson strongly opposed women in the regular Navy, the Navy convinced him to introduce legislation establishing reserves on a permanent basis.[39] He introduced such a bill, which included the Marine Corps Women's Reserve, and it was referred to the Naval Affairs Committee. The Marine Corps had initially opposed retaining women permanently because it felt it did not need them.[40]

The committee held hearings on 9–10 May 1946, and the burden of persuasion fell primarily on Vice Adm. Louis Denfeld, chief of naval personnel, and his assistant, Rear Adm. Felix Johnson. Speaking for the Women's Reserve was Palmer. These witnesses emphasized the continuing postwar need for the WAVES and the importance of maintaining a trained nucleus of women for expansion in an emergency. Vinson steadfastly argued that putting them in the regular Navy was "a nice way for women to get killed." They should, he said, serve only in the reserves.[41]

One prominent member of the Naval Affairs Committee, Margaret Chase Smith (R-Maine), had always been a friend to Navy women. It was she who had introduced legislation in 1944 enabling WAVES to serve overseas. "The Navy either needs these women or they do not," she intoned. If they were needed, then they should be regulars as well as reservists. Smith introduced an amendment giving women regular military status. The committee passed the amended version of the bill, but Congress adjourned for the session before the House acted.[42]

As the congressional machinations continued, Palmer left the Navy in July 1946 and returned to civilian life. She had intended to remain in the Women's Reserve only long enough to oversee demobilization and to help steer the legislation through Congress. She was awarded the Legion of Merit for her executive ability and administrative skill in directing the Women's Reserve.[43]

The dynamic, innovative Joy Bright Hancock replaced Palmer as director. Born in 1898, her naval experience began when she served as a yeoman (F) in World War I. She learned another side of naval life during the 1920s, when she was the wife and then widow of two naval aviators, both killed in dirigible crashes. She began working at the Bureau of Aeronautics in 1930, and from 1934 to 1942 she was the civilian head of the Bureau of Aeronautics editorial and research section. In October 1942 she entered the Women's Reserve as a lieutenant and served as its representative to the Bureau of Aeronautics throughout the war. She moved to the Bureau of Personnel as assistant director for plans, Women's Reserve, and became director in July.[44] In addition to her naval background, Hancock was determined, tactful, and resourceful. She would need these vital attributes in the years ahead.

## *The 1947–1948 Drive*

Hancock had long believed that women should be a permanent and integral part of the Navy, so as director she immediately began working toward this goal. She brought experienced WAVE officers into her office. Cdr. Bess Dunn became assistant director; Lt. Cdr. Winifred Quick and Cdr. Louise Wilde worked with Hancock on legislative proposals.[45] Intensely interested in WAVES' living conditions, training, and possible assignments, Hancock or her representatives crisscrossed the country in late 1946 and 1947 to inspect naval facilities and to buttress her arguments for permanence.[46]

Realizing that she must have the firm support and help of male officers, she began a concerted campaign to secure such backing. Captain Nunn coached her on successful ways to deal with Congress and to improve drafts of the proposed legislation. Next, Rear Adm. Thomas L. Sprague, the new chief of naval personnel, agreed that he and other male officers would present the bill to the congressional committees and argue the Navy's case for retaining women. Their testimony would carry more weight than women's. Sprague assigned Capt. Fred R. Stickney of the Plans Division to help assemble material for the hearings.[47]

Next, Hancock went to the division heads in the bureau and to other naval offices to secure support for women in the Navy. In an era of increased female submissiveness, Hancock was polite and deferential to these officers, but she unhesitatingly manipulated them to win their approval of her plans. She would get one opinion, then go to the next officer and say, "Captain So-and-So thinks this is a good idea." That officer would reply, "Well, if the captain thinks so, I'll go along with it."[48]

As Hancock mustered naval backing, the plan for women in the military widened. After passage of the National Security Act in 1947, all the uniformed services were in a single Department of Defense. It was crucial that the women's services present a unified front. Hancock worked closely with WAC director Col. Mary A. Hallaren and Maj. Julia E. Hamblet, director of the Marine Corps Women's Reserve. In contrast to the interservice rivalries among men, these women worked together harmoniously, always with their larger goal in mind. As the time drew closer for congressional hearings, the directors rehearsed answers to every conceivable question the lawmakers might ask.[49]

The Senate Armed Services Committee began hearings on 2 July 1947. The services had combined their bills into one that included the Army, Navy, and Marine Corps. The military planned its strategy carefully. Gen. of the Army Dwight D. Eisenhower and Fleet Adm. Chester W. Nimitz testified about the necessity of retaining women in permanent status. Their superior work during the war had demonstrated women's manual dexterity, patience, attention to detail, and ability to endure monotonous work. There must be a cadre of women already in place in the regular military in the event the country had to remobilize. For the Navy, Rear Admiral Sprague spoke and added written statements from the top brass of each activity: Vice Adm. Donald B. Duncan, deputy CNO (Air); Rear Adms. W. A. Buck, chief of supplies and accounts; Surgeon General Clifford A. Swanson; and Earl E. Stone, chief of naval communications. Each argued for making women part of the regular and reserve naval forces.[50]

An unexpected question threw the hearings into temporary disarray. Sen. Leverett Saltonstall (R-Mass.) asked if women's incapacitation during menopause would lead to an excessive number of disability retirements. Admiral Sprague noted that there had been only eighteen menopause-related retirements since 1942, and the Army surgeon general quickly pointed out that there were treatments for the condition. Sensing a lingering doubt among committee members, Hancock asked Surgeon General Swanson to write a statement clarifying any medical ramifications. Swanson obligingly wrote, "The commonly held idea that women are invalided in their middle years by the onset of the menopause is largely a popular fallacy. It is well known that men pass through the same physiological change with symptomatology closely resembling that of women."[51] The discussion ended.

Before the hearings concluded, the directors of the women's services presented either oral or written statements supporting the legislation. Hancock emphasized the concept of maintaining a peacetime nucleus that would be readily expandable in an emergency. Such a valuable defense weapon, she noted, "should be developed and kept in good working order and not allowed to rust or to be abolished." In addition, the regular Navy would offer the "permanency, the advancement, and the security of a career."[52] The

Senate committee approved the bill and sent it to the full Senate, which passed it on 23 July 1947. From there the bill went to the House Armed Services Committee, where it languished in subcommittee until the winter of 1948.

During these interim months, the Air Force, born of the Army Air Forces, came into existence in late 1947 and wanted women in its organization. Accordingly, another section of the proposed legislation provided for them. The Navy, anticipating passage of the legislation, announced general policies about enlisting women in the regular Navy.[53]

The world situation worsened, and cold war tensions increased in April 1948 when the Soviets precipitated the Berlin crisis by cutting off that city from the West. The military seriously thought about how to increase personnel and considered a peacetime draft. A permanent place for women in the military would be another way to fill personnel requirements. The sense of tension and crisis undoubtedly played a role in the legislation under consideration.

In February hearings began before the House Armed Services Committee's Organization and Mobilization Subcommittee. Again the services relied on top leaders to testify on the necessity of integrating women into the regulars. General Eisenhower, Defense Secretary Forrestal, CNO Adm. Louis E. Denfeld, and Gen. Omar Bradley argued for permanent status, and the newly established Air Force sent Gen. Hoyt S. Vandenberg to support the measure. The directors of the women's branches—Captain Hancock for the Navy, Colonel Hallaren for the Army, and Major Hamblet for the Marine Corps—fielded questions about their respective services.[54]

Nevertheless, some committee members had predetermined that they would vote only for reserve status. Reportedly, unnamed members of the Navy had met in a secret "off-the-record executive session" with the committee and passed along their objections to giving women permanent status: it would disrupt normal ship-to-shore rotation duties for men and interfere with their qualifying for promotions. The subcommittee voted for reserve status only.[55]

An angry Margaret Chase Smith fired off a letter to Walter G. Andrews (R-N.Y.), chairman of the House Armed Services Committee, protesting the change in intent of the Senate version of the bill and the credence given to off-the-record meetings with naval personnel. She repeated her simple belief: "Either the Armed Services have a *permanent* need of women officers and enlisted women or they don't." If they do, women must receive permanent regular status.[56]

Next came hearings before the full House Armed Services Committee. Beginning on 23 March, committee members queried military leaders about ramifications of the bill; for example, would women officers have command authority over enlisted men? For the Navy, Vice Admiral Sprague and Captain Stickney fielded most questions about implementing any new women's policy. Rep. Dewey Short (R-Mo.) asked Hancock how many pregnancies had occurred among Navy women and if any disciplinary actions had resulted. Hancock perceived the questions as innuendoes that these women were not married. Chivalry was not dead in the committee, for Rep. James E. Van Zandt (R-Pa.) demanded an apology to Hancock.[57]

The Armed Services Committee voted to approve women in the reserves, not the regulars. Margaret Chase Smith was the only member to vote against the final version of the bill. Hancock, seated next to Sprague as the committee voted, heard the decision in stunned silence.[58] The bill then passed the House on 21 April and was referred to a joint committee to resolve differences with the Senate.

Smith and other women in America were not entrusting such important legislation to the male conferees. The representative wrote a heated letter to Defense Secretary Forrestal and detailed the unscrupulous off-the-record meetings between naval personnel and committee members and the pejorative allusions to pregnancy and menopause among servicewomen. Forrestal, in turn, wrote the conferees of his firm support for the Senate bill.[59] From across the country, business and professional women and large organizations flooded the House Armed Services Committee with letters and telegrams supporting the Senate version. Such influential groups as the Business and Professional Women's Club, the Women's Patriotic League, the General Federation of Women's Clubs, the Daughters of the American Revolution, the Women's Overseas League, and the American Association of University Women came out in favor of full integration of women into the military.[60]

Women's support, coupled with continued insistence from top military leaders, caused the House Armed Services Committee to run up a white flag. The joint conference committee endorsed the Senate bill, and on 12 June 1948 both houses of Congress approved the legislation giving women a permanent place in the regular military. President Truman soon signed the act. To assuage fears within the naval establishment, the Bureau of Personnel ran an article in the widely read *All Hands*, reassuring men that permanent WAVES would not interfere with their advancement in ratings or transfer to shore billets. The bureau also described the projected gradual buildup of trained women.[61]

For Hancock, who had worked with such determination to get naval, and then congressional, support, "the victory was sweet." Now the Navy could offer a dignified professional career, attract high-caliber women, and build a strong nucleus for rapid mobilization.[62] In 1953 Secretary of the Navy Robert B. Anderson gave Hancock full credit: "More than any one individual you are responsible for the establishment of the WAVES as a component of the Navy." Years later, Col. Julia E. Hamblet, who had been director of the Marine Corps Women's Reserve during that time, echoed the evaluation: "Joy Hancock *was* the mover and shaker in getting the legislation. Without her, or someone like her, there would have been no permanent status for women."[63]

## *Women's Armed Services Integration Act*

The hard-won legislation gave a permanent place to women in the regular and reserve Army, Navy, Marine Corps, and Air Force. Women could enlist or be commissioned in these services, though they were allowed to comprise no more than 2 percent of each service. Minimum age for enlisted dropped to eighteen years, while new officers had to be between twenty-one and thirty.

Of Navy women, only one could hold the rank of captain, and that was the director, now called assistant to the chief of naval personnel for women (ACNP[W]). Ten percent of officers could be commanders; 20 percent, lieutenant commanders. Officers' promotion lists would be separate from men's lists. The secretary of the Navy would decide the extent of women's command authority and could summarily terminate the service of any woman.

Strictly forbidden was duty in combat aircraft or in any ships except hospital ships and transports. The old restrictions on the dependency of husbands and children remained: they could be dependents only if the Navy woman provided their chief support.[64]

Although the Women's Reserve ceased to exist, the acronym WAVES persisted for another quarter of a century. Similarly, Army women were referred to as WACs, and unlike the other services, were maintained in a separate Women's Army Corps. The newly formed independent Air Force dubbed its women's reserve the WAF, the acronym for Women *in* the Air Force, not Women's Air Force. The Marine Corps Women's Reserve became quite simply the Women Marines.[65]

## The Navy Nurse Corps

The Navy's postwar demobilization affected all its components, including the Bureau of Medicine and Surgery. The number of naval hospitals fell from the wartime high of fifty-four domestic, six overseas, and more than forty temporary base and fleet hospitals to twenty-five domestic and four overseas. There had been fifteen hospital ships at the end of the war, but only one such ship five years later.[66] Similarly, the number of Medical Department personnel plummeted, in spite of vigorous efforts to recruit and retain them. In 1945, there were 12,832 medical officers, 6,218 dental officers, 127,677 Hospital Corps officers and enlisted, and 11,086 Nurse Corps officers. By 1950, these numbers were 2,916 medical, 893 dental, 15,962 Hospital Corps, and 1,942 nurses.[67] A breakthrough for women occurred during these years. In 1948 female physicians were allowed commissions directly into the Medical Corps rather than the wartime process of entering through the Women's Reserve.

The most notable change in the Medical Department was the creation in 1947 of the Medical Service Corps. The new staff corps offered permanent commissioned rank to qualified personnel in allied sciences, which included hospital corpsmen, pharmacists, and optometrists, and to administrative and management specialists trained in nonmedical fields. By 1950, there were 604 officers in this corps.[68] The Nurse Corps director discouraged Navy nurses from transferring to the Medical Service Corps because of the critical shortage of nurses. The Bureau of Medicine and Surgery had even authorized hiring civilian nurses to help in naval dispensaries.[69] The new corps relieved Navy nurses of billets such as dietitian and therapist, said Rear Adm. Alene Duerk. Nurses could now concentrate in specialties such as pediatrics, obstetrics, and operating-room nursing.[70]

The dearth of Navy nurses mirrored the situation in the entire country: some reports estimated a shortage of 40,000 nurses. Low pay, long hours, and lack of status deterred women from a career in hospital nursing. At the same time, the number of nursing students declined, and schools not affiliated with universities dropped to 1,065, down from 1,173 in 1945. One hundred fourteen university-run nursing schools attracted 19,870 students in 1949–50, and 3,269 of them earned bachelor's degrees.[71]

Although nurses were at a premium in American society, Navy nurses, like the women reservists, struggled to solidify their wartime gains. Postwar demobilization, coupled with the nationwide shortage of nurses, decimated the Nurse Corps. No one questioned the Navy's need for nurses, but retaining them was a challenge. Ens. Ann Clendenin, for example, recalled wanting to remain in the corps, but she thought that since physicians were leaving en masse, there were plenty of nurses and she was not needed.[72]

Superintendent Dauser had worked on a draft of legislation giving permanent, rather than temporary, rank to Nurse Corps officers. In October 1945, the Bureau of Medicine and Surgery recommended that nurses become a separate staff corps in the Medical Department. Nurses would be commissioned naval officers with appropriate rank, pay, and allowances.[73] But the chief of naval operations and the chief of naval personnel rejected establishing a separate staff corps, so Surgeon General McIntire had no choice but to withdraw temporarily his suggestion.[74]

As this wrangling continued, on 3 December 1945 Congress provided temporary pay adjustments for the Nurse Corps. Nurses would receive the same pay increases as other naval officers, increased rental and subsistence allowances for dependents, and higher disability retirement allowances.[75]

Before any congressional action on permanent rank occurred, Dauser retired as superintendent in November 1945. Her replacement, Cdr. Nellie

Jane DeWitt, was a veteran of long service in the corps. Born in 1895, DeWitt graduated from the Stamford Hospital Training School in Stamford, Connecticut, and served in the Navy Nurse Corps during World War I. Following two years on inactive status, she returned to active duty in 1922, serving at numerous U.S. stations and overseas before becoming a chief nurse in 1937. Naval Hospital, Aiea Heights, Hawaii, was her last post before returning to the Bureau of Medicine and Surgery in November 1945. Becoming superintendent that same month, DeWitt rose to captain the next April. Others described her as first and foremost a Navy nurse. Gentle and spontaneous, she would need these talents in the years ahead to define the shape and character of the postwar Nurse Corps.[76]

Of paramount importance was passage of legislation giving Navy nurses permanent commissioned rank. Such bills had been pending in Congress since 1946.[77] In early 1947, the Bureau of Medicine and Surgery, now under a new chief, Clifford A. Swanson, submitted a bill to Congress to establish the Nurse Corps as a staff corps, which would carry permanent commissioned rank.[78] The Army Nurse Corps had devised a similar bill. DeWitt kept female members of Congress abreast of progress and hoped that these "champions" of women in the military would continue to support the Nurse Corps.[79]

As the armed forces moved toward unification, the Navy Nurse Corps worked with its counterparts in the Army Nurse Corps to present consistent proposals for legislation. DeWitt prepared a comparison of Navy and Army Nurse Corps bills to help the two services solve their differences and put forward a unified front.[80] She tinkered with material for insertion in the congressional hearings and was firm in requesting a nurse/personnel ratio of .6 percent rather than the current .4 percent.[81] DeWitt and Col. Florence A. Blanchfield, superintendent of the Army Nurse Corps, cooperated in ironing out disparities between the two services' bills and testified, along with their surgeons general, in favor of an Army-Navy Nurse Corps bill.[82] Margaret Chase Smith, again proving to be a friend of Navy women, guided the legislation through the House Armed Services Committee.[83]

On 16 April 1947, the Army-Navy Nurses Act established the Navy Nurse Corps as a staff corps. Its officers held permanent commissioned rank ranging from ensign to commander, with the director a captain while in that position. The act also authorized a Nurse Corps Reserve as a branch of the

Naval Reserve. New appointees were required to be unmarried female citizens between the ages of twenty-one and twenty-eight; reservists could be married and between twenty-two and forty. On the touchy issue of command, the nurses had authority in medical and sanitary matters in naval hospitals and other medical activities next after officers of the Medical, Dental, and Medical Service Corps but could exercise command only over other nurses or those designated as under them. The number of Nurse Corps officers would be .6 percent of the strength of the active-duty Navy and Marine Corps. Current reserve nurses under thirty-five years of age could transfer to the regular Nurse Corps. DeWitt's title changed from superintendent to director of the new Navy Nurse Corps.[84]

An added boost in retirement benefits came for regular and reserve nurses with two measures in 1948. The first equalized the disparities among those who had retired before relative rank was a reality. The second provided the same benefits for reserve nurses as for regulars. At age sixty, reservists with twenty years' federal service could collect retirement benefits. An intricate system awarded points to reservists for such activities as two weeks' training a year, taking correspondence courses, and volunteering in local medical units. Fifty points were the equivalent of a year of federal service.[85]

All these measures solidified the nurses' position as permanent commissioned officers with pay and benefits commensurate with those of regular naval officers. At last, Navy nurses had the prestige and status they had sought since 1920.

## Women in the Regular Navy

### *The WAVES*

Even before Congress passed the Women's Armed Services Integration Act, the Navy had been planning for a permanent role for women. As early as September 1946, Director Hancock had visited all naval districts and discussed potential long-term use of the WAVES.[86] A year later she had drawn up plans to include women in the regular Navy and the Naval Reserve and continued to consult with numerous officials about age requirements, educational and physical qualifications, training, uniforms, and utilization. In another anticipatory move, the chief of naval personnel sent a circular letter about procedures to transfer Reserve officers to the regular Navy. As soon as the legislation passed, the bureau was ready to implement its program of building a nucleus of trained women for future rapid expansion.[87]

At a special ceremony on 7 July 1948, the first six enlisted WAVES to transfer were sworn into the regular Navy. Appropriately, these women represented an assortment of naval activities: Naval Air Transport Service, Communications, the National Naval Medical Center at Bethesda, and the Bureaus of Naval Personnel and Supplies and Accounts. By the end of August, 1,572 enlisted women on active duty had transferred to the regular Navy.[88] By 20 September, the first 288 women officers had been chosen from the Women's Reserve, and 8 were sworn in on 15 October in another symbolic ceremony. With Hancock leading the way, these women included representatives of the Bureaus of Aeronautics, Personnel, Supplies and Accounts, and Medicine and Surgery.[89] They were just the beginning; by the end of the year, there were 502 female officers and 1,909 enlisted on active duty.

The Navy immediately began recruiting more women. First, it sought former WAVES who had left the service and offered them a chance to join the regular Navy. Next, it looked for new recruits from civilian life. Unlike the other services, which had dropped the minimum age to eighteen, the Navy kept the old requirements—twenty years for enlisted and twenty-one for officers. Enlistments could be for two, three, four, or six years until September 1949, when the two- and three-year enlistments ended.[90] Between 1946 and 1949, pay for all enlisted personnel rose: for example, apprentice seamen, from $50 to $75 a month, and chief petty officers, from $138 to $198. All officers' pay rose, such as from $150 to $213 for ensigns, and from $333 to $570 for captains. Allowances also increased.[91]

Training for enlisted women began in early October 1948 at the Naval Recruit Training Center, Great Lakes. Lt. Cdr. Kathryn Dougherty, the officer-in-charge, directed the eleven-week training course for 134 recruits. Additional classes began every six weeks.[92] After recruit training, more than half the enlisted women went to specialized training facilities, including airman, radioman, hospitalman, and yeoman schools. The remaining recruits went directly to billets at major shore stations.[93]

New officers trained in the Officer Indoctrination Unit (W) at the Naval Base, Newport, Rhode Island. Under the direction of Lt. Cdr. Sybil A. Grant, twenty-nine trainees began the five-month program in January 1949. As during World War II, women officers' training remained segregated from men's, although the male Officer Candidate School was also at Newport. Another similarity to wartime training was the continued emphasis on ladylike conduct.[94] Subsequently, all new officer candidates went through the training program at Newport. After the Navy women had completed their indoctrination, they served in numerous billets throughout the country, but on a much smaller scale than in World War II.

A new opportunity, service in Europe, opened to WAVES in 1949. Hancock traveled with WAC director Colonel Hallaren on a European inspection trip in April and May, and Hancock visited Great Britain, the Netherlands, Germany, Austria, France, and Italy. She intended to recommend assigning WAVES to some of these countries and needed to investigate possible billets and housing. She consulted with representatives of women in foreign navies—the WRNS in England, which had become a permanent service in February; the MARVAS in the Netherlands; and the Femmes de la Flotte in France. She toured Army facilities where WACs served. She met Lt. Margaret E. Carver, the first WAVE officer stationed in Europe, who had recently arrived at Frankfort as personnel officer for one of the Navy Air Transport squadrons taking part in the Berlin airlift. In April another WAVE officer reported in London.[95]

Following Hancock's trip, overseas assignments for women came quickly. In June the first women officers to serve in vessels other than hospital ships sailed in transports.[96] Three months later, a group of enlisted WAVES arrived for duty in London. In December the Navy assigned WAVE officers to duty in Guam, Egypt, Alaska, and Germany and decided to station women in Hawaii again the next year.[97]

By the end of the decade, Hancock had led Navy women in their first steps toward permanence. The trained nucleus was in place. There were 515 officers and 2,884 enlisted women and another 315 reservists on active duty, a total of 3,714 women on duty in the peacetime Navy.[98]

## *The Navy Nurse Corps*

During these immediate postwar years, the Nurse Corps's problems were different from those encountered by the WAVES. There was never any doubt about the nurses' continued place in the Navy; they had demonstrated their usefulness many times. Rather, the corps had to attract and retain qualified nurses and secure the status that permanent commissioned rank provided.

Even before demobilization was complete, the Bureau of Medicine and Surgery launched an education program in January 1946 for Nurse Corps officers. Reflecting the emphasis the civilian nursing profession placed on academics, the corps turned to university settings.[99] Ranging from four to eighteen months, postgraduate courses in physical and occupational therapy, anesthesia, neuropsychiatry, teaching and ward administration, and dietetics trained between thirty-four and sixty-two nurses a year. Within a few years, the Nurse Corps phased out courses in occupational and physical therapy, substituting classes in public health and nursing education. In 1948 the corps began sending selected nurses to colleges to complete their undergraduate degrees.[100] The Bureau of Medicine and Surgery considered opening its own school of nursing at the National Naval Medical Center, Bethesda. Captain DeWitt, director of the Nurse Corps, argued against the proposal, which, she felt, would be a needless waste of taxpayer money when plenty of qualified civilian nursing schools could provide military nurses.[101]

Flight nurse training, begun late in World War II and dropped in 1946, resumed two years later at the Air Force's School of Aviation Medicine, Randolph Air Force Base, Texas. Carefully chosen Navy nurses attended the course at this joint school before entering Naval Air Transport Squadrons.[102] After the Air Force established its own nurse corps in 1949, it sent some nurses to train in flight nursing with their Navy counterparts.

Another means of enticing civilian nurses into the Navy was setting up formal indoctrination sites to aid in the transition to military nursing. Lack of such indoctrination during World War II had been a serious shortcoming. The first center to open was the Naval Hospital, St. Albans, New York, in December 1946; others followed at Long Beach, California, and Philadelphia. During the next two years, similar four-week orientation programs began at eleven other naval hospitals.[103]

One advantage of naval nursing sprang from the diverse tasks given Navy nurses. One novel assignment in July 1946 took nine nurses to Kwajalein in the Marshall Islands, where they stood by in two hospital ships during the atomic bomb testing at Bikini. Nurses such as Pauline W. Schmid marveled at the "tremendous mushroom-shaped explosion."[104]

During the postwar years, the number of naval medical facilities dropped precipitously, but nurses served at 161 stations, including 111 in the continental United States, 24 outside the country, 12 civilian institutions (for instruction), and in 1 hospital ship and 13 transports. In December 1949, the Nurse Corps had 2,014 officers—1,770 in the United States, 163 abroad, 63 in ships, and the rest with releases pending.[105]

The schools for young nurses in Samoa and Guam, so successful for many years, continued to operate. After Guam was recovered from the Japanese, the naval hospital became the U.S. Naval Medical Center and operated schools for nurses, medical practitioners, and dental practitioners. These schools instructed young people of Guam and the Trust Territories until the Department of Interior assumed control of them in 1950. The same agency took over the government of Samoa the next year.[106] With the Interior Department's relieving the Navy of administering these islands, one of the Nurse Corps's important roles—training local nurses in the Pacific—ended.

As they had done so often in the past, Navy nurses assisted with civilian catastrophes. In April 1946 a smallpox epidemic swept through Seattle and adjacent areas. Three Navy nurses and six hospital corpsmen helped local health officials vaccinate nearly the entire city.[107] On 16 April 1947, the French freighter *Grandcamp*, while being loaded with nitrate at Texas City, Texas, blew up and triggered a series of explosions, including the steamer *High Flyer* and a nearby chemical plant. Hundreds were killed and thousands injured. Twenty-two Navy nurses were part of medical teams dispatched from the naval hospitals at Houston and Corpus Christi and the naval station at Orange to assist with casualties.[108] Lt. Cdr. Winnie Gibson, who later would become director of the Nurse Corps, was chief nurse at the Houston hospital and had nothing but praise for her nurses sent to Texas City. "Navy nurses are pretty grand people," and you can always count on them in an emergency, she wrote.[109]

Throughout these years of the Nurse Corps's defining its postwar role in the Navy, Captain DeWitt, first as superintendent and then as director, purposefully guided the group with a steady hand. She kept in close contact, either in person or through correspondence, with her nurses and encouraged them to strive for higher professional standing through postgraduate courses and duty rotation. She determinedly pushed for commissioned rank for Navy nurses. Making frequent inspection trips to hospitals in the naval districts, the Potomac River and Severn River Naval Commands, and the Caribbean, she also gathered her chief nurses for conferences and encouraged them to share their successes and problems.[110]

The postwar years saw a major departure from the traditional naval view that women were useful only in wartime.[111] The series of congressional acts, although often grudging, acknowledged both women's wartime performance and their potential importance to the military.

For the WAVES, the Women's Armed Services Integration Act of 1948 represented the culmination of two years' concerted effort, beginning with the fumbling naval approach to Congress in 1946 and succeeding with the multiservice, high-powered drive in 1948. Women now had an unprecedented opportunity for a permanent career as either commissioned officers or enlisted members of the U.S. Navy. That service would now have a nucleus of trained women to ease personnel shortages and would be ready for rapid mobilization in an emergency.

Certainly, there were disadvantages to the act of 1948: limiting females to only 2 percent of all active-duty personnel; restricting their numbers in the higher commissioned grades; maintaining separate promotion lists for men and women; denying benefits for most dependents; giving the secretary of the Navy the responsibility of determining military duty, authority, and even continued service; forbidding any type of combat or sea duty (except in hospital ships and transports); and enforcing an earlier retirement age for women.[112] Nevertheless, the act was an important step in the long campaign for equal career opportunity.

Navy nurses did not have as far to travel as did women in the WAVES. They already held a respected and permanent place in the Navy; their nursing services had been a vital component of the Medical Department since 1908. Permanent commissioned rank, rather than relative rank or no rank at all, was their goal. By joining with their Army counterparts, Navy nurses, with the surgeon general's support, gained permanent commissioned rank with the Army-Navy Nurses Act of 1947. Their new status carried many restrictions on age, marital state, command authority, rank limitations, and dependents' benefits, but the legislation represented a move toward equal status.

For both groups, their foothold, albeit unsteady, was probably as much as the then-current nationwide ideology would tolerate. Women could have a part in a new occupation—naval service—but a prescribed and limited part. After all, women's most important roles were as wives and mothers; there was no need to give them much authority and power in the male-dominated Navy. Their limited permanent status, a major breakthrough for 1947–48, reflected societal ideas about women's roles and place.

Next would come the test of whether the plans and concepts for a readily expandable nucleus of trained women would actually work in a national emergency. Far sooner than expected, and in an unanticipated part of the world, a confrontation between communist and anticommunist forces drew the American military into yet another war. It would be the first test of the Navy's trained nucleus of women.

# 8

# The Korean War and the 1950s

*During the 1950s,* Navy women saw their chances for permanent status imperiled once again. After a brief upsurge of female participation during the Korean War (1950–53), interest in women's programs diminished rapidly. Even the Navy Nurse Corps, always an essential part of naval medical care, dropped to low numbers. Was the fervor of the World War II generation of women merely an aberration, or could women really aspire to dignified careers in the U.S. Navy?

## The Setting

The trends begun during the postwar years intensified in the 1950s. It was a decade of conformity in which suburban domesticity became the standard. There could be no more secure haven from the problems swirling around the country—problems such as the increasing tensions of the cold war, the outbreak of the Korean War, and Sen. Joseph R. McCarthy's (R-Wisc.) communist witch hunt. Gen. Dwight D. Eisenhower's election to the presidency in 1952 helped steer the nation into a more conservative era, a return to "normalcy" after so many unsettling years.

Before joining the ranks of suburban housewives, increasing numbers of young American women were attending college. Their numbers grew from 805,953 in 1950 to 1,339,000 ten years later, and their representation of all college students rose from 30.2 percent to 37 percent.[1] Nevertheless, the prevailing ideology decreed that women should not be educated to compete with men, so many left college to marry, and only 25 percent of female students even considered long-term careers. Generally, their goal was marriage and a family. Of the graduates who did work, most were employed in traditional women's professions: teaching, nursing, and library and social work.[2]

Simultaneously, and paradoxically, even more women entered the work force, albeit in the lower-paying service sector. They dominated such occupations as clerical workers, airline stewardesses, waitresses, nurses' aides, and hotel housekeepers. By 1960, 40 percent of all women worked outside the home; and as in wartime and postwar years, older married women were the main entrants into the labor force. But as if to emphasize the lesser value men accorded their work, women were paid only 61 percent of male wages for comparable jobs.[3]

During the 1950s, social problems did not spark reform movements among women, although groups such as the remnants of the National Women's Party, a small number in the Women's Bureau of the Labor Department, the American Friends Service Committee, and the YWCA kept alive a critique of women's place in the social order. In the late 1950s, concern about radioactive fallout from nuclear testing spawned a renewed peace activism that led to the organization of groups such as the Committee for a Sane Nuclear Policy and the Committee for Non-Violent Action.[4] By and large, however, there were no driving reform movements.

For most women, the lure of home life was enough. The average age for brides dropped to twenty. Wives devoted their lives to suburban households filled with children, for here they supposedly found real feminine fulfillment. Indeed, the fertility rate reached 3.52 children for each woman by 1960.[5] During the baby boom years (1946–64), seventy-six million children were born. Middle-class women's sphere once again revolved around homemaking and motherhood, and women filled their endless days with bearing and raising children, cooking, cleaning, sewing, doing laundry, chauffeuring, volunteering for community and church activities, and entertaining their husbands' work associates. Immersed in prosperous, comfortable suburban living, American housewives were the envy of their sisters around the world.[6]

And yet, beneath the cheerful facade of the 1950s wife-companion-mother festered an unhappiness and longing. These women, cloistered in suburban loneliness and isolation, had lost their identities and purpose in life. Their childlike dependence on the husband-breadwinner and their servant role in child care and housework generated little pride or self-satisfaction. Countless women, especially the college educated, shared this unidentifiable yet widespread problem—"the problem that has no name."[7] By the late

1950s, the domesticity trend slowly began reversing: the marriage age and the divorce rate crept upward while the birthrate slipped. The media began discussing the "trapped housewife" syndrome.

During this decade, the civil rights movement gained momentum. Integrating blacks into mainstream American life had started during World War II and received a boost in 1954, when *Brown v. Board of Education* ended segregation in public schools. The following year Rosa Parks's refusal to sit in the back of a bus in Montgomery, Alabama, paved the way for the movement's boycotts and sit-ins, and the rise of Martin Luther King Jr.[8] Some white women, interested in furthering their own rights, took an avid interest in these techniques for change.

As women struggled to define their roles in society, a thorough reappraisal of American security needs in April 1950 dictated a buildup of military forces to meet the challenges of the cold war. Within months, the cold war turned hot when the United States, as part of the United Nations force, became involved in a "police action" in Korea.[9] For the Navy, this brought a sharp increase from the low of 634 active ships and 381,538 officers and men in June 1950 to 1,122 active ships and 794,440 personnel three years later.[10]

During these years, the Navy continued its postwar mission of maintaining its "presence" in trouble spots wherever communist aggression threatened. It not only maintained a presence but also participated actively. During the Korean War the Navy maintained a strong fleet in the Western Pacific to deter Chinese and Soviet naval involvement. It transported Army and Air Force troops, aircraft, and equipment to the battle area, blockaded and bombarded the North Korean coasts, and launched carrier air strikes.[11] Its most difficult accomplishment was the amphibious landing at Inchon in September 1950.[12]

On the other side of the world, the Sixth Fleet helped the United States keep the peace in the Mediterranean and Middle East. Balancing American support of Israel with the Western need for Arab oil, the United States moved decisively when a communist coup in nearby Iraq seemed to threaten the pro-American government in Lebanon. In July 1958, President Eisenhower directed the fleet to land Marines at Beirut to signal American interest in the area and to support the Lebanese government.[13] That same year, Chinese communists, intent on reclaiming Nationalist-held islands Quemoy, Matsu, and Taiwan just off the Chinese mainland, brought immediate American intervention. At Washington's direction, the Seventh Fleet moved quickly, lending convoys, equipment, and carrier air power to deter communist military activity.[14]

During the 1950s, the Navy achieved vast technological advances. The most spectacular was the perfection of nuclear engineering plants. First came the submarine *Nautilus* (SSN 571), the brainchild of Rear Adm. Hyman G. Rickover, launched in 1955. While other nuclear vessels were under construction, the Navy developed the guided missile Polaris, which could be fired from underwater and soon formed a critical part of U.S. defenses.[15] Simultaneously, jet-propelled aircraft began replacing the Navy's propeller-driven planes, and helicopters aided ground warfare by transporting troops, supplies, and the wounded.

Guiding the Navy through a time of technical and scientific change were Chiefs of Naval Operations Robert B. Carney (1953–55) and Arleigh A. Burke (1955–61). The Defense Reorganization Act of 1958 stripped the service chiefs of their operational authority and gave war-fighting primacy to the unified commands. Admiral Burke feared that steps such as this would lead to a merger of the services or the establishment of a national general staff. Neither happened. For better efficiency within the Navy, the Bureaus of Aeronautics and Ordnance merged into the Naval Weapons Bureau in 1959. Within a few years, other organizational changes would occur.[16]

For Navy women, this period of sweeping change raised many questions about their continuing in the service. Perhaps, in another war, they could again demonstrate their usefulness.

## The Korean War

### *The WAVES*

American entry into the Korean conflict in June 1950 demanded immediate mobilization of the armed services, and the WAVES took the opportunity to employ its trained nucleus concept by efficiently increasing the number of women. Although it failed to meet its quota of 1,000 officers and 10,000 enlisted, it nearly tripled in size from 3,239 to a high of 9,466 by November 1952.[17] Such smooth and rapid mobilization in only eighteen months rested on the well-planned preparations that the director, Capt. Joy Bright Hancock, and her staff had developed in the late 1940s.

To expand the WAVES, the Navy first relied on the voluntary recall of women reservists. When their numbers were insufficient, the Navy turned to their involuntary recall, especially of enlisted hospital corpsmen and supply clerks. It was the first time in history that women reservists were called up, just like the men, and the Navy accepted no excuses, remembered Winifred Quick, who later became director of the WAVES.[18] Next came a change in marriage policies. No longer would WAVES be allowed to resign simply because they were married. Soon the Navy lowered its minimum age to eighteen. The Army and Air Force had accepted eighteen-year-olds since the Armed Services Integration Act of 1948, but the Navy and Marines had resisted, fearing an onslaught of immature schoolgirls.[19]

Despite all these measures and the rapid expansion of the WAVES, there still were not enough women joining. The other services experienced similar shortfalls. In contrast to the patriotic fervor of the two world wars, the Korean conflict did not inspire America's women to rush to sign up. Alarmed, Secretary of Defense George C. Marshall responded to the suggestion of Assistant Secretary of Defense for Manpower Anna Rosenberg and called together fifty prominent civilian women to consider options. The group, known as the Defense Advisory Committee on Women in the Services (DACOWITS), was chaired by Mary Lord, who had led an Army women's advisory committee during the war. When DACOWITS first met in September 1951, it recommended a high-profile recruiting campaign for all the services, which President Harry S. Truman launched in November. This massive drive also failed to meet its goal of 112,000 women. Nevertheless, DACOWITS continued to promote understanding in the civilian world about opportunities for women in the military.[20]

To train its newest members, the WAVES at first sent enlisted women to the Training Center at Great Lakes. Classes had about 135 women and lasted six weeks. When the Navy anticipated a great swell of recruits during the Korean War, it moved the program to the new Naval Training Center at Bainbridge, Maryland, in October 1951.[21] The influx of young women, especially after the minimum age dropped to eighteen, highlighted the shortage of experienced petty officers needed for supervising women's barracks and serving as recruiters and instructors. To solve the problem, Hancock successfully pushed for petty officers leadership schools, which opened at San Diego and Bainbridge in February 1953.[22]

Officer candidates trained at the Officer Indoctrination Unit (W), a part of the General Line Naval School at Newport. To provide more officers, the duration of the training course dropped from five to four months in early 1951.[23] The following year, women were commissioned in the Naval Reserve, a process faster than that required for entering the regular Navy. These reservists could then transfer to the regulars. Still another program available to women was the Reserve Officer Candidate Program (ROC), which ran from 1950 to 1953 at the Great Lakes Training Center. College students trained for eight weeks after their junior and senior years and then received commissions as active duty Reserve officers.[24]

After officers and enlisted finished training, they fanned out across the country, carrying out assignments similar to those they had performed during World War II. Once again, they took over duties in the United States to free men to serve afloat or overseas. As before, they were concentrated in health care, clerical and supply work, and communications. In aviation, for example, 13 percent of WAVES completed basic airman training then went on for specialized training and became Link trainer instructors, parachute riggers, or air traffic controllers.[25] The 1948 Women's Armed Services Integration Act precluded any thoughts of utilizing women in combat ships and aircraft, and no WAVES went to Korea, although they continued to serve in other foreign posts. Generally, WAVES broke no new ground in responsibilities and assignments.[26]

## *The Navy Nurse Corps*

In contrast, Navy nurses, always essential to the nation at war, assumed more important roles. The entire Medical Department expanded to meet wartime needs; and in just one year—by June 1951—the Medical Corps increased from 2,686 officers to 4,341; the Dental Corps, from 896 to 1,777; the Hospital Corps, from 15,855 to 31,081; and the Medical Service Corps, from 612 to 814.[27]

The Nurse Corps, which had dropped to a personnel low of 1,921 in July

1950, peaked at 3,405 in November 1951 and slipped to 2,600 by the time the war ended. In addition to regular Nurse Corps members, the corps relied on Reserve nurses, new appointments, voluntary recalls, and, for the first time, the involuntary recall of 926 former Navy nurses. These latter recalls, affecting single women under age forty, ended in December 1951.[28] One young nurse who was in a ready Reserve unit and recalled to active duty was Alene Duerk, who made a career in the Nurse Corps, later becoming its director.[29] To promote a smooth transition for entering nurses, a five-week course at the central indoctrination center began at the Naval Hospital, St. Albans, in 1952, under the supervision of Lt. Cdr. Rita V. O'Neill. This course and location replaced the dispersed programs at various naval hospitals that had begun during World War II.[30]

A new director, Capt. Winnie Gibson, who succeeded Capt. Nellie Jane DeWitt on 1 May 1950, would oversee the Nurse Corps at war. Born in 1902, Gibson was a graduate of the Seton Hospital School of Nursing in Austin, Texas. After joining the Navy Nurse Corps in 1930 and serving at various U.S. hospitals, she saw duty in the hospital ship *Relief.* Gibson was stationed at the Pearl Harbor Naval Hospital when the Japanese attacked the islands and became a chief nurse in 1942. Her last assignment before returning to the Bureau of Medicine and Surgery was a brief tour at the Naval Medical Center, Guam. In addition to her outstanding professional qualifications, Gibson possessed courage, tact, executive ability, dignity, and a ladylike manner. She inspired confidence and loyalty among her nurses.[31]

During the Korean War, Navy nurses were not in the war zone on the ground, but they contributed their healing talents to military needs. At the height of their deployment in September 1953, they served at 180 stations: 126 in the United States, 25 foreign posts, 3 hospital ships, 8 Military Sea Transport Service (MSTS) ships, 3 MSTS ports, and 15 civilian schools.[32]

In anticipation of escalating casualties, the Bureau of Medicine and Surgery expanded its one-hundred-bed dispensary at Yokosuka, Japan, into a full-scale, five-hundred-bed naval hospital. At first, there were only 8 Navy nurses there, and before the staff expanded, the hospital relied on Japanese civilian nurses to help care for the wounded. By the end of December 1950, there were 201 Navy nurses at the hospital. In that month alone, 5,927 casualties were admitted. During the busy Korean War years, Navy nurses continued teaching English to student nurses at the hospital.[33]

Navy nurses served continuously in hospital ships in Korean waters. Three vessels—the *Consolation, Repose,* and *Haven*—rotated as station hospitals in ports. While one ship was undergoing overhaul or refitting, the other two remained off Korea. Each could accommodate about 800 patients and had a complement of 25 medical officers, 3 dental officers, 4 Medical Service Corps officers, 200 hospital corpsmen, and 30 Navy nurses. The injured arrived onboard by ambulance, then litter hoist, by ship and boat, and by the widely acclaimed helicopter. Such prompt medical attention kept fatalities to a minimum. By September 1952, admissions had totaled 40,662. The Danish hospital ship *Jutlandia* joined the three American vessels in March 1951, caring for United Nations casualties.[34] The peak loads for these ships came in the last quarter of 1950 with the amphibious assault on Inchon and the hasty retreat from Hungnam.

Nurses were aware of the most modern advances in military medicine. In Korea, the innovative use of Mobile Army Surgical Hospitals (MASH), first introduced in the Mediterranean theater during World War II, brought expert care close to the front lines. The most important job of MASH was to save lives by tending to wounds and trauma, leaving reconstructive measures for later treatment. Attached to these MASH units were Army helicopters, which promptly evacuated the wounded to safer hospitals or ships away from the combat area. Air transports, staffed with Air Force and Navy flight nurses and corpsmen, completed the rapid removal of wounded to larger hospitals. These measures dramatically reduced mortality rates of American servicemen.[35] The Navy, too, had four mobile medical teams, each staffed by three doctors and ten hospital corpsmen. Using this "bold new medical technique" at Inchon, the Navy saved the lives of many grievously wounded Marines.[36]

Confronted with assorted casualties, Navy nurses had the unnerving experience of treating patients often only thirty minutes from the battle scene or fresh from a MASH unit. Close fighting produced fragmentation wounds to the head, chest, and limbs, usually accompanied by shock. Many patients also suffered from frostbite. Fortunately, ample supplies of whole blood and penicillin aided in treatment, and less than 2 percent of the injured died from their wounds. Navy nurse Helen Brooks recalled that hospital ship nurses had heavy responsibilities, although they did not realize it at the time.[37]

The *Consolation*, the first American hospital ship to reach the area, arrived at Pusan in August 1950. She participated in operations at Inchon, Wonsan, and Hungnam, and in 1951 became the first hospital ship fitted with a helicopter landing platform. Except for brief returns to the United States, *Consolation* remained off Korea until 1954.[38] The next hospital ship slated for service in Korea was *Benevolence*. Unfortunately, *Benevolence* collided with merchant ship *Mary Luckenback* and sank in San Francisco Bay on 25 August 1950. One of the fifteen Navy nurses onboard, Wilma Ledbetter, died of shock and exposure soon after survivors were plucked from the bay.[39]

Replacing *Benevolence*, the hospital ship *Haven* arrived off Korea in October. So delighted was *Consolation*'s crew when the relief ship came that its band struck up "If I Knew You Were Coming, I'd a Baked a Cake." During the next four years, *Haven* had four tours in Korean waters, primarily at Pusan and Inchon. Under the leadership of Lt. Ruth Cohen, the chief nurse, nurses in *Haven* cared for United Nations troops and Koreans. The more seriously wounded military personnel were taken by plane to hospitals in Japan, then back to the United States. One nurse remembered the satisfaction she felt as she "smooth[ed] a broken body, muster[ed] up a smile." She could only hope, she said, "to match the courage of our youth."[40]

The *Repose*, the third hospital ship at Korea, arrived in September 1950 and remained assigned to the theater throughout the war. Lt. Annette Baer, the chief nurse, directed her staff in caring for wounded at Pusan, Inchon, and as far north as Chinnampo. The *Repose* made numerous trips from Korea to Japan, transporting casualties.[41] Nurses from *Repose* took time out to visit a Korean nursing school in Seoul and hosted a return visit from Korean nurses to the ship.[42]

Occasionally, when there was a lull in the fighting, nurses such as Nancy Crosby from *Haven* went ashore by helicopter to visit forward medical units, where doctors and corpsmen ministered to wounded marines. Unlike Army MASH units, no Navy medical companies had nurses attached to them.[43]

Perhaps the most coveted assignment for Navy nurses was flight nursing, because so few had the opportunity to take their healing skills aloft. Working closely with their Air Force counterparts, Navy flight nurses operated out of Haneda Air Force Base, Tokyo.[44] Lt. (jg) Gizella Papp was the first flight nurse to fly with patients in a C-47, and her picture was on the cover of a national magazine. Another nurse, Lt. (jg) Joan Cordone, continued the Nurse Corps's long tradition of teaching by instructing and supervising flight nurses from Thailand.[45]

Medical evacuation teams consisted of one nurse and two corpsmen, who flew in cargo planes to Korea, loaded patients, and returned to Japan. Such rapid aeromedical evacuation was responsible for lower mortality rates during the Korean War than in World War II.[46] Wounded then were taken to either Tokyo Army Hospital or Yokosuka Naval Hospital, and those requiring long-term rehabilitation later were sent to the United States. Navy nurses from the 1453d Aeromedical Evacuation Squadron at Hickam Field, Hawaii, also played important roles as members of the flight medical teams on these long journeys home in Military Air Transport Service planes. Still other flight nurses served in two fleet logistic air wings in the United States, taking patients to hospitals close to their homes.[47]

A tragic loss of life early in the war took a heavy toll on the Nurse Corps. On 19 September 1950, a four-engine transport plane bound for the Far East crashed off Kwajalein, Marshall Islands. Eleven Navy nurses assigned to the Naval Hospital, Yokosuka, were among the twenty-six people who died.[48] They were not the only fatalities among Navy women during the Korean War. A total of twenty-nine nurses and eighteen enlisted WAVES died. No WAVES officer lost her life. Three nurses received the Bronze Star; six, the Commendation Ribbon; and ninety, the Navy Unit Commendation.[49]

## The WAVES, 1953–1960

### *Changes in Leadership*

After the Korean War ended in July 1953, the strength of the WAVES dropped, in keeping with typical postwar trends and the service's continuing focus on women as a trained nucleus for emergency use. From a peak of 9,466 in November 1952, their numbers declined by May 1958 to 5,122 (673 officers and 4,449 enlisted).[50]

Coinciding with the end of the Korean War, WAVES director Capt. Joy Bright Hancock reached the mandatory retirement age of fifty-five in May 1953. The following month she stepped down as director. Although she recommended that the subsequent tenure of office be no longer than four years, she had served in that capacity for nearly seven.[51] The Navy bestowed the Legion of Merit on Hancock and praised her for overcoming the many varied and complex problems "in establishing the women as an integral part of the naval service." Secretary of the Navy Robert B. Anderson credited her with being the person most responsible for including the WAVES as a component of the Navy. "Your ideals, energy, and enthusiasm are continually reflected in the integration of women into the regular Navy," he added.[52]

Louise Kathleen Wilde, who replaced Hancock, had been in the WAVES since August 1942. Born in New Hampshire in 1910, Wilde graduated from Mount Holyoke College in 1931 and received a master of arts degree from Columbia University ten years later. Her prewar career included newspaper and publicity work, and she was freshman dean at Rockford College, Illinois. As one of the first to join the Women's Reserve, she became coordinator of public relations in Director Mildred McAfee's office. After a postwar tour as district director of WAVES in the Fourteenth Naval District, she was assistant to WAVES director Jean T. Palmer and then deputy director under Hancock. Her last assignment was as assistant director of the Shipping Control Division on the staff of commander, Western Sea Frontier. When she became director and captain on 1 June 1953, she brought long experience and an intimate knowledge of all aspects of women in the Navy. In addition, the lively and decisive Wilde knew well the value of communication and good public relations, and in 1954 she began the *Pers-K Newsletter*, which kept all WAVES informed of events concerning them. When Wilde's tour as director ended in August 1957, the Navy awarded her the Legion of Merit.[53]

Following Wilde, Winifred Redden Quick served as director until August 1962. Like her two predecessors, she was in the first group of women to enter the Women's Reserve in August 1942. She was the second woman sworn in, just after Mildred McAfee. Quick was born in Montana in 1911, graduated from the University of Southern California in 1935, and received a certificate of personnel administration from Radcliffe College three years later. She worked in personnel management before joining the WAVES and continued that same type of work in the Navy. After the war, she became an assistant to Hancock. In 1951 the Navy sent her to Stanford University, where she completed a master of arts degree in personnel administration. When she became director, with the rank of captain, she brought to her post a vast knowledge of the WAVES and the desire to make them a more vital part of the Navy. She was thoroughly aware of utilizing diplomacy and persuasion in accomplishing WAVES' goals. In 1960 Quick married Rear Adm. Howard L. Collins; she retired two years later. The Navy awarded her the Legion of Merit for her five years as director.[54]

## *A Holding Pattern*

Captains Wilde and Collins guided the WAVES through a period of stagnation for women's programs that occurred not only in the Navy but in all the services.[55] Peace and the continuing draft of men caused no real need, and even less public pressure, to draw women into the military. A shift in American policy toward the concept of massive retaliation reinforced this trend: any future war would be a brief exchange of nuclear weapons, and there would be no need for a large mobilization of women—or of men. Another negative factor was the high turnover of enlisted women and the legitimate question of cost-effectiveness of the women's services. It was not surprising, then, that military women took seriously a rumor in 1959 that Congress was considering abolishing their programs.[56]

For the WAVES, slackening interest in promoting women's usefulness took various forms. In spite of the fact that women were as much a part of the regular Navy as men, a reluctance to accept women as commanders persisted. In 1953 Captain Hancock noted that this reluctance followed an old familiar pattern.[57] Lack of enthusiasm for women officers continued for years. It was not until 1962 that a WAVE became a commanding officer, when Cdr. Etta Belle Kitchen assumed that billet for women's recruit training at Bainbridge.[58]

Simultaneously, WAVES officers found limited opportunities for promotions. Bound by law to an officer strength of only 10 percent commanders and 20 percent lieutenant commanders, women had little chance to rise to higher ranks. In 1956 Congress provided some relief by relaxing these limitations, but advancement opportunities for WAVES lagged far behind those of male officers.[59]

Similarly, enlisted women found the door of opportunity steadily closing. Although thirty-six of the sixty ratings were open to women in 1952, the figure fell to twenty-five in 1956 and twenty-one in 1962. Enlisted WAVES continued to cluster in two fields: about 90 percent served in administrative-clerical or health-care billets.[60] In effect, Navy women found themselves performing the same stereotypical jobs they could do in the civilian work force.

Because of the high turnover of enlisted women, in 1954 the Navy tried to cast a military career in a more appealing light by reducing reenlistment tours from four or six to two or three years. Five years later, first enlistments dropped from four or six years to three years, making the Navy more competitive with the other services, which already had shorter enlistment options.[61]

Although turnover rates were high, a number of enlisted WAVES from World War II had made naval service their careers. Chief Radioman Sallie Miller, for example, was on duty at the Naval Air Station, Anacostia; Chief Yeoman Alice Evans served at the Great Lakes Naval Training Center; and Chief Storekeeper Agnes McSkimming was at the Fourteenth Naval District and Hawaiian Sea Frontier. These women, among many others, had become a permanent part of the U.S. Navy.[62]

As opportunities for Navy women narrowed, so too did attitudes concerning them. A series of articles in *Navy Times* in late 1959 vigorously questioned women's usefulness in the military. One declared the WAVES "a military experiment that failed" and suggested that they, like battleships, be placed in mothballs.[63] This was the era of suburban domesticity, and women's proper role was wife and mother. If misguided patriotism lured them into the military, they must be ever mindful of their feminine, ladylike image.

Trying to gain family support, Director Quick wrote to parents of a number of WAVES, asking their opinions about Navy life for their daughters. The Navy wanted to attract only the finest young American women. Most replies were favorable. Quick also generated more positive publicity for the WAVES by informing high schools and colleges that one of their graduates was an outstanding member of the U.S. Navy. So successful were Quick and the WAVES at recruiting offices that by 1962 the Navy could be highly selective and accept only 10 percent of enlisted applicants and 20 percent of officer hopefuls.[64]

The services placed great emphasis on appearance and routinely assigned the best looking women to front offices. Even as late as 1968, WAVES director Rita Lenihan, following male naval tradition of remaining covered, admonished her charges against removing their hats in public. "WAVES are ladies first and always," she said. Women's opportunities in the Navy were still a reflection of acceptable civilian ethos and standards.[65]

## *Positive Changes*

Although this was not a time of great professional advances for Navy women, some positive changes occurred. Following Hancock's initiatives to open overseas posts to WAVES, more and more women served abroad. By late 1951, about 388 WAVES were on duty in Alaska, London, Paris, Heidelberg, Hawaii, and Japan. The following year, women reported in Norway, Naples, Guam, and Puerto Rico. In 1954 the first WAVES arrived in Rome.[66]

WAVES got a taste of duty afloat when, in September 1953, four became hospital corpsmen in Military Sea Transport Service ships carrying Navy dependents. The more than sixty WAVES who eventually served in MSTS transports were supervised by a Navy nurse when onboard. Later, as the Vietnam War got under way, the vessels carried troops rather than dependents. Female corpsmen could no longer go to sea.[67]

Education opportunities slowly became available. A Reserve Officer Candidate (ROC) program for women began in 1950. Patterned after the program for undergraduate college men, the ROC sent women students for six weeks' training at Great Lakes for two summers. After women completed these sessions, earned their degrees, and reached twenty-one years of age, they were commissioned as ensigns. Two years later, this school moved to Bainbridge. The following year, the College Junior program, held at the Officer Indoctrination (Women) School at Newport, replaced the ROC.[68]

An educational innovation designed to help enlisted personnel, both male and female, qualify for commissioned status was the "seaman to admiral" program, begun in 1955. Enlisted women with two years of college study could apply for commissions and, if selected, attend the Women Officers School. Three years later, the Navy allowed officers who could finish a bachelor's degree in five semesters to become full-time students. The first WAVE chosen for both programs was Radioman Lucille Ross Kuhn, who went on to become a captain before she retired in 1985.[69]

As a means of encouraging enlisted men and women to remain in the Navy and giving them the opportunity to become officers, in 1958 the Navy began an enlisted scientific education program, which provided four years of scientific study in civilian colleges and universities. That same year, enlisted women who already held undergraduate degrees could apply for commissions; five became lieutenants (junior grade).[70] Benefiting Reserve line and Supply Corps officers was the policy of augmentation, begun in 1952. Selected junior Reserve officers could transfer to the regular Navy, and by 1956, twenty-six Reserve officers took advantage of the program. Underscoring quality in choosing outstanding women, the augmentation policy increased career opportunities.[71]

Still another means of enhancing careers sprang from Director Wilde's suggestion in 1955 that junior women officers attend the General Line School in Monterey, California. In January 1956, the first class of WAVES officers began a twenty-week course, with similar classes starting in June and September and continuing.[72] Two years later, the Navy offered additional postgraduate education in eight fields to a select few officers. Five WAVES, for example, studied advanced aerology and management at the Navy Postgraduate School in Monterey in 1959. Soon others studied naval intelligence in Washington, business administration at Harvard, or comptrollership at George Washington University.[73] A major breakthrough for women was the appointment of Cdr. Frances E. Biadasz as an instructor in international relations at the Monterey postgraduate school; she was the first woman to teach at that institution.[74]

The Navy not only offered a variety of new education opportunities but also tried to make daily life more appealing for enlisted. Captain Quick spearheaded a drive to make the barracks more attractive. She arranged for most first-class personnel and chiefs to live in their own apartments instead of barracks, and she was responsible for new or remodeled barracks and increased recreational activities.[75]

## The Navy Nurse Corps, 1953–1960

As the Navy reorganized for nuclear age demands, so too did the Bureau of Medicine and Surgery and its medical staff. During the Korean War, medical personnel and facilities expanded to meet the emergency, but afterward the Medical Department suffered cutbacks and shortages of career personnel, including nurses. The surgeon general, Rear Adm. H. Lamont Pugh (1951–55), and his successor, Rear Adm. Bartholomew W. Hogan (1955–61), grappled with these problems.[76] In an effort to make more efficient use of existing personnel, Congress in 1956 revamped the organizational structure of the bureau as well as the rest of the armed forces medical services. Navy health care now fell under the assistant chief for human resources and professional operations. In addition, the Nurse Corps became a branch of the Nursing Division, both under the same director.[77]

The Navy experienced the same shortage of nurses as did the other services and civilian institutions. There just were not enough nurses to satisfy demand. Nurse training, too, was relocating from hospital schools to academic institutions. From 1950 to 1958, for example, the number of diploma-granting hospital schools dropped from 1,190 to 768 while the number of colleges and universities with nursing programs rose. A new source of training, associate degree programs, began. By 1962 there were 192 bachelor's and higher degree programs, 874 diploma programs, and 84 associate degree programs.[78]

Nursing became a more complex profession as medical innovations demanded better-educated nurses. Advances such as heart-lung machines, open-heart surgery, cardiac catheterization, renal dialysis, laser surgery, and an array of new vaccines, medicines, and monitoring devices revolutionized the practice of medicine. By the same token, these changes called for more skilled nurses with sophisticated preparation.[79] Nursing education became increasingly expensive, and the national shortage of nurses continued.

## *Changes in Leadership*

Leading the Navy Nurse Corps through the years of stagnation and higher professional demands called for energetic and imaginative directors. First came Wilma Leona Jackson, who replaced Capt. Winnie Gibson on 1 May 1954. Born in 1909, Jackson graduated from the Nurses Training School of Miami Valley Hospital, Dayton, Ohio, in 1930 and joined the Nurse Corps in 1936. While she was serving at the Naval Hospital, Guam, the Japanese overran the island in December 1941 and took Jackson prisoner. Having endured months in a prisoner-of-war camp in Japan before leaving as part of an exchange of prisoners, she returned to Guam as senior Nurse Corps officer in December 1944. Later, she assumed duty in Washington and in 1950 took advantage of the Navy's willingness to send women for college training. She earned bachelor of science and master of arts degrees from Columbia University. Her last assignment before becoming director was chief nurse at the Naval Hospital, Portsmouth, Virginia.[80]

Following Jackson was Ruth Agatha Houghton. She was born in 1909 and graduated from the St. John's Hospital School of Nursing in Lowell, Massachusetts, in 1932. After joining the Navy Nurse Corps three years later, she was stationed at overseas posts in the Canal Zone, Australia, and New Guinea. Following World War II, Houghton served three years as detail officer for the Nurse Corps. In 1949 she attended Boston College, and two years later she received a bachelor of science degree in nursing education. She then earned a master of science degree in nursing from Catholic University. In 1951 she became senior Nurse Corps officer at Tripler General Hospital in Hawaii and then chief of nursing service at hospitals in San Diego and Bethesda. After Congress removed some rank limitations for the Nurse Corps, Houghton became the first Navy nurse, other than the director, selected as captain, assuming that rank in October 1957. The following May, Houghton became director of the Navy Nurse Corps.[81]

## *A Holding Pattern*

A major problem confronting the directors throughout these years was the persistent difficulty of attracting women to the Navy Nurse Corps.

Competition came from various sources: the civilian sector, where salaries had increased and working hours had fallen to forty a week; other government agencies; and the Army and the Air Force, which ran successful publicity campaigns and awarded nurses higher ranks.[82]

Realizing that the Navy's rank structure deterred many nurses, Captain Gibson had begun pressing for changes as early as 1953. She proposed raising the number of commanders from .6 percent to 2 percent of the actual strength of the corps, and lieutenant commanders from 1.7 percent to 8 percent. Some relief came the following year with a temporary increase in these grades, but it was 1957 before Congress removed any limits on the number of lieutenant commanders, raised the number of commanders to 5 percent, and allowed .2 percent as captains.[83]

The strict physical standards for Navy nurses kept many qualified women with minor physical problems from joining the corps. In 1955 the Nurse Corps reconsidered applicants who had been disqualified between July 1953 and June 1955 and soon appointed twenty nurses from this group.[84]

In an effort to improve the Nurse Corps image and to step up recruiting, the corps sent more nurses to the Offices of Naval Officer Procurement around the country. By 1956 there were twenty-seven officers in recruiting billets, but their numbers soon decreased. Responsible for projecting the advantages of a Navy career, these nurses gave speeches and interviews, went on field trips, made radio and television broadcasts, and issued public relations material.[85]

Opportunities for education offered more incentives to prospective corps members as well as improved the Navy's nursing standards. The Nursing Education Program, established in 1955 to allow Hospital Corps WAVES to attend collegiate nursing schools at Navy expense and subsequently secure commissions in the Nurse Corps, had eighteen enlisted women, and the number remained nearly constant. In 1960 the program expanded to include all enlisted women in the Navy and the Naval Reserve, not just Hospital Corps WAVES.[86]

The Navy Nurse Corps Candidate Program, begun in 1957, also attracted women. It addition to paying for tuition, fees, books, and room and board, the Navy paid seniors in collegiate nursing schools small stipends. When these students completed their undergraduate degrees, they were commissioned ensigns in the Nurse Corps Reserves and had to serve two years on active duty. About fifty young women took advantage of this program annually.[87]

Graduate education for nurses also received a helping hand. Nurses with baccalaureate degrees could pursue either master's or doctoral degrees full time in nursing administration or education, research, and anesthesia. In 1959 the corps began financing off-duty education courses for its officers. All these education benefits mirrored the trend in the private sector and reflected the nursing profession's growing emphasis on collegiate training.[88] Added to these college programs were the Nurse Corps's own in-service short courses, seminars, and workshops, developed by the Nurse Training Branch, established at the Naval Medical School in Bethesda in 1959. The following year the Nursing Research Branch began at the same place.[89]

Naval medical and nursing personnel developed a new field to deal with the atomic age: nuclear nursing. The Nuclear Nursing Division of the Nuclear Medicine Department at Bethesda offered the first course in the country (and perhaps the world) in this evolving specialty. Open to all military nurses, the four-month course began in September 1958 under the direction of Lt. Cdr. Lenore Simon. Fourteen nurses, twelve from the Navy and two from the Air Force, were the first to study, from a military nurse's perspective, the principles of radioisotope therapy and the care of mass casualties from an atomic disaster.[90] So excited was the Nurse Corps about this pioneering program that the director, Capt. Ruth Houghton, enthusiastically greeted the first students. "You are making history!" she said.[91]

As one specialized field opened, another closed. Flight nursing, the glamour billet of the 1940s and early 1950s, seemed no longer necessary, because the country was at peace and the Air Force had an ample number of such nurses. In 1960 the Navy discontinued sending nurses to training courses with Air Force nurses or assigning them to the Military Air Transportation Service.[92]

In spite of the many inducements to attract nurses to the corps, shortages persisted. In July 1953, the corps had 2,600 members; by June 1960 it had 2,198. The racial composition of the corps remained essentially white. There were 13 black nurses in 1953; by 1960 there were only 30.[93] The Army Nurse Corps fared little better in this nationwide shortage of nurses. Even by 1963, it had only 2,928 nurses to serve a much larger force.[94]

The Navy had to assign its nurses carefully. There was so much need and there were so few nurses. By the early 1960s, Navy nurses served in twenty-two continental hospitals, three overseas hospitals, and one hospital ship. Others were in transports or MSTS ships, or at naval recruiting stations. A number were stationed at Marine Corps activities, naval support activities, naval stations at home and abroad, naval air facilities, and dispensaries. Others were active in the Naval Medical and Dental Schools, Bethesda, and of course, they continued their mission of training potential corpsmen at Hospital Corps schools.[95]

### *Humanitarian Aid*

Navy nurses had always volunteered to help with military and civilian disasters, and they continued this tradition. When the aircraft carrier *Bennington* (CV 20) suffered a series of explosions while cruising off Naragansett Bay, Rhode Island, on 26 May 1954, casualties were high: 103 killed, 201 injured. The Naval Hospital, Newport, was the nearest emergency facility. Nurses there helped treat eighty-two severely burned patients from the ship.[96] Living nearby was former Navy nurse Lt. Marion M. Humphreys, who answered the appeal for local volunteers. Working in one of the burn wards, she declared, "I felt as though I was back in the Navy again."[97]

In 1955, during a nationwide polio epidemic, the naval hospital in Chelsea, Massachusetts, opened a ward to care for its own suffering from the disease. Maxine Conder, later director of the Nurse Corps, was charge nurse and recalled a bustling ward filled with iron lungs. A half dozen Navy nurses from Chelsea also went to nearby civilian hospitals to help care for additional polio patients.[98]

The following year, six Navy nurses aided in sealifting European refugees to the United States. Hungarian nationalists had risen up against the Soviet-dominated communist government, and in the blood bath that followed, numerous refugees had fled the country. The transport *General LeRoy Eltinge* (AP 154) picked up 1,750 of these refugees at Bremenhaven on 20 December 1956, carrying them to a new life of freedom in America. The *Eltinge* was the first ship of the three-vessel sealift that carried 5,500 away from Hungary. The sick bay in each had two Navy doctors, two Navy nurses, and ten corpsmen.[99]

## WAVES AND NAVY NURSES: SHARED EXPERIENCES

The indoctrination program at the Women Officers School at Newport was in jeopardy as the 1950s unfolded. During the Korean War, each class had consisted of at least seventy women; in 1956 that number fell to ten. Fearing the program would end, Director Quick soon looked for means of filling these courses and turned to the other Navy women, the nurses. Nurse Corps director Capt. Ruth A. Houghton readily agreed to merging the two indoctrination programs and in January 1959 dispatched ten new Nurse Corps officers, under Lt. Cdr. Dymphna Van Gorp, for a pilot study of the eight-week program. In July Nurse Corps indoctrination became a permanent part of the Women Officers School, and a few months later, the nurses' Indoctrination Center at St. Albans ceased.[100]

Merging programs was not the only example of cooperation between the two groups of women. Nurses had long admired the WAVES' stylish designer uniforms, and after women became a permanent part of the Navy, the uniform board debated identical outfits for all women. A survey of nurses in late 1949 revealed that they preferred the traditional black-blue fabric of male officers and gold sleeve markings. In contrast, WAVES liked their navy blue with light blue stripes. Couturier Mainbocher designed the new dress uniforms to conform with WAVES styling but of the black-blue fabric the nurses preferred.[101] A circular letter in May 1950 announced the changes, which became mandatory in 1951. Nurses, of course, continued to wear their white ward uniforms while on duty. An evening dress uniform was also authorized. In 1959 a light blue service uniform for hot weather broadened the women's options.[102]

Nurses and WAVES shared another feature of naval service: pay and benefits. Women received the same compensation as men of equal rank or rating. The Career Compensation Act of 1949 and the Dependents Assistance Act of 1950 spelled out the provisions. In 1951 enlisted pay ranged from $82.50 a month for seamen to $198.45 for chief petty officers. Among officers, ensigns received $213.75 a month; commanders, $456; and captains, $570.
Quarters allowances varied from $45 to $105 a month; subsistence, from $30 to $45. Subsequent raises by 1960 brought these figures to $99.37 for seamen, $208 for chief petty officers, $222.30 for ensigns, $474.24 for com-

manders, and $592.80 for captains. Allowances had risen to between $51.30 and $136.80 for quarters and $47.88 for subsistence. Restrictions against women's claiming spouses, children, or parents as dependents remained, based on whether such people were in fact dependent on women for more than one half of their support.[103]

As the 1950s ended, a naval career for women, other than nursing, was still uncertain. Aside from the handful of women in the service, no one really seemed interested in promoting women's programs or even their presence. By June 1960, there were 8,071 women, including 5,968 WAVES and 2,103 nurses, out of a total force of 617,984—a scant 1.3 percent of active duty personnel.[104]

For the WAVES, there had been a flurry of activity during the Korean War, a time when the trained nucleus concept worked efficiently.[105] The major problem was, and continued to be throughout the decade, a shortage of women who wanted to join the Navy. Directors Hancock, Wilde, and Quick experimented with a variety of enticements: more overseas posts, lowering the minimum age to eighteen, ROC and College Junior programs, reducing the length of enlistments, the seaman to admiral and the scientific education programs, the augmentation policy, and the chance to attend the General Line School at Monterey.

Women welcomed these innovations, but they were not enough to offset such negatives of naval service as restrictions on officers' advancing through the ranks, fewer ratings open to enlisted women, the narrowly defined dependents' status, and the pervasive feeling that they were not wanted in the Navy. Women's diminished roles were in keeping with the prevailing societal view that women should be wives and mothers, certainly not sailors.

Navy nurses, like their civilian counterparts, became increasingly better trained and educated. Emphasis had shifted to collegiate nursing programs, and the Navy financed various undergraduate and graduate education opportunities for current and prospective Navy nurses. Such specialized education helped Navy nurses pioneer the new field of nuclear nursing. Simultaneously, Congress offered some relief in the logjam of rank increases, and in 1957 allowed more captains, commanders, and lieutenant commanders.

Nurses were subject to less societal criticism than their WAVES sisters; it was all right for women to be nurses. Under the leadership of Captains Gibson, Jackson, and Houghton, the Navy Nurse Corps survived the 1950s with little doubt cast upon its permanence or usefulness.

It had been a difficult decade for all Navy women. Perhaps the upcoming era of activism and another war would again increase opportunities for and interest in military women.

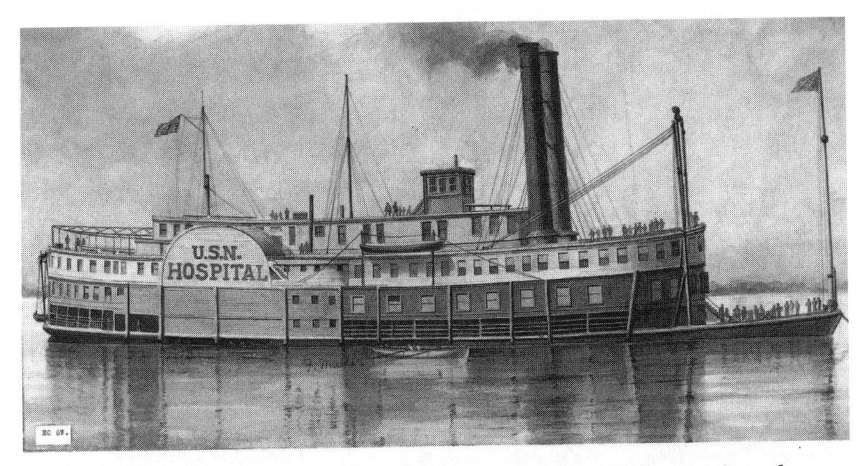


The Navy's pioneer hospital ship *Red Rover* served the Mississippi Squadron during the Civil War. Four nurses from the Catholic order Sisters of the Holy Cross, the forerunner of the Navy Nurse Corps, were on its medical staff.
*Naval Historical Center*

This 1863 *Harper's Weekly* composite sketch depicts life onboard *Red Rover*. *Left to right,* a nurse attends a patient, a lonely grave along the riverbank, and a convalescent ward.
*Naval Historical Center*

After Rear Adm. Presley Marion Rixey lobbied Congress to establish a skilled female nurse corps in 1908, he became known as "father of the Navy Nurse Corps." *Naval Historical Center*

Esther Voorhees Hasson, a former Army nurse, served as the first superintendent of the Navy Nurse Corps from 18 August 1908 to 10 January 1911. Under her leadership, seventy-five nurses were recruited and trained for naval service. *Naval Historical Center*

The "Sacred Twenty," the first group of Navy nurses appointed, poses on the steps of Naval Hospital, Washington, D.C., in 1908. Superintendent Esther Voorhees Hasson, *front row, seventh from the left*, and two future superintendents, J. Beatrice Bowman and Lenah S. Higbee, *front row, fifth and sixth from the left, respectively*, are also shown.
*Naval Historical Center*

Helene Johnson, a business college graduate, responded to Secretary of the Navy Josephus Daniels's call for volunteers to join the Naval Reserve Force. She became a yeoman (F), first class.
*Private Collection*

Bernice Smith Tongate, later chief yeoman (F), modeled for this World War I recruiting poster by artist Howard Chandler Christy in 1917. By the end of the following year, there were more than eleven thousand active yeomen (F).
*Naval Historical Center*

Four companies of yeomen (F) stand in full dress uniform on the Washington Monument grounds, before inspection by the chief of the Bureau of Navigation.
*Naval Historical Center*

Many yeomen (F) filled clerical positions in Navy Department offices such as this one, believed to be a mailroom in Washington, D.C. Others served naval installations across the country, replacing men who were needed at sea.
*Naval Historical Center*

Chief Nurse Sophia V. Kiel supervised six nurses accompanying President Wilson to peace negotiations in *George Washington*, shown here in December 1918. The same month Chief Nurse Mary M. Robinson led six nurses in *Leviathan*, and in May 1919 four seagoing nurses sailed in *Imperator*.
*Bureau of Medicine and Surgery*

The collars of these nurses onboard *George Washington* bear an anchor with a gold oak leaf and acorn, the insignia of the Navy Nurse Corps.
*National Archives*

Navy nurses walk with patients on the deck of the hospital ship *Relief* (AH 1). Commissioned in 1920, *Relief*'s medical staff included the first Navy nurses to serve aboard a hospital ship.
*Naval Historical Center*

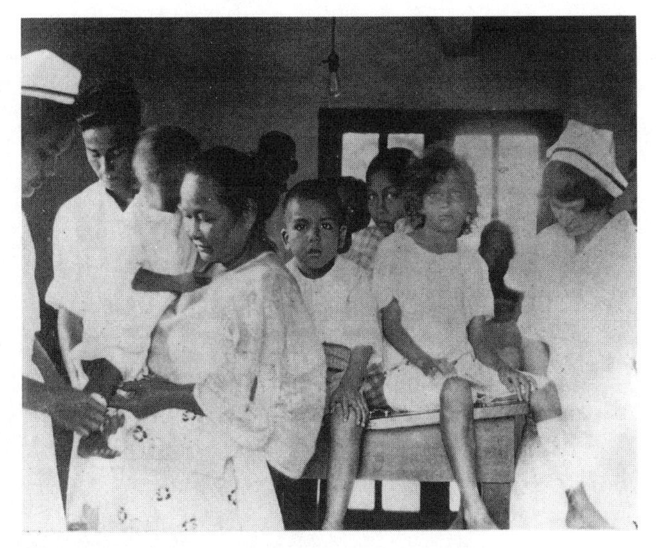

A Navy nurse and her Chamorro student nurse tend to children at a Guam clinic in the 1930s. In an effort to improve the health of the island people, Navy nurses trained young local women in basic nursing care.
*Bureau of Medicine and Surgery*

Civilian nurses, encouraged by World War II recruiting posters, joined the Navy Nurse Corps.
*Bureau of Medicine and Surgery*

The outdoor service dress uniforms of Navy nurses in World War I, *right*, and World War II.
*Naval Historical Center*

When Manila fell to the Japanese in January 1942, eleven nurses were imprisoned in Santo Tomas and Los Baños. Despite their captivity, the nurses continued to care for the sick and wounded until their liberation by American forces in 1945.
*Bureau of Medicine and Surgery*

Sue S. Dauser, superintendent of the Navy Nurse Corps from 1939 to 1946, became the first female naval officer promoted to the rank of captain. Captain Dauser worked tirelessly on legislation that would give permanent rank to Nurse Corps officers.
*Naval Historical Center*

Mildred McAfee, former president of Wellesley College, was sworn in by Secretary of the Navy Frank Knox as the first director of the WAVES on 3 August 1942. Adm. Ernest J. King, *left*, and Rear Adm. Randall Jacobs were also present.
*Naval Historical Center*

Graduates of the WAVES training program at Hunter College in New York City march in review before heading to their Navy assignments. Nearly eighty-one thousand enlisted WAVES revolved through the six-week training program during the war.
*Naval Historical Center*

Lt. (jg) Harriet Ida Pickens and Ens. Frances Elizabeth Wills, the only black WAVES officers commissioned during World War II, graduated from the last class of officer candidates at Smith College in Northampton, Massachusetts.
*Naval Historical Center*

The sign in front of the nurses' quarters at Base Hospital, New Guinea, effectively says, "No men allowed."
*Bureau of Medicine and Surgery*

This cartoon highlights the milestones for Navy women, from President Roosevelt signing legislation authorizing the enlistment and commissioning of women in the U.S. Naval Reserve to the WAVES' first anniversary celebration with twenty-seven thousand women in the service.
*Naval Historical Center*

Aviation metalsmiths and machinist's mates work on an SBD "Dauntless" aircraft in the Assembly and Repair Department at Naval Air Station, Jacksonville, Florida.
*National Archives*

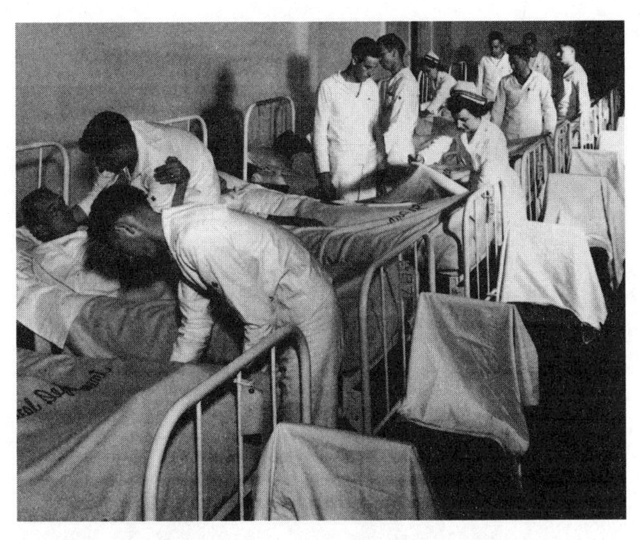

In their customary training role, Navy nurses instruct student hospital corpsmen at the Bainbridge, Maryland, naval training school during the war.
*National Archives*

Specialists (G), Third Class, Florence Johnston, *left*, and Rosamund Small, WAVES gunnery instructors, trained male marksmen at the Naval Air Gunners School in Hollywood, Florida.
*Naval Historical Center*

Artist John Falter portrays a WAVES parachute rigger at work in this painting for a recruiting poster. Riggers ensured the safety of wartime pilots and crewmen by inspecting, mending, and packing their silk parachutes.
*Naval Historical Center*

WAVES specialists, learning to become air navigation instructors, take a practice "flight" at the Navy Link Celestial Navigation School in Seattle, Washington. One Wave, *left*, holds a bubble octant used in night flights over the ocean.
*Naval Historical Center*

A WAVES control tower operator directs aircraft at Floyd Bennett Field, New York.
*Naval Historical Center*

Lt. (jg) B. V. Rivers poses with patients in the hospital ship *Relief* (AH 1), which joined the Pacific Fleet in 1943 to evacuate wounded from the Solomon, Marshall, Mariana, and Caroline Islands.
*Bureau of Medicine and Surgery*

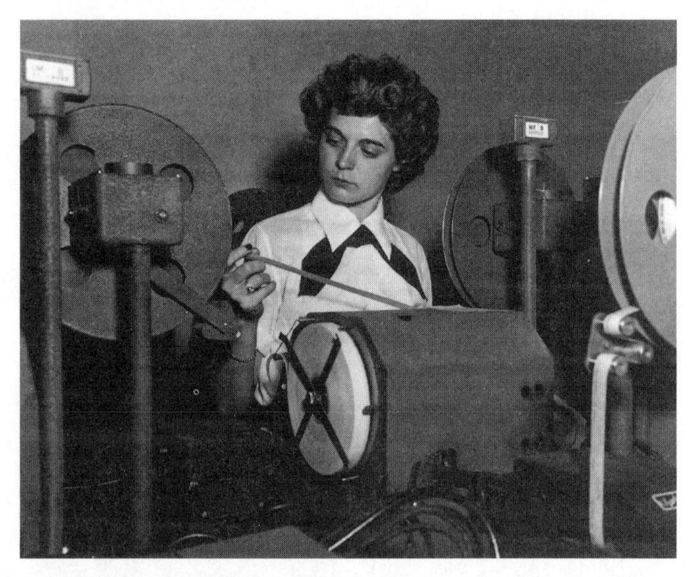

Telegrapher, Third Class, Ida May Rowley checks monitor tape at Naval Communications, Washington, D.C., the heart of the Navy's far-flung communications network.
*Naval Historical Center*

Nurses temporarily wore Army uniforms onboard *Solace* (AH 5) in the Pacific during 1945. Americans wounded in Pacific island campaigns of World War II received emergency treatment in the hospital ship before being transferred to base hospitals.
*Bureau of Medicine and Surgery*

The Navy used air evacuations that included flight nurses. Jane Kendeigh, the first Navy flight nurse to land on a battlefield, cares for a wounded Marine on Iwo Jima in 1945.
*Bureau of Medicine and Surgery*

Capt. Joy Bright Hancock served in the Navy as a Yeoman (F) during World War I, as one of the first WAVES officers during World War II, and as the third WAVES director after the war.
*Naval Historical Center*

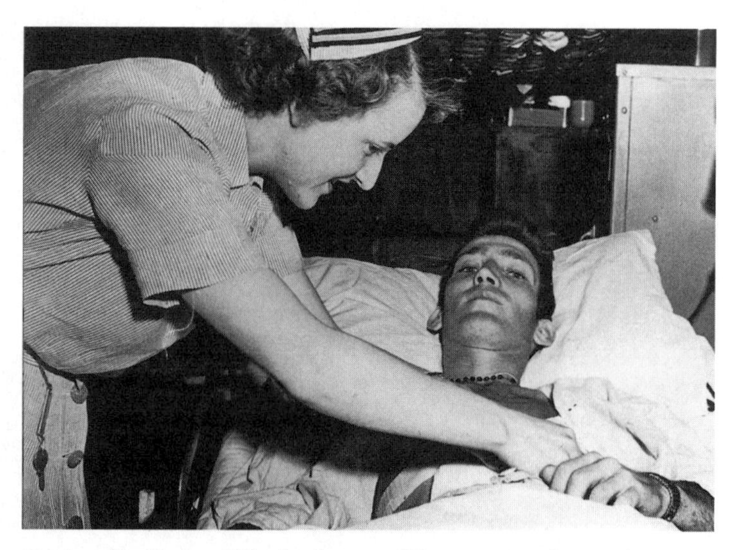

During the Korean War Lt. Loretta Diemert attends a patient onboard *Consolation* (AH 15), the first hospital ship fitted with a landing platform for delivery of casualties by helicopter.
*Bureau of Medicine and Surgery*

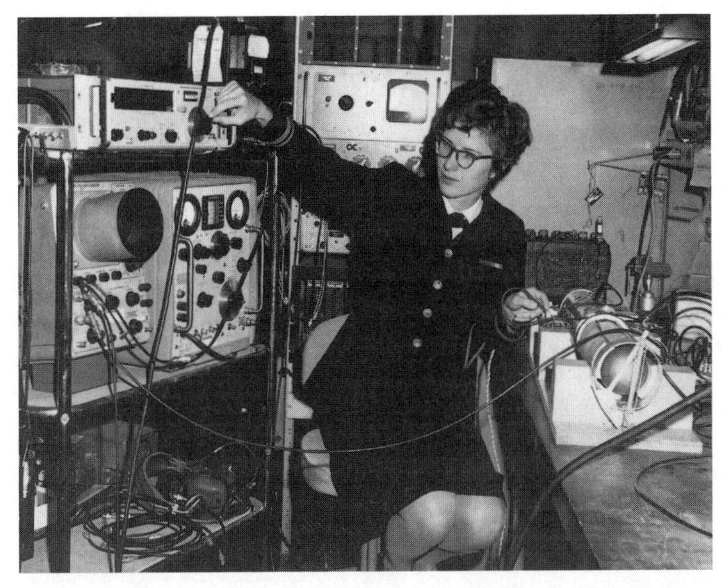

Lt. (jg) Jean Szymanski, one of the Navy's first female electrical engineers, works with aviation electronics equipment in 1968.
*Naval Historical Center*

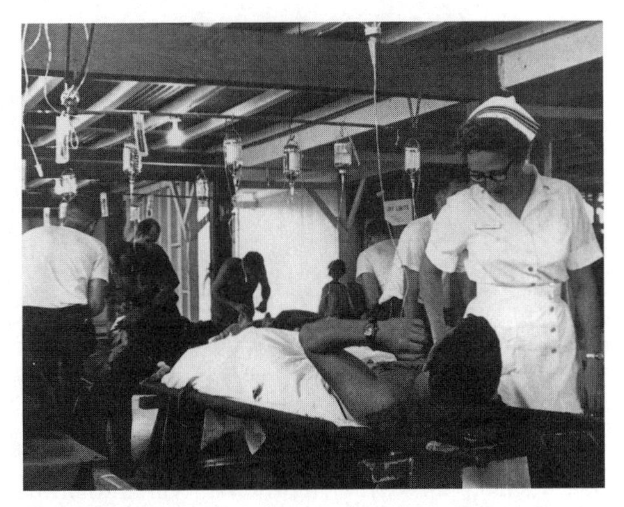

Cdr. Mary F. Cannon, Chief of Nursing Service in Vietnam, comforts a wounded American in the receiving area of the Danang naval hospital. Between 1967 and 1970, ninety-five nurses saw duty at Danang.
*U.S. Navy*

Ens. Arlon P. Peda, a nurse at the naval hospital in Danang, and Lt. Cdr. Joan Brovillette, an operating room nurse, prepare to move a patient from surgery to intensive care. After becoming eligible for the Navy Nurse Corps in November 1964, male nurses served at base hospitals and other stations in Vietnam.
*U.S. Navy*

The hospital ship *Repose* (AH 16) was recommissioned for duty off the coast of Vietnam in October 1965. The ship's proximity to the battlefield, coupled with the use of medical evacuation helicopters, meant that wounded often reached the ship's emergency room within thirty minutes.
*U.S. Navy*

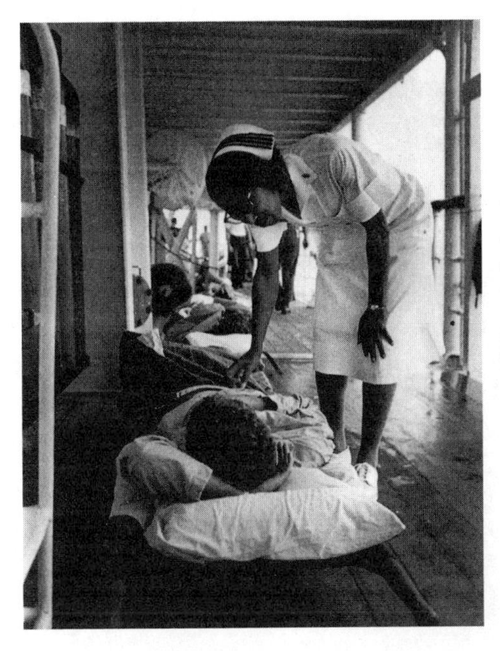

Onboard *Repose,* a Navy nurse checks on a wounded patient waiting for evacuation to the U.S. A total of 145 Navy nurses served on *Repose* before it left Vietnam in March 1970.
*U.S. Navy*

Rear Adm. Alene B. Duerk, director of the Navy Nurse Corps from 1970 to 1975, became the first female naval officer promoted to flag rank. Chief of Naval Operations Adm. Elmo Zumwalt places the admiral's hat on her head during the promotion ceremony in 1972, as Secretary of the Navy John Warner watches.
*U.S. Navy*

Seabee Camella J. Jones was the Navy's first woman to qualify as a heavy equipment operator and to be assigned to the U.S. Navy Construction Battalion.
*U.S. Navy*

Lt. Judith Neuffer, one of the initial group of women pilots selected for aviation training in 1973, engages in a preflight check of her P-3 Orion patrol plane. The 1970s marked rapid changes in career opportunities for women in naval aviation.
*Naval Historical Center*

Fifty-five women joined the crew of the Navy hospital ship *Sanctuary* (AH 17) in a 1972 pilot program that paved the way for sea duty. Seaman Apprentice Anneliese Knapp, one of the first female crew members, handles a line on the deck of *Sanctuary*.
*U.S. Navy*

The Navy's first female diver, Seaman Nancy Garner, prepares to make a dive near San Diego in 1974.
*U.S. Navy*

Ens. Rosemary Mariner (née Conatser) checks the main gear on her S-2 Tracker before taking off for antisubmarine patrol over the Atlantic in 1975. Mariner would become the first woman to command an operational Navy aircraft squadron.
*U.S. Navy*

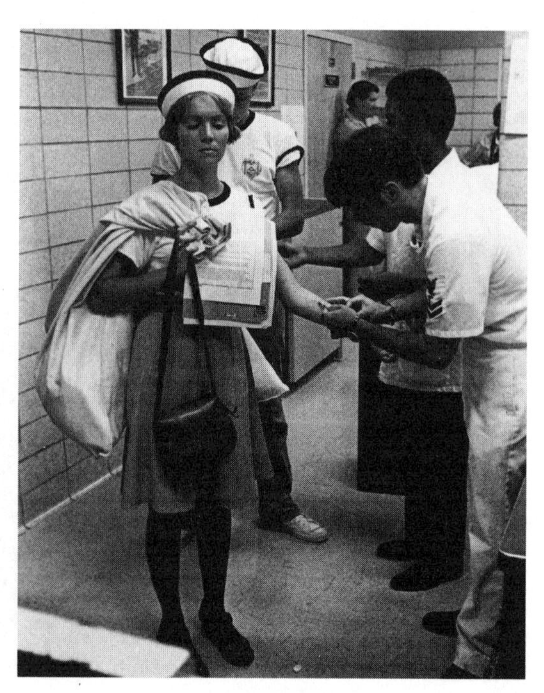

When the service academies opened to women in 1976, Janet Kotovsky was among those entering the U.S. Naval Academy and making her requisite first-day stop at the medical station.
*U.S. Navy*

In 1978 Capt. Joan C. Bynum, assistant director of nursing at the U.S. Naval Regional Medical Center in Yokosuka, Japan, was the first black woman to become a Navy captain.
*U.S. Navy*

Ens. Roberta McIntyre, *left,* and Macushla McCormick, seen here on the bridge of the submarine tender *Dixon* (AS 37) in 1978, were among the first women Navy officers to be assigned for duty aboard ships.
*U.S. Navy*

Midshipman, Second Class, Cindy Mason, a University of Missouri student, watches the altitude dial during pressure chamber tests. Mason took part in an NROTC training program designed to give future naval officers a look at the Navy's warfare communities.
*Courtesy of* Naval Aviation News

Rear Adm. Grace M. Hopper departs USS *Constitution* with Secretary of Navy John Lehman after her retirement ceremony in 1986. Hopper was at the forefront of computer programming development in the U.S. for over four decades.
*Naval Historical Center*

Cdr. Deborah S. Gernes, executive officer of the destroyer tender *Cape Cod* (AD 43), and a petty officer observe activity off Subic Bay, the Philippines, in 1986. A few months later, Gernes would become the first woman to qualify for a command at sea.
*U.S. Naval Institute*

Lt. (jg) Gail Wilkins, a damage control assistant, records information during a general quarters drill on the destroyer tender *Samuel Gompers* (AD 37).
*U.S. Naval Institute*

Interior Communications Electrician, Second Class, Lori Richards operates the fantail phone talker onboard *Grapple* (ARS 53). *Grapple* was towing three ocean minesweepers to the Persian Gulf for tanker escort operations in 1987.
*U.S. Naval Institute*

Lt. Kelly Franke of Helicopter Combat Support Squadron 2 walks to her Sea King helicopter during Operation Desert Shield.
*Defense Visual Information Center*

Airman Ora Howard, plane captain, helps secure a pilot into the cockpit of an A-7 Corsair aircraft in 1988.
*Defense Visual Information Center*

Seabee Lts. Susan Globar and Lynn Bever headed the two construction battalion units that erected Fleet Hospital Five at al-Jubayl, Saudi Arabia, in 1990. The hospital was built to handle casualties of the Persian Gulf War.
*Bureau of Medicine and Surgery*

Flight nurses make sure patient records are complete before the injured leave an aircraft following a medical evacuation from the Persian Gulf.
*Bureau of Medicine and Surgery*

Journalist, Third Class, Wendy Hamme improves her shooting skills while firing her .308-caliber M-14 from a sitting position. Hamme qualified as a marksman on the rifle.
*U.S. Department of Defense*

Lt. Mary Cummings, *left*, and Lt. (jg) Sarah Applegarth were members of Fleet Composite Squadron 5 before its disestablishment in 1992. During training in aerial maneuvers, these women and their squadron mates played the role of enemy pilots.
Courtesy *Naval Aviation News*

In the fall of 1991, following a rigorous screening process and interviews by officials of the U.S. Naval Academy, Midshipman, Second Class, Juliane Gallina became the first woman in Naval Academy history to be named commander of the Brigade of Midshipmen. Aside from serving as chief liaison between the midshipmen and academy officers, she was responsible for the daily military activity of 4,300 midshipmen.
*U.S. Naval Academy*

# 9

# The Vietnam War and the 1960s

*The 1960s was a decade of upheaval and unrest,* exacerbated by an unpopular war in Southeast Asia. Although personnel demands increased markedly, utilization of Navy women did not match this upswing. Stagnation in the WAVES program, so apparent during the 1950s, persisted. The Navy Nurse Corps, on the other hand, enjoyed renewed prestige and the satisfaction of playing an important part in the wartime Navy. The differences between the two branches grew.

## The Setting

During the 1960s, the whole nation seemed to be coming apart at the seams. Sit-ins, demonstrations, and strikes accelerated into antiwar demonstrations, mass arrests, and bombings as many students revolted against American involvement in the Vietnam War. These years of violence saw the assassinations of a president, a senator, and a civil rights leader as well as the downfall of President Lyndon B. Johnson. Some in the hippie culture, heavily into drugs, tried to drop out of American society; others preached violent revolution.

The most widespread and visible protest movement of the 1960s was for civil rights. Its leaders turned from the conciliatory approach of Martin Luther King Jr. and became more strident in enumerating blacks' grievances and more militant in demanding equal opportunities. Activists such as Malcolm X, Stokely Carmichael, and Floyd McKissick advocated black separatism and violence. Demonstrations and marches increased, and riots exploded in one fiery city after another. Measures such as the Civil Rights Act of 1964 and the subsequent Voting Rights Act were too little, too late to pacify many black Americans. Women paid close attention to the protests and tactics of these groups.

American women attended college in record numbers—up from 1,339,000 in 1960 to 3,507,163 ten years later, from 37 percent to 41 percent of all college students.[1] Increasingly large numbers attended graduate schools, and some studied for such male-dominated professions as law and medicine.

Women's presence in the work force climbed, and by 1970, 41 percent of women worked outside the home. Continuing a trend begun during World War II, most new entrants in the labor force were middle-class married women. Women still largely clustered in lower-paying jobs, especially clerical positions. Women's wages decreased, dropping to 59 percent of comparable male pay.[2]

Realizing the inequities confronting American women, newly elected President John F. Kennedy appointed the Presidential Commission on the Status of Women in 1961. Eleanor Roosevelt chaired the commission, while Esther Peterson, head of the Women's Bureau of the Labor Department, directed its activities. Reporting two years later, the commission detailed inequalities in employment, pay, and legal matters, and urged a wide range of social services. The report had two immediate effects: the Equal Pay Act of 1963 and activating professional women to study discrimination against their sex.[3]

During the 1960s, the emphasis on suburban domesticity slackened, although it remained predominate in the lives of white, middle-class women. The age of marriage and the divorce rate rose while the fertility rate dropped. The overwhelming unhappiness of many suburban housewives found a voice in 1963, when writer Betty Friedan eloquently articulated "the problem that has no name" in *The Feminine Mystique.* Her writings were the ideological catalyst for a renewed feminism, and women took inspiration from them.[4]

Even earlier, on 1 November 1961, thousands of women across the country had staged a one-day strike, protesting the radioactive fallout from Soviet nuclear testing, and Women Strike for Peace (WSP) became a national movement. The group soon shifted to antiwar, antidraft activities, which culminated in a march on Washington in September 1967. Overshadowing them were other, more militant women in the peace movement who organized another march on the nation's capital in January 1968, protesting the Vietnam War.[5]

When it became apparent that Title VII of the Civil Rights Act of 1964, which barred discrimination based on race or sex, was not being taken seriously, Friedan and others established the National Organization for Women (NOW) in 1966. Borrowing largely from civil rights organizations, these educated, middle-class individuals wanted to bring women into equal partnership with men in American society. They called for an equal rights amendment to the Constitution; an end to sex discrimination in employment, education, and the professions; child care centers; birth control; and legalized abortion.[6] In addition, the Women's Equity and Action League (WEAL) concentrated on economic and legal problems while the National Women's Political Caucus (NWPC) encouraged greater participation in the political process. The new brand of feminism, fed by the decade of protests and rebellion, spread across the nation. Although the majority of women did not participate in these movements, many watched with interest as fresh voices took up the cry for women's rights.

While women struggled to overcome years of discrimination and to secure a more equitable place in America, the U.S. Navy continued to maintain a presence in areas threatened by communist aggression. Close to home, the 1962 Cuban missile crisis demonstrated the power and efficacy of the Navy as a deterrent. The Soviets had begun setting up nuclear ballistic missile sites in Cuba. Having such weapons poised just ninety miles from the United States led to President Kennedy's announcing a "naval quarantine" of Cuba in October 1962. Eighty-five ships tightened the blockade, stopping and searching some vessels bound for the island. Within days, Soviet premier Nikita Krushchev agreed to halt construction of missile sites and to return the weapons to the Soviet Union.[7]

The largest naval involvement during these years was American participation against communist forces trying to overrun South Vietnam. The United States began sending military "advisers" to that country in 1950, and the practice escalated. Soon after the destroyer *Maddox* (DD 731) was attacked in the Gulf of Tonkin in 1964, President Johnson stepped up American involvement with air strikes in North Vietnam, Laos, and Cambodia, and, eventually, with more than five hundred thousand men. Still later, President Richard M. Nixon expanded the war into neighboring Laos and Cambodia. The Navy had enormous responsibilities during this long war, including air support of ground operations, ship bombardment of ground targets, patrolling the coastlines and rivers, and transporting troops and supplies. The hospital ships *Repose* and *Sanctuary* lay in the war zone, taking on casualties.[8]

To fight the prolonged war, the Navy needed more ships and men. In 1960 there were 812 active vessels. The number rose to 932 in June 1968 and dropped to 743 two years later. Manning these ships required more personnel. They numbered 617,984 in 1960, peaked at 777,326 in July 1969, and fell to 692,660 a year later.[9] Compounding the Navy's personnel difficulties in fighting this unpopular war were rampant drug and alcohol abuse and blatant racial tensions, problems that would not be resolved until the 1970s.

Among the Navy's ships were the new nuclear-powered vessels. After the submarine *Nautilus* (SSN 571) in 1954 came the cruiser *Long Beach* (CGN 9) and attack carrier *Enterprise* (CVAN 65) in 1961, then, in 1962, the guided missile frigate *Bainbridge* (DLGN 25). Others of the nuclear fleet followed. Soon the guided missile Polaris armed forty-one nuclear submarines.[10]

Such vast technological advances made the Navy's administrative structure, especially the old bureau system, outdated, and in 1962 the Dillon Board, appointed to survey naval organization, recommended a complete overhaul. In 1966 Secretary of Defense Robert S. McNamara asked for its reorganization, which the chief of naval operations, Adm. David L. McDonald (1963–67), executed. The bureaus became six functional material commands under the chief of naval material. Medicine and Surgery and Personnel were the only bureaus remaining from the old system. All of these commands reported to the chief of naval operations.[11] Eager to be a part of the rapidly changing Navy and its worldwide commitments, women waited anxiously for definitions of their place in the Navy of the 1960s and in another war.

## The Vietnam Era: The WAVES

With increasing American involvement in Vietnam and the concurrent naval buildup, demand for personnel spiraled upward. Logically, the war and the unpopular draft of young men should have opened greater opportunities for women, but such was not the case. Although the WAVES had received authorization for a 20 percent increase, their numbers remained fairly steady: 5,968 in 1960 and 6,152 in November 1969. This was a drop from .96 percent of active-duty personnel in 1960 to .79 percent ten years later.[12] The Navy was not alone in this lack of interest in women's military service. In 1965 there were only 30,600 women in all the armed services.[13]

Although the Navy had difficulty attracting women to join the WAVES, it turned down one volunteer. American Nazi Party leader George L. Rockwell threatened to sue the WAVES because they rejected one of his storm troopers, Lloyd Brown. He not only exceeded the height and weight limits, he was a male. Rockwell unsuccessfully argued that the Civil Rights Act of 1964 forbade such discrimination.[14]

## *Changes in Leadership*

Guiding the WAVES during these uncertain years were two new directors. First came Viola Brown Sanders, who replaced Capt. Winifred Quick Collins as assistant chief of naval personnel for women on 9 August 1962 and assumed the rank of captain. Born in 1921, she graduated from two Mississippi schools: Sunflower Junior College and Delta State College, from which she earned a bachelor's degree in education. She taught high school before entering the WAVES in August 1943. After completing officer indoctrination and communications schools, Sanders served in various communications billets during the war. She was battalion, then regimental, commander for women's recruit training at Great Lakes, then Bainbridge, followed by a tour in Yokosuka, Japan, from 1953 to 1955. Next she held several administrative posts in Washington, and in 1958 became deputy to the WAVES director. Three years later, she became director of naval personnel on the staff of the commandant, Fifth Naval District. In the summer of 1962, she became WAVES director. When she retired, the Navy awarded her the Legion of Merit.[15] For Sanders and other directors, increased promotion and job opportunities for WAVES were the primary goals.[16]

Following Sanders as director came Rita Lenihan, who also had entered the Women's Reserve during World War II. Born in 1914, she graduated from the College of St. Elizabeth in Morristown, New Jersey, in 1935 with a degree in Latin, and later earned a master of arts degree at George Washington University. Before entering the Navy, she had been a home lighting engineer. After her commissioning in 1943, Lenihan spent the war years in the Plans and Policy Division, Bureau of Personnel. In 1949 she was one of the first WAVES assigned to London and served as administrative assistant and aide to the chief of the Joint Planning Staff. Two years later, she became director of officer personnel in the Potomac River Naval Command and then served as officer in charge of the Women's Officer School, Newport. Lenihan became deputy director of the WAVES in 1961 and two years later joined the staff of the Naval War College. From that billet, she returned to Washington as assistant chief of naval personnel for women in September 1966. She, too, received the Legion of Merit for her service.[17]

A vibrant, enthusiastic woman, Lenihan believed that WAVES had a strong future in oceanography, but only from ashore. Data processing, she believed, was also a natural field for women. She stressed the importance of a thorough mastery of the English language and the art of communication. Conservative in utilizing women, Lenihan was not one to blaze new trails. "I don't think women belong onboard ship," she noted. "Their place is on shore and I don't think the day will come when women will be seagoing as the men. I don't think we'll ever be hearing of service women at Cape Kennedy ready to blast off into outer space."[18]

## *Defending Their Place*

Sanders and Lenihan confronted challenging problems. In addition to routine administration of the WAVES, they had to ward off ill-disguised attempts to end the women's program. In the mid-1960s, there was a spate of activity involving women's permanent status in the service.

Although President Johnson had greeted members of DACOWITS at the White House in April 1964 and noted that military service was becoming an attractive career for women, the Department of Defense still had difficulty justifying women in the Navy.[19] A General Accounting Office preliminary report in 1964 suggested that the services find ways to reduce the high turnover among enlisted women or else hire civil service replacements. Director Sanders rebutted such an idea by pointing out that civilian replacements would cost more than WAVES' turnover expenses. The assistant secretary of defense (manpower) reiterated Sanders's observation. Women formed a nucleus that could expand in wartime to meet military requirements such as mobility, security, watch standing, availability, and responsiveness to command.[20]

Secretary of Defense Robert S. McNamara underscored women's usefulness. "Their record in military service has been . . . exemplary," he declared. Women would, he said, take a greater share in the national defense. In 1966, an interservice group studied women's abilities and concluded that they were highly trainable volunteers who could perform most military jobs.[21]

Interestingly, the Marine Corps, which had fewer women than the other services, led the way in expanding opportunities for women. Beginning in August 1964, Lt. Gen. Robert H. Pepper headed a group to study the Women Marines' program. As a result of the Pepper Board report and recommendations, in 1965 the Marine Corps began more special and postgraduate training, opened more duty stations, emphasized personal development, and authorized increased recruiting to bring the Women Marines up to 1 percent of the corps's total strength.[22]

The WAVES organization, meanwhile, was still protecting its very existence. Captain Sanders issued a fact sheet in April 1965 that explained the need for women in peacetime and as a nucleus from which to expand in a national emergency.[23] Simultaneously, the House held hearings about the expense of maintaining the small women's program. As it had in 1948, the Navy, as well as the other services, called upon top leaders to speak on women's behalf. Vice Adm. Benedict J. Semmes Jr., chief of naval personnel, attested to their value in the Navy.[24] But personnel demands created by the Vietnam War continued while opposition to the draft accelerated. Perforce, the armed services looked again to women to fill noncombat billets. In late 1966, the Army, Navy, and Air Force joined the Marine Corps in agreeing to enlarge their women's components.

For the WAVES, this personnel need was more on paper than in fact. Their numbers actually decreased during the Vietnam War, and their assignments remained what they had always been: primarily clerical, administrative, and health-care related. In 1966 only twenty of the Navy's seventy enlisted ratings were open to women.[25] There was no repeat of the widespread and innovative use of women's skills that World War II had generated.

One woman's talents were vitally needed, however. The Navy recalled retired commander Grace M. Hopper to active duty in 1967. Hopper, an early pioneer in computer development, had joined the WAVES during World War II and had remained in the Reserve until 1966. The Navy once again needed her expertise in computer programs and languages, so she stayed in the service for another nineteen years and eventually achieved flag rank.[26] A few other women received unusual assignments. Ens. Gale Ann Gordon, an experimental psychologist in the Medical Service Corps, underwent basic air training before working at the Naval Aerospace Medical Institute at Pensacola. In 1966 she became the first woman to solo in a Navy training plane.[27]

In spite of the country's antiwar, antimilitary mood by the late 1960s, women continued to join the WAVES. A recruiting conference in May 1967 had ruled against new incentives to attract more young women, but they came anyway and for a variety of reasons. Naval personnel surveys and an informal query at the Newport Naval Base revealed such motivations as the chance to do something different, to learn about the world, to meet more people, and to further an education. One officer found that there were far better career opportunities in her field of dietetics in the Navy.[28]

## The Vietnam Era: The Navy Nurse Corps

The Bureau of Medicine and Surgery also responded to wartime needs. Although the bureau's mission and organization remained unchanged, it grew rapidly. Under the guidance of the Surgeons General Rear Adm. Edward C. Kenney (1961–65) and Vice Adm. Robert B. Brown (1965–69), the Medical Corps grew in personnel from 3,312 to 4,777 between 1960 and 1969; the Dental Corps increased from 1,544 to 1,914. At the same time, the Medical Service Corps expanded from 1,031 to 1,636 personnel, while the Hospital Corps grew from 23,299 to 32,238.[29]

The Navy Nurse Corps had active and important roles in the new conflict. Never reluctant to send nurses into combat areas, the Navy assigned its nurses to hospital ships and to hospitals and other facilities on shore. To meet the emergency, the corps expanded from 2,050 in July 1963 to a high of 2,338 in September 1968 (falling back to 2,050 by June 1970).[30]

Like all of American society in the tumultuous 1960s, the Nurse Corps underwent vast "sea changes" that began transforming the very makeup of the corps. The "Three M's"—males, minorities, and marriage—brought a new look to the organization.[31]

## *Changes in Leadership*

The Nurse Corps was fortunate in its two directors during these difficult years. Ruth Alice Erickson assumed the post in April 1962. A native of Minnesota, she was born in 1913 and graduated from the Methodist Kahler School of Nursing, Rochester, in 1934 and joined the Navy Nurse Corps two years later. Her exciting career included duty in the hospital ship *Relief,* then witnessing the Japanese attack on Pearl Harbor on 7 December 1941. She served at a variety of naval hospitals, then in the hospital ship *Haven* when it started bringing prisoners of war home from Japan in September 1945. Progressively assuming more demanding billets, Erickson had duty as nursing supervisor, senior nurse, assistant chief of nursing service in various naval hospitals, Nurse Corps representative in the Twelfth Naval District and in the Military Sea Transport Service in Seattle. After serving as personnel officer for the corps at the Bureau of Medicine and Surgery, she attended Indiana University and received a degree in nursing education in 1953. Afterward, she was chief of nursing service at three major naval hospitals. Erickson became director of the Navy Nurse Corps on 30 April 1962 and brought twenty-six years of diverse experience to her challenging job.[32]

Veronica M. Bulshefski replaced Erickson as director on 29 April 1966. This Pennsylvania native was born in 1916 and graduated from the Hospital School of Nursing, University of Pennsylvania, in 1937. She received a bachelor's degree in nursing education from Indiana University in 1956 and a master's degree in management from the Naval Postgraduate School at Monterey in 1962. Bulshefski joined the Nurse Corps in 1940 and served at Pearl Harbor and Aiea Heights, Hawaii, during the war. Later, she was chief of nursing service at several naval hospitals, including Guam.[33]

## *Meeting the Needs*

Both directors had to deal with the chronic shortage of nurses and tried various incentives to attract more women. First came an ad hoc panel in 1960–61 to review corps requirements and functions. It considered making the best use of nurses by relieving them of tasks that others could handle: using Hospital Corps WAVES to "stand by" during physical examinations of females, having Medical Service Corps officers deal with administrative duties, employing civilian nurses and ward attendants, and directing senior hospital corpsmen to help with ward administration.[34] Captain Erickson later called a three-day Navy Nurse Corps Directors' Conference at which the chiefs of nursing service of all continental naval hospitals considered these same problems.[35]

The Navy's shortage of nurses reflected a nationwide situation, which had reached dangerous proportions. The federal government stepped in and approved the Nurse Training Act of 1964, which provided $283 million for five years to fund construction of nursing schools and for student loans and scholarships.[36] The following year, the prestigious American Nursing Association adopted a position paper that strongly supported nursing education leading to a college degree rather than a hospital diploma.[37]

To keep in step with civilian nursing opportunities, the Nurse Corps expanded its education programs. Captain Erickson pushed hard for such expansion as soon as she became director by presenting a paper on in-service nursing education at the Naval Medical School in 1962. The following year the Nurse Corps Candidate Program broadened to cover expenses for the junior year in college. The Nursing Research Branch, established at the Medical School in 1960, became a division of the Behavioral Sciences Department five years later. In 1962 an anesthesia program for nurses was introduced at the National Naval Medical Center, Bethesda, in conjunction with George Washington University. Other naval hospitals began offering specialty courses in operating room and orthopedic nursing in 1968.[38]

Navy nurses pioneered in another new field: hyperbaric nursing, using oxygen at high pressures to treat a variety of injuries and diseases. Four Navy nurses completed the first course in hyperbaric nursing at the School of Submarine Medicine, New London, in 1967.[39]

These opportunities still did not attract enough nurses to naval service.[40] In desperation, Surgeon General Brown requested a special selective service call for two hundred registered nurses for the Navy, but nothing came of it. The surgeon general's request probably stemmed from a National Advisory Commission on Selective Service report in 1967 that recommended drafting doctors and dentists but not nurses.[41]

Finally, as a last resort, the Navy did the unthinkable: it allowed male nurses to enter the Nurse Corps. Men had been trying to join since 1942.[42] Congress had authorized their admission to military nurse corps in 1955, and the Army and Air Force Nurse Corps quickly welcomed them. It was not until November 1964, however, that Secretary of the Navy Paul H. Nitze revised requirements for entry into the Navy Nurse Corps to include men.[43] Men were also eligible for the Navy Nurse Corps Candidate program.

Director Erickson was instrumental in bringing about the momentous change. A young man, trained as a nurse, had called on her, expressing his wish to become a Navy nurse. Erickson talked with Surgeon General Edward C. Kenney, pointing out the inconsistency of appealing for nurses and yet rejecting a large pool of male volunteers.[44] That trailblazing young man who called on the director was former hospital corpsman George M. Silver, who had specialized in psychiatric nursing at a civilian nursing school. In August 1965 he received a commission as ensign, Nurse Corps, Naval Reserve. Four more male nurses soon joined the corps, and the five men attended indoctrination classes with line officers at Newport.[45] All entering males were assigned to the Reserves until 1968, when the first officer, Lt. Clarence W. Cote, was augmented to the regular Nurse Corps.[46] Between 1965 and 1972, 379 men served in the Nurse Corps, with their numbers averaging about 168 a year by 1970–71.[47]

In these early years, some resistance to and resentment of male nurses surfaced, recalled two female nurses who later became directors of the corps. At first, older nurses and some physicians viewed male nurses with suspicion. Later, opposition came from senior line officers and Marine Corps officers. As the men quickly proved themselves, resistance faded.[48]

The Nurse Corps's utilization of males paralleled, in reverse, the Navy's own means of buttressing inadequate personnel by admitting women when it established the Nurse Corps itself, the yeomen (F) positions, and the WAVES. Admitting men was a major transition; no longer did "nurse" equate with "female."

## *Humanitarian Aid*

During the 1960s, the Nurse Corps carried on its tradition of rendering aid in civilian disasters. The fall of 1961 was a busy season for hurricanes, and twice Navy nurses helped with relief missions. On 12 September Hurricane Carla buffeted Texas, causing widespread damage and killing at least fifteen people. The Navy dispatched two aircraft carriers, the *Shangri-La* (CVA 38) and *Antietam* (CVS 36), each carrying two Nurse Corps women, to help alleviate suffering from injuries and illness. These nurses also had the distinction of being the first women assigned to combatant ships.[49] On 1 November, Hurricane Hattie battered British Honduras and killed at least one hundred people. Again, the Navy sent *Antietam* on a relief mission, this time with four Navy nurses onboard. In addition to providing emergency treatment ashore, nurses immunized thousands of natives against typhoid.[50]

Two other nurses were part of a naval medical mission to Honduras in June 1962 to combat an epidemic of gastroenteritis. Serving for two weeks in San Pedro Sula, they worked with medical teams trying to curb the epidemic.[51] In October of that year, during the Cuban missile crisis, Navy nurses helped evacuate dependents from the Naval Base, Guantanamo, to the transport *Upshur* (T-AP 198). One nurse even promised a heartbroken child that she would take care of his cat while he was gone.[52]

## Service in the Combat Area

### *The WAVES*

Of the women actually sent to Vietnam, the WAVES were only a token force. The Army began sending WACs to Vietnam in 1966; eventually, about five hundred were there. Women Marines started coming in March 1967, and by war's end thirty-six had served in the combat area. That same year the Air Force dispatched the first WAFs to Vietnam, and by the end of American involvement, between five and six hundred WAFs had seen duty in Vietnam and neighboring Thailand.[53]

As early as 1965, WAVES officers volunteered to serve in Vietnam, but the Navy steadfastly rejected them.[54] Apparently, neither conservative WAVES director Lenihan nor the chief of naval personnel, Vice Adm. Benedict J. Semmes Jr., was receptive to the idea, in spite of women of the other services and nurses of all services being stationed there. Such duty for WAVES was not "appropriate." For whatever reason, Lenihan relented in early 1967, allowing one Wave to go to Saigon in June.

Carefully chosen to personify the best among Navy women, Lt. Elizabeth

G. Wylie brought excellent credentials to her Vietnam assignment. A graduate of Dickinson College, she was also the daughter of Rear Adm. Joseph C. Wylie, deputy commander in chief, U.S. Naval Forces, Europe. After entering the Navy in 1961, she served at posts in the United States and abroad.[55] In Saigon, Wylie impressed her boss, Rear Adm. Kenneth L. Veth, commander, Naval Forces, Vietnam, who wrote that he could use more well-qualified WAVES.[56] She kept Lenihan informed of her work in the Command Information Center and reassured the director that military women in Saigon acted and dressed "discreetly and with propriety." "The WAVES," she continued, "can make much headway in breaking down the barriers of prejudice that still exist within the Navy by sending their sharpest and most capable women volunteers to Saigon."[57]

Other volunteers were slow to go to Vietnam; nine officers and no enlisted served in that country. The Navy had devised a policy that only those WAVES officers requested by name by a commanding officer could go to Vietnam. In February 1968 Lt. Sally L. Bostwick reported for duty as a resources management analyst, and Lt. Susan F. Hamilton came onboard as assistant historian.[58] Others gradually arrived in Saigon: Lt. Cdr. Barbara Bole, Cdr. Carol Adsit, Cdr. Elizabeth Barrett, and Lt. (jg) Kathleen Dugan, all on the commander, Naval Forces, Vietnam staff. Later, Lts. Mary Anderson and Ann Moriarty served at the naval support activity in Cam Ranh Bay.[59] Moriarty, the first female naval adviser in Vietnam, had the unusual task of helping Vietnamese Navy dependents set up barber shops and sewing centers, thereby gaining some independence.[60]

One retired officer did not find WAVES' lack of participation in Vietnam surprising. Women filled predominately clerical or administrative jobs until the early 1970s, recalled Capt. Jo Ann S. Watkins. "The women were not necessarily protected," she said. "The jobs just were not there."[61] In contrast, others believed that enlisted WAVES could have readily filled assorted billets in headquarters, Saigon.

## *The Navy Nurse Corps*

Although reluctant to assign WAVES to Vietnam, the Navy never hesitated to dispatch nurses to the war zone. When American participation in the war began increasing rapidly during 1963, Navy nurses arrived in Saigon in March. They worked in a small dispensary until the Fitzgibbons bachelor enlisted quarters was converted into the seventy-two-bed Saigon Station Hospital later that year. An outpatient clinic operated out of the Metropole Hotel.[62]

Between March 1963 and April 1966, when the Army took over the hospital, twenty-three Navy nurses served in Saigon. These women, under Chief of Nursing Service Cdr. Aline E. Morin, provided medical service to the military and civilian officials and their dependents and functioned as a public health service.[63] They came under Vietcong attack, and four sustained injuries when terrorists bombed the Brink bachelor officer quarters on Christmas Eve 1964. They later were awarded the Purple Heart, the first military women to receive that medal during the Vietnam War.[64]

Other Navy nurses in the war-torn country were sent to Rach Gia on the west coast. In March 1965, two nurses who were part of a Navy Surgical Team on loan to the Agency for International Development (AID) reached Rach Gia. In addition to operating room nurses, the team consisted of two surgeons, a nurse anesthetist (Air Force), a laboratory and X-ray technician, and an Army administrative officer. Charged with training surgical nurses at the Rach Gia Provincial Hospital, the Navy nurses soon organized the nursing service there. Once again, Navy nurses helped locals help themselves. From the hospital, members of the surgical team often made forays into the bush, taking medical care to isolated villages.[65] Between March 1965 and August 1966, eight Navy nurses served with the AID surgical team, and one, Cdr. Ruth M. Pojeky, received the Navy Commendation Medal for her work.[66]

Navy nurses served at stations other than hospitals in Vietnam, and male nurses were exclusively stationed at several. Three male Navy nurses served with Marine Corps divisions; seven others had duty with the commander, Amphibious Force, Western Pacific. Additionally, seven male nurses were at the Military Assistance Command, Saigon.[67] Any resentment from hospital corpsmen toward male nurses usually was directed at those who had been former hospital corpsmen and tried to remain too friendly with their former peers.[68]

By far the largest number of nurses served at the Naval Support Activity Hospital, Danang. Established in 1965, the station hospital grew from sixty to six hundred beds with a staff of more than six hundred doctors, dentists, nurses, and corpsmen.[69] One male nurse, Lt. (jg) Nicholas J. Kachur, an anesthetist, had arrived at the hospital in October 1966.[70] Female nurses had to wait for completion of quarters at Danang. The first four women nurses, led by the chief of nursing service, Cdr. Mary F. Cannon, reached Danang in August 1967. More nurses arrived in subsequent months until the full complement of thirty-four nurses was in place. Ninety-five Navy nurses eventually had duty in Danang before the hospital was decommissioned in May 1970.[71]

Commander Cannon kept the director regularly informed of the nurses' activities in Danang. She soon noticed a recurring problem: hostility toward the nurses from hospital corpsmen, who felt a usurpation of responsibility and status. Two nurses, later directors of the corps, explained the resentment. Hospital corpsmen, who had always served in the field and on training exercises, had set up the hospital in Danang, and it had been running smoothly. They believed they could do very well without female nurses. Furthermore, male corpsmen looked upon nurses as mother figures. It was difficult for them to take orders from women, especially in a war zone.[72] The passage of time and the corpsmen's added maturity eased tensions.

Supportive of her nurses, Captain Bulshefski answered all Cannon's numerous letters.[73] After a year's duty at Danang, the original group was replaced by newly assigned nurses led by Cdr. Helen L. Brooks, chief of nursing service. While directing nursing care at the hospital, Brooks continued corresponding with Bulshefski.[74]

These nurses contended with the busy schedule of attending the wounded and ill. War injuries, often complicated by infections, were predominately caused by shrapnel, fragmentation devices, mines, and booby traps; illnesses included malaria, amebiasis, hepatitis, and helminthiasis (parasitic worms). Helicopter evacuation from the battle scene to the hospital ensured fast medical treatment and the lowest mortality rate of any American war. Of those hospitalized, only 1.5 percent died. Danang Hospital itself cared for more than seventy thousand patients.[75]

A poignant account by Lt. Cdr. Joan Brouillette, a nurse at Danang in 1967–68, captured the emotional and physical stress for nurses in the combat area. Subject to regular Vietcong attacks against the nearby Marine airstrip and in the middle of the Tet Offensive in January 1968, Brouillette cared for most grievously wounded marines and witnessed firsthand the pain and suffering of American forces. Nevertheless, she found her service at Danang "the quintessence of personal fulfillment."[76] Another nurse, Cdr. Anne Steinocher, stationed at Danang in 1969–70, echoed Brouillette's sentiments: "They [the patients] came so quickly, like an avalanche. It was very hard work and the most satisfying nursing experience of my life."[77]

### *Service in Hospital Ships*

Highly visible during the war were the hospital ships *Repose* and *Sanctuary*. Recommissioned in October 1965, *Repose* arrived on line in February 1966 and operated in the area of Danang, Chu Lai, Phu Bai, Dong Ha, and Quang Tri. Under the direction of Cdr. Angelica Vitillo, chief of nursing service, 29 Navy nurses were part of the hospital staff of 24 medical officers, 3 dentists, 2 chaplains, and 250 hospital corpsmen. Nicknamed "Angel of the Orient," the 721-bed hospital treated more than 9,000 casualties and admitted more than 24,000 inpatients before leaving Vietnam in March 1970.[78] At the hub of activity were Navy nurses, and eventually 145 of them served on the ship.[79]

Lt. (jg) Leanna Crosby thrived on such duty. She had joined the Navy, she said, because she could work in her professional field and travel.[80] Years later, two other nurses, Patricia Hildebrand and Roberta J. Grace, reminisced about their shipboard duties: "It called for the best of you or the worst of you. There was so much negative about it, but so much positive."[81]

Soon joining *Repose* in the South China Sea was the hospital ship *Sanctuary*. Modernized, then recommissioned in November 1966, *Sanctuary* arrived at Danang in April 1967 and traveled the same routes off South Vietnam as *Repose*. Her medical staff of 316 included 29 Navy nurses under Cdr. Marcella E. Smith, chief of nursing service.[82] The 750-bed ship stayed off Vietnam until April 1971, treating more than 25,000 patients. Bearing a large burden of attending the injured and sick were her 141 Navy nurses.[83]

It was onboard these ships that the concept of triage was perfected. Mass casualties from high velocity missiles were separated according to the nature and severity of wounds as victims came onboard. Nurse Frances Shea, later to become director of the Nurse Corps, vividly described the procedure on the *Repose*. The walking wounded went to the wards where they were treated.

More severely wounded were triaged (categorized) by the seriousness of their injuries and sent to the operating room in order of medical urgency. Chest and abdominal wounds came first, potential amputees and head wounds next. More often than not, however, soldiers had multiple wounds that required simultaneous treatment. Shea called her year in *Repose* the highlight of her career. "It is what Navy nursing is all about," she said.[84]

Other Navy nurses saw duty in the Military Sea Transportation Service, Pacific, which had carried dependents until the mid-1960s, then transported troops and supplies to Vietnam. Between 1965 and mid-1966, sixteen nurses served in these ships.[85]

Finally, the longest of American wars began to wind down, although there was no peace agreement until 1973. Navy nurses left the region and returned to peacetime assignments. Their valor earned them an assortment of medals and awards: four received the Purple Heart; five, the Navy Commendation Medal; one, the Secretary of the Navy's Commendation for Achievement; and two, the Vietnamese Medal of Honor.[86]

## WAVES and Navy Nurses: Shared Experiences

Although WAVES and Navy nurses were worlds apart in their duties, their experiences in other areas were similar. The impasse in promotion to upper ranks affected both groups. A major breakthrough occurred in 1967 with passage of the act removing percentage restrictions on women's ranks and permitting permanent rather than temporary ranks of captains in the Navy or colonels in the other services. The act authorized but did not mandate flag rank for the Navy or star rank for the other services.[87] With a great flourish, President Johnson signed the act in the East Room of the White House with women representatives of all the services present.[88] In 1968 six WAVES commanders became captains, and Director Rita Lenihan's temporary rank became permanent. The next year, eight more commanders rose to captain. Flag rank for the Navy's women had to wait.[89]

The nurses, also, had been trying for years to ease the restrictions on rank. In 1957 Congress had raised the number of commanders and captains allowed, and four years later Director Ruth Houghton argued persuasively for 1 percent of corps strength as captains and 10 percent as commanders. The director should hold flag rank, she asserted.[90] Nothing came of her proposals until 1966, when three nurses other than the director were temporary captains—Alice Reilly, Burdette Blaska, and C. Edwina Todd—chiefs of nursing service at St. Albans, Great Lakes, and Portsmouth, Virginia, respectively. A year after the legislation of 1967 removed the percentage freezes on ranks and permitted women to hold the permanent rank of captain, CNO Adm. Thomas H. Moorer authorized the Nurse Corps's request for 21 captains and 162 commanders.[91]

Along with the opening of higher ranks came increased pay for officers and enlisted. In 1960, a captain's pay began at $592.80 a month; a commander's, $474.24; a lieutenant's, $326.04; and an ensign's, $222.30. Ten years later, these basic salaries had risen to $894.60 for captains, $715.50 for commanders, and $386.40 for ensigns. Enlisted compensation increased as well, with pay going from $78 to $115.20 for seamen recruits, and from $206.39 to $342.30 for chief petty officers. Quarters allowances ranged from $60 to $160.20, and subsistence was a flat $47.88.[92]

Rules for dependents remained in force. Male nurses, however, had always been allowed to marry and have dependents. The Nurse Corps began granting waivers to permit female nurses to marry and have minor children in the home, remembered Rear Adm. Mary F. Hall, who married in 1964. There was still no colocation policy if both husband and wife were in the Navy.[93]

After WAVES and Navy nurses agreed on identical uniforms in 1950, few basic changes followed—an evening dress uniform and in 1959 a light blue service uniform for warm weather. WAVES director Captain Quick had a hand in bringing about the change to light blue from gray seersucker which, she said, looked like a mattress cover. Wanting her WAVES to look sharp, she also designed two new uniforms and more feminine slacks. She introduced pumps with two-and-a-half-inch heels and new hat covers.[94]

By the time the 1960s ended, Navy women had solidified their preexisting status: the WAVES as young ladies whose presence was merely tolerated and the Navy nurses as useful practitioners of healing arts at home and in the war zone.

The decade of domestic turmoil had made military service less desirable for many women. Under Directors Sanders and Lenihan, the WAVES fought off attempts to substitute civil service workers for enlisted women, whose turnover rates remained high. Officers benefited from Congress's removing rank restrictions and allowing the permanent rank of captain. The door also cracked for attaining flag rank.

As far as active participation in the Vietnam War, women remained in their customary supporting billets. Only nine carefully chosen WAVES officers actually served in Vietnam. The Vietnam War, then, represented no turning point in advancing Navy women. It was, at best, a cautious acknowledgment that WAVES could serve in a combat area without great harm to themselves or to their ladylike image.

The Nurse Corps, on the other hand, served in a variety of posts at home and abroad. Captains Erickson and Bulshefski, both experienced, no-nonsense nurses, worked doggedly to attract and retain nurses for the corps during a nationwide shortage of trained nurses. Finally, the corps admitted males to their previously segregated ranks.

Navy nurses helped during civilian disasters and served in naval hospitals in the United States and overseas. They continued their mission of training hospital corpsmen. Of greater impact was the contribution Navy nurses made to the war in Vietnam. They had duty in Saigon, Rach Gia, Danang, and several other commands. More were in the hospital ships *Repose* and *Sanctuary* while these floating hospitals took on wounded directly from the battlefield.

As the decade ended, the dichotomy between WAVES and Navy nurses remained. Perhaps nurses, whose duties were nurturing and life-sustaining, fit into acceptable roles of appropriate female behavior. They were in no position to challenge the hierarchy of the Medical Department, run by male physicians. The WAVES, on the other hand, filled their traditional billets ashore, releasing men to go to war.

Events in the next ten years would offer expanded opportunities for women in the Navy as well as in all of American society. It would be an exciting era filled with promise and hope.

# 10

# Widening Horizons in the 1970s

*Rapid and wide-sweeping social changes* characterized American society during the 1970s, and women demanded—and received—a more equitable place in that society. Using techniques ranging from demonstrations to legislation to Supreme Court decisions to class action lawsuits, a new brand of feminism propelled many women into ways of life that had been previously dominated by men. Navy women were beneficiaries of some of these philosophical and social upheavals, and their horizons and opportunities broadened to match those of their civilian sisters.

## The Setting

After the turmoil and confrontations of the 1960s, women did not revert to another round of domesticity. So often in the past, an era of upheaval meant a subsequent return to the familiar safety of the home and nest and to the accustomed role of wife-mother-companion.

Instead, a new and noisier form of feminism emphasized woman as person. Dissidents split away from the National Organization for Women (NOW), and in 1970 the Women's Strike for Equality, the largest demonstration ever for women's rights, ushered in a more radical brand of feminism: the women's liberation movement. Women had learned techniques from the civil rights movement and organized themselves around consciousness-raising groups, and "women's libbers" became activists who led the fight for legislative, judicial, and cultural changes.[1] Nurses were active in NOW, and one, Wilma Scott Heide, became president of the organization. There was also a separate nurses' NOW.[2]

A spate of legislation in 1972 began to meet the needs of a generation demanding equality. The Senate approved the equal rights amendment in

March, forty-nine years after its introduction, and rapid ratification by thirty-three states seemed to guarantee that "equality of rights . . . [would] not be denied or abridged . . . on account of sex." Title IX of the Higher Education Act mandated women's inclusion in programs and activities, including sports, at colleges receiving federal funds. The Equal Opportunity Act gave more power to the Equal Employment Opportunity Commission to enforce nondiscriminatory laws. In addition, Congress allowed working married couples tax deductions for child-care expenses.[3] These new laws opened an era of governmental affirmative action to redress longstanding grievances of both women and minorities.

The Supreme Court's decision in *Roe v. Wade* in 1973 represented another victory for equality. The court legalized abortion in the first trimester, thus giving women control over their own reproductive systems. The court even struck down laws that denied military women equal benefits and rights.[4] Women seemed to reach the zenith of their newfound freedom and power in 1975, which, by presidential proclamation, was dubbed the International Women's Year.[5]

The new breed of feminists advocated other far-reaching changes in American culture: open marriage; childcare facilities; an equal distribution of household responsibilities; the sexual revolution; equalized education and employment opportunities; changes in marriage, divorce, and rape laws; and an end to discrimination against lesbians.[6]

The ideas of the women's movement found fertile ground on college campuses, while women's enrollment swelled from 3,507,163 in 1970 to 5,155,000 by 1980, when women made up 50 percent of all college students. More women took graduate degrees, and by the end of the decade, they comprised 23 percent of medical students and 28.5 percent of law students.[7] College women dominated in leading the feminists, and the movement was, as in earlier times, mainly white and middle class.

College women of the 1970s did not embrace the same goals as their mothers had and were in no rush to submerge themselves in domesticity. Their average age of marriage rose from 20.8 years in 1970 to 22 years in 1980. At the same time, divorce rates soared to 50 percent. Women postponed having children, and the birthrate plummeted.[8] In only twenty years, the vision of domestic bliss in suburbia had crumbled.

During the 1970s, women's participation in the work force continued its post–World War II upward trend. Driven by economic necessity (inflation hit 14 percent a year in 1979), fully 50 percent of adult women, including mothers of small children, worked outside the home. Although women made strong inroads into traditionally male occupations and became lawyers, doctors, accountants, chemists, and college professors, few held management positions in industry; but educated women still dominated the teaching, nursing, social work, and library professions. Most nonprofessional women workers gravitated to their stereotypical jobs as clericals or in the services industry. Women continued to earn only 59 percent of the pay that men received for comparable work.[9]

All these changes in women's place in America did not go unchallenged, and an ultraconservative backlash soon targeted the equal rights amendment as the manifestation of evil. Leaders such as Phyllis Schlafly and Jerry Falwell championed homemakers and family values in the total woman movement, which never garnered mainstream support.[10] These opponents, however, contributed significantly to the ultimate defeat of ERA: by 1982 only thirty-five of the necessary thirty-eight states had ratified the amendment.

As women struggled to achieve a more equitable position in American society, the Navy, too, underwent years of upheaval, ultimately assuming a new look. The long Vietnam War had drained naval resources to a dangerous level, even after the withdrawal of American forces and war's end in 1973. During the late 1960s, a diversion of defense spending from naval building to combat operations in Vietnam had left the dwindling fleet outmoded. In June 1970 there had been 743 active duty ships, but nine years later there were only 533.[11]

Simultaneously, the end of the draft in 1973 posed different problems for the Navy. Conscription had kept the ranks filled, but now where would the necessary personnel come from? First-term reenlistments were at a rate of less than 10 percent. There had been 692,660 men and women on active duty in June 1970; there were 588,043 two years later and 524,514 in 1979. Of necessity, the Navy, as well as the other services, relied on an all-volunteer force. Among the many unknowns of such a shift in procurement was women's place in the new military.[12]

Guiding the Navy from 1970 to 1974 was CNO Adm. Elmo R. Zumwalt Jr., who undertook to modernize both the fleet and personnel policies.[13]

Next came Adm. James L. Holloway III, who held the top spot from 1974 until 1978. During these years, defense spending cuts, inflation, and the 1973 Arab oil embargo caused the two CNOs to hasten to maintain the slim margin of American superiority over the expanding Soviet navy. Zumwalt even questioned whether the Navy could win in a confrontation with the Soviet Union.[14]

In spite of the country's curtailed shipbuilding program, the Navy developed an arsenal of highly sophisticated hardware. The Aegis weapons system would soon shield the fleet from incoming missiles, while an array of naval missiles—Talos, Terrier, Tarter, Standard SM-1 and SM-2, Sea Sparrow, Harpoon, and Tomahawk—would better arm warships.[15]

After American withdrawal from Vietnam, the Navy, fortunately, had no wars to fight for the remainder of the decade. There were incidents, such as the Cambodian seizure of the American container ship *Mayaguez* in 1975, but no major engagements.[16] The Navy continued displaying its presence around the world. The Sixth Fleet in the Mediterranean was especially important during the Yom Kippur War in 1973; the Seventh Fleet in the Pacific evacuated Americans and South Vietnamese from Saigon in 1975; the Atlantic Fleet concentrated on means to keep the sea lanes open. By the end of the decade, the Navy maintained a larger force in the Indian Ocean and took on responsibility for defending the oil-rich Persian Gulf.[17]

Altogether, the 1970s were difficult times for the Navy, years fraught with uncertainty and change. The Navy had to deal with the rapidly growing Soviet naval capability, a curtailed shipbuilding program, severely pared budgets, racial discord, and rampant drug and alcohol abuse. In addition, the composition of its personnel changed. Of necessity, the Navy found new ways to employ women as well as other minorities to circumvent the shortcomings of a smaller force.

## Navy Women

### *The End of the WAVES and Z-116*

As CNO, Admiral Zumwalt fully recognized that an all-volunteer force would not produce sufficient personnel to staff the Navy. And he anticipated quick ratification of the equal rights amendment, which could force all the services to expand women's roles.[18] It would be far better for the Navy to act before Congress forced the issue or before class-action lawsuits charged sex discrimination. Hoping to build one Navy with no artificial barriers based on race, religion, or sex, Zumwalt introduced his Programs for People, promulgated in a series of directives known as Z-Grams. Part of this program was to eliminate inequities based on sex. In 1971 he appointed two WAVES retention study groups, which documented the wasted talents of naval women. Zumwalt was, he wrote, "sadly enlightened" by the groups' reports.[19]

Before Zumwalt took any action, a new WAVES director, Capt. Robin Lindsay Quigley, replaced Capt. Rita Lenihan in January 1971. Born in 1929 in Arizona, Quigley graduated from Dominican College, San Rafael, California, in 1951 with a major in music and entered the Navy three years later. After filling billets of progressively more responsibility, she was the youngest to become assistant chief of naval personnel for women and the only one who had not entered the Navy during World War II. Vivacious, attractive, and known for her sense of humor, she seemed ideal for directing the WAVES in the rapidly changing Navy.[20]

But Quigley did not want to direct the WAVES. She strongly believed that women must be accepted as professionals in the Navy and that women must avoid a "forked tongue" approach to their careers: insisting on the one hand that gender have no part in equal professional treatment but claiming on the other that womanhood entitled them to special privileges. Full integration could not occur with women grouped as a separate entity—the WAVES. She slowly but methodically transferred her duties to responsible offices in the Bureau of Naval Personnel and in other appropriate commands and instructed the women's representatives and assistants for women in the field to use regular naval communications and advisory channels rather than go through her office.[21]

In February 1972 Quigley told women to stop using the inaccurate and sentimental acronym "WAVES," which implied a ladies' auxiliary. They were part of the U.S. Navy. Next, she rejected her unofficial title of "director." "I do not *direct* anything," she wrote. Her proper billet was assistant chief of naval personnel for women, and she merely advised on women's matters. In her opinion, this position, too, should end.[22]

Quigley's actions ran afoul of Defense Secretary Melvin R. Laird's opinion that any such change apply to all women's services simultaneously. He withheld his approval to abolish the ACNP(W) billet until early 1973.[23] Taking Quigley's advice, Zumwalt allowed the disestablishment of the WAVES. He later reflected that the move might have been precipitate and that four or five years later would have been better timing.[24] Quigley was detached on 20 March, the same day the ACNP(W) billet was disestablished. An era had ended, and with it the support structure for Navy women. Quigley next became commanding officer, Naval Schools Command, San Diego, then retired from the Navy in 1974.[25] The other services were slower to disestablish their women's branches: the WAF in 1976, the Women Marines in 1977, and the WAC in 1978.[26]

Meanwhile, the CNO dropped another bombshell in August 1972. The month before, he had convened a committee to study existing laws and regulations that discriminated against Navy women and to draft revisions of them. Quigley did not attend the committee meetings, instead dispatching her deputy, Capt. Fran McKee.[27] The committee worked feverishly—"It was a busy and exciting experience," McKee later recalled—and within weeks recommended wide-sweeping changes for women in the Navy.[28]

Adopting the committee's recommendations, Zumwalt issued the famous (or infamous) Z-116 on 7 August, giving equal rights and opportunities to Navy women. Fully expecting ratification of the ERA, Zumwalt authorized preliminary actions that would eventually lead to sending women to service at sea. The Navy would take immediate steps toward equality by assigning women to the ship's company in the hospital ship *Sanctuary* in a pilot program, by allowing enlisted women limited entry into nearly all ratings, by permitting women officers to exercise command ashore, by opening NROTC college programs to women, and by considering women for joint service colleges. In addition, the Navy would open the Chaplain and Civil Engineer Corps to women, provide avenues for progression to flag rank, and assign women to more challenging billets.[29] By inference, these wide-ranging opportunities opened the aviation field as well. Reaction was instantaneous, and Zumwalt held a news conference on 8 August, fielding questions on this new twist to his one-Navy vision.[30] More changes followed. The one that met the most resistance from many old-timers was Zumwalt's October directive that proposed opening the U.S. Naval Academy to women.[31] It took Congress three years to mandate such a change.

Zumwalt and Quigley agreed on the major premise of more opportunities for Navy women but disagreed on the means for attaining them. Quigley, for example, opposed women at sea, in aviation billets, or at the Naval Academy.[32] In spite of her youth and exposure to the feminist movement, she remained essentially conservative. It took Zumwalt's bold leadership to propel far-reaching changes. Her disagreements with Zumwalt and her impasse with Secretary of Defense Laird made her position as senior Navy woman in Washington untenable.

### *An Administrative Vacuum, then Restructuring*

Fortunately, Capt. Fran McKee, now deputy assistant chief of naval personnel for human goals, was on hand to carry out many of Quigley's former duties. Born in 1926, McKee graduated in 1950 from the University of Alabama with a degree in chemistry, receiving her commission as an ensign in December. Her assignments included the Navy Postgraduate School, Monterey, two overseas posts, and officer in charge of the Women Officers School at Newport. In 1969 she was one of the first two women to attend the regular curriculum at the Naval War College, Newport. The following year, she earned a master's degree in international affairs at George Washington University. In 1972 she was the senior Navy woman on the CNO's committee to study equal rights for women. McKee served only a few months after Quigley left in March 1973 and then became commanding officer of the Naval Security Group Activity at Fort Meade, Maryland.[33]

The new chief of naval operations, Adm. James L. Holloway III (1974–78), vowed to continue the advancement toward equal opportunities begun by Zumwalt. Affirmative action would give women a larger role through inclusive and proactive policies, and Holloway called for amending restrictive laws that prohibited duty in all combatant ships or aircraft. This would give the Navy more flexibility in assigning women.[34]

Meanwhile, with no strong hand at the helm to monitor women's affairs, policies for women bounced from one office to another. In practice, the dissolution of the WAVES was a top-down event and, according to one

Women's Representative, had little impact in the field.[35] In 1974 the Equal Opportunity Branch for Women and another billet to oversee enlisted women's assignments provided some help. The next year the chief of naval personnel set up a senior advisory board (Equal Opportunity for Women) to identify policy issues and to study the integration of Navy women into the bureau's structure. This group became the CNO's Advisory Board on Women's Plans and Policy in 1977 and shifted emphasis to accessions and utilization. The new board worked under the direction of Capt. Paul Butcher.[36] In a reorganization of the bureau in 1979, the board was dissolved. At the same time, other boards and billets had tried to fill the void.[37]

High-ranking women officers recognized the need for a means of bringing women's problems to the chief of naval personnel's attention, and they urged establishment of a billet for this purpose.[38] In 1979 the new billet, Special Assistant for Women's Policy (OP-01[W]), first held by Capt. Maria S. Higgins, provided a single office to oversee policies on women and to advise the chief of naval personnel. It was an updated version of the dismantled assistant chief of naval personnel for women slot.[39] Perhaps it was an indication that full integration of women into the Navy had not occurred, but the new OP-01(W) could focus attention on women's place in the service.

## *Women Who Joined the Navy*

As debates over guidance and supervision of Navy women continued throughout the 1970s, the number of women in naval service rose rapidly. In June 1970, there were 6,633 women (excluding nurses) on active duty, .95 percent of total personnel. By September 1979, 24,644 women comprised 4.7 percent of all naval strength. Women came from every state, California providing the most, followed by New York, Pennsylvania, and Texas.[40]

The ethnic composition of Navy women changed as well. Before 1970, most were white, but with the push for equal racial opportunities, more minorities entered the service. By 1979, 91 percent of officers were white, 4 percent were black, and 4.7 percent were Hispanic or members of other ethnic groups. A larger change came among enlisted, with 83 percent white, 12.8 percent black, and 4 percent Hispanic or others.[41]

Standards for Navy women remained higher than those for men. Enlisted women had to be between eighteen and twenty-six years of age, hold a high school diploma or equivalent, and have a clean police record. Potential officers had to be between twenty and twenty-seven and a half, college graduates, and of good character. All had to meet naval physical and mental standards and be U.S. citizens. They could be single or married but could have no dependents under age eighteen.[42]

Feeding into the Navy's recruiting of women was the sex-based affirmative action quota system, set up by the Department of Defense in 1970. Propelled not only by the ERA, which seemed certain of ratification, but also by the Equal Employment Opportunity Act of 1971, the Navy searched for ways to end discrimination in recruiting women—before the courts decided the issues.[43] By 1979, it had revised its recruiting policy to attract more minorities and to provide more upward mobility through skills schools. These minorities, of course, included women.[44]

Naval service attracted women for sundry reasons. The majority (62 percent) wanted new skills to improve their employment prospects; others hoped to travel and meet new people or to perform work that was important enough to make the world a better place. Still others sought opportunities for education. These were conservative motivations in an age of renewed feminism.[45] Less important were the quest for adventure and the patriotic impulses of the yeomen (F) and the WAVES of World War II. The possibilities for WAVES were changing perceptibly from an expandable nucleus to viable careers, and CNO Zumwalt believed that women, like men, wanted to be where the action was.[46]

## *Officers' Education and Training*

Women entering the Navy underwent training for their new roles; and here, too, the mood of the 1970s for equal opportunity affected the process. Female officer candidates attended the sixteen-week indoctrination course at the Women Officers School at Newport. In late 1972 the Navy merged men's and women's orientation schools, and the first mixed class graduated from Officer Candidate School the following November.[47] Women officers were eligible to attend naval postgraduate schools such as the Naval War College at Newport and the General Line School at Monterey.

Next came limited admission to the Naval Reserve Officer Training Corps (NROTC). Even before Z-116 came out, Zumwalt and Secretary of the Navy John H. Chafee had announced, in February 1972, the opening of pilot NROTC scholarship programs for high school seniors entering four universities—Jacksonville in Florida, Purdue in Indiana, Southern University and A&M in Louisiana, and Washington in Seattle. The first year the Navy would accept sixteen women, then gradually grant scholarships to sixty women on all campuses with NROTC programs. In return, women were to serve for four years after graduation and commissioning. The next year, the opportunity expanded to include the two-year contract program for women already in college. These female midshipmen were barred from summer cruises because the law precluded sea duty.[48] A comparable program extended to female high school students in 1972–73, when they could join Navy junior ROTC units, which opened on 223 campuses within the year.[49] Director Quigley disapproved. The Navy did not need women from any NROTC unit, she said, because it got enough women through the Officer Candidate Program.[50]

Finally, the last bastion of male exclusivity toppled, and women began attending the Naval Academy and the other service academies in 1976. It had been a long struggle, which had begun in September 1971, when Sen. Jacob K. Javits (D-N.Y.) wanted to nominate a young woman for appointment to the academy. Quigley was one of the first to disapprove of such a radical departure. Rebuffed by Chafee, Javits and Rep. Jack MacDonald (R-Mich.) nominated two young women in 1972, who were rejected by the academy.[51] Javits promptly submitted a resolution, which the Senate passed but the House did not, that no one should be denied admission solely because of sex.[52] Service personnel representatives met at Quantico in November 1972 and agreed to present a united front if Congress pressed the issue. They would focus on the combat exclusion laws as making women's attendance unnecessary.[53]

Further complicating the issue were lawsuits charging discrimination filed by two women and four congressmen in September 1973 against both the Navy and the Air Force. That same year, the House considered a bill to admit women to the academies. At hearings before the Armed Services Committee, the services argued that they attracted enough educated women, that the academies trained officers for combat, and that women would lower standards. Congress, however, opted for equal access to education and downplayed combat preparation. In 1975 it directed the three service academies to admit women to the classes entering the next year. The Merchant Marine Academy had already begun admitting women, and the Coast Guard Academy made similar plans.[54]

At the Naval Academy, preparations got under way. Determined to make as few changes as possible to accommodate female midshipmen, academy leaders stressed that women would meet the same entrance requirements and pursue the same studies as men. The only differences would be in modified physical training and in barring women from summer cruises on larger ships. Even the women's uniforms closely resembled those of their male counterparts.[55]

Finally, the long-awaited day arrived, and on 6 July 1976, eighty-one women entered the Naval Academy. After the novelty had worn off, the women settled into the routine. They did well academically, and some excelled as athletes. "The women are doing fine," wrote the academy superintendent, Rear Adm. Kinnaird R. McKee, "every bit as well as the men."[56] When the class of 1980 graduated, fifty-five women received commissions.[57] They had often encountered resentment, insults, and sometimes harassment from their male classmates. Nevertheless, women had succeeded in crossing into the citadel that prepared most of the Navy's highest ranking officers.[58]

### *Enlisted Training*

For Navy enlisted women, the nine-week, soon shortened to seven-week, recruit training introduced them to naval customs and history, ships and aircraft identification, and water safety. And they learned how to drill. Until 1972 women trained at the Recruit Training Command (Women) at Bainbridge, Maryland, and then the activity was moved to Orlando, Florida. At first women trained separately, but this duplication led the Navy to combine male and female training in 1973.[59]

Although Z-116 was supposed to have opened all enlisted ratings to women, such was not actually the case, primarily because of the existing combat-restriction laws and sea-shore rotations for men. Before Z-116, only

24 of the 70 ratings were open to women. Z-116 opened all 70, but soon 15 sea-intensive ratings were again closed. By 1979, 76 of the 102 enlisted ratings were open. Enlisted women, however, still clustered in traditional jobs, and about 75 percent of them were in medical, communications, supply, and administration billets.[60]

Specialized training prepared women for new and traditional ratings, and most recently indoctrinated recruits went to schools in fields such as electronics, communications, storekeeping, disbursing, medical and dental technology, air traffic control, personnel, and data processing. Enlisted women could also apply for commissioned status through any of the college programs offered—Navy Enlisted Scientific Education Program, Navy Enlisted Nursing Education Program, and Navy Enlisted Dietetic Education Program. To encourage minorities to take advantage of these opportunities, the Navy provided preparatory instruction through Project Boost.[61]

## *Expanding Opportunities: Line and Staff Officers*

Most female officers entering the Navy had been in the unrestricted line, that is, they were generalists who could form a nucleus in event of mobilization. A reorganization of the system in 1972 kept the warfare communities (surface, air, and submarine) in the unrestricted line and put women officers in this same group. These women developed their own specialty: administration. As time passed, they received important assignments to diverse shore billets. The more technically skilled women found increased opportunities as restricted line officers and used the knowledge and experience they had acquired from graduate, professional, and technical education.[62]

The staff corps, as well, made use of more trained women. Females had always dominated the Nurse Corps, and during and after World War II, they became members of the Medical, Dental, and Medical Service Corps, the Supply Corps, and the Judge Advocate General Corps. Women had served in the Civil Engineer Corps during the war but not afterward. In 1973 Lt. (jg) Jeri Rigoulot led the women's return to the engineering corps, and by the end of the decade fifteen women were in it.[63]

The Chaplain Corps accepted its first woman officer in 1973 when Lt. (jg)

Florence Dianna Pohlman, a Presbyterian minister, received her commission. Pohlman later recalled the frustrations and difficulties in gaining acceptance from her male colleagues. By 1979 there were four women chaplains.[64]

In the early 1970s, the Navy began sending women to more overseas duty stations, and the trend continued. In addition to long-standing posts—Japan, Guam, Bermuda, the United Kingdom, Morocco, Italy, Germany, Spain, and Puerto Rico—women found themselves at such unusual places as Bahrain; Antarctica; Adak, Alaska; Keflavik, Iceland; and Diego Garcia. By 1980, there were about 575 officers and 6,500 enlisted serving overseas. Kathryn A. Ball, the only single enlisted woman at Adak, was a licensed beautician and the barber on the island. She wished that the men did not get so nervous when she cut their hair. "After all," she said in an interview at the time, "I'm a good barber."[65]

### *On the Seas and in the Air: Stumbling Block Removed*

Blocking the way of women's full integration into the whole Navy was Title 10, section 6015 of the 1948 Armed Services Integration Act prohibiting them from duty in combatant ships and aircraft. They could serve in only hospital ships and transports. In 1974 interior communications electrician Yona Owens applied for an assignment on a survey ship, but the Judge Advocate General disapproved. Two years later, Owens and three other enlisted women filed a class action lawsuit, *Owens v. Brown*, charging the Navy and the Defense Department with discrimination against them and all Navy women. Three female officers soon joined the plaintiffs. In 1978 U.S. District Judge John J. Sirica ruled that section 6015 was unconstitutional because it did not provide equal protection under the law for a whole class of women—Navy women.[66]

Perhaps sensing the inevitability of the decision, the Navy had moved to modify the onerous section 6015, but first it had to define "combat." It took many meetings, memos, and labor hours to reach a definition: combat is "engaging an enemy . . . in armed conflict." The Navy wanted Congress to modify the existing law, which it did in October 1978. Women could now have permanent duty on hospital ships, transports, and similar ships, as well as temporary duty on other vessels when not used for combat. They also could serve as crew members in noncombatant aircraft.[67]

In May 1979 the Defense Department mounted an intensive effort to have section 6015 repealed and with it the statutory restrictions on women's assignments in the Navy and the Air Force. The House Armed Services Committee held hearings in mid-November and heard conflicting military and civilian testimony. Among those vehemently against repeal was Adm. Thomas B. Hayward, chief of naval operations since 1978, who was "strongly opposed to the assignment of women to combatant units."[68]

More hearings in January 1980 revealed deep divisions among military leaders, and Congress took no action.[69] Modified section 6015 remained on the books, and women's full utilization and equal opportunity in the Navy had to wait.

## *Sea Duty*

A key provision of Z-116 was to prepare women for ultimate sea duty and to initiate this change by assigning them to the crew of hospital ship *Sanctuary*. This thirty-month pilot program was to determine if women could handle shipboard tasks usually assigned to men. On 8 September 1972, the first of fifty-three enlisted women came aboard, soon followed by Lt. (jg) Ann Kerr, a line officer; Ens. Rosemary Nelson, a Supply Corps officer; and twelve Nurse Corps officers. After several sea trials, *Sanctuary* sailed on the two-and-a-half-month Project Handclasp mission to Columbia and Haiti. After the first year of working with a mixed crew, the commanding officer concluded that women performed every shipboard duty with the same ease, expertise, and dedication as men. They could serve onboard *Sanctuary* "in perpetuity," he said.[70] Altogether, twenty-three officers and ninety-seven enlisted served in *Sanctuary*, which had a maximum of sixty-nine onboard at any one time. The ship was decommissioned in 1975.[71] There were then no hospital ships or transports on active duty, so women had no ships in which to serve.

Even before the *Sanctuary* pilot program began, one zealous female officer suggested to Quigley that women make up half the crew of eighteenth-century frigate *Constitution*, a restored tourist attraction manned by sailors dressed in period costumes (red and white striped jerseys and patent leather hats). The First Naval District commandant explained to Quigley, who had thought such an assignment was innovative, that only one kind of woman, whose activities were legally and socially frowned upon, had come aboard the ship 175 years earlier.[72]

As 1972 progressed, women began to serve in small naval vessels. The judge advocate general had stretched the interpretation of section 6015 that barred women from all ships except hospital ships and transports to allow them in any inshore craft that transported personnel within a harbor.[73] Late that year, eleven enlisted women began serving in the yard patrol craft at the Annapolis Naval Station, and eventually forty were there. Three years later, twenty-three enlisted women became part of tugboat crews at the San Diego Naval Station.[74]

Meanwhile, pressure mounted as more people realized the inequities women endured in professional development. The restrictions further rankled because civilian employees could embark in naval ships, Air Force personnel could serve in Military Sealift Command ships, and in 1977 the Coast Guard assigned female officers and enlisted to permanent sea duty.[75]

Finally, after Congress amended section 6015 in 1978, the Navy introduced its Women in Ships Program. The chief of naval personnel had appointed an Advisory Board for Women—Plans and Policy in May 1977, and this group developed a structured plan to implement the change.[76] Now women could serve permanently in auxiliary and noncombatant ships and up to six months in any ship not slated for combat. Based on the East and West Coasts, four vessels—the repair ship *Vulcan* (AR 5), submarine tender *L.Y. Spear* (AS 36), destroyer tender *Samuel Gompers* (AD 36), and missile test ship *Norton Sound* (AVM 1)—initially had thirteen women officers and 336 enlisted. Reflecting the enthusiasm of women serving in these ships, Personnelman 1st class Vickie Williamson in *Spear* exclaimed, "It's a good feeling knowing you're helping to shape history." Onboard the *Vulcan*, Seaman apprentice Mary Cobb had the distinction of being the only female diver onboard.[77]

During 1979, 55 officers and 375 enlisted became part of the crews of twenty-one ships. So ended a 204-year male-only tradition in U.S. Navy ships. Other spin-off benefits from the Women in Ships Program included five additional ratings for enlisted and training for them, and opening of the Surface Warfare and Special Operations communities to women and appropriate schools for them.[78]

There was opposition, of course, and it emanated from many directions. Arguments against integration came from naval officers who predicted a loss of combat effectiveness (women were not the aggressive predators that men were), a rise in sexual misconduct and pregnancy rates, lack of acceptance by male shipmates, and ridicule from foreign navies.[79] Navy wives felt threatened by their husbands' going to sea with female sailors, but the Navy offered classes and meetings to calm these fears.[80] Many officers watched this vital change with trepidation and concerns about the cost to competency, unity, morale, and retention. Even former WAVES director Capt. Robin Quigley opposed women at sea, as did some other women officers.[81] Many, however, were committed to the change and its benefits to the professionalism of Navy women.[82]

### *In Aviation*

As Navy women gained access to sea duty, so, too, did they enter naval aviation. Although not specifically mentioned in Z-116, aviation came under review in October 1972. Alone of the services, the Navy had a plan to select and train women for aviation billets. The Army followed in 1973 and the Air Force three years later.[83]

Secretary of the Navy John Warner soon announced that women could enter aviation training in a test program. In March 1973, four female officers began training at the Naval Aviation Training Command at Pensacola. Four more civilian women joined the Navy, graduated from Officer Candidate School, and began the same program. Six of these women completed the rigorous eighteen months' training and received the naval aviators' wings of gold in 1974. On 22 February, Lt. Barbara Allen became the first to win her coveted wings, followed by Judith Neuffer a few days later.[84] Two of these women served in helicopters and four in fixed-wing aircraft. After they had been on duty for a year, the Navy declared the test program a success and allowed another eight women to begin aviation training. Still a third group started in 1976.[85]

Newly trained women pilots met the same barrier that had hampered women's sea duty: section 6015 of Title 10. Aviators could not fly in combat planes or land aboard ships. The latter would constitute duty in ships. Hoping for modification of 6015, the Bureau of Naval Personnel had proposed a career development path in 1976, which it implemented two years later when Congress amended 6015: women could serve as crew members on noncombat aircraft.[86]

Women's opportunities expanded from helicopters and propeller aircraft to advanced training in jets. By September 1978, there were nineteen women aviators and fifteen more in training. Barbara Allen led the way and was the first to qualify in jets. Another early flyer was Lucy B. Young, who became a jet pilot in 1978 and went on to become a jet flight instructor. The next year, Lynn Spruill was the first to be carrier qualified.[87]

Not only did women qualify as pilots, but two others broke another barrier when they became the Navy's first female flight surgeons in 1973. Lts. Victoria M. Voge and Jane D. McWilliams graduated from the Naval Aerospace Medical Institute training program and assumed their duties as airborne physicians.[88]

Enlisted women also benefited from the relaxation of prohibitive rules. Ratings, including aircrew, open to them increased to twenty-four, and women in aviation ratings jumped from 700 in 1972 to 4,610 by the end of the decade. One was Seaman Linda Coons, an operation specialist who subsequently trained as an aircrewman. Another was Master Chief Avionics Technician Italia F. Birkinsha, a thirty-year veteran and the Navy's senior enlisted woman, who had been an instructor in radar theory and repair. In 1978 enlisted could also work in four operational antisubmarine patrol squadrons.[89]

## The Navy Nurse Corps

While other women pursued different and expanded roles in the Navy, the Nurse Corps continued its usual steady course. As the country pulled out of the Vietnam War, personnel numbers in most health fields dropped. Within the Medical Department, from 1970 to 1979, the Medical Corps diminished from 4,650 to 3,437; the Dental Corps from 1,959 to 1,640; and the Hospital Corps from 29,282 to 22,081. The Medical Service Corps, with its health-care administrators and allied health scientists, rose from 1,617 to 1,780, as the Nurse Corps increased from 2,290 to 2,551.[90]

Under a series of surgeons general—Vice Adms. George M. Davis Jr. (1969–73), Donald L. Custis (1973–76), and Willard P. Arentzen (1976–80)—the Bureau of Medicine and Surgery underwent reorganizations in 1974 and 1979. To improve management of health-care delivery and to be more responsive to patients' needs in sixty-four facilities in the United States and overseas, the bureau began a regionalization program that attached outlying clinics and dispensaries to central major hospitals, called naval regional medical centers.[91]

Within the bureau, the Nurse Corps and the Nursing Division came under the supervision of one director, who planned and directed nursing services in all medical facilities. She also recommended professional and educational standards for the corps and oversaw personnel actions.[92] The director kept the quality of Navy nurses equal to those in civilian life.

The 1970s produced a bumper crop of registered nurses. Congress helped with a series of nurse training acts, which provided funding to construct new facilities for nursing instruction, student loans, and outright grants.[93] Nursing education had grown increasingly expensive because of the shift from diploma to degree programs. Hospital diploma programs dropped steadily to only 288 by the early 1980s, while associate degree programs rose to 742 and baccalaureate degree training climbed to 402. Clearly, the trend was toward academic preparation. Graduate instruction, both master's and doctoral, provided clinical specialization and training in administration, teaching, or research.[94]

Evolving medical technology included renal dialysis, open-heart surgery, and chemotherapy for cancer, advances that called for increasingly sophisticated nursing skills and more education. Nurses also staffed hospital intensive care units, a 1970s refinement of the concept of postsurgical recovery rooms, and coronary care units for heart and stroke patients.[95]

New roles for nurses gained importance, especially that of the nurse practitioner, who could take over many functions of physicians. Nurse practitioners specialized in various nursing fields—family, school, geriatric, obstetric/gynecologic, pediatric, and emergency—and took medical care to more and more Americans.[96]

But 94 percent of nurses were women and two-thirds of them worked in hospitals. Here they were often relegated to stereotypical female roles as physicians' handmaidens, housewifely managers of nursing units, and committed nurturers. As such, they lacked both freedom and autonomy, which again gave rise to the old question of whether nursing was, in fact, a profession.[97]

## *Leaders*

Navy nurses reflected the status of nursing in America, and their dedicated leaders strove to manage the Nurse Corps by the most modern methods. Capt. Alene Bertha Duerk became director of the corps in May 1970 and brought to her job long and diverse naval experience. The Ohio native was born in 1920, received a diploma from the Toledo Hospital School of Nursing in 1941, and joined the Nurse Corps as a naval reservist two years later. Duerk served in naval hospitals until 1945, when she was part of the nursing staff in the hospital ship *Benevolence,* which cared for wounded from the Third Fleet and took on liberated American prisoners of war. After leaving active duty, she earned a bachelor of science degree from Western Reserve University in 1948. Recalled in 1951, Duerk held progressively more responsible assignments in the United States, the Philippines, and Japan, becoming captain in 1967. Her last assignment was chief of nursing service at Great Lakes Naval Hospital. As director of the Navy Nurse Corps, she made history by becoming the first woman ever to attain flag rank on 1 June 1972, when she was promoted to rear admiral. Duerk served as director for five years and received the Legion of Merit.[98]

Following Duerk as director was Rear Adm. Maxine Conder, who assumed the post in July 1975. A Utah native, Conder was born in 1926 and earned a nursing diploma from St. Marks Hospital School of Nursing, Salt Lake City, in 1947. Shortly after entering the Nurse Corps in 1951, she served in the hospital ship *Haven* off the Korean coast and then went to the Naval Hospital, Guam, before a series of stateside assignments. She subsequently earned a bachelor of science degree from the University of Utah in 1962 and a master's in nursing at the University of Washington in 1966. She had several chief nurse assignments—Guantanamo Bay, Portsmouth, New Hampshire, and Boston—and became captain in 1970. Her last tour of duty was as chief of nursing service at the Naval Regional Medical Center, Philadelphia. When she became director of the Navy Nurse Corps, Conder was the second woman to attain the rank of rear admiral.[99] She, too, received the Legion of Merit.

Both directors were warm, approachable women who wanted Navy nurses to enjoy their service. One of Duerk's greatest satisfactions, she said, was promoting better communication with nurses through correspondence, telephone calls, travel, and an open office door. Like Duerk, Conder listened to nurses' concerns about promotions, education, career patterns, and assignments with spouses.[100]

## *Recruiting and Retaining Nurses*

Duerk and Conder had to find ways to maintain the strength of the Nurse Corps. For most of the decade, there was a chronic shortage of nurses in spite of the fact that more nurses than ever were graduating from civilian nursing programs. In the early 1970s, the Vietnam War had caused such severe antimilitarism that the Navy, as well as the other services, had difficulty recruiting and retaining nurses. Media advertising got off to a bad start when an ad depicted two officers holding hands, under the caption "No one has to take a Navy nurse by the hand—but some people do." Negative reaction was, predictably, instantaneous, and the demeaning ad immediately disappeared.[101]

The Navy acquired its nurses through direct appointment of registered nurses or through its various subsidized education programs. Overseeing all Nurse Corps recruiting was the Procurement and Information Branch of the Nursing Division, which became the Professional Branch of the Nursing Division in 1976. This office assigned nurses to the Navy Recruiting Service, provided recruiting material, prepared audiovisual aids, and supplied high schools, colleges, and nursing schools with information. It also reviewed appointment applications and professional qualifications.[102]

The Navy Nurse Corps Candidate Program subsidized nurses holding associate degrees for two years while they pursued baccalaureate degrees in nursing. This opportunity expanded in 1971 to cover anesthesia courses. The baccalaureate degree subsidy program was phased out in the late 1970s. The four-year Navy Enlisted Nursing Education Program (NENEP) continued until 1979 and gave members of the Hospital Corps the opportunity to earn a college degree in nursing and a Navy commission. Doris J. Safran, for example, had entered the Navy as an operating room technician and Todd Herzog as a hospital corpsman. Both took advantage of the NENEP, completed their degrees, and became Nurse Corps officers. Many more hospital corpsmen followed the same path to commissioned status.[103]

There were other programs for graduate education, such as full-time master's and doctoral studies, the Navy Management course at the Navy Postgraduate School, and specialized instruction in anesthesia, operating-room nursing, and practitioner training.[104] Such programs paralleled civilian emphasis on better nursing education, and these subsidies kept up interest in Navy nursing.

In June 1970, the corps had 2,273 officers on active duty, including 156 males. Nine years later, there were 2,551 nurses, and 648, or 25 percent, were men.[105] Males found military nursing attractive because of better pay and opportunities than in civilian hospitals, better assignments and promotions, and superior educational, medical, and retirement benefits. They were easily assimilated into the corps without any special effort on the part of female nurses.[106]

The corps also grew in racial diversity. The Navy's Equal Opportunity program stressed recruiting blacks and other minorities, and efforts by the Recruiting Command, through advertisements and presentations aimed at the black community and predominately black colleges and nursing schools, produced a wider pool of potential naval talent.[107] In the mid-1970s, there were 63 minority nurses: 51 blacks, 11 Asians, and 1 American Indian. Their numbers steadily increased. In 1978 Joan C. Bynum, assistant director of nursing at the Naval Regional Medical Center, Yokosuka, Japan, became the first black Navy nurse and the first black female naval officer to attain the rank of captain.[108]

Standard requirements for the Navy Nurse Corps remained high. The corps wanted all nurses to hold college degrees, and in 1970 the majority (48 percent) held bachelor of science degrees. Directors Duerk and Conder steadfastly resisted pressure to lower education standards by refusing to admit graduates of nonaccredited nursing schools or nurses with only associate degrees, or to employ more hospital diploma nurses.[109] Other requirements included American citizenship, ages between twenty and thirty-five years, and graduation, or within six months of it, from a three-year academic nursing program. Nurses could be single or married, and until the policy changed in 1975, females could have no dependents under the age of eighteen. Some waivers eased the dependent-child rule. Male nurses were under no such restrictions.[110]

## *Entering the Nurse Corps*

During the 1970s the Nurse Corps still reverberated from changes caused by the "Three M's"—males, minorities, and marriage—that began in the earlier decade. The prime motivation for joining the corps was the opportunity to travel. A close second was the good benefits package, followed by subsidized education, pay, patriotism, experience, security, and family tradition.[111]

After new nurses entered the corps, they underwent indoctrination at Newport, the women at the Women Officers Candidate School, the men at the Naval Officer Training Center. The two facilities merged in 1973. Soon nurses took part in a common six-week core curriculum for all staff corps officers.[112]

## *New Fields for Nurses*

When the draft ended, the Medical Corps found itself acutely short of physicians. As a means of combating this crisis, the Nurse Corps began training and utilizing nurse practitioners.[113] The first practitioners, who had specialized in pediatrics and obstetrics/gynecology, finished training and began practice in June 1972. The program widened to include family practice, anesthesia, midwifery, and ambulatory care. These nurse practitioners relieved doctors of many routine duties at naval hospitals and large dispensaries, and by 1975 there were about one hundred on duty.[114] The expanded sphere of nurse practitioners in the Navy reflected a rapidly growing trend in civilian medicine.

Use of Navy nurses increased in other areas as well. In 1976 the nurses could enter Operational Medicine, which supported operating forces in noncombatant ships, at Marine Headquarters Support Groups, with Construction

Battalions, and with the Fleet Medical Officer.[115] In the late 1970s, nurses trained for roles in Contingency Execution Teams that could respond to rapid mobilization.[116]

### *Deployment of Nurses*

The Navy Nurse Corps maintained its traditional presence wherever naval personnel needed its healing talents. Nurses served at hospitals, regional medical centers, naval stations, clinics, and dispensaries, and at recruiting stations and civilian schools in the United States. Overseas, they were in twelve medical care centers that ranged from the Mediterranean to Newfoundland to the Caribbean to the Pacific.[117] They continued instructing hospital corpsmen at Hospital Corps schools at San Diego and Great Lakes. To every station, nurses carried along the *Nursing Procedures Manual,* updated in 1973 and in 1979, which provided exact directions for patient care.[118]

When the hospital ship *Sanctuary* returned from Vietnam in 1971, she was decommissioned. There were then no ships in which nurses could serve. The next year, *Sanctuary* was recommissioned as a dependent support ship and was the proving ground for the Navy's experiment for women in ships. Director Duerk, speaking at the recommissioning ceremony, referred to *Sanctuary*'s new mission, calling for teamwork.[119] Twelve Navy nurses joined the fifty-five other Navy women as *Sanctuary* sailed on a goodwill mission to Columbia and Haiti. While in port in these countries, nurses ministered to poor and sick natives. Chief Nurse Phyllis A. Butler detailed these activities in correspondence with the director.[120]

After successful completion of the *Sanctuary* pilot program, the ship was decommissioned again in 1975. There were no hospital ships or transports on active duty, so Navy nurses became landlocked. By the late 1970s, the Navy was studying modular, mobile, medical components as feasible alternatives to traditional hospital ships.[121]

### *More New Departures*

In November 1973, Duerk represented the Nurse Corps at the first NATO conference for senior military women, and Conder had the same responsibility when the group met in London in 1975 and 1977.[122] Another new enterprise was the Personnel Exchange Program between the Navy Nurse Corps and Queen Alexandra's Royal Navy Nursing Service. Duerk had begun negotiations with the British matron-in-chief in late 1973; and the following June, Lt. Cdr. Sara Tolar arrived at the Royal Naval School of Nursing at Hasler as a member of the training staff. In exchange, a British nurse served at the Naval Hospital, Portsmouth, Virginia.[123]

As more civilian women trained as physicians, more women became Navy doctors. There were fourteen doctors in 1972, and 223 by the end of the decade. The Dental Corps attracted far fewer women. In fact, Lt. Cdr. Helen M. Paulus had been the only female dentist. By 1979 there were 50 women dentists, and several hundred dental technicians worked in naval dentists' offices. The Medical Service Corps provided such essential specialists as pharmacists, optometrists, dietitians, physical and occupational therapists, and administrators. Women in this corps increased from 76 in 1972 to 130 in 1979. Most medically trained enlisted women were in the hospital corpsman rating, and there were 1,914 providing basic nursing care by the end of the 1970s.[124]

## Navy Women and Navy Nurses: Shared Experiences

All Navy women shared many advances and problems. One of the satisfying experiences was their advance to flag rank—at last. The services were slow to exercise the 1967 statute permitting flag or general officer rank for women. The Army and the Air Force promoted four women to brigadier general in 1970 and 1971. In mid-1972, the Navy promoted Navy Nurse Corps director Alene B. Duerk to rear admiral, then promoted her successor, Capt. Maxine Conder, three years later. There was no opposition to raising nurses to flag rank, remembered Admiral Zumwalt. It was not until 1976 that a line officer achieved flag rank: Capt. Fran McKee became a rear admiral. In 1979 Capt. Frances Shea, another Nurse Corps director, was the fourth woman of the decade to wear an admiral's stars.[125] In another attempt to equalize promotion and pay opportunities, the Nurse Corps proposed upper-half pay for some women rear admirals, but such a change would require later congressional action.[126]

Women's authority over males had always been a touchy and avoided issue, but as more women entered the Navy in the 1970s and more increased in rank and experience, the command problem called for a solution. Over the years, the only permissible command was in billets primarily administering other women.[127] In 1962 Cdr. Etta Belle Kitchen became commanding officer of women's recruit training at Bainbridge, but there were no more such billets until after Z-116. From November 1972 until the following March, Cdr. Elizabeth Barrett served as commanding officer of the Naval Advisory Group's 450 enlisted men at Saigon. When Capt. Robin Quigley left as assistant chief of naval personnel for women in 1973, she took command of the Service School Command in San Diego. Other command assignments came slowly; by 1977 there were only ten, including Capt. Pauline M. Hartington, who became CO of Navy Manpower and Material Analysis Center, Pacific, that year.[128] Male reaction to women commanders was more curiosity than resentment, recalled Admiral McKee, because "the Navy is based on and run by rules and regulations. If the rules are fairly enforced, the sex of the commander is unimportant."[129]

Nurses, too, assumed command duties in the summer of 1975. Capt. Harriet A. Simmons became officer in charge of the Mayport Naval Station dispensary in Mayport, Florida. At the same time, Capt. Bernadette A. McKay became director of administrative services at the Naval Submarine Medical Center, New London. Both posts involved supervision of males as well as females.[130]

All Navy women benefited from promotion and financial increases. Pay depended on rank, and in contrast with the civilian world, Navy men and women received equivalent pay and subsistence allowances. In 1970, officer pay ranged from $386.40 for ensigns to $894.60 for captains. Had there been female rear admirals, they would have earned $1,207.20 a month. Enlisted pay began at $115.20 for seaman recruits and rose to $342.30 for chief petty officers. Basic subsistence was a flat $47.88 a month. During the decade, inflation pushed the pay tables up to $2,354 for rear admirals; $1,745.10 for captains; and $827.40 for ensigns. Enlisted compensation varied from $448.80 for seaman to $741.30 for chief petty officers. Subsistence was $67.21 a month for officers and $3.21 a day for enlisted.[131]

Equity between men and women did not carry over to one important area: dependents' benefits. Female activism led to improvement.[132] Lt. Sandra Doppelheuer, a Medical Service Corps dietitian stationed at Bethesda, Maryland, applied for married basic allowance for quarters, but the Navy turned her down. Although her civilian husband, a full-time medical student, relied on her for support, the Navy could not award the benefit to a female unless her spouse was "in fact" dependent on her because of physical or mental impairment. Her complaint about sex discrimination traveled up the chain of command, and in July 1972 the U.S. comptroller general ruled that physical or mental incapability was no longer a requirement for dependency status.[133]

For Navy women, Doppelheuer's success was representative of a larger drive for equal benefits. In 1970 Air Force lieutenant Sharron Frontiero, whose husband was also a college student, filed a class action lawsuit charging that denial of dependents' benefits was sex discrimination. The case finally ended at the Supreme Court, which in May 1973, decided that if the armed services required females to demonstrate support of their dependents or minor children, they must require males to do the same.[134]

A closely related matter involved pregnancy. It had always been naval policy, reiterated as recently as May 1969 by WAVES director Capt. Rita Lenihan, that all pregnant officers and enlisted should immediately leave the service. The same rule held for women with any children, biological or adopted, under eighteen years of age. The waiver policy, based on individual cases, did make exceptions to this strict regulation, and such uncertainty called for a redefinition of pregnancy and maternal status. Capt. Robin Quigley set in motion a review of the issues. Capt. Alene B. Duerk, the Nurse Corps director, pointed to the loss of valuable Nurse Corps officers because of the outmoded policy.[135] By early 1972, a regulation allowed waivers for women who were pregnant or had dependents to remain in the Navy if the chief of the bureau of naval personnel approved their cases. Women still had the option of leaving the service.[136]

Prodded by yet another lawsuit, the Navy promptly made more changes.[137] By 1975, the Navy routinely retained pregnant women unless they voluntarily requested release, and the service also provided maternity care.[138] In

1978 the Navy became the first of the services to issue a maternity uniform.[139] In less than a decade, the Navy had come full circle, and women, either pregnant or with children, had become routine.

Another family matter, dual careers in the Navy, also received attention. Like their civilian counterparts, many Navy women found that the stringent economic conditions of the 1970s demanded two wage earners in a family. Drawn by shared interests, job security, and financial benefits, Navy couples learned to cope with separate duty stations or child-care difficulties when both parents were at sea. Navy detailers tried to assign husbands and wives to proximate duty stations, and such flexibility markedly reduced marriage-related requests for discharges. By 1979 there were 1,835 couples serving in the Navy.[140]

Navy women were confronted with the problem of sexual harassment, which military women had faced since they first entered the armed services. Largely ignored and unreported, sexual harassment would not be clearly defined until 1980, and little had been done about it. The majority of Navy women had experienced it, and almost all had witnessed it.[141] Whether in the form of verbal abuse, or molestation, or open propositioning, such harassment would leave women without recourse until the 1980s. Few were willing to report offensive male conduct, perhaps realizing that no disciplinary action would follow.[142] Finally, in 1979, one young lieutenant resigned, she wrote the CNO, because of repeated harassment, dehumanization, humiliation, and obstructionism. Many other officers who suffered similar harassment were also quietly leaving the Navy, she said.[143] By this time, harassment was a real, although undefined, problem.

For Navy women, the presence of lesbians caused usually unmentioned difficulties. With the changing civilian moral climate of the 1970s, lesbians became more outspoken about their sexual preferences and women more insistent about their rights. This trend clashed with naval policy of always discharging identified homosexuals, both male and female, as threats to security and discipline and this policy remained. Charges of lesbianism often came from males in units performing jobs that were unfeminine or nontraditional and were leveled against assertive, successful, career-oriented women.[144]

Navy women were proud of their uniforms. For officers, these included the basic service dress blue, which consisted of a dark blue, single-breasted jacket with gold sleeve stripes and line or corps devices, a matching six-gored skirt, a white shirt and black square-knot necktie, black pumps or oxfords, gloves, and a handbag. The hat had detachable covers to match various uniforms. In warm weather, a light blue-and-white striped material provided a more comfortable outfit. There were many options: full dress, formal dress, sport, and working uniforms such as nurses' white dresses or the new pantsuits with dark blue maroon-lined cape. By 1975, enlisted uniforms were the same as officers' except the buttons were pewter rather than gold. Slacks or dungarees could be worn when appropriate. There were other changes: maternity uniforms in January 1978, and khaki work uniforms the next year.[145]

Reflecting the societal turmoil of the 1970s, Navy women grasped at opportunities newly opening to them and carved out a stronger role for themselves in the U.S. Navy. This great change had many causes. First, the drumbeat of an intensified feminism demanded equal employment opportunities and the seemingly certain ratification of the ERA assured such opportunities. Next came a string of lawsuits charging the Navy with sex discrimination. Finally, there was the shortage of male personnel caused by the end of the draft in 1973 and a diminishing pool of eligible young men. The Navy needed women to make up the shortfall. By 1979, there were 4,135 women officers, or 6.5 percent of total officer strength, and 24,815 female enlisted or 5.5 percent of all enlisted.[146]

An increasingly broader spectrum of opportunities opened for women in the Navy: more important assignments for unrestricted line officers and the opening of the restricted line and all staff corps, expanded overseas assignments, command billets, and flag rank. The NROTC and the Naval Academy went coed, as did some officer and enlisted training within the Navy. A great breakthrough, sea duty, occurred with the 1972 *Sanctuary* experiment, which paved the way for the Women in Ships program. Similarly, women entered naval aviation and became pilots. Always receiving the same pay as men, women finally gained full benefits for dependents, and pregnancy and minor children no longer forced women out of the service. The question of whether women could have made more progress if the Navy had not abolished the WAVES and its director's position remains unanswered.[147]

None of women's advances in the Navy would have happened so quickly without the forcefulness and foresight of Chief of Naval Operations

Zumwalt. His Z-116 broke down barriers and created more opportunities for all Navy women. Part of the "loyal opposition" to many of Zumwalt's initiatives was WAVES director Quigley, who opposed most of his policies on women. The two had a common goal: full integration of women, but their means were different.

Obstructing the way of more equality for women was section 6015 of Title 10, which barred women from ships and aircraft. After Congress modified 6015 in 1978, more programs opened, but full professional equality was not achieved. The law perpetuated an institutional sexism that kept women outside the pale of complete integration and acceptance.[148]

During the 1970s, the Navy Nurse Corps, free from wartime responsibilities, grew to 2,551 members; 25 percent were men. Their education, professional competence, and technical advances mirrored the civilian nursing community.

Although the Nurse Corps had perennial difficulty recruiting members, it insisted on high standards and moved toward requiring baccalaureate degrees for its nurses. The Navy subsidized various tracks, including the Navy Nurse Corps Candidate Program and the Navy Enlisted Nursing Education Program, as well as assorted specialized training and graduate education. The new position of nurse practitioner attracted registered nurses who wanted advanced training in preparation for relieving physicians of burdensome routine chores with patients.

Navy nurses, as always, served in hospitals and other medical facilities around the world. Their long-standing task of training hospital corpsmen continued. Fortunate in their directors, Navy nurses thrived under the leadership of Rear Admirals Duerk and Conder, the first female flag officers in the Navy. Both women insisted on maintaining rigorous standards for the corps and fought off outside efforts to lower entrance requirements.

As the 1970s drew to a close, naval women could reflect with pride on the advances and achievements of the decade. But a nagging question remained: Were the momentous changes just the beginning of full integration or had women gone as far as they could? Perhaps the 1980s would yield definitive answers.

# 11

# Women's New Roles in the 1980s

*If widespread social change* characterized the 1970s, retrenchment described the 1980s. Navy women quietly solidified many of the advances they had made during the previous decade, and their numbers swelled along with new job opportunities, command billets, and education options. At the same time, male resistance to and resentment of women in the Navy simmered beneath the surface and occasionally erupted. It was a time of contradictions and uncertainty.

## The Setting

Following a decade of strident protests, demands for equality, and lawsuits, the nation turned away from crusades to embrace conservatism personified in President Ronald Reagan, who led the Republicans to victory in 1980. Economic expansion replaced issues such as affirmative action, women's rights, and social welfare, and, after a short recession, the economy flourished.

Feminists had already effected permanent changes in work-force composition and in women's roles in the family structure, but now they divided over crucial issues. Passage of the equal rights amendment, central to feminism in the previous decade, was a dead issue by the late 1970s because an insufficient number of states had approved it and nothing of such importance had replaced it. Women argued instead about matters such as maternity leave, abortion, and surrogate motherhood.[1]

Ever-increasing numbers of women attended college. In 1980, women's enrollment totaled 5,155,000, then reached 7,302,371—nearly 55 percent of the college population—nine years later. Continuing a trend that had begun in the 1970s, women made greater inroads into traditionally male professions, and 35 percent of medical students, 42 percent of law students, and 31 percent of dental students were women.[2]

These women did not hurry into domestic life. The average marriage age rose from 22 years in 1980 to 23.8 years in 1989, and the divorce rate remained around 50 percent. Nearly one-quarter of all women were opting to remain single. Simultaneously, the birthrate rose in the mid-1980s, skewed by a baby boomlet.[3]

Largely driven by economic necessity, working women, both married and single, were now the norm, not an oddity, in American life. About 75 percent of all women aged twenty-five to fifty-four worked outside the home, and more than half of all married women worked. Even 50 percent of mothers with infants and 70 percent of those with older children were gainfully employed.[4] Although fields such as law and medicine, and those requiring doctorates, became increasingly attractive to women, only about 16 percent of women had professional jobs. These clustered in familiar occupations—teaching, nursing, health, and library science—fields in which women could demonstrate the age-old traits of nurturance and sensitivity. The majority of other women filled stereotypical clerical, sales, service, or factory jobs.[5] In line with the high-consumption life-style of the times, a new phenomenon, the two-income professional family, emerged.[6]

Sex segregation in occupations perpetuated another long-standing discriminatory practice: the wage system. "Comparable worth" rallied the legislators in forty states and hundreds of local governments to raise wages for low-paid female workers.[7] As a result, women earned on the average 70 percent of men's pay for comparable work by 1990—up from 59 percent ten years earlier.[8]

There were no flamboyant old-style crusades in the 1980s, but peace activists joined Women Against Military Madness and participated in a 1984 campaign promoting a freeze on nuclear weapons. Others lobbied as Mothers Against Drunk Driving and advocated stronger laws against drinking and driving.[9]

Although women braced themselves for leaner times in a conservative era, the Navy eagerly anticipated President Reagan's promise to wage an intensified anticommunist campaign and to rebuild the national defenses, which had weakened. Reagan even envisioned a six-hundred-ship fleet, and that would necessitate a concomitant personnel buildup.

In 1980 there were 530 active ships in the U.S. Navy. Thanks to an energetic building program, there were 592 by the end of the decade. Finally armed with the Aegis missile defense system and offensive Harpoon and Tomahawk cruise missiles, new warships brought the surface Navy on parity with the aviation and submarine communities as cohesive parts of a modern fighting force that outclassed the Soviet Navy.[10]

The enlarged fleet called for increased personnel, and the number on active duty rose from 525,096 (including 62,648 officers and 457,459 enlisted; and 4,989 officer candidates) in June 1980 to 605,802 (74,374 officers and 526,018 enlisted; and 5,410 officer candidates) nine years later.[11] The Navy and the other armed services depended on an all-volunteer force to meet their requirements.

Three CNOs guided the Navy during the Reagan era. Adm. Thomas B. Hayward (1978–82) continued his emphasis on "Pride and Professionalism" among naval personnel and began a rigorous drug treatment program to rid the Navy of one of its biggest scourges.[12] Following Hayward in the top job came Adm. James D. Watkins (1982–86) and Adm. Carlisle A. H. Trost (1986–90). Like their commander in chief, both CNOs stressed a naval buildup, which Secretary of the Navy John F. Lehman Jr. and Secretary of Defense Caspar W. Weinberger successfully pushed through Congress.[13] This lasted until late in the 1980s, when naval appropriations dropped because the cold war was over and the military no longer needed such huge appropriations.

There were no other wars to test the Navy's growing preparedness, but the Reagan Doctrine decreed that the United States would counter the Soviets in the Third World, and a number of incidents flared. Among them was the 1986 intervention by U.S. Marines in Lebanon. They were part of a multinational peacekeeping mission in that country long plagued by civil war. That same year, ships of the Sixth Fleet bombed Libyan sites in retaliation for terrorist attacks. The following year, as naval vessels escorted tankers in the Persian Gulf, the frigate *Stark* (FFG 31) suffered heavy damage from an Iraqi missile attack, and in 1988 the frigate *Samuel B. Roberts* (FFG 58) hit an Iranian mine.[14]

Closer to home, the U.S. military invaded the small, independent

Caribbean island of Grenada, overthrowing the communist military government and evacuating American citizens. In less than a week in October 1983, American forces had restored the island's sovereignty and prevented Cuban president Fidel Castro from establishing a foothold there.[15] In December 1989, American forces invaded Panama, toppling the government of strongman Gen. Manuel Antonio Noriega and encouraging the election of a government sympathetic to the United States. Operation Just Cause was to restore democracy to Panama, protect American lives, and capture Noriega and try him for drug trafficking.[16]

The Navy not only demonstrated American power in the Third World but also continued more traditional endeavors. With the aid of its new ships and armaments, the Navy confidently vowed to challenge any Soviet-backed aggression. But the focus of U.S. deterrence began shifting in the late 1980s, when it became increasingly apparent that the Soviet Union was weakening and was unlikely to pose a threat to American dominance on the high seas. Instead, the Navy must be ready for a global response to unrest in and around developing nations and areas. Maintaining carrier battle groups in the Atlantic, the northern flank, the Mediterranean, the Indian Ocean, and the Western Pacific gave the United States the necessary power and flexibility to counter any potential conflict.[17]

At home, organizational changes during the decade streamlined the Navy's administrative tasks. The last remnant of the old bureau system, which had been founded in the 1840s, was eliminated in 1982, when the Bureau of Medicine and Surgery temporarily became the Naval Medical Command. Three years later, the Naval Material Command, which had been established in 1966 to unify the technical bureaus, burdened naval management with an unnecessary bureaucratic layer, so Secretary of the Navy Lehman disestablished it. The five remaining systems commands then reported to the secretary and to the CNO. In 1989 the systems commands gave way to program executive officers controlling all facets of acquisitions.[18]

As the Navy took on a new, more aggressive, look in the 1980s, it had to keep its personnel in a high state of readiness. The old nagging question returned: Would there be ways to utilize women more equitably and effectively in the revitalized Navy?[19]

## Navy Women

### *Women Who Joined*

As the 1980s unfolded, the all-volunteer-force concept and fewer eligible men (reflecting the end of the baby boom in the 1960s) produced a personnel crunch for the Navy and all military services. Of necessity, the Navy turned to women to help build the force required for its projected six-hundred-ship fleet. Female participation grew from 29,981 personnel (excluding nurses) on active duty in 1980 to 57,847 nine years later. Women's representation rose from 5.7 percent to 9.5 percent of total naval strength. California, the most populous state, led in providing new women, followed by New York, Florida, and Texas.[20]

Minorities grew disproportionately. By 1989, white female officers had fallen to 85 percent, while black officers had increased to 7.4 percent and Hispanic officers to 2.3 percent. Other minorities made up the remainder. More striking were the numbers in the enlisted force, where blacks comprised 26.4 percent and Hispanics 7 percent of the total. Far more black women than men joined the Navy. There were twice as many black female officers as male officers (7.4 percent vs. 3.6 percent) and 10 percent more enlisted (26.4 percent vs. 16.5 percent).[21] Some officers thought that black women found naval service attractive because it gave them improved opportunities for upward mobility.[22]

As in earlier years, standards for Navy women remained higher than for their male counterparts. Nearly all were high school graduates, and many scored at the upper range in mental exams. Enlisted had to be seventeen years of age, with parental consent, or eighteen years without such consent. They had to meet the Navy's physical standards and serve six years in either the regular Navy or the Reserves.[23]

Women continued to join the Navy for a myriad of reasons. There were the usual ones—adventure, education opportunities, new friends, travel, job training, and financial security—and patriotic commitment to their country was another motivation. Some, such as Ens. Lynn Schrage, followed in family footsteps: her father and three brothers saw naval service.[24]

## A Resurgence of Resistance

Although the numbers of women in the Navy rose, the 1980s did not present a completely warm and welcoming scenario. Resistance to women resurfaced with the advent of the Reagan presidency, when some in the military hoped the new administration would encourage a conservative backlash against women's intrusion into a male profession. In early 1981, the Army announced plans to curtail recruitment of women until it studied their influence on combat effectiveness. Critics charged that this was a move to reduce the number of new volunteer recruits and would lead to a personnel shortfall because the services wanted to reinstate the draft.[25]

The Air Force jumped on the Army bandwagon and announced that it, too, would impose a moratorium. As if to reinforce the services' position, in June 1981 the Supreme Court ruled that in the event of a new military draft, Congress could exclude women from registering or serving. But the Reagan administration shot down the concerted attempts to get rid of women. In January 1982, Defense Secretary Weinberger announced that women were a critical component of the armed forces and directed the services to expand their numbers and utilization.[26] Navy women as well were distressed when in 1982, Secretary Lehman emphasized operational experience for promotions and minimized the career potential of women unrestricted line officers.[27]

Although the Navy had not joined the initial attempt to turn back the clock, in 1986 it issued its own proposals. Outgoing CNO Adm. James D. Watkins stated that the Navy had recruited enough women; more would adversely affect readiness. Women had taken many of the better shore billets and therefore interfered with men's ship-to-shore rotation. Reaction from women was predictable and instantaneous.[28] On 2 February 1987, the new CNO, Adm. Carlisle A. H. Trost, implemented Watkins's suggestion by freezing the number of enlisted women through 1991. The next day, Weinberger interceded and overruled Trost, saying the Navy must keep its goal of increasing the number of enlisted by 10 percent by 1991.[29]

Navy women hardly had time to breathe a sigh of relief before the next blow fell. Secretary of the Navy Lehman resigned, and his replacement, James H. Webb Jr., was well known for his opposition to women in combat and at the service academies. Webb announced a new promotion policy stressing combat performance.[30] Many women wondered if they were truly not wanted in the Navy.

## *Combat Exclusion*

Underlying much of the resistance to more women in the Navy and the other services was the combat exclusion law stemming from the 1948 Women's Armed Services Integration Act. Section 6015 of Title 10 barred women from serving on ships, other than temporarily on hospital ships and transports, and in combatant aircraft. In 1978 the Navy convinced Congress to modify the act. Women now could have permanent duty on hospital ships and transports and temporary duty on other noncombatant ships. They could also act as crew in aircraft not on combat missions. Nevertheless, the narrow parameters of service hindered women's advancement and created difficulties for the Navy's personnel deployment system.

Uncertainty emanated from the lack of a clear definition of combat and its uneven application by the various services. Direct combat was "seeking out, reconnoitering, or engaging hostile forces in offensive action," but each service interpreted this definition differently. Finally, in 1988, the Department of Defense tried to standardize the definition with its Risk Rule: women could be barred from jobs carrying "risks of exposure to direct combat, hostile fire, or capture." For the Navy, problems multiplied. Women could serve in supply ships such as destroyer or submarine tenders that could be deployed in combat areas, but not in combatant ships. Where should the Navy draw the line in protecting women?[31]

## *Administrative Restructuring*

Advising the Navy on how to make use of women was the Office of Special Assistant for Women's Policy (OP-O1[W]) within the Bureau of Naval Personnel. Established in 1979, this office oversaw policies and activities of Navy women. Capt. Barbara R. Nyce replaced Capt. Maria S. Higgins as OP-01(W) in 1980 and was in turn succeeded by Capt. Sarah Watlington and Capt. Julia J. DiLorenzo. A major drawback was that the billet was collateral, and all OP-01(W)s spent only part of their time in this advisory work.[32] In 1988 the post became a full-time, primary duty with Capt. Kathleen Byerly Bruyere as the incumbent. Two years later, she also headed the Women's Policy Branch (OP-13W), which actively devised and supervised policies for women. Finally, in a reorganization of the Bureau of Naval Personnel in 1991, OP-01(W) became Pers-00W, with the same functions.[33]

This central oversight office reintroduced the support structure that had ended for women in 1973. Charged with monitoring and reviewing policies affecting women, OP-01(W) advised the chief of naval personnel on everything pertaining to Navy women: "accessions, classifications, training, assignment, promotion, utilization, and career development."[34] Such a billet was necessary, Captain Nyce later recalled, so that women had access to the chief of naval personnel.[35] As always, the role of this senior woman officer remained advisory with no command authority. Nevertheless, the return to one office's oversight of women's policy gave women a sense of cohesiveness and structure in a predominately male environment.

## *Officer Education and Training*

The avenues for coeducational training of women officers that had opened or expanded during the 1970s became the norm for the 1980s. Potential officers of both sexes attended the indoctrination program at the Officer Candidate School, Newport. More women took advantage of the college scholarship funds provided by the NROTC programs.[36] Others in the restricted line or staff corps entered the Navy by direct appointment.

The greatest education plum of all was, of course, the Naval Academy. Women had begun attending the prestigious institution in 1976, and by 1980, fifty-five had graduated. Throughout the 1980s, about one hundred women entered the academy each year. They distinguished themselves academically. Elizabeth Belzer, for example, graduated in 1980 as a Trident Scholar, and Kristin Holderied graduated first in the class of 1984. Others, such as all-American swimmer and volleyball player Cheryl Dolyniuk, excelled in athletics. Still others held leadership positions within the brigade.[37] Academy superintendent Rear Adm. R. F. Marryott in an interview said women with high technical and athletic ability were the most successful as midshipmen.[38]

In 1986, the superintendent appointed a study group to evaluate the progress of women midshipmen and to make recommendations for improving their integration into the brigade. The ensuing report pinpointed the continuing lack of acceptance by male midshipmen who charged favoritism and inadequate preparation and who expressed resentment that women were even at the academy. The ongoing resistance to female midshipmen contributed to their high attrition rate—35 percent compared to less than 23 percent for males.[39]

Male hostility manifested itself in various forms of harassment, often dismissed as pranks. Such offensive behavior culminated on 8 December 1989, when two male midshipmen handcuffed Midshipman Gwen M. Dreyer to a urinal while others jeered and photographed her. She resigned a few months later, noting that the men's resentment crushed women's spirits. The two perpetrators were punished but remained at the academy. After the press picked up the story, the ensuing uproar generated congressional and naval investigations of the episode.[40]

After women received their commissions through one of these preparatory routes, they were eligible to continue their education at the Navy's postgraduate schools: the Naval War College at Newport and the Naval Postgraduate School at Monterey, as well as at the Industrial College of the Armed Forces. New for women was preparation for joint military operations. An increasingly large number of more senior officers undertook Joint Professional Military Education.[41]

## *Enlisted Training*

As officers prepared for naval careers, so too did enlisted recruits, who reported to the Naval Training Center, Orlando, for eight grueling weeks of boot camp. The integrated center supervised two women's and five men's divisions simultaneously. Divided into companies of eighty women, the recruits were bombarded with rules and regulations, history and tradition, drill and fitness training. Molding individuals from all walks of life into a cohesive, disciplined military unit challenged the company commanders, but team spirit prevailed. Recruit Michelle G. Bucarich described the metamorphosis: "When I graduate, it won't be with 80 women; it will be with 80 shipmates."[42]

Following recruit training, many enlisted women attended "A" schools to develop necessary skills for advancement in their ratings. As more sea billets opened for women, training in necessary skills was imperative. To help hone technical abilities, the Navy encouraged women to take advantage of the Job Oriented Basic Skills (JOBS) program. Advanced technical training could be acquired in "C" schools. So successful was the Navy's drive to put women in nontraditional ratings that by 1990 about 60 percent of rated women held such billets.[43]

## *Expanding Opportunities for Line and Staff Officers*

A major breakthrough for women officers was passage of the Defense Officer Personnel Management Act (DOPMA) in 1980. It had taken the measure seven years to get through Congress, and among its provisions was integration of men's and women's promotion lists for the Navy, the Army, and the Marine Corps. The Air Force had always had integrated promotion lists.[44] Subsequent naval selection boards discounted the effects of legal restrictions on women's careers, and by the late 1980s, promotion rates for male and female officers were roughly equal.[45] Navy nurses were not as fortunate because DOPMA severely limited promotions in the upper grades for them.[46]

Most women officers had been in the unrestricted line—generalists who specialized mainly in administration. In 1980, the chief of naval personnel, Vice Adm. Robert B. Baldwin, described added career opportunities for these women, directing attention to the recently opened surface warfare and aviation warfare communities and to increasing numbers of women in the restricted line and staff corps.[47] Progress was uneven, but by the end of the decade there were 555 women in the restricted line and 3,867 in staff corps. Their opportunities were "excellent."[48]

The staff corps utilized more trained women with varying degrees of acceptance by their male peers. The Nurse Corps had always been a female bailiwick and continued to be. There were other health-care professionals as well. By 1989, there were 453 women in the Medical Corps, 566 in the Medical Service Corps, and 170 in the Dental Corps. Another 163 women served in the Judge Advocate General Corps, 290 in the Supply Corps, and 120 in the Civil Engineer Corps.[49] Professional opportunities had multiplied.

Oddly, perhaps the greatest resistance to women was in the Chaplain Corps. Beginning with Florence Dianna Pohlman, the first female chaplain, women repeatedly reported that male chaplains were generally reluctant to accept their female colleagues. Perceived as curiosities and novelties, these idealistic young women were frequently treated with condescension and disrespect.[50] Lt. Janell O. Nickols, who entered the corps in 1981, recalled that some male chaplains did not know how to behave around female chaplains and were patronizing and standoffish.[51] Nevertheless, by 1989 there were forty-eight women in the Chaplain Corps.[52]

Another path for advancing to officer status came through the chief warrant officer (CWO) and limited duty officer (LDO) communities. "Excelling—that's what warrants are all about," said CWO4 Dorothy J. Stowe, a thirty-year Navy veteran. The number of CWOs grew from 16 in 1981 to 42 nine years later, and there were 8 command master chiefs. Still others answered the demand for technical specialists through the LDO program, which opened to women in 1980. Ens. Jeri D. Ezell, for example, became a photographic officer, while Lt. (jg) Jannine M. Weiss, an aviator, trained students in turboprop aircraft. By 1989, there were 130 LDOs.[53]

## *Sea Duty*

After Congress modified section 6015 of Title 10 in 1978, women could have permanent duty on hospital ships, transports, and like vessels and temporary duty on other ships not expected to engage in combat.[54] The Navy immediately launched its Women in Ships Program, and by 1980, 56 officers were serving in 14 ships and 396 enlisted had duty in 5 of these. These vessels were Mobile Logistic Support Force tenders, tugs, and repair ships—and soon the training carrier *Lexington* (AVT 16).[55]

Guiding the Women in Ships Program during its formative years was Cdr. Roberta L. Hazard, who initially had strong reservations about the concept. She soon realized that training women, men, and officers and assigning senior enlisted women to ships were keys to success. Her shop, Career Opportunity in OP-13, was responsible for the entire program—training, assignment, reconfiguring ships, and overseeing the smooth assimilation of women in ships. She attributed the overall success of the program to ships' commanding officers, who were able to mold their crews into teams regardless of gender.[56]

During the 1980s, the number of ships modified for women's use and of women assigned to sea duty increased dramatically. CNO Watkins encouraged and supported this expanded deployment of women. When he was chief of naval personnel, he had, in fact, helped draft the 1978 legislation opening the door for the change. He later remarked that placing women in naval ships was "extremely successful" and that the women were "doing a superb job."[57]

Following the CNO's example, male shipmates exhibited positive attitudes, and women had no detrimental effect on ship efficiency. Women's primary shortcoming was that they lacked the necessary physical strength to perform some strenuous shipboard jobs. But generally women were more easily integrated into ship crews than into shore stations.[58]

Demographics, of course, influenced the Navy's decision to send women to sea. The declining pool of eligible men for staffing the rapidly growing fleet made it necessary to use those available for combatant ships and rely more and more on women for noncombatants. Whatever the underlying reason, Navy women eagerly embraced the evolving opportunities.[59]

These new opportunities came in rapid succession. In 1986 Secretary of the Navy Lehman opened seventeen replenishment ships of the Military Sealift Command (MSC) to women.[60] The next year twenty-four Combat Logistics Force ships opened with a potential of women's filling one-half of the billets onboard. Such changes meant seventy naval ships and thirty-seven MSC vessels could accommodate women by 1990, when 331 officers and 7,803 enlisted served at sea.[61] Along with this expansion came a change that put women's ship-shore rotation on the same basis as men's. Earlier, women had accrued sea duty credit for time in any overseas post; now they would have to serve shipboard duty for that credit.[62]

Navy women had glimpses of duty in danger zones. In May 1987, an Iraqi jet fired two missiles into the guided missile frigate *Stark* while she sailed in the Persian Gulf. Thirty-seven men were killed, and *Stark* was badly damaged. The Navy sent the destroyer tender *Acadia* (AD 42) to make temporary repairs at Bahrain. Among *Acadia*'s crew were 248 women who worked alongside their male shipmates, readying *Stark* to sail home.[63]

American forces moved into Panama in 1989, and about 770 Army and Air Force women took part in Operation Just Cause. Army captain Linda L. Bray commanded the 988th Military Policy Company and led it to capture a kennel for attack dogs. A prolonged fight ensued, and Bray became the subject of a media blitz. Once again, women in combat moved to center stage and would soon be a major issue.[64] At the time of the invasion, there were thirty-five Navy women stationed in Panama, but apparently they had no role in the operation.[65]

Monitoring women's assimilation into the seagoing Navy was the Women at Sea Working Group, established in 1988. Representatives of major commands discussed such issues as embarkation training, medical care, wider roles for senior enlisted women, and unexpected losses because of pregnancy. The group continued to implement policy for women in ships.[66]

There were problems such as those described by a seagoing female lieutenant. Fraternization undermined the crew's discipline and morale; perceived preferential treatment created hostility; unplanned pregnancies affected readiness. Limitations of physical strength and of professional development caused more difficulties.[67]

But women themselves rejoiced that their expanded roles included such unlikely jobs as handling cranes, rigging ships, hauling lines, or weighing anchors. Machinery repairman Sharon Cameron praised the equality she had found onboard her ship. "A shipmate is a shipmate," she said. Damage Controlman 2d Class Robin Kaler believed she had learned more from four years in the Navy than she would have in college. Instrumentman 2d Class Patricia A. White Bear considered her job in the calibration lab to be vital.[68]

Although women's participation in the seagoing Navy increased dramatically, section 6015 continued to block women in combatant ships. While this barrier remained, women could never be equal participants in the male-dominated Navy. Even so, their seafaring ancestors—those nineteenth-century women who had sailed in war ships, and whaling, privateer, merchant, and clipper ships—were probably smiling.

### *In Aviation*

Paralleling women's expanded service at sea was a comparable increase in the aviation community. Aviation training had opened to women in 1973 and the naval flight officer program six years later. Sadly, Lt. Cdr. Barbara Allen Rainey, the first woman to earn the wings of gold and the first to qualify as a jet pilot, died in a training accident in 1982, leaving behind her husband and two young daughters.[69]

As the 1980s unfolded, women made more progress in naval aviation specialties. In 1982 the jet training pipeline opened to five women a year, and the following year test piloting became available. Lt. Colleen Nevius was the first woman to complete the rigorous studies at the Naval Test Pilot School at Patuxent River. The school "was 150 percent demanding . . . but most satisfying to complete," she recalled.[70] Other women became naval flight officers and performed onboard duties such as navigation, intelligence, and communications. Still others went into air traffic control, engineering duty, or flight instruction. Some became flight surgeons, aviation supply officers, or maintenance officers.[71]

One of the most exciting jobs resulted from a 1983 policy change authorizing temporary duty to the Sixth and Seventh Fleets for female helicopter pilots. "Carrier aviation is a finger-tingling kind of excitement," said Cdr. Jane Odea. "Landing on an aircraft carrier is clearly one of the most challenging flight evolutions that any pilot could ever face," emphasized Cdr. Lin Hutton. In fact, several women helicopter pilots landed on carriers during the bombing of Libya in 1986. By the early 1990s ninety women shared in the task of landing helicopters on carriers.[72]

Enlisted women also enjoyed opportunities in the expanding field of naval aviation. In 1984 all operational VP squadrons opened to enlisted women, and by 1990, 4,892 of the 7,733 women in aviation ratings served in these squadrons. Others filled aircrew billets in noncombatant planes.[73]

An impressive tribute to Navy women came from the achievements of Lt. Cdr. Kathryn D. Sullivan, a Reserve officer who had been in NASA's space program since 1978. She was not a naval aviator but held a doctorate in geology. In 1984 she became the first woman to walk in space and subsequently was a mission specialist on two more shuttle flights.[74]

Like their sisters serving in ships, women in naval aviation encountered the same barrier, the combat exclusion law. The prohibition would continue to curtail their progress.

### *Reports on Progress*

DACOWITS, the watchdog of women's assimilation into the military, continued its involvement by visiting bases and meeting with service members to learn of their problems and concerns. The group reported directly to the secretary of defense and was a strong lobbying force within Congress. During a fact-finding visit to naval and marine bases in the Pacific in August 1987, DACOWITS members unearthed low morale, sexual harassment, little communication between enlisted women and their commanders, and job discrimination. Upon receiving the DACOWITS report, Secretary of the Navy Webb instructed Chief of Naval Operations Trost to conduct a study on utilization of women in the Navy.[75]

The study group's intensive investigation of ships and shore commands resulted in the *Navy Study Group's Report on Progress of Women in the Navy* in December 1987. The document led to widespread changes, including opening more ships, as well as fleet reconnaissance squadrons, to women and generating another ten thousand billets for them. In 1990 Rear Adm. Roberta L. Hazard directed a follow-up study. *An Update Report on the Progress of Women in the Navy* concluded that the continuing combat restrictions and the institutional character of the Navy had a negative impact on women's careers and perpetuated the belief that women are not "equal contributors."[76] Another concurrent study focused on a theme that had been present since the early 1970s—equal opportunity for minorities. *CNO Study Group's Report on Equal Opportunity in the Navy*, issued in 1988, revealed that the Navy had assimilated blacks more successfully than it had women.[77]

## The Navy Nurse Corps

As Navy women coped with the changes of the 1980s, the Navy Nurse Corps continued to care for Navy and Marine personnel and their families at disparate spots around the globe. To meet the demands of the growing fleet, the Medical Corps grew from 3,575 in 1980 to 3,885 nine years later; the Medical Service Corps, from 1,853 to 2,531; the Hospital Corps, from 21,759 to 26,487; and the Nurse Corps, from 2,628 to 3,010. Only the Dental Corps slipped slightly lower, from 1,708 to 1,677.[78]

Reorganization was a way of life for the Bureau of Medicine and Surgery, and this routine continued in the 1980s. Guided by three successive surgeons general—Vice Adms. J. William Cox (1980–83), Lewis H. Seaton (1983–87), and James A. Zimble (1987–91)—the bureau underwent two major changes. In 1982 it became the Naval Medical Command, and the surgeon general took on a new title: director of naval medicine. Command of hospitals and other activities remained with medical officers who reported to geographic or mission-specific commanders, who in turn reported to the Naval Medical Command.[79]

Navy medicine lost its cutting edge in nationwide medical excellence, and by 1987, Surgeon General Zimble characterized it as "in extremis." A Medical Blue Ribbon Panel recommended overhauling the system. Zimble began a revitalization program, part of which involved ending the cumbersome Naval Medical Command in 1989 and reestablishing the Bureau of Medicine and Surgery. Line officers would have command responsibility for medical and dental facilities while the bureau provided medical and dental care and personnel. The National Naval Medical Center at Bethesda, after several years as Naval Hospital, Bethesda and National Capital Region, resumed its old name.[80]

The Nurse Corps was a critical element within the Medical Department, and its director was also head of the Nursing Division. Her responsibilities encompassed planning and advising on administrative policy, devising and enforcing professional standards for the corps, and supervising procurement, education, training, and assignment of Navy nurses.[81] The director's duties also temporarily included serving as commanding officer, Health Sciences, Education, and Training, and deputy commander, Naval Medical Command, Personnel Management Directorate. So, for a few months the director wore three hats.[82]

The 1970s had produced a plethora of trained nurses, but the pendulum swung the other way during the 1980s, and national shortages of nurses were "massive and pervasive." The trend toward academic degree preparation rather than hospital diploma programs and increased emphasis on graduate education, especially in the field of nursing service administration, continued, but enrollment dropped by 25 percent. A dry-up of federal money curtailed education programs.[83] At the same time, nurses' increased education and professional training often put them at odds with physicians, many of whom still regarded nurses as doctors' subservient handmaidens.[84]

New or revitalized diseases such as acquired immune deficiency syndrome (AIDS) and tuberculosis brought forth new treatments and medications that were just a part of burgeoning medical technology. Nurses had to stay current with the rapidly changing scene. Intensive care units, typical of modern hospitals, expanded from solely coronary care to units for medical and surgical, stroke, respiratory, burn, renal, neonatal, and pediatrics patients. Technological innovations such as magnetic resonance imaging (MRI) and computerized axial tomography (CAT) scanning became routine procedures.[85] All these advances called for an educated and dedicated cadre of nurses for health-care teams.

### *Nurse Corps Leaders*

The first director guiding Navy nurses in the 1980s was Rear Adm. Frances Teresa Shea. Born in Massachusetts in 1929, she received a bachelor of science degree from St. Joseph College, Hartford, Connecticut, in 1950. She joined the Navy Nurse Corps the following year and left active duty in 1954, but stayed in the Reserve. After earning a master of science degree in nursing service administration from DePaul University, Chicago, in 1960, she returned to active duty. In 1968, she became operating room supervisor in the *Repose*, stationed off Vietnam.[86]

Afterward, she held billets of progressively more responsibility until becoming director of the Nurse Corps with the rank of rear admiral in July 1979. Shea soon held other commands: in 1980 she also became commanding officer, Naval Health Sciences Education and Training Command. Two years later, she took on still another job, deputy commander for Personnel Management, Naval Medical Command. She was the first Nurse Corps director to fill additional billets, beginning a trend that subsequent directors followed.[87]

Succeeding Shea was Commo. Mary Joan Nielubowicz, who was born in Pennsylvania in 1929 and earned a nursing diploma from Misericordia Hospital, Philadelphia, in 1950. After joining the Nurse Corps the next year, she continued her education, earning a bachelor of science degree from the University of Colorado in 1961 and a master of science degree in nursing from the University of Pennsylvania four years later.

Nielubowicz's Navy nursing career included diverse assignments in and out of the country, and in 1967 she became senior nurse at the branch clinic, Iwakuni, Japan. After returning to the United States in 1969 and continuing her upward career path, Nielubowicz became the director of nursing service at the Naval Regional Medical Center at Portsmouth, Virginia, in 1979. Rising to the rank of commodore, the first and only nurse to hold that rank, she replaced Shea as director of the Nurse Corps in October 1983. She, too, had other duties: first as deputy commander for Personnel Management, then as deputy commander for Health Care Operations. In 1985, Nielubowicz's rank of commodore changed to rear admiral.[88]

The last of the 1980s triumvirate was Rear Adm. Mary Fields Hall, who became director of the Nurse Corps in September 1987. Born in Pennsylvania in 1934, Hall received a nursing diploma from Episcopal Hospital School of Nursing, Philadelphia, in 1955. She joined the Nurse Corps in 1959 and subsequently earned a bachelor of science degree in nursing from Boston University in 1966 and a master of science in nursing service administration from the University of Maryland in 1973.

Hall's naval service encompassed duty in various hospitals and regional medical centers in the United States and in Guam. She became the first Navy nurse, as well as the first military nurse, to assume command of a hospital when she took over as commanding officer at the Naval Hospital, Guantanamo Bay, Cuba, in July 1983. Two years later, she held a similar post at the Naval Hospital, Long Beach. With such demonstrated executive ability, it was natural that Hall would become director of the Navy Nurse Corps. She also served as deputy commander, Personnel Management, Naval Medical Command and continued the dual role until 1991.[89]

All three directors built on the work of their predecessors and pursued the same goals of ensuring the smooth operation of the Nurse Corps's mission and of enhancing the status of Navy nurses. They kept in touch with nurses in the field through letters, visits to facilities at home and abroad, conferences, and, eventually, informational videos. They encouraged nurses to write or phone about their problems and concerns. "I am extremely proud of the professionalism displayed and accomplishments made around the world by our dedicated and totally committed officers," wrote Director Nielubowicz.[90]

The various surgeons general either helped or hindered the efforts of the directors. Vice Admiral Cox, remembered Shea, was supportive and backed up Nurse Corps programs. Vice Admiral Seaton, on the other hand, was so involved with establishing and running the Naval Medical Command that he paid scant attention to Nurse Corps problems, confirmed both Shea and Nielubowicz. When Vice Admiral Zimble took over in 1987, his energy and enthusiasm in rebuilding the Bureau of Medicine and Surgery radiated to the Nurse Corps.[91]

### *Recruiting and Retention*

A major problem common to all three directors was the extreme difficulty in recruiting a sufficient number of nurses, especially as the decade progressed. In an era of a nationwide shortage of professional nurses and stiff competition from other employers, the Navy experimented with assorted enticements.[92]

In 1984 the Medical Enlisted Commissioning Program began, filling the void left by the termination of the Navy Enlisted Nursing Education Program five years earlier. Enlisted hospital corpsmen and dental technicians were eligible for nursing education and commissioning as officers. In 1989 the program expanded to include any active-duty enlisted.[93]

By 1986, shortfalls in both active-duty and reserve nurses prompted Admiral Nielubowicz to appeal to directors of Nursing Service and officers in education programs to help with recruiting efforts. But by the following year the situation had become so serious for the Nurse Corps of all the services that their directors formed a joint task force to address the problem.[94]

The Navy itself introduced a number of initiatives. In December 1987, it raised the maximum age for entering nurses from thirty-five to forty for active duty and from forty to forty-seven for reservists. In January 1988, it established the Cooperative Nursing Program in which the Navy paid minority students' tuition for the last two years of a four-year nursing degree program. In return, students had to serve either as military or civil service nurses. A few months later, a nursing leaders conference convened following a three-year hiatus.[95]

The Nurse Corps reevaluated its nurse recruiters and sent more experienced members to recruiting districts across the country. It dispatched direct mailings to student nurses and to nurses already in the work force, and it stepped up advertising.[96]

In early 1989, fifteen universities established NROTC programs for nursing students. An even more important step was to reinstitute the Nurse Corps Candidate Program, which had been so successful in the late 1960s and

1970s. The revitalized program for junior and senior nursing students, introduced in 1990, included an accession bonus of five thousand dollars and a five-hundred-dollar monthly stipend. After completing the baccalaureate, the nurse had a four-year service obligation in the Reserve.[97]

The Nurse Corps not only sought to recruit and retain active duty members but also exerted similar efforts toward its reservists. So important did they become that in 1987 Director Nielubowicz set up a full-time position on her staff for a Reserve officer to monitor this vital group.[98]

Finally, as the Nurse Corps still fell short of its quotas, the Navy turned to contracting civilian nurses to fill empty billets. These contract nurses came under Navy supervision. By 1989, there were 885 civilian registered nurses and 521 licensed practical nurses serving in naval hospitals, clinics, and branch clinics.[99]

Closely paralleling recruiting was retention of nurses already in the corps. Many decided against remaining after their initial three-year obligation. To find out what factors were relevant to keeping its nurses, the corps sent questionnaires to all nurses in 1986 and again in 1989. The survey revealed that better nursing management practices, more flexibility in assignments and work hours, treatment as adult professionals, and more pay would appeal to them. Yet the same study showed that nurses stayed in the corps because of nonmonetary rewards such as personal fulfillment, retirement benefits, job and education opportunities, and good pay.[100]

## *Who Joined?*

Registered nurses between twenty and thirty-five years of age (raised to forty years in 1987) who were American citizens meeting the Navy's physical qualifications were eligible to join. The corps's long desire for an all-degree force came closer to reality: by 1989, only 28 percent of the nurses had come from hospital diploma programs, while 69 percent held bachelor's degrees. Twenty-seven percent had earned master's degrees; a few had earned doctorates.[101]

Although nursing remained predominately a women's profession, more men entered the field in spite of stereotyping and labeling of male nurses. Generally, the assimilation of males into the Navy Nurse Corps went smoothly, although sometimes there was discrimination against them, recalled Admiral Nielubowicz; and they were often precluded from areas such as obstetrics, pediatrics, and operating room. Consequently, they gravitated toward specialized rather than traditional nursing roles. On the other hand, Director Shea recalled reverse discrimination: male nurses could accept operational and geographical assignments forbidden to women. The men thus provided the opening wedge in billets such as in aircraft carriers for all Navy nurses.[102] Rear Adm. Mary Hall called a meeting with about forty male nurses in 1989 to explore the problems that twenty-five years' experience had presented from a male perspective and to offer solutions to ongoing difficulties.[103]

Navy nurses could be married or single, and 57 percent were married. Gone was the prohibition against minor dependents, and 42 percent had children at home. The corps remained predominately white, although minorities accounted for more significant numbers.[104]

Nurses entered the Navy for many reasons. During the 1980s the most attractive features, in descending order, were thirty days' paid vacation a year, funded advanced education, comprehensive retirement and benefits, good pay and allowances, travel opportunities, career security, and wider nursing experience.[105]

## *Education and Training*

Navy nurses had the prerequisite professional training before they entered the service, so the Navy emphasized additional academic and specialized education. Each year, full-time duty under instruction (DUINS) provided the opportunity for about twenty-nine diploma nurses to complete their undergraduate education in civilian institutions. Another sixty-three pursued master's degrees in various specialties, and this advanced degree became required for higher level billets and for nurse practitioners.[106]

Other opportunities for nurses opened in the early 1980s, including the Army/Baylor University's master's program in health-care administration and the computer systems program at the Naval Postgraduate School, Monterey. Education of another sort began for selected nurses in October 1981, when the operational readiness course, held at Quantico, taught casualty care in the event of a sudden mobilization. Training for flight nurses, which had been discontinued in 1957, resumed in 1982. Four years later, nurses began attending the Marine Corps Command and Staff College at Quantico.[107]

A multitude of short courses sharpened nurses' skills and kept them abreast of modern professional advances. These included operational readiness, operating-room orientation, education and training management, executive medicine, holistic health care, advanced anesthesia, and field nursing. The Shea-Arentzen Symposium, begun in 1981, presented timely matters for senior nurse officers.[108]

Utilizing nurses' academic training and research, the Nurse Corps set up a resource pool of theses written by Navy nurses at the medical library at Naval Hospital, Bethesda. To further encourage scholarly efforts, in 1986 the Navy Nurse Corps; Reserve, established the Mary J. Nielubowicz Award for the best advanced nursing essay.[109]

## *Deployment of Nurses*

Throughout their history, Navy nurses served where the need arose. By the late 1980s, 85 percent had duty in the United States at twenty-three naval hospitals, twenty-two clinics, and twenty-nine branch clinics, at recruiting or headquarters commands, at Marine Corps facilities, or in DUINS at civilian universities.[110]

A major responsibility for nurses continued to be training hospital corpsmen. Training schools at Great Lakes and San Diego taught basic skills in programs that increased from ten to fourteen weeks by 1989. Nurses continued vigorous preparation on naval hospital wards.[111] Nurse Corps training of corpsmen paid off in operations such as the Grenada invasion and the terrorist attack on the Marine barracks in Beirut, both in 1983.[112]

Overseas, Navy nurses served in fifteen medical facilities around the world, ranging from one nurse at the small clinic in Diego Garcia, to twelve at the branch hospital at Keflavik, Iceland, to seventy-four at the large hospital at Okinawa.[113]

Shipboard service offered some Navy nurses duty on the high seas. A male nurse anesthetist led the way in 1980 when he reported onboard aircraft carrier *Constellation* (CV 64). By the end of the 1980s, male nurses (of necessity males because of the lingering combat exclusion law) were on fourteen carriers. At first, these nurses were anesthetists, but in 1989 general duty officers became the norm. "Traditional nursing in a nontraditional setting . . . [makes] an effective contribution to the healthcare team," said one such officer.[114]

Female nurses had their chance to go to sea when two new hospital ships, USNS *Mercy* (T-AH 19) and USNS *Comfort* (T-AH 20), entered naval service. Both could accommodate one thousand patients. Two nurses, Cdr. Judith Lombardi and Lt. Cdr. Suzan Mazer, described the last stages of fitting out *Mercy* as "incredibly awesome."[115] The *Mercy* went through an unusual shakedown cruise. In February 1987, she began a five-month humanitarian mission for bringing badly needed medical care to people at seven ports in the Philippines and at several small South Pacific islands. The mission was a reflection of American character: "reaching out to help people who need it desperately," recalled the hospital's commander.[116]

This same tradition of humanitarian aid had recurred during the decade. In 1980, fourteen Navy nurses joined in caring for Cuban refugees at the Refugee Receiving Center, Key West.[117] When a devastating earthquake hit the San Francisco Bay area on 18 October 1989, Navy nurses were on the scene again. An estimated 270 people were killed, more than 1,400 injured. Among the fifteen ships sent to provide relief was the hospital ship *Mercy*, with nurses onboard.[118]

## Navy Women and Female Navy Nurses: Shared Experiences

Both nurses and other Navy women achieved higher rank and experienced problems unique to naval service. Four women—three Nurse Corps and one line—had received appointments to flag rank during the previous decade, and in 1981 the second woman line officer, Pauline M. Hartington, became a rear admiral. She had entered the Navy in 1954 and enjoyed a career that culminated in her appointment as commanding officer, Navy Manpower and Material Analysis Center, Pacific in 1977.[119] In 1983, the redoubtable Grace M. Hopper was appointed commodore and then rear admiral two years later when the Navy changed its nomenclature and designated commodores as rear admirals, lower half. In 1986 this Reserve restricted line officer retired at the age of seventy-nine. She always maintained that her highest award was "serving proudly in the U.S. Navy."[120] During the 1980s, directors of the Navy Nurse Corps each held flag rank. Rear Adms. Frances T. Shea, Mary J. Nielubowicz, and Mary F. Hall assumed that rank with their directorships.[121]

Law prevented the logical next step for female flag officers: promotion to rear admiral, upper half. For men, such action was based on seniority and about three and a half years in lower-half status. In January 1980, Capt. Maria S. Higgins OP-01(W), began pushing for more equitable treatment of women, and the Navy soon proposed the necessary legislation.[122] In July, Sen. Nancy Kassebaum (R-Kans.) successfully sponsored such an amendment, which became part of the Defense Officer Personnel Management Act in 1980.[123] But laws do not always mean immediate action. Nurse Corps director Frances T. Shea became rear admiral upper half in 1983, but it was not until 1988 that a line officer, Roberta L. Hazard, was selected by a promotion board for rear admiral, upper half.

Going hand in hand with higher rank went command opportunities, and more women became commanding officers (COs) and executive officers (XOs). First came Cdr. Louise C. Wilmot, CO, Navy Recruiting District, Omaha, in late 1979. The following year, Capt. Roberta Hazard took over as CO, Naval Technical Training Center, followed by Rear Adm. Pauline M. Hartington as CO, Naval Training Center, Orlando. Among other notable commands of the decade were those of Hazard at the Naval Training Center, Great Lakes; Capt. Elizabeth Wylie at the Atlantic Military Sealift Command; and Wilmot at Navy Recruiting Area Five, Great Lakes, all in 1985. Wilmot went on to become CO, Naval Training Center, Orlando, in 1989. Cdr. Rosemary Mariner, an aviator, became a squadron XO at Point Magu, California, in 1988 and two years later took over as CO.[124] Another first occurred when Lt. Cdr. Deborah Gernes reported as XO of the destroyer tender *Cape Cod* (AD 43) in June 1987. This was, she said, "one of the most challenging jobs I've had in the Navy." A few months later, she was the first woman to qualify for command at sea.[125]

Navy nurses, as well, assumed CO and XO billets. The first was Rear Adm. Frances T. Shea, director of the Nurse Corps, who also took over the Health Sciences Education and Training Command in 1980. Three more senior officers screened for command in October. The next CO was Capt.

Mary F. Hall, later to become Nurse Corps director, who was commander of the Naval Hospital at Guantanamo Bay, Cuba, in July 1983—the first nurse to hold such a command.[126] Capt. Phyllis J. Elsass became CO of the School of Health Sciences at Bethesda; Capt. Jo Ann Jennett the CO of the Naval Medical Command, Northeast Region.[127]

By the end of the decade, women commanded naval hospitals, recruiting districts and processing stations, Military Sealift Command offices, security groups, training stations, communications stations, and NROTC units. At the end of 1987, five nurses, forty-nine general unrestricted line, and thirty-seven restricted line/staff officers held command, and their numbers were growing.[128]

Was there resentment from men as women made inroads in attaining CO and XO billets? One high-ranking officer recalled hearing about growing resistance, especially at the Naval Academy and in operational commands. It began as an undercurrent that would swell as time passed. Another said that resentment toward a female CO did not matter because that woman was the boss at that particular command.[129]

As always, Navy women received the same pay and subsistence as their male counterparts. In 1980, basic monthly compensation for officers ranged from $3,210.60 for rear admiral to $827.40 for ensign; for enlisted, from $741.30 for chief petty officer to $448.80 for seaman recruit. Subsistence was $67.21 a month for all officers and $3.63 a day for enlisted. Quarters allowance varied, ranging from $479.10 a month for rear admiral to $92.40 for seaman recruit. By 1989, the spiraling cost of living pushed these rates ever higher. A rear admiral began at $4,584.30 a month; an ensign, $1,338.90. A chief petty officer earned $1,227.30; a seaman recruit, $646.20. Subsistence was $119.61 a month for officers, $6.44 a day for enlisted. Quarters allowances were $613 for rear admirals; $150.30 for seaman recruits.[130]

The high cost of living prompted many Navy women, like civilians, to continue working after marriage, and dual career families became commonplace. By 1989, 46 percent of female officers and 40 percent of female enlisted were married. Forty-six percent of these women married military men.[131] Illustrative of this trend was a young chaplain, Lt. (jg) Janell Osborne, who met and married another Navy chaplain. She left active duty after four years, primarily because of anxiety over whether she and her husband would be transferred together.[132]

Pregnancy no longer brought immediate discharge; this issue had been resolved in the 1970s. By the end of the 1980s, 17.6 percent of officers were married and had children, and 4.6 percent were single parents. Fifteen percent of enlisted were married mothers, and 11.2 percent were single parents.[133] One single parent, Yeoman 1st Class Connie Bishop, took her eleven-year-old son with her to the naval base at Yokosuka, Japan. Dealing with raising a child in a foreign culture helped Bishop "reach a little deeper within [herself] to draw upon [hidden] talents."[134] Chief PO Mary Prise, another single parent, who had entered the Navy in 1976, remained stationed in Norfolk or afloat so that her son would have stability in living and schooling arrangements.[135]

Assignment of pregnant women evolved during the decade. At first, expectant mothers could not serve overseas or in ships. Later, policy changes ended discharge upon request, lengthened postchildbirth leave from thirty days to forty-two days, allowed new mothers to return to sea duty after four months, and permitted pregnant women to stay onboard while underway if medevac could get them ashore in three hours.[136] Thus pregnant Navy women could continue to work until delivery as could women in civilian society.

A problem common to many Navy women was sexual harassment. Previously undefined, unreported, or ignored, sexual harassment moved into the spotlight during the 1980s. In 1980 the Navy issued a policy statement defining it and outlining appropriate disciplinary action. Two years later, the definition of offensive conduct expanded to include creating an offensive or hostile work environment.[137] Prevention of such harassment came under mandatory equal opportunity training for all personnel, except aviators and officers in executive or CO billets.

Nevertheless, the problem continued. So much was a matter of perspective: women thought that harassment was rampant and blatant; men thought it was an infrequent occurrence. Few women reported incidents because they believed that no action would ensue.[138] By 1988, 73 percent of women had experienced some form of uninvited and unwanted sexual talk or behavior; the most common victims were vulnerable young enlisted serving their first tour. More blacks than whites were harassed. The usual perpetrators, in descending order, were military coworkers, other military, and immediate military supervisors.[139]

The situation did not improve. DACOWITS inspection trips to Europe in 1986 and to Pacific military installations in 1987 revealed pervasive and demoralizing sexual harassment. Their report triggered congressional hearings and a call for stronger disciplinary action.[140] Simultaneously, the secretary of the Navy appointed a study group to examine the problem, along with other issues pertaining to women in the Navy.

Three years later, after harassment incidents and rapes at the Naval Academy and at the Naval Training Center, Orlando, a follow-up study revealed that still women often did not file complaints, usually because they feared retaliation, or they believed no action would follow, or they were pressured not to hurt the command or careers of others. Lack of acceptance as equal members of the Navy—women had "second class status"—abetted harassment.[141] And so the long-standing, pervasive problem of sexual harassment remained unsolved; the Navy's efforts to address the problem proved "largely ineffective."[142]

Closely related to harassment was fraternization—overfamiliarity between officers and enlisted or between senior and junior personnel when there was a supervisory relationship. Widespread fraternization prompted the Navy, which had no formal, written policy, to prohibit the practice in 1989. But uneven enforcement and lack of understanding precluded effective execution of the policy, and fraternization continued to undermine "good order and discipline."[143]

Another seemingly unsolvable situation involved lesbians in the Navy. In 1981 a change in military policy broadened the grounds for discharge to include desire or intent as well as homosexual acts.[144] Always viewed as incompatible with naval service, homosexuals, of necessity, tried to conceal their activities because disclosure would lead to dismissal. There were some incidents of lesbian sexual harassment of heterosexuals, but fear of reprisal usually kept victims from reporting them.[145]

Uniforms for all Navy women remained essentially the same: the basic service dress made of authorized navy blue fabric or white for summer. Aviation green was available, and work khaki had joined the options by 1980. The occasion dictated the appropriate uniform: full dress, formal, dinner dress, service, or working. Brown shoes and handbags could now be worn with khaki and aviation green uniforms. A full array of maternity uniforms was required for expectant women, and dungarees could be worn when necessary. In 1981 white gloves became optional rather than mandatory with the service dress blue uniform.[146]

Navy nurses experienced the most radical uniform change. In 1982 they could no longer wear their traditional white ward uniforms, tunic pantsuits, nurses' caps, or white stockings while on duty. Instead, they would wear the uniform of the day—summer whites, summer khakis, or winter blues—without ribbons. Black sweaters could be worn indoors with summer whites. Nurses continued to wear their trademark blue cape with maroon lining.[147]

Although the 1980s was a conservative era, women did not give up the advances they had made during the previous decade. There was no rush to return to the domesticity of the 1950s and 1960s. Navy women's activities reflected these societal trends, and they persisted in increasing their presence and importance in this service.

President Reagan's naval buildup called for more personnel to staff the fleet, but the continuing shortage of eligible males forced the Navy to use the available men in combatant ships and aircraft. It needed women to make up the difference, and by 1989 their numbers soared to 57,847, or 9.5 percent of total naval strength.

To guide Navy women was the reinstituted oversight office, now called OP-01(W), which filled the void left by the disestablishment of the ACNP(W) in 1973. Responsible for all policies affecting women, OP-01(W) advised the Chief of Naval Personnel on women's affairs. Once again, women had a sense of supervision and structure.

Women continued to benefit from the earlier opening of NROTC programs, the Naval Academy, coed Officer Candidate School, and enlisted boot camp as well as postgraduate education. The DOPMA legislation in 1980 integrated promotion lists, equalized promotion rates, and allowed women to be selected by board rather than appointment for flag rank.

More and more women made the leap from the unrestricted line to restricted line and staff corps and thus to more specialized billets. At the same time, the chief warrant officer and limited duty officer communities offered added opportunities for advancement.

The Women in Ships Program saw more women deployed to sea duty, and by the end of the decade some 8,134 women served in 107 ships. Similarly, women's roles in naval aviation increased dramatically, and by 1990, 5,407 officers and enlisted served in the aviation community.

As women's experience increased, they rose in rank; and in the 1980s two unrestricted line officers (Pauline Hartington and Roberta Hazard), one restricted line officer (Grace Hopper), and three Nurse Corps staff officers (Frances Shea, Mary Nielubowicz, and Mary Hall) wore admiral's stars. Simultaneously, women moved into command positions, both as COs and XOs. Wielding such authority was new for women and helped entrench them in the naval hierarchy.

Although Navy women enjoyed much improvement in their military calling, problems persisted. As always, section 6015 of Title 10 barred women from service in combatant ships and aircraft and thus curtailed normal career progression. Resistance and resentment toward women's presence and growing visibility simmered and often erupted. Even two CNOs tried to curtail their numbers, and a secretary of the Navy was openly opposed to female fighting sailors. Sexual harassment and fraternization continued unabated.

In contrast, no one questioned the importance of the Navy Nurse Corps, and its members steadily carried out its duties of ministering to naval and marine personnel and their families and of training hospital corpsmen. The corps grew to 3,010 nurses, 25 percent of whom were male.

Reflecting a nationwide trend, the Nurse Corps became increasingly short of nurses and took various steps to improve recruiting and retention. It raised the maximum age for entering nurses, worked with other military nurse corps, established the Medical Enlisted Commissioning Program and the Cooperative Nursing Program, reinstituted the Nurse Corps Candidate Program, encouraged the NROTC for nursing students, and sent more vibrant recruiters into the field. Retention received a boost from the corps's education programs such as financing undergraduate and graduate degrees and providing short courses and seminars.

Although the Nurse Corps had difficulty maintaining its numerical strength, such was not the case for its professional strength. Determined to have an all-degree corps, Navy nurses became increasingly better trained, rivaling civilian standards.

Sea duty opened again for nurses, and deployment of male nurse anesthetists to carriers expanded to fourteen ships. Women served in two new hospital ships, the *Mercy* and *Comfort.*

Fortunate in its three directors—Rear Admirals Shea, Nielubowicz, and Hall—the Navy Nurse Corps emerged from the 1980s scarcely touched by the problems that plagued other naval women. It continued to administer its healing talents wherever the Navy needed them. Navy nurses, said Rear Admiral Hall, must be like the telephone company—prepared to reach out and touch someone every day.[148]

Altogether, the 1980s provided for all Navy women more advances than setbacks. Nevertheless, no definitive answers to the questions of full utilization of these women emerged. Uncertainty still hung heavy.

# Epilogue

The recent past presents difficulties for any historian. Vital source materials are not yet available, and insufficient time has passed to place events in historical perspective. Nevertheless, the 1990s, chock-full of fast-moving actions, saw old barriers crumble and new opportunities open. At the same time, long-standing problems persisted or intensified. A brief summary of major events from 1990 to 1995 can indicate roads traveled by Navy women and perhaps offer a glimpse of possibilities yet to come.

## Navy Women

With the collapse of the Soviet Union in the late 1980s, the United States had no major cold war adversary, and the military buildup slowed.[1] All the services began downsizing, and the Navy reduced its active ships from 570 in 1990 to 392 in 1995. Concurrently, personnel requirements dropped, and the 604,562 on active duty fell to 444,661, which included 55,548 women, or 12.5 percent of total strength. Although the number of women decreased from 60,411, their percentage of the active-duty force rose.[2]

### *Desert Storm*

The defining test for Navy, as well as all military, women came in 1990–91 with American participation in the Persian Gulf War. Ensuring the flow of Middle Eastern oil to the West had long been a keystone of American policy, and that flow was jeopardized in August 1990, when President Saddam Hussein sent the Iraqi army to invade the tiny emirate Kuwait.[3] When neighboring Saudi Arabia requested American help, President George Bush dispatched a massive military force as part of a thirty-three-nation coalition to drive Saddam from Kuwait. Vital components were the 167 ships and more than 75,000 naval personnel deployed to the area.[4]

Eventually, more than 1 million military men and women took part in the Persian Gulf War, including more than 37,000 American women. Of naval personnel, women accounted for about 3,700.[5] This largest deployment of women in history included, for the first time, military mothers. The war revealed how completely women had become integrated into the armed forces and how essential their services were. Military women suffered casualties: thirteen Army women died; two were captured by the Iraqis.[6]

Navy women filled a variety of roles in the combat area. Hundreds served in support ships—ammunition, supply, tenders, and oilers—and in Military Sealift and Combat Logistics Force vessels. Others were in two helicopter combat support squadrons, in Construction Battalions at Al Jubayl, and in a cargo-handling and port unit at Bahrain.[7]

For the Medical Department, the operational readiness concept, a part of planning and training for years, worked efficiently. About 250 nurses, both females and males, served in the hospital ships *Comfort* (T-AH 20) and *Mercy* (T-AH 19), dispatched to the gulf in September 1990. These state-of-the-art one-thousand-bed floating hospitals were prepared to care for massive casualties that, fortunately, never materialized.[8] Twenty-one male nurses staffed amphibious assault ships *Guam* (LPH 9) and *Iwo Jima* (LPH 2). The First Marine Amphibious Brigade and the First and Second Force Service Support Groups utilized thirty-one additional male nurses.[9]

Far busier were the three fleet hospitals erected in the region. Fleet Hospital Five, composed largely of active-duty personnel, including 152 nurses, reached Saudi Arabia in August 1990, and Fleet Hospitals Six and Fifteen, staffed mainly by reservists, arrived a few months later. Designed to handle battle casualties, these hospitals instead dealt primarily with illnesses or injuries not caused by combat.[10] Navy nurses played vital roles in these medical facilities, all located within range of Iraqi Scud missiles. Reserve nurses became critically important, recalled Nurse Corps director Rear Adm. Mary F. Hall, to staff fleet hospitals and to backfill in stateside hospitals for nurses deployed to the gulf.[11]

For all Navy women and nurses, the Gulf War demonstrated women's capabilities in a combat zone and exposed them to enemy fire. "We could not have won without them," said Secretary of Defense Richard Cheney. Their service, along with that of Army, Air Force, and Marine Corps women, brought to the forefront that old prohibition, combat exclusion.

## *Combat Exclusion Repealed*

Women's superior performance during the war elicited immediate demands to reexamine the outmoded 1948 combat exclusion law and triggered vigorous debate.[12] In April 1991, DACOWITS pushed for an end to the restrictions. By the end of the year, at the urging of Rep. Patricia Schroeder (D-Colo.) and others, both houses of Congress had debated the issue, authorized women to fly in combat planes, and mandated a presidential commission to study women's roles in the military.[13]

In November 1992, after eight months of acrimonious debate, the Presidential Commission on the Assignment of Women in the Armed Forces issued its report. The document recommended reenacting section 8549 of Title 10, barring women from combatant aircraft, but suggested allowing women to serve in all combatant ships except submarines and amphibious vessels. It also recommended exclusion of women from direct land combat.[14]

Following this contradictory and divisive report, Secretary of Defense Les Aspin took matters into his own hands and in April 1993 ordered the services to assign women to combat air squadrons. The services, he declared, must also offer more specialties to women, and the Navy must open additional ships to them. In November Congress repealed section 6015 of Title 10 and thereby opened combatant ships to women. Aspin went further still in January 1994 when he announced that the Defense Department was rescinding the risk rule of 1988 and instituting a new policy that barred women only from direct ground combat.[15] There was opposition from service women as well as men.[16]

It had taken since 1948 to remove most combat restrictions for women. The repeal of section 6015 and changes in Defense Department policy put women on more equal footing with men for career and promotion opportunities. By 1995, Navy women could serve in twenty-four of the twenty-six officer communities and in ninety-one of the ninety-four enlisted ratings.[17] It is far too soon to assess the long-term impact of these sweeping changes, but at least the full assimilation of women into the Navy and the other services moved forward, although military women continued to fill only a low number of combat-related jobs.[18]

### *Sea Duty*

Nowhere was progress more apparent than with women on ships. In 1990, 331 officers and 7,803 enlisted served on 117 ships.[19] Although downsizing the Navy during the early 1990s reduced the number of billets available to women, the 1993 repeal of the combat exclusion law opened a whole array of opportunities, most notably permanent assignment in combatant ships. The *Dwight D. Eisenhower* (CVN 69) was the first combatant with a mixed crew and air wing, and in October 1994 more than four hundred women sailed on the aircraft carrier on a six-month deployment to the Caribbean, the Middle East, and the Adriatic. "I've waited my whole career to go on a carrier," exclaimed CPO Chris Jackson. The *Eisenhower* successfully completed her mission with no diminution of readiness or performance. There was some resistance from male crew, recalled CPO2 Sandra Plunkett, who was told, "This is our world. This is a man's world." But the commanding officer, Capt. Alan M. Gemmill, called the deployment a success. "I think we've become a little more civilized," he added.[20]

As more combatants were reconfigured to accommodate female crew members, more women were assigned permanently to these warships. By the end of 1995, 374 officers and 2,332 enlisted were serving on 40 combat ships. An additional 218 officers and 5,425 enlisted were on 72 noncombatants. Altogether, 8,349 women were serving on 112 naval vessels.[21] The Navy wisely insisted on assigning sufficient female officers and enlisted to ships to prevent women's feeling isolated. The only combat ships that remained closed to them were submarines and mine warfare vessels.

Duty afloat, especially in combatants, was important to women, not only because of equal opportunity but also because it made them more competitive in promotions. "It was vital to have the same experiences as men," recalled Senior Chief PO Mary B. Prise, who served on four ships.[22]

### *In Aviation*

The crumbling of the combat exclusion law had an equally positive effect on women in naval aviation. In 1990, there had been 173 qualified female pilots and 80 naval flight officers, with more in the training pipeline, as well as 7,733 enlisted in aviation ratings.[23] Two years after Congress repealed the ban on female pilots for all the services in 1991, the Navy began assigning women aviators to combat aircraft squadrons.[24]

Aviators such as Lt. Sharron Workman, the first to qualify for carrier operations, was one of six female pilots assigned to the *Eisenhower* in the fall of 1994. While deployed in 1994–95, female fliers from the ship took part in 156 of the 2,856 sorties over Iraq and Bosnia.[25] Another pioneering combat pilot was Lt. Kara S. Hultgreen, the first woman F-14 pilot to qualify for combat duty. Her plane crashed during a training flight from the carrier *Abraham Lincoln* (CVN 72) in the Pacific in October 1994. Although later investigations unearthed mechanical problems as the cause of the crash, other aviators started a whisper campaign discrediting her qualifications, raising anew questions about women in combat aviation.[26]

Lt. (jg) Carey Lohrenz, another F-14 pilot and close friend of Hultgreen assigned to *Abraham Lincoln,* later told of being ostracized and derided, a fate the three remaining female pilots shared. Never a part of the squadron "jockdom," all these women eventually left the carrier.[27] Reinforcing such rejection was a naval helicopter commander's refusal to fly with women on combat missions during the American deployment ashore in Haiti in the summer of 1994. He cited his religious belief that men are to protect women.[28]

In spite of lack of acceptance by their male peers, the number of women in aviation continued to increase. By 1995, there were 206 pilots, including 82 combat aviators, 77 naval flight officers, and 9,502 enlisted.[29]

Attesting to the competence of naval women, NASA selected three for its space shuttle program. In 1992, Lt. Cdr. Wendy B. Lawrence, a CH-46/SH-2 pilot, started training as an astronaut. Three years later, Lt. Cdr. Susan L. Still, an F-14 pilot, and Cdr. Kathryn P. Hire began preparations to become astronauts.[30]

### *Naval Academy*

The U.S. Naval Academy, that bellwether of women's progress and acceptance, admitted even more budding female officers. In spite of a number of incidents that put the Academy on the defensive, women continued to apply for admission, especially after the 1993 repeal of the combat exclusion law. By 1995, there were 571 women at the Academy, 14 percent of the brigade. Still blocking women's true acceptance was the resentment festering even after twenty years of women's attendance.[31]

## Navy Nurse Corps

After participating in the Persian Gulf War, the Nurse Corps returned to its peacetime activities. There had been 3,102 active duty nurses, including 790 men, in 1990. Five years later, there were 3,319. The corps had ample nurses, which was a marked change from the shortage in the late 1980s. In fact, recruiting goals for 1994 included only 20 nursing specialists. The Navy soon instituted a reduction of strength that would gradually cost the corps 199 billets.[32]

### *Nurse Corps Leaders*

Replacing Rear Adm. Mary F. Hall was Rear Adm. Mariann Stratton, who became Nurse Corps director and deputy commander for personnel management in September 1991. Born in 1945, Stratton, a Houston, Texas, native, entered naval service in 1964 with a Navy Nurse Corps Candidate Scholarship and graduated from Sacred Heart Dominican College with nursing and English degrees. She later earned master's degrees in human resource management and nursing. Beginning active duty in 1966, Stratton served in a variety of hospitals overseas, including Japan, Ethiopia, Greece, and Italy, and stateside. Her last assignment was director of nursing services, Naval Hospital, San Diego.[33]

Although the 1990s saw downsizing and budget cuts, Stratton advocated a philosophy of "total quality leadership" and encouraged her nurses to devise innovative means of advancing patient care such as nursing case management programs. She emphasized research and publishing to spread innovations in nursing. Reflecting her vision, in 1993 she devised *Nurse Corps Strategic Plan—Charting New Horizons*, an organization plan and course of action.[34]

Following Stratton came Rear Adm. Joan Marie Engel, who became director of the Navy Nurse Corps in September 1994. The following year, the Health Sciences, Education and Training Command was disestablished and with it Engel's collateral job of deputy commander for personnel management. In its place came the billet of assistant chief for Education, Training, and Personnel.

Born in 1940 in St. Mary's, Pennsylvania, Engel received a diploma from Mercy Hospital School of Nursing, Buffalo, in 1961, then a bachelor's degree in public school nursing from Pennsylvania's Clarion University eight years later. After entering the Nurse Corps in 1969, Engel served in naval hospitals stateside and in Japan and Sardinia, holding progressively more responsible administrative posts. She was deputy director of the corps under Stratton.[35]

These two leaders maintained that "Navy Nursing IS Nursing Excellence." They kept Navy nursing in the mainstream of American nursing, which now emphasized disease prevention and health promotion. Similarly, Navy nurses encouraged good health practices with such programs as smoking cessation, prenatal and infant clinics, and women's health clinics. Ambulatory care included home health visits and same-day surgery, while a holistic approach to pregnancy provided multidiscipline services. Teams of nurses staffed family practice clinics, and others conducted education programs.[36] To assist with these changes, eighteen specialty advisers, a new means to address specifically matters in each subspecialty, became active.

During the early 1990s, Navy nurses in the United States continued to either attend civilian universities or serve at hospitals, clinics, branch clinics, recruiting commands, or Marine Corps stations. Abroad, they were in hospitals and clinics, on hospital ships, in aircraft carriers, and with fleet surgical teams of the Fleet Marine Force. In March 1994, twenty-three Navy nurses staffed the Fleet Hospital in Zagreb, Croatia, in support of United Nations peacekeeping forces. Two years later, five Navy nurses served in the amphibious assault ship *Wasp* (LHD 1) off the coast of Bosnia-Herzegovina.[37] As always, nurses trained hospital corpsmen.

They continued their tradition of rendering humanitarian aid in sundry disasters such as Operation Fiery Vigil in July 1991, when nurses helped evacuate twenty-two hundred Air Force and naval personnel and their dependents from Subic Bay after Mt. Pinatubo erupted. On the other side of the world, Navy nurses at Guantanamo Bay gave medical care to hundreds of Haitian refugees.[38] During the Los Angeles riots of April 1992, nurses at Naval Hospital, Long Beach, helped provide medical support for the ten thousand federal and military personnel activated in the area. In that same year, Navy nurses helped in the aftermath of Typhoon Omar in the Pacific and of Hurricane Andrew in Florida. In 1994 nurses from Naval Hospital, Long Beach, volunteered to assist victims of an earthquake at Los Angeles.[39]

## Shared Experiences

### *Rank and Command*

As the 1990s unfolded, more line and Nurse Corps officers rose to flag rank with commensurate command responsibilities. Rear Adm. Marsha J. Evans became superintendent of the Naval Postgraduate School at Monterey, and Rear Adm. Katherine L. Laughton took over the Naval Space Command at Dahlgren, Virginia. Rear Adm. Veronica Z. Froman became director for Manpower and Personnel, J-1, Joint Staff, while Rear Adm. Barbara E. McGann served as ACNP for Total Programming for Manpower at the Bureau of Naval Personnel. Patricia A. Tracey became a rear admiral in 1993 and commanded the Naval Training Center, Great Lakes. Three years later, she became the first woman promoted to vice admiral.[40]

Simultaneously, directors of the Nurse Corps also held flag rank. Rear Adm. Mariann Stratton began serving as director as well as assistant chief for Personnel Management in 1991. Three years later, Rear Adm. Joan M. Engel took over these two commands. The first Reserve Nurse Corps member, Maryanne I. Ibach, gained flag rank in 1990, followed by Nancy A. Fackler.[41]

More novel commands became available to women, as a few examples will illustrate. In late 1990, Lt. Cdr. Darlene Iskra assumed command of the rescue and salvage ship *Opportune* (ARS 41). The following year Lt. Cdr. Deborah Gernes became CO of the fleet oiler *Cimarron* (AO 177). Rear Adm. Louise C. Wilmot became the first woman to command a naval base when she took over at the Philadelphia Navy Base in 1993, and in 1994 Capt. Susan Brooker assumed command of Naval Readiness Command 22. The following year Capt. Linda V. Hutton became commander of the Naval Air Station, Key West.[42]

In addition to the directors, other Navy nurses took on positions of more responsibility. Eight captains were selected as commanding officers in 1992. One, Capt. Barbara A. Mencik, became CO, Naval Hospital, Long Beach, and another, Capt. Ann Langley, served as CO, Naval School of Health Sciences, Bethesda. By 1995 four Navy nurses were commanding officers.[43]

## *Pregnancy and Motherhood*

Until the 1970s, pregnancy and dependent children usually meant an automatic end to a woman's naval career. As working mothers became the norm in the American labor force, the Navy relaxed its prohibitions during the 1980s, and by the 1990s, it had accepted pregnancy as a normal female condition. Even so, the Navy had to grapple with issues such as the effect on readiness, lost time, workload of shipmates, and hazards in the work environment. Secretary of the Navy John H. Dalton announced the Navy's new pregnancy policy in February 1995, which concluded that pregnancy and parenthood do not preclude a naval career and stipulated various medical and counseling options available.[44]

## *Sexual Harassment and Tailhook*

Although Navy women made progress professionally in the early 1990s, some things stayed the same. The longtime problem of sexual harassment exploded with a fury at the Tailhook Association convention in September 1991. The Navy had decreed "zero tolerance" for sexual harassment the previous year, but apparently this message had not reached naval and Marine aviators. Their annual professional meetings often degenerated into drunken brawls with attendant lewd behavior.

As they made inroads into naval aviation, female pilots began going to these affairs, including the 1991 convention, held at the Hilton Hotel in Las Vegas. After attending panels and symposia by day, many male pilots partied at hospitality suites where alcohol was plentiful. Soon drunken men lined the hotel hallway outside the suites, groping and pawing any women who passed through this "gauntlet." At least twenty-six women, half of them naval officers, were molested in the gauntlet. Such behavior might have been brushed aside except that one victim was Lt. Paula Coughlin, a helicopter pilot and an admiral's aide. She reported the frightening episode to the admiral, who took no action. Determined that women should not suffer such indignities to protect their naval careers, she next notified Vice Adm. Richard M. Dunleavy, assistant CNO for Air Warfare, and her complaint soon reached the highest levels. By now the press had picked up portions of the story.

Chief of Naval Operations Frank B. Kelso II launched a Naval Investigative Service investigation, and simultaneously the Navy inspector general began another. Both groups reported in the spring of 1992; neither investigation resulted in charges against any of the seventy perpetrators and identified only two suspects. Exasperated, Coughlin went public with her story, and the Navy received a hailstorm of bad publicity. The Department of Defense inspector general began still another investigation amid charges of cover-ups and scapegoating. Accepting full responsibility, Lawrence Garrett resigned as secretary of the Navy in June. The summer of 1992 brought revocation of two nominations for high commands and postponing promotions for about five thousand officers until they could show they had not been at the Tailhook convention. In those same summer months, the Navy ordered all naval personnel and civilian employees to attend a one-day conference about sexual harassment.[45]

The DOD inspector general's reports, released in September 1992 and February 1993, were sharply critical of the unproductive investigations of the Naval Investigative Service and the Navy inspector general. The admirals at the top of these offices were held responsible. The DOD report raised the number of officers for possible discipline to 117 and the number of women assaulted to 83.[46]

Three aviators were eventually tried at Legal Services in Norfolk in December 1993, but the charges against them were dismissed. The Marine captain who had allegedly assaulted Coughlin was acquitted of criminal charges at Quantico, and eventually all charges against him were dropped. About fifty other officers received administrative penalties. No one was punished for sexual harassment or assault. Finally, CNO Kelso took early retirement in April 1994.[47]

And what of Lieutenant Coughlin? She did not receive accolades for courageously turning the spotlight on blatant sexual harassment and molestation. Almost from the beginning, rumors vilifying her circulated in the Navy, and other naval aviators ostracized her. In February 1994 Coughlin submitted a letter of resignation stating that "the covert attacks on me . . . have stripped me of my ability to serve." She could later take comfort in the $6.7 million awarded her in punitive and compensatory damages by a federal jury in a lawsuit against the Las Vegas Hilton and Hilton Hotels.[48]

The Tailhook scandal had rocked the entire naval establishment, turning searing attention to the persistent harassment problem, and everyone hoped Navy men had learned from the experience. Unfortunately, this was not the case. Glaring newspaper headlines revealed a continuing pattern of sexual misconduct.

In Orlando, for example, three instructors pushed an enlisted woman into a steaming shower, then beat and kicked her. In San Diego, ten instructors harassed communications trainees. The careers of two admirals ended because of adulterous relationships. Two officers—one at Norfolk, the other at Pearl Harbor—faced charges of sexual harassment. A drunken chief petty officer repeatedly groped an enlisted woman while on a cross-country commercial flight. In response, CNO Adm. Jeremy M. Boorda ordered more instruction for the entire Navy. Then the head of the U.S. Pacific Command uttered an impolitic remark, trivializing the rape of a twelve-year-old girl by a sailor and two marines. It ended that admiral's career.[49] Nevertheless, sexual misconduct continued.[50]

In spite of repeated incidents, Navy women reported in a survey that from 1988 to 1995 sexual harassment had fallen from 66 percent to 53 percent of all Navy women who had experienced or heard of such conduct during the past year. But the American public remained pessimistic and thought that harassment would always be present in the military.[51]

Another unresolved problem was that of lesbians in the Navy. Homosexuals, both male and female, had been barred from military service, but newly elected President William Clinton urged lifting the ban. The "don't ask, don't tell" policy, implemented in 1994, permitted homosexuals to serve as long as they did not openly engage in homosexual activities or unless the military discovered their orientation. In operation, the policy has, in fact, led to the discharge of more gays than before.[52] How the military will resolve this long-standing problem is unknown.[53]

Over the years, women have made great strides in the U.S. Navy. The unthinkable—women's permanent military service—had become possible. Theirs is the story of uneven and often uncertain progress. Their advancement in the Navy generally mirrored the situation of women in American society; the avenues that opened for all women soon had parallels in the Navy.

The Navy's personnel requirements governed its acceptance of women. It needed clericals in World War I, hence the yeomen (F). It needed women to fill stateside desk jobs in World War II, hence the WAVES. Even after the 1948 Women's Armed Forces Integration Act made women a permanent part of the military, the Navy had little use for them. Few took women's service seriously, and women fought an uphill battle for two decades just to survive in the Navy.

The 1970s brought massive changes for Navy women. The end of the draft and the beginning of the all-volunteer force once again caused personnel shortages, and once again the Navy needed women. It might not want women, but it needed them. Then Z-116 opened the floodgates of increased professional opportunities and the real possibility of a viable career in the Navy. As women rose in rank and assumed command responsibilities, more and more jobs became available. Finally, the Persian Gulf War and the repeal of the combat exclusion law added impetus to career potential for women. Still, Navy women encountered resentment, opposition, harassment, and sexism. There was always a lingering doubt about whether they were wanted in the U.S. Navy.

On the other hand, there was never any doubt about the acceptance of Navy nurses. The Navy needed nurses to care for sailors and marines, and few questioned their value or usefulness. Navy men did not fear competition from these professionals. Perhaps such strong support fostered an atmosphere of security that kept the Nurse Corps outside the turmoil that often affected other Navy women.

Since the Sacred Twenty first donned the blue capes of Navy nurses in

1908, the corps has grown in numbers, composition, training, and expertise. It has kept abreast of currents in the wider field of American nursing and has, in fact, surpassed civilian nursing in such areas as college degree requirements for its members. In wartime and peacetime, Navy nurses have served at home and abroad, caring for naval personnel and their dependents and carrying out their vital function of training hospital corpsmen. The Navy Nurse Corps enters the new century as its first superintendent, Esther V. Hasson, had envisioned it: "a dignified and respected body."

The story of all Navy women is one of dedication and valor. They proudly chose to serve their country as part of the U.S. Navy and pursued their goal with dogged determination. They would not be denied such an honorable calling. As in the eighteenth and nineteenth centuries, women's familiarity with maritime matters and their nursing skills have made them essential to the naval service.

Tributes to their service have been many. One of the most touching came in 1996, when the Navy named the guided missile destroyer *Hopper* (DDG 70) in honor of Rear Adm. Grace Hopper, who had led the Navy into the computer age. And in the fall of 1997, a lasting monument to Navy woman, as well as to all 1.8 million women who have served in the military, was dedicated: the Women in Military Service for America Memorial at the entrance to Arlington National Cemetery, which stands as a fitting reminder of all women who have volunteered to defend American freedom.

# Notes

### *Chapter 1. The Eighteenth and Nineteenth Centuries*

1. Carol Klaver, "An Introduction to the Legend of Molly Pitcher," *Minerva: Quarterly Report on Women and the Military* (summer 1994): 35–61; Ida C. Selavan, "Nurses in American History: The Revolution," in *Pages from Nursing History: A Collection of Original Articles from the Pages of "Nursing Outlook," the "American Journal of Nursing" and "Nursing Research"* (New York: American Journal of Nursing, 1984), 19–21; Mary Beth Norton, *Liberty's Daughters: The Revolutionary Experience of American Women, 1750–1800* (Boston: Little, Brown, 1980), 174; Linda Grant DePauw, "Women in Combat: The Revolutionary War Experience," *Armed Forces and Society* 7 (winter 1981): 209, 215–22; Nancy B. Samuelson, "Revolutionary War Women and the Second Oldest Profession," *Minerva: Quarterly Report on Women and the Military* 7 (summer 1989): 16–25; Wilma L. Vaught, "Women of the Revolution—Celebrating Heroines of Earlier Times," *Pentagram*, 9 July 1992. Sampson was the only woman to be recognized as a Revolutionary veteran, a pensioner, and later the official heroine of Massachusetts. See "Deborah Sampson, (1760–1827)," in *Liberty's Women*, ed. Robert McHenry (Springfield, Mass.: G. & C. Merriam, 1980), 367; Patrick L. Leonard, "Deborah Samson: Official Heroine of the State of Massachusetts," *Minerva: Quarterly Report on Women and the Military* 6 (fall 1988): 61–66. Leonard maintains that the correct spelling of Deborah's surname was "Samson."

2. Linda Grant DePauw, *Seafaring Women* (Boston: Houghton Mifflin, 1982), 91–92; Linda Grant DePauw, comment on "Women in a Warship, 1813," *USNIP* 110 (April 1984): 104.

3. Samuel Eliot Morison, *John Paul Jones: A Sailor's Biography* (Boston: Little, Brown, 1959), 159, 166. Jones took the cook and his wife to France and later exchanged them, along with his other prisoners, for American sailors held in British jails. The *Ranger's* Logbook, 24–26 April 1778, makes no mention of these prisoners, in Logbook 98, Mariners' Museum Library, Newport News, Va.; *Ranger*, in *Dictionary of American Naval Fighting Ships*, 8 vols, ed. James L. Mooney et al. (Washington, D.C.: GPO, 1959–) (hereafter cited as *DANFS*), 6:30.

4. *Rules for the Regulation of the Navy of the United Colonies of North America* (1775; reprint, Washington, D.C.: Naval Historical Foundation, 1944), article 16; Louis

H. Roddis, *A Short History of Nautical Medicine* (New York: Paul B. Hoeber, 1941), 70, 161–62; "History of the Hospital Corps, United States Navy: 1814–1975," typescript, Hospital Corps folder, box 5, ZV Files, OA, NHC.

5. Christopher McKee, *A Gentlemanly and Honorable Profession: The Creation of the U.S. Naval Officer Corps, 1794–1815* (Annapolis, Md.: Naval Institute Press, 1991), passim; Nathan Miller, *The U.S. Navy: An Illustrated History* (Annapolis, Md.: Naval Institute Press, 1977), 35, 38–39, 41–43; Robert W. Love Jr., *History of the U.S. Navy*, vol. 1, *1775–1941* (Harrisburg, Pa.: Stackpole Books, 1992), 52–55, 59–62; Julius A. Furer, *Administration of the Navy Department in World War II* (Washington, D.C.: GPO, 1959), 3.

6. Miller, *U.S. Navy*, 48–49, 52–54, 59–60; Love, *History of the U.S. Navy* 1:74–85; Spencer C. Tucker, *The Jeffersonian Gunboat Navy* (Columbia: University of South Carolina Press, 1993), 10, 13.

7. Department of the Navy, *Naval Regulations, Issued by Command of the President of the United States of America*, 25 January 1802, article 36.

8. N. A. M. Rodger, *The Wooden World: The Anatomy of the Georgian Navy* (Annapolis, Md.: Naval Institute Press, 1986), 68–70, 76–77. The eighteenth-century Navy "combined the disciplined efficiency of a man-of-war with large elements of the playground, the farmyard, and the travelling circus" (ibid., 71).

9. *Chesapeake*, in *DANFS* (1963) 2:95; Beverly F. Stoughton, "Women at Sea," *American History Illustrated* 15 (June 1980): 40; "Brief Account of Women in Naval Ships," 23 February 1951, Women in the Navy folder, box 13, ZV Files, OA, NHC; DePauw, *Seafaring Women*, 93–94. DePauw cites the journal of Midshipman Henry Wadsworth for the story of the infant's christening and the subsequent brawl.

10. Tucker, *Jeffersonian Gunboat Navy*, 83, 91; Miller, *U.S. Navy*, 76–78; Edward K. Eckert, *The Navy Department in the War of 1812* (Gainesville: University of Florida Press, 1973), 12–13.

11. Roddis, *Nautical Medicine*, 258–59, 277; Martha L. Crawley, "The Navy Medical Department, 1890–1916" (Ph.D. diss., George Washington University, 1989), 149.

12. J. Beatrice Bowman, "History of Nursing in the Navy," *AJN* 28 (September 1928), typed copy in Published Materials folder, box 37, Records of the Office of the Director, Navy Nurse Corps: 1881–1981 (hereafter cited as NNC Records), OA, NHC; Eckert, *War of 1812*, 47.

13. Rodger, *Wooden World*, 110–11; Selavan, "Nurses in American History," 20–21.

14. Roddis, *Nautical Medicine*, 188, 285–87, points to E. Cutbush and his book *Observations on the Means of Preserving the Health of Sailors and Soldiers, with Remarks on Hospitals and Their Internal Administration*, as the first American to write on naval medicine. Cutbush had called for hospital ships with sailors' wives as nurses. Secretary of the Navy Paul Hamilton had given Barton instructions to devise these regulations in July 1811, and he hastily compiled them during a tempestuous voyage in *Hornet* from Norfolk to New York. The report, sent to Congress on 16 March 1812, was signed by naval surgeons E. Cutbush, George Davis, Samuel R. Marshall, and Thomas Ewell, although Barton

had drafted it. In Report on Naval Hospitals, 16 March 1812, and addendum, 17 March 1812, in U.S. Congress, *American State Papers* (Washington, D.C.: Gales and Seaton, 1834) 1:270–73; William P. C. Barton, *A Treatise Containing a Plan for the Internal Organization and Government of Marine Hospitals in the United States: Together with a Scheme for Amending and Systematizing the Medical Department of the Navy* (Philadelphia: printed for the author, 1814), ix–x.

15. Barton, *Marine Hospitals*, sec. 26, p. 99.

16. Barton, *Marine Hospitals*, sec. 27, pp. 100–101.

17. Eckert, *War of 1812*, 15, 20, 23.

18. Harold D. Langley, "Women in a Warship, 1813," *USNIP* 110 (January 1984): 124–25; *United States*, in *DANFS* (1981) 7:415.

19. Langley, "Women in a Warship," 124–25.

20. Dianne Dugaw, "'Wild Beasts' and 'Excellent Friends': Gender, Class and the Female Warrior, 1750–1830," in *Jack Tar in History: Essays in the History of Maritime Life and Labour*, ed. Colin Howell and Richard J. Twomey (Fredericton, New Brunswick: Acadiensis Press, 1991), 132–33; Dianne Dugaw, "'Rambling Female Sailors': The Rise and Fall of the Seafaring Heroine," *International Journal of Maritime History* 4 (June 1992): 180–83.

21. Rodger, *Wooden World*, 77. For a recent account of women in RN ships, see Suzanne J. Stark, *Female Tars: Women Aboard Ship in the Age of the Sail* (Annapolis, Md.: Naval Institute Press, 1996).

22. Tyrone G. Martin, *A Most Fortunate Ship: A Narrative History of "Old Ironsides"* (Chester, Conn.: Globe Pequot Press, 1980), 144.

23. Dugaw, "Wild Beasts," 134–35; DePauw, *Seafaring Women*, 89–91. *The Female Soldier* was written by Robert Walker and published in 1750. For accounts of women warriors worldwide, see David E. Jones, *Women Warriors: A History* (Washington, D.C.: Brassey's 1997).

24. [Mary Ann Talbot], *The Life and Surprising Adventures of Mary Ann Talbot, in the Name of John Taylor, A Natural Daughter of the Late Earl Talbot* (London: R. S. Dirby, [1809]); DePauw, *Seafaring Women*, 60, 87–89.

25. Lucy Brewer, *The Female Marine, or Adventures of Miss Lucy Brewer* (printed 1 January 1816), 7–28; DePauw, *Seafaring Women*, 96–98.

26. Brewer, *Female Marine*, 28–29. The mean height of seafarers was 66.85 inches. See Ira Dye, "Physical and Social Profiles of Early American Seafarers, 1812–1815," in Howell and Twomey, *Jack Tar*, 226.

27. Brewer, *Female Marine*, 29–30. See Thomas C. Gillmer, *Old Ironsides: The Rise, Decline, and Resurrection of the USS "Constitution"* (Camden, Me.: International Marine, 1993), 69–79, for the battles.

28. Erika Nau, *Angel in the Rigging* (New York: Berkly Publishers, 1976), carries on the tale. Gillmer, *Old Ironsides*, makes no mention of Lucy Brewer; but Martin, *Most Fortunate Ship*, 144–46, thoroughly debunks the story.

29. Vern L. Bullough with Bonnie Bullough, *The Subordinate Sex: A History of Attitudes toward Women* (Urbana: University of Illinois Press, 1973), 299, 303; William H. Chafe, *Women and Equality: Changing Patterns in American Culture* (New York: Oxford University Press, 1977), 15–16; Sara M. Evans, *Born for Liberty: A History of Women in America* (New York: Free Press, 1989), 61–62, 68–69.

30. Norton, *Liberty's Daughters*, 298; Bullough and Bullough, *Subordinate Sex*, 310. The idea of separate spheres had first been eloquently described by Alexis de Tocqueville in *Democracy in America* (1840). Mid-twentieth-century historians picked up the terminology and ideology and propagated it. See Betty Friedan, *The Feminine Mystique* (New York: W. W. Norton, 1963); Barbara Welter, "The Cult of True Womanhood," *American Quarterly* 18 (summer 1966): 151–74; Aileen S. Kraditor, ed., *Up from the Pedestal: Selected Writings in the History of American Feminism* (Chicago: Quadrangle Books, 1968); and Gerda Lerner, "The Lady and the Mill Girl: Changes in the Status of Women in the Age of Jackson," *Midcontinent American Studies Journal* 10 (spring 1969): 5–15. More recent historians have questioned these earlier concepts; for example, Rosalind Rosenberg, *Beyond Separate Spheres: Intellectual Roots of Modern Feminism* (New Haven: Yale University Press, 1982); and Linda K. Kerber, "Separate Spheres, Female Worlds, Woman's Place: The Rhetoric of Women's History," *JAH* 75 (June 1988): 9–39.

31. Evans, *Born for Liberty*, 72–76.

32. Harold D. Langley, *Social Reform in the United States Navy: 1798–1862* (Urbana: University of Illinois Press, 1967), 39, 52, 59, 61–63, 67, 77, 131–32, 146, 168, 192, 209–10, 217, 227, 229, 238, 266, 274–75; Hugh H. Davis, "The American Seamen's Friend Society and the American Sailor, 1828–1838," *American Neptune* 39 (January 1979): 45–47, 49–52, 56; Mary P. Ryan, *Womanhood in America: From Colonial Times to the Present*, 3d ed. (New York: Franklin Watts, 1983), 153; Lisa Norling, "The Sentimentalization of American Seafaring: The Case of the New England Whalefishery, 1790–1870," in Howell and Twomey, *Jack Tar*, 171.

33. William H. Chafe, *The Paradox of Change: American Women in the 20th Century* (New York: Oxford University Press, 1991), 4–6; Ryan, *Womanhood*, 163–64; Evans, *Born for Liberty*, 93–95, 101–4. Led by Elizabeth Cady Stanton and Susan B. Anthony, the women's rights movement of the 1850s focused on public and civic life and emphasized women's property rights.

34. Miller, *U.S. Navy*, 111, 114, 118; Stephen Howarth, *To Shining Sea: A History of the United States Navy, 1775–1991* (New York: Random House, 1991), 127–28, 130, 134, 137, 167.

35. Furer, *Administration*, 5–6; Miller, *U.S. Navy*, 107–8, 127–28; Donald L. Canney, *The Ironclads, 1842–1885*, vol. 2 of *The Old Steam Navy* (Annapolis, Md.: Naval Institute Press, 1993), passim; Howarth, *To Shining Sea*, 145–48; Langley, *Social Reform*, 16, 28; Charles O. Paullin, *Paullin's History of Naval Administration: 1775–1911* (Annapolis, Md.: U.S. Naval Institute, 1968), 165–73, 179–80, 210. The bureaus set up in

1842 were Provisions and Clothing; Navy Docks and Yards; Ordnance and Hydrography; Medicine and Surgery; and Construction, Equipment and Repair.

36. Paullin, *History of Naval Administration*, 199, 240, 299–300.

37. Howarth, *To Shining Sea*, 159–63; Miller, *U.S. Navy*, 115, 131–34.

38. Miller, *U.S. Navy*, 134–36.

39. Love, *History of the U.S. Navy* 1:222–23.

40. U.S. Congress, *Report of the Secretary of the Navy: 1843* (hereafter cited as *SecNav Report*, followed by the date of the report); and John Rodgers to SecNav Mahlon Dickerson, 18 March 1836, with Board of Navy Commissioners Report on Hospitals, both in U.S. Congress, *American State Papers* (Washington, D.C.: Gales and Seaton, 1861), Class VI: Naval Affairs, 4:606, 866; Roddis, *Nautical Medicine*, 184, 262; Crawley, "Navy Medical Department," 149. See also Richmond C. Holcomb, *A Century with Norfolk Naval Hospital, 1830–1930* (Portsmouth, Va.: Printcraft Publishing, 1930). For an overview, see Harold D. Langley, *A History of Medicine in the Early U.S. Navy* (Baltimore: Johns Hopkins, 1995).

41. Cutbush had mentioned hospital ships in his *Observations . . . of 1808*, cited in Roddis, *Nautical Medicine*, 285, 288.

42. Bowman, "History of Nursing"; "History of the Hospital Corps."

43. Roddis, *Nautical Medicine*, 208–9; Jan K. Herman, *A Hilltop in Foggy Bottom: Home of the Old Naval Observatory and the Navy Medical Department* (Washington, D.C.: Bureau of Medicine and Surgery, 1991), 67.

44. Herman, *Hilltop*, 67; Paullin, *History of Naval Administration*, 196.

45. Bowman, "History of Nursing"; Roggis, *Nautical Medicine*, 211–12; Jan K. Herman, "Welcome Back BUMED," *U.S. Navy Medicine* 80 (July–August 1989): 10–11. The chief of the bureau did not gain the title of surgeon general until 1869.

46. *SecNav Report*, 1861, 377; Paullin, *History of Naval Administration*, 237.

47. Philip A. Kalisch and Beatrice J. Kalisch, *The Advance of American Nursing*, 2d ed. (Boston: Little, Brown, 1986), 89–92; Evans, *Born for Liberty*, 105–6.

48. Lavinia L. Dock and Isabel M. Stewart, *A Short History of Nursing: From Earliest Times to the Present Day*, 4th ed. (New York: G. P. Putnam's Sons, 1938), 144–45. See Joseph L. Dirvin, *Mrs. Seton: Foundress of the American Sisters of Charity* (New York: Farrar, Straus and Cudahy, 1962), 276, 303–6; Leonard Feeney, *Mother Seton: Saint Elizabeth of New York*, rev. ed. (Cambridge: Ravengate Press, 1975), 150–69.

49. M. Patricia Donahue, *Nursing: The Finest Art: An Illustrated History* (St. Louis: C. V. Mosby, 1985), 312.

50. Elspeth J. G. Huxley, *Florence Nightingale* (New York: G. P. Putnam's Sons, 1975), 11, 29, 44, 47, 50, 59, 63–64, 71, 76, 79, 101, 109–10, 117, 141, 188, 191; Linda S. Smith, "History of American Military Nursing," *Advancing Clinical Care* 6 (November–December 1991): 31–32; Dock and Stewart, *History of Nursing*, 118–27; Kalisch and Kalisch, *American Nursing*, 2d ed., 41–52. In 1856 Nightingale's official title became "General

Superintendent of the Female Nursing Establishment in Turkey." For a recent collection of Nightingale's letters, see Sue M. Goldie, ed., *I Have Done My Duty: Florence Nightingale in the Crimean War* (Iowa City: University of Iowa Press, 1989).

51. John C. Reilly Jr., *Ships of the United States Navy: Christening, Launching and Commissioning,* 2d ed. (Washington, D.C.: Naval History Division, 1976), 9.

52. Langley, *Social Reform,* 32. For a delightful account of one such voyage, see Elizabeth Douglas Van Denburgh, *My Voyage in the United States Frigate "Congress"* (New York: Desmond Fitzgerald, 1913). Elizabeth was the daughter of Joel Turrill, whom President Polk sent to the Sandwich Islands in 1845. The twelve civilians onboard included diplomats, wives, children, a friend, and a maid.

53. Department of the Navy, *Naval Regulations Issued by Command,* January 25, 1802; U.S. Congress, *Rules and Regulations for the Government of the Navy of the United States,* 23d Cong., 1st sess., 1833, H. Doc. 20; Department of the Navy, *Orders and Instructions for the Direction and Government of the Naval Service of the United States,* February 15, 1853 (Washington, D.C.: Robert Armstrong, 1853); Department of the Navy, *Regulations for the Government of the Navy of the United States: 1876* (Washington, D.C.: GPO, 1876); Department of the Navy, *Regulations for the Government of the Navy of the United States: 1893* (Washington, D.C.: GPO, 1893); Department of the Navy, *Regulations for the Government of the Navy of the United States: 1896* (Washington, D.C.: GPO, 1896).

54. Stoughton, "Women at Sea," 40–41; Women in Ships.

55. U.S. Congress, *Rules and Regulations for the Government of the Navy of the United States,* 27th Cong., 3d sess., 1843, H. Doc. 148, with accompanying transmittal letter.

56. Department of the Navy, *Regulations for the Government of the United States Navy: 1893,* 55; Dermott V. Hickey, "Women in the Navy," 4, seminar paper, George Washington University, 1961, in Historical Information folder, box 31, NNC Records.

57. Writers such as Julia C. Bonham, "Feminist and Victorian: The Paradox of American Seafaring Women of the Nineteenth Century," *American Neptune* 37 (July 1977): 205–7, believed that women went to sea primarily to be with their men. More pragmatic reasons came from Basil Greenhill and Ann Giffard, *Women Under Sail: Letters and Journals Concerning Eight Women Travelling or Working in Sailing Vessels between 1829 and 1949* (Newton Abbot: David and Charles, 1970), 9, who maintained that women went to sea as cabin passengers, wives or daughters of the captains, stewardesses working their passage, or emigrants. For a brief overview, see Diane E. Cooper, "She Dressed Herself in Sailors' Clothes," *Sea Letter* 49 (fall/winter 1994): 2–9.

58. DePauw, *Seafaring Women,* 40–43.

59. Ibid., 57–59.

60. Ibid., 162–63, 174, 179, 183, 196.

61. Ibid., 197–99.

62. Stoughton, "Women at Sea," 10; DePauw, *Seafaring Women,* 199–203.

63. Joan Druett, *Petticoat Whalers: Whaling Wives at Sea, 1820–1920* (Auckland,

New Zealand: Collins, 1991), 18–19, 29; Margaret S. Creighton, "'Women' and Men in American Whaling, 1830–1870," *International Journal of Maritime History* 4 (June 1992): 206; Margaret S. Creighton, "American Mariners and the Rites of Manhood, 1830–1870," in Howell and Twomey, *Jack Tar,* 143; and in recent book form, Margaret S. Creighton, *Rites and Passages: The Experience of American Whaling, 1830–1870* (New York: Cambridge University Press, 1995).

64. Locally available diaries include the Diary of Mrs. Daniel Taber, 25 September 1848–26 August 1855, Logbook 3; Diary of Asemath P. Taber, daughter of the master of *Alice Frazier,* Logbook 2, both at Mariners' Museum Library, Newport News, Va.

65. Druett, *Petticoat Whalers,* 26, 120, 139, 141–42, 148, 154–56.

66. Norling, "American Seafaring," 166, 168–70, 173, 178. Margaret S. Creighton, "The Private Life of Jack Tar: Sailors at Sea in the Nineteenth Century" (Ph.D. diss., Boston University, 1985), 184–202, stressed the heavy responsibilities placed on women by their husbands' long absences at sea.

67. See John D. Hayes, "Sea Power in the Civil War," *USNIP* 87 (November 1961): 60–69. For broad overviews, see William M. Fowler Jr., *Under Two Flags: The American Navy in the Civil War* (New York: W. W. Norton, 1990); and Bern Anderson, *By Sea and By River: The Naval History of the Civil War* (New York: Alfred A. Knopf, 1962).

68. Miller, *U.S. Navy,* 155–56; Paullin, *History of Naval Administration,* 250, 260.

69. Kalisch and Kalisch, *American Nursing,* 2d ed., 55.

70. American officials were well aware of the usefulness of female nurses in British general hospitals in Crimea. See *United States Sanitary Commission: Bulletin (1863–1865),* 3 vols. in 1 (New York: n.p., 1866), 1:213.

71. McHenry, *Liberty's Women,* 102; Kalisch and Kalisch, *American Nursing,* 2d ed., 56–57.

72. Kalisch and Kalisch, *American Nursing,* 2d ed., 62, 79.

73. Among the most famous of the Confederate nurses was Ella K. Newsom, who organized hospitals for the Army. In Barbara Duffey, "The Nurse: Ella K. Newsom Trader," in *Valor and Lace: The Roles of Confederate Women, 1861–1865,* ed. Mauriel P. Joslyn (Murfreesboro, Tenn.: Southern Heritage Press, 1996), 91–114; Anne L. Austin, "Nurses in American History: Wartime Volunteers—1861–1865," *AJN* 75 (May 1975), reprinted in *Pages from Nursing History,* 24; Smith, "Military Nursing," 31.

74. Ishbel Ross, *Angel of the Battlefield: The Life of Clara Barton* (New York: Harper & Brothers, 1956), 28–41, 55; Elizabeth B. Pryor, *Clara Barton: Professional Angel* (Philadelphia: University of Pennsylvania Press, 1987), 78–90, 92–100, 105–7. See also Stephen B. Oates, *A Woman of Valor: Clara Barton and the Civil War* (New York: Free Press, 1994).

75. See Nina B. Smith, "Men and Authority: The Union Army Nurse and the Problem of Power," *Minerva: Quarterly Report on Women and the Military* 6 (winter 1988): 25–41; Smith, "Military Nursing," 31; Marilyn M. Culpepper and Pauline G. Adams, "Nursing in the Civil War," *AJN* 88 (July 1988): 982.

76. Bickerdyke had the firm support of Gens. Ulysses S. Grant and William T. Sherman. She was adept at cutting through bureaucratic red tape and dismissing the protests of incompetent officers. In Culpepper and Adams, "Nursing in the Civil War," 984; Smith, "Men and Authority," 34–36; Mary A. Livermore, *My Story of the War: A Woman's Narrative of Four Years Personal Experience as a Nurse in the Union Army, and in Relief Work at Home, in Hospitals, Camps, and at the Front, during the War of the Rebellion* (Hartford, Conn.: A. D. Worthington, 1889), 476–98.

77. Harold E. Straubing, comp., *In Hospital and Camp: The Civil War through the Eyes of Its Doctors and Nurses* (Harrisburg, Pa.: Stackpole Books, 1993), 133; Evans, *Born for Liberty*, 114; William Q. Maxwell, *Lincoln's Fifth Wheel: The Political History of the United States Sanitary Commission* (New York: Longmans, Green, 1956), 1–2, 5, 8.

78. Straubing, *In Hospital and Camp*, 134; Austin, "Wartime Volunteers," 23; Maxwell, *Lincoln's Fifth Wheel*, 152–53. For a detailed description of the hospital transports during the Peninsula Campaign, see [Frederick Law Olmstead, comp.], *Hospital Transports: A Memoir of the Embarkation of the Sick and Wounded from the Peninsula of Virginia in the Summer of 1862* (Boston: Ticknor and Fields, 1863); and excerpts in Straubing, *In Hospital and Camp*, 132–47.

79. *Sanitary Commission: Bulletin*, 15 February 1864, 1:228, 237; 1 April 1864, 1:339.

80. George W. Grupp, "Navy Used First Hospital Ship to Treat Civil War Wounded," *Navy Times*, 5 December 1953, in Published Materials folder, box 37, NNC Records, OA, NHC; *ORN*, ser. 1, 6:603, 7:13, 184, 237, 469, 531, 650; ser. 2, 1:44; *Ben Morgan*, in *DANFS* (1959), 1:115.

81. Maxwell, *Lincoln's Fifth Wheel*, 98, 101, 104; Austin, "Wartime Volunteers," 22–23.

82. Reuben E. Stivers, *Privateers and Volunteers: The Men and Women of Our Reserve Naval Forces, 1766–1866* (Annapolis, Md.: Naval Institute Press, 1975), 331.

83. See Mary Denis Maher, *To Bind Up the Wounds: Catholic Sister Nurses in the U.S. Civil War* (Westport, Conn.: Greenwood Press, 1989); Cheryl Ellefson, "Servants of God and Man: The Sisters of Charity," in Joslyn, *Valor and Lace*, 175–83.

84. Stivers, *Privateers and Volunteers*, 329–30; Sister M. Eleanor, *On the King's Highway: A History of the Sisters of the Holy Cross of St. Mary of the Immaculate Conception* (New York: D. Appleton, 1931), 233–34.

85. *ORN*, ser. 1, 23:153–54.

86. *ORN*, ser. 1, 23:179; Louis H. Roddis, "The U.S. Hospital Ship *Red Rover* (1862–1865)," *Military Surgeon* 77 (August 1935): 93–94; William M. Fowler Jr., "Relief on the River: The *Red Rover*," *Naval History* 5 (fall 1991): 17.

87. "Civil War Hospital Ship," *All Hands*, book supplement, February 1962, 60; Eleanor, *King's Highway*, 239; Fowler, "Relief," 17–18.

88. "Civil War Hospital Ship," 60; Roddis, "*Red Rover*," 91; Fowler, "Relief," 18.

89. Roddis, "*Red Rover*," 94–95.

90. "Civil War Hospital Ship," 60, 62; Roddis, "*Red Rover*," 95; Fowler, "Relief," 19; "*Red Rover*," in *DANFS* (1976), 6:51–52.

91. Eleanor, *King's Highway*, 234; Stivers, *Privateers and Volunteers*, 330–31; "Civil War Hospital Ship," 60.

92. For operational details, see *ORN*, ser. 1, 24:100, 323, 518, 532, 658, 682; 25:91, 125, 336, 609, 692; 26:222, 242, 261, 517, 731, 750.

93. "Civil War Hospital Ship," 63; Stivers, *Privateers and Volunteers*, 332.

94. Stivers, *Privateers and Volunteers*, 337.

95. Hospital Ships, folder 312.180, RG 52, NARA; Fowler, "Relief," 19; "Civil War Hospital Ship," 63; Grupp, "Navy Used First Hospital Ship," 13. *Idaho* arrived at Nagasaki on 18 May 1868 and remained there until August 1869. In *Idaho*, in *DANFS* (1968): 3:415.

96. Roddis, "*Red Rover*," 98; Kalisch and Kalisch, *American Nursing*, 2d ed., 58.

97. Robley D. Evans, *A Sailor's Log: Recollections of Forty Years of Naval Life* (New York: D. Appleton, 1901), 98–105; Holcomb, *Norfolk Naval Hospital*, 298–301. Evans was able to continue his naval career and eventually took part in the blockade, then bombardment of Cuba during the Spanish-American War. He later commanded the Great White Fleet on its around-the-world cruise.

98. *ORN*, ser. 2, 1:264; reports of Cdr. Edward T. Nichols to Gideon Welles, 29 January 1863 and 15 February 1863, in *ORN*, ser. 1, 2:65–66, 84–85.

99. C. Kay Larson, "Bonny Yank and Ginny Reb," *Minerva: Quarterly Report on Women and the Military* 8 (spring 1990): 39; DePauw, *Seafaring Women*, 100–101. This account differs from Nichols's reports, which say that two men in charge of the prize crew decided to recapture *Ellicott* and sail her to New York. They were overcome by other crew members, who returned the vessel to St. Thomas.

100. C. Kay Larson, "Bonny Yank and Ginny Reb Revisited," *Minerva: Quarterly Report on Women and the Military* 10 (summer 1992): 47–48; Mary L. Clifford, *Women Who Kept the Lights: An Illustrated History of Female Lighthouse Keepers* (Vancouver, Wash.: Cypress Publications, 1993), passim.

101. Richard Hall, *Patriots in Disguise: Women Warriors of the Civil War* (New York: Paragon House, 1993), passim; Larson, "Yank and Reb Revisited," 35–56; Larson, "Bonny Yank and Ginny Reb," 33–48; "Mary Edwards Walker," in McHenry, *Liberty's Women*, 427.

102. Larson, "Yank and Reb Revisited," 50, 56; Evans, *Born for Liberty*, 115–18.

103. Miller, *U.S. Navy*, 191–95; "The Medical Department during the Period of Naval Decline (1866–1880)," typed MS, Overview—Naval Medical History, 1866–1898 folder, box 5, RG 52, NARA.

104. Miller, *U.S. Navy*, 196–98; Howarth, *To Shining Sea*, 232, 234. See also Mark R. Shulman, *Navalism and the Emergence of American Sea Power, 1882–1893* (Annapolis, Md.: Naval Institute Press, 1995).

105. Miller, *U.S. Navy*, 200–203; *SecNav Report*, 1897, 3. For rebuilding the Navy, see Peter Karsten, *The Military in America: From the Colonial Era to the Present* (New York: Free Press, 1986), 239–74.

106. Paullin, *History of Naval Administration*, 370–72, 414–16.

107. U.S. Congress, Report of the Surgeon General, U.S. Navy, *SecNav Report*, 1896,

54th Cong. 2d sess., 1 October 1896, H. Doc. 3, 575. In 1897 BuMed had 170 medical officers and 17 vacancies. In *SecNav Report*, 1897, 55th Cong., 2d sess., 29, 37.

108. Report of the Surgeon General, *SecNav Report*, 1896, 563–65, 576, 585; U.S. Congress, Report of the Surgeon General, U.S. Navy, *SecNav Report*, 1897, H. Doc. 3, 536–42, 553, 555; Holcomb, *Norfolk Naval Hospital*, 334.

109. Report of the Surgeon General, U.S. Navy (1896), 581–83; Report of the Surgeon General, U.S. Navy (1897), 554.

110. Monthly reports of Naval Asylum, entry 71.3, RG 71, NARA; Clothing factory file, entry 80.5, RG 80, NARA; Journals and Daybooks, Washington Navy Yard, entry 181.2, RG 181, NARA, all cited in Charlotte P. Seeley, comp., *American Women and the U.S. Armed Forces: A Guide to the Records of Military Agencies in the National Archives Relating to American Women* (Washington, D.C.: NARA, 1992).

111. Robert G. Albion, "A Brief History of Civilian Personnel in the U.S. Navy Department," typed manuscript, 1943, Navy Department Library, 6.

112. Secretary of the Interior, comp., *Official Register of the United States, Containing a List of Officers and Employees in the Civil, Military, and Naval Service*, 1879 (Washington, D.C.: GPO, 1879) (hereafter cited as *Official Register*, followed by the date in parentheses), 1:279. "Writer" was synonymous with clerk or scribe. Women possibly worked for the Navy earlier, but the *Official Register* often used only initials and the surname. In the early 1880s, this register began using either first names of women or the honorifics "Mrs." or "Miss."

113. *Official Register* (1881), 1:441–42; (1883), 1:433–35; (1885), 1:406–7, 409; (1887), 1:419–25; (1889), 1:470–75; (1891), 1:521; (1899), 1:694–704. The bureaus employing women were Yards and Docks, Navigation, Provisions and Clothing, Equipment and Recruiting, Construction and Repair, Medicine and Surgery, and Supplies and Accounts.

114. Eleanor Flexner, *Century of Struggle: The Woman's Rights Movement in the United States*, rev. ed. (Cambridge: Belknap Press, 1975), 222–31; Evans, *Born for Liberty*, 122–24, 153.

115. Ryan, *Womanhood*, 203–4; Evans, *Born for Liberty*, 125–29; "Frances Elizabeth Caroline Willard," in McHenry, *Liberty's Women*, 446–47.

116. Bullough and Bullough, *Subordinate Sex*, 316; Sheila M. Rothman, *Woman's Proper Place: A History of Changing Ideals and Practices, 1870 to the Present* (New York: Basic Books, 1978), 74–75; Evans, *Born for Liberty*, 140–41.

117. Patrick Gilbo, *The American Red Cross* (New York: Chelsea House, 1987), 27–33; Pryor, *Clara Barton*, 204–5, 210; Foster R. Dulles, *The American Red Cross: A History* (Westport: Greenwood Press, 1950), 15–17.

118. Chafe, *Women and Equality*, 28; Rothman, *Proper Place*, 5, 14, 64–70.

119. Lynn Y. Weiner, *From Working Girl to Working Mother: The Female Labor Force in the United States, 1820–1980* (Chapel Hill: University of North Carolina Press, 1985), 27–29; Evans, *Born for Liberty*, 134–35; Bullough and Bullough, *Subordinate Sex*, 332; Rothman, *Proper Place*, 14, 18, 42.

120. Evans, *Born for Liberty*, 130–31, 133–37.

121. Bullough and Bullough, *Subordinate Sex*, 323, 330–31; Ryan, *Womanhood*, 201, 205; Rothman, *Proper Place*, 106; Chafe, *Women and Equality*, 26–27, 37. Rosalind Rosenberg, "The Limits of Access: The History of Coeducation in America," in *Women and Higher Education in American History*, ed. John M. Faragher and Florence Howe (New York: W. W. Norton, 1988), 109, argues that coeducation, the prevalent form of women's education, was inferior to eastern male colleges.

122. Evans, *Born for Liberty*, 141, 148–50; "Jane Addams," in McHenry, *Liberty's Women*, 3–4.

123. Carl N. Degler, "Charlotte Perkins Gilman on the Theory and Practice of Feminism," in *Our American Sisters: Women in American Life and Thought*, by Jean E. Friedman and William G. Shade (Boston: Allyn and Bacon, 1973), 197–218.

124. Kalisch and Kalisch, *American Nursing*, 2d ed., 96–97; Donahue, *Finest Art*, 308–10.

125. Donahue, *Finest Art*, 313–14; Kalisch and Kalisch, *American Nursing*, 2d ed., 94–95, 100–101; Dock and Stewart, *History of Nursing*, 147, 151.

126. Kalisch and Kalisch, *American Nursing*, 2d ed., 101–4; Dock and Stewart, *History of Nursing*, 151–52; Donahue, *Finest Art*, 314–16.

127. Josephine Dolan, "Nurses in American History: Three Schools—1873," *AJN* 75 (June 1975), reprinted in *Pages from Nursing History*, 34–36; Dock and Stewart, *History of Nursing*, 152, 155; Kalisch and Kalisch, *American Nursing*, 2d ed., 161.

128. Doris M. Sterner, *In and Out of Harm's Way: A History of the Navy Nurse Corps* (Seattle: Peanut Butter Publishing, 1996), 8–9; Kalisch and Kalisch, *American Nursing*, 2d ed., 110.

129. Dock and Stewart, *History of Nursing*, 160, 176; Donahue, *Finest Art*, 316, 333, 335.

130. Teresa E. Christy, "Nurses in American History: The Fateful Decade, 1890–1900," *AJN* 75 (July 1975), reprinted in *Pages from Nursing History*, 37–38; Donahue, *Finest Art*, 360–61, 369. The society became the National League of Nursing Education in 1912, then the National League for Nursing in 1952.

131. Christy, "Nurses in American History," 38–39. In 1911 the Associated Alumnae changed its name to the American Nurses Association.

132. Kalisch and Kalisch, *American Nursing*, 2d ed., 266–71.

133. For a recent account of the failed diplomacy that led to war, see John L. Offner, *An Unwanted War: The Diplomacy of the United States and Spain over Cuba, 1895–1898* (Chapel Hill: University of North Carolina Press, 1992).

134. Miller, *U.S. Navy*, 203–4. Although the United States blamed Spain for the *Maine* disaster, the cause of the explosion was not determined. In 1976, Adm. Hyman G. Rickover, *How the Battleship* Maine *Was Destroyed* (Washington, D.C.: Naval History Division, 1976), concluded that the blast probably resulted from spontaneous combustion in a coal bunker which ignited nearby ammunition. More recently, Peggy and

Harold Samuels, *Remembering the* Maine (Washington, D.C.: Smithsonian Institution Press, 1995), have argued that a primitive mine probably destroyed the ship. See also Michael Blow, *A Ship to Remember: The* Maine *and the Spanish-American War* (New York: William Morrow, 1992).

135. David F. Trask, *The War with Spain in 1898* (New York: Macmillan, 1981), 101–7; Miller, *U.S. Navy*, 208–9, 211; Gerald R. Anderson, *Subic Bay: From Magellan to Mr. Pinatubo, A History of the U.S. Naval Station, Subic Bay* (N.p.: n.p., 1992), 12–15.

136. Trask, *War with Spain*, 225–48, 286–319; Miller, *U.S. Navy*, 211–12, 215, 217–20.

137. "Splendid little war" in John Hay to Theodore Roosevelt, 27 July 1898, in William R. Thayer, *The Life and Letters of John Hay*, 2 vols. in 1 (Boston: Houghton Mifflin 1929) 2:37.

138. Donahue, *Finest Art*, 327; Kalisch and Kalisch, *American Nursing*, 2d ed., 230–31, 234, 255; Philip A. Kalisch and Margaret Scobey, "Female Nurses in American Wars: Helplessness Suspended for the Duration," paper presented at Inter-University Seminar on Armed Forces and Society, 1980, 3–4, in Historical Information folder, box 31, NNC Records, OA, NHC.

139. Dulles, *Red Cross*, 52–54; Gilbo, *American Red Cross*, 34.

140. Kalisch and Kalisch, *American Nursing*, 2d ed. 244–47; "*Relief*," in *DANFS* (1976) 6:68. *Relief* was transferred to the U.S. Navy in 1902.

141. Kalisch and Kalisch, *American Nursing*, 2d ed., 253; Smith, "Military Nursing," 36.

142. *SecNav Report*, 1898, 23; Report of the Surgeon General (1898), 787; Statistical Report of the Health of the Navy and Marine Corps, 21 April–12 August 1898, in appendix, Report of the Surgeon General (1898), 805; Surgeon General's Office, memorandum, 16 December 1914, Spanish-American War—General no. 1 folder, box 8, ZO Files, OA, NHC.

143. Report of the Surgeon General (1898), 770.

144. U.S. Congress, SecNav Report, *Annual Reports of the Navy Department: 1898*, 55th Cong., 3d sess., H. Doc. 3, 43; *Surgeon General's Report: 1898*, 772; "History of the Hospital Corps."

145. Report of the Surgeon General (1897), 536–42; *1898*, 775; *Register of the . . . Navy of the U.S. . . . to Jan. 1, 1898* (Washington, D.C.: GPO, 1898), 116–20; Department of the Navy, *Hospital Corps Handbook: United States Navy, 1923* (Washington, D.C.: GPO, 1923), 2; "History of the Hospital Corps."

146. Holcomb, *Norfolk Naval Hospital*, 326; Report of the Surgeon General (1898), 772. The women at Brooklyn were Margaret Long, Dorothy Reed, Mable P. Simis, and Mable F. Austin. Those at Norfolk were Emilyn Mann, Wilhelmine Geisemann, Lula M. Plant, Lucy N. White, Rebecca Jackson, Caroline Patterson, and Sisters Magdalen Kelleher, Chrysostom Moneyhan, Cecelia Beck, Victorine Salazar, and Mary Larkin, all in Spanish War folder, box 5, entry 48D, RG 52, NARA.

147. Report of the Surgeon General (1898), 772; Crawley, "Navy Medical Department," 202–3.

148. Log Book of USS *Solace,* 1 August 1898–9 February 1899, NARA; *SecNav Report,* 1898, 42; Report of the Surgeon General (1898), 770–71; "*Solace,*" in *DANFS* (1976), 6:543; Holcomb, *Norfolk Naval Hospital,* 328–33; Richard A. Douglas, "Treating the Enemy: Santiago, Cuba, 1898," *U.S. Navy Medicine* 80 (July–August 1989): 20–21. Movements of *Solace* in *Report of the Chief of the Bureau of Navigation* in *SecNav Report,* 1898, 352–53. Any lingering doubts about whether the trained nurses onboard were male or female are resolved by a letter of 16 October 1898 and signed by eight men who had been rated as cooks for nurse duty. They requested discharges from the Navy since there was no longer any need for nurses. In file 44975, RG 52, NARA, and Feeney Notebooks, folder 1, box 24, NNC Records, OA, NHC.

## *Chapter 2. The Navy Nurse Corps, 1900–1915*

1. See Robert H. Wiebe, *The Search for Order: 1877–1920* (New York: Hill and Wang, 1967), passim.

2. Lynn D. Gordon, *Gender and Higher Education in the Progressive Era* (New Haven: Yale University Press, 1990), 2, 7; Mabel Newcomer, *A Century of Higher Education for American Women* (Washington, D.C.: Zenger, 1959), 19, 46; Ryan, *Womanhood,* 201; Rothman, *Proper Place,* 106.

3. Chafe, *Women and Equality,* 31, 35; Nell Irvin Painter, *Standing at Armageddon: The United States, 1877–1919* (New York: W. W. Norton, 1987), 235; Ryan, *Womanhood,* 169; Weiner, *Working Girl,* 4.

4. Rothman, *Proper Place,* 5, 97–99; Wiebe, *Search for Order,* 169.

5. Evans, *Born for Liberty,* 160; McHenry, *Liberty's Women,* 234–35. Lathrop was the first woman to be appointed by a president and confirmed by the Senate to head a federal bureau.

6. Evans, *Born for Liberty,* 148–50; Ryan, *Womanhood,* 202.

7. Evans, *Born for Liberty,* 157–60.

8. William H. Chafe, *The American Woman: Her Changing Social, Economic, and Political Roles, 1920–1970* (London: Oxford University Press, 1972), 16–17; Evans, *Born for Liberty,* 150; Ryan, *Womanhood,* 204. See also Mildred W. Wells, *Unity in Diversity: The History of the General Federation of Women's Clubs* (Washington, D.C.: General Federation of Women's Clubs, 1953), and Karen Blair, *The Clubwoman as Feminist: True Womanhood Redefined, 1868–1914* (New York: Holmes and Meier, 1980).

9. Wiebe, *Search for Order,* 122, 293; Evans, *Born for Liberty,* 152–54, 164–68; McHenry, *Liberty's Women,* 67–68; Rothman, *Proper Place,* 127–28. Eleanor Flexner, *Century of Struggle: The Woman's Rights Movement in the United States* (Cambridge: Harvard University Press, 1959), remains the comprehensive account of the movement.

10. Wyoming gave women the vote in 1890, Colorado in 1893, and Utah and Idaho in 1896. Next came Washington in 1910, California in 1911, and Kansas, Oregon, and Arizona in 1912.

11. Gordon C. O'Gara, *Theodore Roosevelt and the Rise of the Modern Navy* (1943; reprint, New York: Greenwood Press, 1969), passim.

12. Figures from "U.S. Navy Active Ship Force Levels, 1900–1989," Ships History Branch, OA, NHC.

13. See Robert A. Hart, *The Great White Fleet: Its Voyage around the World, 1907–1909* (Boston: Little, Brown, 1965); James R. Reckner, *Teddy Roosevelt's Great White Fleet* (Annapolis, Md.: Naval Institute Press, 1988). Karsten, *Military in America,* 239–74, has a summary of changes in military reorganization.

14. *SecNav Report,* 1915, 21; *Navy Registers: 1900,* 6–39; *Navy Registers: 1915,* 8–74; Frederick S. Harrod, *Manning the New Navy: The Development of a Modern Naval Enlisted Force, 1899–1940* (Westport, Conn.: Greenwood Press, 1978), 5–6, 35, 58, 78, 89. Harrod sees the decade after the Spanish-American War as revolutionary in establishing a naval recruiting and training system that saw few changes before World War II (3, 6, 166).

15. Robert W. Love Jr., ed., *The Chiefs of Naval Operations* (Annapolis, Md.: Naval Institute Press, 1980), xv–xvii, 3; Miller, *U.S. Navy,* 241, 257, 260; Karsten, *Military in America,* 256; Paullin, *History of Naval Administration,* 232–37.

16. Henry P. Beers, *American Naval Occupation and Government of Guam, 1898–1902* (Washington, D.C.: Office of Records Administration, Navy Department, 1944), 11; J. A. C. Gray, *Amerika Samoa: A History of American Samoa and Its United States Naval Administration* (Annapolis, Md.: U.S. Naval Institute, 1960), ix.

17. *Surgeon General's Report: 1909,* 858–67; Herman, *Hilltop,* 67–68, 71–73; Roddis, *Nautical Medicine,* 234.

18. Holcomb, *Norfolk Naval Hospital,* 334–35; Crawley, "Navy Medical Department," 163, 165–66, 169.

19. Kalisch and Kalisch, *American Nursing,* 2d ed., 299, 377; Donahue, *Finest Art,* 377, 380; Dock and Stewart, *History of Nursing,* 160; Dermott V. Hickey, "First Ladies in the Navy: A History of the Navy Nurse Corps, 1908–1939" (Master's thesis, George Washington University, 1963), 37.

20. Donahue, *Finest Art,* 358, 374–75; Kalisch and Kalisch, *American Nursing,* 2d ed., 290–94. The first four states to pass licensing laws were North Carolina, New Jersey, New York, and Virginia.

21. Kalisch and Kalisch, *American Nursing,* 2d ed., 297–98. Sponsored by the Carnegie Foundation, Abraham Flexner investigated all medical schools in the U.S. and Canada. His 1910 report describing the shocking conditions he found precipitated nationwide reform. Medical education became a part of university programs demanding strict standards.

22. Donahue, *Finest Art,* 353, 355, 366–69; Kalisch and Kalisch, *American Nursing,* 2d ed., 292.

23. Dock and Stewart, *History of Nursing,* 299, 320.

24. Teresa Christy, "Equal Rights for Women: Voices from the Past," in *Pages from Nursing History,* 62–67 (reprinted from *AJN* 71 [February 1971]).

25. Barbara B. Tomblin, *G.I. Nightingales: The Army Nurse Corps in World War II* (Lexington: University Press of Kentucky, 1996), 2–3; William K. Van Reypen to SecNav, 3 February 1899, with draft of provision to be included in the Naval Appropriations Bill, file 47147, box 110, RG 52, NARA.

26. Kalisch and Kalisch, *American Nursing*, 2d ed., 255–57; *United States Statutes at Large* 31 (1901): 753; Tomblin, *G.I. Nightingales*, 3.

27. Biographical data, Presley M. Rixey, OA, NHC; William C. Braisted, William H. Bell, and Presley M. Rixey, *The Life Story of Presley Marion Rixey: Surgeon General, U.S. Navy, 1902–10* (Strasburg, Va.: Shenandoah Publishing House, 1930), 31, 89, 92, 95, 101, 123, 125, 137, 296–307; *Relief*, in *DANFS* (1976) 6:68; *Solace*, in *DANFS* (1976) 6:543.

28. *Surgeon General's Report: 1902*, 913; *Surgeon General's Report: 1903*, 1197; *Surgeon General's Report: 1904*, 1168–69; *Surgeon General's Report: 1905*, 1219; *Surgeon General's Report: 1906*, 1033–34; *Surgeon General's Report: 1907*, 1176–78.

29. Surgeon General to Norfolk Hospital, 3 May 1907, file 112009; Surgeon General to Naval Hospital, Chelsea, telegram and letter, 18 August 1908, both in file 115880, box 267, entry 11, all in RG 52, NARA.

30. Hickey, "Navy Nurse Corps," 36, 38–40; Bowman, "History of Nursing," 6; J. S. Taylor, "The Hospital Corpsman and the Trained Nurse," *U.S. Naval Medical Bulletin*, supplement (July 1919): 7–8.

31. Presley M. Rixey to Victor H. Metcalf, 29 February 1908, and Metcalf to George E. Foss, 3 March 1908, both attached to U.S. Congress, *An Act Making Appropriations for the Naval Service for the Fiscal Year Ending June 30, 1909*, 60th Cong., 1st sess., H. Rept. 1309, chap. 166.

32. *United States Statutes at Large* 35 (1908): 146; *Navy Regulations: 1909*, 241–42.

33. *Surgeon General's Report: 1908*, 863.

34. Julia E. Woods to surgeon general, 30 January 1903; and Laura A. C. Hughes to Theodore Roosevelt, 7 July 1908, both in folder 3, Subject Files, 1898–1978, box 8, NNC Records, OA, NHC.

35. Esther V. Hasson to SecNav, 16 July 1903; letters of recommendation for Hasson from J. M. Kennedy, 17 January 1903; from George H. Torney, 7 February 1903; from S. B. M. Young, 20 April 1903, all in file 80896, box 169, RG 52, NARA; Biographical data, Esther Voorhees Hasson, OA, NHC; "The Navy Nurse Corps," editorial comment, *AJN* 9 (November 1908): 91.

36. Records of Proceedings of Examining Board, 3 August 1908, file 80896, box 169, RG 52, NARA; *Surgeon General's Report: 1908*, 865; Hickey, "Navy Nurse Corps," 45–46. The three members of the examining board were medical directors W. S. Dixon, C. E. H. Harmon, and surgeon W. C. Braisted.

37. Rixey, Duties of the Superintendent of the Nurse Corps (female), 28 October 1909, Feeney notebooks, folder 1, box 24, NNC Records; Department of the Navy, *Manual for the Medical Department of the United States Navy*, 1917 (Washington, D.C.: GPO, 1917), 46–47.

38. *Surgeon General's Report: 1908*, 865–66; Rixey, Circular Letter, 24 August 1908, Feeney notebooks, folder 1, box 24, NNC Records.

39. Esther V. Hasson, "The Navy Nurse Corps," *AJN* 9 (March 1909): 413.

40. "Sacred 20" folder, box 3, entry 48D, RG 52, NARA; "First Twenty Nurses," Feeney notebooks, folder 1, box 24, NNC Records; "Nurse Corps," *AJN* 9 (November 1908): 91.

41. Daybook, May 1908–April 1930, box 4, NNC Records.

42. Bound volume, "Monthly Rooster [*sic*], Nurses at Navy Medical School, Washington, DC, Sept. 17, 1908–June 1915," box 4, entry 48D, RG 52, NARA; Department of the Navy, *Regulations and Instructions for the Nurse Corps, U.S. Navy: 1909* (Washington, D.C.: GPO, 1909) (hereafter cited as *Nurse Corps Regulations*), 7; *Surgeon General's Report: 1908*, 865–66.

43. *Surgeon General's Report: 1909*, 872.

44. For example, medical officer, Mare Island, to BuMed, 14 September 1910, folder 1, box 24, NNC Records.

45. Letterbook, Semi-Official, NNC Records, August 1909–December 1911, box 1, entry 20, RG 52, NARA.

46. Hasson to Bowman, 16 April 1910, correspondence 1903–11 folder, box 1, Bowman Papers, NNC Records, OA, NHC.

47. *Nurse Corps Regulations*, 5–6, 8–10; Crawley, "Navy Medical Department," 216–17, 234.

48. Hasson, "Nurse Corps," 414; Hasson to DeCeu, 7 September 1910, Semi-Official Letterbook.

49. *Nurse Corps Regulations*, 10–11, 13. After *Muller v. Oregon* in 1908 limited factory work for women to ten hours a day, a federal investigation of women's occupations found that nursing involved "moral risk" and was a dangerous profession. Nursing demanded long hours of physical labor and mental strain, made drugs and liquor readily available, and made nurses easy targets for male patients. Between 1908 and 1917, 39 states passed or strengthened laws regulating women's working hours. In 1913 California extended its eight-hour day, six-day week to student nurses. Because of opposition from doctors and hospitals, the law went to the Supreme Court, which ruled in 1915 that it was constitutional. See Kalisch and Kalisch, *American Nursing*, 2d ed., 313–17.

50. *Nurse Corps Regulations*, 16; Rixey, Circular Letter; Crawley, "Navy Medical Department," 230.

51. Hasson to J. Beatrice Bowman, 16 April 1910, Correspondence, 1903–11 folder, box 1, J. B. Bowman Papers, NNC Records, OA, NHC.

52. *United States Statutes at Large* 36 (1910): 249; SecNav General Order 65, 4 May 1910; Pay Table, Pay and Allowances folder 1, box 15, NNC Records, OA, NHC.

53. Hasson to Bowman, 16 April 1910; *Nurse Corps Regulations*, 4–5.

54. Hasson to Surgeon General, 27 November 1908; Braisted to Hasson, 28 November 1908, with Surgeon General's approval, both in file 116262, box 270, RG 52, NARA; *Nurse Corps Regulations*, 16; "Uniforms of the United States Navy, 1905–1913," History

of Uniforms folder, box 19; BuMed Circular Letter, 9 March 1910, Feeney notebooks, folder 1, box 24, both in NNC Records, OA, NHC.

55. Hasson to Surgeon General, 7 November 1910, and 23 November 1910, both in Letterbook: Letters Sent by the Superintendent, NNC Records, August 1909–December 1911, box 1, entry 20, RG 52, NARA.

56. Crawley, "Navy Medical Department," 202.

57. U.S. Fleet Surgeon Albert M. D. McCormick to SecNav, 6 May 1910; Surgeon General to CINC, Atlantic Fleet, 7 May 1910; McCormick to SecNav and BuMed, 11 May 1910, all in folder 1, box 24, NNC Records, OA, NHC.

58. Hasson to [Clare L.] DeCeu, 7 September 1909; Hasson to [Adah M.] Pendleton, 25 August 1910, both in Feeney notebooks, folder 2; Surgeon General to commanding officer, Annapolis Naval Hospital, 17 August 1909, and 2 May 1910, both in Feeney notebooks, folder 6 (Dependents and Navy nurses); BuMed Circular Letter, 23 December 1910, folder 1, all in box 24, NNC Records; *Surgeon General's Report: 1909*, 875. *Nurse Corps Regulations*, 8, expressly prohibited Navy nurses from providing services to the families of officers and enlisted men.

59. *Nurse Corps Regulations*, 10–11.

60. Hasson, "Navy Nurse Corps," 412–13.

61. Taylor, "Hospital Corpsman," 8, 10–12. Women's sphere, continued Taylor, provided them with an "innate delicacy of touch, silent steps, deft movements, speed without haste, efficiency without officiousness, solicitude without persecution, the apt word on occasion, or golden silence."

62. Surgeon General to Naval Hospitals, New York, Annapolis, Washington, Norfolk, and Mare Island, 22 January 1910, folder 1, box 24, NNC Records, OA, NHC.

63. Stokes to Hasson, 27 September 1910; Hasson to Stokes, 29 September 1910; Hasson to SecNav, 14 January 1911 and Stokes's endorsement, all in file 80896, box 169, RG 52, NARA. Hasson later returned to the Army as a nurse during World War I and served at base hospitals in Europe and was chief nurse at two Army hospitals. She was honorably discharged in June 1919. Hasson died on 8 March 1942 and was buried in Arlington National Cemetery.

64. Biographical data, Lenah Sutcliffe Higbee, OA, NHC; Stokes letter regarding Higbee cited in Hickey, "Navy Nurse Corps," 64.

65. Daybook, May 1908–April 1930, box 4; J. Beatrice Bowman, "Comment on Navy Nursing," report to ANA Annual Convention, 25 April 1914, folder 3, box 24, both in NNC Records, OA, NHC; some correspondence regarding appointing nurses in NNC Records: Letters Sent by Superintendent, November–December 1911, entry 20, RG 52, NARA.

66. BuMed memo to Department, 28 January 1914; and Travel Allowances, NNC Records, 16 April 1914, both in Travel Allowances folder, box 19, NNC Records, OA, NHC.

67. Department of the Navy, *Hospital Corps Handbook*, 2; "History of the Hospital Corps"; *Surgeon General's Report: 1914*, 361; *Surgeon General's Report: 1915*, 701.

68. Bowman, "Comment on Navy Nursing"; [Katrina] Hertzer, "Comments on Navy

Nursing," report to ANA Annual Convention, 25 April 1914, folder 3, box 24, NNC Records, OA, NHC; letter to editor, *AJN* 17 (November 1916): 159.

69. *Surgeon General's Report: 1912*, 471; *Surgeon General's Report: 1915*, 684–87.

70. Acting commandant, Norfolk Naval Hospital, to BuMed, telegram, 23 May 1914; BuMed to Commandant, Portsmouth, Va., telegram, 23 May 1914; BuMed to Commandants, Naval Hospitals, Circular Letter, 26 May 1914, all in folder 6 (Dependents and Navy Nurses), box 24, NNC Records, OA, NHC.

71. *Relief*, in *DANFS* (1976) 6:68; *Solace*, in *DANFS* (1976) 6:543. Beatrice Van H. Stevenson, Secretary, New York State Committee on Red Cross Nursing Service, gave a vivid account of the workings of the hospital ship in "A Visit to the *Solace*, the Hospital Ship of the United States Navy," *AJN* 11 (December 1910).

72. "Navy Nurse Corps Chronology"; *Mayflower*, in *DANFS* (1969) 4:281–82; *Dolphin*, in *DANFS* (1963) 2:285; Logbooks, USS *Mayflower*, 6–27 March 1913, and USS *Dolphin*, 6–30 March 1913, both at NARA; E. David Cronon, ed., *The Cabinet Diaries of Josephus Daniels, 1913–1921* (Lincoln: University of Nebraska Press, 1963), 13.

73. Paullin, *History of Naval Administration*, 484; *Surgeon General's Report: 1899*, 882; *Surgeon General's Report: 1902*, 939; *Surgeon General's Report: 1906*, 1045.

74. *Surgeon General's Report: 1905*, 1205; Surgeon General to E. R. Stitt, 10 August 1910, file 120850, box 305; Stitt to Stokes, 4 November 1910, file 121683, box 310, both in RG 52, NARA.

75. Hasson to Surgeon General, 27 September 1910; Hasson to BuNav, 24 September 1910, both in Feeney notebooks, folder 2, box 24, NNC Records, OA, NHC.

76. Edward R. Stitt to Surgeon General, 6 December 1910; Surgeon General to Stitt, 16 January 1911, both in file 121921, box 312; Stitt to Surgeon General, 4 January 1911, file 122150, box 314, all in RG 52, NARA.

77. C. S. Butler to Stokes, 31 October 1911, file 124134, box 327, entry 11, RG 52, NARA.

78. "Guam, Mariana Islands," in *United States Navy and Marine Corps Bases, Domestic*, ed. Paolo E. Coletta and K. Jack Bauer (Westport, Conn.: Greenwood Press, 1985), 140. For a thorough account of the early years of American administration, see Beers, *American Naval Occupation and Government of Guam*.

79. Crawley, "Navy Medical Department," 245–53, 261; *Surgeon General's Report: 1906*, 1042–44; Charles M. Oman, *Doctors Aweigh: The Story of the United States Naval Medical Corps in Action* (Garden City, N.Y.: Doubleday, Doran, 1943), 104–5. Gangosa (rhino-pharyngitis mutilans) caused ulceration of the upper part of the face and extensive disfigurement. Medical officers finally determined that gangosa was a form of yaws and that isolation was unnecessary.

80. *Surgeon General's Report: 1906*, 1042–43.

81. Crawley, "Navy Medical Department," 264; Hickey, "Navy Nurse Corps," 54; Medical Director, Guam to Surgeon General, 1 September 1910, and 23 January 1911; Surgeon General to CO, Guam, 13 March 1911, all in Feeney notebooks, folder 8, box 24, NNC Records, OA, NHC.

82. *Surgeon General's Report: 1914*, 362; *Surgeon General's Report: 1915*, 701; E. L. [Elizabeth Leonhardt], letters from Navy nurses, *AJN* 14 (November 1913): 126–29; 14 (January 1914): 295–96; 14 (May 1914): 655–56; 14 (August 1914): 987–88; 15 (November 1914): 151–52; 15 (April 1915): 595–97. This series of letters provides colorful descriptions of conditions in Guam and of the nurses' work there.

83. This entire episode is in Feeney notebooks, folder 8, box 24, NNC Records, OA, NHC.

84. Della V. Knight, "Maria Roberta—A Tribute," *AJN* 22 (June 1922): 736–37.

85. "Tutuila, Samoa," in Coletta and Bauer, *Navy and Marine Corps Bases, Domestic*, 332–35; T. F. Darden, *Historical Sketch of the Naval Administration of the Government of American Samoa, April 17, 1900–July 1, 1951* (Washington, D.C.: GPO, 1952), ix–xi.

86. Gray, *Amerika Samoa*, 164–67, 170–71; *Surgeon General's Report: 1906*, 1044–45. F. W. Ryan, "The Samoan Hospital," Appendix C.1, Annual Report of the Governor of American Samoa, 30 June 1926, Samoa folder 1, box 17, NNC Records, OA, NHC, has an account based on interviews with a chief pharmacist's mate who had been in Samoa since 1902.

87. *American Samoa: A General Report by the Governor* (Washington, D.C.: 1927), 75, in Samoan Islands folder, box 5, ZE files, OA, NHC; C. F. Stokes letter, 26 August 1913, and Stokes to commandant, Naval Station, Tutuila, 9 September 1913, both in Feeney notebooks, folder 8, box 24, NNC Records, OA, NHC.

88. M. H. H. [Mary H. Humphrey], "Samoa," *AJN* 14 (September 1914): 1069–73. Draft is dated November 1913, in Samoa folder 1, box 17, NNC Records, OA, NHC.

89. Crawley, "Navy Medical Department," 309–29; Higbee to Surgeon General, 21 March 1914; Josephus Daniels to Commandant, Naval Station, Tutuila, 26 March 1914; C. D. Stearns to SecNav, 4 May 1914, all in Samoa folder 1, box 17, NNC Records, OA, NHC.

90. Senior Medical Officer to Surgeon General, n.d., in Feeney notebooks, folder 8, box 24, NNC Records, OA, NHC; Darden, *Historical Sketch*, 15; "Care Procedure Book, Samoan Hospital," in Samoa folder 2, box 17, NNC Records, OA, NHC.

91. H. [Humphrey], "Letters from Navy Nurses, Samoa," *AJN* 15 (June 1915): 760–63.

92. Humphrey letter, 3 August 1914; Surgeon General's and SecNav's approval, n.d., all in Feeney notebooks, folder 8, box 24, NNC Records, OA, NHC.

93. *Surgeon General's Report: 1914*, 362; *Surgeon General's Report: 1915*, 702.

94. Crawley, "Navy Medical Department," 330–31.

95. Dulles, *Red Cross*, 130–33; Gilbo, *American Red Cross*, 43–44. The neutrality policy ended in 1916 when the British halted Red Cross shipments of medical supplies to the Central Powers.

96. Higbee to Bowman, 22 April 1914; Stokes to Mabel Boardman, Chairman of American Red Cross, 19 August 1914; Stokes to Jane Delano, Chairman of American Red Cross Nurse Service, 19 August 1914, all in Correspondence 1914–15 folder, box 1,

Bowman Papers. The Navy did not encourage its nurses to go with the Red Cross; it would need them in its own hospitals. Higbee, writing in *AJN* 14 (September 1914): 1041.

97. C. L. Magee, Secretary, American Red Cross, to Bowman, 8 June 1915, Correspondence 1914–15 folder, box 1, Bowman Papers; *AJN* 15 (October 1914): 38; 15 (November 1914): 127; 15 (December 1914): 209; Sterner, *Harm's Way*, 39. J. Beatrice Bowman described her overseas service in an article, "Experiences of Unit D at Haslar, England," *AJN* 15 (September 1915): 1112.

98. *AJN* 15 (October 1914): 38, 65; "Navy Nurse Corps," *AJN* 17 (December 1916): 256.

## *Chapter 3. The World War I Era, 1916–1920*

1. Figures from Gordon, *Gender and Higher Education*, 2; Newcomer, *Higher Education*, 46.

2. Ryan, *Womanhood*, 205; Rothman, *Proper Place*, 107; Evans, *Born for Liberty*, 182. Barbara Sickerman, "College and Careers: Historical Perspectives on the Lives and Work Patterns of Women College Graduates," in Faragher and Howe, *Women and Higher Education*, 147, 154–55; John L. Rury, *Education and Women's Work: Female Schooling and the Division of Labor in Urban America, 1870–1930* (Albany: State University of New York Press, 1991), 94.

3. Evans, *Born for Liberty*, 170–71; Dorothy Schneider and Carl J. Schneider, *American Women in the Progressive Era, 1900–1920* (New York: Facts on File, 1993), 196–204; McHenry, *Liberty's Women*, 340.

4. Plan of Organization Adopted by the Woman's Committee of the Council of National Defense, 23 May 1917, Josephus Daniels Papers, LC, MSS Division, Microfilm Reel 35; Dulles, *Red Cross*, 181; Schneider and Schneider, *American Women*, 213–24, 232; Evans, *Born for Liberty*, 171–72; McHenry, *Liberty's Women*, 379; Cronon, *Diaries of Josephus Daniels*, 138, 303, 307. For a pictorial essay on women's wartime work, see Nancy E. Milan, "How Ya Gonna Keep 'Em Down? Women and World War I," *Prologue*, 25th Anniversary Issue (1994): 112–17. See also Maurine W. Greenwald, *Women, War, and Work: The Impact of World War I on Women Workers in the United States* (Westport, Conn.: Greenwood Press, 1980).

5. Figures from Ryan, *Womanhood*, 204.

6. Painter, *Armageddon*, 248; Christy, "Equal Rights," 66; Evans, *Born for Liberty*, 166–70; Rothman, *Proper Place*, 127–32. Although Dock was a highly visible suffragist, most nurses were conservative and had little use for reform movements. See Jo Ann Ashley, "Nurses in American History: Nursing and Early Feminism," in *Pages from Nursing History*, 68–69. Women were often their own worst enemies in the suffrage drive. See Jane J. Camhi, *Women against Women: American Anti-Suffragism, 1880–1920* (Brooklyn, N.Y.: Carlson Publishing, 1994).

7. Interestingly, in 1893 New Zealand became the first country to grant women the vote, followed by Australia in 1902. Britain did not enfranchise women until 1928.

8. Historians continue to differ on the ramifications of the nineteenth amendment.

Flexner, *Century of Struggle*, 222–37, remains the most thorough coverage. In the revised edition (1975), she argues that the vote was essential for human dignity and for awareness that women could perform as responsible citizens (xi). In contrast, Chafe, in *American Woman*, 46–47, and in *Paradox of Change*, 43, sees the amendment as a reform that did not change women's status or political power.

9. *United States Statutes at Large* 39 (1916): 587, 592.

10. Although writers usually blame the German's unrestricted submarine warfare policy for America's entry into the war, another historian maintains that Wilson wanted to enter the war so that he could dictate the peace. See David F. Trask, "The American Navy in a World at War, 1914–1919," in *In Peace and War: Interpretations of American Naval History, 1775–1978*, ed. Kenneth J. Hagan, 2d ed. (Westport, Conn.: Greenwood Press, 1984), 209.

11. Paul G. Halpern, A *Naval History of World War I* (Annapolis, Md.: Naval Institute Press, 1994), 343–44, 351–70, 436; William S. Sims, *The Victory at Sea* (New York: Garden City, 1920), passim; Dean C. Allard, "Anglo-American Naval Differences during World War I," *Military Affairs* 44 (April 1980): 75–81. See also Lewis P. Clephane, *History of the Naval Overseas Transportation Service in World War I* (Washington, D.C.: GPO, 1969); and Robert G. Albion and Jennie B. Pope, *Sea Lanes in Wartime: The American Experience, 1775–1942* (New York: W. W. Norton, 1942), 187–88, 190, 199.

12. "U.S. Navy Active Ship Force Levels, 1900–1989," Ships' History Branch, OA, NHC; "U.S. Navy Ship Force Levels, 1917–1989," in Statistics Vertical File, Navy Department Library; Miller, *U.S. Navy*, 270; William J. Williams, "Josephus Daniels and the U.S. Navy's Shipbuilding Program during World War I," *JMH* 60 (January 1996): 7–38. Daniels explained the Navy's five-year building program to many; for example, Daniels to Paul E. Faust (Union League Club, Chicago), 24 January 1916, Josephus Daniels Papers, Navy Department Library.

13. *SecNav Report*, 1919, 363; *BuNav Report*, 1919, in *SecNav Report*, 1919, 367–68. See William J. Williams, *The Wilson Administration and the Shipbuilding Crisis of 1917* (New York: Edwin Mellen, 1992).

14. Kenneth J. Hagan, *This People's Navy: The Making of American Sea Power* (New York: Free Press, 1991), 250–51; Furer, *Administration*, 6; Love, *History of the U.S. Navy* 1:458–60.

15. Miller, *U.S. Navy*, 242; Love, *History of the U.S. Navy* 1:423, 462–65; Hagan, *This People's Navy*, 246. See Donald A. Yerza, *Admirals and Empire: The United States Navy and the Caribbean, 1898–1945* (Columbia: University of South Carolina Press, 1991).

16. Cronon, *Diaries of Josephus Daniels*, 249, 303, 370, 448, 506, 511, 547, 552–53; Harold T. Wieand, "The History of the Development of the United States Naval Reserve, 1889–1941" (Ph.D. diss., University of Pittsburgh, 1952), 131.

17. *United States Statutes at Large* 39 (1916): 587, 592. The six classes of the Naval Reserve Force were the Fleet Naval Reserve, Naval Reserve, Naval Auxiliary Reserve, Naval Coast Defense Reserve, Volunteer Naval Reserve, and Naval Reserve Flying Corps.

18. Josephus Daniels, *Our Navy at War* (Washington, D.C.: Pictorial Bureau, 1922),

328–29; Cronon, *Diaries of Josephus Daniels*, 119; Daniels, writing in the *Note Book*, March 1935, September 1939, October 1942. The *Note Book* is the newsletter of the National Yeomen (F), and the Smithsonian has the complete set of them . Over the years, others have taken credit for the suggestion. Lt. Cdr. Frederick R. Payne, USN (Ret.), who was executive officer at the Naval Home, Philadelphia, and in charge of recruiting in the 4th Naval District, later said that he had suggested to Daniels that the Navy enlist women. In the *Note Book*, November 1928 and March 1937. Biographical data in *Navy Register: 1917*, 194; and ZB files, OA, NHC. Rear Adm. Leigh C. Palmer, chief, BuNav, wrote to Daniels on 7 March 1917, asking if women could be enlisted. It is possible that Payne wrote to Palmer who then wrote to Daniels, but neither the index to SecNav General Correspondence, 1916–26, M-1052, rolls 67 and 68, RG 80, NARA, nor Daniels's correspondence with Palmer in February and March 1917, Reel 58, Daniels Papers, LC, reflects such an exchange.

19. SecNav to Chief BuNav, 14 March 1917, file 28550-45, box 2525, RG 80, NARA; BuNav Circular letter, to commandants of all districts, 19 March 1917, in Women in the Navy folder, box 13, ZV Files, OA, NHC; also in Women in the USNR Force—Employment as Yeomen (F) folder, box 277, RG 45, NARA.

20. The *Note Book*, September 1929, March 1937, December 1937; Harrod, *Manning the New Navy*, 65; "And to the Sugar 'n' Spice, Too," *American Legion Magazine* 103 (November 1977): 9. Other women claimed to be first; for example, Irma M. Alloway (obit in *St. Petersburg Times*, 14 September 1986). Belle V. Dunn and Helen O'Shaughnessy were the first to enlist onboard a ship, the USS *Hartford*, on 6 April. See Eunice C. Dessez, *The First Enlisted Women* (Philadelphia: Dorrance, 1955), 23–24.

21. Figures from Employment of Women in the U.S. Naval Reserve Force as Yeomen (F), Women in the Navy folder, box 13, ZV Files, OA, NHC.

22. Figures from Personnel of the United States Navy on Active Duty During the War—Number Furnished by Each State, in General Information—Enlisted Personnel, NA-3, subject file 1911–1927, box 277, RG 45, NARA.

23. Naval Reserve Act of 1916; Susan H. Godson, "Womanpower in World War I," *USNIP* 110 (December 1984): 60.

24. Capt. Joy Bright Hancock [Ofstie], interview with author, 4 August 1981; Mrs. Henry F. Butler, *I Was a Yeoman (F)* (Washington, D.C.: Naval Historical Foundation, 1967), 2–3.

25. *Baltimore American*, 18 March 1918 [?]; Committee on Public Information news release, 14 June 1918; newspaper article about three socialites who had joined the Navy, no name, n.d., all in Women in the USNR Force—Employment as Yeomen (F), NA-3 folder, subject file 1911–1927, box 277, RG 45, NARA.

26. The *Note Book*, December 1978, June 1980; *[Baltimore?] Sun*, 4 February 1918, in Women in the USNR Force—Employment as Yeomen (F), NA-3 folder, subject file 1911–1927, box 277, RG 45, NARA; Elizabeth A. Andrews letter, n.d., in Miscellaneous Articles folder 3, box 21, NNC Records, OA, NHC.

27. Lt. Col. Helen O'Neill, interview with author, 25 August 1981; Yeoman (F) Helene

Johnson Coxhead, interview with author, 6 February 1994; Joy Bright Hancock, *Lady in the Navy: A Personal Reminiscence* (Annapolis, Md.: Naval Institute Press, 1972), 23.

28. Some historians, for example, Morris J. MacGregor and Bernard C. Nalty, eds., *Blacks in the United States Armed Forces: Basic Documents* (Wilmington, Del.: Scholarly Resources, 1977), 4:462, 510; Regina T. Akers, "The Integration of Afro-Americans into the WAVES, 1942–1945" (Master's thesis, Howard University, 1993), 10–11, maintain that there were about twenty-four black Yeomen (F) in a segregated office in the Navy Department. They base their conclusion on C. W. Nimitz to Hamilton Fish, 17 June 1937, approximating this figure. Writers Jean Ebbert and Marie-Beth Hall, *Crossed Currents: Navy Women from WW I to Tailhook* (Washington, D.C.: Brassey's, 1993), n. 13, 280–81, found no evidence supporting this assertion. Also, the fact that Daniels was still receiving letters late in the war protesting the Navy's excluding black women would seem to refute these claims. John R. Schillady, Secretary NAACP, to Daniels, 16 August 1918; and James R. Posey Daniels, 5 September 1918, both in Daniels Papers, Reel 62, LC. Helen O'Neill, in an interview with the author, remembered that there were black landsmen (males) who did filing for white yeomen in the Washington bureaus.

29. Coxhead interview; Hancock interview; Andrews letter; Mrs. John Winne, who had lost her husband in a torpedoed ship, told the *Baltimore Sun*, 4 February 1918, "I shall be happy in doing my duty for the country."

30. Anna Hagen Etzler, interview with author, 22 August 1981.

31. "Sugar 'n' Spice," 9.

32. Ruth Styffe Paull, in the *Note Book*, September 1979.

33. Mary E. Dwyer, in the *Note Book*, December 1962.

34. Hancock, *Lady in the Navy*, 25.

35. Daniels, *Navy at War*, 329; Daniels's address, 27 September 1939, in the *Note Book*, September 1939; Committee on Public Information press release, 27 March 1918, in Women in the USNRF, Employment as Yeomen (F)—NA-3 folder, subject file 1911–1927, box 277, RG 45, NARA.

36. Department of the Navy, *The Bluejacket's Manual: United States Navy*, 5th ed. (Baltimore: Franklin Printing, 1917); Ebbert and Hall, *Crossed Currents*, 11.

37. The *Note Book*, March 1934; Hancock, *Lady in the Navy*, 25; Dessez, *First Enlisted Women*, 55; John A. Stacey, "What Happened to This Man's Navy? A Brief History of the Yeomanettes," *Military Images* (July–August 1989): 5.

38. The *Note Book*, June 1934; "Growth of the Naval Reserve Force," *Army and Navy Register* 63 (18 May 1918): sec. 2—Navy sec.): 38; "Will Navy Commission Women?" *Army and Navy Journal* 55 (8 June 1918): 1569; Butler, *Yeoman (F)*, 8.

39. Etzler interview; Dessez, *First Enlisted Women*, 7; Daniels, in the *Note Book*, October 1942. Ebbert and Hall, *Crossed Currents*, 7, found no record of protests.

40. Harrod, *Manning the New Navy*, 65–66; "About Women," *Our Navy* 11 (March 1918): 21. "Women wearing rating badges," continued the writer, "and sailors wearing corsets impresses us about the same—only the other way."

41. Butler, *Yeomen (F)*, 3; Dessez, *First Enlisted Women*, 13.

42. Ebbert and Hall, *Crossed Currents*, 186; Coxhead interview. Coxhead worked at the Naval Medical Supply Depot, Mare Island, Calif.

43. SecNav to Paymaster, USN, 19 April 1917, file 26254-2225; and JAG to Disbursing Officer, Navy Yard, Charleston, 2 July 1917, file 26254-2225:4, both in box 1577, RG 80, NARA; *SecNav Report*, 1918, 66.

44. Press release, Committee on Public Information, Navy Department, 18 June 1917; *Baltimore American*, 19 June 1917, both in Women in the USNR Force—Employment as Yeomen (F)—NA-3 folder, subject file 1911–1927, box 277, RG 45, NARA. Daniels gave the same reassurance to Mary Anderson, Assistant Director, Women in Industry Service, 23 October 1918, file 27470-165:1, box 2485, RG 80, NARA.

45. *Navy Register: 1917*, 361; *Baltimore Sun*, 4 February 1918, in Women in the USNR Force—Employment as Yeomen (F)—NA-3 folder, 1911–1927 subject file, box 277, RG 45, NARA.

46. JAG to BUS&A, 10 June 1918, file 26254-2225:34, box 1577, RG 80, NARA.

47. Coxhead interview; Ebbert and Hall, *Crossed Currents*, 10–11; Hancock, *Lady in the Navy*, 24.

48. Change in Uniform Regulations, no. 15: Garments and Articles of Equipment of Enrolled Women of the Naval Reserve Force [with illustrations], Washington, D.C.: GPO, 1918, in National Yeomen (F) material folder, box 1, Helen G. O'Neill Papers, OA, NHC. Although one Yeoman (F) remembered that the uniforms looked like her father's business suits, Daniels described them as "natty and beautiful." Butler, *Yeomen (F)*, 6; Daniels, *Navy at War*, 329.

49. Cronon, *Diaries of Josephus Daniels*, 253; SecNav to CO, USNTS, Newport, 26 March 1918, file 27217-2648, box 2152; JAG to Chief BuNav, 25 March 1919, file 27217-3544; and SecNav to CO, Fleet Supply Base, South Brooklyn, 25 March 1919, file 27217-3626, both in box 2153, all in RG 80, NARA. Harrod, *Manning the New Navy*, 66, believes that such a protective attitude, coupled with the lack of sea duty, showed that the Navy did not consider women as true enlisted persons.

50. Lou M. Guthrie, "I Was a Yeomanette," *USNIP* 110 (December 1984): 58; "Yeomanettes: Navy Women of World War One," *All Hands*, July 1972, 14–15; "Women in the Navy: A Historical Perspective," *Deckplate* 10 (January–February 1990): 11–12; Wieand, "Naval Reserve," 131–32; Committee on Public Information, press release, 16 February 1918, subject file 1911–1927, Women in the USNRF—Employment as Yeomen (F)—NA-3 folder, box 277, RG 45, NARA.

51. Commandant, Washington Navy Yard, to Assistant SecNav, n.d., file 4488-882, box 2485, RG 80, NARA.

52. There was no central office dealing with Yeomen (F), nor was there a commander for women reservists. Consequently, records are scattered and few firm figures emerge. There was no list, such as the NNC had, of women. In 1921 the assistant SecNav tried to determine the number of women who had served at various stations and their ratings but had limited success. Assistant SecNav to commandants of Navy Yards

and Ordnance Plants, 21 January 1921. The replies were often vague and sometimes unclear about whether women workers were reservists or civilians. All in file 4488-882, box 2485, RG 80, NARA. The SecNav tried also. Despatch, 7 February 1921, file 4488-913, box 119, RG 80, NARA, asked for reports of women employed between 1 April 1917 and 11 November 1918 and their ratings. The answers indicated that the records of these women were kept in Boston, so the individual stations could not determine the number of Yeomen (F). Complements of stations in naval districts during the war gave the number of yeomen but did not differentiate between the sexes. In Subject File 1911–1927, NF-1, folder 15, box 363, RG 45, NARA.

53. The *Note Book,* June 1981; Ebbert and Hall, *Crossed Currents,* 12; Patricia J. Thomas, "From Yeomanettes to WAVES to Women in the U.S. Navy," in *Life in the Rank and File: Enlisted Men and Women in the Armed Forces of the United States, Australia, Canada, and the United Kingdom,* ed. David R. Segal and H. Wallace Sinaiko (Washington, D.C.: Pergamon-Brassey, 1986), 98; *Washington Times,* 3 March 1918, and *Times Herald,* 26 May 1918, both in Women in the USNRF—NA-3 folder, subject file 1911–1927, box 277, RG 45, NARA.

54. SecNav to Pay Director, 1st Naval District, 26 January 1918, file 26254-2488, box 1580, RG 80, NARA. Rose Lowther had been cooking for naval lookouts at the lighthouse in Providence section; Daniels authorized enrolling her as ship's cook, class 4 of the Naval Reserve, with commensurate pay and allowances.

55. "The Yeomanettes of World War I," *USNIP* 83 (December 1957), pictorial section; Daniels, *Navy at War,* 330; quotation in Josephus Daniels, *The Navy and the Nation: War-Time Addresses* (New York: George H. Doran, 1919), 324.

56. Andrews letter; Donna J. Fournier, "The Forgotten Enlisted Women of World War I," *Retired Officer* 40 (October 1984): 31.

57. Assorted newspaper clippings with city names but no names of papers and no dates, in Women in the USNRF-NA-3 folder, subject file 1911–1927, box 277, RG 45, NARA.

58. The young woman was Bernice Smith Tongate; the artist, Howard Chandler Christy. Tongate did join the Navy and became a chief Yeoman (F). She later enlisted in the Army in WWII. Feature article in *Memphis Commercial Appeal,* 3 July 1977; "Bernice Tongate," obit in *Washington Post,* 27 January 1990, p. B7.

59. Hancock, *Lady in the Navy,* 24–25; Stacey, "This Man's Navy," 5; Daniels, *Navy at War,* 329; Godson, "Womanpower," 63.

60. List of Hospital Corps and nonmedical personnel nominated for duty with Base Hospital no. 5; CO, Naval Base Hospital no. 5 to BuMed, 30 November 1917, monthly report, both in Red Cross Base Hospital no. 5 folder, file 127046, box 502B, entry 12, RG 52, NARA; Stacey, "This Man's Navy," photo captions, 5; "People: Navy Women," *All Hands,* bicentennial issue, 1975, 70; Mary E. Dwyer, in the *Note Book,* December 1962.

61. Hancock, *Lady in the Navy,* 28; Ebbert and Hall, *Crossed Currents,* 12; Fournier, "Enlisted Women," 31.

62. Maj. Gen. George Barnett memos, 18 July 1918; Barnett to Daniels, 2 August

1918, both cited in Linda L. Hewitt, *Women Marines in World War I* (Washington, D.C.: History and Museums Division, USMC, 1974),4; SecNav to Maj. Gen. Commandant, USMC, 12 August 1918, file 28550-402, box 2527, RG 80, NARA.

63. "What's What in the Marine Corps," *Marines Magazine* 3 (September 1918): 20.

64. Fact Sheet: Women in the USMC; Fact Sheet: WW I Marine Reservists (F); Marine Corps Reserve (F); Brief History of Women Marines; USMC Women's Reserve: History—World War I, all in box 7, RG 127-79-27, Marine Corps Research Center, Quantico, Va. In this same collection is a good paper by Dawn A. Tepe, "Women Marines in World War I." See also Erika S. Nau, "The Spirit of Molly Marine," *Minerva: Quarterly Report on Women and the Military* 8 (winter 1990): 23; Katherine A. Towle, "Women Marines: The Feminine Side," *MCG* 34 (November 1950): 111.

65. Hewitt, *Women Marines*, 16; "Introducing Some Fair Marines," *Marines Magazine* 3 (October 1918): 23.

66. Etzler interview.

67. Fact Sheet: WW I Marine Reservists (F); Casualties of Women (Yeomen F) in the Naval Service (USNF) during the World War and Subsequently, 3 October 1925, subject file 1911–1927, NC-1, folder (2), box 362, RG 45, NARA. The 1925 list put the deaths at 51, but a new count in 1932 raised it to 57. Twenty-five died between 6 April 1917 and 11 November 1918. Another 29 died between the armistice and 1920.

68. Personnel of the United States Navy, on Active Duty, during the War, in General Information, Enlisted Personnel—NA-3 folder, subject file 1911–1927, box 277, RG 45, NARA; *United States Statutes at Large* 41 (1920): 138; Bess Glenn, *Demobilization of Civilian Personnel by the U.S. Navy after the First World War* (Washington, D.C.: Office of Records Administration, Navy Department, 1945), 11.

69. JAG to Chief BuNav, 3 December 1920, file 28550-1397, box 2533, RG 80, NARA.

70. Harrod, *Manning the New Navy*, 66; Ebbert and Hall, *Crossed Currents*, 16.

71. "People: Navy Women," 70–71; Demobilization of Yeowomen, *Army and Navy Register* (26 April 1919): 522; Tepe, "Women Marines," 10; "Marine Corps Reserve (F)," 4–5.

72. *SecNav Report*, 1918, 66; Barnett quotation in Tepe, "Women Marines," 9.

73. For an overview, see Katherine B. Johnson, "Called to Serve: American Nurses Go to War, 1914–1918" (Master's thesis, University of Louisville, 1993).

74. Kalisch and Kalisch, *American Nursing*, 2d ed., 329–30, 339–42, 344–45, 369; Donahue, *Finest Art*, 397–402, 407; Dulles, *Red Cross*, 139; Katherine D. Dreves, "Nursing in American History: Vassar Training Camp for Nurses," in *Pages from Nursing History*, 93.

75. Gabriel and Metz, *Military Medicine* 2:241–43; Kalisch and Kalisch, *American Nursing*, 2d ed., 350–51, 358–62; Kalisch and Scobey, "Helplessness Suspended," 6–7; David Watkins, "In Remembrance," *Nursing Times* 82 (November 1986): 48–49.

76. *SecNav Report*, 1918, 85.

77. Ibid.; *Surgeon General's Report: 1920*, 751–52; Department of the Navy, *Hospital Corps Handbook*, 2–3; Sterner, *Harm's Way*, 54.

78. Elizabeth W. Neil, "The Experiences of an Ex-Navy Nurse on Recruiting Duty,"

*AJN* 18 (May 1918): 625, described having to pursue qualified nurses for the NNC and then having to counter objections: "I get seasick"; "Will I have to go on battleships?"; "I want to go to France."

79. World War I Statistics—NNC, Statistics—NC-75—WW I folder, box 34, NNC Records, OA, NHC. Figures vary, depending on whether the count is until the armistice or until the official end of the war—1,835 had served by then. Editorial Comment, *AJN* 14 (September 1914): 1041; Dulles, *Red Cross*, 180. There is a complete roster of these nurses in Statistics—NC-75—List of Nurses Who Served during the World War, 6 April 1917–11 November 1918 folder, box 34, NNC Records, OA, NHC.

80. World War Nurses—Number Represented from States, Statistics—NC-75—List of States folder, box 34, NNC Records, OA, NHC.

81. Bowman to Anita McGee, 22 October 1923, Spanish War Nurses folder, box 5, entry 48D, RG 52, NARA. The chief nurses were Sara M. Cox, Alice Gillett, Elizabeth M. Hewitt, Mary J. McCloud, and reservist Olla R. Hazelton.

82. Editorial Comment, *AJN* 18 (May 1918): 598; Department of the Navy, *Manual for the Medical Department of the United States Navy*, 1917, 47, 57; Navy Nurse Corps sec., *AJN* 17 (May 1917): 739; Red Cross sec., *AJN* 17 (August 1917): 1095.

83. Pay Table, Pay and Allowances folder 1, box 15, NNC Records, OA, NHC; Department of the Navy, *Manual for the Medical Department of the United States Navy*, 1917, 55; NNC sec., *AJN* 20 (August 1920): 921. Lenah S. Higbee to J. Beatrice Bowman, 22 July 1918, J. B. Bowman Papers, Correspondence (1918) folder, box 1, NNC Records, OA, NHC, explains the congressional error in reducing chief nurses' compensation.

84. Department of the Navy, *Manual for the Medical Department of the United States Navy*, 1917, 49, 53; "War Insurance," *AJN* 18 (December 1917): 242.

85. Department of the Navy, *Manual for the Medical Department of the United States Navy*, 1917, 56; "Uniforms—1917–1918," History of Uniforms folder, box 19 NNC Records, OA, NHC. Higbee to Bowman, 9, 12, 15 October, and 2 November 1918, Bowman Papers, Correspondence (1918) folder, box 1, NNC Records, OA, NHC. A pamphlet, "All Honor to the American War Nurse" (Washington, D.C.: American Red Cross, n.d.), Nurse Corps folder, box 8, ZV Files, OA, NHC, has photographs of uniforms of nurses in the Army, Navy, and Red Cross.

86. Red Cross sec., *AJN* 18 (January 1918): 318. The superintendent disapproved of the Red Cross handouts to Navy nurses—they were "an appearance of charity"—but had to accept them. Higbee to Bowman, 15 October and 2 November 1918, Bowman Papers, Correspondence (1918) folder, box 1, NNC Records, OA, NHC.

87. Kay Hickox, "WW I Navy Nurse Looks Back," *All Hands*, August 1983, 17.

88. The College Equal Suffrage League asked for the rank of second lieutenant for Army nurses. The ANA asked for adequate authority, which implied rank, for military nurses. In Editorial Comment, *AJN* 17 (September 1917): 1151.

89. War Department memo, n.d., but c. December 1916, folder 127267, box 510, entry 12, RG 52, NARA; Excerpts from Military Affairs Hearings, *AJN* 20 (October 1919): 37.

90. SecNav to Congressman Daniel J. Riordan, 19 October 1917, folder 127267, box

510; W. C. Braisted to BuNav, 17 January 1918; Braisted to Congressman Frederick C. Hicks, 31 January 1918, both in folder 125786, box 430, all in entry 12, RG 52, NARA; Samuel McGowan, Paymaster General, to all officers of the Pay Corps, 13 June 1918, Pay and Allowances folder, box 15, NNC Records, OA, NHC.

91. *SecNav Report*, 1918, 87; *Surgeon General's Report: 1918*, 1347; *Surgeon General's Report: 1919*, 2068; NNC sec. *AJN* 18 (February 1918): 425.

92. Higbee, "Work of the Navy Nurse Corps," report given to 25th Annual Convention of the National League of Nursing Education, [1919?], folder 4, box 24, NNC Records, OA, NHC.

93. Information on dietitians in folder 3, box 24, NNC Records, OA, NHC; *Surgeon General's Report: 1919*, 2071.

94. *Surgeon General's Report: 1918*, 1348; *Surgeon General's Report: 1919*, 2073; Bowman, "The Pharmacist's Mates School," *Hospital Corps Quarterly* 11 (July 1927): 303; *SecNav Report*, 1918, 85.

95. Mary G. Wood, "Naval Nursing Service," *AJN* 19 (October 1918): 100; Higbee, "Nursing as It Related to the War: The Navy," paper read at 21st annual convention of the ANA, 9 May 1918, folder 4, box 24, NNC Records, OA, NHC; Bowman, "The Great Lakes Training Station," *AJN* 18 (May 1918): 691.

96. I. Grace Kline, "The Naval Hospital at Charleston, South Carolina," *AJN* 18 (May 1918); quotation from Bowman to Higbee, 28 August 1918, Bowman Papers, Correspondence (1918) folder, box 1, NNC Records, OA, NHC.

97. Higbee to Bowman, 24 August 1918, Bowman Papers, Correspondence (1918) folder, box 1, NNC Records, OA, NHC.

98. Taylor, "Hospital Corpsman," 12.

99. WW I Statistics, Statistics folder 1, box 19; List of Nurses, Statistics—NC-75—List of Nurses folder, box 34, both in NNC Records, OA, NHC.

100. Braisted to CO, U.S. Naval Hospital, Great Lakes, 4 November 1918; Bowman to Higbee, 12 October 1918; Higbee to Bowman, 2 November 1918, all in Bowman Papers, Correspondence (1918) folder, box 1, NNC Records, OA, NHC.

101. Higbee to Members of the Navy Nurse Corps Going Overseas, 21 September 1918, Statistics—NC-75—WW I folder, box 34, NNC Records, OA, NHC; Kalisch and Kalisch, *American Nursing*, 2d ed., 352.

102. William S. Sims to OPNAV, n.d., Red Cross Army and Navy Hospital—London folder, file 127046, box 502B, entry 12, RG 52, NARA; Dulles, *Red Cross*, 181; *Surgeon General's Report: 1918*, 1347; Higbee to Bowman, 25 June 1918, Bowman Papers, Correspondence (1918) folder, box 1, NNC Records, OA, NHC.

103. Higbee, "Work," 130; Hickey, "Navy Nurse Corps," 68; Organization of Navy Base Hospital Units, Statistics—NC-75—WW I folder, box 34, NNC Records, OA, NHC. Sterner, *Harm's Way*, 42–48, has a long account of these base hospitals.

104. CO, Naval Base Hospital no. 5, to BuMed, various monthly reports, Red Cross Base Hospital no. 5 folder, file 127046, box 502B, entry 12, RG 52, NARA; WW I

Statistics—NNC, Statistics—NC-75—WW I folder, box 34; and Maj. Gen. Charles H. Muir, General Orders 1, 16 May 1919, commending the nurses at Cohen, WW I—Letters of Commendation folder, box 8, both in NNC Records, OA, NHC; Higbee, "Work," 130–31; Hickey, "Navy Nurse Corps," 68, 70.

More on Base Hospital no. 5 in Esther V. Hasson folder, box 1, entry 48D, RG 52, NARA. Depending on the source, the number of nurses assigned to each hospital unit varies, so I have consistently used the figures in the NNC Statistics folder. A delightful series of letters written by a Navy nurse to her sister from Base Hospital no. 1 is in WW I Nurse Esther N. ("Essie") Behr Papers, box 1, OA, NHC.

105. Higbee, "Work," 131–32; WW I Statistics—NNC, Statistics—NC-75—WW I folder, box 34, NNC Records, OA, NHC; *SecNav Report*, 1918, 86. Recollections of a nurse who served there in Hickox, "WW I Nurse Looks Back," 16–17.

106. *Surgeon General's Report: 1919*, 2067; WW I Statistics—NNC, Statistics—NC-75—WW I folder, box 34, NNC Records, OA, NHC; Hickey, "Navy Nurse Corps," 69. For a poignant account, based on diaries and letters of a Scottish nurse who served and died in the front lines of the British Army, see Margaret McConnell, "Living on the Front Line," *Nursing Times* 85 (August 1989): 50–52.

107. WW I Statistics—NNC, Statistics—NC-75—WW I folder, box 34, NNC Records, OA, NHC; Hickey, "Navy Nurse Corps," 69–70.

108. Dulles, *Red Cross*, 194, stresses that such charges were not true, although, he says, they may have been more true in WWII!

109. *Surgeon General's Report: 1919*, 2067–68; Hickey, "Navy Nurse Corps," 71; Sterner, *Harm's Way*, 59; Bowman, "History of Nursing"; *George Washington*, in *DANFS* 3:81–82. Chief nurses in transports carrying aliens were Grace Kline in *Princess Matoika*, Frida Krook in *Martha Washington*, Lela Coleman in *Powhatan*, and Martha E. Pringle in *Pocahontas*. In NNC sec., *AJN* 20 (November 1919). Apparently, transports did not use hull numbers in WW I.

110. Chief BuNav to Bowman, orders, 31 December 1915, Bowman Papers, Orders, Travel, Pay folder, box 2, NNC Records, OA, NHC; Braisted to BuNav, 27 March 1916, folder 127334, box 517, entry 12, RG 52, NARA; Dept. of Health and Charities, report to Governor of Guam, in Reports of the Governor of Guam, folder 8, box 24, NNC Records.

111. "Navy Nurses Detailed to the United States Insular Possessions"; "Three Tropical Stations of the U.S. Navy and Their Native Nurses," both in Overseas Duty Stations folder, box 14, NNC Records, OA, NHC; Frederica Braun, "Duty and Diversion in Guam," *AJN* 18 (May 1918): 650; Letters from Navy Nurses, *AJN* 17 (December 1916): 248.

112. Letters from Navy Nurses, *AJN* 17 (December 1916): 248; *Surgeon General's Report: 1916*, 49; "Three Tropical Stations."

113. *Surgeon General's Report: 1919*, 2068–69; *SecNav Report*, 1918, 137–38; "Insular Possessions."

114. "Insular Possessions"; Letters from Navy Nurses, *AJN* 17 (December 1916): 248;

Ada Chew, "U.S. Naval Hospital, Canacao, P.I.," c. 1918, in Overseas Duty Stations folder, box 14, NNC Records, OA, NHC. Chew was in the Nurse Corps from 1917 to 1919.

115. *Surgeon General's Report: 1919*, 2068; "Insular Possessions"; NNC News, *AJN* 19 (November 1918):159.

116. Braisted to BuNav, 30 July 1917; Braisted to C.S. Butler, 17 September 1917, both in folder 1917, file 128527, box 547, entry 12, RG 52, NARA; NNC sec., *AJN* 18 (December 1917):251.

117. *SecNav Report*, 1918, 138; Surgeon General's Report: 1918, 1347; *Surgeon General's Report: 1919*, 2069. Nurses stationed in the Virgin Islands wrote profusely about their experiences, and draft copies are in Virgin Islands folder, box 20, NNC Records, OA, NHC; for example, H. M. Workman, untitled article about St. Croix; Kathleen O'Brien, "The Tropics and Native Nurses"; also, "Three Tropical Stations of the U.S. Navy and Their Native Nurses," Overseas Duty Stations folder, box 14, NNC Records, OA, NHC.

118. Jennie M. Jason, "The Leper Colony of the Virgin Islands of the United States," Virgin Islands folder, box 20, NNC Records, OA, NHC.

119. Gov. J. W. Oman to BuMed, 15 August 1919; Braisted to Oman, 29 August 1919, both in 1919 folder, file 128527, box 546, entry 12, RG 52, NARA.

120. Lucia D. Jordan, "The First Training School for Native Nurses in Haiti"; Jordan, biographical sketch, 25 February 1946, both in Haiti folder, box 11; Jordan, "A Year in Haiti," folder 4, box 24, all in NNC Records, OA, NHC; Foreign Department sec., *AJN* 19 (January 1919): 292; NNC sec., *AJN* 19 (May 1919): 642; *Surgeon General's Report: 1918*, 1347; *Surgeon General's Report: 1919*, 2069.

121. SecNav to Secretary of State, 23 July 1919, folder 8, box 24, NNC Records, OA, NHC; *Surgeon General's Report, 1920*, 746.

122. Kalisch and Kalisch, *American Nursing*, 2d ed., 360–62; Carla R. Morrisey, "The Influenza Epidemic of 1918," *U.S. Navy Medicine* 77 (May–June 1986): 11–17; Higbee to Bowman, 15 March 1919, Bowman Papers, Correspondence (1919) folder, box 1, NNC Records, OA, NHC. For complete accounts, see A. A. Hoehling, *The Great Epidemic* (Boston: Little Brown, 1961), and G. Marks and W. K. Beatty, *Epidemic* (New York: Charles Scribner's Sons, 1976).

123. Hickey, "Navy Nurse Corps," 74; quotation from Services Rendered by Navy Nurses, *AJN* 19 (December 1918): 188.

124. *Surgeon General's Report: 1919*, 2071; Acting Quartermaster General of the Army to Chief BuMed, 28 September 1918, Statistics—NC-9 folder, box 34, NNC Records, OA, NHC.

125. Awards WW I—Navy Cross folder; Awards WW I—Letters of Commendation folder; Awards WW I—Victory Medal folder, all in box 8, NNC Records, OA, NHC.

126. *Surgeon General's Report: 1919*, 2070; WW I Statistics—NNC, Statistics—NC-75—WW I folder, box 34, NNC Records, OA, NHC. Numbers vary from one source to another.

127. "Chronological History: Navy Nurse Corps," typescript, ND Records, BuMed, 1962, 14–16.

128. William Howard Taft, in *Philadelphia Public Ledger*, quoted in *AJN* 18 (September 1918): 1135; Grace E. Allison, "Rank for Nurses," *AJN* 19 (April 1919): 515. Throughout 1919, the *AJN* threw its support behind legislation for relative rank.

129. Excerpts from Military Affairs Hearings, *AJN* 20 (October 1919): 30–38; Kalisch and Scobey, "Helplessness Suspended," 8–10.

130. Higbee to Bowman, 6 February 1919; Bowman to Higbee, 18 February 1919, both in Bowman Papers, Correspondence (1919) folder, box 1, NNC Records, OA, NHC.

131. *Surgeon General's Report, 1920*, 746; Chief BuMed to SecNav, 15 September and 28 November 1921, both in Rank/Status folder, box 16, NNC Records, OA, NHC; JAG to Chief BuMed, 26 December 1921, file 125686 (2), box 428, entry 12, RG 52, NARA; NNC sec., *AJN* 22 (February 1922): 383.

132. For example, Bowman Papers, Correspondence (1918) and (1919) folders, box 1, NNC Records, OA, NHC; *Surgeon General's Report: 1919*, 2072; *AJN*, 1916–1920, passim. Fortunately for historians, NNC Records are full of draft articles written by nurses with Higbee's comments on them.

## *Chapter 4. The Interwar Years, 1921–1940*

1. Evans, *Born for Liberty*, 175–78, 186, 195; Rothman, *Proper Place*, 177–81, 213–14, 218; Bullough and Bullough, *Subordinate Sex*, 333.

2. Gordon, *Gender and Higher Education*, 2; Newcomer, *Higher Education*, 37, 46.

3. Chafe, *Paradox of Change*, 100; Newcomer, *Higher Education*, 179; Rury, *Education and Women's Work*, 95.

4. Chafe, *American Woman*, 53–54, 60; Chafe, *Paradox of Change*, 67, 100.

5. Evans, *Born for Liberty*, 182; Rothman, *Proper Place*, 224; Bullough and Bullough, *Subordinate Sex*, 333. For more, see Margery W. Davies, *Woman's Place Is at the Typewriter: Office Work and Office Workers, 1870–1930* (Philadelphia: Temple University Press, 1982); Weiner, *Working Girl*, 4, 78–79.

6. Evans, *Born for Liberty*, 187–88, 190–91; Ryan, *Womanhood*, 218; McHenry, *Liberty's Women*, 67–68.

7. Donahue, *Finest Art*, 339–40; Evans, *Born for Liberty*, 192–93; Kalisch and Kalisch, *American Nursing*, 2d ed., 438–46.

8. Kalisch and Kalisch, *American Nursing*, 2d ed., 446, 460; McHenry, *Liberty's Women*, 368. For the work of this pioneer, see Margaret Sanger, *Margaret Sanger: An Autobiography* (New York: W. W. Norton, 1938); David Kennedy, *Birth Control in America: The Career of Margaret Sanger* (New Haven: Yale University Press, 1970); Ellen Chesler, *Woman of Valor: Margaret Sanger and the Birth Control Movement in America* (New York: Simon & Schuster, 1992); Madeline Gray, *Margaret Sanger: A Biography of the Champion of Birth Control* (New York: R. Marek, 1979); Linda Gordon, *Woman's Body: Woman's Right: A Social History of Birth Control in America* (New York: Grossman, 1976).

9. McHenry, *Liberty's Women*, 319–20; Christy, "Equal Rights," 66–67; Chafe,

*American Woman*, 112–31; Letters to the Editor, signed by the superintendents, *AJN* 24 (May 1924): 665. There have been resolutions for an Equal Rights Amendment presented to each Congress since 1923; the measure was approved by Congress in 1972, only to be rejected in the ratification process.

10. McHenry, *Liberty's Women*, 324, 354; Ryan *Womanhood*, 219, 225, 250; Evans, *Born for Liberty*, 205–8. For more on Roosevelt, see Blanche N. Cook, *Eleanor Roosevelt*, vol. 1 (New York: Viking, 1992), and Doris K. Goodwin, *No Ordinary Time: Franklin and Eleanor Roosevelt: The Home Front in World War II* (New York: F. Watts, 1994). For Perkins, see George W. Martin, *Madam Secretary: Frances Perkins* (Boston: Houghton Mifflin, 1976).

11. Harold Sprout and Margaret Sprout, *Toward a New Order of Sea Power: American Naval Policy and the World Scene, 1918–1922* (Princeton, N.J.: Princeton University Press, 1940), 107–10. This book remains the classic coverage.

12. In the Four-Power Treaty, the United States, Britain, France, and Japan pledged to maintain the status quo in the Pacific; in the Nine-Power Treaty, these four nations and Italy, Belgium, the Netherlands, Portugal, and China agreed to preserve the territorial integrity of China. Miller, *U.S. Navy*, 275–77; Love, *History of the U.S. Navy* 1:530–33; Hagan, *This People's Navy*, 264–67; Sprout and Sprout, *New Order*, 286, 292.

13. Figures from "U.S. Navy Ship Force Levels, 1917–1989." Thomas C. Hone, "The Effectiveness of the 'Washington Treaty' Navy," *Naval War College Review* 32 (November–December 1979): 35–59, maintains that in spite of treaty limitations, the U.S. Navy took advantage of technological innovations while staying within treaty limitations, constructing a fleet that was effective for defensive strategic functions. See also Thomas C. Hone and Mark D. Mandeles, "Managerial Style in the Interwar Navy: A Reappraisal," *Naval War College Review* 33 (September–October 1980): 88–101.

14. Miller, *U.S. Navy*, 280–81, 284–86. See also Stephen Roskill, *Naval Policy Between the Wars* (New York: Walker, 1968).

15. BuPers, "Navy and Marine Corps Military Personnel Statistics," 30 June 1959, in Vertical File, Navy Department Library.

16. Philip T. Rosen, "The Treaty Navy, 1919–1937," in Hagan, *In Peace and War*, 223–24, 233. Rosen felt that by abiding by treaty limitations and concentrating on technological improvements, the U.S. Navy actually benefited.

17. Hagan, *This People's Navy*, 283–84; Miller, *U.S. Navy*, 288; number of ships from "U.S. Navy Ship Force Levels, 1917–1989"; number of personnel from BuPers, "Personnel Statistics."

18. Hancock interview; O'Neill interview; Etzler interview. Hancock recalled that in the beginning the American Legion in Washington would not allow women to join.

19. SecNav Memo, 7 July 1923; JAG to BuNav, 26 July 1923, both in file 28553-510, box 2544, RG 80, NARA.

20. *Miscellaneous Hearings*, Soldiers' Adjusted Compensation, 68th Cong., 1st sess; Harrod, *Manning the New Navy*, 67; Helen O'Neill, a brief history of the USS *Jacob Jones Post*, given to author. The bill was introduced by Rep. John McKenzie (R-Ill.).

21. *United States Statutes at Large* 43 (1924): 121–31.

22. *United States Statutes at Large* 43 (1924): 607–30; the *Note Book*, December 1929.

23. *United States Statutes at Large* 43 (1925): 1080–90.

24. *United States Statutes at Large* 45 (1929): 1090; and *United States Statutes at Large* 46 (1930): 991–1002; the *Note Book*, April 1930.

25. The *Note Book*, June 1934, June 1981; "Case of the Missing Yeoman Portrait," *Navy Times*, 16 November 1981, 16; Ebbert and Hall, *Crossed Currents*, 17–18. The three models for the composite were Helen O'Neill, Charlotte Berry Winters, and Ulla Tracy. There is a color negative of the portrait in Photographic Material folder, box 1, O'Neill Papers, OA, NHC.

26. The *Note Book*, November 1928, June 1936, September 1939, December 1985; "Milestones," and "The Fourth of March in 1929," both in the *Note Book*, September 1929; Dwyer, "Who and What is the NYF?", in the *Note Book*, December 1962. NYF constitution and bylaws in folder with same name, box 1, O'Neill Papers, OA, NHC.

27. *SecNav Report*, 1921, 10; appendix H, 46–47; *SecNav Report*, 1932, 62; *BuNav Report*, in *SecNav Report*, 1940, 43; *Surgeon General's Report: 1921*, 72–73.

28. *U.S. Naval Medical Bulletin* 29 (October 1931): 677; K. C. Melhorn, "Aspects of the Personnel Division of the Bureau of Medicine and Surgery," *U.S. Naval Medical Bulletin* 30 (January 1932): 31.

29. *Surgeon General's Report: 1921*, 72; *Surgeon General's Report: 1929*, 295–96; *Surgeon General's Report: 1930*, 298–99; *SecNav Report*, 1932, 63; Louis H. Roddis, "Organization of the Navy Medical Department," *Surgical Clinics of North America* (December 1941): 1538; Herman, *Hilltop*, 76.

30. *Surgeon General's Report: 1922*, 261; (*Surgeon General's Report: 1921*, 262, had the figures for 1920 rather than 1921); *SecNav Report*, 1932, 63; *Medical Department at War*, 106.

31. There were 470 in the NNC in 1921; 504 in 1932; 488 in 1940. In Statistics—NC-75 folder, box 34, NNC Records, OA, NHC; postgraduate training in Reports of the Superintendent, 1922–30, passim.

32. Kalisch and Kalisch, *American Nursing*, 2d ed., 369, 377–81, 484, 497.

33. Sterner, *Harm's Way*, 63, 84.

34. Donahue, *Finest Art*, 370, 380, 456; Annie W. Goodrich, "Yale University School of Nursing," *AJN* 25 (May 1925): 360. For an overview of the profession's growth, see M. Adelaide Nutting, "Thirty Years of Progress in Nursing," read at National League of Nursing Education Meeting, 19 June 1923 and printed in *AJN* 23 (September 1923): 1027–35.

35. Helen M. Fitzgerald, "A History of the United States Navy Nurse Corps from 1934 to the Present," M.S. thesis (Ohio State University, 1968), 17.

36. Kalisch and Kalisch, *American Nursing*, 2d ed., 412, 416, 418, 484; "The Nurse Question," *AJN* 25 (July 1925): 601, and 25 (August 1925): 704.

37. Kalisch and Kalisch, *American Nursing,* 2d ed., 383–84, 457–58, 462–63, 476–80, 483–84.

38. Kalisch and Kalisch, *American Nursing,* 2d ed., 429–30, 433–34, 443–44, 450–53, 523.

39. Alvin M. Owsley, Assistant National Director, American Legion to Edwin Denby, with attachments, 5 April 1921; Denby to Owsley, with attachments, 15 April 1921, all in file 125686, box 428, entry 12, RG 52, NARA; Letters to Editor, *AJN* 21 (June 1921).

40. Higbee to SecNav, via Surgeon General, 23 November 1922, file 125686, box 428, entry 12, RG 52, NARA. Editorial Comments sec., *AJN* 23 (January 1923): 293, paid tribute to Higbee's long years of selfless leadership.

41. Bowman to SecNav, 11 February 1922; Higbee to Surgeon General, 1 March 1922; Stitt to Bowman, 29 March 1922; Stitt to Higbee, 29 March 1922; Stitt to SecNav, 27 November 1922, all in Bowman Papers, Correspondence (1922–25) folder, box 1, NNC Records, OA, NHC; SecNav to Bowman, 28 November 1922, file 125686, box 428, entry 12, RG 52, NARA.

42. Biographical information from OA, NHC; and J. Beatrice Bowman folder, box 1, entry 48D, RG 52, NARA; Bowman Papers, Orders, Travel, Pay folder (1), box 1, NNC Records, OA, NHC; NNC sec., *AJN* 23 (January 1923): 328–29.

43. W. T. Gildberg, USN Hospital, Ft. Lyon, CO, to J. A. Murphy, BuMed, 28 February 1920; Murphy to Gildberg, 10 April 1920, both in file 125686, box 428, entry 12, RG 52, NARA. Gildberg said that he knew that NNC members were hard to handle and that Bowman's manner had caused discontent among doctors and hospital corpsmen. Murphy declined to act because BuMed was pleased with the hospital.

44. Figures from Statistics folder (1), box 19; Bowman to All Members of the Nurse Corps, 23 March 1934, Bowman Papers, Correspondence (1930–38) folder, box 1, all in NNC Records, OA, NHC; Superintendent's Reports: 1933, 1934.

45. Hickey, "Navy Nurse Corps," 103. Between 1917 and 1926, 1,071 women had entered the NNC through the Reserves.

46. *Surgeon General's Report: 1920,* 744; *Surgeon General's Report: 1921,* 73–74; *Surgeon General's Report: 1922,* 260; *Surgeon General's Report: 1926,* 262–63; *Surgeon General's Report: 1929,* 297; *Surgeon General's Report: 1930,* 298; Superintendent's Report, 10 July 1922, Personnel—NC-78—Annual Reports folder, box 32, NNC Records, OA, NHC. Bowman made no mention of any less qualified nurses in her annual reports.

47. Superintendent's Reports: 1923–30, passim; *Surgeon General's Report: 1924,* 365; *Surgeon General's Report: 1925,* 315; *Surgeon General's Report: 1927,* 283; *Surgeon General's Report: 1929,* 296; *AJN* 21 (March 1921): 410; 21 (August 1921): 886; 23 (April 1923): 576; 28 (July 1928): 722; 29 (January 1929): 213; 30 (January 1930): 224; "The Navy Nurse Corps and What It Offers to Nurses," *AJN* 29 (May 1929): 595–99.

48. Pay Table, 1922; Pay Table 1909–29; BUS&A, Pay and Allowances of Female Nurses, U.S. Navy, [June 1922]. Private-duty nurses earned an average of $6 for a twelve-hour day; $8 for mental or addiction cases, in Graduate Nurses Association of D.C., Scale

of Charges, March 1924, and May 1927. All in Pay and Allowances folders 1 and 2, box 15, NNC Records, OA, NHC.

49. Hickey, "Navy Nurse Corps," 118; *United States Statutes at Large* 47 (1932): 382–419. The cuts were restored by 1935.

50. *United States Statutes at Large* 43 (1924): 607–30; Superintendent's Report: 1923; Red Cross sec., *AJN* 24 (July 1924), and 25 (December 1924).

51. Related correspondence and Notes about British Military Nursing Service in Retirement folder (1), box 17, NNC Records, OA, NHC; *United States Statutes at Large* 44 (1926): 531–32; Editorial sec., *AJN* 26 (April 1926): 298; and *AJN* 26 (August 1926): 637. The first Navy nurse to retire under this act was Chief Nurse Martha Pringle, one of the Sacred Twenty. In *AJN* 26 (September 1926): 726.

52. *United States Statutes at Large* 45 (1928): 366; and *United States Statutes at Large* 46 (1930): 790; Red Cross sec., *AJN* 28 (January 1928): 72; Bowman, "Disability Bill for Army and Navy Nurses," *AJN* 30 (August 1930): 1016; "Disabled Ex-Service Women to be Admitted to Soldiers' Homes," *AJN* 24 (November 1923): 109.

53. Chief BuMed to Chief BuNav, 1 June 1940, Retirement folder 1, box 17, NNC Records, OA, NHC.

54. Cdr. Mary J. Lindner, interview with author, 2 May 1995; quotation from Mrs. Milford Bristol, interview with author, 4 March 1983; Bowman, "The History and Development of the Navy Nurse Corps," *AJN* 25 (May 1925): 359; "The Navy Nurse Corps and What It Offers," 595–99.

55. Stitt to all Naval Hospitals and Stations, 8 September 1924, file 125686, box 428, entry 12, RG 52, NARA; Superintendent's Report, 21 March 1924; *Surgeon General's Report: 1924*, 365.

56. Department of the Navy, *Uniform Regulations: United States Navy Nurse Corps* (Washington, D.C.: GPO, 1923); complete specifications in file 125786, RG 52, NARA, cited in Feeney, 1922–35 folder, box 24, NNC Records, OA, NHC; NNC sec., *AJN* 24 (April 1924); P. S. Rossiter, memo re NNC, n.d., but c. 1935, 1922–35 folder, box 24, NNC Records, OA, NHC. For a painstakingly detailed description, see William A. Edwards, "A History of United States Uniforms for the Sea Services," unpublished typescript, c. 1980, Navy Department Library, chap. 9, 1–54.

57. Braisted to all Medical Officers and Hospital Corpsmen, 11 June 1920, Miscellaneous Articles folder (3), box 21, and in Rank/Status folder, box 16, both in NNC Records, OA, NHC.

58. Superintendent's Annual Report: 1923. Surgeon General Stitt expressed the same sentiments, in *Surgeon General's Report: 1923*, 349.

59. Chief BuNav, to COs, *Chaumont, Henderson, Kittery, Gold Star*, 6 November 1924, file 125686, box 428, entry 12, RG 52, NARA; Superintendent's Report: 1925; *Surgeon General's Report: 1925*, 315.

60. Stitt, Circular Letter to All Naval Hospitals, 24 January 1925, file 125686, box 428, entry 12, RG 52, NARA.

61. Hickey, "Navy Nurse Corps," 106–7.

62. Department of the Navy, *Manual for the Medical Department of the United States Navy*, 1927 (Washington, D.C.: GPO, 1927), 34–35; Department of the Navy, *Manual for the Medical Department of the United States Navy*, 1939, 28; Superintendent's Report: 1923; The Nursing Service of the United States Navy (1924), Personnel—NC-78 folder, box 32, NNC Records, OA, NHC; "The Navy Nurse Corps," *AJN* 37 (December 1937); NNC sec., *AJN* 21 (March 1921): 410. Reserve nurses had more latitude for age: 22 to 40 in 1927 and 22 to 45 in 1939.

63. Superintendent's Reports: 1923–35, passim.

64. All in file 125686, box 428, entry 12, RG 52, NARA; Bowman's summons in Bowman Papers, Correspondence (1922–25) folder, box 1, NNC Records, OA, NHC.

65. "Postgraduate Instruction for Members of the Medical Department of the Navy in the Calendar Year 1932," *U.S. Naval Medical Bulletin* (April 1933); Superintendent's Report: 1924; "Present Trends in Nursing," radio address, 17 February 1932, J. Beatrice Bowman folder, box 1, entry 48D, RG 52, NARA.

66. Nurse Anna Redding Krapp (interview with author, 4 March 1983) recalled that the Navy had sent her to Columbia to complete a B.S. in Nursing Education. NNC Officer Program History folder, box 14, NNC Records, OA, NHC; NNC sec., *AJN* 22 (May 1922): 599; 22 (September 1922): 1099; 23 (April 1923): 576; and 24 (December 1923): 228; Della V. Knight, "Care and Treatment of Tuberculosis Patients"; "Physiotherapy from the Viewpoint of a Nurse," both in Nursing Specialties folder, box 14, NNC Records, OA, NHC; *Surgeon General's Report: 1923*, 349; *Surgeon General's Report: 1924*, 364; Superintendent's Reports: 1923, 1924.

67. NNC sec., *AJN* 26 (April 1926): 336; 27 (August 1927): 688; Superintendent's Reports: 1925–1929, 1934–1939; *Surgeon General's Report: 1926*, 263; *Surgeon General's Report: 1931*, 3; *SecNav Report*, 1932, 63; Ethelyn Everman, "The Art of Anesthesia," *U.S. Naval Medical Bulletin* 27 (April 1929); Joanna Ferris, "A Summer Session at Columbia University," *U.S. Naval Medical Bulletin* 28 (April 1930); related correspondence about physical therapy in Physical Therapy Courses (1931–37) folder, box 15, NNC Records, OA, NHC. Some nurses took courses in accounting that taught efficient hospital management. See Mabel T. Cooper, "The Lectures on Accounting from a Nurse's Point of View," *U.S. Naval Medical Bulletin* 25 (1927).

68. Superintendent's Reports: 1923, 1924; *Surgeon General's Report: 1924*, 364–65; NNC sec., *AJN* 24 (December 1923): 228. Initially, BuMed intended to assign the assistants to the Hospital Corps Training Schools and make these into centers where nurses would get an indoctrination course when they entered the Navy. This was similar to the procedure followed by new officers entering the Medical Corps and receiving training at the Medical School. But the plans changed.

69. Superintendent's Reports: 1925–1929; NNC sec., *AJN* 28 (July 1928): 841; Sterner, *Harm's Way*, 73.

70. *SecNav Report*, 1921, appendix H, 46; *SecNav Report*, 1929, 22; Higbee's paper

given at Veterans' Bureau meeting, 18 January 1922, printed in *AJN* 22 (April 1922): 524–25; Hickey, "Navy Nurse Corps," 94.

71. NNC sec., *AJN* 21 (November 1920): 112; Bowman, "Pharmacist's Mates School," 301–5; *Surgeon General's Report: 1920*, 748–49; *Surgeon General's Report: 1921*, 76; *Surgeon General's Report: 1922*, 261; *Surgeon General's Report: 1928*, 327.

72. *U.S. Naval Medical Bulletin*, supplement (January and April 1924): 65; Superintendent's Report: 1923; *Surgeon General's Report: 1924*, 365; I. Grace Kline, "Hospital Corpsmen of the Navy," *AJN* 21 (January 1921): 226. Chief Pharmacist W. H. MacWilliams wrote of members of the Graduate Nurses' Association visiting the Portsmouth facility in "Visit of Virginia Nurses to the Pharmacist's Mates School, Portsmouth, VA," *Hospital Corps Quarterly* 11 (October 1927): 268–70.

73. *Surgeon General's Report: 1930*, 299; Bowman, "History and Development of the Navy Nurse Corps," 357; J. Beatrice Bowman, "The Hospital Training School of the Navy," *AJN* 23 (February 1923): 489; J. Beatrice Bowman, "The Navy Nurse Corps and Its Relation to the Advancement of Nursing Education," paper presented to ANA convention, 1924.

74. Braisted to Medical Director, *Mercy*, 2 February 1918, folder 3, box 24, NNC Records, OA, NHC; NNC sec., *AJN* 21 (October 1920): 53; *Surgeon General's Report: 1919*, 2068; *Surgeon General's Report: 1920*, 744; *Surgeon General's Report: 1921*, 74; *Mercy*, in *DANFS* 4:331.

75. *Relief*, in *DANFS* 6:68; Sterner, *Harm's Way*, 60; Letters from Navy Nurses, *AJN* 22 (November 1921): 120, describes the quarters. Bowman to Higbee, 21 February 1921, 2 March 1921, 4 March 1921, 29 March 1921, 31 March 1921, 16 April 1921, 20 April 1921; Higbee to Bowman, 12 February 1921 (suggesting that Bowman write a series of articles), all in Bowman Papers, Correspondence (1920–21) folder, box 1, NNC Records, OA, NHC. The articles followed: J. B. B. [Bowman], Letters from Navy Nurse from U.S.S. *Relief*, 21 (February 1921): 485; (June 1921): 644; (July 1921): 732–33; (August 1921): 816; (September 1921): 901.

76. For more on nurses in *Relief* from its commissioning through WW II, see Christine Curto, "Nurse Pioneers and the Hospital Ship *Relief*," *U.S. Navy Medicine* 83 (May–June 1992): 20–25.

77. Capt. Ruth A. Erickson to author, 13 March 1995; Lindner interview.

78. Lindner interview.

79. *Surgeon General's Report: 1921*, 74–75; Activities of the Navy Nurse Corps from January 1, 1921, 21 March 1924, NNC History folder, box 14; The Nursing Service of the United States Navy, Personnel—NC-78 folder, box 32, both in NNC Records, OA, NHC; *Mercy*, in *DANFS* 4:331.

80. BuNav to BuMed, 10 November 1921; Stitt to BuNav, 23 November 1921, both in file 125686, box 428, entry 12, RG 52, NARA.

81. The Nursing Service of the United States Navy, Personnel—NC-78 folder, box 32,

NNC Records, OA, NHC; Susie I. Fitzgerald, "A Transport Trip," *AJN* 23 (October 1922): 141, and (December 1922): 222–25. Fitzgerald never mentioned the name of the transport.

82. BuNav to COs, *Chaumont, Henderson, Kittery, Gold Star,* 6 November 1924, file 125686, box 428, entry 12, RG 52, NARA; Superintendent's Report: 1927, cites Chief Nurses Mary B. Gainey and Mabel Powell for their excellent service.

83. *Henderson,* in *DANFS* 3:295–96; Sue S. Dauser, "President Harding's Alaskan Trip," and "President Harding's Last Illness"; Ruth A. Houghton to F. Kent Loomis, 28 July 1961, enclosing biographical information on Ruth Powderly, all in President Warren G. Harding folder, box 11, NNC Records, OA, NHC. Powderly also nursed President Wilson during his last illness in 1924.

84. *Surgeon General's Report: 1921,* 74; *Surgeon General's Report: 1924,* 365; CO, Naval Hospital, Guam, to BuMed, 5 December 1924; Native Graduate Nurses in Guam, March 1927, both in Guam folder (2), box 11; J. Beatrice Bowman, "Nursing in the Islands"; and Sue S. Dauser, who preceded Workman as chief nurse, wrote of her impressions of the island in "Guam and the Philippines," both in Overseas Duty Stations folder, box 14, all in NNC Records, OA, NHC.

85. Superintendent's Report: 1925; *Surgeon General's Report: 1925,* 315.

86. Hannah M. Workman to CO, Naval Hospital, Guam, 25 August 1927; CO to BuMed, 25 August 1927 (first endorsement), Guam folder (2); Workman letters, 10 June 1927, and 6 February 1928, Guam folder (1), all in box 11, NNC Records, OA, NHC.

87. Program: Graduation Ceremony, 5 April 1929; chief nurse's introductory remarks, in Workman to Bowman, 6 April 1929; Program: Commencement Exercises, 1934; Henrietta Wiltzius to Bowman, 6 April 1934, all in Guam folder (2); Workman's letter, 14 January 1929, Guam folder (1), all in box 11, NNC Records, OA, NHC.

88. Emily J. Cunningham, Native School of Nursing, Guam, 18 January 1934, Guam folder (2), NNC Records, OA, NHC.

89. E. S. Kellogg to Commandant-Governor, 10 December 1924, Samoa folder (1), box 17, NNC Records, OA, NHC; Bowman, "Nursing in the Islands"; *SecNav Report,* 1921, 14; *Surgeon General's Report, 1920,* 745; *Surgeon General's Report: 1921,* 74; *Surgeon General's Report: 1924,* 365.

90. B.D.M. [Bernice Mansfield], letter to editor, *AJN* 22 (January 1922): 296; Bowman, "Advancement of Nursing Education." One nurse, Laura Hartwell, "Impressions of Samoa," *AJN* 23 (February 1923): 397–98, wrote of her experiences with the Samoans. Another described the elaborate farewell from them when she left Samoa in 1923 and her return to the U.S. via Europe. No name, "Halfway Round the World," Overseas Duty Stations folder, box 14, NNC Records, OA, NHC.

91. Superintendent's Report: 1928. Chief Nurse Ellen M. Hodgson received a letter of commendation for assisting Mead.

92. Chief Nurse Mary Elizabeth Hand, Report of Samoan Nurses, 30 June 1932; Address by Hand to Graduating Class, 3 November 1932; Chief Nurse Theresa E. Wilkins to Bowman, detailed report, 10 January 1934; Mary L. Benner, "Life in

American Samoa as Seen by Local Nurse," (1935), all in Samoa folder (1), box 17, NNC Records, OA, NHC; *SecNav Report*, 1941, 56.

93. Dauser, "Guam and the Philippines"; Dauser, "China and Japan," Overseas Duty Stations folder, box 14, NNC Records, OA, NHC; Superintendent's Report: 1925; *Surgeon General's Report: 1925*, 315.

94. Figures in untitled paper, 1 March 1934, Guam folder (2), box 11, NNC Records, OA, NHC; Superintendent's Report: 1925; *Surgeon General's Report: 1925*, 315.

95. Sterner, *Harm's Way*, 58; E.N.L. [Elizabeth Leonhardt] and N.E.T. [unidentified], "The Earthquake in Japan," History—Articles Published folder, box 20, NNC Records, OA, NHC, give a vivid account of the destruction caused by the earthquake and of the Americans' departure from Japan.

96. Bowman, "Nursing in the Islands"; Graduation Exercises, Municipal Hospital, St. Thomas, 1923; lists of graduates from all three schools [1924] and similar lists in 1927, all in Virgin Islands folder, box 20, NNC Records, OA, NHC.

97. *Surgeon General's Report, 1920*, 746, first mentioned such an affiliation. Superintendent's Report: 1925; *Surgeon General's Report: 1925*, 315; relevant correspondence in Bowman to John Harper, CO, Municipal Hospital, St. Thomas, 24 April 1925; E. R. Stitt to Gov. Philip Williams, Virgin Islands, 24 April 1925, both in box 20, NNC Records, OA, NHC.

98. Myn M. Hoffman to Bowman, 11 March 1931, Virgin Islands folder, box 20, NNC Records, OA, NHC; Bowman, "Advancement of Nursing Education."

99. Hoffman to Bowman, 11 March 1931; Jennie W. Jason, "The District Welfare Nursing in St. Croix, Virgin Islands"; other information from Notes on Training Schools—a compilation of letters written by Nurses Harkins (26 February 1926), Gainey (23 May 1926 and 26 February 1927), and Dr. Stopps's report for 1925–26, all in Virgin Islands folder, box 20, NNC Records, OA, NHC.

100. Press release: Executive Order of 27 February 1931; BuNav to Commandant, Naval Station, St. Thomas, 14 May 1931; Joseph M. Dixon, Acting Secretary of the Interior, to SecNav, 6 July 1931; T. W. Reed, Commissioner of Public Health, Virgin Islands, to BuMed, 25 July 1931, all in Virgin Islands folder, box 20, NNC Records, OA, NHC.

101. Red Cross sec., *AJN* 25 (September 1925): 781–82; *Surgeon General's Report: 1921*, 74; *SecNav Report*, 1922, 21.

102. Superintendent's Report: 1925; Virginia A. Rau, "In the Capital of Haiti," 29 September 1925; another unidentified nurse left a handwritten account of her experiences, both in Haiti folder, box 11, NNC Records, OA, NHC.

103. CO, Naval Hospital, Washington, to BuMed, 30 January 1922; Stitt to CO, Naval Hospital, 2 February 1922, both in file 126472 (1922), box 466, entry 12, RG 52, NARA; Hickey, "Navy Nurse Corps," 88.

104. Altogether, burn victims totaled about 150, and 53 died. "The *Mackinac* Disaster"; M. Nirvinia Bailey, "Factors in Emergency Nursing: Methods Used in the *Mackinac* Disaster," both in History—Articles Published folder, box 20; Anna E. Manning, Red Cross

field director, "Report of Hospital Worker in the *Mackinac* Disaster," Disasters folder (1), box 10, all in NNC Records, OA, NHC; Red Cross sec., *AJN* 26 (January 1926): 53.

105. Nurses who were there wrote eyewitness accounts: M. J. McCloud, "The Pensacola Hurricane"; L. A. MacFarland, no title but about the hurricane; Ellen E. Wells and M. Hennemeier, "A Hurricane Thrill," all in Disasters folder (2), box 10, NNC Records, OA, NHC.

106. Biographical information from OA, NHC; "Mainly about People," *AJN* 35 (1935): 185.

107. *AJN* 39 (January 1939): 90; "A Nurses' Monument in Arlington," *AJN* 37 (June 1937): 623.

108. Biographical information from Myn M. Hoffman folder, box 1, entry 48D, RG 52, NARA; *AJN* 38 (1938): 1280.

109. Biographical information from BuMed History; Virginia Rau, "The Tide and Trend of the NNC," 20 January 1932, in Esther V. Hasson folder, box 1, entry 48D, RG 52, NARA.

110. For a good account of naval preparations, see John Major, "The Navy Plans for War," in Hagan, *In Peace and War*, 235–62.

111. BuPers, "Personnel Statistics"; *United States Statutes at Large* 52 (1938): 1175–86. The Naval Reserve consisted of four classes: Fleet Reserve, Organized Reserve, Merchant Marine Reserve, and Volunteer Reserve.

112. Biographical information from BuMed Archives; NNC sec., *AJN* 39 (March 1939): 324, and 39 (April 1939): 441.

113. Correspondence about nurses in Specialist Units in Procurement History, 1938–40 folder—Enrollment of Naval Reserve Nurses in Medical Specialists Units, box 7, entry 48D, RG 52, NARA. Hickey, "Navy Nurse Corps," 120; "The Decentralization Plan," *AJN* 36 (1936): 181; "Red Cross Nursing and the Navy," *AJN* 40 (September 1940): 981; NNC sec., *AJN* 41 (April 1941): 385. Although males could not join the Army Nurse Corps or the Navy Nurse Corps, the Red Cross started enrolling qualified men nurses as technologists, who could later serve in auxiliary positions to the Nurse Corps.

114. Donahue, *Finest Art*, 371–72.

## *Chapter 5. The WAVES in World War II*

1. D'Ann Campbell, *Women at War with America: Private Lives in a Patriotic Era* (Cambridge: Harvard University Press, 1984), 20.

2. See Leila J. Rupp, *Mobilizing Women for War: German and American Propaganda, 1939–1945* (Princeton, N.J.: Princeton University Press, 1978), passim.

3. Gordon, *Gender and Higher Education*, 2; Newcomer, *Higher Education*, 46; Chafe, *Women and Equality*, 70; Bureau of the Census, *Statistical Abstract of the United States: 1947* (Washington, D.C.: GPO, 1947), 136 (hereafter cited as *Statistical Abstract*, followed by the date in parentheses).

4. Ryan, *Womanhood*, 281; table of occupational status, 1940–47, in Campbell, *Women at War*, 239.

5. Ruth H. Howes and Caroline L. Herzenberg, "Women in Weapons Development: The Manhattan Project," in *Women and the Use of Military Force*, ed. Ruth H. Howes and Michael R. Stevenson (Boulder: Lynne Rienner, 1993), 95–109.

6. Chafe, *American Woman*, 137, 141; Susan M. Hartmann, *The Home Front and Beyond: American Women in the 1940s* (Boston: Twayne Publishers, 1982), 21.

7. Ryan, *Womanhood*, 256; Michael C. C. Adams, *The Best War Ever: America and World War II* (Baltimore: Johns Hopkins University Press, 1994), 71, 134; Maureen Honey, *Creating Rosie the Riveter: Class, Gender and Propaganda during World War II* (Amherst: University of Massachusetts Press, 1984). For a contemporary view of women working in shipyards, the difficulties they encountered, and their efficiency, see Fred M. Earle, "Employment of Women in Navy Yards," *USNIP* 71 (September 1945): 1050–57; and more recently, "Women Shipbuilders," *Sea Letter* (fall/winter 1994): 20–13.

8. Hartmann, *Home Front*, 23, 43; Karen Anderson, *Wartime Women: Sex Roles, Family Relations, and the Status of Women during World War II* (Westport, Conn.: Greenwood Press, 1981), 62; "Women's Place is in the Shop," *BNPIB* (November 1943): 33–35. For more on postwar women in the work force, see chapter 7.

9. Community Facilities Act [Lanham Act], 1941; Campbell, *Women at War*, 13; Ryan, *Womanhood*, 258; Anderson, *Wartime Women*, 6, 123, 125.

10. Chafe, *American Woman*, 152–53.

11. William L. O'Neill, *A Democracy at War: America's Fight at Home and Abroad in World War II* (New York: Free Press, 1993), 242; Evans, *Born for Liberty*, 225; Chafe, *Paradox of Change*, 161–62; Chafe, *American Woman*, 144. The figures are slightly different in Adams, *Best War Ever*, 123–24.

12. Ryan, *Womanhood*, 254, 258; Campbell, *Women at War*, 65–72.

13. See Gerhard Weinberg, *A World at Arms: A Global History of World War II* (New York: Cambridge University Press, 1995), for a recent and comprehensive account; and Robert W. Love Jr., "Fighting a Global War, 1941–1945," in Hagan, *In Peace and War*, 263–89, for a brief summary.

14. Miller, *U.S. Navy*, 296–300; O'Neill, *Democracy*, 31–32, 72; Nathan Miller, *War at Sea: A Naval History of World War II* (New York: Scribner, 1995). There is a vast literature on the naval history of World War II, but Samuel Eliot Morison, *History of United States Naval Operations in World War II*, 15 vols. (Boston: Little, Brown, 1947–1962), remains the best starting point.

15. Miller, *U.S. Navy*, 294. Figures from "U.S. Navy Ship Force Levels, 1917–1987."

16. BuPers, "Personnel Statistics"; *SecNav Report*, 1945, A-15. *SecNav Report*, 1940, 43, 47, gives different figures: 10,817 officers and 139,554 enlisted in 1940.

17. Both are covered in Paolo E. Coletta, ed., *American Secretaries of the Navy* (Annapolis, Md.: Naval Institute Press, 1980), 2:677–727 for Knox, 2:729–43 for Forrestal. See Townsend Hooper, *Driven Patriot: The Life and Times of James Forrestal* (New York: Knopf, 1992).

18. Furer, *Administration*, 15–19. The bureaus were Yards and Docks, Ships (a merger of Construction and Repair, and Engineering), Supplies and Accounts, Ordnance,

Medicine and Surgery, Naval Personnel (formerly Navigation), and Aeronautics. For King's role, see Ernest J. King, *The United States Navy at War: Official Reports to the Secretary of the Navy* (Washington, D.C.: GPO, 1946), and Ernest J. King and Walter M. Whitehill, *Fleet Admiral King: A Naval Record* (New York: Norton, 1952).

19. Memo: Women's Royal Naval Service, n.d., folder 28, box 4, ser. 1, ACNP(W), OA, NHC; M. H. Fletcher, *The WRNS: A History of the Women's Royal Naval Service* (Annapolis, Md.: Naval Institute Press, 1989), 26–30, 80. The WRNS grew from 275 officers and 3,086 ratings in 1939 to 4,646 officers and 69,309 ratings in December 1944. D'Ann Campbell, "Women, Combat, and the Gender Line," *Quarterly Journal of Military History* 6 (Autumn 1993): 88–97, surveys how the British, Germans, and Soviets utilized women warriors.

20. "Edith Nourse Rogers," in McHenry, *Liberty's Women,* 352; Mattie E. Treadwell, *United States Army in World War II: Special Studies: The Women's Army Corps* (Washington, D.C.: Department of the Army, 1954), 15–29, 42–45; Cecilia Hock, "Creation of the WAC Image and Perception of Army Women, 1942–44," *Minerva: Quarterly Report on Women and the Military* 13 (spring 1995): 41–44; Jeanne Holm, *Women in the Military: An Unfinished Revolution,* rev. ed. (Novato, Calif.: Presidio, 1992; paperback reprint, 1993), 24. More recently, Leisa Meyer, *Creating G.I. Jane: The Women's Army Corps During World War II* (New York: Columbia University Press, 1996); and Bettie Morden, "Women's Army Corps: WAAC and WAC," in *In Defense of a Nation: Servicewomen in World War II,* ed. Jeanne M. Holm (Washington, D.C.: Military Women's Press, 1998), 39–55.

21. The Bureau of Navigation became the Bureau of Naval Personnel in 1942, but for consistency, that bureau will be referred to by the latter name throughout.

22. Chief BuNav, to Chief BuAer, 12 December 1941; CNO to all Bureaus and Offices, 30 December 1941, both in folder 9, box 1, Joy Bright Hancock Papers, no. 854, Hargrett Rare Book and Ms Library, University of Georgia, Athens.

23. Chief BuAer to Chief BuNav, 1 January 1942, folder 9, box 1, Hancock Papers; Bureau of Naval Personnel, *U.S. Naval Administration in World War II: Women's Reserve,* 2 vols., typescript, Washington, D.C., 1946–47, 1:3–7, 57; Sue Fischer, ed., *Navy Women, 1908–1988: A Pictorial History* (n.p., WAVES National, 1990), 22; Hancock, *Lady in the Navy,* 49–52.

24. BuPers, *Women's Reserve* 1:9–12; U.S. Congress, *Hearings on H.R. 6807,* 15 April 1942; *Hearings on S. 2527,* 19 May and 23 June 1942, both in folder 8, box 33, ser. 4, ACNP(W), OA, NHC; Hancock, *Lady in the Navy,* 53–56; quotation from Virginia C. Gildersleeve, *Many a Good Crusade: Memoirs of Virginia Crocheron Gildersleeve* (New York: Macmillan, 1954), 271. Margaret Chung was a San Francisco physician who had befriended many naval aviators, who called themselves the "sons of Mom Chung."

25. Quotation from Gildersleeve, *Crusade,* 267. For a useful summary, see Jean Ebbert and Marie-Beth Hall, "Navy Women's Reserve: WAVES," in Holm, *In Defense of a Nation,* 57–75.

26. Randall Jacobs to Gildersleeve, 24 April 1942, asking her to chair the council; Gildersleeve to Jacobs, 28 April 1942, reporting on conference at Barnard, with list of

women educators attending, both in folder QR-8, box 2328, RG 24, NARA; and in folder 2, box 1, ser. 1, ACNP(W), OA, NHC. In addition to Gildersleeve, the council included Dr. Meta Glass of Sweet Briar College; Dr. Lillian Gilbreth, an efficiency expert; Dr. Ada Comstock, president of Radcliffe College; Harriet Elliot, dean of women at the University of North Carolina; Dean Alice Lloyd, University of Michigan; Mrs. Malbone Graham, a West Coast lecturer; and Mrs. Thomas Gates, wife of the president of the University of Pennsylvania. After Elliot resigned, Dr. Alice Baldwin, dean of women at Duke University, replaced her. Susan H. Godson, "The WAVES in World War II," *USNIP* 107 (December 1981): 46; Hancock, *Lady in the Navy*, 60; Ebbert and Hall, *Crossed Currents*, 32; Gildersleeve, *Crusade*, 268–70.

27. Gildersleeve, *Crusade*, 270–71.

28. Capt. Mildred McAfee Horton, official bio, OA, NHC; Recollections of Capt. Mildred McAfee, USNR (Ret.), USNI Oral History series, 1971, 6; "Mildred McAfee (Horton)," in *Women and the Military: Over 100 Notable Contributors, Historic to Contemporary*, by John P. Dever and Maria C. Dever (Jefferson, N.C.: McFarland, 1995), 83–84. Capt. Winifred Q. Collins gave a touching eulogy at McAfee's funeral, 29 September 1994, copy at OA, NHC.

29. McAfee Recollections, 18–19; Hancock, *Lady in the Navy*, 61.

30. BuPers, *Women's Reserve* 1:10; Chief BuNav to All Bureaus and Offices of Navy Department, and Commandants, All Naval Districts, less 10th, 14th, and 15th, 20 April 1942, folder QR-8, box 2328, RG 24, NARA. Answers are in the same folder and also in QR-8 folder, box 2329, RG 24, NARA.

31. BuPers, *Women's Reserve* 1:12–13; C. Mildred Thompson to Franklin Roosevelt, 1 June 1942; Herman Davis to Roosevelt, telegram, 11 June 1942; Forrestal to Eleanor Roosevelt, 10 June 1942, all in folder QR-8, box 2329, RG 24, NARA.

32. Knox to C. Mildred Thompson, 17 June 1942; Knox to Sen. David Walsh, 18 June 1942, both in folder QR-8 5-79, box 2329, RG 24, NARA; BuPers, *Women's Reserve* 1:13; Hancock, *Lady in the Navy*, 56.

33. *United States Statutes at Large* 56 (1942): 730–31; U.S. Navy Press release, 30 July 1942.

34. Campbell, *Women at War*, 20; Mary E. McWilliams, "Women in the Coast Guard: SPARS," in Holm, *In Defense of a Nation*, 97–110. For an overview, Judy B. Litoff and David C. Smith, "The Wartime History of the WAVES, Spars, Women Marines, Army and Navy Nurses, and Wasps," in *A Woman's War Too: U.S. Women in the Military in World War II*, ed. Paula M. Poulos (Washington, D.C.: NARA, 1996), 47–67.

35. The WASPs have enjoyed extensive coverage. See Byrd H. Granger, *On Final Approach: The Women Airforce Service Pilots of W.W. II* (Scottsdale, Ariz.: Falconer, 1991); Sally Van Wagenen Keil, *Those Wonderful Women in Their Flying Machines: The Unknown Heroines of World War II*, rev. ed. (New York: Four Directions Press, 1990); Jacqueline Cochran, *The Stars at Noon* (Boston: Little, Brown, 1954); Dean Jaros, *Heroes Without Legacy: American Airwomen, 1912–1944* (Niwot: University of Colorado Press, 1993), 61–66; Helen F. Collins, "Fifinella and Friends," *Naval Aviation News* (July 1977): 21–23.

36. Gildersleeve, *Crusade*, 274–75; BuPers, *Women's Reserve* 1:33, 35; McAfee, Recollections, 50–51; Godson, "WAVES," 48.

37. Hancock, report of Canadian Inspection Trip, 6–12 September 1942, folder 9, box 1, Hancock Papers; Hancock, *Lady in the Navy*, 49.

38. Recollections of Jean Palmer, 6; of Dorothy Stratton, 2, 4, 10, USNI Oral History series; official bios of Palmer, Winifred Quick Collins, and Louise K. Wilde, OA, NHC; Ebbert and Hall, *Crossed Currents*, 40–41. By 30 September 1942, there were 108 officers and 16 enlisted, in BuPers, "Personnel Statistics."

39. BuPers, *Women's Reserve* 1:37–41; Hancock, *Lady in the Navy*, 66; Palmer, Recollections, 12–13.

40. BuPers Memo to all Divisions, 16 September 1942, folder 28, box 4, and folder 39, box 5, both in ser. 1, ACNP(W), OA, NHC.

41. Memo to Assistant Chief BuPers, 14 December 1942, folder 1, box 18, ser. 2, ACNP(W), OA, NHC; BuPers, *Women's Reserve* 1:33, 158–59; Wilde and Palmer bios, OA, NHC; Elizabeth A. Butler, *Navy WAVES* (Charlottesville: Wayside Press, 1988), 9.

42. McAfee to Fechteler, 31 December 1942; Requests for Officers W-V(S), 25 September 1942, both in folder 20, box 3; District Directors Conferences (1943–46), folder 14, box 2; Jacobs to All Shore Stations in Continental U.S., 8 April 1943; Jacobs to chiefs of various naval air training commands, 24 April 1943, both in folder 30, box 4; Annual Report of Director of WR for 1943–44, folder 88, box 14, all in ser. 1, ACNP(W), OA, NHC; BuPers, *Women's Reserve* 1:51–53.

43. Hancock, *Lady in the Navy*, 62, 143; BuPers, *Women's Reserve* 1:63–68. For a first-hand account of a WAVE officer's recruiting duties in Pittsburgh, see Florence C. McLaughlin, "Down to the Sea in Slips," *Western Pennsylvania Historical Magazine* 51 (October 1968): 377–87.

44. *Chicago Daily Tribune*, 6 April 1943; Chief BuPers to all Directors of Naval Officer Procurement and O-in-Cs of All Branch Offices, 1 May 1943, both in folder 1, box 18, ser. 2, ACNP(W), OA, NHC; McAfee to J. A. Mayer, 7 December 1943, folder 2, box 18, ser. 2, ACNP(W), OA, NHC.

45. Public Relations Correspondence and Policies, folder 2, box 18, ser. 2; Publicity and Advertising pamphlets (1943–1947), folder 6, box 19, ser. 2; Louise K. Wilde's correspondence in General Publicity, folder 4, box 19, ser. 2, all in ACNP(W), OA, NHC; BuPers, *Women's Reserve* 1:69–73; Fischer, *Navy Women*, 25. Typical of recruiting booklets were *How to Serve Your Country in the WAVES or SPARs*, 1943, folder 9, ser. 4, ACNP(W), OA, NHC, and "Enlist in the WAVES: Serve in the Hospital Corps," n.d.

46. Figures from BuPers, "Personnel Statistics."

47. Chief of Naval Personnel, Commandants USMC and USCG, to SecNav, 20 November 1942; Directors of WR of NR and of WR of CGR to Chief of Naval Personnel and Commandant of CG, 30 November 1942; report of meeting of Jacobs and representatives of USCG and USMC, 12 November 1942, all in folder 28, box 4, ser. 1, ACNP(W), OA, NHC.

48. Mary V. Stremlow, *Free a Marine to Fight: Women Marines in World War II* (Washington, D.C.: Marine Corps Historical Center, 1994), 25; Mary V. Stremlow, "Marine Corps Women's Reserve: Free a Man to Fight," in Holm, *In Defense of a Nation*, 77–95. For other detailed accounts, see Peter A. Soderbergh, *Women Marines: The World War II Era* (Westport: Praeger, 1992); Ruth C. Streeter and Katherine A. Towle, *History of the Marine Corps Women's Reserve: A Critical Analysis of Its Development and Operation, 1943–1945* (Washington, D.C.: 1945); and Pat Meid, *Marine Corps Women's Reserve in World War II* (Washington, D.C.: USMC, 1968).

49. Mary C. Lyne and Kay Arthur, *Three Years Behind the Mast: The Story of the United States Coast Guard, SPARs* (Washington, D.C.: 1946), is the standard work. For general accounts of the Coast Guard, see Malcolm F. Willoughby, *The U.S. Coast Guard in World War II* (Annapolis, Md.: USNI, 1957); and U.S. Coast Guard, *The Coast Guard at War, Dec. 7, 1941–Apr. 12, 1944* (Washington, D.C.: U.S. Coast Guard, 1944–1954), 30 vols.

50. Treadwell, *Women's Army Corps*, 281; Holm, *Women in the Military*, 98. For an overview in one state, see Marie B. Alsmeyer, "Those Unseen, Unheard Arkansas Women: WACs, WAVES, and Women Marines of World War II," *Minerva: Quarterly Report on Women and the Military* 12 (summer 1994): 15–33.

51. Treadwell, *Women's Army Corps*, 193; Holm, *Women in the Military*, 51–53; Melissa S. Herbert, "Amazons or Butterflies: The Recruitment of Women into the Military during World War II," *Minerva: Quarterly Report on Women and the Military* 9 (summer 1991): 56–57; Cecilia Hock, "Creation of the WAC Image and Perception of Army Women: 1942–44," *Minerva: Quarterly Report on Women and the Military* 13 (spring 1995): 49–53; Campbell, *Women at War*, 37, 57, 223; D'Ann Campbell, "Women in Combat: The World War II Experience in the United States, Great Britain, Germany, and the Soviet Union," *JMH* 57 (April 1993): 320–22. Typical of the scurrilous propaganda was a memo, Specifications of WAVES, 1 January 1943, in Vertical Files, Navy Dept. Library.

52. Naval Personnel . . . by State of Residence, folder 42 (8), box 35, NNC Records, OA, NHC.

53. BuPers, *Women's Reserve* 1:76–77; Basic Requirements for Classes V-10, V-9, W-V (S), n.d. [1944], folder 79 A, box 12, ser. 1, ACNP(W), OA, NHC.

54. Palmer to McAfee, 30 June 1943, folder 37, box 5, ser. 1, ACNP(W), OA, NHC. The average age was twenty-one. "Happy 30th Anniversary," *All Hands*, July 1972, 13.

55. BuPers, *Women's Reserve* 1:76–77; Ebbert and Hall, *Crossed Currents*, 58.

56. Specialist (T) Doris Locke Grady, interview with author, 8 July 1995.

57. Jacobs to Victoria McCall, 27 October 1942, folder 28, box 4, ser. 1, ACNP(W), OA, NHC; McAfee to Jacobs, 3 April and 23 April 1943, folder QR-8, RG 24, NARA. QR-8 folders in boxes 2329, 2330, and 2331 are full of letters and petitions from blacks wanting to join the WAVES or protesting the segregation policy. Other letters, for example, Thomasina W. Johnson to members of Alpha Kappa Alpha Sorority, July 1943, are in the NAACP Papers, LC. This letter was quoted in Judy B. Litoff and David C. Smith,

*We're in This War, Too: World War II Letters from American Women in Uniform* (New York: Oxford University Press, 1994), 78–79.

58. Dennis D. Nelson, *The Integration of the Negro into the U.S. Navy* (New York: Farrar, Straus, and Young, 1951), 12, 134–37. For a good account of blacks in the WAVES, see Akers, "Integration of Afro-Americans." One black WAVE wrote of the smoothness of integration in boot training at Hunter. In Clemintine B. Forsyth to Walter White, n.d. [1945], quotation in Litoff and Smith, *We're in This War, Too*, 79.

59. Mary E. Heckathorn, "The Navy WAVES the Rules," *USNIP* 69 (August 1943): 1082. Another contemporary, Nancy Ross Wilson, *The WAVES: The Story of the Girls in Blue* (New York: Henry Holt, 1943), 2, echoed this evaluation.

60. "Uncle Sam Needed Me!" in *Old WAVES Tales: Navy Women: Memories of World War II*, comp. Marie B. Alsmeyer (Conway, Ark.: Hamba Books, 1982), 33.

61. Eunice to Mom and Dad, 20 June and 4 August 1943, in Litoff and Smith, *We're in This War, Too*, 96–97.

62. Jacqueline Van Voris, "Quiet Victory: The WAVES in World War II" (unpublished MS, n.d., OA, NHC), 120, 124.

63. Mary Jo Shelley, *Navy Service: A Short History of the United States Naval Training School (WR), Bronx, New York* ([New York]: Public Relations Office, USNTS [WR], n.d.), 23; Ebbert and Hall, *Crossed Currents*, 58; Butler, *Navy WAVES*, 10; Louanne Johnson, *Making WAVES: A Woman in This Man's Navy* (New York: St. Martin's Press, 1986), 16.

64. Based on composite of author interviews with WW II WAVES Jean Klinefelter Nakhnikian, 22 July 1995; Margaret Lucas Montgomery, 22 July 1995; Doris Locke Grady; and Dorothy Ditter Beers, 11 September 1995.

65. Louise T. Stockly, "History of the Naval Reserve Midshipman's School (WR), Northampton, Mass.," in BuPers, *Women's Reserve* 1:231, appendix B; BuPers, *Women's Reserve* 1:85–86.

66. More records of the Smith operation are in the War Service Collection, Smith College Archives, Northampton, Mass.

67. Herbert W. Underwood, official bio, OA, NHC; Hancock, *Lady in the Navy*, 77.

68. "Naval Training of Women," [summary-type paper, 1947], folder 102, box 16, ser. 1, ACNP(W), OA, NHC; J. L. Woodruff, "Wave Training," *USNIP* 71 (February 1945): 151; Ebbert and Hall, *Crossed Currents*, 48–49.

69. Stockly, "Midshipman's School," 242–43.

70. Author interview with Capt. Winifred Quick Collins, 15 July 1996.

71. Stockly, "Midshipman's School," 247–48; Regulations of the Naval Reserve Midshipmen's School (WR), Northampton, Mass., 10 April 1943; Naval Reserve Midshipmen's School (WR), report for December 1944—final report, both in folder 58, box 8, ser. 1, ACNP(W), OA, NHC. A contemporary popular account of life at Smith was Helen H. Jacobs, *By Your Leave, Sir* (New York: Dodd, Mead, 1943).

72. BuPers, *Women's Reserve* 1:247–49; Hancock, *Lady in the Navy*, 79.

73. Hancock, *Lady in the Navy*, 80–81; Woodruff, "WAVE Training," 152.

74. Ebbert and Hall, *Crossed Currents,* 52–54; Hancock, *Lady in the Navy,* 88.

75. Hancock, *Lady in the Navy,* 82, 90.

76. Capt. Joy Bright Hancock, interview with author, 8 January 1982. Hancock voiced these same sentiments in *Lady in the Navy,* 187.

77. Quotation in Litoff and Smith, "Wartime History," 50.

78. Claire E. Brou, "WAVES: Twenty-Five Years in Retrospect" (Naval Historical Foundation [1967]), 14, in folder 16, ser. 4, ACNP(W), OA, NHC; "Naval Training of Women."

79. Shelley, *Navy Service,* 5–6; Jacobs to SecNav, 30 December 1942, folder 28, box 4, ser. 1, ACNP(W), OA, NHC; BuPers, "U.S. Naval Training School (WR): The Bronx, New York," in *U.S. Naval Administration in World War II: Women's Reserve* 2:1–4, 7.

80. William F. Amsden, official bio, OA, NHC; Shelley, *Navy Service,* 6–7.

81. H. G. Hopwood to Jacobs, 25 May 1943, folder 28, ser. 1, ACNP(W), OA, NHC; Hancock, *Lady in the Navy,* 104–5; Heckathorne, "Navy WAVES," 1083–84; BuPers, *Women's Reserve* 2:64–65. For an overview, see E. Louise Stewart, "Women in Uniform," *Sea Power* 3 (November 1943): 45, 61–63. A useful contemporary book on etiquette and customs is Mary V. Harris, *Guide Right: A Handbook for WAVES and SPARs* (New York: Macmillan, 1944).

82. Figure is for September 1943, in History of the Field Administration Division—Women's Reserve [a critical evaluation], n.d., folder 102, box 16, ser. 1, ACNP(W), OA, NHC. This percentage dropped to between 45 and 50, in Shelley, *Navy Service,* 140.

83. "Naval Training of Women"; BuPers, *Women's Reserve* 1:82.

84. BuPers, *Women's Reserve* 1:84; J. M. Lewis, "WAVES Forecasters in World War II," *Bulletin of the American Meteorological Society* 76 (November 1995): 2187; Hancock, *Lady in the Navy,* 127–43. Hancock gives a thorough description of the training for these ratings.

85. Ebbert and Hall, *Crossed Currents,* 68–69; Hancock, *Lady in the Navy,* 145–46.

86. Van Voris, "Quiet Victory," 127; "Equal Pay," in Alsmeyer, *Old WAVES Tales,* 45; Pay of Officers and Warrant Officers, 15 July 1942, folder 71, ser. 1, ACNP(W), OA, NHC. Pay tables in *Navy Register: 1945,* 587, 589.

87. R. H. Hillenkoetter (Director of Planning and Control) to Jacobs, 6 September 1944; WR Circular Letter no. 4-44, 16 September 1944, both in folder 30, box 4, ser. 1, ACNP(W), OA, NHC.

88. Knox to ALSTACON, 12 November 1943; Memo re: Quarters Allowances for Officers in the WR, n.d., both in folder 71, box 10, ser. 1, ACNP(W), OA, NHC; BuPers, *Women's Reserve* 1:27–28; *United States Statutes at Large* 57 (1943): 586–87.

89. Jacobs to Rear Adm. Ben Moreell, 15 January 1943, folder 28, box 4, ser. 1, ACNP(W), OA, NHC; Marie B. Alsmeyer, "Those Navy WAVES," *All Hands,* July 1983, 3; BuPers, *Women's Reserve* 1:111–12; Hancock, *Lady in the Navy,* 173–76. Specialist (S) was the rating for personnel supervisor—barracks administration.

90. Jean T. Palmer to Jacobs, 6 October 1942, folder 28, box 4, ser. 1; Jacobs, Procurement Directive, 28 October 1942; Jacobs to McAfee, 21 November 1942; Jacobs

to Directors of Naval Officer Procurement, 8 December 1942; McAfee to Jacobs, 19 February 1943; Jacobs to SecNav, 6 March 1943; L. E. Denfeld to WR Representatives, 8 March 1943; Jacobs to COs, USNR Training Schools, 26 August 1943, all in folder 37, box 5, ser. 1, all in ACNP(W), OA, NHC; "Automatic Discharge," in Alsmeyer, *Old WAVES Tales*, 28.

91. McAfee memos, 16 November and 18 November 1942, folder 13 (Discipline), box 2, ser. 1, ACNP(W), OA, NHC.

92. Chief of Naval Personnel, "Principles of Discipline for Women's Reserve," 14 December 1942, cited in Hancock to Capt. Mewhinney, 7 September 1948; Tova F. Wiley to CO, Naval Barracks, Washington, 16 July 1945, both in folder 13, box 2, ser. 1, ACNP(W), OA, NHC.

93. Miriam A. Shelden to Director, WR, statement on discipline, 19 May 1947; Memo—Discipline of WAVE Officers, 4 June 1947, both in folder 13, box 2, ser. 1, ACNP(W), OA, NHC.

94. Note re termination of service, n.d., folder 12, box 2, ser. 1, ACNP(W), OA, NHC; McAfee to Thomas H. Binford, 10 March 1943, folder QR-8, box 2335, RG 24, NARA; BuPers, *Women's Reserve* 1:117.

95. WR Circular Letters no. 3-44, 11 May 1944; no. 1-45, 5 March 1945; and no. 8-45, 5 September 1945, all in folder 30, box 4, ser. 1, ACNP(W), OA, NHC; BuMed and BuPers, Joint Letter, to all Ships and Stations, 28 August 1945, folder 34, box 13, ser. 3, NNC Records, OA, NHC; BuPers, *Women's Reserve* 1:155–56.

96. Ebbert and Hall, *Crossed Currents*, 189; Mary Liskow to "Dear Folks," 3 January 1944, in Litoff and Smith, *We're in This War, Too*, 63.

97. Allan Berube, *Coming Out Under Fire: The History of Gay Men and Women in World War II* (New York: Free Press, 1990), 33. Berube gave no figures on the number of lesbians in any of the women's services.

98. Grady interview; Nakhnikian interview; Montgomery interview; Beers interview.

99. Johnson, *Making WAVES*, 28–29, 82–83.

100. *United States Statutes at Large* 56 (1942): 730–31; *United States Statutes at Large* 57 (1943): 586–87; Hearings before the Committee on Naval Affairs, U.S. Senate, 29 September 1943; and before House Committee, 4 June 1943; Senate report 426, 1 October 1943.

101. McAfee to Jacobs, 20 April 1943; BuPers memo, 5 May 1943, both in folder 39, box 5, ser. 1, ACNP(W), OA, NHC.

102. McAfee to Jacobs, 21 August 1943; A. M. Bledsoe to Jacobs, 6 September 1943. H. G. Hopwood to Jacobs, n.d., echoed the sentiment. All in folder 30, box 4, ser. 1, ACNP(W), OA, NHC.

103. Lt. Elsa Scharles Diduk, interview with author, 8 March 1996.

104. Hancock Recollections, 88; Palmer Recollections, 15, 35.

105. McAfee speech, 27 October 1944, folder 101, box 16, ser. 1, ACNP(W), OA, NHC. McAfee was citing Psalm 88, 7th verse.

106. "Here to Stay?" *Our Navy* (1 September 1943): 1.

107. Montgomery, Grady, and Nakhnikian interviews.

108. McAfee Recollections, 52. McAfee was still telling this story thirty years later, in "Goblets," in Alsmeyer, *Old WAVES Tales*, 4.

109. Van Voris, "Quiet Victory," 36–39; Ross, *WAVES*, 130–35; Fischer, *Navy Women*, 33.

110. Changes in uniform regulations, in folder 27, box 4, ser. 1, ACNP(W), OA, NHC.

111. Rates and Ratings . . . WW II, in BuPers Utilization report, March 1954, folder 107, box 17, ser. 1, ACNP(W), OA, NHC; Hancock, *Lady in the Navy*, appendixes, 271–80; BuPers, *Women's Reserve* 1:93–97.

112. Forrestal message, WAVES News Letter, August 1945, in folder 110, box 17, ser. 1, ACNP(W), OA, NHC.

113. Author interview with Lt. Dorothy Brown Hurt, 30 July 1996; William O. Foss, "How WAVES Succeeded in a Man's Navy," *Our Navy* (July 1962): 5; Hancock, *Lady in the Navy*, 210; "Navy Women," *All Hands*, August 1975, 72. Author interview with Margaret Lucas Montgomery, who described the monotony of communications work in Norfolk.

114. Lt. Susan Davis Roy, interview with author, 10 July 1996.

115. McAfee to William J. C. Agnew, 24 October 1942; Ross T. McIntire to McAfee, 28 October 1942, both in folder 28, box 4, ser. 1, ACNP(W), OA, NHC; Mary T. Sarnecky, "Women, Medicine, and War," in Poulos, *Woman's War Too*, 73–74; *SecNav Report*, 1945, A-90; BuPers, *Women's Reserve* 1:17; *United States Statutes at Large* 57 (1943): 65. The American Medical Women's Association had campaigned vigorously for this legislation. Campbell, *Women at War*, 55.

116. Ebbert and Hall, *Crossed Currents*, 68–69. Marie B. Alsmeyer, *The Way of the WAVES: Women in the Navy* (Conway, Ark.: Hamba Books, 1981), describes her experiences as a member of the Hospital Corps. Especially useful were her duties as an occupational therapist, 114–26.

117. Kathleen B. Williams, "Women Ashore: The Contribution of WAVES to US Naval Science and Technology in World War II," *Northern Mariner* 8 (April 1998): 7; Lewis, "Forecasters," 2187.

118. WAVES News Letters, April 1943, December 1943; Hancock, *Lady in the Navy*, 185–94, 210, 271, 275–76; Deborah G. Douglas, *United States Women in Aviation: 1940–1986* (Washington, D.C.: Smithsonian Institution Press, 1991), 17, 38. A firsthand account by a WAVES who was an antiaircraft gunnery instructor is in Josette D. Wingo, *Mother Was a Gunner's Mate: World War II in the WAVES* (Annapolis, Md.: Naval Institute Press, 1994).

119. Letters cited in Litoff and Smith, "Wartime History," 53.

120. Beers interview; WAVES News Letters, April 1943, August 1943, November 1943, December 1943, January 1944; Hancock, *Lady in the Navy*, 80–84, 272, 275; Van Voris, "Quiet Victory," 99. More on WAVES work in the bureaus in Godson, "WAVES," 50–51. For an account by a Supply Corps officer, see Joan B. Crawford, "Making

WAVES," *Naval History* 2 (winter 1988): 25–29. Information on Hopper from Charlene W. Billings, *Grace Hopper: Navy Admiral and Computer Pioneer* (Hillside, N.J.: Enslow Publishers, 1989), 39, 48–49.

121. Hancock, *Lady in the Navy*, 51.

122. WAVES News Letters, April 1943, November 1943; Foss, "WAVES Succeeded," 6; *SecNav Report*, 1945, A-11. Women would not be eligible for the Chaplain's Corps as ministers until 1973, in Van Voris, "Quiet Victory," 114.

123. House Committee on Naval Affairs, *Hearings on H.R. 5067*, 21 and 22 June 1944, in folder 8, box 33, ser. 4; Memo for Chief BuPers, 22 August 1944, folder 30, box 4, ser. 1, both in ACNP(W), OA, NHC; McAfee Recollections, 99; *United States Statutes at Large* 58 (1944): 754; Margaret Chase Smith, *Declaration of Conscience* (New York: Doubleday, 1972), 85.

124. Notes on Meeting with Members of the WAC, 24 June 1944; CNO to Chief BuPers, 23 June 1944; Tova P. Wiley to McAfee, 19 September 1944; McAfee to Director, Planning and Control, 25 September 1944, all in folder 68, box 10, ser. 1, ACNP(W), OA, NHC.

125. Chief BuPers to All Naval Activities in Continental U.S., etc., 29 September 1944; L. E. Denfeld, Bureau Policy and Procedures series, no. 92, 24 October 1944, both in folder 68, box 10, ser. 1, ACNP(W), OA, NHC. Three Women's Reserve officers served on this board, along with two male members.

126. Collins interview; Hancock, *Lady in the Navy*, 199–206, has a graphic description. More in WAVES News Letters, December 1944, February 1945; BuPers, *Women's Reserve* 1:146–47. More instructions in McAfee to WR Officers . . . Hawaii, 2 January 1945; William M. Fechteler, Assistant Chief BuPers to All Naval Activities in Continental U.S., 27 April 1945, both in folder 68, box 10, ser. 1, ACNP(W), OA, NHC.

127. Hancock to Louise Wilde, 19 June 1945, folder 68, box 10, ser. 1; Calendar of WAVE History, folder 33, box 5, ser. 1; WAVES News Letters, January 1945, February 1945, all in ACNP(W), OA, NHC.

128. Chief of Information, SecNav's Office, to Assistant Secretary of Defense (Public Affairs), 13 March 1963, folder 33, box 5, ser. 1, ACNP(W), OA, NHC.

129. Ibid.; McAfee bio, OA, NHC.

130. Quoted in WAVES News Letters, August 1945 and September 1945. For a brief overview of WAVES' service, see Maria T. Armas, "Women at War," *Naval History* 8 (March/April 1994): 10–14.

131. The Navy Poll, *All Hands*, October 1946, 26, showed that 94 percent of enlisted surveyed thought that women had performed well. Only 6 percent believed that they did not help much.

132. Fantail Forum, *All Hands*, January 1946, 80.

133. Nakhnikian and Montgomery interviews; Helen C. Gunter, *Navy WAVE: Memories of World War II* (Ft. Bragg, Calif.: Cypress House Press, 1992), 134.

134. Lt. Cdr. Mary Josephine Shelly, USNR (Ret.), interview, USNI Oral History series, 1970, 64.

135. Dean F. Johnson, Carolyn M. Wells, and Robert Breckenridge, "Implications for

Aging: Service as a Female Naval Officer," *Minerva: Quarterly Report on Women and the Military* 7 (spring 1989): 15, 17–18, 27. The authors go on to suggest that naval experience prepares women for life enhancement, a broader outlook, and increased independence (33).

136. This debate continues; for example, historians such as Chafe, *American Woman,* 136, and *Paradox of Change,* 172, and June A. Willenz, *Women Veterans: America's Forgotten Heroines* (New York: Continuum, 1983), 29, see WWII service and work as a watershed for women. Others take the more negative view that the war was but an interruption in women's usual role; for example, Rothman, *Proper Place,* 224; Campbell, *Women at War,* 236; Hartmann, *Home Front,* 212; Anderson, *Wartime Women,* 178; Evans, *Born for Liberty,* 223.

## *Chapter 6. The Navy Nurse Corps in World War II*

1. Donahue, *Finest Art,* 371; Philip A. Kalisch and Beatrice J. Kalisch, *The Advance of American Nursing,* 3d ed. (Philadelphia: J. B. Lippincott, 1995), 324. (This edition will be used for the remainder of the manuscript.)

2. Bonnie Bullough, "The Lasting Impact of World War II on Nursing," in *Pages from Nursing History,* 128; Kalisch and Kalisch, *American Nursing,* 325–26; *United States Statutes at Large* 55 (1941): 466–97.

3. Beatrice J. Kalisch and Philip A. Kalisch, "The Cadet Nurse Corps in World War II," in *Pages from Nursing History,* 103–4; Smith, "Military Nursing," 32; Donahue, *Finest Art,* 413; Elizabeth A. Shields, ed., *Highlights on the History of the Army Nurse Corps* (Washington, D.C.: U.S. Army Center of Military History, 1981), 23–24. Although the Cadet Nurse Corps did not finish training many nurses in time for wartime service, federal aid to nursing education had begun, and with it federal requirements that upgraded nursing schools.

4. Figures for 1940 from *Statistical Abstract* (1947), 138; for 1945, from Department of Health, Education, and Welfare, *Biennial Survey of Education in the United States: 1944–46* (Washington, D.C.: GPO, 1950), 1:3, 6.

5. The ANA supported the draft but only as a first step to selective service for all women. In editorial, *AJN* 45 (January 1945): 85–86; "ANA Testimony on Proposed Draft Legislation," *AJN* 45 (March 1945): 1–3. Campbell, *Women at War,* 54; Kalisch and Kalisch, *American Nursing,* 344–47; Shields, ed., *Army Nurse Corps,* 25. BuMed had begun joint planning with the Army for common physical and professional qualifications and induction stations, if the bill passed. Louis H. Roddis to Surgeon General, 9 March 1945, folder 44, box 14, ser. 3, NNC Records, OA, NHC.

6. Donahue, *Finest Art,* 415–16; Gabriel and Metz, *Military Medicine* 2:254; Kalisch and Kalisch, *American Nursing,* 331–33, 336–37.

7. Department of the Navy, *The History of the Medical Department of the United States Navy, 1945–1955* (Washington, D.C.: GPO, 1958), 29.

8. *SecNav Report,* 1945, A-85.

9. *SecNav Report,* 1942, 25; Herman, *Hilltop,* 81–82.

10. *SecNav Report,* 1945, A-86, A-87, A-90; Census—Nurse Corps, folder 42, box 34, ser. 6, NNC Records, OA, NHC.

11. *SecNav Report,* 1944, 35; Department of the Navy, *The History of the Medical Department of the United States Navy in World War II,* 3 vols. (Washington, D.C.: GPO, 1953), 1:37.

12. In addition to five nurses, the Harvard Field Hospital Unit's housemother, Mrs. Ruth Breckinridge, also died. For a detailed account of this episode, see Susan H. Godson, "Red Cross Nurses: German U-Boat Victims," *Retired Officer* 38 (June 1982): 24–26. Other material in Fragmentary Personal Documents Files: Marion Blissett Stafford material and manuscript, OA, NHC. More information from Red Cross: Hospitals, Service in Military, Red Cross Library, Washington, D.C. The story is also told in Walter Karig et al., *Battle Report: The Atlantic War* (New York: Rinehart, 1946), 2:52–54.

13. Mary Ellen Condon-Rall, "The U.S. Army Medical Department and the Attack on Pearl Harbor," *JMH* 53 (January 1989): 67. For an overview, see Mary T. Sarnecky, "Army Nurse Corps," in Holm, *In Defense of a Nation,* 9–28.

14. Barbara B. Tomblin, "Beyond Paradise: The U.S. Navy Nurse Corps in the Pacific in World War II," pt. 1, *Minerva: Quarterly Report on Women and the Military* 11 (spring 1993): 33–34; "*Solace,*" in *DANFS* 6:544. Brief sketches of Navy nurses under fire in the Pacific in folder 4, box 25, ser. 6, NNC Records, OA, NHC.

15. Miller, *U.S. Navy,* 300; Gordon W. Prange, *At Dawn We Slept: The Untold Story of Pearl Harbor* (New York: McGraw-Hill, 1981), 539. Prange, 517–40, gives a vivid account of the carnage at Pearl Harbor.

16. Tomblin, "Beyond Paradise," pt. 1, 36–38.

17. Capt. Ruth Erickson, interview with author, 11 December 1995; Prange, *At Dawn We Slept,* 567; Sterner, *Harm's Way,* 108. More of Erickson's comments in Jan K. Herman, *Battle Station Sick Bay: Navy Medicine In World War II* (Annapolis, Md.: Naval Institute Press, 1997), 25–27.

18. Condon-Rall, "Attack on Pearl," 77.

19. USS *Solace,* Action Report, no ser., 12 December 1941, OA, NHC; Tomblin, "Beyond Paradise," pt. 1, 34–36; Herman, *Battle Station Sick Bay,* 27–28; Grace B. Lally, "On Being a Chief Nurse," *R.N.* (September 1943): 22. An account of Lally's wartime career is in Jessie F. Evans, "Lt. Lally, Chief of Nurses at Bethesda, Saw Much Action," folder 1 (1), box 20, ser. 4, NNC Records, OA, NHC.

20. Leona Jackson, "I Was on Guam," *AJN* 42 (December 1942): 96; Mary E. V. Frank, "Army and Navy Nurses Held as Prisoners of War during World War II," *Minerva: Quarterly Report on Women and the Military* 6 (summer 1988): 83.

21. Jackson, "I Was on Guam," and "Woman Prisoner of Japan" [memoir-type accounts], folder 1 (6), box 21, ser. 4, NNC Records, OA, NHC; Sterner, *Harm's Way,* 130–31. The other three imprisoned NNC nurses were Doris M. Yetter, Virginia J. Fogarty, and Lorraine Christiansen. From *Nurse Corps Chronology,* 23.

22. Tomblin, "Beyond Paradise," pt. 1, 39–40; Frank, "Prisoners of War," 83. Another brief account is "Experience in Guam," folder 1 (2), box 20, ser. 4, NNC Records, OA, NHC.

23. Mary Ellen Condon-Rall, "U.S. Army Medical Preparations and the Outbreak of War: The Philippines, 1941–6 May 1942," *JMH* 56 (January 1992): 40–43; Tomblin, *G.I. Nightingales*, 20–21.

24. Michele Manning, "Angels of Mercy and Life amid Scenes of Conflict and Death: The Combat Experience and Imprisonment of American Military Nurses in the Philippines, 1941–1945," student paper, Marine Corps Command and Staff College, Quantico, 1985, 11.

25. Condon-Rall, "Philippines," 43–44; Philip A. Kalisch and Beatrice J. Kalisch, "Nurses Under Fire: The World War II Experience of Nurses on Bataan and Corregidor," in *Pages from Nursing History*, 105.

26. Manning, "Angels of Mercy," 12; Frank, "Prisoners of War," 83; Kalisch and Kalisch, "Bataan and Corregidor," 106. Dorothy Still shared her memories in Herman, *Battle Station Sick Bay*, 53–55.

27. Kalisch and Kalisch, "Bataan and Corregidor," 108; Manning, "Angels of Mercy," 22–23; "Reminiscences of a Nurse POW," *U.S. Navy Medicine* 83 (May–June 1992): 37. For a civilian description, see Emily Van Sickel, *The Iron Gates of Santo Tomas: The Firsthand Account of an American Couple Interned by the Japanese in Manila, 1942–45* (Chicago: Academy Chicago Publishers, 1992).

28. J.M.G., "Nurses Stood By to the End," *Trained Nurse and Hospital Review* (March 1945): 182–83; "Nurse POW," 38–39; Manning, "Angels of Mercy," 48–56, 59; Frank, "Prisoners of War," 84. There are fifteen folders on these prisoners of war in boxes 6 and 7, entry 48D, RG 52, NARA. One nurse POW has written of her experiences: Dorothy Still Danner, *What a Way to Spend a War: Navy Nurse POWs in the Philippines* (Annapolis, Md.: Naval Institute Press, 1995).

29. Kalisch and Kalisch, "Bataan and Corregidor," 123; "Nurse POW," 39–40; Tomblin, "Beyond Paradise," pt. 1, 39. The nurses who had started at the Cañacao Naval Hospital and survived Japanese prison camps were Chief Nurse Laura M. Cobb and Nurses Mary Chapman, Bertha R. Evans, Helen C. Gorzelanski, Mary R. Harrington, Margaret A. Nash, Goldia O'Haver, Eldene E. Paige, Susie Pitcher, Dorothy Still, and C. Edwina Todd. Listed in *Nurse Corps Chronology*, 23.

30. Condon-Rall, "Philippines," 46; Kalisch and Kalisch, "Bataan and Corregidor," 108–9, 111, 113. More on Bernatitus's experiences in Herman, *Battle Station Sick Bay*, 55–60.

31. Condon-Rall, "Philippines," 54–55; Kalisch and Kalisch, "Bataan and Corregidor," 115–18.

32. Kalisch and Kalisch, "Bataan and Corregidor," 119–20; *Nurse Corps Chronology*, 23; Frank, "Prisoners of War," 86; Kalisch and Scobey, "Helplessness Suspended," 17–18; Shields, ed., *Army Nurse Corps*, 21. In an address, 25 November 1942, Ann Bernatitus

told the poignant story of valiant fighting men and medical personnel—all desperately short of ammunition and supplies—in the last days of Bataan and Corregidor. Address in folder 1 (3), box 20, ser. 4, NNC Records, OA, NHC.

33. *SecNav Report,* 1942, 56.

34. Dauser, interview with Jean DeWitt, n.d. [1943], Biography: Sue S. Dauser folder, box 1, entry 48D, RG 52, NARA. For an overview of the NNC in WW II, see Susan H. Godson, "Navy Nurse Corps," in Holm, *In Defense of a Nation,* 27–35.

35. Page Cooper, *Navy Nurse* (New York: Whittlesey House, 1946), 40, 121.

36. Papers prepared by Mary G. Lynch, 1–5, folder 1 (5), box 21, ser. 4, NNC Records, OA, NHC; *AJN* 43 (March 1943): 220. Lynch was secretary to the superintendent.

37. American Red Cross . . . new procedure, 24 January 1944, folder 55 (1), box 15; National Nursing Council for War Service, Army and Navy Needs, 1 March 1945, folder 37, box 13, both in ser. 3, NNC Records, OA, NHC.

38. Digest of Information on Nurse Procurement, folder 55 (6), box 16, ser. 3, NNC Records, OA, NHC; correspondence between the commission and Dauser and McIntire in War Manpower Commission folder, box 7, entry 48D, RG 52, NARA.

39. Sue S. Dauser to Edith N. Lindquist, 7 December 1944, folder 37, box 13, ser. 3, NNC Records, OA, NHC. More on mobilization in Personnel Policies—Mobilization—WW II folder, box 6, entry 48D, RG 52, NARA.

40. Surgeon General, USN, to Nursing Council for War Service of Metropolitan Philadelphia, 29 November 1944, folder 37, box 13, ser. 3; BuPers, Procurement Directive 4-45, 24 January 1945; and Procurement and Assignment Service, War Manpower Commission, to State Chairmen for Nurses, 1 February 1945, both in folder 55 (2), box 15, ser. 3; Digest of Information, all in NNC Records, OA, NHC. Naval support for the draft was lukewarm and only because the Army needed more nurses. Statement of Rear Adm. W. J. C. Agnew, Acting Chief of BuMed, 7 February 1945, folder 42 (8), box 35, ser. 6, NNC Records, OA, NHC.

41. Problems [Procurement], folder 55 (6), box 16, ser. 3; E. L. Ballard, "Navy Nurse Outlines Role in Officer Procurement," *Service Woman,* 27 August 1943, in folder 1 (1), box 20, ser. 4; BuMed Memo [re procurement], 19 April 1948, folder 55 (1), box 15, ser. 3, all in NNC Records, OA, NHC.

42. Survey of Cadet Nurses, 31 July 1945; WW II Statistics: Navy Nurse Corps; Assignment Dates for ONOP Applicants, all in folder 55 (6), box 16, ser. 3, NNC Records, OA, NHC.

43. Dauser to Capt. McMillan, 9 October 1945; McIntire to Thomas Parran, 21 November 1945, both in Education—Cadet Nurses folder; more correspondence in Cadet Nurse Corps, 1944–48 folder, all in box 3, entry 48D, RG 52, NARA.

44. BuMed, Memo, 19 April 1948, folder 55 (1), box 15, ser. 3, NNC Records, OA, NHC; Digest of Information.

45. BuPers, "Personnel Statistics"; Nurse Corps Monthly Census, folder 42 (6), box

35, ser. 6, NNC Records, OA, NHC; Shields, ed., *Army Nurse Corps*, 25. Tomblin, *G.I. Nightingales*, 186, puts the figure at 52,000.

46. "Nurse Total Tops War's Volunteers," *New York Times*, 17 September 1945, p. 16.

47. Department of the Navy, *Manual for the Medical Department of the United States Navy*, 1939 (Washington, D.C.: GPO, 1939), 28–29; Department of the Navy, *Manual for the Medical Department of the United States Navy, 1945* (Washington, D.C.: GPO, 1945), 76–77; Qualifications for Appointment, enclosure 5, BuPers, Procurement Directive 4-45, folder 55 (2), box 15, ser. 3, NNC Records, OA, NHC.

48. Personnel . . . by State of Residence, folder 42 (8), box 35, ser. 6, NNC Records, OA, NHC.

49. ONOP Applicants, folder 55 (6), box 16, ser. 3, NNC Records, OA, NHC; "Nurse Corps Personnel," *Statistics of Navy Medicine* 2 (May 1946): 5.

50. Dauser and McIntire denied any policy of discrimination, saying that each application was considered on its merits. Dauser personally answered all letters from black nurses. All in Negro Nurses folder, box 6, entry 48D, RG 52, NARA. Litoff and Smith, *We're in This War, Too*, 65–66; Shields, ed., *Army Nurse Corps*, 22; "Negro Nurses Ban by Services Cited," *New York Times*, 14 January 1945, p. 26; Joyce Ann Elmore, "Black Nurses: Their Service and Their Struggle," in *Pages from Nursing History*, 32; Mary E. Carnegie, *The Path We Tread: Blacks in Nursing, 1854–1984* (Philadelphia: J. B. Lippincott, 1986), 177.

51. In April 1945, Phyllis M. Daley and Ivy B. Montgomery entered the NNC; in June, Helen F. Turner and Edith M. Devoe. Negro Nurses in Navy, folder 42 (8), box 35, ser. 6, NNC Records, OA, NHC. "Enters Navy Nurse Corps," *Dallas Express*, 26 May 1945, n.p., listed a fifth nurse, Eula L. Stimley, as a corps member. NNC Nursing Information, 15 June 1945, folder 68 (1), box 19, ser. 3, NNC Records, OA, NHC, counts five black nurses.

52. L. Sheldon Jr. to Julia C. Stimson, 17 April 1944; Dauser to W. S. Douglass, 20 May 1944, both in folder 33 (3), box 13; ANA, Registered Men Nurses, folder 44, box 14, all in ser. 3, NNC Records, OA, NHC; Lawrence W. Martin, "Men Nurses Are Available for Military Nursing," *Trained Nurse and Hospital Review* (May 1944): 357; "Men Nurses and the Armed Forces," *AJN* 43 (December 1943): 1069.

53. Reba K. W. Hartley, "A Nurse Looks at the Navy," *AJN* 45 (April 1945): 294.

54. Lally, "Chief Nurse," 23.

55. Krapp interview and Bristol interview; Lindner interview.

56. Catherine K. Williams to Dauser, 2 December 1944, folder 37, box 13, ser. 3, NNC Records, OA, NHC.

57. Rear Adm. Alene Duerk, interview with author, 11 October 1996.

58. W. E. Eaton to All Navy Nurses, U.S. Naval Hospital, Great Lakes, 5 August 1942; Indoctrination of Navy Nurses, 24 March 1943, both in folder 29 (1), box 11, ser. 3, NNC Records, OA, NHC.

59. *Nurse Corps Chronology*, 26; information from folder 29 (1), box 11, ser. 3, NNC Records, OA, NHC; "Indoctrination Course," *AJN* 43 (December 1943): 1144.

60. *Navy Nurses Guide*, n.d., copy in folder 29 (2), box 11, ser. 3, NNC Records, OA, NHC.

61. Hartley, "A Nurse Looks at the Navy," 294.

62. Superintendent's Annual Reports: 1941–43, folder 35 (1), box 32, ser. 6, NNC Records, OA, NHC. The superintendent's reports for the war years are very sketchy and contain only the barest recital of numbers. The reports for 1944 and 1945 are not there.

63. Leora B. Stroup, "Aero-Medical Nursing and Therapeutics," *AJN* 44 (June 1944): 575–77; Shields, ed., *Army Nurse Corps*, 22; *SecNav Report*, 1945, A-85; Kalisch and Kalisch, *American Nursing*, 331–33.

64. Procurement (Regular Navy) paper, n.d., folder 27 (1), box 31, ser. 6; BuMed to Detail Officer, BuMed, 21 November 1944, box 10, ser. 3, both in NNC Records, OA, NHC; "Navy Nurses Fly," *Professional Nursing* (January 1945): 3; Emily G. Purvis, "Nursing Care in Air Ambulances," *AJN* 47 (March 1947): 158; draft in folder 19 (3a), box 10, ser. 3, NNC Records, OA, NHC.

65. Dauser memo, 27 November 1944, folder 19 (3a); roster of WW II Flight Nurses, folder 19 (2); Training Syllabus, n.d., folder 19 (3a), all in box 10, ser. 3, NNC Records, OA, NHC.

66. Mary Ellen O'Connor to Dauser, 29 December 1944, 25 January, 20 March, 6 April 1945; Dauser to O'Connor, 9 January, 11 April 1945, all in folder 19 (1), box 10, ser. 3, NNC Records, OA, NHC.

67. Annual Pay and Allowances of Female Nurses, USN and USNR, *Navy Register: 1945*, 590; Department of the Navy, *Manual for the Medical Department of the United States Navy*, 1939, 35–36.

68. Department of the Navy, *Manual for the Medical Department of the United States Navy*, 1939, 32–33, 40–42.

69. *United States Statutes at Large* 57 (1943): 80–81.

70. Department of the Navy, *Manual for the Medical Department of the United States Navy*, 1939, 28; McIntire to SecNav, 9 January 1945; SecNav to ALNAV, 19 January 1945; W. J. C. Agnew to SecNav, 15 February 1945, all in folder 34, box 13, ser. 3, NNC Records, OA, NHC.

71. McIntire to SecNav, 23 August 1945; W. M. Fechteler to SecNav, 10 September 1945, and approved 17 September 1945; Dauser, draft of ALNAV, released 11 October 1945, all in folder 34, box 13, ser. 3, NNC Records, OA, NHC; Dauser to McIntire, 12 October 1945, Personnel Policies—Marriage folder, box 5, entry 48D, RG 52, NARA.

72. W. M. Fechteler to All Activities in Continental U.S., 11 May 1944; W.J.C. Agnew to All Ships and Stations, 23 January 1945; BuMed and BuPers, Joint Letter, 28 August 1945, all in folder 34, box 13, ser. 3, NNC Records, OA, NHC.

73. Quotation in *Army and Navy Journal*, 4 April 1942. Chief BuMed to SecNav, 8 February 1942, folder 58 (E), box 16, ser. 3, NNC Records, OA, NHC.

74. *United States Statutes at Large* 56 (1942): 1074; SecNav to ALNAV, n.d. [July 1942], folder 1 (2), box 20, ser. 4, NNC Records, OA, NHC; "Navy Nurses Have Relative Rank," *AJN* 42 (August 1942): 954.

75. *United States Statutes at Large* 56 (1942): 1072–74; SecNav to ALNAV, 12 January 1943, folder 58, box 16, ser. 3, NNC Records, OA, NHC. The Army Nurse Corps acquired similar rank increases—from colonel through second lieutenant—by this same act.

76. Dauser bio; *AJN* 43 (March 1943): 305; *Nurse Corps Chronology*, 25; "Four Stripes on Her Sleeve," *BNPIB* (February 1943): 31.

77. Dever and Dever, *Women and the Military*, 130.

78. *United States Statutes at Large* 58 (1944): 324–26; SecNav to ALNAV no. 65, 22 March 1944; Dauser memo, 27 March 1944; L. Sheldon Jr., Acting Chief BuMed to various hospitals, naval and Marine activities, 18 May 1944, all in folder 58 (E), box 16, ser. 3, NNC Records, OA, NHC. The Army gained similar privileges in June 1944.

79. Thelma F. Laird, "R.H.I.P. and the Navy Nurse," folder 1 (2), box 20, ser. 4, NNC Records, OA, NHC. (R.H.I.P. = Rank Has Its Privilege.)

80. *United States Statutes at Large* 59 (1945): 594–95; BuS&A to SecNav, n.d. [1946]; Proposed ALNAV, n.d., both in folder 50 (1), box 15, ser. 3, NNC Records, OA, NHC.

81. Laird, "R.H.I.P.," 2; Bullough, "Lasting Impact," 128; Sarah O'Toole, "They Pioneered on Tinian," *AJN* 45 (December 1945): 1015; Campbell, *Women at War*, 57.

82. Dauser, memo to surgeon general, 28 May 1945, folder 35 (4), box 33, ser. 6, NNC Records, OA, NHC.

83. Department of the Navy, *Uniform Regulations, United States Navy: 1941* (Washington, D.C.: GPO, 1941), 50–51; *AJN* 41 (April 1941): 440; Fischer, *Navy Women*, 11; Sterner, *Harm's Way*, 106.

84. *Nurse Corps Chronology*, 28, 31; Dauser memo, 27 March 1944, folder 58 (E), box 16, ser. 3, NNC Records, OA, NHC. More on uniforms in folder 72 (2), box 19, ser. 3, NNC Records, OA, NHC.

85. *Nurse Corps Chronology*, 35; *SecNav Report*, 1945, A-93.

86. Navy Nurses Assigned in Each State, May 1945, folder 42 (5), box 35, ser. 6; NNC, Nursing Information, 15 June 1945, folder 68 (1), box 19, ser. 3, both in NNC Records, OA, NHC.

87. Carolyn Valentine, "The Navy Faces Rehabilitation," *R.N.* (January 1945): 28–32, 80; Frances G. Gustafson, "Navy Nurse Physical Therapist," folder 46, box 14, ser. 3, NNC Records, OA, NHC.

88. Olive Boyer and Mary E. Felder, "The Navy Cares for Its Own," *Trained Nurse and Hospital Review* (February 1943): 97–99.

89. Ens. Ann Clendenin Paroubek, interview with author, 12 August 1996. Pedical skin grafts involved scraping skin from the arm, attaching it to the abdomen, and allowing it to grow and generate new skin to use for wounds.

90. Genevieve Albers, "Malaria," *Trained Nurse and Hospital Review* (February 1945): 110–12; "The Navy Nurse and Her Responsibilities in the Rehabilitation Program of Returning Naval War Veterans," folder 1 (3), box 20, ser. 4, NNC Records, OA, NHC.

91. *SecNav Report,* 1945, A-93.

92. BuPers, *Naval Administration: The United States Navy Medical Department at War, 1941–1945* 2:404–9; BuMed, *Medical Department . . . WW II,* 1:35.

93. Commandant, 12th Naval District and NOB, San Francisco to Chief BuMed, 13 January and 23 January 1942; Chief BuMed to Commandant, 17 January 1942, all in folder 19 (1), box 10, ser. 3, NNC Records, OA, NHC. The three nurses who volunteered were Josephine M. Constantino, Mildred K. Lindquist, and Pauline M. Metzger.

94. *SecNav Report,* 1945, A-85; "History of the Hospital Corps"; Dorothy M. Davis, "The Navy Nurse Teaches as She Serves," *Pacific Coast Journal of Nursing* 38 (September 1942): 544–45, and copy in folder 1 (1), box 20, ser. 4, NNC Records, OA, NHC; Cooper, *Navy Nurse,* 133.

95. Davis, "Navy Nurse Teaches," 545; *AJN* 41 (November 1941), and 42 (May 1942); *SecNav Report,* 1944, 35; Helen H. Johnson, "The Training of Operating Room Technicians by Navy Nurses in Australia," folder 67, box 18, ser. 3, NNC Records, OA, NHC.

96. Cooper, *Navy Nurse,* 137.

97. NNC, Nursing Information, 15 June 1945, folder 68 (1), box 19, ser. 3, NNC Records, OA, NHC; *Nurse Corps Chronology,* 35. For an overview, see Kathi Jackson, "50 Years Ago—World War II and the Navy Nurse," *U.S. Navy Medicine* 86 (July–August 1995): 18–22.

98. Nellie M. Quinn, "Navy Nurses in Alaska," folder 1 (1), box 20, ser. 4, NNC Records, OA, NHC; Coletta and Bauer, *United States Navy and Marine Corps Bases, Domestic,* 269–72.

99. Coletta and Bauer, *U.S. Bases, Domestic,* 3–6, 32–33, 188–89; Fitzgerald, "Navy Nurse Corps," 42. Lt. (jg) Judy N. Wilson was the first chief nurse at Attu; Lt. (jg) Mildred Terrell, the first at Adak. In *Nurse Corps Chronology,* 26. Jessie F. Evans, no title, folder 49, box 14, ser. 3, NNC Records, OA, NHC, wrote of the experiences of the first group of eleven nurses at Adak.

100. "The Task Force in White," *BNPIB* (March 1945): 24, and in folder 1 (3), box 20, ser. 4, NNC Records, OA, NHC.

101. *Nurse Corps Chronology,* 23–25, 27; BuMed, *Medical Department . . . WW II* 1:13, 22, 38.

102. *Nurse Corps Chronology,* 26–27; "Lt. Dymphna Van Gorp, (NC), USNR," folder 1 (3), box 20, ser. 4, NNC Records, OA, NHC. More information on the Brazilian training program in folder 19 (4), box 10, ser. 3, NNC Records, OA, NHC.

103. *Refuge,* in *DANFS* 6:60–61; Sterner, *Harm's Way,* 169.

104. BuMed, *Medical Department . . . WW II* 1:42; Fitzgerald, "Navy Nurse Corps," 52; Cooper, *Navy Nurse,* 129–32. For firsthand accounts, see Eleanor M. McDonnell,

"Nursing on Barbary Coast in 1944," folder 49; and Genevieve E. Repper, "Nursing in the E.T.O.," folder 48, both in box 14, ser. 3, NNC Records, OA, NHC.

105. BuMed, *Medical Department . . . WW II* 1:38; *SecNav Report*, 1945, A-93; *Nurse Corps Chronology*, 27; "The Task Force in White," 23; Cooper, *Navy Nurse*, 121–28.

106. Herman, *Battle Station Sick Bay*, 206–7.

107. BuMed, *Medical Department . . . WW II* 1:38. Nurse-anesthetist Mary V. Desmarais, "Navy Nursing on D-Day Plus 4," *AJN* 45 (January 1945): 12, described the round-the-clock activity in caring for the wounded.

108. *SecNav Report*, 1945, A-93; BuMed, *Medical Department . . . WW II* 1:22; Fitzgerald, "Navy Nurse Corps," 49.

109. Lindner interview; *SecNav Report*, 1941, 55–57; *SecNav Report*, 1942, 56; BuMed, *Medical Department . . . WW II* 1:21.

110. In an interview with the author, Anna Redding Krapp described her service in hospitals in the New Hebrides. Tomblin, "Beyond Paradise," pt. 1, 44–47; BuMed, *Medical Department . . . WW II* 1:22.

111. BuMed, *Medical Department . . . WW II* 1:30.

112. O'Toole, "Tinian," 1013–15. Draft in folder 49, box 14, ser. 3, NNC Records, OA, NHC.

113. Theresa V. Chapas, article with no title, folder 48, box 14, ser. 3, NNC Records, OA, NHC.

114. Martha E. Page, "With the Navy Nurses at a Base Hospital in the South Pacific," folder 49, box 14, ser. 3, NNC Records, OA, NHC.

115. Mary H. Staats, "Navy Nurses in the Solomons," folder 49, box 14, ser. 3, NNC Records, OA, NHC.

116. Alice A. Goudreau, "Nursing at an Advance Naval Base Hospital," *AJN* 45 (November 1945): 884–86; Olivine B. St. Peter, "In the Southwest Pacific: The Marianas," *AJN* 45 (December 1945): 1012–13.

117. Ruth B. Dunbar, "Return to the Philippines," *AJN* 45 (December 1945): 1015–18.

118. BuMed, *Medical Department . . . WW II* 1:1, 30. Lt. (jg) Georgia Reynolds described the actions aboard one such ship in a letter to the *AJN* 45 (March 1945): 234–35, and reprinted in Litoff and Smith, *We're in This War, Too*, 200.

119. *Solace*, in *DANFS* 6:544; Fitzgerald, "Navy Nurse Corps," 41.

120. *Relief*, in *DANFS* 6:68–69; Christine Curto, "Nurse Pioneers and the Hospital Ship *Relief*," *U.S. Navy Medicine* 83 (May–June 1992): 24–25; Barbara B. Tomblin, "Beyond Paradise: The U.S. Navy Nurse Corps in the Pacific in World War II," pt. 2, *Minerva: Quarterly Report on Women and the Military* 11 (fall/winter 1993): 38–42.

121. Quoted in Litoff and Smith, "Wartime History," 61.

122. BuMed, *Medical Department . . . WW II* 1:30; *Nurse Corps Chronology*, 34. One nurse described Christmas aboard *Refuge* in a letter in *AJN* 45 (December 1945): 1,063, and reprinted in Litoff and Smith, *We're in This War, Too*, 201. For more on nurses' experiences in hospital ships, see Herman, *Battle Station Sick Bay*, 170–75.

123. Duerk interview.

124. *SecNav Report*, 1944, 38.

125. Press release, USNAS, Olathe, KS, 20 January 1945; news article on flight nurses, n.d.; historical supplement, Air Transport Squadron 11, WW II, all in folder 19 (3a), box 10, ser. 3, NNC Records, OA, NHC; "Navy Flight Nurses," *AJN* 45 (June 1945): 487.

126. *BUMED Newsletter: Aviation Supplement*, 20 July 1945, 1–2, in folder 19 (3b); O'Connor to Dauser, 6 April 1945, folder 19 (1), both in box 10, ser. 3, NNC Records, OA, NHC; Purvis, "Air Ambulances," 159–60.

127. *AJN* 45 (April 1945): 318; *Nurse Corps Chronology*, 32; Tomblin, "Beyond Paradise," pt. 2, 48; Kalisch and Scobey, "Helplessness Suspended," 21; Herman, *Battle Station Sick Bay*, 104–6.

128. Evelyn Schretenthaler Wisner, interview with James Brady, in "We Remember the Sands of Iwo Jima," *Parade*, 22 January 1995.

129. For another account, see J. K. Herman, "Flight Nurse at Iwo," *U.S. Navy Medicine* 86 (March–April 1995): 8–12.

130. *Nurse Corps Chronology*, 33; Tomblin, "Beyond Paradise," pt. 2, 47–48.

131. WW II Statistics—NNC, folder 55 (6), box 16; WW I and WW II Statistics—NNC, folder 68, box 19, both in ser. 3, NNC Records, OA, NHC. In contrast, 201 Army nurses died, 16 from enemy action. Shields, ed., *Army Nurse Corps*, 25–26.

132. BuMed, *Medical Department . . . WW II* 2:91, 119, 154–55, 215–17; WW I and WW II Statistics—NNC, folder 68 (1), box 19, ser. 3, NNC Records, OA, NHC. The WW II Statistics says that 40 received Letters of Commendation with Ribbon, while *Medical Department . . . WW II*, 2:215–17, lists 44 by name.

133. *Nurse Corps Chronology*, 29.

134. Quotation in *Goodnow's History of Nursing*, 10th ed., 258.

135. Quotations in Jackson, "50 Years Ago," 22.

136. Dauser, memo, 21 February 1946, folder 40, box 14, ser. 3, NNC Records, OA, NHC.

137. Bullough, "Lasting Impact," 128.

138. The NNC Records are full of firsthand accounts by the nurses. Dauser sent many of these drafts on to the *AJN* and other professional journals for publication. The nurses' stories are a boon to historians.

139. Lindner interview pointed to Dauser's administrative skills.

## *Chapter 7. The Fight for Permanence, 1945–1950*

1. Evans, *Born for Liberty*, 236–37; William L. O'Neill, *American High: The Years of Confidence, 1945–1960* (New York: Free Press, 1986), 74, 85–87.

2. Ryan, *Womanhood*, 281; Newcomer, *Higher Education*, 46; *Statistical Abstract* (1947), 136; *Statistical Abstract* (1952), 126.

3. Chafe, *Paradox of Change*, 180.

4. Newcomer, *Higher Education*, 179; Ryan, *Womanhood*, 281.

5. Hartmann, *Home Front*, 24; Rothman, *Proper Place*, 224; Evans, *Born for Liberty*, 236, 240.

6. Susan Lynn, *Progressive Women in Conservative Times: Racial Justice, Peace, and Feminism, 1945 to the 1960s* (New Brunswick, N.J.: Rutgers University Press, 1992), 11, 39. For more, see Leila Rupp, *Survival in the Doldrums: The American Women's Rights Movement, 1945–1960* (New York: Oxford University Press, 1987).

7. Chafe, *American Woman*, 187–88; Evans, *Born for Liberty*, 233; Hartmann, *Home Front*, 22.

8. Rothman, *Proper Place*, 221; Evans, *Born for Liberty*, 237–38; Ryan, *Womanhood*, 268, 275.

9. Ferdinand Lundberg and Marynia F. Farnham, *Modern Woman: The Lost Sex* (New York: Harper and Brothers, 1947), 364–68, 376; Ryan, *Womanhood*, 262–64, 272–75; Bullough and Bullough, *Subordinate Sex*, 334, 337.

10. "U.S. Navy Ship Force Levels, 1917–1989."

11. BuPers, "Personnel Statistics."

12. Miller, *U.S. Navy*, 380; *SecNav Report*, 1946, 26.

13. *SecNav Report*, 1946, 26. See Jonathan M. Weisgall, *Operation Crossroads, The Atomic Test at Bikini Atoll* (Annapolis, Md.: Naval Institute Press, 1994); Miller, *U.S. Navy*, 381–82, 388–89. For more on Rickover, see Clay Blair Jr., *The Atomic Submarine and Admiral Rickover* (New York: Henry Holt, 1954); Richard G. Hewlett and Francis Duncan, *The Nuclear Navy: 1946–1962* (Chicago: University of Chicago Press, 1974); Norman Polmar and Thomas B. Allen, *Rickover* (New York: Simon and Schuster, 1982).

14. For general studies, see Norman Friedman, *The Postwar Naval Revolution* (Annapolis, Md.: Naval Institute Press, 1986); and Michael T. Isenberg, *Shield of the Republic: The United States Navy in an Era of Cold War and Violent Peace, 1945–1962* (New York: St. Martin's Press, 1993).

15. Dean C. Allard, "An Era of Transition, 1945–1953," in Hagan, *In Peace and War*, 290–92; Miller, *U.S. Navy*, 379–80, 385; Adams, *Best War*, 141. See Edward J. Sheehy, *The U.S. Navy, the Mediterranean, and the Cold War, 1945–47* (New York: Greenwood, 1992).

16. Miller, *U.S. Navy*, 379–82; *SecNav Report*, 1948, 1. For more, see Paolo E. Coletta, *The United States Navy and Defense Unification, 1947–1953* (Newark: University of Delaware Press, 1981).

17. Allard, "Era of Transition," 293–94. For the complete story, see Jeffrey G. Barlow, *The Revolt of the Admirals: The Fight for Naval Aviation, 1945–1950* (Washington, D.C.: NHC, 1994).

18. W. R. Terrell, Assistant Director of Demobilization, to McAfee, 2 June 1944; McAfee to Terrell, 9 June 1944, both in folder 23, box 3, ser. 1, ACNP(W), OA, NHC.

19. WR Circular Letter no. 4-45, 20 June 1945, folder 31, box 5; WAVES Newsletter, July 1945, folder 110, box 17, both in ser. 1, ACNP(W), OA, NHC.

20. Male officers had to have 49 points; enlisted, 44. ALNAV 252, 9 September 1945, Personnel Policies—Demobilization folder, box 5; revision no. 1, 24 September 1945,

Demobilization—1945 folder, box 3, both in entry 48D, RG 52, NARA; Annual Report of the WR for 1946, folder 88, box 14, ser. 1, ACNP(W), OA, NHC; WAVES Newsletter, October 1945.

21. BuPers, "Personnel Statistics"; *SecNav Report*, 1946, 22–23; Ebbert and Hall, *Crossed Currents*, 93.

22. Sue S. Dauser to Katherine E. Payne, Chairman, State Postwar Planning Committee, New York State Nurses Association, 24 August 1944; Dauser to Katharine [*sic*] J. Densford, president, ANA, 28 August 1944, both in Personnel Policies—Demobilization folder, box 5, entry 48D, RG 52, NARA.

23. Dauser to Chief Nurses, 24 September 1945, Personnel Policies—Demobilization folder, box 5; Nellie Jane DeWitt, report of Nurse Corps, 22 November 1946, Demobilization—1945 folder, box 3, both in entry 48D, RG 52, NARA, and in folder 35 (1), box 32, ser. 6, NNC Records, OA, NHC.

24. DeWitt, report of Nurse Corps, 1946; *SecNav Report*, 1946, 23; BuPers, "Personnel Statistics."

25. Duerk interview; Diduk interview; Beers interview.

26. Jean Palmer, Acting Director, WR, to Director, Planning and Control Division, 9 January 1946; W. M. Fechteler, Directive 150, 9 January 1946; SecNav memo, 5 January 1946, all in folder 30, box 4, ser. 1; Louise K. Wilde to D. R. McLean, 21 June 1946, folder 71, box 10, ser. 1, all in ACNP(W), OA, NHC.

27. WAVES Newsletter, April 1946; BuPers, "Personnel Statistics"; Ebbert and Hall, *Crossed Currents*, 99, 101–2.

28. DeWitt, report of Nurse Corps, 1946; BuPers, "Personnel Statistics."

29. McAfee to Director of Planning and Control, 29 December 1943, folder 23, box 3, ser. 1, ACNP(W), OA, NHC.

30. G. J. Grimm to L. N. Miller, 8 January 1944, and 10 January 1944, folder 23, box 3, ser. 1, ACNP(W), OA, NHC.

31. McAfee to Chief of Naval Personnel, 11 July 1944, folder 23, box 3, ser. 1, ACNP(W), OA, NHC.

32. Randall Jacobs to assistant SecNav for Air, 6 September 1945; McAfee to Jacobs, 17 September 1945, both in folder 30, box 4, ser. 1, ACNP(W), OA, NHC.

33. McAfee bio, OA, NHC; WAVES Newsletter, February 1946; McAfee to Chief BuPers, 17 September 1945, folder 30, box 4, ser. 1, ACNP(W), OA, NHC; McAfee to District and Air Command Directors, 4 February 1946, folder 9, box 1, Hancock Papers.

34. Palmer bio, OA, NHC; Palmer Recollections, 2, 6, 30; WAVES Newsletter, February 1946.

35. Palmer to Director of Plans and Operations, Planning and Control Activity, 16 January 1946; Palmer to CNP, 27 February 1946, Palmer to J. H. Nevins Jr., 8 March 1946; all in folder 30, box 4, ser. 1, ACNP(W), OA, NHC.

36. The Navy Poll, *All Hands*, October 1946, 26; Fantail Forum, *All Hands*, April 1946, 80. One WAVE went so far as to say that any woman staying in the peacetime Navy was "mentally deficient."

37. Hancock interview, 8 January 1982. Cf. Beers interview; Diduk interview; Hurt interview. None had heard of any feelings from women about staying in the Navy.

38. Hancock, *Lady in the Navy*, 220, 222; Hancock bio, OA, NHC; memo to Chief of Naval Personnel, n.d. [after 31 January 1946], folder 30, box 4, ser. 1, ACNP(W), OA, NHC.

39. Palmer to CNP, 25 March 1946, reporting on meeting with Carl Vinson, folder 30, box 4, ser. 1, ACNP(W), OA, NHC.

40. Col. Julia Hamblet, interview with author, 28 November 1995; Mary V. Stremlow, *A History of the Women Marines, 1946–1977* (Washington, D.C.: History and Museums Division, USMC, 1986), 15. Marine Corps commandant, General Alexander A. Vandergrift, envisioned an inactive WR of 500 officers and 4,500 enlisted, with 200 officers and 1,000 enlisted on active duty during summer training. Vandergrift to Chief of Naval Personnel, 12 March 1946, folder 30, box 4, ser. 1, ACNP(W), OA, NHC.

41. House Committee on Naval Affairs, *Hearings on H.R. 5915, To Amend the Naval Reserve Act of 1938, as Amended, so as to Establish the Women's Reserve on a Permanent Basis*, 79th Cong., 2d sess., 9–10 May 1946. Copies of postwar hearings also in folder 8, box 33, ser. 4, ACNP(W), OA, NHC.

42. Smith, *Declaration of Conscience*, 85–86; Janann Sherman, "'They Either Need These Women or They Do Not': Margaret Chase Smith and the Fight for Regular Status for Women in the Military," *JMH* 54 (January 1990): 63–66.

43. Palmer bio, OA, NHC.

44. Hancock bio, OA, NHC. More on Hancock's background in *Lady in the Navy*, 4–45. For overviews of Hancock's life and career, see Susan H. Godson, "Capt. Joy Bright Hancock and the Role of Women in the U.S. Navy," *New Jersey History* 105 (spring/summer 1987): 1–17; and Godson, "Capt. Joy Bright Hancock—Builder of the Co-Ed Navy," *Retired Officer* 38 (December 1982): 14–17.

45. Ebbert and Hall, *Crossed Currents*, 104–6.

46. Reports on these trips in folder 89 (2), box 14, ser. 1, ACNP (W), OA, NHC.

47. Hancock, *Lady in the Navy*, 223–24. Hancock, "Recollections," 115–16, described pushing Sprague into getting naval support for the bill.

48. Hancock interview, 8 January 1982.

49. Hamblet interview; Holm, *Women in the Military*, 106; Stremlow, *Women Marines*, 16; Hancock, *Lady in the Navy*, 225–26. This cooperation continued. Hancock to T. F. Darden, 18 September 1947, folder 113, box 18, ser. 1, ACNP(W), OA, NHC.

50. House Committee on Naval Affairs, *Hearings on H.R. 5915, To Amend the Naval Reserve Act of 1938, as Amended, So as to Establish the Women's Reserve on a Permanent Basis*, 79th Cong., 2d sess., 9–10 May 1946. Senate Committee on Armed Services, *Hearings on S. 1103, S. 1527, S. 1641, Women's Armed Services Integration Act*, 80th Cong., 1st sess., 2, 9, 15 July 1947; Sherman, "Regular Status," 68–69; Ebbert and Hall, *Crossed Currents*, 107–8.

51. Senate *Hearings*, 94–95; Hancock, *Lady in the Navy*, 226–27.

52. Hancock statement, Senate *Hearings*, 68–69; Hancock, *Lady in the Navy*, 228.

53. CNP to All Ships and Stations, 13 November 1947, folder 3, box 9, ser. 3, Pers 00W Records, OA, NHC.

54. House Subcommittee on Organization and Mobilization, *Hearings on S. 1641*, 80th Cong., 2d sess., 18, 23, 25, 27 February, 2, 3 March 1948.

55. Sherman, "Regular Status," 70–72; Smith, *Declaration of Conscience*, 86–87.

56. Smith to W. G. Andrews, 14 February 1948, quoted in Smith, *Declaration of Conscience*, 87–88.

57. Hancock, *Lady in the Navy*, 229; Ebbert and Hall, *Crossed Currents*, 110.

58. Full House committee hearings on various bills, including S. 1641, 80th Cong., 2d sess., 23 March 1948; Smith, *Declaration of Conscience*, 88–89; Hancock, *Lady in the Navy*, 230.

59. Sherman, "Regular Status," 76 and note 89; Smith to Forrestal, 22 April 1948, quoted in Smith, *Declaration of Conscience*, 96–97.

60. Holm, *Women in the Military*, 117; Stremlow, *Women Marines*, 17; Hancock, *Lady in the Navy*, 230–31.

61. "WAVES Will Not Interfere with Opportunities Offered Navy Men," *All Hands*, May 1948, 42–43; "Permanent WAVES Plan Gradual Build-Up of Trained Personnel," *All Hands*, July 1948, 53.

62. Hancock, *Lady in the Navy*, 110; Hancock, "Recollections," 131–32.

63. Hamblet interview; Robert B. Anderson to Hancock, May 1953, quoted in Hancock, *Lady in the Navy*, 262–63, copy in folder 4, box 8, Hancock Papers;

64. *U.S. Code*, Title 10, sec. 6015; and *United States Statutes at Large* 62 (1948): 356–75; Annual Report of the WR for 1948, folder 88, box 14, ser. 1, ACNP(W), OA, NHC.

65. Holm, *Women in the Military*, 121–22; Stremlow, *Women Marines*, 18.

66. *SecNav Report*, 1945, A-85; BuMed, *History of Medical Department, 1945–1955*, 103.

67. *SecNav Report*, 1945, A-86, A-87, A-90; Medical Department Material for SecDef Report, folder 69, box 19, ser. 3, NNC Records, OA, NHC.

68. BuMed, *History of the Medical Department, 1945–1955*, 56; *Handbook of the Hospital Corps: 1953*, 4–5; *United States Statutes at Large* 61 (1947): 734–38. For a full account, see Edward L. Costello, "Establishment of the Medical Service Corps," typescript, BuMed Archives.

69. Nellie Jane DeWitt to J. B. Logue, 28 December 1948; H. L. Pugh memo, 5 December 1947, both in folder 35 (4), box 33, ser. 6, NNC Records, OA, NHC.

70. Duerk interview.

71. Kalisch and Kalisch, *American Nursing*, 350–52, 355, 364; Department of Health, Education, and Welfare, *Biennial Survey of Education in the United States: 1948–50* (Washington, D.C.: GPO, 1954), 4:38, 64.

72. Ann Clendenin Paroubek, interview with author, 15 March 1996.

73. Sue S. Dauser to W. S. Douglass, 29 May 1945; Ross T. McIntire to SecNav, 15 October 1945, both in folder 4, box 8, ser. 3, NNC Records, OA, NHC.

74. William M. Fechteler, Assistant CNP, to CNO, 28 November 1945, with enclo-

sures Louis Denfeld to SecNav, n.d., and CNO to Chief BuMed, n.d., folder 4, box 8; McIntire to CNO, 19 December 1945, folder E58, box 16, both in ser. 3, NNC Records, OA, NHC.

75. *United States Statutes at Large* 59 (1945): 594–95.

76. Nellie Jane DeWitt bio, OA, NHC; DeWitt bio, press release, and tributes all in DeWitt folder, box 2, entry 48D, RG 52, NARA.

77. DeWitt to Elmira B. Wickenden, National Nursing Council, 5 April 1946, folder 37, box 13, ser. 3, NNC Records, OA, NHC; DeWitt memo, 16 April 1946, Personnel Policies folder, box 5, entry 48D, RG 52, NARA.

78. "Navy Nurse Corps," *Army-Navy Journal*, 11 May 1946; statements of C. A. Swanson, Chief BuMed, 20 December 1946, and 30 January 1947, folder 4, box 8, ser. 3; various copies of bills as prepared by BuMed in folder 27 (1), box 31, ser. 6, and folder 4, box 8, ser. 3, all in NNC Records, OA, NHC; House Committee on Armed Services, *Hearings on H.R. 1373, to Reorganize the Nurse Corps of the Navy and of the Naval Reserve*, 80th Cong., 1st sess., 20 January 1947.

79. DeWitt to Frances P. Bolton, 30 January 1947, and 4 February 1947; DeWitt to Margaret Chase Smith, 30 January 1947, all in folder 4, box 8, ser. 3, NNC Records, OA, NHC.

80. DeWitt to surgeon general, 5 February 1947, folder 4, box 8, ser. 3, NNC Records, OA, NHC.

81. DeWitt memo, 13 February 1947, folder 4, box 8, ser. 3, NNC Records, OA, NHC.

82. Senate Committee on Armed Services, *Hearings on H.R. 1943*, 80th Cong., 1st sess., 24 March 1947.

83. Sherman, "Regular Status," 67.

84. *United States Statutes at Large* 61 (1947): 41–52; highlights in "Utilization of Women in Department of Defense: Nurse Corps, U.S. Navy and U.S. Naval Reserve," n.d., folder 4, box 8, ser. 3, and folder 27 (1), box 31, ser. 6; Procurement Bulletin no. 12-47, 18 April 1947, folder 55 (3), box 15, ser. 3, all in NNC Records, OA, NHC; Smith, "Military Nurses," 36. The act had similar provisions for the Army Nurse Corps. The *AJN* quickly contacted DeWitt about explaining provisions for Navy nurses for a forthcoming article about the act. Nell V. Beeby, associate editor, to DeWitt, 29 April 1947; DeWitt to Beeby, 1 May 1947, both in folder 1 (2), box 20, ser. 4, NNC Records, OA, NHC.

85. *United States Statutes at Large* 62 (1948): 211–12; and *United States Statutes at Large* 62 (1948): 1081–91. Title III, chap. 708 applies to reserve nurses of all services; Dorothy E. Jones, "The Nurse Corps of the U.S. Naval Reserve," reprinted from *AJN* 50 (May 1950).

86. Jean T. Palmer to District and Air Commands and Washington Bureaus, 6 February 1946, folder 9, box 1; Hancock to C. A. Heil Jr., 23 September 1946, folder 2, box 8, both in Hancock Papers.

87. Hancock to T. F. Darden, 18 September 1947; CNP to All Ships and Stations,

Circular Letter no. 231-47, 26 November 1947; CNP to SecNav, 18 July 1948, all in folder 113, box 18, ser. 1, ACNP(W), OA, NHC.

88. These women were Kay L. Langdon, Wilma J. Marchal, Edna E. Young, Doris R. Robertson, Frances R. Devaney, and Ruth Flora. Listed in Hancock, *Lady in the Navy*, 235–36; Fischer, *Navy Women*, 37; Ebbert and Hall, *Crossed Currents*, 117. Figures in BuPers, "Personnel Statistics."

89. The first eight officers were Hancock, Lt. Cdrs. Winifred R. Quick, Ann King, and Frances L. Willoughby; Lts. Ellen Ford and Doris Cranmore; and Lts. (j.g.) Doris A. Defenderfer and Betty Rae Tennant. In Hancock, *Lady in the Navy*, 238; Ebbert and Hall, *Crossed Currents*, 117.

90. Hancock, Review of Program for Women in U.S. Navy, 5 March 1953, folder 9, box 1, Hancock Papers; Ebbert and Hall, *Crossed Currents*, 118.

91. Your Pay as a Navy WAVE, March 1946; Tables I and II, Monthly Pay, October 1949, both in folder 71, box 10, ser. 1, ACNP(W), OA, NHC.

92. Hancock, *Lady in the Navy*, 237; Fischer, *Navy Women*, 37.

93. Ebbert and Hall, *Crossed Currents*, 121. For a good description of recruit training, see Robert A. Rogers, III, "These Boots Wear Skirts," *USNIP* 75 (September 1949): 1025–27.

94. Hancock, *Lady in the Navy*, 239; Fischer, *Navy Women*, 37; Ebbert and Hall, *Crossed Currents*, 122.

95. Fletcher, *WRNS*, 88–89; *All Hands*, April 1949, 39. Hancock gives a thorough account of her trip in *Lady in the Navy*, 245–54. Her report of the trip is in folder 10, box 1, Hancock Papers.

96. The Navy had recommended assigning women to transports two years earlier, especially those carrying women and children dependents. CNP to CNO, 31 July 1947, folder 20, box 3, ser. 1, ACNP(W), OA, NHC.

97. Chronology in "Calendar of WAVE History," folder 33, box 5, ser. 1, ACNP(W), OA, NHC.

98. BuPers, "Personnel Statistics."

99. W. Leona Jackson, "We've Reached the Golden Year," *AJN* 58 (May 1958): 672; Report of Nurse Corps: 1946, folder 35 (1), box 32, ser. 6, NNC Records, OA, NHC. The 1948 report written by Esther L. Brown, *Nursing for the Future*, advocated concentrating nursing education in colleges and universities and phasing out hospital schools of nursing. This Brown Report generated adverse reactions from doctors and hospital administrators, although nursing associations favored such increased professionalization. Kalisch and Kalisch, *American Nursing*, 361–63.

100. Colleges and universities included the Medical College of Virginia, University of Utah School of Medicine, University Hospital at Cleveland, Baylor, the Boston and Philadelphia Schools of Occupational Therapy, and George Washington University. *Nurse Corps Chronology*, 37–38, 40; *Surgeon General's Report: 1947, 1948, 1949, 1950.*

101. DeWitt to Chief BuMed, 23 December 1947; DeWitt to J. B. Logue, 15 March 1948, both in folder 35 (4), box 33, ser. 6, NNC Records, OA, NHC.

102. *Nurse Corps Chronology*, 38; DeWitt to Nell V. Beeby, 18 September 1946, folder 19 (3a), box 10, ser. 3, NNC Records, OA, NHC; Mary C. Grimes, "Aero-Medical Nursing—A New Specialty," *Trained Nurse and Hospital Review* (November 1949): 211, 243. Lists of 1948 and 1949 Nurse Corps graduates in folder 19 (2), box 10, ser. 3, NNC Records, OA, NHC.

103. Report of Nurse Corps: 1946; list of indoctrination locations, and "Indoctrination Course for Nurse Corps Officers," both in folder 29 (1), box 11, ser. 3, NNC Records, OA, NHC. Nurse Ellen H. Connelly, "Shipmates in White," *AJN* 49 (April 1949): 204, describes such a course.

104. Quotation in Sterner, *Harm's Way*, 208.

105. Current Statistics, 1 January 1950, folder 68 (2), box 19, ser. 3; Calendar Year Statistics: 1949, folder 42 (9), box 35, ser. 6, both in NNC Records, OA, NHC. In a talk before the Medico-Military Symposium, 23–28 October 1950, C. I. Bailey, NC, "Aboard a Hospital Ship," described her duty in *Consolation*, folder 1 (5), box 21, ser. 4, NNC Records, OA, NHC.

106. Extracts from Files of U.S. Naval Hospital, Guam, folder 22, box 11, ser. 3, NNC Records, OA, NHC; *Nurse Corps Chronology*, 39; Lt. Ganey to R. Pickis, 3 January 1962, Samoan Islands folder, box 5, ZE files, OA, NHC.

107. Ens. Marguerite E. Green's account in folder 15 (1), box 10, ser. 3, NNC Records, OA, NHC.

108. Series of articles in *New York Times*, pp. 17, 18, 19, 20 April 1947; Sterner, *Harm's Way*, 214. True to form, many nurses sent to Texas City wrote of their experiences. These included accounts by Grace L. Barrett, Hazel L. Delk, Jesse D. Hodge, D. M. Bacon, Nellie E. Morrison, and Evelyn T. Stotz, all in folder 15 (1), box 10, ser. 3, NNC Records, OA, NHC.

109. Winnie Gibson to Evelyn T. Stotz, 25 April 1947; DeWitt to Gibson, 28 April 1947, both in folder 15 (1), box 10, ser. 3, NNC Records, OA, NHC.

110. DeWitt to Chief BuMed, 1 July 1947, 30 July 1947; Conference of Chief Nurses, 30 July 1947; report of inspection of nursing service in the Caribbean, 26 April 1948; schedule of inspection trip of Committee on Medical and Hospital Services of the Armed Forces, n.d., all in Nellie Jane DeWitt folder, box 2, entry 48D, RG 52, NARA.

111. Willenz, *Women Veterans*, 104.

112. Holm, *Women in the Military*, 119–27, analyzes each section of the legislation.

## *Chapter 8. The Korean War and the 1950s*

1. *Statistical Abstract* (1952), 126; *Statistical Abstract* (1961), 124; Gordon, *Higher Education*, 2.

2. Bullough and Bullough, *Subordinate Sex*, 338; Evans, *Born for Liberty*, 261;

O'Neill, *American High*, 41; Ryan, *Womanhood*, 281. For the contemporary thinking on the purposes of higher education, see Lynn White Jr., *Educating Our Daughters: A Challenge to the Colleges* (New York: Harper, 1950).

3. Evans, *Born for Liberty*, 253; O'Neill, *American High*, 43–44; Chafe, *Women and Equality*, 94–95; Weiner, *Working Girl*, 4, 89.

4. O'Neill, *American High*, 238; Lynn, *Conservative Times*, 39, 139, 168–69; Evans, *Born for Liberty*, 268.

5. Ryan, *Womanhood*, 268, 275; Friedan, *Feminine Mystique*, 16, 18.

6. Evans, *Born for Liberty*, 246–47, 250; Friedan, *Feminine Mystique*, 24, 43–44; Ryan, *Womanhood*, 267.

7. Rothman, *Proper Place*, 225–27, 231; Chafe, *Paradox of Change*, 195–96; Friedan, *Feminine Mystique*, 15, 19–20, 26, 32.

8. Evans, *Born for Liberty*, 259–60; Chafe, *Women and Equality*, 88–90.

9. For a historiographical survey, see Allan R. Millett, "A Reader's Guide to the Korean War," *JMH* 61 (July 1997): 583–97.

10. "U.S. Navy Ship Force Levels, 1917–1989"; BuPers, "Personnel Statistics," 1950 and 1960.

11. Floyd D. Kennedy Jr., "The Creation of the Cold War Navy, 1953–1962," in Hagan, *In Peace and War*, 305. More on naval operations in James A. Field Jr., *History of United States Naval Operations: Korea* (Washington, D.C.: GPO, 1962); and Richard P. Hallion, *The Naval Air War in Korea* (Baltimore: Nautical & Aviation Publishing, 1985). A general account of the war is Clay Blair, *The Forgotten War: America in Korea, 1950–1953* (New York: Times Books, 1987), and a broader view is William Stueck, *The Korean War: An International History* (Princeton, N.J.: Princeton University Press, 1995). For surveys of recent historiography, see Philip West, "Interpreting the Korean War," *AHR* 94 (February 1989): 80–96; and James I. Matray, "Civil Is a Dumb Name for War," *SHAFR Newsletter* 26 (December 1995): 1–15.

12. For the Navy's role, see Curtis A. Utz, *Assault from the Sea: The Amphibious Landing at Inchon* (Washington, D.C.: NHC, 1994).

13. Miller, *U.S. Navy*, 390–91; Kennedy, "Cold War Navy," 320–22.

14. David A. Rosenberg, "Arleigh Albert Burke: 17 August 1955–1 August 1961," in Love, *Chiefs of Naval Operations*, 288–91; Miller, *U.S. Navy*, 391–93; Kennedy, "Cold War Navy," 316–17.

15. Miller, *U.S. Navy*, 388–90; Kennedy, "Cold War Navy," 309.

16. Thomas C. Hone, *Power and Change: The Administrative History of the Office of the Chief of Naval Operations, 1946–1986* (Washington, D.C.: NHC, 1989), 36, 38–40; Gail Mason, *Organization of the Navy Department: A History from 1947 to 1970* (Washington, D.C.: OA, Naval History Division 1970), 50–54; Rosenberg, "Burke," 287–88; "The Men at the Helm: The Last Nine CNOs and Their Portraits," *All Hands*, August 1986, 14.

17. In June 1950, there were 493 women officers and 2,746 enlisted for a total of

3,239. Figures from BuPers, "Personnel Statistics," 1950. Failure to meet quotas in Hancock memo, 20 March 1952, folder 88, box 14, ser. 1, ACNP(W), OA, NHC.

18. Collins interview; Hancock, *Lady in the Navy*, 222, 258.

19. Hancock memo, 6 June 1951, folder 9, box 9, ser. 3, Records of the Bureau of Personnel, Special Assistant for Women's Policy [Pers 00W]; Hancock, *Lady in the Navy*, 258; Ebbert and Hall, *Crossed Currents*, 129; Stremlow, *Women Marines*, 53; Hancock memo, 6 August 1952, folder 88, box 14, ser. 1, ACNP(W), OA, NHC. More on recruiting in folders 85 and 86, box 13, ser. 1, ACNP(W), OA, NHC.

20. Holm, *Women in the Military*, 150–53; Hancock, *Lady in the Navy*, 241–42; M. C. Devilbiss, *Women and Military Service: A History, Analysis, and Overview of Key Issues* (Maxwell Air Force Base, Ala.: Air University Press, 1990), 10.

21. Hancock, *Lady in the Navy*, 237; Ebbert and Hall, *Crossed Currents*, 129; Hancock memo, 20 March 1952, folder 88, box 14, ser. 1, ACNP(W), OA, NHC. More on training at Bainbridge in folder 10, box 11, and folder 1, box 12, both in ser. 3, Pers 00W Records, OA, NHC.

22. Hancock, Program for Women, 5 March 1953, folder 9, box 1, Hancock Papers, Special Collections Division, University of Georgia Libraries; Hancock, *Lady in the Navy*, 258–59; Department of the Navy, *History of Administrative Problems, Korean War* (Washington, D.C.: OA, Naval History Division, n.d. [1953]), 5:37.

23. Folders 6 and 7, box 12, ser. 3, Pers 00W Records, OA, NHC.

24. Hancock, *Lady in the Navy*, 239–41; Ebbert and Hall, *Crossed Currents*, 131.

25. "Coed Airmen Training," *All Hands*, November 1950, 24–25; "Women in the Navy: Jills of All Trades," *All Hands*, July 1952, 20–21; Douglas, *Women in Aviation*, 72.

26. Cf., Stremlow, *Women Marines*, 57, who says that the Korean War was a turning point that opened new career fields.

27. Figures in On Board Navywide (1940–1968), folder 35 (6), box 33, ser. 6, NNC Records, OA, NHC; BuMed, *History of the Medical Department . . . 1945–55*, 102.

28. Calendar Year Statistics: 1950, 1951, 1953, folder 42 (9); Statistics—Census, 24 April 1951, folder 42 (6), both in box 35, ser. 6; Chief BuMed to Chief BuPers, 7 February 1951, folder 55 (3), box 15, ser. 3, all in NNC Records, OA, NHC; *Administrative Problems* 3:6–8. Rosters of involuntary recalls in Involuntary Recalls folder, box 5, RG 52, entry 48D, NARA. For a brief summary, see BuPers, "Medical Department Orientation," n.d., 181, folder 21, box 30, ser. 6, NNC Records, OA, NHC.

29. Duerk interview. During the war, Duerk was charge nurse on a neurosurgical unit at Portsmouth, Virginia, then taught at the Hospital Corps school there for five years.

30. Rita V. O'Neill and Elizabeth B. Seidl, "Indoctrination Program for Navy Nurses," *AJN* 54 (May 1954) describes the program at St. Albans.

31. Capt. Winnie Gibson Palmer bio, Officers Bio Files, OA, NHC; biographical sketch prepared by Mary G. Lynch, 1951, folder 1 (5), box 21, ser. 4, NNC Records, OA, NHC; Sterner, *Harm's Way*, 229.

32. Calendar Year Statistics: 1953, folder 42 (9), box 35, ser. 6, NNC Records, OA, NHC; "The Military Sea Transport Service," *All Hands*, August 1951, 24–27.

33. Narrative on Yokosuka Hospital, 1 March 1951; Lt. Cdr. Alberta Burk to Winnie Gibson, 13 April 1951, both in folder 31 (1), box 12, ser. 3, NNC Records, OA, NHC. Lts. Mary D. Shanks and Faith A. Salden supervised the Japanese nurses and wrote of them in "Nursing Trends in Japan," History folder (1), box 20, ser. 4, NNC Records, OA, NHC. For English classes, see Zoe Gilmore, "A Navy Nurse Teaches in Japan," folder 1 (4), box 21, ser. 4, NNC Records, OA, NHC.

34. E. R. Coyl, "Hospital Ships in Korea," folder 1, box 37, ser. 7., NNC Records, OA, NHC.

35. Arthur M. Smith, "Getting Them Out Alive," *USNIP* 115 (February 1989): 41–42; Kalisch and Kalisch, *American Nursing*, 382–84; Kalisch and Scobey, "Helplessness Suspended," 20, 27–28; Donahue, *Finest Art*, 421–22; Gabriel and Metz, *Military Medicine* 2:257–59; Carmelita Schimmenti and Maureen A. Darmody, "Taking Flight," *AJN* 87 (November 1987): 1422.

36. "Mobile Medical Teams Saving More Lives," *All Hands*, December 1951, 12–13.

37. Sterner, *Harm's Way*, 236; "The Role of the Navy Nurse on the U.S.S. *Repose*," folder 31 (1), box 12, ser. 3, NNC Records, OA, NHC; "Women in White Help Guard Your Health," *All Hands*, February 1953, 20.

38. *Consolation*, in *DANFS* 2:169; Coyl, "Hospital Ships."

39. "Nurse Corps Chronology," 39; Coyl, "Hospital Ships"; *Benevolence*, in *DANFS* 1:116; Sterner, *Harm's Way*, 231–34, gives a graphic account.

40. *Haven*, in *DANFS* 3:271; "Nurse Corps Chronology," 39; Eleanor Harrington, "Nursing Aboard a Hospital Ship," folder History (3), box 20, ser. 4; Ruth Cohen to Gibson, 12 April 1951, folder 31 (1), box 12, ser. 3, both in NNC Records, OA, NHC. A civilian nurse visited *Haven* and had high praise for its Navy nurses. No name, no title, report on two-week trip to Pearl Harbor, folder 1 (3), box 21, ser. 4, NNC Records, OA, NHC.

41. *Repose*, in *DANFS* 6:77–78; Coyl, "Hospital Ships"; Roberta Ohrman to Gibson, 14 April 1951, folder 31 (1), box 12, ser. 3, NHC Records, OA, NHC. Annette Baer described duty in *Repose* in "Nursing Aboard a Hospital Ship," folder 1 (4), box 21, ser. 4, NNC Records, OA, NHC; History of Our Ship, in *Cruise Book: Repose, 1969–1970*, Navy Department Library.

42. Thelma B. Hase, "Korean and American Nurses Exchange Visits," folder 1 (4), box 21, ser. 4, NNC Records, OA, NHC.

43. Sterner, *Harm's Way*, 247–48.

44. Contributions of Navy Flight Nurses during the Korean Phase, folder 31 (1), box 12, ser. 3, NNC Records, OA, NHC, describes activities in the holding ward at Haneda.

45. Contributions of Navy Flight Nurses, folder 31 (1), box 12, ser. 3, NNC Records, OA, NHC.

46. Carmelita Schimmenti and Maureen A. Darmody, "Taking Flight," *AJN* 87 (November 1987): 1422.

47. Flight Nurses, folder 31 (1), box 12, ser. 3; "Precious Cargo," folder 49, box 14, ser. 3; Melva Stankovich, "Interservice Coordination, Relationship, and Communication in Air Evacuation by Military Air Transport Service," folder 19 (3b), box 10, ser. 3, all in NNC Records, OA, NHC. For details on the hospital at Yokosuka, see Alberta Burk to Gibson, 13 April 1951, folder 31 (1), box 12, ser. 3, NNC Records, OA, NHC. Nurses also handled special problems such as described by Mary E. Headly, "Nursing the Respirator Patient during Flight," folder 1 (7), box 22, ser. 4, NNC Records, OA, NHC. A new air evacuation plane, C-54M, was put into use by MATS in December 1950 and was readily convertible from an air cargo transport to a 32-litter air evacuation plane. Descriptions in Press release, 27 December 1950, and The New MATS C-54M, both in folder 19 (3b), box 10, ser. 3, NNC Records, OA, NHC; "Flying Ambulances," *All Hands*, June 1951, 25.

48. "Nurse Corps Chronology," 39.

49. Chief of Information, Executive Office of SecNav, 13 March 1963, re Servicewomen Casualties, folder 33, box 5, ser.1, ACNP(W), OA, NHC; Awards to Navy Nurses, folder 8 (12), box 9, ser. 3, NNC Records, OA, NHC. Nurses receiving the Bronze Star were Ruth Cohen and Eleanore Harrington, who had served in *Haven*, and Estelle K. Lange, who had been in *Consolation*.

50. BuPers, "Personnel Statistics"; W. R. Quick, Memo, 8 January 1958, folder 4, box 1, ser. 3, Pers 00W Records, OA, NHC.

51. Hancock, *Lady in the Navy*, 257–58; Hancock bio, OA, NHC; Hancock to Chief BuPers, 26 January 1953, folder 34 (k), box 5, ACNP(W), OA, NHC. For an overview of Hancock's career, see Catherine Fellows, "First Lady of the Navy," *All Hands*, July 1978, 33–35.

52. Citation for Legion of Merit, 25 May 1953; Robert B. Anderson to Hancock, 18 May 1953, both in folder 4, box 8, Hancock Papers.

53. Capt. Louise K. Wilde bio, Officers Bio File, OA, NHC; obituaries, *Washington Star*, 10 December 1979, and *Washington Post*, 11 December 1979; *Women of the U.S. Navy*, Public Information folder (Washington, D.C.: Department of the Navy, 1955), 19–20; Ebbert and Hall, *Crossed Currents*, 136–37; *Who's Who in America: 1960–1961* (Chicago: A. N. Marquis, 1960), 3125. The Newsletters had started in 1953 as Memos and continued through Wilde's and Quick's tenures. All in folder 5, box 4, ser. 3, Pers 00W Records, OA, NHC.

54. Collins interview; Tom Philpott, "Making WAVES," *Washingtonian* 32 (March 1997): 48, 50, 53–54; Capt. Winifred Quick Collins bio, Officers Bio File, OA, NHC; Ebbert and Hall, *Crossed Currents*, 40, 104, 117, 145; *Who's Who in America: 1960–1961*, 2352.

55. Holm, *Women in the Military*, 157–58; Stremlow, *Women Marines*, 62–63, 68. Stremlow refers to the 1954–1964 years as a decade of status quo.

56. Holm, *Women in the Military*, 158, 161–63.

57. Hancock, Program for Women, 5.

58. Cdr. Etta Bell Kitchen Oral History Interview (USNI, 1969), 2:18–19; Ebbert and Hall, *Crossed Currents*, 145.

59. *United States Statutes at Large* 62 (1948): 356–75; PL 585, 84th Cong., 2d sess., *An Act . . . to Provide Flexibility in the Distribution of Women Officers.*

60. Ebbert and Hall, *Crossed Currents,* 141. The WACs, WAFs, and Women Marines experienced a similar trend. Holm, *Women in the Military,* 160–61, 173–74; Stremlow, *Women Marines,* 62–63, 68.

61. Collins interview; "Calendar of WAVE History," folder 33, box 5, ser. 1, ACNP(W), OA, NHC; M. J. Luosky to Vice Adm. Harold P. Smith, 30 January 1958; Smith to Luosky, 30 January 1958; Smith to SecNav Thomas S. Gates Jr., 17 April 1958, all in folder 9, box 9, ser. 3, Pers 00W Records, OA, NHC.

62. "WAVES 'Gold Hash Mark' Anniversary," *All Hands,* July 1954, 14–16.

63. "No Women Regulars," *Navy Times,* 15 August 1959, 11; "Wants No WAVES," *Navy Times,* 12 September 1959, 10, 36; "Gals but 1 Factor," *Navy Times,* 3 October 1959, 10, 15.

64. Collins interview; correspondence between Quick and parents in folder 70, box 10, ser. 1, ACNP(W), OA, NHC; Collins, My Work as ACNP(W), 1957–1962, transcript given to author.

65. Devilbiss, *Military Service,* 32; Holm, *Women in the Military,* 177, 179, 181–83.

66. Hancock to Assistant SecDef, 25 July 1951; WAVES in Foreign Areas, 19 December 1951, both in folder 69, box 10, ser. 1, ACNP(W), OA, NHC. Correspondence in this folder shows Hancock's persistent efforts to get overseas assignments for WAVES.

67. Fischer, ed., *Navy Women,* 38; *WAVES of the U.S. Navy,* 6; "Calendar of WAVE History; Fact Sheet: 1955, folder 29, box 4, ser. 1, ACNP(W), OA, NHC; "Sea-Going WAVES? It's True—Here's a Sample," *All Hands,* August 1958, 20–21.

68. Hancock, *Lady in the Navy,* 239–40; Ebbert and Hall, *Crossed Currents,* 131.

69. "Service Is Scheduled for Lucille Ross Kuhn," *Richmond Times Dispatch,* 26 September 1995, p. B3. Ebbert and Hall, *Crossed Currents,* 148–51, has a long write-up on Kuhn.

70. Quick, Annual Report, 1959; "Calendar of WAVE History."

71. Louise K. Wilde, Annual Report, 18 June 1956, folder 88, box 14; Quick to Margaret E. Tracy, 7 April 1958, folder 3, box 1, both in ser. 1; Quick Memo 33, 8 March 1958, folder 5, box 4, ser. 3, all in ACNP(W), OA, NHC.

72. Wilde, Annual Report, 18 June 1956, folder 88, box 14; curricula and more on Monterey in folder 103, box 16, both in ser. 1, ACNP(W), OA, NHC.

73. Quick, Annual Report, 6 August 1959, folder 88, box 14, ser. 1, ACNP(W), OA, NHC; Quick, Memo 33, 8 March 1958, folder 5, box 4, ser. 3, Pers 00W Records, OA, NHC.

74. Charlotte L. Safford, "U.S. Lady of the Month: Cdr. Frances E. Biadasz, USN," *U.S. Lady* (September 1963): 12, 47. Biadasz earned a doctorate at Georgetown University in 1961.

75. Collins interview; Collins, My Work as ACNP(W).

76. BuMed, *History of the Medical Department, 1945–1955,* 100–103, 149, 159, 189–90, 207, 214–15.

77. PL 1028, 84th Cong., 2d sess., Title 10; Department of the Navy, *Manual of the*

*Bureau of Medicine and Surgery, U.S. Navy*, typescript, 1956, 00-1, 32-1, 32-2, folder 7, box 25, ser. 6, NNC Records, OA, NHC; Jackson, "Golden Year," 673.

78. Kalisch and Kalisch, *American Nursing*, 370, 386, 411–12, 419, 447.

79. Donahue, *Finest Art*, 446–48.

80. Capt. W. Leona Jackson bio, Officers Bio Files, OA, NHC; Sterner, *Harm's Way*, 257.

81. Capt. Ruth A. Houghton bio, Officers Bio Files, OA, NHC; "Nurse Corps Chronology," 43–44; *Who's Who in America: 1960–1961*, 1394; Sterner, *Harm's Way*, 275–76.

82. Procurement Problems, prepared for Gibson, 21 September 1953, folder 55 (6), box 16, ser. 3, NNC Records, OA, NHC.

83. Gibson memo, 1 May 1953, Proposed legislation to increase the number of commanders and lieutenant commanders folder, box 7, RG 52, entry 48D, NARA; PL 85-155, 85th Cong., 1st sess., *An Act to Improve the Career Opportunities of Nurses and Medical Specialists in the Army, Navy, and Air Force.*

84. Waivers for height, weight, vision, teeth, spinal, and skin deficiencies eased the physical requirements. Procurement and Retention of Nurse Corps Personnel, 1 August 1961, 3, folder 1 (2), box 8, ser. 3, NNC Records, OA, NHC, and in Personnel Polices—Retention folder, box 5, RG 52, entry 48D, NARA; Historical Summary of Nurse Corps Procurement, February 1961, folder 55 (4), box 15; Chief BuMed to Chief BuPers, 21 June 1955, folder 55 (6), box 16, both in ser. 3, NNC Records, OA, NHC; *Surgeon General's Report: 1957.*

85. Procurement and Retention, 3; Chief BuMed to Chief BuPers, 7 February 1951, folder 55 (4), box 15; D. L. Ellis to Pers B6232, 9 February 1956; H. W. Hall to W. L. Jackson, [8 February 1956], both in folder 55 (6), box 16, all in ser. 3, NNC Records, OA,NHC.

86. Summary of . . . Procurement, February 1961; "Nurse Corps Chronology," 42, 46; Procurement and Retention, 3; *Surgeon General's Report: 1959, 1960*; BuPers, "Medical Department," 182.

87. Procurement and Retention, 3; Navy Nurse Corps Candidate Program, 30 June 1958, folder 55 (4), box 15, ser. 3, NNC Records, OA, NHC; *Surgeon General's Report: 1959, 1960.*

88. Ruth A. Houghton to Code 3, 21 October 1959; BuMed Instruction 1520.14, 7 September 1960, both in folder 41, box 14, ser. 3, NNC Records, OA, NHC; "Nurse Corps Chronology," 44, 46.

89. "Nurse Corps Chronology," 45–46.

90. Department of Defense (hereafter cited as DOD), *Fact Sheet: Nuclear Nursing*, n.d.; Nuclear Nursing Course: A Navy First, n.d.; A New Navy Nurse Corps Career Horizon, all in folder 43, box 14, ser. 3; Lenore Simon, "The Nuclear Age and Nursing Technology," paper presented at convention of the Association of Military Surgeons, 31 October 1960, folder 1 (4), box 21, ser. 4, all in NNC Records, OA, NHC; "Nuclear Nurses," *All Hands*, April 1959, 7. Zoe Gilmore, "The Navy Nurse Corps," *Bulletin of the California State Nurses Association* 51 (October 1955): 312–13, anticipated such a program.

91. Houghton's remarks to nuclear nursing students, 3 September 1958, folder 43, box 14, ser. 3, NNC Records, OA, NHC.

92. List of Nurse Corps women sent for training at Gunter Air Force Base, Montgomery, Alabama, folder 19 (2), box 10, ser. 3, NNC Records, OA, NHC; "Nurse Corps Chronology," 46.

93. Calendar Year Statistics: 1953, 1960, folder 42 (9), box 35, ser. 6, NNC Records, OA, NHC.

94. Shields, ed., *Army Nurse Corps,* 51.

95. Nurse Staffing, 1955 and 1961, folder 1 (1), box 8, ser. 3, NNC Records, OA, NHC.

96. Frances E. Quebbeman, "Nursing Service in an Emergency," folder 1 (3), box 21, ser. 4; more in folder 26, box 11, ser. 3, both in NNC Records, OA, NHC; "Bennington," *DANFS* 1:118.

97. Sterner, *Harm's Way,* 263.

98. Ibid., 264–65.

99. Lucille F. Finney, "Voyage #62"; Daily Account of the Navy's Hungarian Refugee Sealift; Catherine Recicar, "I Nursed Aboard a Refugee Ship," all in folder 1 (3), box 21, ser. 4, NNC Records, OA, NHC; "Nurse Corps Chronology," 42; "*General LeRoy Eltinge,*" *DANFS* 3:49–50.

100. "Nurse Corps Chronology," 44–45; Quick, Annual Report: 1959.

101. Hancock, *Lady in the Navy,* 157–58; Nellie J. DeWitt to All Nurses, 2 December 1949 and results of survey, both in folder 72 (8), box 20, ser. 3, NNC Records, OA, NHC. The survey showed that 1,522 nurses wanted the traditional black-blue uniform with gold sleeve markings; 117 preferred the lighter blue of the WAVES' uniform with gold sleeve markings; none wanted WAVES' blue with light blue sleeve markings.

102. Collins interview; Circular Letter no. 63-50, 11 May 1950, folder 27, box 4, ser. 1, ACNP(W), OA, NHC; Uniforms folder 72(2), box 19, ser. 3, NNC Records, OA, NHC. Capt. Quick designed the new formal and service dress uniforms.

103. *Navy Register: 1951,* xiv; *Navy Register: 1959,* xv; PL 20, 84th Cong., 1st sess., *Career Incentive Act of 1955;* and PL 85-422, 85th Cong., 2d sess., *Armed Forces Salary Increase;* Personal Affairs Branch, Welfare Division, BuPers, Directive no. 2, 17 October 1950; SecNav to All Ships and Stations, 27 April 1951, both in folder 71, box 10, ser. 1, ACNP(W), OA, NHC.

104. BuPers, "Personnel Statistics," 1960; Calendar Year Statistics: 1960.

105. Collins interview. Collins has recently published her own book telling of her naval career. See Winifred Quick Collins, with Herbert M. Levin, *More than a Uniform: A Navy Woman in a Navy Man's World* (College Station: University of North Texas Press, 1997).

## *Chapter 9. The Vietnam War and the 1960s*

1. *Statistical Abstract* (1961), 124; *Statistical Abstract* (1971), 127.
2. Ryan, *Womanhood,* 319; Weiner, *Working Girl,* 4.

3. Evans, *Born for Liberty*, 274–75; "American Women: Report of the President's Commission of the Status of Women: 1963." The wide-ranging report was generalized and somewhat patronizing. A progress report the next year described advances during the previous twelve months, in First Annual Report of the Interdepartmental Committee and Citizens' Advisory Council on the Status of Women, 12 October 1964, both reports in folder 107, box 17, ser. 1, ACNP(W), OA, NHC. WAVES Director Viola B. Sanders provided information on the status of the Navy's women, in Memo to Executive Secretary, DACOWITS, 15 January 1963, folder 4, box 1, ser. 1, Pers 00W Records, OA, NHC.

4. Friedan, *Feminine Mystique*, passim; O'Neill, *American High*, 44; Helen Z. Lopata, *Occupation: Housewife* (New York: Oxford University Press, 1971). More recently, Joanne Meyerwitz, "Beyond the Feminine Mystique: A Reassessment of Postwar Mass Culture, 1946–58," *JAH* 79 (March 1993): 1455–82, takes issue with Friedan, primarily on Friedan's interpretation of her sources. Meyerwitz found that popular media also stressed women's individual accomplishments as well as her domestic abilities.

5. Amy Swerdlow, *Women Strike for Peace: Traditional Motherhood and Radical Politics in the 1960s* (Chicago: University of Chicago Press, 1993), 1, 70, 130, 178, 264, 268; Evans, *Born for Liberty*, 284.

6. Rothman, *Proper Place*, 232, 235; Evans, *Born for Liberty*, 275–77; Chafe, *Women and Equality*, 96–97; Ryan, *Womanhood*, 309–10.

7. Kennedy, "Cold War Navy," 322–25; Curtis A. Utz, *Cordon of Steel: The U.S. Navy and the Cuban Missile Crisis* (Washington, D.C.: NHC, 1993), 14–15, 22–33, 36–39; Isenberg, *Shield of the Republic* 1:782–819. Also, Robert A. Divine, *The Cuban Missile Crisis* (Chicago: Quadrangle Books, 1971).

8. Miller, *U.S. Navy*, 395–401. For the complete naval story, see Edwin B. Hooper, Dean C. Allard, and Oscar P. Fitzgerald, *Setting the Stage*, vol. 1 of *The United States Navy and the Vietnam Conflict* (Washington, D.C.: Naval History Division, 1976); Marolda and Fitzgerald, *From Military Assistance to Combat: 1959–1965*, vol. 2 of *The United States Navy and the Vietnam Conflict* (Washington, D.C.: NHC, 1986); Frank Uhlig Jr., ed., *Vietnam: The Naval Story* (Annapolis, Md.: Naval Institute Press, 1988), and more recently, Edward J. Marolda, *By Sea, Air, and Land: An Illustrated History of the U.S. Navy and the War in Southeast Asia* (Washington, D.C.: NHC, 1994). In addition there are numerous specialized studies such as Edward J. Marolda, ed., *Operation End Sweep: A History of Minesweeping Operations in North Vietnam* (Washington, D.C.: NHC, 1993).

9. "U.S. Ship Force Levels, 1917–1989"; BuPers, "Personnel Statistics," 1960, 1969, and 1970.

10. Miller, *U.S. Navy*, 388–90; Kennedy, "Cold War Navy," 309, 314.

11. Floyd D. Kennedy Jr., "David Lamar McDonald: 1 August 1963–1 August 1967," in Love, *Chiefs of Naval Operations*, 346; "CNO—Since 1915, A Naval Career at Its Zenith," *All Hands*, July 1974, 5; Hone, *Power and Change*, 46, 48–49, 53–54, 67–68; Muir, *Black Shoes*, 153; Mason, *Organization*, 58–61. The six subcommands—Air

Systems, Ship Systems, Ordnance Systems, Supply Systems, Electronic Systems, and Faculties Engineering—made up the Naval Material Command.

12. BuPers, "Personnel Statistics." For a history of the draft, see George Q. Flynn, *The Draft: 1940–1973* (Lawrence: University Press of Kansas, 1993).

13. Holm, *Women in the Military*, 177.

14. "Nazi May Sue Navy's WAVES," *Washington Post*, 8 September 1965, p. B11.

15. Capt. Viola Brown Sanders, bio, Officer Bios, OA, NHC; folder 4 (bio data on Sanders), box 1, ser. 1, Pers 00W, OA, NHC; DOD News Release, 13 March 1962, Vertical File, Navy Dep't. Library; Fischer, ed., *Navy Women*, 42.

16. Capt. Viola Sanders to Jean Ebbert, 3 March 1986, copy in folder 1, box 1, CNO Study Group, OA, NHC.

17. Capt. Rita Lenihan bio, Officer Bios, OA, NHC; "Senorita Takes to the WAVES," *Washington Post*, 11 June 1966, p. C1; Leniham Oral History (USNI, 1970), 2–3, 7; folder 2 (bio data on Lenihan), box 1, ser. 1, Pers 00W Records, OA, NHC.

18. "The Captain Sets Her Sights on Arts, Oceanography," *Navy Times*, 19 July 1967, W1, W3.

19. Remarks of President Johnson, 28 April 1964; W. V. Combs to Rear Adm. John L. Alford, 24 September 1964, both in folder 34 (k), box 5, ser. 1, ACNP(W), OA, NHC.

20. Holm, *Women in the Military*, 163–64; The Role of Women as Military Persons—Why They Have to Be Military Instead of Civilians: Excerpts from Navy Reply to GAO Report, n.d., folder 34 (k), box 5, ser. 1, ACNP(W), OA, NHC; Sanders memo, 7 January 1965; Norman S. Paul, Assistant SecDef, to Harold H. Rubin, GAO, 2 March 1965, both in folder 4, box 9, ser. 3, Pers 00W Records, OA, NHC.

21. Memo for Deputy Under Secretaries of Military Departments, 13 October 1966, re Report of Inter-service Working Group on the Utilization of Women in the Armed Services, 31 August 1966, folder 106, box 17, ser. 1, ACNP(W), OA, NHC.

22. Stremlow, *Women Marines*, 71–72; Holm, *Women in the Military*, 188.

23. Sanders, Fact Sheet, April 1965, folder 34 (m), box 5, ser. 1, ACNP(W) Records, OA, NHC.

24. Excerpt from House Hearings, 15 February 1965, folder 34 (h), box 5, ser. 1, ACNP (W) Records, OA, NHC.

25. Enlisted Utilization, 1966, folder 106, box 17, ser. 1, ACNP(W) Records, OA, NHC.

26. Billings, *Grace Hopper*, 85–90; *Government Computer News*, 4 July 1986.

27. Helen F. Collins, "From Plane Captains to Pilots," *Naval Aviation News* (July 1977): 9.

28. Cdr. Sandra Doppelheuer House, interview with author, 26 February 1996; Personnel survey and Navy WAVE Recruit survey, 1965, folder 76, box 11, ser. 1, ACNP(W) Records, OA, NHC; Lenihan comments on agenda for recruiting conference, 26 April 1967, folder 9, box 9, ser. 3, Pers 00W Records, OA, NHC; "Girls, Too, Have Many Reasons for Choosing Service in the Navy," *Newport News Daily News*, 25 October 1967.

29. Herman, "Welcome Back BUMED," 15; BuPers, "Personnel Statistics," 1979; On-Board Navywide Statistics, folder 35 (6), box 33, ser. 6, NNC Records, OA, NHC; Hospital Corps Statistics, H.C. History folder, BuMed Archives.

30. Calendar Year Statistics: 1963, 1968; BuPers, "Personnel Statistics," 1963 and 1969. More details in Statistics for Surgeon General's Budget Back-Up Book (later called Black Book), 1962–1970, folder 44, box 36, ser. 6, NNC Records, OA, NHC.

31. Author phone conversation with Rear Adm. Mary F. Hall, 31 May 1998.

32. Erickson interview, 11 December 1995; Erickson bio, BuMed Archives.

33. Capt. Veronica M. Bulshefski bio, Officer Bios, OA, NHC; General Information—NNC, folder 27 (2), box 31, ser. 6, NNC Records, OA, NHC; *Who's Who in America: 1968–1969* (Chicago: A. N. Marquis, 1968), 329.

34. W. R. Smedberg III to Richard W. Parker, n.d., [after 7 November 1960]; same to same, 23 October 1961, both in folder 1 (1), box 8, ser. 3, NNC Records, OA, NHC.

35. Director, NNC, Conference, 14–16 October 1962, folder 27(2), box 31, ser. 6, NNC Records, OA, NHC.

36. Kalisch and Kalisch, *American Nursing*, 421–23; PL 88-581, 88th Cong., 2d sess., *Nurse Training Act of 1964;* Summary Provisions of the Nurse Training Act of 1964, folder 45, box 14, ser. 3, NNC Records, OA, NHC.

37. Kalisch and Kalisch, *American Nursing*, 432.

38. *Surgeon General's Report: 1962, 1963;* Medical Department Activities, October 1966, folder 1 (5), box 21, ser. 4, NNC Records, OA, NHC.

39. *Mediscope*, May 1967; Patricia Fellenz, "Nurses under the Sea," *U.S. Navy Medical News Letter* 51 (April 1968): 19–21; Alice L. Gaul, Robert E. Thompson, and George B. Hart, "The Nurse in Hyperbaric Medicine," all in folder 27, box 11, ser. 3, NNC Records, OA, NHC.

40. BuMed, "A Study of the Requirements for Registered Nurses in the Navy: 1965," folder 55 (7), box 16, ser. 3, NNC Records, OA, NHC.

41. "In Pursuit of Equity: Who Serves When Not All Serve," February 1967, 55, folder 64, box 18, ser. 3, NNC Records. In contrast, the ANA had supported legislation for drafting nurses in an emergency since 1952. Burke Marshall to Judith G. Whitaker, executive director, ANA, 15 September 1966; Whitaker to Marshall, 11 October 1966, both in folder 5, box 8, ser. 3, NNC Records, OA, NHC.

42. Folders 33 (2) and 33 (3) box 13, ser. 3, NNC Records, OA, NHC, are full of letters questioning why the NNC did not admit men nurses or charging the corps with discrimination.

43. PL 294, 84th Cong., 1st sess., *An Act to Authorize Male Nurses and Medical Specialists to Be Appointed as Reserve Officers*; P. G. Saylor, memo re: male nurses, 3 September 1964, folder 55 (7), box 16, ser. 3, NNC Records, OA, NHC.

44. Capt. Ruth Erickson, interview with author, 5 February 1996; New Horizons for Men Nurses in the NNC, n.d. [1964], folder 27 (2), box 31, ser. 6, NNC Records, OA, NHC.

45. Picture and clippings of George Silver, folder 33 (2); B. J. Semmes Jr., Chief

BuPers to Chief BuMed, 25 November 1964, folder 33 (1), both in box 13, ser. 3, NNC Records, OA, NHC.

46. History of the Nurse Corps; "Epochal Event," *Navy Times*, 3 January 1968, 12.

47. Memo, folder 33 (2), box 13, ser. 3; Profile—NNC, 1970 and 1971, folder 27 (7), box 31, ser. 6, all in NNC Records, OA, NHC.

48. Rear Adm. Maxine Conder, telephone interview with author, 2 November 1996, and Rear Adm. Ailene Duerk, telephone interview with author, 20 May 1998.

49. "Nurse Corps Chronology," 47; "Tornadoes Lash Hurricane Area," *New York Times*, 13 September 1961, p. A-1; Sterner, *Harm's Way*, 288. Lt. Cdr. Mariam Frank and Lt. (jg) Joan Helgendorff served in *Shangri-La;* Lt. Janice Langley and Lt. (jg) Mary Freeman were in *Antietam*, Always prolific writers, all these nurses wrote of their experiences—Langley and Freeman, "Texas Hurricane," and Frank and Hilgendorff, "Texas Hurricane," both in folder 15, box 10, ser. 3, NNC Records, OA, NHC.

50. "Storm Hits British Honduras; Winds and Tides Batter Belize," *New York Times*, 1 November 1961, p. A8; "99 Are Left Dead in British Honduras in Wake of Hurricane, *New York Times*, 2 November 1961, p. A1; *BUMED Newsletter*, 6 December 1961; "Navy Nurse Corps Officers Serve on Aircraft Carriers in Hurricane Disaster Relief Missions," both in folder 15, box 10, ser. 3, NNC Records, OH, NHC. Lt. Cdr. Audrey Fellabaum, Lt. (jg) Mary McArdle, Lt. (jg) Patricia Cope, and Ens. Joan Beasley were the nurses in *Antietam*. The four collaborated in "Report on Hurricane Hattie Disaster Relief: British Honduras," folder 15, box 10, ser. 3, NNC Records, OA, NHC.

51. "Nurse Corps Chronology," 47. Lt. (jg) Fesina E. Paradis and Lt. (jg) Lois L. McCue described their experiences in "Nursing Aspects of a Special U.S. Navy Medical Mission to the Republic of Honduras," folder 15, box 10, ser. 3, NNC Records, OA, NHC.

52. Information submitted to DACOWITS, n.d., folder 27 (2), box 31, ser. 6, NNC Records, OA, NHC; "You Have 15 Minutes to Pack," *All Hands*, December 1962, 6–10.

53. Holm, *Women in the Military*, 214, 216–17, 220, 223; Stremlow, *Women Marines*, 87.

54. For example, W. A. Lamm to Ora A. McKenzie, 7 September 1965, answering her letter of 26 August 1965; H. H. Epes Jr., memo, 2 December 1966, both in folder 7, box 11, ser. 3, Pers 00W Records, OA, NHC.

55. Assistant SecDef, press release, 10 February 1967, folder 7, box 11, ser. 3, Pers 00W Records, OA, NHC.

56. Kenneth L. Veth to M. F. Weisner, 24 July 1967; Weisner to Veth, 4 August 1967, both in folder 7, box 11, ser. 3, Pers 00W Records, OA, NHC.

57. Elizabeth G. Wylie to Lenihan, 5 August 1967; Lenihan to Wylie, 28 August 1967, both in folder 7, box 11, ser. 3, Pers 00W Records, OA, NHC.

58. Lenihan to DACOWITS Secretariat, 22 January 1968, folder 7, box 11, ser. 3, Pers 00W Records, OA, NHC; Ebbert and Hall, *Crossed Currents*, 158.

59. Information on other WAVES in Vietnam in Ebbert and Hall, *Crossed Currents*, 157–58.

60. "First Woman U.S. Navy Advisor Aids Dependents of Vietnamese Navymen," *All Hands*, July 1972, 53.

61. Author conversation with Capt. Jo Ann Watkins, 11 October 1996.

62. History of the Nurse Corps; Marolda and Fitzgerald, *Vietnam Conflict* 2:258; "Navy Hospital, Saigon," *All Hands*, May 1966, 13.

63. J. William Cox, memo re Nurse Officer Assignments in Vietnam, n.d. [after 12 May 1981]; N.C. Officers Assigned to Hedsuppact, Saigon, 5 December 1966, both in folder 46 (6); Alvina M. Harrison, "Military Nursing in Vietnam" folder 46 (5), all in box 36, ser. 6, NNC Records, OA, NHC. Bobbi Hovis, *Station Hospital, Saigon: A Navy Nurse in Vietnam*, 1963–1964 (Annapolis, Md.: Naval Institute Press, 1991), describes her 13 months in Saigon.

64. History of the NNC; Director, NNC, Activities Report, October 1965, folder 27 (2), box 31, ser. 6, NNC Records, OA, NHC; Kalisch and Scobey, "Helplessness Suspended," 29. Recipients of the Purple Heart were Lt. Ruth Ann Mason, Lt. Frances L. Crumpton, Lt. Barbara J. Wooster, and Lt. (jg) Ann D. Reynolds.

65. Bernadette A. McKay, "Surgical Team," folder 46(3); Winifred Copeland to Bulshefski, 30 March 1967, folder 46 (5), both in box 36, ser. 6, NNC Records, OA, NHC; H. H. Epes Jr. to Chief BuPers, 6 December 1966, folder 7, box 11, ser. 3, Pers 00W Records, OA, NHC; Elizabeth M. Norman, *Women at War: The Story of Fifty Military Nurses Who Served in Vietnam* (Philadelphia: University of Pennsylvania Press, 1990), 92.

66. Cox memo, folder 46 (6), box 36, ser. 6; BuMed Report [1967], folder 1 (5), box 21, ser. 4, both in NNC Records, OA, NHC.

67. Cox memo, folder 46 (6), box 36, ser. 6, NNC Records, OA, NHC. One male nurse, Lt. (jg) Roger Kline, wrote an interesting end-of-tour report on his duty at Cong Hoa General Hospital, in folder 46 (4), box 36, ser. 6, NNC Records, OA, NHC.

68. Conder telephone interview.

69. Edward J. Marolda, *By Sea, Air, and Land*, 251; *U.S. Naval Support Activity, Danang—1969*, 152.

70. BuMed Report, n.d. [1967], folder 1 (5), box 21, ser. 4, NNC Records, OA, NHC.

71. Bulshefski to Surgeon General, 27 April 1967; Background Information on Danang, n.d. [1967]; Nurse Corps Officers . . . Danang, n.d. [1968], all in folder 46 (2); Cox memo, folder 46 (6), all in box 36, ser. 6, NNC Records, OA, NHC. For a vivid account of the hospital during the Tet offensive, see Sterner, *Harm's Way*, 340.

72. Duerk interview; Conder telephone interview; Mary Cannon to Bulshefski, 6 November 1967, folder 46 (2), box 36, ser. 6, NNC Records, OA, NHC.

73. Cannon's letters, 8 August 1967 through 27 August 1968, and Bulshefski's replies all in folder 46 (2), box 36, ser. 6, NNC Records, OA, NHC.

74. Helen L. Brooks to Bulshefski, 27 August 1968 and ff., folder 46 (2), box 36, ser. 6, NNC Records, OA, NHC

75. F. J. Linehan to Surgeon General R. B. Brown, 8 April 1967, folder 46 (2), box 36, ser. 6, NNC Records, OA, NHC; Kalisch and Kalisch, *American Nursing*, 437–38.

For a good summary of Navy medical activities in Vietnam, see F. O. McClendon Jr., "Doctors and Dentists, Nurses and Corpsmen in Vietnam," *Naval Review: 1970* 96 (May 1970): 276–89.

76. "I Was There Too," interview, *Biarritz* (July 1980): 56–58; and "Joan Brouillette Recalls Vietnam," *NNCA News* 3 (March 1990): 12–13.

77. "Steinocher Shares VN Memories," *NNCA News* 3 (March 1990): 13–14.

78. History of the Nurse Corps; Director, NNC, Activities Report, October 1965; General Information—NNC, both in folder 27 (2), box 31, ser. 6, NNC Records, OA, NHC; *Repose*, in *DANFS* 6:78; History of Our Ship, in *Cruise Book—Repose, 1969–70;* McClendon, "Doctors," 283–84; "Angel of the Orient Returns," *All Hands*, April 1966, 5.

79. Cox memo; list of NC officers assigned to *Repose*, both in folder 46(6), box 36, ser. 6, NNC Records, OA, NHC.

80. "Navy Nurse at Sea," *All Hands*, July 1966, 21.

81. "The Angels of Vietnam," *Washington Post*, 11 November 1993, p. C-1.

82. *Sanctuary*, in *DANFS* 6:305; History of the USS *Sanctuary*, folder 62 (2), box 18, ser. 3; Erickson, General Information—NNC, 21 April 1966, folder 27 (2), box 31; list of NC officers scheduled for *Sanctuary*, 2 November 1966, folder 46 (6), box 36, both in ser. 6, all in NNC Records, OA, NHC. Following Marcella Smith as chiefs of nursing service were Cdr. Patricia Hurst (1968–69), Cdr. Ann O. Watson (1969–70), and Cdr. Janice M. Burcham (1970–71). Correspondence between Bulshefski and these nurses in folders 62 (2) and 62 (3), box 18, ser. 3, NNC Records, OA, NHC.

83. Cox memo, folder 46 (6), box 36, ser. 6, NNC Records, OA, NHC; McClendon, "Doctors," 284, 286. A good account of life aboard the hospital ships is in Norman, *Women at War*, 82–84. An interesting study found the highest rate of shipboard psychiatric cases (1,936 per 100.000 a year during the Vietnam War) occurred not in combatants but among the crews and medical staffs of hospital ships. E. K. Eric Gunderson, "Health and Adjustment of Men at Sea," in *The Social Psychology of Military Service*, ed. Nancy L. Goldman and David R. Segal (Beverly Hills: Sage Publications, 1976), 67–80.

84. Rear Adm. Frances Shea-Buckley, interview with author, 21 April 1997; R. R. Henderson, history written for 75th anniversary of NNC, n.d., "History" folder, ND Records, BuMed, 10–11.

85. Marolda, *By Sea, Air, and Land*, 235–39; Cox memo, folder 46 (6), box 36, ser. 6, NNC Records, OA, NHC; "Our Number One Mover," *All Hands*, October 1967, 2–6. For an interesting account by a nurse in *General W. A. Mann* in 1964, see Sterner, *Harm's Way*, 307–8.

86. Bulshefski memo, 6 November 1967; Military Awards to Navy Nurses, both in folder 8 (12), box 9, ser. 3, NNC Records, OA, NHC.

87. PL 90-130, 90th Cong., 1st sess., *An Act to Remove Restrictions on the Careers of Female Officers in the Army, Navy, Air Force, and Marine Corps*; Holm, *Women in the Military*, 200.

88. President's Remarks, 8 November 1967, in *Weekly Compilation of Presidential Documents,* folder 18 (6), box 28, ser. 6, NNC Records, OA, NHC.

89. The first six captains were Dorothy Council, Marie Kelleher, Alma Ellis, Mary Kate Bonds, Winifred Love, and Beatrice Truitt. In Ebbert and Hall, *Crossed Currents,* 162.

90. Ruth A. Houghton to Director, Bolte Task Force, 7 February 1961, folder 12, box 33, ser. 6, NNC Records, OA, NHC.

91. Medical Department Activities for October 1966, folder 1 (5), box 21, ser. 4, NNC Records, OA, NHC; PL 9-130, 90th Cong., 1st sess.; History of the Nurse Corps.

92. Pay and Allowances, *Navy Register,* 1960, xv; 1970, xvii–xviii.

93. Author phone conversation with Rear Adm. Mary F. Hall, 31 Mary 1998; Ebbert and Hall, *Crossed Currents,* 139.

94. Collins interview; Uniforms, Uniforms folder no. 72 (2), box 19, NNC Records, OA, NHC.

## *Chapter 10. Widening Horizons in the 1970s*

1. Ethel Kline, *Gender Politics: From Consciousness to Mass Politics* (Cambridge: Harvard University Press, 1984), 1, 2, 22; Evans, *Born for Liberty,* 278–79, 282–83; Ryan, *Womanhood,* 309–17; Chafe, *Women and Equality,* 98; Rothman, *Proper Place,* 245.

2. Ashley, "Nursing and Early Feminism," 70.

3. Evans, *Born for Liberty,* 291; Chafe, *Paradox of Change,* 215.

4. Evans, *Born for Liberty,* 291–92; Chafe, *Paradox of Change,* 216; Holm, *Women in the Military,* 290–91.

5. Material on International Women's Year in folders 9–12, box 5, ser. 3, Pers 00W Records, OA, NHC.

6. Chafe, *Paradox of Change,* 211; Rothman, *Proper Place,* 243.

7. *Statistical Abstract* (1971), 127; *Statistical Abstract* (1982–83), 160; Evans, *Born for Liberty,* 300. In 1970, only 8.4 percent of medical students and 5.4 percent of law students were women.

8. Bureau of Census, *Population Profile of the United States* (June 1981): 19; Evans, *Born for Liberty,* 302.

9. Ryan, *Womanhood,* 317–20; Weiner, *Working Girl,* 4, 96. Dee Ann Spencer, "Public Schoolteaching: A Suitable Job for a Woman," in *The Worth of Women's Work: A Quantitative Synthesis,* ed. Anne Statham, Eleanor M. Miller, and Hans O. Mauksch (Albany: State University of New York, 1988), 167–68, characterized careers such as school teaching and nursing as semiprofessional because women still lacked control and autonomy in their occupations.

10. Chafe, *Women and Equality,* 134; Chafe, *Paradox of Change,* 217–19.

11. Miller, *U.S. Navy,* 401–2; "U.S. Ship Force Levels, 1917–1989"; Norman

Friedman, "Elmo Russell Zumwalt, Jr., 1 July 1970–1 July 1974," in Love, *Chiefs of Naval Operations*, 371.

12. BuPers, "Personnel Statistics," 30 June 1970, 30 June 1972, 30 June 1979; *SecNav Report*, 1970, 61–62.

13. See Malcolm Muir Jr., *Black Shoes and Blue Water: Surface Warfare in the United States Navy, 1945–1975* (Washington, D.C.: NHC, 1996), 195–229, for a good summary of Zumwalt's tenure. Also, Elmo R. Zumwalt Jr., *On Watch: A Memoir* (New York: Quadrangle, 1976), for the CNO's version.

14. "The 20th CNO: Adm. James L. Holloway III, *All Hands*, July 1974, 6–7; Muir, *Black Shoes*, 203; Lawrence J. Korb, "The Erosion of American Naval Preeminence, 1962–1978," in Hagan, *In Peace and War*, 329, 331, 344.

15. Love, *History of the U.S. Navy* 2:645, 684; Muir, *Black Shoes*, 211–12, 214–20.

16. See John F. Guilmartin Jr., *A Very Short War: The "Mayaguez" and the Battle of Koh Tang* (College Station: Texas A & M University Press, 1995).

17. Love, *History of the U.S. Navy* 2:662–69, 676, 693, 698; Korb, "Erosion," 328. For more background, see Michael A. Palmer, *On Course to Desert Storm: The United States Navy and the Persian Gulf* (Washington, D.C.: NHC, 1992), 75–100.

18. Legal Interpretation of Equal Rights Amendment as reported in *Yale Law Review*, folder 17 (a), box 10, ser. 3, NNC Records; Mary Ann Tetreault, "Gender Belief Systems and the Integration of Women in the U.S. Military," *Minerva: Quarterly Report on Women and the Military* 6 (spring 1988): 62.

19. Elmo R. Zumwalt Jr., *On Watch* (New York: Quadrangle, 1977), 262; WAVE Retention Study Group, folder 4, box 13, ser. 3, Pers 00W Records, OA, NHC. For a brief summary of Zumwalt's accomplishments, see "Fair Winds and Following Seas: Admiral Zumwalt Retires as Chief of Naval Operations," *All Hands*, June 1974, 2–9.

20. Robin L. Quigley bio, Officer Bios, OA, NHC; other bio information in folder 3, box 1, ser. 1, Pers 00W Records, OA, NHC; "New WAVE Commander," *Washington Post*, 6 November 1970, B-3; "Air Force to Salute the Navy," *Washington Evening Star*, 16 December 1970, C-1; "Next WAVES Boss: Brunette and Shipshape," *Los Angeles Times*, 20 November 1970, IV-1, 6.

21. Quigley, memo from the director, no. 2, 31 March 1971, folder 1, box 9, ser. 3, Pers 00W Records; CNP to All Ships and Stations, 16 February 1972, folder 1, box 1, CNO Study Group on Women in the Navy Records; Quigley, Point Paper: Integration of Women in the Navy, n.d. [ca. July 1972], folder 4, box 1, ser. 2, Pers 00W Records, all at OA, NHC.

22. Quigley, memo 5, 23 February 1972, folder 1, box 1, CNO Study Group, and in folder 1, box 9, ser. 3, Pers 00W Records, both at OA, NHC; "Director of WAVES Doesn't Like Title," *Navy Times*, 1 December 1971, 39.

23. Melvin R. Laird, memo, 23 January 1973, folder 4, box 1, ser. 2, Pers 00W Records, OA, NHC; Zumwalt, *On Watch*, 262–63.

24. Adm. Elmo Zumwalt, interview with author, 23 September 1996.

25. Quigley, memo to DCNP, 13 March 1973, folder 4, box 1, ser. 2, Pers 00W

Records, OA, NHC. Quigley (to author, 21 September 1996) declined to be interviewed about her role.

26. Holm, *Women in the Military*, 283, 285, 287; "In the Military, War of Sexes Is All but Won," *Los Angeles Times*, 18 December 1978, 1.

27. Zumwalt memo for SecNav, 17 July 1972, folder 7, box 16, ser. 3, Pers 00W Records; and 3 September 1972, folder 1, box 3, CNO Study Group; R. L. Hazard memo, items for Ad Hoc Committee, 3 July 1972, folder 5, box 1, CNO Study Group, all at OA, NHC. Ebbert and Hall, *Crossed Currents*, 168, say that Quigley declined to attend committee meetings. Cf., Holm, *Women in the Military*, 281, who maintains that Quigley was deliberately excluded.

28. Rear Adm. Fran McKee, interview with author, 26 August 1996; Ad Hoc CNO Informal Study Group on Equal Rights for Women: Proposals for Consideration, n.d., folder 9, box 3, ser. 3, Pers 00W, OA, NHC.

29. Z-116, 7 August 1972, Navy Department Library, and in Congressional Quarterly, comp., *Historic Documents: 1972* (Washington, D.C.: Congressional Quarterly, 1973), 628–29; draft in folder 9, box 3, ser. 3, Pers 00W Records, OA, NHC; Zumwalt, *On Watch*, 263–64. For a summary of the results on women's opportunities from Z-116, see Georgia C. Sadler, "Women in the Sea Services: 1972–1982," *USNIP/Naval Review* 109 (May 1983): 144–45.

30. Transcript of news conference, 8 August 1972, Navy Department Library.

31. Zumwalt to SecNav, 1 September 1972, with enclosed plan of action; James E. Johnson to VCNO, 5 December 1972, both in folder 1, box 3, CNO Study Group Records, OA, NHC.

32. Quigley, Alternative Proposals Relative to Career Planning, 3 April 1972, folder 4, box 1, ser. 3, Pers 00W Records, OA, NHC; Ebbert and Hall, *Crossed Currents*, 168.

33. McKee interview; Rear Adm. Fran McKee bio, Officer Bio Files, OA, NHC; Shirley Wilson, "Selected for Line Rear Admiral," *All Hands*, March 1976, 22–23.

34. "An Interview with Your CNO," *All Hands*, December 1974, 4–5; draft of CNO Policy on Female Naval Personnel, n.d. [October 1976]; CNO to SecNav, 30 November 1976, both in folder 3 (2), box 6, ser. 3, Pers 00W Records, OA, NHC. More background in "The 20th CNO: Adm. James L. Holloway, III, *All Hands*, July 1974, 6–7. One wonders if this was merely lip service to the vague concept of equal opportunity. Holloway caused a flap when he appeared on the "Today Show," 13 October 1975, and said that the main Navy role for women was as wives of those who go to sea and as mothers of their children. Excerpt from "Today Show"; Josette L. Maxwell to President Gerald Ford, 14 October 1975; Holloway to Maxwell, 20 November 1975; L. C. Wilmot to DCNP, 3 December 1975, all in folder 4, box 1, ser. 2, Pers 00W Records, OA, NHC.

35. Author conversation with Capt. Jo Ann S. Watkins, 11 October 1996.

36. T. J. Kilcline to Women Line Officers, 21 October 1974, folder 6, box 16, ser. 3; W. L. McDonald memo, 9 May 1977; Vice Adm. James D. Watkins to Capt. Paul Butcher, 13 June 1977; Watkins to CNO, 14 November 1977; Butcher memo, 25 June

1977, 12 January 1978, and 21 March 1978, all in folder 5, box 1, ser. 3, Pers 00W Records, OA, NHC; Department of the Navy, *Navy Study Group's Report on Progress of Women in the Navy*, 5 December 1987, 1-35–1-36.

37. These included the Women's Policy Coordination Board, the Women's Career Pattern, Programs, and Policy Branch, and the Assistant to the DCNP for Human Resource Management.

38. Rear Adm. Roberta Hazard, telephone interview with author, 2 December 1996. Hazard credits Rear Adm. Fran McKee and Capt. Barbara Nyce with masterminding this change.

39. J. J. DiLorenzo to DCNO, 24 January 1985, Historical Perspective of OP-01W Position, folder 5, box 2, CNO Study Group, OA, NHC.

40. BuPers, "Personnel Statistics," 1970, 1979, and 1980.

41. A similar pattern occurred among male personnel. Officer/Enlisted Population by Sex/Ethnic, folder 1, box 4, ser. 3; M. L. Turner, Equal Opportunity in the Navy, February 1973, folder 2, box 9, ser. 3, both in Pers 00W Records, OA, NHC. A higher percentage of blacks were enlisted in the Army (33 percent) and Marines (22 percent) than in the Navy and Air Force, which had about 12 percent each. In Martin Binkin, *America's Volunteer Military: Progress and Prospects* (Washington, D.C.: Brookings Institution, 1984), 25. The pattern continued throughout the 1970s. L. E. Zierdt to CNO, 2 April 1980, folder 1, box 4, ser. 3, Pers 00W Records, OA, NHC.

42. John G. Finneran, memo, CO, Navy Recruiting Command, 8 May 1972, folder 9, box 9, ser. 3; G. E. R. Kinnear II, memo, Assistant Chief Enlisted Personnel Control, 13 January 1973, folder 1, box 1, ser. 2; T. O. Nutt Jr., memo, CO, Navy Recruiting Command, 8 November 1972, folder 1, box 1, ser. 2; Quigley, Fact Sheet, June 1972, box 1, ser. 1; J. William Middendorf II to Assistant SecDef, 23 June 1976, folder 4, box 6, ser. 3, all in Pers 00W Records, OA, NHC. By the end of the decade, the Navy was reconsidering the disparity of standards based on sex. J. R. Hogg to Special Assistant for Legal Affairs, 8 August 1979, folder 11, box 4, ser. 3, Pers 00W Records, OA, NHC.

43. Holm, *Women in the Military*, 262, 274. All the services were scurrying to follow a DOD directive, "Equal Opportunity Within the Dept. of Defense," December 1970; M. O. Wade to Deputy CNP, 11 September 1972, folder 2, box 6, ser. 3, Pers 00W Records, OA, NHC; Devilbiss, *Military Service*, 33–34.

44. New Release, 29 August 1979, and other documents on equal opportunity and race relations in folder 1, box 4, ser. 3, Pers 00W Records, OA, NHC.

45. Thomas, "Yeomenettes to WAVES," in Segal and Sinaiko, *Life in the Rank and File*, 100–101; Edna J. Hunter and Carol B. Million, "Women in a Changing Military," *USNIP* 103 (July 1977): 53.

46. Zumwalt interview.

47. Quigley, Fact Sheet, June 1972; Ebbert and Hall, *Crossed Currents*, 198.

48. SecNav Press Release, 8 February 1972; CNO to SecNav, n.d. [11 February 1972]; Emmett H. Tidd to CNP, 6 June 1972, all in folder 14, box 7, ser. 3, Pers 00W

Records, OA, NHC. Linda Rutledge was one early appointment to the NROTC at Penn State. She also wore the crown of Miss Junior Miss America for 1973. In "Miss Junior Miss Joins NROTC," *All Hands*, February 1974, 48–49.

49. R. W. Kennedy, "Navy Blue and Blond," *USNIP* 99 (August 1973): 50.

50. Quigley to CNP, 11 February 1972, folder 14, box 7, ser. 3, Pers 00W Records, OA, NHC.

51. Jacob K. Javits to SecNav, 22 September 1971; Quigley memo, 19 October 1971; Navy Press Release, 8 February 1972; DOD Press Conference, 8 February 1972, all in folder 13, box 7, ser. 3, Pers 00W Records, OA, NHC.

52. S. Concurrent Resolution 71, 92d Cong., 2d sess., 28 March 1972.

53. David H. Bagley to Deputy Chiefs of Staff, 13 November 1972, folder 1, box 1, ser. 2, Pers 00W Records, OA, NHC.

54. PL 94-106, 94th Cong., 1st sess., *Appropriations Act for FY 1976*, Title VIII, sec. 803; U.S. Naval Academy, Press Release, 9 October 1975, folder 73 (a), box 20, ser. 3, NNC Records, OA, NHC; "Coed Service Academies," editorial, *Retired Officer* (September 1975). See Holm, *Women in the Military*, 305–12, and Ebbert and Hall, *Crossed Currents*, 200–206, for good accounts.

55. "Naval Academy Class of 1980 Will Be Fully Integrated," *USNIP* 102 (April 1976): 117–19; "Here's What Female Mids Will Wear," *Navy Times*, 17 December 1975, 14, has photos.

56. Kinnaird R. McKee to William L. Maloy, 22 December 1976, in Utilization of Women in the Military, pt. 1, folder 2, box 13, ser. 3, Pers 00W Records, OA, NHC.

57. NAVPERS, *Women in the Navy Information Book* (1979), 56–58, folder 7, box 1, CNO Study Group, OA, NHC; "So Far, So Good: A Report Card on Coed Military Academies," *U.S. News & World Report*, 11 July 1977, 26–31; Ebbert and Hall, *Crossed Currents*, 202–4. Rick Atkinson, *The Long Gray Line* (Boston: Houghton Mifflin, 1989), 403, 408–10, 413, 522, describes experiences of the first class with women at West Point. Carol Barkalow, *In the Men's House* (New York: Poseidon, 1990), gives a more graphic account.

58. One member of that first class has recently written of her experiences. Sharon Hanley Disher, *First Class: Women Join the Ranks at the Naval Academy* (Annapolis, Md.: Naval Institute Press, 1998). Disher served in the Civil Engineer Corps for ten years before retiring to raise her family.

59. Training—Bainbridge, folder 3, box 12; Quigley, Women in the Navy, 1 May 1972, folder 2, box 9, both in ser. 3, Pers 00W Records, OA, NHC; "Navy News," *All Hands*, July 1972, 48.

60. BuPers, "Personnel Statistics," June 1979; BuPers, Women in the Navy by Rate, 31 March 1979; *Report on Progress* (1987), 1-10–1-11; Hunter and Million, "Women," 54.

61. Quigley, Fact Sheet, June 1972; C. E. Mackey, memo re School Guarantee Program, 28 April 1972, folder 9, box 9, ser. 3; Zumwalt, memo re minority WAVE participation, 13 March 1972, folder 11, box 7, ser. 3, both in Pers 00W Records, OA, NHC.

62. *Report on Progress* (1987), 2-29–2-34, 2-40–2-45; Martin Binkin and Shirley J. Bach, *Women and the Military* (Washington, D.C.: Brookings Institution, 1977), 26. As early as 1967, the Navy had begun considering revamping the designator system so that all women officers without staff corps specialties would fall into the unrestricted line officer designation. D. B. Bell to VCNO, 1 March 1967, folder 4, box 1, ser. 3, Pers 00W Records, OA, NHC.

63. Ebbert and Hall, *Crossed Currents*, 206–7; BuPers, "Personnel Statistics," 1979.

64. William F. R. Gilroy and Timothy J. Demy, *A Brief Chronology of the Chaplain Corps of the United States Navy* (Washington, D.C.: NAVPERS, 1983), 35; "Women in Naval Chaplaincy," *Navy Chaplain* 1 (winter 1987): 3; BuPers, "Personnel Statistics," 1979. More on the chaplains in John Coleman, "Navy Chaplains: Nearly Two Centuries of Providing Encouragement, Comfort, and Inspiration," *All Hands*, April 1974, 22–27; Bruce Friedland, "For God and Country," *Military Lifestyle* (February 1986): 38–39, 65–66.

65. *Report on Progress* (1987), 1-12–31-13; "Kathy's Here at Adak," *All Hands*, February 1974, 50; Bill Wedertz, "Women in the Navy: Jobs They Do," *All Hands*, July 1972, 11. One station, Roosevelt Roads, became top-heavy with enlisted women, and the Atlantic Fleet commander questioned the wisdom of assigning so many to the station. CINCLANTFLT to CNO, 29 June 1979, folder 11, box 4, ser. 3, Pers 00W Records, OA, NHC.

66. Holm, *Women in the Military*, 329–32; Assistant SecDef (Manpower), America's Volunteers: A Report on the All-Volunteer Armed Forces, 31 December 1978, 301–3, folder 7, box 18, ser. 4; Lt. (jg) Joellen M. Drag to SecNav, 4 March 1976, requesting sea duty as a helicopter pilot; Louise C. Wilmot to Assistant Head, Sea Assignment Supervisor, 13 July 1976, both in folder 4, box 6, ser. 3, all in Pers 00W Records, OA, NHC; DOD, *Background Study: Use of Women in the Military*, 2d ed., September 1978, d, 38, folder 43 (3), box 35, ser. 6, NNC Records, OA, NHC.

67. James D. Watkins to CNO, 12 April 1976, 6 May 1976, folder 3 (1); CNO to SecNav, July 1976, folder 4, all in box 6, ser. 3, Pers 00W Records, OA, NHC; Mitzi Wertheim to SecNav, 30 August 1977, folder 2; C. W. Duncan Jr. to Walter F. Mondale, 14 February 1978, folder 1, both in box 3, CNO Study Group, OA, NHC; draft of bill, 11 January 1978, folder 5, box 13; SecNav Instruction 1300.1, folder 1 (2), box 16, both in ser. 3, Pers 00W Records, OA, NHC.

68. Adm. Thomas B. Hayward, memo to SecNav, 11 December 1979, folder 2, box 4, CNO Study Group, OA, NHC.

69. Maria S. Higgins to NMPC-03, 26 July 1979; Higgins to OP-13, 1 August 1979; J. R. Hogg to Director, Management Control, 23 February 1980, all in folder 4, box 6, ser. 3; CNO to Deputy SecNav, n.d. [December 1979], folder 1, box 4, ser. 3, all in Pers 00W Records, OA, NHC; Congressional Hearings Resumes, 13, 14, 15, 16 November 1979, folder 2, box 3, CNO Study Group Records, OA, NHC; and summaries in P. M. Gormley to Chief, Legislative Affairs, 21 November 1979, folder 11, box 4, ser. 3, Pers 00W Records, OA, NHC. DACOWITS had come out strongly for repeal at its fall meeting, recommendations in folder 2, box 3, CNO Study Group, OA, NHC.

70. "Women Line Officers Assigned to Duty in Hospital Ship," *USNIP* 98 (November 1972): 118–19; T. A. Rodgers, Report on the Evaluation of the Assignment of Women to the USS *Sanctuary* (AH 17), 1 October 1972–31 October 1973, 19 November 1973; Susan B. Canfield memo, 3 January 1974, both in folder 1, box 3, CNO Study Group, OA, NHC; C. F. Rauch Jr. to CNP, Evaluation of Women in USS *Sanctuary*, 9 September 1974, folder 3, box 10, ser. 3, Pers 00W Records, OA, NHC; Binkin and Bach, *Women and the Military*, 93–99.

71. L. C. Wilmot, Effects of Decommissioning USS *Sanctuary*, 31 March 1975, folder 4, box 6, ser. 3, Pers 00W Records, OA, NHC.

72. J. C. Wylie to Quigley, 3 May 1972, 3 May 1972, folder 1, box 3, CNO Study Group, OA, NHC; Quigley to Wylie, 9 May 1972, folder 7, box 3, ser. 3, Pers 00W Records, OA, NHC.

73. JAG to CNP, 7 November 1972, folder 1, box 3, CNO Study Group, OA, NHC.

74. JAG to Vice Adm. Bagley, 28 March 1975, folder 6, box 16, ser. 3, Pers 00W Records, OA, NHC; Ebbert and Hall, *Crossed Currents*, 218–19; Holm, *Women in the Military*, 330.

75. H. E. Reichert to CNO, 31 January 1975, folder 6, box 16; G. L. Hurt to Commander Air Force Eastern Test Range, 9 May 1975, folder 4, box 6, both in ser. 3, Pers 00W Records, OA, NHC; "Gals: Join the AF and Go to Sea!" *Navy Times*, 31 December 1975, 17; "Coast Guard Names Second Group of Women for Sea Duty," *Navy Times*, 8 August 1977, 3.

76. T. H. Miller, WIN Structured Plan, 28 November 1977, folder 9, box 4; ADCNO (Manpower), to Implement Navy-Sponsored Amendment, 12 April 1978, folder 1 (2), box 16, both in ser. 3, Pers 00W Records, OA, NHC.

77. "Women Aboard *Spear*," *All Hands*, February 1980, 12; "She Changed Her Wardrobe: SA Mary Cobb," *All Hands*, December 1980, 44–45.

78. Assistant SecDef News Release, 24 October 1978; "Women on Sea Duty," *All Hands*, November 1978, 7; SecNav Instruction 1300.12, 18 April 1979, folder 5, box 1, CNO Study Group, OA, NHC; *Report on Progress* (1987), 1-23–1-24.

79. For example, Douglas R. Burnett, "The Sexually-Integrated Warship Can't Be the Most Combat-Effective Warship," *USNIP* 103 (April 1977): 90–91; letters to editor, *USNIP*, from John L. Byron, February 1979, 82–84; Charles O. Cook Jr., February 1979, 84; Jeffrey P. Simpson, March 1979, 79–80.

80. Rodgers, Report on the Evaluation of the Assignment of Women to the USS *Sanctuary*, 13–2; *Information Book*, 82–83.

81. Quigley, "Women Aboard Ships: A Few Observations," *Sea Power* 20 (May 1977): 16–18; excerpted in *USNIP* 104 (October 1978): 52–53, as "A Requirement to Serve." Also, Dimity L. Graichen, "Some Drawbacks to Women at Sea," *Navy Times*, 11 April 1977, 15.

82. For example, James F. Kelly Jr., "Women in Warships: A Right to Serve," *USNIP* 104 (October 1978): 44–52; "First Women Report to Navy Ships," *Wifeline* (winter 1979): 1–2.

83. The Army, the Air Force, and the Marine Corps had no similar programs in

1972. Memo to CNP with paper on Women in Military Aviation, 21 October 1972, folder 1, box 1, ser. 2, Pers 00W Records, OA, NHC; CHINFO Newsgram, November 1972; Holm, *Women in the Military*, 317, 319, 321.

84. Collins, "Captains to Pilots," 9, 12–13; Sandy Russell, "Womanpower in Naval Aviation: 20 Years of Progress," *Naval Aviation News* (September–October 1992): 13, 19; Douglas, *Women in Aviation*, 99–100. The other four pioneering women were Jane Skiles, JoEllen Drag, Rosemary Conatser, and Anna Scott.

85. *Report on Progress* (1987), 1-25, 1-27, 1-29; Collins, "Captains to Pilots," 13–14. The third group skipped the Officer Candidate School at Newport and was instead sent to Aviation Officer Candidate School at Pensacola.

86. F. D. Koon, CNO's office, to CNP, 16 March 1976; James D. Watkins to CNO, 19 May 1976, both in folder 3 (1), box 6, ser. 3, Pers 00W Records, OA, NHC; "Combat Laws Clip Wings of Navy's Women Pilots," *Navy Times*, 16 January 1978, 2.

87. A. A. Bradick to Fay Marles, 19 September 1978, folder 1 (2), box 14, ser. 3, Pers 00W Records, OA, NHC; Lee W. Coleman, "Getting the Good Things in Life," *All Hands*, April 1981, 46–47; Ebbert and Hall, *Crossed Currents*, 245, 249.

88. Collins, "Captains to Pilots," 9.

89. DACOWITS, 30th Anniversary Meeting, 26–30 April 1981, F-7; Russell, "20 Years," 13; "Flight Wings for Linda," *All Hands*, July 1974, 44–45; *Report on Progress* (1987), 1-28–1-30; Collins, "Captains to Pilots," 16.

90. BuPers, "Personnel Statistics," 1979, and 30 September 1990, with summaries; Hospital Corps Data, H.C. History, Manpower, and Staffing folder, BuMed Archives; Melvin Museles, "Current Status of Medical Department Manpower," *U.S. Navy Medicine* 70 (November 1979): 9–12; John E. Carr, "Medical Corps Status Report," *U.S. Navy Medicine* 70 (November 1979): 12–15.

91. By 1979, there were 17 naval hospitals, 32 regional medical centers, 3 regional medical clinics, and 22 regional dental centers. Listed in BuPers Directory, May 1979, BuMed Archives; "BUPERS Completes Reorganization," *U.S. Naval Medicine* 70 (May 1979): 10–17.

92. Department of the Navy, *Organization Manual*, 1976, 32-1–32-2; "Naval Regional Medical Center," *Navy in Newport*, 20–21; Organization—BuMed, 4 August 1975, folder 7, box 25, ser. 6, NNC Records, OA, NHC.

93. PL 92-158, 92d Cong., 1st sess., *Nurse Training Act of 1971*; PL 94-63, 94th Cong., 1st sess., *Nurse Training of 1975*; PL 96-76, 96th Cong., 1st sess., *Nurse Training Amendments of 1979*.

94. Kalisch and Kalisch, *American Nursing*, 446–51.

95. Ibid., 458–59.

96. Ibid., 453–57. The Nurse Training Act of 1975 provided funding to train nurse practitioners.

97. Mary C. Corley and Hans O. Mauksch, "Registered Nurses, Gender, and

Commitment," in Statham, Miller, and Mauksch, *Worth of Women's Work*, 136–37, 146–47; Ada M. Gugenheim, "Nursing Focuses on Education," *Hospitals* (1 April 1980): 151.

98. Duerk interview; Duerk bio, Officers Bio Files, OA, NHC; Sterner, *Harm's Way*, 351–52; Robert Neil, "Navy's First Lady Admiral," *All Hands*, July 1972, 2–5; "Alene B. Duerk," in Dever and Dever, *Women and the Military*, 130; Robert J. Boylan, "The Admiral with the Healer's Hands," *Sea Power* (June 1972): 36.

99. Rear Adm. Maxine Conder bio, Officers Bio Files, OA, NHC; Sterner, *Harm's Way*, 377–78; "Rear Admiral Conder Retires," *U.S. Navy Medicine* 70 (May 1979): 6–8. For Conder's views on the NNC, see Maxine Conder, "Open Letter to Nurse Corps Officers," *U.S. Navy Medicine* 68 (May 1977): 2–5.

100. Duerk interview; "Nurse Corps Chief Finds White Shoes Navy Healthy," *Navy Times*, 19 July 1976, 4, 40.

101. The text promised nurses they could go where they wanted, live as they wanted, do what they wanted in nursing fields because "most females get their way." Sharron Frontiero to [BuMed], 25 September 1972; Elizabeth M. Pfeffer to Naval Recruiting Command, 3 October 1972; Patricia Reuss ltr., 16 October 1972; Pfeffer to Reuss, 31 October 1972, all in folder 32, box 12, ser. 3, NNC Records, OA, NHC. By 1973, Grey Medical Advertising had taken over advertising for the corps. Material in folder 21, box 11, ser. 3, NNC Records, OA, NHC.

102. Procurement and Information Branch, Nursing Division, 19 December 1973; Professional Branch, Nursing Division, 17 March 1976, both in folder 29, box 32, ser. 6, NNC Records, OA, NHC.

103. Duerk, Status of the ADN Graduate in the United States Navy Nurse Corps, 4 March 1971, folder 2 (1), box 25, ser. 6, NNC Records, OA, NHC; "Nurse Corps Chronology"; Margaret Barton, "The Navy Nurse Corps: Eighty Years of Service, Professionalism, and Spirit," *U.S. Navy Medicine* 79 (May–June 1988): 14–15.

104. Summary of Education Programs, *All Hands*, July 1972, 28.

105. Calendar Year Statistics: 1970, folder 5, box 25, ser. 6, NNC Records, OA, NHC. Figures vary according to source. BuPers, "Personnel Statistics," 30 June 1970, lists 2,050 nurses. BuPers, "Personnel Statistics," 1979; Profile: Navy Nurse Corps, 1970, folder 27 (7), box 31; Professional Health Manpower Personnel, FY 79, folder 19 (8), box 29, both in ser. 6, NNC Records, OA, NHC.

106. Duerk telephone interview and Shea telephone interview.

107. CNP to Chief BuMed, 3 May 1971; Surgeon General G. M. Davis to CNO, 4 October 1971; Anna M. Byrnes to R. L. Toney, 23 June 1971; "The Navy Nurse: Honored . . . Respected" [aimed at the black community], all in folder 4, box 16a, ser. 3, NNC Records, OA, NHC. These efforts continued throughout the 1970s: "A Plan to Boost Minority Recruiting," *Navy Times*, 19 July 1976, 54; W. P. Arentzen, BuPers Instruction 1500.12B, 11 July 1977, folder 8a, box 9, ser. 3, NNC Records, OA, NHC.

108. Nurse Corps Chronology; Duerk to CNP, 9 April 1974, folder 12, box 7, ser. 3, Pers 00W Records, OA, NHC; Jerry Acthison, "Captain Joan Bynum: A Matter of Setting Goals," *All Hands*, February 1979, 14–19; Carnegie, *Path We Tread*, 177–78.

109. Nurse Corps Profile, 1970. Duerk resisted proposals to admit graduates of nonaccredited nursing schools and to procure associate degree nurses. In VCNO to Chief BuPers, 20 September 1971, folder 4, box 16(a) ser. 3; Duerk to Code 34, 26 May 1971; G. M. Davis to Assistant SecDef, 1 July 1971, both in folder 2 (1), box 25, ser. 6, all in NNC Records, OA, NHC. The defense of degreed nurses continued in NNC Position Paper, 1973, folder 15 (a), box 10, ser. 3; Duerk to Code 3, 10 January 1974, folder 55 (5), box 15, ser. 3; Abstracting Position Paper, 1976, folder 2 (3), box 25, ser. 6, all in NNC Records, OA, NHC.

110. *U.S. Navy Recruiting Manual*, with change no. 5 (1970); NAVPERS 15838 (1963).

111. Study on the Recruitment of Medical Professionals for the Military Services, April 1976, V-7, folder 38 (5), box 34, ser. 6, NNC Records, OA, NHC.

112. Student Regulations for Naval Women Officers School, 1971, folder 38, box 13, ser. 3; Chief Naval Training, to Chief BuPers, 4 May 1973; Duerk to Chief Naval Technical Training, 15 April 1974, both in folder 13 (2), box 13, ser. 6, all in NNC Records, OA, NHC.

113. Nurse practitioners differ from physicians' assistants in that the latter worked under the supervision and direction of a licensed physician—in effect, physician extenders, not substitutes. The Navy began utilizing them in the early 1970s. CO, Naval Medical School, to Surgeon General, 13 November 1970; Robert Jewett, "Characteristics of Physician's Assistant Programs," photocopy; The Navy's Physician's Assistant, all in folder 31, box 32, ser. 6, NNC Records, OA, NHC.

114. "The Navy PNP: Pediatric Nurse Practitioner," and "The OB-GYN Nurse Practitioner," both in *U.S. Navy Medicine* 59/60 (May 1972): 4–7, 8–9; "The Nurse Practitioner," *U.S. Navy Medicine* 69 (October 1978): 8–13; Duerk to Surgeon General, 5 February 1974, folder 55 (5), box 15, ser. 3; Naval Hospital and NRMC . . . Staffing Shortfalls, October 1975, folder 19 (4), box 29, ser. 6, both in NNC Records, OA, NHC; Sterner, *Harm's Way*, 360–61. More in folder 6550.5a (Nurse Practitioners), ND Records, BuPers.

115. Mary Nielubowicz to Code 0011, 1 October 1976; Nurse Corps Operational Medicine Workshop, n.d., both in folder 13 (6), box 27, ser. 6, NNC Records.

116. Maxine Conder to Code 0011, 18 October 1977, folder 13 (2), box 13; R. G. Williams Jr. to BuPers Codes, 2 March 1978, folder 9, box 25; F. T. Shea to Med-11, 22 August 1979, folder 13 (7), box 27, all in ser. 6, NNC Records, OA, NHC.

117. NC Yearly On Board Strength, 1964–1978, folder 35 (7), box 33, ser. 6, NNC Records, OA, NHC.

118. *U.S. Navy Medicine* 70 (September 1979): 28.

119. Duerk speech, 18 November 1972, folder 62 (2), box 18, ser. 3, NNC Records, OA, NHC.

120. Phyllis A. Butler to Duerk, 6 November 1973, folder 62 (1), box 18, ser. 3, NNC Records, OA, NHC. An account by Butler also in Sterner, *Harm's Way*, 362–63.

121. CNO to Distribution List, 27 February 1978, folder 43 (4), box 35, ser. 6, NNC Records, OA, NHC.

122. Nurse Corps Chronology; Conder, presentation at conference, 29 October 1975, folder 32a, box 12, ser. 3, NNC Records, OA, NHC; "Top Navy Nurse," *Stars and Stripes*, 7 May 1977, 1.

123. E. J. Carroll to L. R. Bell Davies, 4 December 1973; K. C. D. Watson to ADCNO, 20 December 1973; Janice A. Emal to Sara Tolar, 10 April 1974; Carroll to Davies, 19 April 1974; letter from "Sara" [Tolar], 15 January 1975, all in folder 36, box 33, ser. 6, OA, NHC.

124. "Women in Navy Medicine": "Doctors"; "Nurses"; "Hospital Corps"; "Dentists"; "Medical Service Corps," 5-part article, *All Hands*, July 1972, 22–33; Carr, "Medical Corps," 13; BuPers, "Personnel Statistics," September 1979.

125. Zumwalt interview; PL 90-130,, 90th Cong., 1st sess.; Holm, *Women in the Military*, 202–3; material on these admirals in Officer Bios Files, OA, NHC.

126. Nancy L. Lundquist to Mary A. Gore, 29 January 1979, with summary of events; JAG opinion, 30 July 1979, all in folder 5, box 1, CNO Study Group, OA, NHC.

127. The JAG had always supported this interpretation; for example, JAG to Chief of Information, 22 October 1959; JAG to CO, Naval Hospital, Charleston, 15 November 1963, both in folder 5, box 16, ser. 3, Pers 00W Records, OA, NHC.

128. *Navy News*, 2 May 1975; Ebbert and Hall, *Crossed Currents*, 145, 158, 198–99, 209–10; Rear Adm. Pauline M. Hartington bio, Officers bios, OA, NHC. Other early commanding officers included Capt. Ruth Tomsuden of the Navy Food Service System; Capt. Sarah Koestline of Personnel Accounting Machine Installation, Norfolk; Capt. Fran McKee of the Naval Security Group Activity, Fort Meade; Capt. Mary Gore of a Navy Recruiting District; and Capt. Lucille Kuhn of the Officer Candidate School, Newport. In 1979 Kuhn became commander of the recruit training center at Orlando.

129. McKee interview.

130. Information in NNC Personnel folder, BuMed Archives.

131. *Navy Register: 1970*, xvii–xviii; Monthly Basic Pay, 1 October 1979, *All Hands*, November 1979, 28.

132. Lt. (jg) Sharon K. Lieblich filed suit, *Sharon K. Lieblich v. United States*, in 1968 to recover expenses she incurred supporting her husband, who was a full-time law student, but the GAO rejected her claims. In O. R. Carpenter to Edwin L. Weial Jr., 15 November 1968, folder 2, box 1, CNO Study Group, OA, NHC.

133. House interview; Sandra B. Doppelheuer to Comptroller General, 17 February 1972; Chief BuMed endorsement, 13 March 1972; CNP endorsement, 13 April 1972, all in Sandra Doppelheuer House private collection; comptroller general's decision, 3 July 1972; W. S. Thompson to CNP, 18 July 1972, both in folder 2, box 6, ser. 3, Pers 00W Records, OA, NHC; DOD had been trying since 1971 to have the law changed to permit spouses of female service members to be presumptive dependents. J. Fred Buzhardt to F. Edward Hebert, Chairman House Armed Services Committee, March 1971; Buzhardt to John C. Stennis, Chairman Senate Armed Services Committee, 30 November 1971, both in folder 2, box 6, ser. 3, Pers 00W Records, OA, NHC.

134. Edna J. Hunter and Carol B. Million, "Women in a Changing Military," *USNIP* 103 (July 1977): 54–55; Holm, *Women in the Military,* 290–91; Devilbiss, *Women and Military Service,* 13–14.

135. Quigley to CNP, 23 February 1971; various BuPers responses during March–June 1971; Duerk to Quigley, 3 June 1971, all in folder 1 (1), box 3, ser. 3, Pers 00W Records, OA, NHC.

136. BuPers Notice, with enclosure, 10 February 1972; Quigley memo, 5 July 1972, both in folder 1 (3), box 3, ser. 3, Pers 00W Records, OA, NHC; Sadler, "Sea Services," 146.

137. *Cook v. Arentzen.* Lt. Cdr. Alice C. Cook, a Navy nurse, had been unwillingly released from the Navy in 1967 after she learned she was pregnant. She reentered the Nurse Corps as a lieutenant in the Reserves in 1971. After exhausting administrative remedies, in 1973 Cook filed suit for reinstatement in the regular Navy, the rank of commander, and back pay. In January 1976 a federal district judge dismissed her suit. C. R. Davis, JAGC, enclosing interrogatories, *Cook v. Arentzen,* 20 November 1974, folder 3 (1); JAG to CNP, enclosing opinion, 15 January 1976, folder 3 (2), all in box 6, ser. 3, Pers 00W Records, OA, NHC. The Cook case was but one of several in the early 1970s challenging military pregnancy/dependency discharge regulations.

138. BuPers Notice 1900, 1 August 1975; section 3810170, BuPers Manual, January 1976, both in folder 5, box 9, ser. 3, Pers 00W Records, OA, NHC.

139. Devilbiss, *Women and Military Service,* 15.

140. Quigley memo, 1 May 1972, folder 9; N. J. Hampson, Counseling Guidance for Female Enlistees, 5 February 1976, folder 5, both in box 9, ser. 3, Pers 00W Records, OA, NHC; Pete Sundberg, "Sharing Life . . . on and off the Job," *All Hands,* June 1979, 6–13.

141. *Report on Progress* (1987), 3–1; Sandra H. Carey, *Sourcebook on Sexual Harassment* (Washington, D.C.: Naval Military Personnel Command, 1982), 3, folder 3, box 19, ser. 4, Pers 00W Records, OA, NHC.

142. Louanne Johnson, "This Man's Navy," *Minerva: Quarterly Report on Women and the Military* 6 (fall 1988): 12–25; Carey, *Sourcebook,* 20; Holm, *Women in the Military,* 70.

143. Joyce Z. Fessler to Thomas B. Hayward, 16 April 1979; Hayward to Fessler, 10 July 1979, both in folder 5, box 1, CNO Study Group, OA, NHC.

144. Tracy Timmons, "We're Looking for a Few Good Men": The Impact of Gender Stereotypes on Women in the Military," *Minerva: Quarterly Report on Women and the Military* 10 (summer 1992): 25–26; Ebbert and Hall, *Crossed Currents,* 188–90. So far, naval records have revealed no figures on actual numbers of lesbians or on their rate of discharge from the Navy.

145. Department of the Navy, *Uniform Regulations, United States Navy: 1975* (Washington, D.C.: GPO, 1975), and changes of 30 June 1976, 3-1–3-6, 3-13, 3-29–3-33; "A Change in the Service Dress Uniform for Enlisted Women," *All Hands,* July 1972, 53; Department of the Navy, *Uniform Regulations, United States Navy: 1978* (Washington, D.C.: GPO, 1978), 2-17–2-28, 2-85–2-88.

146. R. L. Hazard, Talking Paper on Women in the Navy, 31 August 1979, folder 2, box 3, CNO Study Group, OA, NHC.

147. Beth F. Coye, "We've Come a Long Way, But . . . ," *USNIP* 105 (July 1979): 48, calls the time wrong and points to a resulting fragmented administration and management.

148. Coye, "Long Way," 46, 48.

## *Chapter 11. Women's New Roles in the 1980s*

1. Evans, *Born for Liberty*, 306, 312.

2. *Statistical Abstract* (1982–83), 160; National Center for Education Statistics, *Digest of Education Statistics: 1991* (Washington, D.C.: GPO, 1991), 167; National Center for Education Statistics, *Digest of Education Statistics: 1993* (Washington, D.C.: GPO, 1993), 174; Ryan, *Womanhood*, 318.

3. Bureau of the Census, *Marital Status and Living Arrangements: March 1989*, Current Population Reports, ser. P-20, no. 445 (Washington, D.C.: GPO, 1990); and Bureau of the Census, *Fertility of American Women: June 1990*, Current Population Reports, ser. P-20, no. 454 (Washington, D.C.: GPO, 1991).

4. "Women Gaining at Work," *Newport News Daily Press*, 3 January 1997, C7; Chafe, *Paradox of Change*, 222.

5. Kline, *Gender Politics*, 167; Ruth Needleman and Anne Nelson, "Policy Implications: The Worth of Women's Work," in Statham, Miller, and Mauksch, *Worth of Women's Work*, 294, 296; Sheila K. Collins, "Women at the Top of Women's Fields: Social Work, Nursing, and Education," in Statham, Miller, and Mauksch, *Worth of Women's Work*, 200.

6. Evans, *Born for Liberty*, 307–8, 310; Ryan, *Womanhood*, 328. Yuppie = young, upwardly mobile professional.

7. Kline, *Gender Politics*, 166, 169; Evans, *Born for Liberty*, 310.

8. Weiner, *Working Girl*, 36; "Women's Pay Still Trails Men's," *Newport News Daily Press*, 30 July 1996, p. C5.

9. Evans, *Born for Liberty*, 311.

10. "U.S. Ship Force Levels, 1917–1989"; Muir, *Black Shoes*, 231–33.

11. BuPers, "Personnel Statistics," June 1980 and June 1990; BuPers, Annual Report, 30 September 1990. The Navy and the other armed services depended on an all volunteer force to meet their requirements.

12. "The Men at the Helm," *All Hands*, August 1986, 16–17; "CNO Shares His Thoughts," *All Hands*, April 1981, 3, 5, 7.

13. Thomas C. Hone, *Power and Change: The Administrative History of the Office of the Chief of Naval Operations, 1946–1986* (Washington, D.C.: NHC, 1989), 113–25; Floyd K. Kennedy Jr., "From SLOC Protection to a National Maritime Strategy: The U.S. Navy under Carter and Reagan, 1977–1984," in Hagan, *In Peace and War*, 354, 366–67; Love, *History of the U.S. Navy* 2:704–7.

14. Muir, *Black Shoes*, 234; Kennedy, "Maritime Strategy," 364–66; Love, *History of the U.S. Navy* 2:729, 731; Howarth, *To Shining Sea*, 537–40, 545–46, 549–50. For a recent account of American involvement with Libya, see Joseph T. Stanik, *"Swift and Effective Retribution": The U.S. Sixth Fleet and the Confrontation with Quaddafi* (Washington, D.C.: NHC, 1996).

15. For a brief but exciting account, complete with combat art, see William Berry, "Urgent Fury," *All Hands*, May 1984, 19–27. Also, Timothy J. Christmann, "TacAir in Grenada," *Naval Aviation News* (November–December 1985): 6–9.

16. "President Calls Panama Slaying a Great Outrage," *New York Times*, 19 December 1989, pp. A1, A12; "U.S. Troops Move in Panama in Effort to Seize Noriega; Gunfire Heard in Capital," *New York Times*, 20 December 1989, pp. A1, A8; "Troops Gain Wide Control in Panama; New Leaders Put In, but Noriega Gets Away," *New York Times*, 21 December 1989, pp. A1, A18.

17. Howarth, *To Shining Sea*, 708, 720; John F. Morton, "The U.S. Navy in 1989," *USNIP* (1990): 166.

18. Herman, "Welcome Back BuMed," 15; Norman Polmar, "The U.S. Navy: Command Changes," *USNIP* 111 (December 1985): 157; Morton, "Navy in 1989," 169.

19. Capt. Georgia C. Sadler describes the growing feeling of concern in "Women in the Sea Service: 1972–1982," *USNIP* 109 (May 1983): 154.

20. BuPers, "Personnel Statistics," 1980 and 1990.

21. Distribution by . . . Ethnic Group, Vertical File: Statistics, Navy Dept. Library; Department of the Navy, Navy Women's Study Group, *An Update Report on the Progress of Women in the Navy, 1990* (hereafter cited as *Update Report*) I-68–I-69; Navy-Wide Demographics, 26 September 1987, folder 6, box 1, CNO Study Group, OA, NHC.

22. For an overview of black women in all services, see Brenda L. Moore, "African-American Women in the U.S. Military," *Armed Forces and Society* 17 (April 1991): 363–84.

23. *Update Report*, I-52; Department of the Navy, BuPers, *Naval Military Personnel Manual: 1987*, 10–41.

24. Dale Hewey, "They Found a Career," *All Hands*, July 1983, 16–17; "Women in the Navy," *All Hands*, June 1988, 27–28, 35–36.

25. Many conservative congressmen and senators supported reinstating the draft. Barbara Oganesoff, "Women in the Military: It Is Really a Matter of Human Power," *Government Executive* (February 1982): 25–26. Lt. Col. David Evans, USMC, argued persuasively against continued use of women in the Fleet Marine Force, in "No Place for Women," *USNIP* 107 (March 1981): 53–56.

26. Holm, *Women in the Military*, 377–78, 385, 387–92, 395–96; Sadler, "Sea Services," 154.

27. Capt. Mary A. Gore to Lehman, 7 January 1982; John S. Herrington to Gore, 8 March, 1982, both in folder 4, box 1, ser. 2, Pers 00W Records, OA, NHC.

28. "Watkins: Navy Has All the Women It Needs," *Navy Times*, 23 June 1986, 4, 20;

"Watkins Says Navy Now Has a Few Too Many Women," *Minerva: Quarterly Report on Women and the Military* 4 (winter 1986): 49; memos to OP-13, n.d. [after 16 June 1986], folder 4, box 15, ser. 3, Pers 00W Records, OA, NHC.

29. Holm, *Women in the Military*, 410–11; "Navy Freezes Number of Women on Duty for Next Five Years," *Washington Post*, 3 February 1987, p. A19; Chronology of Events Leading to CNO Decision, 4 February 1987, folder 3, box 4, CNO Study Group Records, OA, NHC.

30. Holm, *Women in the Military*, 411–12.

31. Ibid., 416, 433–34.

32. Julia J. DiLorenzo memo, Historical Perspective of OP-O1(W) Position, 24 January 1985, folder 5, box 2, CNO Study Group Records, OA, NHC; description of duties in Special Assistant for Women's Policy, OP-O1 (W), OPNAVIST 5430.48B, 21 March 1985.

33. Information from Pers-00W, BuPers; Ebbert and Hall, *Crossed Currents*, 174–75; "Capt. Kathleen D. Byerly," *Minerva: Quarterly Report on Women and the Military* 6 (spring 1988): 5.

34. *Update Report*, I-49–I-50.

35. Capt. Barbara Nyce, interview with author, 2 March 1997.

36. Holm, *Women in the Military*, 392.

37. Jo Jones, "Women of Annapolis," *All Hands*, July 1983, 34–35; Ebbert and Hall, *Crossed Currents*, 204; "Naval Academy's Top Woman," *Minerva: Quarterly Report on Women and the Military* 3 (fall 1985): 57.

38. Stephen E. Becker, "Integration of Women in the Brigade: Interview with Rear Admiral R. F. Marryott," *Shipmate* (June 1988): 16.

39. Ebbert and Hall, *Crossed Currents*, 203–4.

40. "Taunted Woman Quits Academy," *New York Times*, 14 May 1990, p. B9; "Navy, Congress Open Probes of Harassment at Annapolis," *Washington Post*, 18 May 1990, p. A1; Ebbert and Hall, *Crossed Currents*, 205–6.

41. *Update Report*, I-53–I-55.

42. J. D. Leipold, "Women Recruits: Sharp and Together," *All Hands*, July 1983, 21–23, 26–27.

43. *Update Report*, I-55–I-58; Ebbert and Hall, *Crossed Currents*, 196–97.

44. DOPMA for Women, folder 4 (1), box 2, ser. 3, Pers 00W Records, OA, NHC.

45. Holm, *Women in the Military*, 276–77; *Update Report*, I-59; chart with promotion rate percentages on I-60. The Navy had not been optimistic about the passage of DOPMA and had proposed its own legislation to end sex discrimination in appointments, enlistments, promotions, benefits, entitlements, and separation/retirement. In Rear Adm. Hugh A. Benton to OP-O9 BL, 9 June 1980, folder 12, box 4, ser. 3, Pers 00W Records, OA, NHC.

46. "DOPMA Grade Relief," *Navy Nurse Corps: Director's Update* (January 1997): 7. This inequity continued until late 1996.

47. Vice Adm. Robert B. Baldwin memo, 21 April 1980, folder 12, box 4, ser. 3, Pers 00W Records, OA, NHC.

48. Officer Career Development: Problems of Three Unrestricted Line Communities, August 1988, folder 12, box 19, ser. 4, Pers 00W Records, OA, NHC; *Update Report*, II-65. Figures from Navy Military Personnel Statistics, 30 September 1989.

49. Personnel Statistics, 30 September 1989; Fact Sheet: CEC, 1 April 1987, folder 3, box 1, CNO Study Group Records, OA, NHC.

50. Friedland, "For God and Country," 65; "Women in Naval Chaplaincy," 18–19.

51. Lt. Janell Osborne Nickols, interview with author, 14 September 1996. *Update Report*, II-65–II-67, also pinpointed the lack of acceptance in the Chaplain Corps and urged redress of the problems.

52. More background data in R. F. Meyer, Historical Chronology, 13 October 1987 and revised 19 October 1987, folder 3, box 1, CNO Study Group Records, OA, NHC.

53. Limited Duty and Chief Warrant Officer Community, 9 October 1987, folder 3, box 1, CNO Study Group Records, OA, NHC; Russell L. Coons, "Women CWOs and LDOs: Larger Horizons and Brighter Sunsets," *All Hands*, December 1983, 4–7; *Update Report*, I-11, I-22, I-B-1.

54. SecNav Instruction 1300.12, 18 April 1979, folder 1, box 2, CNO Study Group Records, OA, NHC.

55. SecNav to Melvin Price, and SecNav to John C. Stennis, 8 November 1979, folder 2, box 4, CNO Study Group Records, OA, NHC; *Report on Progress* (1987), 1-16. *Lexington* changed from CVT 16 to AVT 16, which permitted women crew onboard.

56. Rear Adm. Roberta Hazard, interview with author, 8 April 1997.

57. John Coleman, "Admiral Watkins: CNO Outlines Goals and Objectives," *All Hands*, October 1982, 5.

58. Patricia J. Thomas and Carol S. Greebler, "Men and Women in Ships: Attitudes of Crews after One to Two Years of Integration," November 1983, folder 7, box 19, ser. 4, Pers 00W Records, OA, NHC.

59. Ebbert and Hall, *Crossed Currents*, 226; Cdr. G. C. Sadler, Expansion of Women in Ships Program, 23 March 1981, folder 2, box 4, CNO Study Group Records, OA, NHC.

60. James D. Watkins to SecNav, 28 April 1986, folder 3, box 4, CNO Study Group Records, OA, NHC; *Report on Progress* (1987), 1-21.

61. *Update Report*, I-23–I-25; Women in Ships, 24 April 1987, folder 1, box 2, CNO Study Group Records, OA, NHC.

62. Vice Adm. Dudley L. Carlson, CNP, to CNO, Women in Ships Program, 10 April 1987, folder 1, box 2, CNO Study Group Records, OA, NHC; "More Sea Duty Required for Navy Women," *Minerva: Quarterly Report on Women and the Military* 5 (fall 1987): 66; Navy Currents: Women's Sea/Shore Rotation, *All Hands*, October 1987, 2–3.

63. "Women Sailors Go to Persian Gulf on Destroyer Tender *Acadia*," *Minerva: Quarterly Report on Women and the Military* 5 (summer 1987): 17–18; Ebbert and Hall, *Crossed Currents*, 235–36.

64. Holm, *Women in the Military*, 434–36; Donna Miles, "The Women of Just Cause," *Soldiers* 45 (March 1990): 21–24; Francine D'Amico, "Women at Arms: The Combat Controversy," *Minerva: Quarterly Report on Women and the Military* 8 (summer 1990): 3–4. D'Amico puts the number of women at 1,206. For more on the invasion, see Malcolm McConnell, *Just Cause: The Real Story of America's High-Tech Invasion of Panama* (New York: St. Martin's, 1991), and Thomas Donnelly, Margaret Roth, and Caleb Baker, *Operation Just Cause: The Storming of Panama* (New York: Lexington Books, 1991).

65. BuPers has no record of Navy women participating in Just Cause. Since they could not serve as SEALS or in combatant ships, it is doubtful that any were involved. No documents show that any were evacuated prior to the operation; such action would have tipped off the enemy. Capt. Barbara L. Brehm to author, 19 June 1997.

66. *Update Report*, I-26.

67. Roberta Spillane, "Women in Ships: Can We Survive?" *USNIP* 113 (July 1987): 44–45.

68. Dave Fraker, "A Shipmate is a Shipmate," *All Hands*, June 1988, 5–8; Ron Bayles, "IM2 Patricia White Bear," in "Women in the Navy" section, *All Hands*, June 1988, 31–32.

69. Lt. Cdr. Barbara A. Rainey, bio data; casualty reports, 13 July 1982, all in folder 2, box 2, CNO Study Group Records, OA, NHC.

70. Women in Naval Aviation Chronology, folder 2, box 2, CNO Study Group Records, OA, NHC. Colleen Nevius became a project manager for testing helicopters. Quotation in Timothy J. Christmann, "Navy's First Female Test Pilot," *Naval Aviation News* (November–December 1985): 26.

71. Sandy Russell, "High Flying Ladies," *Naval Aviation News* (February 1981): 8–9; Russell, "20 Years," 14.

72. Russell, "20 Years," 15–17; Association of the Bar of the City of New York, Committee on Military Affairs and Justice, "The Combat Exclusion Laws: An Idea Whose Time Has Gone," *Minerva: Quarterly Report on Women and the Military* 9 (winter 1991): 18. More on Odea in Milinda D. Jensen, "Women Fliers Continuing the Tradition," *Naval Aviation News* (November–December 1989): 12.

73. *Report on Progress* (1987), 1-30; *Update Report*, I-37.

74. NASA, "Information Summaries: Astronaut Fact Book," 5 May 1996, 10, 57; "Kathryn Sullivan," in *Who's Who in Space: The First 25 Years*, by Michael Cassutt (Boston: G. K. Hall, 1987), 116–17; Gregory Vogt, *The Space Shuttle* (Brookfield, Conn.: Millsbrook Press, 1991), 97, 101; "Kathryn Sullivan," in *Women Astronauts Aboard the Shuttle*, by Mary V. Fox (New York: Julian Messner, 1984), 79–83. Actually, the first female in space was a one-pound monkey named "Miss Baker," who went on a flight in 1959. In *Fly-By* (spring 1992): 3.

75. Robin Barnette, "DACOWITS: A Focus on Issues," *All Hands*, June 1988, 17; Briefing for DACOWITS, May 1987, folder 5, box 2, CNO Study Group Records, OA, NHC; Holm, *Women in the Military*, 412; "DACOWITS," folder 5420.3a, ND Records, BuMed.

76. *Report on Progress* (1987); *Update Report,* ES-3, ES-38, VI-2–VI-3; news briefing by James H. Webb Jr., 21 December 1987, folder 5, box 5, ser. 3, Pers 00W Records, OA, NHC.

77. *CNO Study Group's Report on Equal Opportunity in the Navy,* December 1988, 1-1. The Navy had made progress, though. Summarized in Robert C. Rucker, "Navy Women: Ready for the '90s," *All Hands,* June 1991, 6–9.

78. BuPers, "Personnel Statistics," Annual Report, 30 September 1990; HC Statistics, HC History, Manpower and Staffing folder, BuMed Archives.

79. Department of the Navy, BuMed, *Organization Manual: Naval Medical Command: 1988,* NC Notebook; Navy Medical Department, NNC Almanac, 1987 ed., both in ND Records, BuMed.

80. Annual Report of the Surgeon General, 1 August 1988, 1–2; Blue Ribbon Panel in folders 6000.3i, ND Records, BuMed; "Medical Department Reorganization," *U.S. Navy Medicine* 80 (July–August 1989): 8–9; Herman, "Welcome Back BUMED," 10, 15; John F. Morton, "The U.S. Navy in 1989," *USNIP* (1990): 172; "BUMED Update: Navy Surgeon General Discusses Efforts to Improve Medical Care," *All Hands,* December 1989, 15.

81. Department of the Navy, *Manual for the Medical Department of the United States Navy,* changes, 25 November 1980 (Washington, D.C.: GPO, 1980), 8-3.

82. Shea to Nurses, 10 December 1982, folder 5727.7, ND Records, BuMed.

83. Connie R. Curran, "The Nursing Shortage: Facts and Fallacies," 1989, Factual Data folder, ND Records, BuMed; Kalisch and Kalisch, *American Nursing,* 447, 451, 476; Gugenheim, "Nursing Focuses," 151–52; Linda E. Demkovich, "The Nurses Shortage—Do We Need to Train More or Just Put Them to Work?" *National Journal* (9 May 1981): 837, 839.

84. Carol J. Peterson, "The New Nurse and the New Physician," *Annals of Internal Medicine* 96 (March 1982): 374–75.

85. Kalisch and Kalisch, *American Nursing,* 458–59, 474–75; "BUMED Update," 17.

86. Shea-Buckley interview; Rear Adm. Frances Shea bio, 6 September 1979, Bio files, OA, NHC.

87. Shea bio, 1 July 1983, NC History/Articles folder; Shea to Nurses, 22 August 1980, and 10 December 1982, folder 5727.7, all in ND Records, BuMed.

88. Rear Adm. Mary J. Nielubowicz, interview with author, 8 April 1997; Commo. Mary Joan Nielubowicz bio, 26 October 1984, Bio files, OA, NHC; *Nurse Corps Chronology,* 23. For a brief time in the early 1980s, the Navy used the title "commodore" to signify the most junior flag officers. By 1985, another change grouped all junior flag officers as rear admirals—either lower or upper half to denote one or two stars.

89. Rear Adm. Mary F. Hall, interviews with author, 23 June 1997, 12 October 1997; Rear Adm. Mary F. Hall bio, Bio files, OA, NHC; *Nurse Corps Chronology,* 25; Jan K. Herman, "A Conversation with RAdm Hall," *U.S. Navy Medicine* 79 (May–June 1988): 8–9.

90. Nielubowicz quotations in letters to Nurses, July 1985 and June 1986. All other

information from directors' letters, 1980–88, passim, folder 5727.7, ND Records, OA, NHC.

91. Shea-Buckley interview and Nielubowicz interview.

92. "BUMED Update," 17.

93. *Nurse Corps Chronology*, 23; Shea to Nurses, 30 March 1983, and 2 December 1983; Program Authorization 116A; Nielubowicz to Nurses, May 1987, all in folder 5727.7, ND Records, BuMed; *Update Report*, I-49.

94. *Nurse Corps Chronology*, 27; Nielubowicz to Directors of Nursing Service, 5 June 1986; Nielubowicz to NC Officers in DUINS, 9 June 1986, both in folder 5727.7, ND Records, BuMed.

95. *Nurse Corps Chronology*, 26; *Surgeon General's Report: 1988.*

96. FY 89 NC Billet File, Nurse Recruiters folder; Anne P. Flynn to Lt. Cdr. Margaret Barton, 8 November 1988, folder 1100.1, both in ND Records, BuMed. Perhaps reinforcing the concept of dynamic recruiters was an article by W. David Melancon, "A Duo That's Taking the City by Storm," *Navy Recruiter* (October 1989): 11–14, describing the effectiveness of two energetic Navy medical recruiters.

97. *Nurse Corps Chronology*, 29; M. F. Hall, memo, 6 July 1988; James A. Zimble, memo, 8 August 1988; J. M. Boorda to Director, Naval Medicine, 1 November 1989; Program Authorization: 116C, revised April 1990, all in folder 1520.15, ND Records, BuMed.

98. Nielubowicz to Nurses, September 1987, folder 5727.7, ND Records, BuMed; *Nurse Corps Chronology*, 26. Capt. Margaret Armstrong was the first to fill the billet.

99. Surgeon General's Report: 1988, 5; Devilbiss, *Women and Military Service*, 26.

100. Nielubowicz to Nurses, March 1986, and October 1986, folder 5727.7; Timothy W. Cooke, "Navy Nurse Corps Retention: FY 1974 to FY 1988," July 1989, 3; 1989 Navy Nurse Corps Survey: Summary of Findings, both in folder 1040.6, all in ND Records, BuMed.

101. BuPers, *Naval Military Personnel Manual: 1987*, 10-2–10-3; NNC Survey, 1989.

102. Nielubowicz interview; Hall interview, 23 June 1997; Rear Adm. Frances Shea-Buckley, telephone interview with author, 20 May 1998, and Rear Adm. Mary J. Nielubowicz, telephone interview with author, 1 June 1998.

103. Report of Meeting on 29 June 1989 . . . Men in the Nurse Corps, folder 5354.1, ND Records, BuMed; Rear Adm. Mary F. Hall, telephone interview with author, 31 May 1998.

104. NNC Survey, 1989.

105. Donna M. Haase, "Uncle Sam Needs You: The Factors That Keep Eligible Nurses from Entering the Military," Bachelor's thesis, Indiana University of Pennsylvania, 1989, 17–18; M. F. Hall to Haase, 28 December 1989, attached to thesis; NNC Survey, table 7.

106. Summary of Training Requirements: NC, 12 August 1981, 9–10, folder 13 (2), box 13, ser. 6, NNC Records, OA, NHC; Nielubowicz, FY 87 NC Training Plan, 30 December 1986; Hall, Program Goals, 10 December 1987; Medcom 534 to Medcom 53B, 15 November

1988, all in folder 1520.10a; Hall to Nurses, April 1988, folder 5727.7, all in ND Records, BuMed. Specialized studies for master's degrees included nursing administration and health care administration; medical-surgical, maternal-child, psychiatric, community health, emergency trauma, operating room, critical care, and nurse anesthesia.

107. *Nurse Corps Chronology*, 22–24; "Nurse Corps Continuing Education," *U.S. Navy Medicine* 73 (January 1982): 14–16; "Operational Readiness Course Trains Nurses," *U.S. Navy Medicine* 73 (July 1982): 24–25; Training Requirements, 4, 8, 13; Shea to Nurses, 21 May 1980, and 22 August 1980, folder 5727.7, ND Records, BuMed.

108. *Nurse Corps Chronology*, 22–23, 25; Shea to Nurses 5 February 1982, and 27 September 1982; Nielubowicz to Nurses, 6 August 1984, July 1985, March 1986, July 1986; Hall to Nurses, December 1987, all in folder 5727.7, ND Records, BuMed.

109. Shea to Nurses, 28 June 1983, folder 5727.7, ND Records, BuMed.

110. NC Survey, 1989, table 1; NC Officers per Duty Station; Naval Medical Facilities, both in NNC Almanac, 1987 ed., ND Records, BuMed.

111. Shea-Buckley interview; Fred Frailey, "Navy Medicine Maintains Tradition of Caring," *All Hands*, November 1987, 41; "History of the Hospital Corps, United States Navy," n.d., History folder, ND Records, BuMed; Surgeon General's Report: 1988, 4; Hall to Nurses, December 1987, folder 5727.7, ND Records, BuMed.

112. "History of the Hospital Corps"; Frailey, "Tradition of Caring," 41; Berry, "Urgent Fury," 27.

113. NC Officers per Duty Station; Naval Medical Facilities; Classification of Naval Hospitals, December 1988, Ambulatory Care Nurse folder, ND Records, BuMed.

114. Ships with NC Officers, October 1988, folder 5727.7, ND Records, BuMed; Russell S. Poyner, "Carrier Nursing," *U.S. Navy Medicine* 83 (May–June 1992): 14–15, 19.

115. In Nielubowicz to Nurses, October 1986, folder 5727.7, ND Records, BuMed.

116. Surgeon General's Report: 1988, 7; quotation is Rear Adm. Donald Sturtz, in Deborah Burnette, "Angels of Mercy," *All Hands*, November 1987, 22.

117. Shea to Nurses, 21 May 1980, and 27 June 1980, folder 5727.7. ND Records, BuMed.

118. Morton, "Navy in 1989," 174; "Quake Dead Put at 270, Damage at a Billion as Californians Strive to Restore Order," *New York Times*, 19 October 1989, pp. A1, B11; "The Shock of 6.9," *New York Times* editorial, 19 October 1989, p. A28; "San Francisco Inches Toward Normalcy," *New York Times*, 20 October 1989, pp. A1, A18.

119. Rear Adm. Pauline M. Hartington bio, Officers bios, OA, NHC.

120. Rosario M. Rausa, "In Profile: Grace Murray Hopper," *Naval History* 6 (fall 1992): 60; Steve John, "Grace Hopper—A Living Legend," *All Hands*, September 1982, 6; Candace Sams, "RAdm. Grace Hopper, USNR (Ret.): Looking Ahead," *All Hands*, November 1986, 26–27; "ICP Interview: Grace M. Hopper," *ICP Interface* (spring 1980): 18–23.

121. *Update Report*, I-1.

122. M. S. Higgins to OP-O1, 29 January 1980; Higgins to OP-13, 9 May 1980; Vice

Adm. Robert B. Baldwin memo, 19 May 1980, all in folder 2, box 7, ser. 3, Pers 00W Records, OA, NHC.

123. *Congressional Record,* 96th Cong., 2d sess., 1 July 1980; PL 96-513, 96th Cong., 2d sess., *Defense Officer Personnel Management Act,* 12 December 1980.

124. "Women in the Navy: History and Firsts of Women in the Navy," Navy Public Affairs Library, 6–7; Milinda D. Jensen, "Women Fliers Continuing the Tradition," *Naval Aviation News* (November–December 1989): 12; Ebbert and Hall, *Crossed Currents,* 210, 259; Russell, "20 Years," 15.

125. Ronald W. Bayles, "Lt. Cmdr. Deborah Gernes," *All Hands,* June 1988, 33; Tracy Berry, "Command at Sea," *All Hands,* April 1989, 4.

126. Shea-Buckley interview; Rear Adm. Mary F. Hall to Nurses, 5 April 1988, folder 5727.7, ND Records, BuMed; *Nurse Corps Chronology,* 23.

127. Sterner, *Harm's Way,* 371.

128. J. M. Welch memo, 18 November 1987, folder 4, box 15, ser. 3, Pers 00W Records, OA, NHC; *Update Report,* I-A-2–I-A-3. For a complete list of CO and XO billets in 1990, see *Update Report,* I-F-1–I-F-6.

129. Hazard interview; Shea-Buckley interview.

130. Lee E. Sharff and Sol Gordon, eds. and comps., *Uniformed Services Almanac: 1980* (Washington, D.C.: Uniform Services Almanac, 1980), 5, 9, 11, 14, 19–20; *Uniformed Services Almanac: 1989* (Washington, D.C.: Uniform Services Abstract, 1989), 8–9, 21–23, 25.

131. *Update Report,* I-70–I-71.

132. Lt. Janell Osborne Nichols, interview with author, 14 September 1996.

133. *Update Report,* I-71.

134. Gary L. Martin, "Single Parent in Japan," *All Hands,* February 1980, 30–31.

135. Author interview with SCPO Mary S. Prise, 15 July 1997; "A Long Career of Firsts for Prise," Naval Weapons Station Yorktown, *Booster,* June 1997, 1, 5.

136. Dept. of Defense, *Background Review: Women in the Military,* October 1981, 121–22; *Update Report,* II-70–II-71. A good summary is in Marie D. Thomas et al., "Pregnant Enlisted Women in Navy Work Centers," *Minerva: Quarterly Report on Women and the Military* 9 (fall 1991): 1–32. An unofficial study by a San Diego Navy nurse revealed that 41 percent of pregnant women were unmarried, which the researcher called "astonishing and overwhelming." About 6 percent to 7 percent of Navy women were pregnant at any one time, with higher rates for women in ships. Such rates concerned commanders about the readiness of the fighting Navy. In *Washington Times,* 2 February 1988, pp. A1, A12.

137. SecNav Instruction 5300.26 with enclosure, 25 August 1980, and OPNAV Instruction 5350.5, 12 November 1982, in Sandra H. Carey, "Sourcebook on Sexual Harassment," 1982, appendix A, folder 3, box 19, ser. 4, Pers 00W Records, OA, NHC. Sexual harassment was "(1) influencing, offering to influence, or threatening the career, pay, or job of another person in exchange for sexual favors; or (2) deliberate or repeated

offensive comments, gestures, or physical contact of a sexual nature in a work or work-related environment."

138. *Report on Progress* (1987), 3-5, 3-9–3-10, 3-13.

139. Juanita M. Firestone and Richard J. Harris, "Sexual Harassment in the U.S. Military: Individualized and Environmental Contexts," *Armed Forces and Society* 21 (fall 1994): 31–36. Although this article was published in 1994, data came from the "1988 Survey of Sex Roles in the Active-Duty Military." Also, *Report on Progress* (1987), 3–12; Nancy G. Wilds, "Sexual Harassment in the Military," *Minerva: Quarterly Report on Women and the Military* 8 (winter 1990): 5–6, 8.

140. William Proxmire to Caspar W. Weinberger, 18 September 1987, folder 5, box 5; HASC Hearings, 1 October 1987, folder 1, box 2, both in ser. 3, Pers 00W Records, OA, NHC.

141. *Update Report*, III-7, III-16, III-22–III-24; "Sex Harassment Called Pervasive in Navy," *Washington Post*, 4 April 1991, p. A4.

142. Wilds, "Sexual Harassment," 1.

143. OPNAVIVST 5370.2 and NAVOP 011/89; *Update Report*, IV-2–IV-14.

144. Tracy Timmons, "'We're Looking for a Few Good Men': The Impact of Gender Stereotypes on Women in the Military," *Minerva: Quarterly Report on Women and the Military* 10 (summer 1992): 26; BuPers, *Naval Military Personnel Manual: 1987*, 36-42–36-44.

145. *Report on Progress* (1987), 3-9; *Update Report*, IV-25–IV-30.

146. NDWINST 1020.5G CH-1, 21 April 1980, folder 45(2), box 36, ser. 6, NNC Records, OA, NHC; Department of the Navy, *Uniform Regulations, United States Navy: 1981* (Washington, D.C.: GPO, 1981), iii–v, 2-15–2-16, 3-21–3-22; Department of the Navy, *Uniform Regulations, United States Navy: 1985* (Washington, D.C.: GPO, 1985), iii–iv, 4-24–4-36, table 8-1-1; Department of the Navy, *Uniform Regulations, United States Navy: 1987* (Washington, D.C.: GPO, 1987), iii, v, 4-25–4-37, 8-4.

147. Rear Adm. Frances T. Shea to Stanley L. Spero, 8 October 1982, folder 1020; Shea to Nurses, 27 September 1982, 10 December 1982; Rear Adm. Mary J. Nielubowicz to Nurses, 6 August 1984, all in folder 5727.7, all in ND Records, BuMed; Department of the Navy, *Uniform Regulations, United States Navy: 1981*, 2-15, 2-22; Department of the Navy, *Uniform Regulations, United States Navy: 1985*, 4-30; Department of the Navy, *Uniform Regulations, United States Navy: 1987*, 4-27.

148. Herman, "Conversation with RAdm Hall," 11.

## *Epilogue*

1. CNO Adm. Carlisle A. H. Trost stressed the continued importance of naval preparedness for deterrence, forward deployments, and crisis management. In "Maritime Strategy for the 1990s," *Naval Review*, 1990, 92–98.

2. BuPers, "Personnel Statistics," 1990; figures on active ships from Ships History

Branch, NHC; Pers 00W, Facts on Women in the Navy, 31 December 1995. See Deborah L. Rogers, "The Force Drawdown and Its Impact on Women in the Military," *Minerva: Quarterly Report on Women and the Military* 10 (spring 1992): 1–13.

3. For a survey of evolving U.S. involvement in the area, see Palmer, *On Course to Desert Storm.*

4. For the official Navy history, see Edward J. Marolda and Robert Schneller, *Shield and Sword: The United States Navy and the Persian Gulf War* (Washington, D.C.: NHC, 1998).

5. DOD, *Conduct of the Persian Gulf War: Final Report to Congress,* April 1992, R-1. Numbers of Navy women who served in the Gulf range from 2,600 to 3,700. I have chosen the latter, from the DOD *Report.*

6. Holm, *Women in the Military,* 456–61.

7. Ebbert and Hall, *Crossed Currents,* 262–65; DOD, *Gulf War,* R-2.

8. "Navy Medicine: Deploying the Best to Prepare for the Worst," *All Hands,* special edition no. 892, 49–51; Bruce M. Meth et al., "Critical Care Medicine Aboard the Hospital Ship, USNS *Comfort,*" Desert Shield/Storm folder, BuMed Archives; William Matthews, "Hospital Ships Ready to Begin Work," *NNCA News* 3 (March 1990): 1.

9. Figures from ND Records, BuMed.

10. Alfred A. Bove, T. G. Patel, and Raphael F. Smith, "Fleet Hospitals: Full Service Care," *USNIP* 118 (October 1992): 77–79. Navy nurse Raelene K. Hoogendorn, "Deployed to Desert Storm: The First 40 Hours," *Journal of Emergency Nursing* 17 (August 1991): 26A–29A, described the anxieties of the first nurses deployed. More critical assessments of naval medical care in Dana C. Covey, "Fleet Hospitals Could Be Better," *USNIP* 118 (June 1992): 60–63; GAO, *Operation Desert Storm: Improvements Required in the Navy's Wartime Medical Care Program,* Report, July 1993, 1–12.

11. Hall interview, 23 June 1997.

12. "Combat Role to be Sought for Women," *Washington Post,* 4 January 1990, p. A25. Combat exclusion generated a welter of articles; for example, M. C. Devilbiss, "Women in Combat: A Quick Summary of the Arguments on Both Sides," *Minerva: Quarterly Report on Women and the Military* 8 (spring 1990): 29–31; Paul E. Roush, "Combat Exclusion: Military Necessity or Another Name for Bigotry?" *Minerva: Quarterly Report on Women and the Military* 8 (fall 1990): 1–15; Marilyn A. Gordon and Mary Jo Ludvigson, "A Constitutional Analysis of the Combat Exclusion for Air Force Women," *Minerva: Quarterly Report on Women and the Military* 9 (summer 1991): 1–34; D'Ann Campbell, "Combatting the Gender Gap," *Temple Political and Civil Rights Law Review* 2 (fall 1992): 63–91; a series of articles in *USNIP* 118 (February 1992), including A. DiLucente, "Equality: A Step Backward," 46–48; Douglas M. Norton, "It's Time," 48–50; Lori Bolebruch, "And the Walls Come Tumblin' Down," 42–44; T. M. Downing, "Just Say No!!" 45–46.

13. Karen S. Geraci, "Women in Combat?" *Minerva: Quarterly Report on Women and the Military* 13 (spring 1995): 22; Ebbert and Hall, *Crossed Currents,* 267–68.

14. Presidential Commission on the Assignment of Women in the Armed Forces,

*Report to the President, 15 November 1992* (Washington, D.C.: GPO, 1992), 24, 28, 31–33; William P. Lawrence, "The Commission," *USNIP* 119 (February 1993): 49.

15. Navy Public Affairs Library, DOD press release, 13 January 1994.

16. Only a few examples will suffice: "Women Unfit for Combat, Marine Says," *Washington Post,* 14 August 1995, p. A15; John L. Olliges, "No Double Standards," in "Nobody Asked Me, but . . . ," *USNIP* 119 (January 1993): 94–95; Kathleen G. Bergeron, "The Right Agenda for Military Women," in "Nobody Asked Me Either, but . . . ," *USNIP* 119 (January 1993): 95–96.

17. Pers 00W, Career Fields Open to Women, 31 December 1995. Sherman Baldwin, "Creating the Ultimate Meritocracy," *USNIP* 119 (June 1993): 33–36, argues persuasively that eliminating sexism and offering women the chance to compete for all billets will strengthen the Navy.

18. A RAND National Defense Research Institute study in late 1997 revealed that women fill only 815 of the 47,544 combat-related jobs open to them. Story in "Women Fill Few Jobs Tied to Combat," *Washington Post,* 21 October 1997, pp. A1, A8.

19. *Update Report,* I-24–I-25.

20. "Women's Sea Billets to Shrink," *Navy Times,* 9 March 1992, 22; Douglas Waller, "Life on the Coed Carrier," *Time* (17 April 1995): 36; "Women Eager to Sail on Ike," *Newport News Daily Press,* 8 March 1994, pp. B1–B2; "A New Ike Returns," *Newport News Daily Press,* 14 April 1995, pp. A1–A2.

21. Pers 00W, Facts on Women in the Navy, 31 December 1995; "Women's Navy Blues: Don't Rock the Boat," *Washington Post,* 22 September 1992, pp. B1, B4; "New Navy Chief Wants Women in All Ships, Subs," *Newport News Daily Press,* 4 May 1994, pp. A1–A2; "Nearly 2,000 Women in Combat," *Newport News Daily Press,* 11 March 1996, pp. B1–B2. These combatants included amphibious assault ships, guided missile destroyers, dock landing ships, destroyers, and aircraft carriers.

22. SCPO Mary B. Prise, interview with author, 15 July 1997.

23. *Update Report,* I-35, I-37.

24. "Senate Votes to Remove Ban on Women as Combat Pilots," *New York Times,* 1 August 1991, pp. A1, A13; Pers 00W, Women Assignment Policy, 14 March 1996.

25. "Stretching Their Wings," *Washington Post,* 8 November 1994, pp. E1–E2; "Ike Shapes Up as Navy Women Ship Out," *Newport News Daily Press,* 21 February 1994, pp. A1–A2.

26. "Female Combat Pilot Is Believed Dead," *Washington Post,* 27 October 1994, p. A9; "Pilot's Death Renews Women-in-Combat Debate," *Newport News Daily Press,* 30 October 1994, p. A4; "Female Pilot's Crash Blamed on Engine Stall," *Washington Post,* 1 March 1995, p. A7; "Vindication for a Flier," editorial, *Newport News Daily Press,* 2 March 1995, p. A10.

27. Evan Thomas and Gregory L. Vistica, "Falling Out of the Sky," *Newsweek* (17 March 1997): 26–28.

28. "Officer Who Refused to Fly with Women Still in Navy," *Newport News Daily Press,* 20 August 1995, p. A9.

29. Pers 00W, Navy Women in Aviation, 31 December 1995.

30. "New Naval Astronauts: First Female Naval Aviator Selected," *Wings of Gold* (summer 1992): 56–57; "Pilot Headed for Space," *Newport News Daily Press*, 20 December 1994, pp. A1–A2; NASA, "Information Summaries," 8, 10, 22, 24, 30.

31. "2 of 3 Female Midshipmen Cite Harassment at Academy," *Washington Times*, 10 October 1990, p. 1; "Academy Weighs New Tailor for the Female Sailor," *Washington Post*, 28 October 1995, pp. A1, A6; "The Academy," editorial, *Newport News Daily Press*, 16 May 1996, p. A9; "Treading Water in Annapolis," *Washington Post*, 24 May 1997, pp. B1, B5; "No 'Systemic Flaw' Found at Naval Academy," *Washington Post*, 31 May 1997, p. A7.

32. BuPers, "Personnel Statistics," 30 September 1990; *Director's Update* 3 (January 1994): 47–48; 1995 stats from NHC home page.

33. Rear Adm. Mariann Stratton bio, BuMed Archives; Sterner, *Harm's Way*, 386.

34. "A Conversation with RAdm Stratton," *U.S. Navy Medicine* 83 (May–June 1992): 7–8; Stratton to Nurse Corps, in *Director's Update* 1 (January 1992): 1–2; 2 (November 1992): 1; 2 (April 1993): 1; 2 (August 1993): 1, 31. The complete *Strategic Plan* is in *Director's Update* 3 (January 1994).

35. Rear Adm. Joan M. Engel bio, BuMed Archives.

36. Kalisch and Kalisch, *American Nursing*, 3d ed., 473; "Conversation," 7; *Director's Update* 2 (April 1993): 4; Nursing Innovations, Factual Data–Current Information folder, ND Records, BuMed.

37. *Director's Update* 3 (August 1994): 4; 5 (January 1995): 4; "USS *Wasp* Medical Team Ready to Help off Bosnia," *Flagship*, 15 February 1996, A7.

38. Reports in *Director's Update* 1 (January 1992): 23–26; and 1 (April 1992): 16.

39. Reports in *Director's Update* 1 (August 1992): 27; 2 (November 1992): 3; 3 (August 1994): 5.

40. Female Flag Officers, 1996, Ready Reference File, OA, NHC; Pers 00W, History and "Firsts" of Women in the Navy, 31 December 1995, 7–8; "Work Hard," [re: Marsha Evans], *Parade Magazine*, 21 April 1996, 4.

41. Mariann Stratton and Joan M. Engel bios, BuMed Archives; *Update Report*, I-1.

42. Rear Adm. Louise C. Wilmot bio, Officers bios, OA, NHC; Ebbert and Hall, *Crossed Currents*, 238–39; "First Woman Takes Command of Ship," *Navy Times*, 14 January 1991, 4; "Through Top-Brass Ceiling," *Newport News Daily Press*, 21 September 1993, p. C1; Pers 00W, History and "Firsts," 8.

43. *Director's Update* 1 (January 1992): 17; 2 (November 1992): 13, 25; 3 (August 1994): 30; statistics from ND Records, BuMed.

44. Georgia C. Sadler and Patricia J. Thomas, "Rock the Cradle, Rock the Boat?" *USNIP* 121 (April 1995): 51–56; Julia T. Cadenhead, "Pregnancy on Active Duty: Making the Tough Decisions," *USNIP* 121 (April 1995): 52–53; Patricia J. Thomas and Marie D. Thomas, "Impact of Pregnant Women and Single Parents upon Navy Personnel Systems," *Minerva: Quarterly Report on Women and the Military* 10 (fall/winter 1992): 41–75.

45. Information for this section came primarily from Jean Zimmerman, *Tailspin:*

*Women at War in the Wake of Tailhook* (New York: Doubleday, 1995), 3–19, 23–27, 42, 62, 69–85, 90–92, 133, 213, 252–53, 261, 272–74; Ebbert and Hall, *Crossed Currents,* 253–55, 270–73; Richard B. Linnekin, "Tailhook 1991 and Other Perplexities," *USNIP* 118 (September 1992): 36–40; "She Stood Alone: The Tailhook Scandal," ABC television documentary, 22 May 1995; K. A. Krohne, "Conduct Unbecoming," *USNIP* 118 (August 1992): 53–56.

46. DOD Inspector General, "Report of Investigation: Tailhook 1991, Pt. 1, Review of Navy Investigations," September 1992; and Pt. 2, "Events of the 35th Annual Tailhook Symposium," February 1993, OA, NHC.

47. All from *Newport News Daily Press:* "Aviator Cleared of Assault Charges," 22 October 1993, p. A1; "Admiral Blasts Dalton for Tailhook Penalty," 29 October 1993, p. A5; "Lack of Evidence Cited, Last Tailhook Case Tossed," 10 February 1994, p. A3; "Kelso to Retire Early Due to Tailhook," 16 February 1994, pp. A1, A8; "Tailhook's Lessons," 18 August 1996, pp. H4–H5. A recent writer, William H. McMichael, *The Mother of All Hooks: The Story of the U.S. Navy's Tailhook Scandal* (New Brunswick, N.J.: Transaction Publishers, 1997), characterizes Tailhook as a gross failure of naval leadership.

48. "Tailhook Accuser to Leave Navy," *Newport News Daily Press,* 11 February 1994, p. A1; "Jury Awards $5 Million in Tailhook Damages," *Newport News Daily Press,* 1 November 1994, pp. A1–A2. The treatment of Coughlin was typical: those who complained were subject to "notoriety and embarrassment . . . possibility of retaliation . . . repraisals for being 'troublemakers and boat rockers.'" In Wilds, "Sexual Harassment," 9.

49. All in *Newport News Daily Press:* "Navy Addresses New Sex Scandal," 16 December 1994, p. A9; "Tailhook-Tainted Navy Facing New Harassment Case," 19 December 1994, p. B3; "Admiral Convicted of Adultery," 9 December 1995, p. A4; "Navy Looks at New Assault Incident," 9 November 1995, p. A9; "Navy Admiral Orders New 'Stand Down,'" 10 November 1995, p. A3; "Navy Charges 2 with Sexual Harassment," 14 December 1995, pp. C1–C2; "Navy Finds 4 Guilty of Harassing Women," 26 April 1995, p. A6; "Woman Details Groping by Drunken Officer," 30 December 1995. Also, "Navy Admiral Accused of Sexual Misconduct," *Washington Post,* 25 July 1996, p. A27; "Remarks on Rape Case Sink Officer," *Washington Post,* 18 November 1995, pp. A1, A23.

50. "Outside Review of Sexual Misconduct Charges Sought at Navy Base," *Washington Post,* 9 May 1998, p. A5, details misconduct cases at the Great Lakes Naval Training Center.

51. "Sexual Harassment Dips in Military," *Newport News Daily Press,* 3 July 1996, p. A3; "Poll: Harassment in Military Inherent," *Newport News Daily Press,* 1 March 1997, p. A5; John L. Byron, "End Sexism, *USNIP* 122 (February 1996): 27–31. Byron equates today's sexism with the racism of earlier years.

52. "Administration Rewords Military Rules on Gays," *Washington Post,* 11 February 1994, p. A4; "Military, Despite Policy Shift, Discharged More Gays in '95," *Washington Post,* 28 January 1996, p. A7; "Military Still Hounding Gays, Group Says," *Newport News Daily Press,* 27 February 1996, pp. A1–A2; Susan Warshauer, "Living under the Debated

Homosexuality Regulations: Lesbians in the U.S. Military Challenge a Policy of Containment," *Minerva: Quarterly Report on Women and the Military* 10 (summer 1992): 8–19. Numbers of discharges on homosexuality charges rose from 597 in 1994 to 850 two years late. Story in "Cohen: More Leaving Military by Saying They're Homosexual," *Newport News Daily Press*, 7 April 1998, p. A3.

53. Predictably, writers have come down on both sides of the issue. For example, *USNIP* 119 (April 1993): 88–102, carried a series of articles, pro and con, in "Gays in the Military." Navy Chaplain Eugene T. Gomulka, "Why No Gays?" *USNIP* 118 (December 1992): 44–46; and Senior Chief Yeoman John M. Tucker, "The Gay Issue," *USNIP* 119 (January 1993): 109, argue emphatically against a change in policy.

# Bibliography


## Manuscript and Archival Sources

### *Bureau of Medicine and Surgery, Washington, D.C.*

Costello, Edward L. "Establishment of the Medical Service Corps." Typescript. N.d.
Navy Nurse Corps Records.
Nursing Division. "Chronological History, Navy Nurse Corps." Typescript. 1962.

### *Hargrett Rare Book and Manuscript Library. University of Georgia, Athens.*

Hancock, Joy Bright. Papers. MS 854.

### *Library of Congress, Washington, D.C.*

Daniels, Josephus. Papers.

### *Marine Corps Research Center, Quantico, Virginia*

Women Marines. Records. Record Group 127-79-27.

### *Mariner's Museum Library, Newport News, Virginia*

Logbooks: *Ranger* (1777–78), *Alatamaha* (1855–57), *Alice Frazier* (1848–55).

### *National Archives and Records Administration, Washington, D.C.*

Record Group 24. Bureau of Naval Personnel. Records.
Record Group 45. Naval Records Collection of the Office of Naval Records and Library.
Record Group 52. Bureau of Medicine and Surgery. Records.
Record Group 80. Secretary of the Navy General Correspondence, 1916–26.

### *Navy Department Library, Washington, D.C.*

Albion, Robert G. "A Brief History of Civilian Personnel in the U.S. Navy Department." Typescript. October 1943.
Cruise Books: *Repose* (1967, 1970), *Sanctuary* (1967, 1968, 1970, 1973).

Daniels, Josephus. Papers.
Edwards, William H. "A History of United States Uniforms for the Sea Services." 4 vols. Typescript, ca. 1980
Mason, Gail. "Organization of the Navy Department: A History from 1947 to 1970." Typescript. Washington, D.C.: Naval History Division, 1970.

*Operational Archives, Naval Historical Center. Washington, D.C.*

Assistant Chief of Naval Personnel for Women. Records.
Behr, Nurse Esther N. Papers.
Bowman, J. Beatrice. Papers. Navy Nurse Corps Records.
Bureau of Medicine and Surgery. Records, 1824–1970.
Bureau of [Naval] Personnel, Special Assistant for Women's Policy (Pers 00W). Records.
Chief of Naval Operations Study Group on Women in the Navy. Records.
"CNO Study Group's Report on Equal Opportunity in the Navy." December 1988.
Early Records. ZC Files.
Early Records: Wars. ZO Files.
Early Records: Women in the Navy. ZV Files.
"History of the Hospital Corps: United States Navy, 1814–1975." Typescript. Box 5, ZV Files.
Office of the Director, Navy Nurse Corps. Records.
O'Neill, Helen G. Papers.
Ready Reference Files.

*Private Collection, Williamsburg, Virginia.*

House, Sandra Doppelheuer. Papers.

*Ships History Branch. Naval Historical Center, Washington, D.C.*

U.S. Navy Ship Force Levels, 1917–1989.

## Oral and Written Interviews by Author. (Copies in Operational Archives, Naval Historical Center, Washington, D.C.)

Beers, Lt. Dorothy Ditter. USNR. 11 September 1995.
Bristol, Mrs. Milford. NC. 4 March 1983.
Collins, Capt. Winifred Quick. USNR; USN. 15 July 1996.
Coxhead, Helene Johnson. Yeoman (F). 6 February 1994.
Diduk, Lt. Elsa Scharles. USNR. 8 March 1996.

Duerk, Rear Adm. Alene. NC, USN. 11 October 1996.
Erickson, Capt. Ruth. NC, USN. October 1995.
Etzler, Anna Hagen. NC. 22 August 1981.
Grady, Doris Locke. Specialist (T), USNR. 8 July 1995.
Hall, Rear Adm. Mary F. NC, USN. 23 June 1997.
Hamblet, Col. Julia. Women Marines. 28 November 1995.
Hancock, Capt. Joy Bright. Yeoman (F); USNR; USN. 4 August 1981, 8 January 1982, 6 September 1982.
Hazard, Rear Adm. Roberta L. USN. 2 December 1996, 8 April 1997.
House, Cdr. Sandra Doppelheuer. MSC, USN. 26 February 1996.
Hurt, Lt. Dorothy Brown. USNR. 30 July 1996.
Krapp, Anna Redding. NC. 4 March 1983.
Lindner, Cdr. Mary J. NC, USN. 2 May 1995.
McKee, Rear Adm. Fran. USN. 26 August 1996.
Montgomery, Lt. Margaret Lucas. USNR. 22 July 1995.
Nakhnikian, Lt. Jean Klinefelter. USNR. 22 July 1995.
Nickols, Lt. Janell Osborne. Chap. Corps, USN. 14 September 1996.
Nielubowicz, Rear Adm. Mary F. NC. 8 April 1997.
Nyce, Capt. Barbara. USN. 2 March 1997.
O'Neill, Lt. Col. Helen G. Yeoman (F). 25 August 1981.
Paroubek, Ens. Ann Clendenin. NC. 15 March 1996.
Porter, S.Sgt. Mary Stedman. Women Marines. 8 August 1995.
Prise, SCPO Mary S. USN. 15 July 1997.
Roy, Lt. Susan Davis. USNR. 7 June 1996, 10 July 1996.
Shea-Buckley, Rear Adm. Frances T. NC. 21 April 1997.
Zumwalt, Adm. Elmo. USN. 23 September 1996.

## Other Oral Histories. (Copies in Operational Archives, Naval Historical Center, Washington, D.C.)

Hancock, Recollections of Capt. Joy Bright, USN (Ret.). Naval Institute Oral History Series, 1971.
"ICP Interview—Grace M. Hopper." *ICP Interface* (spring 1980): 18–23.
McAfee, Recollections of Capt. Mildred, USNR (Ret.) Naval Institute Oral History Series, 1971.
Palmer, Recollections of Capt. Jean, USNR (Ret.). Naval Institute Oral History Series, 1971.
Shelly, Lt. Cdr. Mary Josephine, USNR (Ret.). Naval Institute Oral History Series, 1970.
Stratton, Recollections of Capt. Dorothy, USCG (Ret.). Naval Institute Oral History Series, 1971.

## U.S. Government Documents and Reports


Congressional Quarterly, comp. *Historic Documents: 1972*. Washington, D.C.: Congressional Quarterly, 1973.

Department of Defense. *Conduct of the Persian Gulf War: Final Report to Congress.* Report in 3 vols. April 1992.

——. Office of the Assistant Secretary of Defense (Manpower, Reserve Affairs, and Logistics). *Background Study: Use of Women in the Military*. Report. 2d ed. September 1978.

Department of Health, Education, and Welfare. *Digest of Educational Statistics, 1962.* Washington, D.C.: GPO, 1962.

——. *Digest of Educational Statistics, 1966*. Washington, D.C.: GPO, 1966.

——. *Digest of Educational Statistics, 1967*. Washington, D.C.: GPO, 1967.

——. *Digest of Educational Statistics, 1968*. Washington, D.C.: GPO, 1968.

——. *Digest of Educational Statistics, 1969*. Washington, D.C.: GPO, 1969.

——. *Digest of Educational Statistics, 1970*. Washington, D.C.: GPO, 1970.

——. *Digest of Educational Statistics, 1971*. Washington, D.C.: GPO, 1971.

——. *Digest of Educational Statistics, 1972*. Washington, D.C.: GPO, 1972.

Department of the Navy. *The Bluejacket's Manual: United States Navy, 1917*. 5th ed. Baltimore: Franklin Printing, 1917.

——. *History of Administrative Problems, Korean War*. 5 vols. Washington, D.C.: OA, Naval History Division, [1953].

——. *Naval Regulations, Issued by Command of the President of the United States of America*, January 25, 1802. Washington, D.C., 1802.

——. *Orders and Instructions for the Direction and Government of the Naval Service of the United States*. Washington, D.C.: Robert Armstrong, 1853.

——. *Regulations and Instructions for the Nurse Corps, U.S. Navy: 1909*. Washington, D.C.: GPO, 1909.

——. *Regulations for the Government of the United States Navy: 1865*. Washington, D.C.: GPO, 1865.

——. *Regulations for the Government of the United States Navy: 1869*. Washington, D.C.: GPO, 1869.

——. *Regulations for the Government of the United States Navy: 1870*. Washington, D.C.: GPO, 1870.

——. *Regulations for the Government of the United States Navy: 1876*. Washington, D.C.: GPO, 1876.

——. *Regulations for the Government of the United States Navy: 1893*. Washington, D.C.: GPO, 1893.

——. *Regulations for the Government of the United States Navy: 1896*. Washington, D.C.: GPO, 1896.

——. *Regulations for the Government of the United States Navy: 1900*. Washington, D.C.: GPO, 1900.

——. *Rules, Regulations, and Instructions for the Naval Service of the United States*. Washington, D.C.: E. DeKnafft, 1818.

——. *Rules, Regulations, and Instructions for the Naval Service of the United States*. Washington, D.C.: Gales and Seaton, 1821.

——. *Uniform Regulations: United States Navy Nurse Corps*. Washington, D.C.: GPO, 1923.

——. "The United States Navy in 'Desert Shield'–'Desert Storm.'" 15 May 1991.

Department of the Navy. Bureau of Medicine and Surgery. *The History of the Medical Department of the United States Navy, 1945–1955*. Washington, D.C.: GPO, 1958.

——. *The History of the Medical Department of the United States Navy in World War II*. 3 vols. Washington, D.C.: GPO, 1953.

——. *Hospital Corps Handbook: United States Navy, 1923*. Washington, D.C.: GPO, 1923.

——. *Manual of the Bureau of Medicine and Surgery, U.S. Navy*. Typescript. 1976, 1980.

——. *Manual of the Medical Department of the United States Navy*. Washington, D.C.: GPO, 1914, 1917, 1927, 1939, 1945, 1971, 1980.

——. *Organization Manual: Naval Medical Command: 1988*.

——. *White Task Force: History of the Nurse Corps, United States Navy*. Washington, D.C.: GPO, 1945.

Department of the Navy. Bureau of Naval Personnel. *Uniform Regulations, United States Navy: 1941*. Washington, D.C.: GPO, 1941.

——. *Uniform Regulations, United States Navy: 1975*. Washington, D.C.: GPO, 1975.

——. *Uniform Regulations, United States Navy: 1978*. Washington, D.C.: GPO, 1978.

——. *Uniform Regulations, United States Navy: 1981*. Washington, D.C.: GPO, 1981.

——. *Uniform Regulations, United States Navy: 1985*. Washington, D.C.: GPO, 1985.

——. *Uniform Regulations, United States Navy: 1987*. Washington, D.C.: GPO, 1987.

——. "U.S. Naval Administration in World War II: Women's Reserve." 2 vols. Typescript. Washington, D.C., 1946–47.

Department of the Navy. Navy Women's Study Group. *An Update Report on the Progress of Women in the Navy*. 1990.

Department of the Navy. Office of Naval Personnel. "Annual Report: Navy Military Personnel Statistics." Typescript. 30 September 1989 and 1990.

——. *Naval Military Personnel Manual: 1987*. Photocopy.

Federal Security Agency. Office of Education. *Biennial Survey of Education in the United States: 1944–1946*. Washington, D.C.: GPO, 1950.

——. *Biennial Survey of Education in the United States: 1948–1950*. Washington, D.C.: GPO, 1954.

General Accounting Office. *Operation Desert Storm: Improvements Required in the Navy's Wartime Medical Care Program*. Report. Washington, D.C.: The Office, July 1993.

——. *Women in the Military: Deployment in the Persian Gulf War.* Report. Washington, D.C.: The Office, July 1993.

National Center for Education Statistics. *Digest of Education Statistics: 1981.* Washington, D.C.: GPO, 1981.

——. *Digest of Education Statistics: 1991.* Washington, D.C.: GPO, 1991.

——. *Digest of Education Statistics: 1993.* Washington, D.C.: GPO, 1993.

*Official Records of the Union and Confederate Navies in the War of the Rebellion.* Ser. 1, vols. 23, 24, 25. Washington, D.C.: GPO, 1910–12.

Presidential Commission on the Assignment of Women in the Armed Forces. *Report to the President, November 15, 1992.* Washington, D.C.: GPO, 1992.

*United States Sanitary Commission: Bulletin (1863–1865).* 3 vols. in 1. New York: N.p., 1866.

U.S. Bureau of the Census. *Fertility of American Women: June 1990.* Population Characteristics, series P-20, no. 454.

——. *Marital Status and Living Arrangements: March 1989 and March 1990.* Population Characteristics, series P-20, no. 445 and no. 450.

——. *Population Profile of the United States.* June 1981. Washington, D.C.: GPO, 1982.

——. *Statistical Abstract of the United States: 1945.* Washington, D.C.: GPO, 1945.

——. *Statistical Abstract of the United States: 1947.* Washington, D.C.: GPO, 1947.

——. *Statistical Abstract of the United States: 1952.* Washington, D.C.: GPO, 1952.

——. *Statistical Abstract of the United States: 1958.* Washington, D.C.: GPO, 1958.

——. *Statistical Abstract of the United States: 1960.* Washington, D.C.: GPO, 1960.

——. *Statistical Abstract of the United States: 1961.* Washington, D.C.: GPO, 1961.

——. *Statistical Abstract of the United States: 1962.* Washington, D.C.: GPO, 1962.

——. *Statistical Abstract of the United States: 1971.* Washington, D.C.: GPO, 1971.

——. *Statistical Abstract of the United States: 1972.* Washington, D.C.: GPO, 1972.

——. *Statistical Abstract of the United States: 1982–1983.* Washington, D.C.: GPO, 1982–83.

U.S. Coast Guard. *The Coast Guard at War: Women's Reserve.* Washington, D.C.: Historical Section, Public Information Division, 1946.

U.S. Congress. *American State Papers. Documents, Legislative and Executive, of the Congress of the United States.* Vol. 1. Washington, D.C.: Gales and Seaton, 1834.

——. *Annual Reports of the Navy Department: 1898.* 55th Cong., 3d sess., H. Doc. 3.

——. *Report of the Secretary of the Navy.* In *Executive Documents.* 36th Cong., 1st sess., 1 December 1860.

——. *Report of the Secretary of the Navy.* In *Executive Documents.* 37th Cong., 2d sess., 2 December 1861.

——. *Report of the Secretary of the Navy.* In *Executive Documents.* 40th Cong., 1st sess., 1 December 1864.

——. *Report of the Secretary of the Navy: 1896.* 54th Cong., 2d sess., 1 October 1896. H. Doc. 3.

——. *Report of the Secretary of the Navy: 1897.* 55th Cong., 2d sess. H. Doc. 3.

——. *Rules and Regulations for the Government of the Navy of the United States.* 23d Cong., 1st sess., 1833. H. Doc. 20.

——. *Rules and Regulations for the Government of the Navy of the United States.* 27th Cong., 3d sess., 1843. H. Doc. 148.

U.S. Congress. House Committee on Armed Services. *Hearings on H.R. 1373, To Reorganize the Nurse Corps of the Navy and of the Naval Reserve.* 80th Cong., 1st sess., 20 January 1947.

U.S. Congress. House Committee on Naval Affairs. *Hearings on H.R. 5915, To Amend the Naval Reserve Act of 1938, as Amended, So as to Establish the Women's Reserve on a Permanent Basis.* 79th Cong., 2d sess., 9–10 May 1946.

——. *Report no. 1309, to Accompany H.R. 15438.* 60th Cong., 1st sess., 25 March 1908.

U.S. Congress. House Committee on Ways and Means. *Hearings on Soldiers' Adjusted Compensation.* 68th Cong., 1st sess, 1924.

U.S. Congress. Senate Committee on Armed Services. *Hearings on H.R. 1943.* 80th Cong., 1st sess., 24 March 1947.

——. *Hearings on S. 1103, S. 1527, S. 1641, Women's Armed Services Integration Act.* 80th Cong., 1st sess., 2, 9, 15 July 1947.

——. Senate Subcommittee on Organization and Mobilization, *Hearings on S. 1641.* 80th Cong., 2d sess., 18, 23, 25, 27 February, 2, 3 March 1948.

U.S. Secretary of the Interior, comp. *Official Register of the United States, Containing a List of Officers and Employees in the Civil, Military, and Naval Service.* Washington, D.C.: GPO, 1879–99.

## Books

Adams, Michael C. C. *The Best War Ever: America and World War II.* Baltimore: Johns Hopkins University Press, 1994.

Albion, Robert G., and Jennie B. Pope. *Sea Lanes in Wartime: The American Experience, 1775–1942.* New York: W. W. Norton, 1942.

Alsmeyer, Marie Bennett, comp. *Old WAVES Tales: Navy Women: Memories of World War II.* Conway, Ark.: Hamba Books, 1982.

——. *The Way of the WAVES: Women in the Navy.* Conway, Ark.: Hamba Books, 1981.

Anderson, Bern. *By Sea and By River: The Naval History of the Civil War.* New York: Alfred A. Knopf, 1962.

Anderson, Gerald R. *Subic Bay: From Magellan to Mt. Pinatubo, A History of the U.S. Naval Station, Subic Bay.* N.p., 1992.

Anderson, Karen. *Wartime Women: Sex Roles, Family Relations, and the Status of Women during World War II.* Westport, Conn.: Greenwood Press, 1981.

Angel, Joan. *Angel in the Navy: The Story of a WAVE.* New York: Hasting House, 1943.

Art, Robert J., Vincent Davis, and Samuel P. Huntington, eds. *Reorganizing America's Defenses: Leadership in War and Peace.* Washington, D.C.: Pergamon-Brassey, 1985.

Atkinson, Rick. *The Long Gray Line.* Boston: Houghton Mifflin, 1989.

Baer, George W. *One Hundred Years of Sea Power: The U.S. Navy, 1890–1990*. Stanford, Calif.: Stanford University Press, 1994.

Barkalow, Carol. *In the Men's House*. New York: Poseidon, 1990.

Barlow, Jeffrey G. *The Revolt of the Admirals: The Fight for Naval Aviation, 1945–1950*. Washington, D.C.: Naval Historical Center, 1994.

Barton, William P. C. *A Treatise Containing a Plan for the Internal Organization and Government of Marine Hospitals in the United States: Together with a Scheme for Amending and Systematizing the Medical Department of the Navy*. Philadelphia: Printed for author, 1814.

Beers, Henry P. *American Naval Occupation and Government of Guam, 1898–1902*. Washington, D.C.: Navy Department, Office of Records Administration, 1944.

Berube, Allan. *Coming Out Under Fire: The History of Gay Men and Women in World War II*. New York: Free Press, 1990.

Bidwell, Shelford. *The Women's Royal Army Corps*. London: N.p., 1977.

Billings, Charlene W. *Grace Hopper: Navy Admiral and Computer Pioneer*. Hillside, N.J.: Enslow Publishers, 1989.

Binkin, Martin. *America's Voluntary Military: Progress and Prospects*. Washington, D.C.: Brookings Institution, 1984.

Binkin, Martin, and Mark J. Eitelberg. *Blacks and the Military*. Washington, D.C.: Brookings Institution, 1982.

Binkin, Martin, and Shirley J. Bach. *Women and the Military*. Washington, D.C.: Brookings Institution, 1977.

Bird, Caroline, with Sara Welles Briller. *Born Female: The High Cost of Keeping Women Down*. Rev. ed. New York: Pocket Book edition, Simon and Schuster, 1971.

Blair, Clay, Jr. *The Atomic Submarine and Admiral Rickover*. New York: Henry Holt, 1954.

———. *The Forgotten War: America in Korea, 1950–1953*. New York: Times Books, 1987.

Blair, Karen. *The Clubwoman as Feminist: True Womanhood Redefined, 1868–1914*. New York: Holmes and Meier, 1980.

Blow, Michael. *A Ship to Remember: The* Maine *and the Spanish-American War*. New York: William Morrow, 1992.

Braisted, William C., William H. Bell, and Presley M. Rixey. *The Life Story of Presley Marion Rixey: Surgeon General, U.S. Navy, 1902–1910*. Strasburg, Va: Shenandoah Publishing, 1930.

Brewer, Lucy. *The Female Marine, or Adventures of Miss Lucy Brewer*. N.p., 1 January 1816.

Bullough, Vern, with Bonnie Bullough. *The Subordinate Sex: A History of Attitudes toward Women*. Urbana: University of Illinois Press, 1973.

Butler, Elizabeth A. *Navy WAVES*. Charlottesville: Wayside Press, 1988.

Butler, Mrs. Henry F. *I Was a Yeoman (F)*. Washington, D.C.: Naval Historical Foundation Publication, ser. 2, no. 7, 1967.

Byerly, Dorothea J. *Up Came a Ripple*. N.p., 1945.

Camhi, Jane J. *Women against Women: American Anti-Suffragism, 1880–1920.* Brooklyn, N.Y.: Carlson Publishing, 1994.

Campbell, D'Ann. *Women at War with America: Private Lives in a Patriotic Era.* Cambridge: Harvard University Press, 1984.

Canney, Donald L. *The Ironclads, 1842–1885.* Vol. 2 of *The Old Steam Navy.* Annapolis, Md.: Naval Institute Press, 1993.

Carnegie, Mary E. *The Path We Tread: Blacks in Nursing, 1854–1984.* Philadelphia. J. B. Lippincott, 1986.

Cassutt, Michael. *Who's Who in Space: The First 25 Years.* Boston: G. H. Hall, 1987.

Chafe, William Henry. *The American Woman: Her Changing Social, Economic, and Political Roles, 1920–1970.* London: Oxford University Press, 1972.

———. *The Paradox of Change: American Women in the 20th Century.* New York: Oxford University Press, 1991.

———. *Women and Equality: Changing Patterns in American Culture.* New York: Oxford University Press, 1977.

Chesler, Ellen. *Woman of Valor: Margaret Sanger and the Birth Control Movement in America.* New York: Simon and Schuster, 1992.

Clephane, Lewis P. *History of the Naval Overseas Transportation Service in World War I.* Washington, D.C.: GPO, 1969.

Clifford, Mary L. *Women Who Kept the Lights: An Illustrated History of Female Lighthouse Keepers.* Vancouver, Wash.: Cypress Publications, 1993.

Cochran, Jacqueline. *The Stars at Noon.* Boston: Little, Brown, 1954.

Coletta, Paola E., *The United States Navy and Defense Unification, 1947–1953.* Newark: University of Delaware Press, 1981.

———, ed. *American Secretaries of the Navy.* 2 vols. Annapolis, Md.: Naval Institute Press, 1980.

Coletta, Paola E., and K. Jack Bauer, eds. *United States Navy and Marine Corps Bases, Domestic.* Westport, Conn.: Greenwood Press, 1985.

Collins, Winifred Quick, with Herbert M. Levine. *More than a Uniform: A Navy Woman in a Navy Man's World.* College Station: University of North Texas Press, 1997.

Cook, Blanche N. *Eleanor Roosevelt.* 2 vols. New York: Viking, 1992.

Cooper, Page. *Navy Nurse.* New York: Whittlesey House, 1946.

———. *White Task Force.* New York: Whittlesey House, 1945.

Copeland, Peter. *She Went to War: The Rhonda Cornum Story.* Novato, Calif.: Presidio, 1992.

Costello, John. *Virtue Under Fire: How World War II Changed Our Social and Sexual Attitudes.* Boston: Little, Brown, 1985.

Creighton, Margaret S. *Rites and Passages: The Experience of American Whaling, 1830–1870.* New York: Cambridge University Press, 1995.

Cronon, David E., ed. *The Cabinet Diaries of Josephus Daniels, 1913–1921.* Lincoln: University of Nebraska Press, 1963.

Daniels, Josephus. *The Navy and the Nation: War-Time Addresses.* New York: George H. Doran, 1919.

——. *Our Navy at War.* Washington, D.C.: Pictorial Bureau, 1922.

Danner, Dorothy Still. *What a Way to Spend a War: Navy Nurse POWs in the Philippines.* Annapolis, Md.: Naval Institute Press, 1995.

Darden, T. F. *Historical Sketch of the Naval Administration of the Government of American Samoa: April 17, 1900–July 1, 1951.* Washington, D.C.: GPO, 1952.

Davies, Margery W. *Woman's Place Is at the Typewriter: Office Work and Office Workers, 1870–1930.* Philadelphia: Temple University Press, 1982.

DePauw, Linda Grant. *Baptism of Fire.* Pasadena, Md.: Minerva Center, 1993.

——. *Seafaring Women.* Boston: Houghlin Mifflin, 1982.

Dessez, Eunice C. *The First Enlisted Women: 1917–1918.* Philadelphia: Dorrance, 1955.

Dever, John P., and Maria C. Dever. *Women and the Military: Over 100 Notable Contributors, Historic to Contemporary.* Jefferson, N.C.: McFarland, 1995.

Devilbiss, M. C. *Women and Military Service: A History, Analysis, and Overview of Key Issues.* Maxwell Air Force Base, Ala.: Air University Press, 1990.

Dirvin, Joseph L. *Mrs. Seton: Foundress of the American Sisters of Charity.* New York: Farrar, Straus and Cudahy, 1962.

Disher, Sharon Hanley. *First Class: Women Join the Ranks at the Naval Academy.* Annapolis, Md.: Naval Institute Press, 1998.

Divine, Robert A. *The Cuban Missile Crisis.* Chicago: Quadrangle Books, 1971.

Dock, Lavinia L., and Isabel M. Stewart. *A Short History of Nursing: From Earliest Times to the Present Day.* 4th ed. New York: G. P. Putnam's Sons, 1938.

Donahue, M. Patricia. *Nursing: The Finest Art: An Illustrated History.* St. Louis: C. V. Mosby, 1985.

Donnelly, Thomas, Margaret Roth, and Caleb Baker. *Operation Just Cause: The Storming of Panama.* New York: Lexington Books, 1991.

Douglas, Deborah G. *United States Women in Aviation: 1940–1985.* Washington, D.C.: Smithsonian Institution Press, 1991.

Druett, Joan. *Petticoat Whalers: Whaling Wives at Sea, 1820–1920.* Auckland, New Zealand: Collins, 1991.

DuBois, Ellen Carol. *Feminism and Suffrage: The Emergence of an Independent Women's Movement in America, 1848–1869.* Ithaca: Cornell University Press, 1978.

Dulles, Foster Rhea. *The American Red Cross: A History.* Westport, Conn.: Greenwood, 1950.

Ebbert, Jean, and Marie-Beth Hall. *Crossed Currents: Navy Women from WW I to Tailhook.* Washington, D.C.: Brassey's, 1993.

Eckert, Edward K. *The Navy Department in the War of 1812.* Gainesville: University of Florida Press, 1973.

Eleanor, Sister M. *On the King's Highway: A History of the Sisters of the Holy Cross of St. Mary of the Immaculate Conception.* New York: D. Appleton, 1931.

Evans, Robley D. A *Sailor's Log: Recollections of Forty Years of Naval Life*. New York: D. Appleton, 1901.
Evans, Sara M. *Born for Liberty: A History of Women in America*. New York: Free Press, 1989.
Faragher, John M., and Florence Howe, eds. *Women and Higher Education in American History*. New York: W. W. Norton, 1988.
Feeney, Leonard. *Mother Seton: Saint Elizabeth of New York (1774–1821)*. Rev. ed. Cambridge: Ravengate Press, 1975.
Field, James A., Jr. *History of United States Naval Operations: Korea*. Washington, D.C.: GPO, 1962.
Fischer, Sue, ed. A *Pictorial History: Navy Women, 1908–1988*. N.p.: WAVES National, 1990.
Fletcher, M. H. *The WRNS: A History of the Women's Royal Naval Service*. Annapolis, Md.: Naval Institute Press, 1989.
Flexner, Eleanor. *Century of Struggle: The Woman's Rights Movement in the United States*. Cambridge: Harvard University Press, 1959.
Flynn, George Q. *The Draft: 1940–1973*. Lawrence: University Press of Kansas, 1993.
Fowler, William M., Jr. *Under Two Flags: The American Navy in the Civil War*. New York: W. W. Norton, 1990.
Fox, Mary V. *Women Astronauts Aboard the Shuttle*. New York: Julian Messner, 1984.
Friedan, Betty. *The Feminine Mystique*. New York: W. W. Norton, 1963.
———. *It Changed My Life: Writings on the Women's Movement*. 1963. Reprint, New York: Random House, 1976.
Friedl, Vicki L. *Women in the United States Military, 1901–1995: A Research Guide and Annotated Bibliography*. Westport, Conn.: Greenwood Press, 1996.
Friedman, Joan E., and William G. Shade. *Our American Sisters: Women in American Life and Thought*. Boston: Allyn and Bacon, 1973.
Friedman, Norman. *The Postwar Naval Revolution*. Annapolis, Md.: Naval Institute Press, 1986.
Furer, Julius A. *Administration of the Navy Department in World War II*. Washington, D.C.: GPO, 1959.
Gabriel, Richard A., and Karen S. Metz. *From the Renaissance through Modern Times*. Vol. 2 of A *History of Military Medicine*. Westport, Conn.: Greenwood, 1992.
Gilbo, Patrick. *The American Red Cross*. New York: Chelsea House, 1987.
Gildersleeve, Virginia Crocheron. *Many a Good Crusade: Memoirs of Virginia Crocheron Gildersleeve*. New York: Macmillan, 1954.
———. *The "WAVES" of the Navy: How They Began*. New York: Macmillan, 1956.
Gillmer, Thomas C. *Old Ironsides: The Rise, Decline, and Resurrection of the USS "Constitution."* Camden, Maine: International Marine, 1993.
Gilroy, William F. R., and Timothy J. Demy. A *Brief Chronology of the Chaplain Corps of the United States Navy*. Washington, D.C.: Naval Personnel, 1983.

Glenn, Bess. *Demobilization of Civilian Personnel by the U.S. Navy after the First World War.* Washington, D.C.: Office of Records Administration, Navy Department, 1945.

Goldie, Sue M., ed. *I Have Done My Duty: Florence Nightingale in the Crimean War.* Iowa City: University of Iowa Press, 1989.

Goldman, Nancy L., ed. *Female Soldiers—Combatants or Non-Combatants? Historical and Contemporary Perspectives.* Westport, Conn.: Greenwood, 1982.

Goldman, Nancy L., and David R. Segal, eds. *The Social Psychology of Military Service.* Beverly Hills: Sage Publications, 1976.

Goodnow, Minnie. *Nursing History.* 1916. Reprint, Philadelphia: W. B. Saunders, 1948.

Goodwin, Doris K. *No Ordinary Time: Franklin and Eleanor Roosevelt: The Home Front in World War II.* New York: F. Watts, 1994.

Gordon, Linda. *Woman's Body: Woman's Right: A Social History of Birth Control in America.* New York: Grossman, 1976.

Gordon, Lynn D. *Gender and Higher Education in the Progressive Era.* New Haven: Yale University Press, 1990.

Granger, Byrd H. *On Final Approach: The Women Airforce Service Pilots of W.W. II.* Scottsdale, Ariz.: Falconer Publishing, 1991.

Gray, Colin S. *The Navy in the Post Cold-War World: The Uses and Value of Strategic Sea Power.* University Park: Pennsylvania State University Press, 1994.

Gray, J[ohn] A. C. *Amerika Samoa: A History of American Samoa and Its United States Naval Administration.* Annapolis, Md.: U.S. Naval Institute, 1960.

Gray, Madeline. *Margaret Sanger: A Biography of the Champion of Birth Control.* New York: R. Marek, 1979.

Green, Blanche. *Growing Up in the WAC: Letters to My Sister, 1944–1946.* New York: Vantage Press, 1987.

Greenhill, Basil, and Ann Giffard. *Women Under Sail: Letters and Journals Concerning Eight Women Travelling or Working in Sailing Vessels between 1829 and 1949.* Newton Abbot: David and Charles, 1970.

Greenwald, Maurine W. *Women, War, and Work: The Impact of World War I on Women Workers in the United States.* Westport, Conn.: Greenwood, 1980.

Grossman, Mark. *Encyclopedia of the Persian Gulf War.* Santa Barbara, Calif.: ABC-CLIO, 1995.

Guilmartin, John F., Jr. *A Very Short War: The "Mayaguez" and the Battle of Koh Tang.* College Station: Texas A & M University Press, 1995.

Gunter, Helen C. *Navy WAVE: Memories of World War II.* Ft. Bragg, Calif.: Cypress House, 1992.

Hagan, Kenneth J., ed. *In Peace and War: Interpretations of American Naval History, 1775–1978.* 2d ed. Westport, Conn.: Greenwood Press, 1984.

———. *This People's Navy: The Making of American Sea Power.* New York: Free Press, 1991.

Hall, Richard. *Patriots in Disguise: Women Warriors of the Civil War.* New York: Paragon House, 1993.

Hallion, Richard P. *The Naval Air War in Korea*. Baltimore: Nautical & Aviation Publishing, 1985.

Halpern, Paul G. *A Naval History of World War I*. Annapolis, Md.: Naval Institute Press, 1994.

Hancock, Joy Bright. *Lady in the Navy: A Personal Reminiscence*. Annapolis, Md.: Naval Institute Press, 1972.

Harris, Mary Virginia. *Guide Right: A Handbook for WAVES and SPARS*. New York: Macmillan, 1944.

Harrod, Frederick S. *Manning the New Navy: The Development of a Modern Naval Enlisted Force, 1899–1940*. Westport, Conn.: Greenwood, 1978.

Hart, Robert A. *The Great White Fleet: Its Voyage around the World, 1907–1909*. Boston: Little, Brown, 1965.

Hartmann, Susan M. *The Home Front and Beyond: American Women in the 1940s*. Boston: Twayne Publishers, 1982.

Herman, Jan K. *Battle Station Sick Bay: Navy Medicine in World War II*. Annapolis, Md.: Naval Institute Press, 1997.

———. *A Hilltop in Foggy Bottom: Home of the Old Naval Observatory and the Navy Medical Department*. Washington, D.C.: Department of the Navy, Bureau of Medicine and Surgery, 1991.

Hewitt, Linda L. *Women Marines in World War I*. Washington, D.C.: History and Museums Division, Headquarters, USMC, 1974.

Hewlett, Richard G., and Francis Duncan. *The Nuclear Navy: 1946–1962*. Chicago: University of Chicago Press, 1974.

Hoehling, A. A. *The Great Epidemic*. Boston: Little Brown, 1961.

Holcomb, Richmond C. *A Century with Norfolk Naval Hospital: 1830–1930*. Portsmouth, Va.: Printcraft Publishing, 1930.

Hole, Judith, and Ellen Levine. *Rebirth of Feminism*. New York: Quadrangle Books, 1971.

Holm, Jeanne. *Women in the Military: An Unfinished Revolution*. Rev. ed. Novato, Calif.: Presidio, 1992.

———, ed. *In Defense of a Nation: Servicewomen in World War II*. Washington, D.C.: Military Women's Press, 1998.

Hone, Thomas C. *Power and Change: The Administrative History of the Office of the Chief of Naval Operations, 1946–1986*. Washington, D.C.: Naval Historical Center, 1989.

Honey, Maureen. *Creating Rosie the Riveter: Class, Gender and Propaganda during World War II*. Amherst: University of Massachusetts Press, 1984.

Hooper, Edwin B., Dean C. Allard, and Oscar P. Fitzgerald. *The Setting of the Stage*. Vol. 1 of *The United States Navy and the Vietnam Conflict*. Washington, D.C.: Naval History Division, 1976.

Hooper, Townsend. *Driven Patriot: The Life and Times of James Forrestal*. New York: Knopf, 1992.

Hovis, Bobbi. *Station Hospital Saigon: A Navy Nurse in Vietnam, 1963–1964*. Annapolis, Md.: Naval Institute Press, 1991.

*How to Serve Your Country in the WAVES or SPARS.* Recruiting booklet. N.p., 1943.

Howarth, Stephen. *To Shining Sea: A History of the United States Navy, 1775–1991.* New York: Random House, 1991.

Howell, Colin, and Richard J. Twomey, eds. *Jack Tar in History: Essays in the History of Maritime Life and Labour.* Fredericton, New Brunswick: Acadiensis Press, 1991.

Howes, Ruth H., and Michael R. Stevenson, eds. *Women and the Use of Military Force.* Boulder, Colo.: Lynne Rienner, 1993.

Huxley, Elizabeth. *Florence Nightingale.* New York: G. P. Putnam's Sons, 1975.

Isenberg, Michael T. *Shield of the Republic: The United States Navy in an Era of Cold War and Violent Peace, 1945–1962.* New York: St. Martin's, 1993.

Jacobs, Helen H. *By Your Leave, Sir.* New York: Dodd, Mead, 1943.

Jaros, Dean. *Heroes without Legacy: American Airwomen, 1912–1944.* Niwot: University of Colorado Press, 1993.

Johnson, Jesse J. *Black Women in the Armed Forces, 1942–1974: A Pictorial History.* Hampton, Va.: Hampton Institute Press, 1974.

Johnson, Louanne. *Making WAVES: A Woman in This Man's Navy.* New York: St. Martin's Press, 1986.

Jones, David E. *Women Warriors: A History.* Washington, D.C.: Brassey's, 1997.

Joslyn, Mauriel P., ed. *Valor and Lace: The Roles of Confederate Women, 1861–1865.* Murfreesboro, Tenn.: Southern Heritage Press, 1996.

Kalisch, Philip A., and Beatrice J. Kalisch. *The Advance of American Nursing.* 2d ed., Boston: Little, Brown, 1986; 3d ed., Philadelphia: J. B. Lippincott, 1995.

Karig, Walter, et al. *Battle Report.* Vol. 2, *The Atlantic War.* New York: Farrar & Rinehart, 1946.

Karsten, Peter. *The Military in America: From the Colonial Era to the Present.* Rev. ed. New York: Free Press, 1986.

———. *The Naval Aristocracy: The Golden Age of Annapolis and the Emergence of Modern American Navalism.* New York: Free Press, 1972.

Keil, Sally Van Wagenen. *Those Wonderful Women in Their Flying Machines: The Unknown Heroines of World War II.* New York: Rawson, Wade, 1979; New York: Four Directions Press, 1990.

Kennedy, David. *Birth Control in America: The Career of Margaret Sanger.* New Haven: Yale University Press, 1970.

King, Ernest J. *The United States Navy at War: Official Reports to the Secretary of the Navy.* Washington, D.C.: GPO, 1946.

King, Ernest J., and Walter M. Whitehill. *Fleet Admiral King: A Naval Record.* New York: Norton, 1952.

Kline, Ethel. *Gender Politics: From Consciousness to Mass Politics.* Cambridge: Harvard University Press, 1984.

Kraditor, Aileen S., ed. *Up from the Pedestal: Selected Writings in the History of American Feminism.* Chicago: Quadrangle Books, 1968.

Krichmar, Albert. *The Women's Movement in the Seventies: An International English-Language Bibliography.* Metuchen, N.J.: Scarecrow, 1977.

Langley, Harold D. *A History of Medicine in the Early U.S. Navy.* Baltimore: Johns Hopkins University, 1995.

———. *Social Reform in the United States Navy: 1798–1862.* Urbana: University of Illinois Press, 1967.

Lerner, Gerda. *The Female Experience: An American Documentary.* Indianapolis: Bobbs-Merrill Educational Publishing, 1977.

Litoff, Judy B., and David C. Smith. *We're in This War, Too: World War II Letters from American Women in Uniform.* New York: Oxford University Press, 1994.

Livermore, Mary A. *My Story of the War: A Woman's Narrative of Four Years Personal Experience as a Nurse in the Union Army, and in Relief Work at Home, in Hospitals, Camps, and at the Front, during the War of the Rebellion.* Hartford, Conn.: A. D. Worthington, 1889.

Lopata, Helen Z. *Occupation: Housewife.* New York: Oxford University Press, 1971.

Love, Robert W., Jr. *History of the U.S. Navy.* 2 vols. Harrisburg, Pa.: Stackpole Books, 1992.

———. ed. *The Chiefs of Naval Operations.* Annapolis, Md.: Naval Institute Press, 1980.

Lundberg, Ferdinand, and Marynia F. Farnham. *Modern Woman: The Lost Sex.* New York: Harper & Brothers, 1947.

Lyne, Mary C., and Kay Arthur. *Three Years Behind the Mast: The Story of the United States Coast Guard, SPARs.* Washington, D.C.: N.p., 1946.

Lynn, Susan. *Progressive Women in Conservative Times: Racial Justice, Peace, and Feminism, 1945 to the 1960s.* New Brunswick, N.J.: Rutgers University Press, 1992.

MacGregor, Morris J., and Bernard C. Nalty, eds. *Segregation Entrenched, 1917–1940.* Vol. 4 of *Blacks in the United States Armed Forces: Basic Documents.* Wilmington, Del.: Scholarly Resources, 1977.

Maher, Sister Mary Denis. *To Bind Up the Wounds: Catholic Sister Nurses in the U.S. Civil War.* Westport, Conn.: Greenwood Press, 1989.

Marks, G., and W. K. Beatty. *Epidemic.* New York: Charles Scribner's Sons, 1976.

Marolda, Edward J. *By Sea, Air, and Land: An Illustrated History of the U.S. Navy and the War in Southeast Asia.* Washington, D.C.: Naval Historical Center, 1994.

———, ed. *Operation End Sweep: A History of Minesweeping Operations in North Vietnam.* Washington, D.C.: Naval Historical Center, 1993.

Marolda, Edward J., and Oscar P. Fitzgerald. *From Military Assistance to Combat: 1959–1965.* Vol. 2 of *The United States Navy and the Vietnam Conflict.* Washington, D.C.: Naval Historical Center, 1986.

Marolda, Edward J., and Robert Schneller. *Shield and Sword: The U.S. Navy and the Persian Gulf War.* Washington, D.C.: Naval Historical Center, 1998.

Martin, George W. *Madam Secretary: Frances Perkins.* Boston: Houghton Mifflin, 1976.

Martin, Tyrone G. *A Most Fortunate Ship: A Narrative History of "Old Ironsides."* Chester, Conn.: Globe Pequot Press, 1980.

Mason, Gail. *Organization of the Navy Department: A History from 1947 to 1970.* Washington, D.C.: OA, Naval History Division, 1970.

Maxwell, William Quentin. *Lincoln's Fifth Wheel: The Political History of the United States Sanitary Commission.* New York: Longmans, Green, 1956.

McConnell, Malcolm. *Just Cause: The Real Story of America's High-Tech Invasion of Panama.* New York: St. Martin's, 1991.

McHenry, Robert, ed. *Liberty's Women.* Springfield, Mass.: G. & C. Merriam, 1980.

McKee, Christopher. *A Gentlemanly and Honorable Profession: The Creation of the U.S. Naval Officer Corps, 1794–1815.* Annapolis, Md.: Naval Institute Press, 1991.

McMichael, William H. *The Mother of All Hooks: The Story of the U.S. Navy's Tailhook Scandal.* New Brunswick, N.J.: Transaction Publishers, 1997.

Meid, Pat. *Marine Corps Women's Reserve in World War II.* Washington, D.C.: U.S. Marine Corps, 1968.

Meyer, Leisa. *Creating G.I. Jane: The Women's Army Corps During World War II.* New York: Columbia University Press, 1996.

Milkman, Ruth. *Gender at Work: The Dynamics of Job Segregation by Sex during World War II.* Urbana: University of Illinois Press, 1987.

Miller, Nathan. *The U.S. Navy: An Illustrated History.* Annapolis, Md.: Naval Institute Press, 1977.

——. *War at Sea: A Naval History of World War II.* New York: Scribner, 1995.

Morison, Elting E., ed. *The Letters of Theodore Roosevelt.* 8 vols. Cambridge: Harvard University Press, 1951–54.

Morison, Samuel Eliot. *History of United States Naval Operations in World War I.* 15 vols. Boston: Little, Brown, 1947–62.

——. *John Paul Jones: A Sailor's Biography.* Boston: Little, Brown, 1959.

Muir, Malcolm, Jr. *Black Shoes and Blue Water: Surface Warfare in the United States Navy, 1945–1975.* Washington, D.C.: Naval Historical Center, 1996.

National Aeronautics and Space Administration. *Information Summaries: Astronaut Fact Book,* 5 May 1996.

National Yeomen (F). *The Note Book, 1926–1983.* Smithsonian Institution, Washington, D.C.

Nau, Erika. *Angel in the Rigging.* New York: Berkly, 1976.

Naval History Division [Center]. *Dictionary of American Naval Fighting Ships.* 8 vols. Edited by James L. Mooney et al. Washington, D.C.: GPO, 1959–91.

Nelson, Dennis D. *The Integration of the Negro into the U.S. Navy.* New York: Farrar, Straus, and Young, 1951.

Newcomer, Mabel. *A Century of Higher Education for American Women.* Washington, D.C.: Zenger, 1959.

Noble, Dennis L. *Lighthouses and Keepers: The U.S. Lighthouse Service and Its Legacy.* Annapolis, Md.: Naval Institute Press, 1998.

Norman, Elizabeth M. *Women at War: The Story of Fifty Military Nurses Who Served in Vietnam.* Philadelphia: University of Pennsylvania Press, 1990.

Norton, Mary Beth. *Liberty's Daughters: The Revolutionary Experience of American Women, 1750–1800*. Boston: Little, Brown, 1980.

Oates, Stephen B. *A Woman of Valor: Clara Barton and the Civil War*. New York: Free Press, 1994.

Offner, John L. *An Unwanted War: The Diplomacy of the United States and Spain over Cuba, 1895–1898*. Chapel Hill: University of North Carolina Press, 1992.

O'Gara, Gordon C. *Theodore Roosevelt and the Rise of the Modern Navy*. 1943. New York: Greenwood Press, 1969.

[Olmstead, Frederick Law], comp. *Hospital Transports: A Memoir of the Embarkation of the Sick and Wounded from the Peninsula of Virginia in the Summer of 1862*. Boston: Ticknor and Fields, 1863.

Oman, Charles M. *Doctors Aweigh: The Story of the United States Medical Corps in Action*. Garden City, N.Y.: Doubleday, Doran, 1943.

O'Neill, William L. *American High: The Years of Confidence, 1945–1960*. New York: Free Press, 1986.

———. *A Democracy at War: America's Fight at Home and Abroad in World War II*. New York: Free Press, 1993.

*Pages from Nursing History: A Collection of Original Articles from the Pages of "Nursing Outlook," the "American Journal of Nursing" and "Nursing Research."* New York: American Journal of Nursing, 1984.

Painter, Nell Irvin. *Standing at Armageddon: The United States, 1877–1919*. New York: W. W. Norton, 1987.

Palmer, Michael A. *On Course to Desert Storm: The United States Navy and the Persian Gulf*. Washington, D.C.: NHC, 1992.

Pateman, Yvonne C. *Women Who Dared: American Test Pilots, Flight-Test Engineers, and Astronauts, 1912–1996*. Laguna Hills, Calif.: Norstahr, 1997.

Paullin, Charles O. *Paullin's History of Naval Administration: 1775–1911*. Annapolis, Md.: U.S. Naval Institute, 1968.

Polmar, Norman, and Thomas B. Allen. *Rickover*. New York: Simon and Schuster, 1982.

Poulos, Paula N., ed. *A Woman's War Too: U.S. Women in the Military in World War II*. Washington, D.C.: NARA, 1996.

Prange, Gordon. *At Dawn We Slept: The Untold Story of Pearl Harbor*. New York: McGraw-Hill, 1981.

Pryor, Elizabeth B. *Clara Barton: Professional Angel*. Philadelphia: University of Pennsylvania Press, 1987.

Reckner, James R. *Teddy Roosevelt's Great White Fleet*. Annapolis, Md.: Naval Institute Press, 1988.

Reilly, John C., Jr. *Ships of the United States Navy: Christening, Launching and Commissioning*. 2d ed. Washington, D.C.: Naval History Division, 1976.

Rickover, Hyman. *How the Battleship* Maine *Was Destroyed*. Washington, D.C.: Naval History Division, 1976.

Roddis, Louis H. *A Short History of Nautical Medicine.* New York: Paul B. Hoeber, 1941.

Rodger, N. A. M. *The Wooden World: The Anatomy of the Georgian Navy.* Annapolis, Md.: Naval Institute Press, 1986.

Rosenberg, Rosalind. *Beyond Separate Spheres: Intellectual Roots of Modern Feminism.* New Haven: Yale University Press, 1982.

Roskill, Stephen. *Naval Policy between the Wars.* New York: Walker, 1968.

Ross, Ishbel. *Angel of the Battlefield: The Life of Clara Barton.* New York: Harper, 1956.

Ross, Nancy Wilson. *The WAVES: The Story of the Girls in Blue.* New York: Henry Holt, 1943.

Rothman, Sheila M. *Woman's Proper Place: A History of Changing Ideals and Practices, 1870 to the Present.* New York: Basic Books, 1978.

*Rules for the Regulation of the Navy of the United Colonies of North America.* 1775. Reprint, Washington, D.C.: Naval Historical Foundation, 1944.

Rupp, Leila M. *Mobilizing Women for War: German and American Propaganda 1939–1945.* Princeton, N.J.: Princeton University Press, 1978.

——. *Survival in the Doldrums: The American Women's Rights Movement, 1945–1960.* New York: Oxford University Press, 1987.

Rury, John L. *Education and Women's Work: Female Schooling and the Division of Labor in Urban America, 1870–1930.* Albany: State University of New York Press, 1991.

Ryan, Mary P. *Womanhood in America: From Colonial Times to the Present.* 3d ed. New York: Franklin Watts, 1983.

Samuels, Peggy, and Harold Samuels. *Remembering the* Maine. Washington, D.C.: Smithsonian Institution Press, 1995.

Sanger, Margaret. *Margaret Sanger: An Autobiography.* New York: W. W. Norton, 1938.

Schneider, Dorothy, and Carl J. Schneider. *American Women in the Progressive Era.* New York: Facts on File, 1993.

Scott, Anne Firor. *The Southern Lady: From Pedestal to Politics, 1830–1930.* Chicago: University of Chicago Press, 1970.

Seeley, Charlotte P., comp. *American Women and the U.S. Armed Forces: A Guide to the Records of Military Agencies in the National Archives Relating to American Women.* Washington, D.C.: NARA, 1992.

Segal, David R., and H. Wallace Sinaiko, eds. *Life in the Rank and File: Enlisted Men and Women in the Armed Forces of the United States, Australia, Canada, and the United Kingdom.* Washington, D.C.: Pergamon-Brassey, 1986.

Sharff, Lee E., and Sol Gordon, eds. and comps. *Uniformed Services Almanac: 1980, 1989, 1990.* Falls Church, Va.: Uniformed Services Almanac, 1980, 1989, 1990.

Sheehy, Edward J. *The U.S. Navy, the Mediterranean, and the Cold War, 1945–1947.* Westport, Conn.: Greenwood Press, 1992.

Shelley, Mary J. *Navy Service: A Short History of the United States Naval Training School (WR) Bronx, New York.* [New York]: Public Relations Office, USNTS (WR), n.d.

Shields, Elizabeth Q., ed. *Highlights in the History of the Army Nurse Corps.* Washington, D.C.: U.S. Army Center of Military History, 1981.

Shulman, Mark R. *Navalism and the Emergence of American Sea Power, 1882–1893.* Annapolis, Md.: Naval Institute Press, 1995.

Sims, William S. *The Victory at Sea.* Garden City, N.Y.: Doubleday, Page, 1920.

Smith, Margaret Chase. *Declaration of Conscience.* Edited by William C. Lewis Jr. New York: Doubleday, 1972.

Smith, Page. *Daughters of the Promised Land: Women in American History.* Boston: Little, Brown, 1970.

Soderbergh, Peter A. *Women Marines: The World War II Era.* Westport, Conn.: Praeger, 1992.

Sprout, Harold, and Margaret Sprout. *Toward a New Order of Sea Power: American Naval Policy and the World Scene, 1918–1922.* Princeton, N.J.: Princeton University Press, 1940.

Stanik, Joseph T. *"Swift and Effective Retribution": The U.S. Sixth Fleet and the Confrontation with Quaddafi.* Washington, D.C.: NHC, 1996.

Stark, Suzanne J. *Female Tars: Women Aboard Ship in the Age of Sail.* Annapolis, Md.: Naval Institute Press, 1996.

Statham, Anne, Eleanor M. Miller, and Hans O. Mauksch, eds. *The Worth of Women's Work: A Quantitative Synthesis.* Albany: State University of New York Press, 1988.

Staubing, Harold E., comp. *In Hospital and Camp: The Civil War through the Eyes of Its Doctors and Nurses.* Harrisburg, Pa.: Stackpole Books, 1993.

Sterner, Doris M. *In and Out of Harm's Way: A History of the Navy Nurse Corps.* Seattle: Peanut Butter Publishing, 1996.

Stiehm, Judith Hicks. *Bring Me Men and Women: Mandated Change at the U.S. Air Force Academy.* Berkeley and Los Angeles: University of California Press, 1981.

Stivers, Reuben E. *Privateers and Volunteers: The Men and Women of Our Reserve Naval Forces: 1766–1866.* Annapolis, Md.: Naval Institute Press, 1975.

Streeter, Ruth C., and Katherine A. Towle. *History of the Marine Corps Women's Reserve: A Critical Analysis of Its Development and Operation, 1943–1945.* Washington, D.C.: GPO, 1945.

Stremlow, Mary V. *Free a Marine to Fight: Women Marines in World War II.* Washington, D.C.: Marine Corps Historical Center, 1994.

———. *A History of the Women Marines, 1946–1977.* Washington, D.C.: History and Museums Division, Headquarters, U.S. Marine Corps, 1986.

Stueck, William. *The Korean War: An International History.* Princeton, N.J.: Princeton University Press, 1995.

Swerdlow, Amy. *Women Strike for Peace: Traditional Motherhood and Radical Politics in the 1960s.* Chicago: University of Chicago Press, 1993.

[Talbot, Mary Ann]. *The Life and Surprising Adventures of Mary Ann Talbot, in the Name of John Taylor, A Natural Daughter of the Late Earl Talbot.* London: R. S. Kirby, [1809].

Thayer, William R. *The Life and Letters of John Hay*. 2 vols. in 1. Boston: Houghton Mifflin, 1929.

Tomblin, Barbara B. *G.I. Nightingales: The Army Nurse Corps in World War II*. Lexington: University Press of Kentucky, 1996.

Towle, Katherine A. *History of the Marine Corps Women's Reserve: A Critical Analysis of Its Development and Operation, 1943–1945*. Washington, D.C.: 1945.

Trask, David F. *The War with Spain in 1898*. New York: Macmillan, 1981.

Treadwell, Mattie E. *United States Army in World War II: Special Studies*. The Women's Army Corps. Washington, D.C.: Dept. of the Army, 1954.

Tucker, Spencer C. *The Jeffersonian Gunboat Navy*. Columbia: University of South Carolina Press, 1993.

Uhlig, Frank, Jr., ed. *Vietnam: The Naval Story*. Annapolis, Md.: Naval Institute Press, 1988.

Utz, Curtis A. *Assault from the Sea: The Amphibious Landing at Inchon*. Washington, D.C.: Naval Historical Center, 1994.

———. *Cordon of Steel: The U.S. Navy and the Cuban Missile Crisis*. Washington, D.C.: Naval Historical Center, 1993.

Van Denburgh, Elizabeth Douglas. *My Voyage in the United States Frigate "Congress."* New York: Desmond Fitzgerald, 1913.

Van Sickel, Emily. *The Iron Gates of Santo Tomas: The Firsthand Account of an American Couple Interned by the Japanese in Manila, 1942–1945*. Chicago: Academy Chicago Publishers, 1992.

Vogt, Gregory. *The Space Shuttle*. Brookfield, Conn.: Millsbrook Press, 1991.

Weinberg, Gerard L. *A World at Arms: A Global History of World War II*. New York: Cambridge University Press, 1995.

Weiner, Lynn Y. *From Working Girl to Working Mother: The Female Labor Force in the United States, 1820–1980*. Chapel Hill: University of North Carolina Press, 1985.

Weisgall, Jonathan M. *Operation Crossroads: The Atomic Tests at Bikini Atoll*. Annapolis, Md.: Naval Institute Press, 1994.

Wells, Mildred W. *Unity in Diversity: The History of the General Federation of Women's Clubs*. Washington, D.C.: General Federation of Women's Clubs, 1953.

White, Lynn. *Educating Our Daughters: A Challenge to the Colleges*. New York: Harper, 1950.

*Who's Who in America: 1960–1961*. Chicago: A. N. Marquis, 1960.

*Who's Who in America: 1962–1963*. Chicago: A. N. Marquis, 1962.

*Who's Who in America: 1964–1965*. Chicago: A. N. Marquis, 1964.

*Who's Who in America: 1966–1967*. Chicago: A. N. Marquis, 1966.

*Who's Who in America: 1968–1969*. Chicago: A. N. Marquis, 1968.

*Who's Who in America: 1970–1971*. Chicago: A. N. Marquis, 1970.

Wiebe, Robert H. *The Search for Order: 1877–1920*. New York: Hill and Wang, 1967.

Willenz, June A. *Women Veterans: America's Forgotten Heroines*. New York: Continuum, 1983.

Williams, Kathleen B. *Secret Weapon: U.S. High-Frequency Direction Finding in the Battle of the Atlantic*. Annapolis, Md.: Naval Institute Press, 1996.

Williams, William J. *The Wilson Administration and the Shipbuilding Crisis of 1917*. New York: Edwin Mellen, 1992.

Willoughby, Malcolm F. *The Coast Guard in World War II*. Annapolis, Md.: U.S. Naval Institute, 1957.

Wilson, Nancy R. *The WAVES: The Story of the Girls in Blue*. New York: Henry Holt, 1943.

Wingo, Josette D. *Mother Was a Gunner's Mate: World War II in the WAVES*. Annapolis, Md.: Naval Institute Press, 1994.

*Women in War Service*. Compiled by Headquarters Research Office, General Federation of Women's Clubs, Washington, D.C.: n.p. [1944?].

Yerxa, Donald A. *Admirals and Empire: The United States Navy and the Caribbean, 1898–1945*. Columbia: University of South Carolina Press, 1991.

Yianilos, Theresa Koras. *Woman Marine: A Memoir of a Woman Who Joined the U.S. Marine Corps in World War II to "Free a Marine to Fight."* La Jolla, Calif.: La Jolla Book Publishing, 1994.

Zimmerman, Jean. *Tailspin: Women at War in the Wake of Tailhook*. New York: Doubleday, 1995.

Zumwalt, Elmo R., Jr. *On Watch*. New York: Quadrangle, 1977.

## Newspapers, Magazines, and Journals

*Advancing Clinical Care*. 1991.

*All Hands*. 1945–91.

*Armed Forces and Society*. 1980–94.

*Armed Forces Talk*. Special Issue: "Women in the Armed Forces." 7 November 1952.

*Army and Navy Register*. 1918–19.

*Bulletin of the American Meteorological Society*. 1995.

*Bureau of Naval Personnel Information Bulletin*. 1942–45. Became *All Hands*, June 1945.

*Hospital Corps Quarterly*. 1927.

*International Journal of Maritime History*. 1992.

*Journal of Emergency Nursing*. 1991.

*Marines Magazine*. 1918.

*Minerva: Quarterly Report on Women and the Military*. 1982–95.

*Naval Aviation News*. 1977–92.

*Navy Nurse Corps Association News* (*NNCA News*). 1990.

*Navy Nurse Corps: Director's Update*. 1992–97.

*Navy Times*. 1967–92.

*Newport News Daily Press*. 1992–98.

*New York Times*. 1945–91.

*Nursing Times*. 1986–89.

*Pacific Coast Journal of Nursing*. 1942.
*Proceedings* (*USNIP*), U.S. Naval Institute. 1943–96.
*R.N.* 1943–45.
*Sea Letter.* 1994.
*Sea Power.* 1943–77.
*Soldiers.* 1990.
*Trained Nurse and Hospital Review.* 1943–49.
*U.S. Naval Medical Bulletin.* 1919–33.
*U.S. Navy Medicine.* 1979–95.
*Washington Post.* 1917–97.
*Washington Times.* 1988–90.
*Wings of Gold.* 1992.

## Articles and Book Chapters

"About Women." *Our Navy* 11 (March 1918): 21.

Acthison, Jerry. "Captain Joan Bynum: A Matter of Setting Goals." *All Hands* (February 1979): 14–19.

Akers, Regina T. "Female Naval Reservists during World War II: A Historiographical Essay." *Minerva* 8 (summer 1990): 55–61.

Allard, Dean C. "Anglo-American Naval Differences during World War I." *Military Affairs* 44 (April 1980): 75–81.

——. "An Era of Transition, 1945–1953." In Hagan, *In Peace and War*, 290–303.

Alsmeyer, Marie Bennett. "Those Navy WAVES." *All Hands* (July 1983): 2–7.

——. "Those Unseen, Unheard Arkansas Women: WACs, WAVES, and Women Marines of World War II." *Minerva* 12 (summer 1994): 22–33.

"And to the Sugar 'n' Spice, Too." *American Legion Magazine* 103 (November 1977): 9.

Armas, Maria T. "Women at War." *Naval History* 8 (March/April 1994): 10–14.

Ashley, Jo Ann. "Nursing and Early Feminism." In *Pages from Nursing History*, 68–70.

Association of the Bar of the City of New York Committee on Military Affairs and Justice. "The Combat Exclusion Laws: An Idea Whose Time Has Gone." *Minerva* 9 (winter 1991): 1–55.

Austin, Anne L. "Wartime Volunteers—1861–1865." In *Pages from Nursing History*, 22–24.

Bainder, Herman C. "WOTC." *Marine Corps Gazette* 34 (September 1950): 47–51.

Baker, Mary. "War Memories." *Nursing Times* 82 (January 1986): 46–47.

Baldwin, Sherman. "Creating the Ultimate Meritocracy." United States Naval Institute *Proceedings* 119 (June 1993): 33–36.

Barnette, Robin. "DACOWITS: A Focus on Issues." *All Hands* (June 1988): 17.

——. "Looking Ahead: The Navy's Senior Woman Line Officer Talks about What a Woman Needs to Succeed in Today's Navy, and the Navy of Tomorrow." *All Hands* (June 1988): 10–11.

Barton, Margaret. "The Navy Nurse Corps: Eighty Years of Service, Professionalism, and Spirit." *Navy Medicine* 79 (May–June 1988): 12–15.

Beck, Lois M. "Sexual Harassment in the Army: Roots Examined." *Minerva* 9 (spring 1991): 29–40.

Becker, Stephen E. "Integration of Women in the Brigade." *Shipmate* (June 1988): 15–16.

Becraft, Carolyn, and Lisa Zurmuhlen. "Military Women in the 80's." *Minerva* 5 (winter 1987): 28–32.

Bergeron, Kathleen G. "Nobody Asked Me Either, but . . . The Right Agenda for Military Women." U.S. Naval Institute *Proceedings* 119 (January 1993): 95–96.

Berry, Tracy. "Command at Sea." *All Hands* (April 1989): 4.

Berry, William. "Ten Days of Urgent Fury." *All Hands* (May 1984): 18–27.

Bolebruch, Lori. "And the Walls Came Tumblin' Down." United States Naval Institute *Proceedings* 118 (Febuary 1992): 42–44.

Bonham, Julia C. "Feminist and Victorian: The Paradox of the American Seafaring Women of the Nineteenth Century." *American Neptune: A Quarterly Journal of Maritime History* 37 (July 1977): 203–18.

Booher, Alice A. "American Military Women as Prisoners of War." *Minerva* 10 (fall/winter 1992): 76–80; 11 (spring 1993): 17–22.

Bove, Alfred A., T. G. Patel, and Raphael F. Smith. "Fleet Hospitals: Full-Service Care." United States Naval Institute *Proceedings* 118 (October 1992): 77–79.

Bowman, J. Beatrice. "Comment on Navy Nursing." In *Report of 17th Annual Convention of ANA, 25 April 1914. American Journal of Nursing* 14 (July 1914): 837–39.

———. "Disability Bill for Army and Navy Nurses." *American Journal of Nursing* 30 (August 1930): 1016.

———. "Experiences of Unit D at Haslar, England." *American Journal of Nursing* 15 (September 1915): 1112.

———. "The Great Lakes Training Station." *American Journal of Nursing* 18 (May 1918): 691–94.

———. "The History and Development of the Navy Nurse Corps." *American Journal of Nursing* 25 (May 1925): 356–60.

———. "History of Nursing in the Navy." *American Journal of Nursing* 28 (September 1928).

———. "The Hospital Corps Training School of the Navy." *American Journal of Nursing* 23 (March 1923): 489.

———. "The Navy Nurse Corps and Its Relation to the Advancement of Nursing Education." *American Journal of Nursing* 24 (1924): 78–83. Also presented at the twenty-fourth annual convention of the ANA.

———. "The Pharmacist's Mates School." *Hospital Corps Quarterly* 11 (July 1927): 301–5.

———. "Present Trends in Nurses' Training." *U.S. Navy Medical Bulletin* (July 1932): 390. Also presented as a radio address, 17 February 1932.

Boyer, Olive, and Mary E. Felder. "The Navy Cares for Its Own." *Trained Nurse and Hospital Review* (February 1943): 97–99.

Boylan, Robert J. "The Admiral with the Healer's Hands." *Sea Power* (July 1972): 36.

Boyle, Ron. "SA Mary Cobb: She Changed Her Wardrobe." *All Hands* (December 1980): 44–45.

Braun, Frederica. "Duty and Diversion on Guam." *American Journal of Nursing* 18 (May 1918): 650–52.

Broe, Ruth. "Women Marines Celebrate a Triple Anniversary." *Navy Magazine* (November 1968): 34–36.

Brooks, Mary. "The Naval Hospital, Newport, RI." *American Journal of Nursing* 18 (May 1918): 627–33.

Brou, Claire E. "WAVES: Twenty-Five Years in Retrospect." Washington, D.C.: Naval Historical Foundation, 1967.

Bullough, Bonnie. "The Lasting Impact of World War II on Nursing." In *Pages from Nursing History*, 126–28.

"BuMed Completes Reorganization." *U.S. Navy Medicine* 70 (May 1979): 10–17.

"BuMed Update: Navy Surgeon General Discusses Efforts to Improve Medical Care." *All Hands* (December 1989): 15–17.

Burgess, Ann C., and Janet Burns. "Partners in Care." *American Journal of Nursing* 90 (June 1990): 73–75.

Burlage, John. "After 32 Years in Navy, Hazard Goes Out on Top." *Navy Times*, 14 September 1992, 8.

Burnett, Douglas R. "The Sexually-Integrated Warship Can't Be the Most Combat-Effective Warship." U.S. Naval Institute *Proceedings* 103 (April 1977): 90–91.

Burnette, Deborah. "Angels of Mercy." *All Hands* (November 1987): 18–22.

Bush, Ted. "Watkins: Navy Has All the Women It Needs." *Navy Times*, 23 June 1986, 4, 20.

Byron, John L. "End Sexism." U.S. Naval Institute *Proceedings* 122 (February 1996): 27–31.

JFC. "New Emphasis on Pride: CNO Shares His Thoughts." *All Hands* (April 1981): 2–7.

Cadenhead, Julia T. "Pregnancy on Active Duty: Making the Tough Decisions." U.S. Naval Institute *Proceedings* 121 (April 1995): 52–53.

"Call Them Marines." U.S. Naval Institute *Proceedings* 101 (November 1975): 68.

Campbell, D'Ann. "Combatting the Gender Gap." *Temple Political and Civil Rights Law Review* 2 (fall 1992): 63–91.

———. "Servicewomen and the Academies: The Football Cordon and Pep Rally as a Case Study of the Status of Female Cadets at the United States Military Academy." *Minerva* 13 (spring 1995): 1–14.

———. "Servicewomen of World War II." *Armed Forces and Society* 16 (winter 1990): 263–66.

———. "Women, Combat, and the Gender Line," *MHQ: Quarterly Journal of Military History* 6 (Autumn 1993): 88–97.

———. "Women in Combat: The World War II Experience in the United States, Great Britain, Germany, and the Soviet Union." *Journal of Military History* 57 (April 1993): 301–23.

Campbell, Jeannie. "Vice Admiral Zimble: Surgeon General of the Navy." *All Hands* (November 1987): 4–9.

Carr, John E. "Medical Corps Status Report." *U.S. Navy Medicine* 70 (November 1979): 12–15.

Christmann, Timothy J. "Navy's First Female Test Pilot." *Naval Aviation News* (November–December 1985): 24–26.

——. "TacAir in Grenada." *Naval Aviation News* (November–December 1985): 6–9.

Christy, Teresa. "Equal Rights for Women: Voices from the Past." In *Pages from Nursing History*, 62–67.

——. "The Fateful Decade, 1890–1900." In *Pages from Nursing History*, 37–39.

"Civil War Hospital Ship." *All Hands*, book supplement (February 1962): 59–63.

"CNO—Since 1915, A Naval Career at Its Zenith." *All Hands* (July 1974): 2–5.

"The Coast Guard's Women at Sea." *Times Magazine*, 20 February 1978.

Coleman, John. "Admiral Watkins: CNO Outlines Goals and Objectives." *All Hands* (October 1982): 2–6.

——. "Nearly Two Centuries of Providing Encouragement, Comfort, and Inspiration." *All Hands* (April 1974): 22–27.

Collins, Helen F. "Fifinella and Friends." *Naval Aviation News* (July 1977): 21–23.

——. "From Plane Captains to Pilots." *Naval Aviation News* (July 1977): 8–18.

Collins, Sheila K. "Women at the Top of Women's Fields: Social Work, Nursing, and Education." In Statham, Miller, and Mauksch, *Worth of Women's Work*, 187–201.

Conder, Maxine. "Open Letter to Nurse Corps Officers." *Navy Medicine* 68 (May 1977): 2–5.

Condon-Rall, Mary Ellen. "The U.S. Army Medical Department and the Attack on Pearl Harbor." *Journal of Military History* 53 (January 1989): 65–78.

——. "U.S. Army Medical Preparations and the Outbreak of War: The Philippines, 1941–6 May 1942." *Journal of Military History* 56 (January 1992): 35–56.

Connelly, Ellen H. "Shipmates in White." *American Journal of Nursing* 49 (April 1949): 204.

"A Conversation with RAdm. Stratton." *U.S. Navy Medicine* 83 (May–June 1992): 5–8.

Coons, Russell L. "Larger Horizons and Brighter Sunsets: Women CWOs and LDOs." *All Hands* (December 1983): 3–7.

Cooper, Diane E. "She Dressed Herself in Sailors' Clothes." *Sea Letter* 49 (fall/winter 1994): 2–9.

Copeland, Mary, Jewell Derryberry, Dorothy Eaton, and Margaret Harper. "A Projective Technique for Investigating How Nurses Feel about the Use of Authority." *Nursing Research* 4 (October 55): 79–86.

Corley, Mary C., and Hans O. Mauksch. "Registered Nurses, Gender, and Commitment." In Statham, Miller, and Mauksch, *Worth of Women's Work*, 135–49.

Covey, Dana C. "Fleet Hospitals Could Be Better." U.S. Naval Institute *Proceedings* 118 (June 1992): 60–63.

Coye, Beth F. "The Restricted Unrestricted Line Officer: The Status of the Navy's Woman Line Officer." *Naval War College Review* 24 (March 1972): 53–63.

——. "We've Come a Long Way, But . . ." U.S. Naval Institute *Proceedings* 105 (July 1979): 41–49.

Coye, Beth F., Sara P. Denby, C. Cort Hooper, and Kathleen A. Mullen. "Is There Room for Women in Navy Management: An Attitudinal Survey." *Naval War College Review* 25 (January–February 1973): 69–87.

Coyl, E. R. "Hospital Ships in Korea." Paper presented at 59th Annual Convention of the Association of Military Surgeons of the United States, 17–19 November 1952.

Crawford, Joan B. "Making WAVES." *Naval History* 2 (winter 1988): 25–29.

Creighton, Margaret S. "American Mariners and the Rites of Manhood, 1830–1870." In Howell and Twomey, *Jack Tar in History*, 143–63.

——. "'Women' and Men in American Whaling, 1830–1870." *International Journal of Maritime History* 4 (June 1992): 195–218.

Culbertson, Sharon Marie. "Women Veterans Opens Membership to Veterans of All Services." *Minerva* 3 (fall 1985): 37–38.

Culpepper, Marilyn M., and Pauline G. Adams. "Nursing in the Civil War." *American Journal of Nursing* 88 (July 1988): 981–84.

Curto, Christine. "Nurse Pioneers and the Hospital Ship *Relief*." *Navy Medicine* 83 (May–June 1992): 20–25.

D'Amico, Francine. "Women at Arms: The Combat Controversy." *Minerva* 8 (summer 1990): 1–19.

Davis, Dorothy M. "The Navy Nurse Teaches as She Serves." *Pacific Coast Journal of Nursing* 38 (December 1942): 544–45.

Davis, Hugh H. "The American Seamen's Friend Society and the American Sailor, 1828–1838." *American Neptune: A Quarterly Journal of Maritime History* 39 (January 1979): 45–57.

DePauw, Linda Grant. "Women in Combat: The Revolutionary Experience." *Armed Forces and Society* 7 (winter 1981): 209–26.

Desmarais, Mary V. "Navy Nursing on D-Day Plus 4." *American Journal of Nursing* 45 (January 1945): 12.

Devilbiss, M. C. "Women in Combat: A Quick Summary of the Arguments on Both Sides." *Minerva* 8 (spring 1990): 29–31.

DiLucente, A. "Equality: A Step Backward." U.S. Naval Institute *Proceedings* 118 (February 1992): 46–48.

Dock, Lavinia. "Foreign Department." *American Journal of Nursing*, editorial, 19 (January 1919): 292.

Dohlie, Britt. "Women in the Military of Foreign Countries." *Minerva* 6 (winter 1988): 73–78.

Dolan, Josephine. "Three Schools—1873." In *Pages from Nursing History*, 33–36.

Douglas, Richard A. "Treating the Enemy: Santiago, Cuba, 1898." *Navy Medicine* 80 (July–August 1989): 20–21.

Downing, T. M. "Just Say No!!" U.S. Naval Institute *Proceedings* 118 (February 1992): 45–46.

Doyle, Brian. "The Admiral." *Boston College Magazine* (1990?): 42–49.

Dreves, Katharine D. "Vassar Training Camp for Nurses." In *Pages from Nursing History*, 93–95.

Duffey, Barbara. "The Nurse: Ella K. Newsom Trader." In Joslyn, *Valor and Lace*, 91–114.

Dugaw, Dianne. "'Rambling Female Sailors': The Rise and Fall of the Seafaring Heroine." *International Journal of Maritime History* 4 (June 1992): 179–94.

———. "'Wild Beasts' and 'Excellent Friends': Gender, Class and the Female Warrior, 1750–1830." In Howell and Twomey, *Jack Tar in History*, 132–42.

Dunbar, Ruth B. "Return to the Philippines." *American Journal of Nursing* 45 (December 1945): 1015–18.

Dunivin, Karen O. "There's Men, There's Women, and There's Me: The Role and Status of Military Women." *Minerva* 6 (summer 1988): 43–68.

Dye, Ira. "Physical and Social Profiles of Early American Seafarers, 1812–1815." In Howell and Twomey, *Jack Tar in History*, 220–35.

Earle, Fred M. "Employment of Women in Navy Yards." United States Naval Institute *Proceedings* 71 (September 1945): 1050–57.

Ebbert, Jean. "Honoring WAVES: Not Just Nostalgia." *Navy Times*, 31 August 1981.

———. "Keeping 'Magic' a Secret for 40 Years." *Navy Times*, 25 July 1983.

Ebbert, Jean, and Marie-Beth Hall. "Navy Women's Reserve: WAVES." In Holm, *In Defense of a Nation*, 57–75.

Ellefson, Cheryl. "Servants of God and Man: The Sisters of Charity." In Joslyn, *Valor and Lace*, 175–85.

Elmore, Joyce A. "Black Nurses: Their Service and Their Struggle." In *Pages from Nursing History*, 30–32.

Enloe, Cynthia. "The Politics of Constructing the American Woman Soldier as a Professionalized 'First Class Citizen': Some Lessons from the Gulf War." *Minerva* 10 (spring 1992): 14–31.

Evans, David. "No Place for Women." U.S. Naval Institute *Proceedings* 107 (November 1981): 53–56.

"Fair Winds and Following Seas: Admiral Zumwalt Retires as Chief of Naval Operations." *All Hands* (June 1974): 2–9.

Fellenz, Patricia. "Nurses under the Sea." *U.S. Navy Medical News Letter* 51 (April 1968): 19–21.

Fellows, Catherine. "First Lady of the Navy." *All Hands* (July 1978): 33–35.

Firestone, Juanita M., and Richard J. Harris. "Sexual Harassment in the U.S. Military: Individualized and Environmental Contexts." *Armed Forces and Society* 21 (fall 1994): 25–43.

Fletcher, Jean W., Joyce S. McMahon, and Aline O. Quester. "Tradition, Technology, and the Changing Roles of Women in the Navy." *Minerva* 11 (fall/winter 1993): 57–85.

"Flight Wings for Linda." *All Hands* (July 1974): 44–45.

"Flying Ambulances." *All Hands* (June 1951): 25.

Forrester, D. Anthony, and Pamela M. Grandinetti. "Nurses on Stamps: A Distinguished History." *American Journal of Nursing* 92 (May 1992): 62–65.

Foss, William O. "How WAVES Succeeded in a Man's Navy." *Our Navy* (July 1962): 4–6, 59.

Fournier, Donna J. "The Forgotten Enlisted Women of World War I." *Retired Officer* 40 (October 1984): 30–32.

Fowler, William M., Jr. "Relief on the River: The *Red Rover*." *Naval History* 5 (fall 1991): 14–19.

Frailey, Fred. "Navy Medicine Maintains Tradition of Caring." *All Hands* (November 1987): 40–43.

Fraker, Dave. "A Shipmate Is a Shipmate." *All Hands* (June 1988): 4–9.

Frank, Mary E.V. "Army and Navy Nurses Held as Prisoners of War during World War II." *Minerva* 6 (summer 1988): 82–90.

Friedman, Norman. "Elmo Russell Zumwalt, Jr., 1 July 1970–1 July 1974." In Love, *Chiefs of Naval Operations*, 365–79.

"Gays in the Military." U.S. Naval Institute *Proceedings* 119 (April 1993): 88–102.

Geraci, Karen S. "Women in Combat?" *Minerva* 13 (spring 1995): 19–35.

Gilbert, Michael H. "Women in Combat: Who Should Make the Policy." *Minerva* 10 (summer 1992): 1–7.

Gilmore, Zoe. "The Navy Nurse Corps." *Bulletin of the California State Nurses' Association* 51 (October 1955): 312–13.

Godson, Susan H. "Capt. Joy Bright Hancock and the Role of Women in the U.S. Navy." *New Jersey History* 105 (spring/summer 1987): 1–17.

———. "Capt. Joy Bright Hancock—Builder of the Co-Ed Navy." *Retired Officer* 38 (December 1982): 14–17.

———. "Navy Nurse Corps." In Holm, *In Defense of a Nation*, 29–37.

———. "Red Cross Nurses: German U-Boat Victims." *Retired Officer* 38 (June 1982): 24–26.

———. "The WAVES in World War II." U.S. Naval Institute *Proceedings* 107 (December 1981): 46–51.

———. "Womanpower in World War I." U.S. Naval Institute *Proceedings* 110 (December 1984): 60–64.

Gomulka, Eugene T. "Why No Gays?" U.S. Naval Institute *Proceedings* 118 (December 1992): 44–46.

Goodrich, Annie W. "Yale University School of Nursing." *American Journal of Nursing* 25 (May 1925): 360.

Gordon, Marilyn A., and Mary Jo Ludvigson. "A Constitutional Analysis of the Combat Exclusion for Air Force Women." *Minerva* 9 (summer 1991): 1–34.

Goudreau, Alice A. "Nursing at an Advance Naval Base Hospital." *American Journal of Nursing* 45 (November 1945): 884–86.

"Growth of the Naval Reserve Force." *Army and Navy Register* 63 (18 May 1918): 38.

Grupp, George W. "The First: Navy Used First Hospital Ship to Treat Civil War Wounded." *Navy Times*, 5 December 1953, 13.

Guthrie, Lou MacPherson. "I Was a Yeomanette." U.S. Naval Institute *Proceedings* 110 (December 1984): 57–64.

Hancock, Eleanor. "Employment in Wartime: The Experience of German Women during the Second World War." *War and Society* 12 (October 1994): 43–68.

"Happy 30th Anniversary." *All Hands* (July 1972): 12–13.

Hartley, Reba K. W. "A Nurse Looks at the Navy." *American Journal of Nursing* 45 (April 1945): 294.

Hartwell, Laura. "Impressions of Samoa." *American Journal of Nursing* 23 (February 1923): 397–98.

Hasson, Esther V. "The Navy Nurse Corps." *American Journal of Nursing* 9 (March 1909): 410–15.

Hayes, John D. "Sea Power in the Civil War." U.S. Naval Institute *Proceedings* 87 (November 1961): 60–69.

Heckathorn, Mary E. "The Navy Waves the Rules." U.S. Naval Institute *Proceedings* 69 (August 1943): 1082–84.

Herbert, Melissa S. "Amazons or Butterflies; the Recruitment of Women into the Military during World War II." *Minerva* 9 (summer 1991): 50–68.

Herman, Jan K. "A Conversation with RAdm Hall." *U.S. Navy Medicine* 79 (May–June 1988): 8–11.

——. "Flight Nurse at Iwo." *U.S. Navy Medicine* 86 (March–April 1995): 8–12.

——. "Welcome Back BuMed." *U.S. Navy Medicine* 80 (July–August 1989): 10–15.

Hertzer, R. "Comments on Navy Nursing." Report of 17th Annual Convention of ANA, 25 April 1914. *American Journal of Nursing* 14 (July 1914): 840–41.

Hewey, Dale. "They Found a Career." *All Hands* (July 1983): 16–17.

Hickox, Kay. "WW I Navy Nurse Looks Back." *All Hands* (August 1983): 16–18.

Higbee, Lenah S. Editorial comment on Navy Nurse Corps requirements. *American Journal of Nursing* 18 (May 1918): 598.

——. "Nursing as It Relates to the War: The Navy." *American Journal of Nursing* 18 (May 1918): 661–64. Also paper presented to 21st Annual Convention of ANA, May 1918.

——. "Nursing in Government Services." *American Journal of Nursing* 22 (April 1922): 524–26. Also paper presented to Veterans' Bureau meeting.

Hirsch, Erwin F. "Were Naval Medical Forces Prepared?" U.S. Naval Institute *Proceedings* 118 (July 1992): 93–95.

Hock, Cecilia. "Creation of the WAC Image and Perception of Army Women: 1942–44." *Minerva* 13 (spring 1995): 40–62.

Hone, Thomas C. "The Effectiveness of the 'Washington Treaty' Navy." *Naval War College Review* 32 (November–December 1979): 35–59.

Hone, Thomas C., and Mark D. Mandeles. "Managerial Style in the Interwar Navy: A Reappraisal." *Naval War College Review* 33 (September–October 1980): 88–101.

Hoogendorn, Raelene K. "Deployed to Desert Storm: The First 40 Hours." *Journal of Emergency Nursing* 17 (August 1991): 26A–29A.

Hoover, William D. "The Disadvantaged Navy Woman." U.S. Naval Institute *Proceedings* 103 (July 1977): 118–21.

Howes, Ruth H., and Caroline L. Herzenberg. "Women in Weapons Development: The Manhattan Project." In Howes and Stevenson, *Women and the Use of Military Force*, 95–109.

Humphrey, Mary. "Letters from Navy Nurses, Samoa." *American Journal of Nursing* 15 (June 1915): 760–63.

Humphrey, Mary H. [M. H. H.]. "Samoa." *American Journal of Nursing* 14 (September 1914): 1069–73.

Hunter, Edna J., and Carol B. Million. "Women in a Changing Military." U.S. Naval Institute *Proceedings* 103 (July 1977): 50–58.

"An Interview with Your CNO." *All Hands* (December 1974): 2–9.

"Introducing Some Fair Marines: Ninety-nine Men Have Already Been Released for Field Service Through Enrollment of Women Reservists." *Marines Magazine* 3 (October 1918): 23.

"I Was There Too." *Biarritz* (July 1980): 56–58.

Jackson, Kathi. "50 Years Ago—World War II and the Navy Nurse." *U.S. Navy Medicine* 86 (July–August 1995): 18–22.

Jackson, Leona. "I Was on Guam." *American Journal of Nursing* 42 (December 1942): 95–99.

———. "We've Reached the Golden Year." *American Journal of Nursing* 58 (May 1958): 671–73.

Jensen, Milinda D. "Women Military Aviators 1989 Convention: Women in Naval Aviation, 15 Years." *Naval Aviation News* (November–December 1989): 10–12.

John, Steve. "Grace Hopper—A Living Legend." *All Hands* (September 1982): 2–6.

Johnson, Dean Frazier, Carolyn M. Wells, Robert Breckenridge. "Implications for Aging: Service as a Female Naval Officer." *Minerva* 7 (spring 1989): 15–46.

Johnson, Louanne. "This Man's Navy." *Minerva* 6 (fall 1988): 12–25.

Jones, Dorothy E. "The Nurse Corps of the U.S. Naval Reserve." Reprinted from *American Journal of Nursing* 50 (May 1950).

Jones, Jo. "Women of Annapolis." *All Hands* (July 1983): 32–36.

Kalisch, Beatrice J., and Philip A. Kalisch. "The Cadet Nurse Corps in World War II." In *Pages from Nursing History*, 102–4.

Kalisch, Philip A., and Beatrice J. Kalisch. "Nurses under Fire: The World War II Experience of Nurses on Bataan and Corregidor." In *Pages from Nursing History*, 105–25.

Kalisch, Philip A., and Margaret Scobey. "Female Nurses in American Wars: Helplessness Suspended for the Duration." *Armed Forces and Society* 9 (winter 1983): 215–44.

Katzenstein, Mary F. "The Spectacle as Political Resistance: Feminist and Gay/Lesbian Politics in the Military." *Minerva* 11 (spring 1993): 1–16.

Kelly, James F., Jr. "Women in Warships: A Right to Serve." U.S. Naval Institute *Proceedings* 104 (October 1978): 44–53.

Kennedy, Floyd D., Jr. "The Creation of the Cold War Navy, 1953–1962." In Hagan, *In Peace and War*, 304–26.

———. "David Lamar McDonald: 1 August 1963–1 August 1967." In Love, *Chiefs of Naval Operations*, 333–49.

———. "From SLOC Protection to a National Maritime Strategy: The U.S. Navy under Carter and Reagan, 1977–84." In Hagan, *In Peace and War*, 346–70.

Kennedy, R. W. "Navy Blue and Blonde." U.S. Naval Institute *Proceedings* 99 (August 1973): 49–55.

Kerber, Linda K. "Separate Spheres, Female Worlds, Woman's Place: The Rhetoric of Women's History." *Journal of American History* 75 (June 1988): 9–39.

Klaver, Carol. "An Introduction to the Legend of Molly Pitcher." *Minerva* 12 (summer 1994): 35–61.

Kline, I. Grace. "Hospital Corpsmen of the Navy." *American Journal of Nursing* 21 (January 1921) 226–28.

———. "The Naval Hospital at Charleston, South Carolina." *American Journal of Nursing* 18 (May 1918): 668–72.

Knight, Della V. "Maria Roberta—A Tribute." *U.S. Naval Medical Bulletin* 17 (September 1922): 515–18.

Korb, Lawrence J. "The Erosion of American Naval Preeminence, 1962–1978." In Hagan, *In Peace and War*, 327–46.

Krohne, K. A. "Conduct Unbecoming." U.S. Naval Institute *Proceedings* 118 (August 1992): 53–56.

Lally, Grace B. "On Being a Chief Nurse." *R.N.* (September 1943): 22–24.

Langdon, Mildred L. "A Moment to Remember." U.S. Naval Institute *Proceedings* 103 (July 1977): 59.

Langley, Harold D. "Women in a Warship, 1813." U.S. Naval Institute *Proceedings* 110 (January 1984): 124–25.

Larson, C. Kay. "Bonny Yank and Ginny Reb." *Minerva* 8 (spring 1990): 33–48.

———. "Bonny Yank and Ginny Reb Revisited." *Minerva* 10 (summer 1992): 35–61.

Lawrence, William P. "The Commission." U.S. Naval Institute *Proceedings* 119 (February 1993): 48–51.

LeDonne, Diane M. "Trends in Morbidity and Use of Health Services by Women Veterans of Vietnam." *U.S. Navy Medicine* 79 (May–June 1988): 22–25.

Leonard, Patrick L. "Deborah Samson: Official Heroine of the State of Massachusetts." *Minerva* 6 (fall 1988): 61–66.

Leonhardt, Elizabeth [E. L.]. "Letters from Navy Nurses." *American Journal of Nursing* 14 (November 1913): 126–29; (January 1914): 294–95; (May 1914): 655–56; (August 1914): 987–88; 15 (November 1914): 151–52; (April 15): 595–97; (June 1915): 760.

Lerna, Gerda. "The Lady and the Mill Girl: Changes in the Status of Women in the Age of Jackson." *Midcontinent American Studies Journal* 10 (spring 1969): 5–15.

Lewis, J. M. "WAVES Forecasters in World War II." *Bulletin of the American Meteorological Society* 76 (November 1995): 2187–2202.

Linnekin, Richard B. "Tailhook 1991 and Other Perplexities." U.S. Naval Institute *Proceedings* 118 (September 1992): 36–40.

Litoff, Judy B., and David C. Smith. "The Wartime History of the Waves, Spars, Women Marines, Army and Navy Nurses, and Wasps." In Poulos, *Woman's War Too*, 47–67.

Love, Robert W., Jr. "Fighting a Global War, 1941–1945." In Hagan, *In Peace and War*, 263–89.

MacWilliams, W. H. "Visit of Virginia Nurses to the Pharmacist's Mates School, Portsmouth, VA." *Hospital Corps Quarterly* 11 (October 1927): 268–70.

Major, John. "The Navy Plans for War." In Hagan, *In Peace and War*, 235–62.

Malan, Nancy E. "How Ya Gonna Keep 'Em Down? Women and World War I." *Prologue*, 25th Anniversary Issue (1994): 112–17.

Mallison, Mary B. "Ninety Years Through Nursing's Lens." *American Journal of Nursing* 90 (October 1980): 14–15.

Martin, Gary. "Single Parent in Japan." *All Hands* (February 1980): 30–31.

Martin, Lawrence W. "Men Nurses Are Available for Military Nursing." *Trained Nurse and Hospital Review* (May 1944): 357.

Matray, James I. "Civil Is a Dumb Name for War." *SHAFR Newsletter* 26 (December 1995): 1–15.

McConnell, John P. "Women Reserves." *Leatherneck* 34 (November 1951): 36–39.

McConnell, Margaret. "Living on the Front Line." *Nursing Times* 85 (2 August 1989): 50–52.

McDowell, Denise. "Navy Nursing—1992: 84 Years of Caring." *Navy Medicine* 83 (May–June 1992): 9–13.

McLaughlin, Florence C. "Down to the Sea in Slips." *Western Pennsylvania Historical Magazine* 51 (October 1968): 377–87.

McWilliams, Mary E. "Women in the Coast Guard: SPARS." In Holm, *In Defense of a Nation*, 97–110.

"Medical Department Reorganization." *U.S. Navy Medicine* 80 (July–August 1989): 8–9.

Melancon, W. David. "A Duo That's Taking the City by Storm." *Navy Recruiter* (October 1989): 10–15.

Melhorn, K. C. "Some Aspects of the Personnel Division of the Bureau of Medicine and Surgery." *U.S. Naval Medical Bulletin* 30 (January 1932): 31.

"The Men at the Helm: The Last Nine CNOs and Their Portraits." *All Hands* (August 1986): 14–17.

Meriwether, Walter S. "The Many Sided Naval Reserve: Plumber's Helpers, Naval Architects, College Professors, Yachtsmen and a Corps of Able Women." *Sea Power* 4 (March 1918): 196–200.

Meyerowitz, Joanne. "Beyond the Feminine Mystique: A Reassessment of Postwar Mass Culture, 1946–1958." *Journal of American History* 79 (March 1993): 1455–82.

"Mildred McAfee (Horton)." In Dever and Dever, *Women and the Military: Over 100 Notable Contributors, Historic to Contemporary*, 83–87. Jefferson, N.C.: McFarland, 1995.

Miles, Donna. "The Women of Just Cause." *Soldiers* 45 (March 1990): 21–24.

Milhon, William. "Women Marines." *Leatherneck* 33 (November 1950): 60–63.

"The Military Sea Transportation Service." *All Hands* (August 1951): 24–27.

Millett, Allan R. "A Reader's Guide to the Korean War" (review essay), *Journal of Military History* 61 (July 1997): 583–97.

Moore, Brenda L. "African-American Women in the U.S. Military." *Armed Forces and Society* 17 (spring 1991): 363–84.

Morden, Bettie. "Women's Army Corps: WAAC and WAC." In Holm, *In Defense of a Nation*, 39–55.

Morrisey, Carla R. "The Influenza Epidemic of 1918." *U.S. Navy Medicine* 77 (May–June 1986): 11–17.

Morton, John F. "The U.S. Navy in 1989." U.S. Naval Institute *Proceedings, Naval Review, 1990*, 166–69, 172, 174, 176.

Museles, Melvin. "Current Status of Medical Department Manpower." *U.S. Navy Medicine* 70 (November 1979): 9–12.

Mussi, Chuck. "Navy Chaplain." *All Hands* (May 1988): 13–17.

Nau, Erika S. "The Spirit of Molly Marine." *Minerva* 8 (winter 1990): 23–29.

"Naval Academy Class of 1980 Will Be Fully Integrated." U.S. Naval Institute *Proceedings* 102 (April 1976): 117–19.

"Navy Medicine: Deploying the Best to Prepare for the Worst." *All Hands*, Special Issue no. 892, 49–51.

"The Navy Nurse Corps." *American Journal of Nursing* 9 (November 1908): 91–92.

"The Navy Nurse Corps and What It Offers to Nurses." *American Journal of Nursing* 29 (May 1929): 595–99.

"Navy Women." *All Hands* (August 1975): 70–73.

Neil, Elizabeth Wells. "The Experience of an Ex-Navy Nurse on Recruiting Duty." *American Journal of Nursing* 18 (May 1918): 623–26.

Neil, Robert. "Navy's First Lady Admiral." *All Hands* (July 1972): 2–5.

"New Naval Astronauts: First Female Naval Aviator Selected," *Wings of Gold* (summer 1992): 56–57.

Norling, Lisa. "The Sentimentalization of American Seafaring: The Case of the New England Whalefishery, 1790–1870." In Howell and Twomey, *Jack Tar in History*, 164–78.

Norris, Catherine M. "The Work of Getting Well." *American Journal of Nursing* 90 (July 1990): 47–50.

Norton, Douglas M. "It's Time." U.S. Naval Institute *Proceedings* 118 (February 1992): 48–50.

"Nurse Corps Chief Finds White Shoes Navy Healthy." *Navy Times*, 19 July 1976, 4.

"Nurses Stood By to the End." *Trained Nurse and Hospital Review* (March 1945): 182–83.

Nutting, M. Adelaide. "Thirty Years of Progress in Nursing." *American Journal of Nursing* 23 (September 1923): 1027–35.

Nye, Sandy. "Up Front with Judy." *Naval Aviation News* (July 1977): 18–20.

O'Connor, Patricia M. "Bearings: Taking Risks Earns New Position for Woman Officer." *All Hands* (September 1989): 42.

Oganesoff, Barbara. "Women in the Military: It Is Really a Matter of Human Power." *Government Executive* (February 1982): 22–26.

Olliges, John L. " Nobody Asked Me, but . . . No Double Standards." U.S. Naval Institute *Proceedings* 119 (January 1993): 94–95.

Olmstead, Frederick Law. "Hospital Transports: A Memoir of the Embarkation of the Sick and Wounded from the Peninsula of Virginia in the Summer of 1862." In Staubing, *In Hospital and Camp*, 133–47.

O'Toole, Sarah. "They Pioneered on Tinian." *American Journal of Nursing* 45 (December 1945): 1013–15.

"Our Number One Mover." *All Hands* (October 1967): 2–6.

A. J. P. "The Navy Nurse at Portsmouth." *American Journal of Nursing* 18 (May 1918): 706.

Parker, John. "Sexual Harassment in Our Navy?" U.S. Naval Institute *Proceedings* 118 (August 1992): 57.

Peterson, Carol J. "The New Nurse and the New Physician." *Annals of Internal Medicine* 96 (March 1982): 374–75.

Philpott, Tom. "Making WAVES." *Washingtonian* 32 (March 1997): 47–55.

Polmar, Norman. "The U.S. Navy: Command Changes." U.S. Naval Institute *Proceedings* 111 (December 1985): 156–57.

Poyner, Russell S. "Carrier Nursing." *U.S. Navy Medicine* 83 (May–June 1992): 14–19.

Purvis, Emily G. "Nursing Care in Air Ambulances." *American Journal of Nursing* 47 (March 1947): 158–60.

Quigley, Robin. "A Requirement to Serve." U.S. Naval Institute *Proceedings* 104 (October 1978): 52–53.

——. "Women Aboard Ships: A Few Observations." *Sea Power* 20 (May 1977): 16–18.

"Rank for Army Nurses." *American Journal of Nursing* 18 (September 1918): 1135.

Rausa, Rosario M. "In Profile: Grace Murray Hopper." *Naval History* 6 (fall 1992): 58–60.

"Rear Admiral Conder Retires." *U.S. Navy Medicine* 70 (May 1979): 6–8.

"Reminiscences of a Nurse POW." *U.S. Navy Medicine* 83 (May–June 1992): 36–40.

Richie, Sharon I. "Combat Nurses and You Won't Be Alone." *Military Review* 69 (January 1989): 87–97.

Roddis, Louis H. "Organization of the Navy Medical Department." *Surgical Clinics of North America* (December 1941): 1533–43.

——. "The U.S. Hospital Ship *Red Rover* (1862–1865)." *Military Surgeon* 77 (August 1935): 91–98.

Rogers, Deborah L. "The Force Drawdown and Its Impact on Women in the Military." *Minerva* 10 (spring 1992): 1–13.

Rogers, Robert A., III. "The Boots Wear Skirts." U.S. Naval Institute *Proceedings* 75 (September 1949): 1022–27.

Rosen, Philip T. "The Treaty Navy, 1919–1937." In Hagan, *In Peace and War*, 221–36.

Rosenberg, David A. "Arleigh Albert Burke: 17 August 1955–1 August 1961." In Love, *Chiefs of Naval Operations*, 263–319.

Roush, Paul E. "Combat Exclusion: Military Necessity or Another Name for Bigotry?" *Minerva* 8 (fall 1990): 1–15.

Rucker, Robert C. "Navy Women: Ready for the '90s." *All Hands* (June 1991): 6–9.

Russell, Sandy. "High Flying Ladies." *Naval Aviation News* (February 1981): 6–15.

——. "Womanpower in Naval Aviation: 20 Years of Progress." *Naval Aviation News* (September–October 1992): 12–19.

Sadler, Georgia Clark. "Women in the Sea Services: 1972–1982." U.S. Naval Institute *Proceedings* 109 (May 1983): 140–55.

Sadler, Georgia C., and Patricia J. Thomas. "Rock the Cradle, Rock the Boat?" U.S. Naval Institute *Proceedings* 121 (April 1995): 551–56.

Safford, Charlotte L. "U.S. Lady-of-the-Month: Cdr. Frances E. Biadasz, USN." *U.S. Lady* (September 1963): 12–13, 47.

Sams, Candace. "RAdm. Grace Hopper, USNR (Ret.): Looking Ahead." *All Hands* (November 1986): 26–27.

Samuelson, Nancy B. "Revolutionary War Women and the Second Oldest Profession." *Minerva* 7 (summer 1989): 16–25.

Sarnecky, Mary T. "Army Nurse Corps." In Holm, *In Defense of a Nation*, 9–28.

——. "Women, Medicine, and War." In Poulos, *Woman's War Too*, 71–81.

Schimmenti, Carmelita, and Maureen A. Darmody. "Taking Flight." *American Journal of Nursing* 87 (November 1987): 1420–23.

"Seawomen: A New Breed." *Sealift* 29 (July 1979): 8–11.

Segal, Mady W. "Women in the Armed Forces." In Howes and Stevenson, *Women and the Use of Military Force*, 81–93.

Selavan, Ida C. "The Revolution." In *Pages from Nursing History*, 19–21.

"She Changed Her Wardrobe: SA Mary Cobb." *All Hands* (December 1980): 44–45.

Sherman, Janann. "'They Either Need These Women or They Do Not': Margaret Chase Smith and the Fight for Regular Status for Women in the Military." *Journal of Military History* 54 (January 1990): 47–78.

"She's in the Navy Now." *American Journal of Nursing* 18 (December 1918): 168.

"She Stood Alone: The Tailhook Scandal." ABC television documentary, 22 May 1995.

Shields, Patricia M., Landon Curry, and Janet Nichols. "Women Pilots in Combat: Attitudes of Male and Female Pilots." *Minerva* 8 (summer 1990): 21–35.

Sickerman, Barbara. "College and Careers: Historical Perspectives on the Lives and Work Patterns of Women College Graduates." In Faragher and Howe, *Women and Higher Education in American History.*

Smith, Arthur M. "Getting Them Out Alive." U.S. Naval Institute *Proceedings* 115 (February 1989): 40–46.

Smith, Linda S. "History of American Nursing." *Advancing Clinical Care* 6 (November–December 1991): 31–32, 36.

Smith, Nina B. "Men and Authority: The Union Army Nurse and the Problem of Power." *Minerva* 6 (winter 1988): 25–41.

Spencer, Dee Ann. "Public Schoolteaching: A Suitable Job for a Woman." In Statham, Miller, and Mauksch, *Worth of Women's Work,* 167–86.

Spillane, Roberta. "Women in Ships: Can We Survive?" U.S. Naval Institute *Proceedings* 113 (July 1987): 43–46.

Stacey, John A. "What Happened to This Man's Navy? A Brief History of the Yeomanettes." *Military Images* (July–August 1989): 4–5, 7.

Stewart, E. Louise. "Women in Uniform." *Sea Power* 3 (November 1943): 45, 61–63.

Stockly, Louise T. "History of the Naval Reserve Midshipman's School (WR), Northampton, Mass." Appendix B in BuPers, *Women's Reserve.*

Stoddard, Ellwyn R. "Female Participation in the U.S. Military: Gender Trends by Branch, Rank and Racial Categories." *Minerva* 11 (spring 1993): 23–40.

Stoughton, Beverly F. "Women at Sea." *American History Illustrated* 15 (June 1980): 8–11, 40–43.

St. Peter, Olivine B. "In the Southwest Pacific." *American Journal of Nursing* 45 (December 1945): 1012–13.

Stremlow, Mary V. "Marine Corps Women's Reserve: Free a Man to Fight." In Holm, *In Defense of a Nation,* 77–95.

Summers, Harry G., Jr. "Women's Role in Military Is Old Story, Contrary to 'News,'" *Navy Times* (22 January 1990): 21.

Sundberg, Pete. "Sharing Life . . . on and off the Job." *All Hands* (June 1979): 6–13.

"The Task Force in White." *Bureau of Naval Personnel Information Bulletin* (March 1945): 22–25.

Taylor, J. S. "The Hospital Corpsman and the Trained Nurse." *Naval Medical Bulletin,* supplement (July 1919): 7–14.

Tein-Geddes, Barb. "Women Aboard *Spear.*" *All Hands* (February 1980): 12–15.

Tetreault, Mary Ann. "Gender Belief Systems and the Integration of Women in the U.S. Military." *Minerva* 6 (spring 1988): 44–71.

"They Are Enlisting Girls in the Navy—Why not the Marine Corps?" *Marines Magazine* 2 (June 1917): 19.

Thomas, Evan, and Gregory L. Vistica. "Falling Out of the Sky." *Newsweek* (March 17, 1997): 26–28.

Thomas, Marie D., Patricia J. Thomas, and Virginia McClintock. "Pregnant Enlisted Women in Navy Work Centers." *Minerva* 9 (fall 1991): 1–32.

Thomas, Patricia J. "Women in the Military: America and the British Commonwealth." *Armed Forces and Society* 4 (August 1978): 623–46.

———. "From Yeomanettes to WAVES to Women in the U.S. Navy." In Segal and Sinaiko, *Life in the Rank and File*, 98–115.

Thomas, Patricia J., and Marie D. Thomas. "Impact of Pregnant Women and Single Parents upon Navy Personnel Systems." *Minerva* 10 (fall/winter 1992): 41–75.

Timmons, Tracy. "'We're Looking for a Few Good Men': The Impact of Gender Stereotypes on Women in the Military." *Minerva* 10 (summer 1992): 20–33.

Tomblin, Barbara B. "Beyond Paradise: The U.S. Navy Nurse Corps in the Pacific in World War II." Pt. 1: *Minerva* 11 (spring 1993): 33–53; pt. 2: *Minerva* 11 (fall/winter 1993): 37–56.

Towle, Katherine A. "Women Marines: The Feminine Side." *Marine Corps Gazette* 34 (November 1950): 110–15.

Trask, David J. "The American Navy in a World at War, 1914–1919." In Hagan, *In Peace and War*, 205–20.

Trippet, Josephine. "Sketch of a Naval Emergency Hospital." *American Journal of Nursing* 18 (May 1918): 683–87.

Trost, Carlisle A. H. "Maritime Strategy for the 1990s." U.S. Naval Institute *Proceedings* 116 (May 1990): 92–98.

Tucker, John M. "The Gay Issue." U.S. Naval Institute *Proceedings* 119 (January 1993): 109.

"The 20th CNO: Adm. James L. Holloway III." *All Hands* (July 1974): 6–7.

Valentine, Carolyn. "The Navy Faces Rehabilitation." *R.N.* (January 1945): 28–32, 80.

Vaught, Wilma L. "Women of the Revolution—Celebrating Heroines of Earlier Times." *Pentagram*, 9 July 1992.

Waller, Douglas. "Life on the Coed Carrier." *Time*, 17 April 1995, 36.

Warshauer, Susan. "Living Under the Debated Homosexuality Regulations: Lesbians in the U.S. Military Challenge a Policy of Containment." *Minerva* 10 (summer 1992): 8–19.

Watkins, David. "In Remembrance." *Nursing Times* 82 (November 1986): 48–49.

Wedertz, Bill. "Women in the Navy: Jobs They Do." *All Hands* (July 1972), 6–11.

Welter, Barbara. "The Cult of True Womanhood." *American Quarterly* 18 (summer 1966): 151–74.

West, Philip. "Interpreting the Korean War." *American Historical Review* 94 (February 1989): 80–96.

"What's What in the Marine Corps." *Marines Magazine* 3 (September 1918): 20.

Wheelwright, Julie. "An Officer and A Gentleman." *Nursing Times* 85 (29 March 1989): 61–63.

Wilchinski, Martha L. "The Marinette." *Marines Magazine* 3 (October 1918): 14.

Wilds, Nancy G. "Sexual Harassment in the Military." *Minerva* 8 (winter 1990): 1–16.

Willenz, June A. "VA's Advisory Committee on Women Veterans is Launched." *Minerva* 1 (winter 1983): 11.

——. "Women Veterans from the Vietnam War through the Eighties." *Minerva* 6 (fall 1988): 44–60.

Williams, Kathleen B. "Women Ashore: The Contribution of WAVES to US Naval Science and Technology in World War II." *Northern Mariner* 8 (April 1998): 1–20.

Williams, William J. "Josephus Daniels and the U.S. Navy's Shipbuilding Program during World War I." *Journal of Military History* 60 (January 1996): 7–38.

"Will Navy Commission Women?" *Army and Navy Journal* 55 (8 June 1918): 1569.

Wilson, Shirley. "Selected for Line Rear Admiral." *All Hands* (March 1976): 22–23.

"A Winding Sheet and a Wooden Box." *U.S. Navy Medicine* 77 (May–June 1986): 18–19.

"Women Aboard Spear." *All Hands* (February 1980): 12–15.

"Women in Combat." U.S. Naval Institute *Proceedings* 118 (February 1992): 42–50.

"Women in Combat." U.S. Naval Institute *Proceedings* 119 (February 1993): 47–58.

"Women in Naval Chaplaincy." *Chaplain Corps* 1 (winter 1987): 2–25.

"Women in Navy Medicine." 5-pt. article. *All Hands* (July 1972): 22–33.

"Women in the Navy." *All Hands* (June 1988): 26–37.

"Women in the Navy." *Shipmate* 45 (March 1982), 14–15.

"Women in the Navy: A Historical Perspective." *Deckplate* 10 (January–February 1990): 11–14.

"'Women in White' Help Guard Your Health." *All Hands* (February 1953): 20–24.

"Women Line Officers Assigned to Sea Duty on Hospital Ships." U.S. Naval Institute *Proceedings* 98 (November 1972): 118–19.

"Women on Sea Duty." *All Hands* (November 1978): 6–11.

"Women Shipbuilders." National Maritime Museum Association, *Sea Letter* (fall/winter 1994): 20–23.

Wood, Mary G. "Naval Nursing Service." *American Journal of Nursing* 19 (October 1918): 100–105.

Woodruff, J. L. "WAVE Training." U.S. Naval Institute *Proceedings* 71 (February 1945): 151–55.

"Yeomanettes: Navy Women of World War One." *All Hands* (July 1972): 14–15.

"The Yeomanettes of World War I." U.S. Naval Institute *Proceedings*, Pictorial Section, 83 (December 1957): 1338–45.

Zimble, James A. "Navy Meets Call of Desert Shield." *U.S. Navy Medicine* (January 1991).

## Theses, Dissertations, and Research Papers

Akers, Regina T. "The Integration of Afro-Americans into the WAVES, 1942–1945." Master's thesis, Howard University, 1993.

Crawley, Martha L. "The Navy Medical Department, 1890–1916." Ph.D. diss., George Washington University, 1989.

Creighton, Margaret S. "The Private Life of Jack Tar: Sailors at Sea in the Nineteenth Century." Ph.D. diss., Boston University, 1985.

Fitzgerald, Helen M. "A History of the United States Navy Nurse Corps from 1934 to the Present." Master's thesis, Ohio State University, 1968.

Haase, Donna M. "Uncle Sam Needs You: The Factors that Keep Eligible Nurses from Entering the Military." Bachelor's thesis, Indiana University of Pennsylvania, 1989.

Hickey, Dermott V. "First Ladies in the Navy: A History of the Navy Nurse Corps, 1908–1939." Master's thesis, George Washington University, 1963.

Johnson, Katherine B. "Called to Serve: American Nurses Go to War, 1914–1918." Master's thesis, University of Louisville, 1993.

Manning, Michele. "Angels of Mercy and Life Amid Scenes of Conflict and Death: The Combat Experience and Imprisonment of American Military Nurses in the Philippines, 1941–1945." Student paper, Marine Corps Command and Staff College, Quantico, Va., 1985.

Tepe, Dawn A. "Women Marines in World War I." N.d. Marine Corps Research Center, Quantico, Va.

Van Voris, Jacqueline. "Quiet Victory: The WAVES in World War II." N.d. Operational Archives, Naval Historical Center, Washington, D.C.

Wieand, Harold T. "The History of the Development of the United States Naval Reserve, 1889–1941." Ph.D. diss., University of Pittsburgh, 1952.

# Index

# About the Author

Susan H. Godson attended the College of William and Mary, received her undergraduate degree from George Mason University and earned master's and doctoral degrees in history from The American University. She is the author of *Viking of Assault: Admiral John Lesslie Hall, Jr., and Amphibious Warfare*, and a co-author of *The College of William and Mary: A History*. She has also contributed to *The D-Day Encyclopedia*; *Assault from the Sea: Essays on the History of Amphibious Warfare*; and *In Defense of a Nation: Servicewomen in World War II*. Dr. Godson has written many articles on naval, educational, and women's history for such publications as the U.S. Naval Institute *Proceedings*, *William and Mary Magazine*, *New Jersey History*, *Virginia Cavalcade*, *Retired Officer*. She lives in her native Williamsburg, Virginia, where she is president of the local historical society and historian of Bruton Parish Church.

**The Naval Institute Press** is the book-publishing arm of the U.S. Naval Institute, a private, nonprofit, membership society for sea service professionals and others who share an interest in naval and maritime affairs. Established in 1873 at the U.S. Naval Academy in Annapolis, Maryland, where its offices remain today, the Naval Institute has members worldwide.

Members of the Naval Institute support the education programs of the society and receive the influential monthly magazine *Proceedings* and discounts on fine nautical prints and on ship and aircraft photos. They also have access to the transcripts of the Institute's Oral History Program and get discounted admission to any of the Institute-sponsored seminars offered around the country.

The Naval Institute also publishes *Naval History* magazine. This colorful bimonthly is filled with entertaining and thought-provoking articles, first-person reminiscences, and dramatic art and photography. Members receive a discount on *Naval History* subscriptions.

The Naval Institute's book-publishing program, begun in 1898 with basic guides to naval practices, has broadened its scope to include books of more general interest. Now the Naval Institute Press publishes about one hundred titles each year, ranging from how-to books on boating and navigation to battle histories, biographies, ship and aircraft guides, and novels. Institute members receive significant discounts on the Press's more than eight hundred books in print.

Full-time students are eligible for special half-price membership rates. Life memberships are also available.

For a free catalog describing Naval Institute Press books currently available, and for further information about subscribing to *Naval History* magazine or about joining the U.S. Naval Institute, please write to:

Membership Department
**U.S. Naval Institute**
291 Wood Road
Annapolis, MD 21402-5034
Telephone: (800) 233-8764
Fax: (410) 269-7940
Web address: www.navalinstitute.org